KU-522-262

James Russell Lowell

Emery Walker Ph. sc.

POEMS OF
JAMES RUSSELL LOWELL

CONTAINING

THE VISION OF SIR LAUNFAL, A FABLE FOR CRITICS
THE BIGLOW PAPERS, UNDER THE WILLOWS
AND OTHER POEMS

LONDON: HENRY FROWDE
OXFORD UNIVERSITY PRESS, AMEN CORNER, E.C.
NEW YORK: 35 WEST 32ND STREET
TORONTO: 25-27 RICHMOND STREET WEST
MELBOURNE: CATHEDRAL BUILDINGS
BOMBAY: HORNBY ROAD

1912

HERTFORDSHIRE
COUNTY LIBRARY
811/LOW

10538

C60891882

CONTENTS

CONTENTS

EARLIER POEMS

THRENODIA

Gone, gone from us ! and shall
  we see
Those sibyl-leaves of destiny,
Those calm eyes, nevermore ?
Those deep, dark eyes so warm and
  bright,
Wherein the fortunes of the man
Lay slumbering in prophetic light,
In characters a child might scan ?
So bright, and gone forth utterly !
O stern word—Nevermore !   9

  The stars of those two gentle eyes
Will shine no more on earth ;
Quenched are the hopes that had
  their birth,
As we watched them slowly rise,
Stars of a mother's fate ;
And she would read them o'er and o'er,
Pondering, as she sate,
Over their dear astrology,
Which she had conned and conned
  before,   18
Deeming she needs must read aright
What was writ so passing bright,
And yet, alas ! she knew not why,
Her voice would falter in its song,
And tears would slide from out her eye,
Silent, as they were doing wrong.
O stern word—Nevermore !

  The tongue that scarce had learned
  to claim
An entrance to a mother's heart
By that dear talisman, a mother's
  name,
Sleeps all forgetful of its art !
I loved to see the infant soul   30
(How mighty in the weakness
Of its untutored meekness !)

Peep timidly from out its nest,
His lips, the while,
Fluttering with half-fledged words,
Or hushing to a smile
That more than words expressed,
When his glad mother on him stole
And snatched him to her breast !
O, thoughts were brooding in those eyes,
That would have soared like strong-
  winged birds   41
Far, far into the skies,
Gladding the earth with song,
And gushing harmonies,
Had he but tarried with us long !
O stern word—Nevermore !

  How peacefully they rest,
Crossfolded there
Upon his little breast,
Those small, white hands that ne'er
  were still before,   50
But ever sported with his mother's hair,
Or the plain cross that on her breast
  she wore !
Her heart no more will beat
To feel the touch of that soft palm,
That ever seemed a new surprise
Sending glad thoughts up to her eyes
To bless him with their holy calm,—
Sweet thoughts ! they made her eyes
  as sweet.
How quiet are the hands   59
That wove those pleasant bands !
But that they do not rise and sink
With his calm breathing, I should
  think
That he were dropped asleep.
Alas ! too deep, too deep
Is this his slumber !
Time scarce can number

The years ere he will wake again.
O, may we see his eyelids open then !
O stern word—Nevermore !

   As the airy gossamere,   70
Floating in the sunlight clear,
Where'er it toucheth clingeth tightly,
Round glossy leaf or stump unsightly,
So from his spirit wandered out
Tendrils spreading all about,
Knitting all things to its thrall
With a perfect love of all :
O stern word—Nevermore !

  He did but float a little way
Adown the stream of time,   80
With dreamy eyes watching the
    ripples play,
Or hearkening their fairy chime ;
His slender sail
Ne'er felt the gale ;
He did but float a little way,
And, putting to the shore
While yet 't was early day,
Went calmly on his way,

To dwell with us no more !
No jarring did he feel,   90
No grating on his vessel's keel ;
A strip of silver sand
Mingled the waters with the land
Where he was seen no more :
O stern word—Nevermore !

   Full short his journey was ; no
    dust
Of earth unto his sandals clave ;
The weary weight that old men must,
He bore not to the grave.
He seemed a cherub who had lost his
    way   100
And wandered hither, so his stay
With us was short, and 't was most
    meet
That he should be no delver in earth's
    clod,
Nor need to pause and cleanse his feet
To stand before his God :
O blest word—Evermore !
    1839.

THE SIRENS

THE sea is lonely, the sea is dreary,
The sea is restless and uneasy ;
Thou seekest quiet, thou art weary,
Wandering thou knowest not whi-
    ther :—
Our little isle is green and breezy,
Come and rest thee ! O come hither,
Come to this peaceful home of ours,
    Where evermore
The low west-wind creeps panting up
    the shore   9
To be at rest among the flowers ;
Full of rest, the green moss lifts,
  As the dark waves of the sea
Draw in and out of rocky rifts,
  Calling solemnly to thee
With voices deep and hollow,—
    ' To the shore
    Follow ! O, follow !

To be at rest forevermore !
    Forevermore ! '   19

  Look how the grey old Ocean
From the depth of his heart rejoices,
Heaving with a gentle motion,
When he hears our restful voices ;
List how he sings in an undertone,
Chiming with our melody ;
And all sweet sounds of earth and
    air
Melt into one low voice alone,
That murmurs over the weary sea,
And seems to sing from every-
    where,—   29
' Here mayst thou harbour peacefully,
Here mayst thou rest from the aching
    oar ;
  Turn thy curvèd prow ashore,

And in our green isle rest forevermore!
Forevermore !'
And Echo half wakes in the wooded
hill,
And, to her heart so calm and deep,
Murmurs over in her sleep,
Doubtfully pausing and murmuring
still,
'Evermore !'   39
Thus, on Life's weary sea,
Heareth the marinere
Voices sweet, from far and
near,
Ever singing low and clear,
Ever singing longingly.

Is it not better here to be,
Than to be toiling late and soon ?
In the dreary night to see
Nothing but the blood-red moon
Go up and down into the sea ;
Or, in the loneliness of day,   50
To see the still seals only
Solemnly lift their faces grey,
Making it yet more lonely ?
Is it not better than to hear
Only the sliding of the wave
Beneath the plank, and feel so near
A cold and lonely grave,
A restless grave, where thou shalt lie
Even in death unquietly ?
Look down beneath thy wave-worn
bark,   60
Lean over the side and see
The leaden eye of the sidelong shark
Upturnèd patiently,
Ever waiting there for thee :
Look down and see those shapeless
forms,
Which ever keep their dreamless
sleep
Far down within the gloomy deep,
And only stir themselves in storms,
Rising like islands from beneath,
And snorting through the angry spray,
As the frail vessel perisheth   71
In the whirls of their unwieldy play ;
Look down ! Look down!
Upon the seaweed, slimy and dark,

That waves its arms so lank and
brown,
Beckoning for thee !
Look down beneath thy wave-worn
bark
Into the cold depth of the sea !
Look down ! Look down !
Thus, on Life's lonely sea,
Heareth the marinere   81
Voices sad, from far and near,
Ever singing full of fear,
Ever singing drearfully.

Here all is pleasant as a dream ;
The wind scarce shaketh down the
dew,
The green grass floweth like a stream
Into the ocean's blue ;
Listen ! O, listen !
Here is a gush of many streams,
A song of many birds,   91
And every wish and longing seems
Lulled to a numbered flow of words,—
Listen ! O listen !
Here ever hum the golden bees
Underneath full-blossomed trees,
At once with glowing fruit and flowers
crowned ;—
The sand is so smooth, the yellow sand,
That thy keel will not grate as it
touches the land ;   99
All around with a slumberous sound,
The singing waves slide up the strand,
And there, where the smooth, wet
pebbles be,
The waters gurgle longingly,
As if they fain would seek the shore,
To be at rest from the ceaseless roar,
To be at rest forevermore,—
Forevermore.
Thus, on Life's gloomy sea,
Heareth the marinere
Voices sweet, from far and
near,   110
Ever singing in his ear,
'Here is rest and peace for
thee !'

NANTASKET, July 1840.

IRENÉ

HERS is a spirit deep, and crystal-clear;
Calmly beneath her earnest face it lies,
Free without boldness, meek without a fear,
Quicker to look than speak its sympathies;
Far down into her large and patient eyes
I gaze, deep-drinking of the infinite,
As, in the mid-watch of a clear, still night,
I look into the fathomless blue skies.

So circled lives she with Love's holy light,
That from the shade of self she walketh free;   10
The garden of her soul still keepeth she
An Eden where the snake did never enter;
She hath a natural, wise sincerity,
A simple truthfulness, and these have lent her
A dignity as moveless as the centre;
So that no influence of our earth can stir
Her steadfast courage, nor can take away
The holy peacefulness, which night and day,
Unto her queenly soul doth minister.

Most gentle is she; her large charity   20
(An all unwitting, childlike gift in her)
Not freer is to give than meek to bear;
And, though herself not unacquaint with care,
Hath in her heart wide room for all that be,—
Her heart that hath no secrets of its own,
But open is as eglantine full blown.
Cloudless forever is her brow serene,
Speaking calm hope and trust within her, whence
Welleth a noiseless spring of patience,
That keepeth all her life so fresh, so green   30
And full of holiness, that every look,
The greatness of her woman's soul revealing,
Unto me bringeth blessing, and a feeling
As when I read in God's own holy book.

A graciousness in giving that doth make
The small'st gift greatest, and a sense most meek
Of worthiness, that doth not fear to take
From others, but which always fears to speak
Its thanks in utterance, for the giver's sake;—
The deep religion of a thankful heart,   40
Which rests instinctively in Heaven's clear law

With a full peace, that never can depart
From its own steadfastness ;—a holy awe
For holy things,—not those which men call holy,
But such as are revealèd to the eyes
Of a true woman's soul bent down and lowly
Before the face of daily mysteries ;—
A love that blossoms soon, but ripens slowly
To the full goldenness of fruitful prime,
Enduring with a firmness that defies   50
All shallow tricks of circumstance and time,
By a sure insight knowing where to cling,
And where it clingeth never withering ;—
These are Irené's dowry, which no fate
Can shake from their serene, deep-builded state.

In-seeing sympathy is hers, which chasteneth
No less than loveth, scorning to be bound
With fear of blame, and yet which ever hasteneth
To pour the balm of kind looks on the wound,
If they be wounds which such sweet teaching makes   60
Giving itself a pang for others' sakes ;
No want of faith, that chills with sidelong eye,
Hath she ; no jealousy, no Levite pride
That passeth by upon the other side ;
For in her soul there never dwelt a lie.
Right from the hand of God her spirit came
Unstained, and she hath ne'er forgotten whence
It came, nor wandered far from thence,
But laboureth to keep her still the same,
Near to her place of birth, that she may not   70
Soil her white raiment with an earthly spot.

Yet sets she not her soul so steadily
Above, that she forgets her ties to earth,
But her whole thought would almost seem to be
How to make glad one lowly human hearth ;
For with a gentle courage she doth strive
In thought and word and feeling so to live
As to make earth next heaven ; and her heart
Herein doth show its most exceeding worth,
That, bearing in our frailty her just part,   80
She hath not shrunk from evils of this life,
But hath gone calmly forth into the strife,
And all its sins and sorrows hath withstood
With lofty strength of patient womanhood :
For this I love her great soul more than all,
That, being bound, like us, with earthly thrall,
She walks so bright and heaven-like therein,—
Too wise, too meek, too womanly, to sin.

Like a lone star through riven storm-clouds seen
By sailors, tempest-tost upon the sea,
Telling of rest and peaceful heavens nigh,
Unto my soul her star-like soul hath been,
Her sight as full of hope and calm to me ;—
For she unto herself hath builded high
A home serene, wherein to lay her head,
Earth's noblest thing, a Woman perfected.

90

SERENADE

FROM the close-shut windows gleams
      no spark,
The night is chilly, the night is dark,
The poplars shiver, the pine-trees
      moan,
My hair by the autumn breeze is
      blown,
Under thy window I sing alone,
Alone, alone, ah woe ! alone !

The darkness is pressing coldly
      around,
The windows shake with a lonely
      sound,
The stars are hid and the night is
      drear,
The heart of silence throbs in thine ear,

In thy chamber thou sittest alone,
Alone, alone, ah woe ! alone !

The world is happy, the world is wide,
Kind hearts are beating on every side ;
Ah, why should we lie so coldly curled
Alone in the shell of this great world ?
Why should we any more be alone ?
Alone, alone, ah woe ! alone !

O, 't is a bitter and dreary word,
The saddest by man's ear ever heard !
We each are young, we each have
      a heart,
Why stand we ever coldly apart ?
Must we forever, then, be alone ?
Alone, alone, ah woe ! alone !

WITH A PRESSED FLOWER

THIS little blossom from afar
Hath come from other lands to thine ;
For, once, its white and drooping star
Could see its shadow in the Rhine.

Perchance some fair-haired German
      maid
Hath plucked one from the selfsame
      stalk,
And numbered over, half afraid,
Its petals in her evening walk.

'He loves me, loves me not,' she cries;
'He loves me more than earth or
      heaven !'
And then glad tears have filled her eyes
To find the number was uneven.

And thou must count its petals well,
Because it is a gift from me ;
And the last one of all shall tell
Something I 've often told to thee.

But here at home, where we were
      born,
Thou wilt find blossoms just as true,
Down-bending every summer morn,
With freshness of New England dew.

For Nature, ever kind to love,
Hath granted them the same sweet
      tongue,
Whether with German skies above,
Or here our granite rocks among.

THE BEGGAR

A BEGGAR through the world am I,—
From place to place I wander by.
Fill up my pilgrim's scrip for me,
For Christ's sweet sake and charity!

A little of thy steadfastness,
Rounded with leafy gracefulness,
Old oak, give me,—
That the world's blasts may round me blow,
And I yield gently to and fro,   9
While my stout-hearted trunk below
And firm-set roots unshaken be.

Some of thy stern, unyielding might,
Enduring still through day and night
Rude tempest-shock and withering blight,—
That I may keep at bay
The changeful April sky of chance
And the strong tide of circumstance,—
Give me, old granite grey.

Some of thy pensiveness serene,
Some of thy never-dying green,   20
Put in this scrip of mine,—
That griefs may fall like snow-flakes light,

And deck me in a robe of white,
Ready to be an angel bright,—
O sweetly mournful pine.

A little of thy merriment,
Of thy sparkling, light content,
Give me, my cheerful brook,—
That I may still be full of glee   29
And gladsomeness, where'er I be,
Though fickle fate hath prisoned me
In some neglected nook.

Ye have been very kind and good
To me, since I've been in the wood;
Ye have gone nigh to fill my heart;
But good-bye, kind friends, every one,
I've far to go ere set of sun;
Of all good things I would have part,
The day was high ere I could start,
And so my journey's scarce begun.

Heaven help me! how could I forget
To beg of thee, dear violet!   42
Some of thy modesty,
That blossoms here as well, unseen,
As if before the world thou 'dst been,
Oh, give, to strengthen me.

MY LOVE

I

NOT as all other women are
Is she that to my soul is dear;
Her glorious fancies come from far,
Beneath the silver evening-star,
And yet her heart is ever near.

II

Great feelings hath she of her own,
Which lesser souls may never know;
God giveth them to her alone,
And sweet they are as any tone
Wherewith the wind may choose to blow.

III

Yet in herself she dwelleth not,
Although no home were half so fair;
No simplest duty is forgot,
Life hath no dim and lowly spot
That doth not in her sunshine share.

IV

She doeth little kindnesses,
Which most leave undone, or despise:
For naught that sets one heart at ease,
And giveth happiness or peace,
Is low-esteemèd in her eyes.

V

She hath no scorn of common things,
And, though she seem of other birth,
Round us her heart intwines and
    clings,
And patiently she folds her wings
To tread the humble paths of earth.

VI

Blessing she is : God made her so,
And deeds of week-day holiness
Fall from her noiseless as the snow,
Nor hath she ever chanced to know
That aught were easier than to bless.

VII

She is most fair, and thereunto
Her life doth rightly harmonize ;
Feeling or thought that was not
    true
Ne'er made less beautiful the blue
Unclouded heaven of her eyes.

VIII

She is a woman : one in whom
The spring-time of her childish years
Hath never lost its fresh perfume,
Though knowing well that life hath
    room
For many blights and many tears.

IX

I love her with a love as still
As a broad river's peaceful might,
Which, by high tower and lowly mill,
Goes wandering at its own will,
And yet doth ever flow aright.

X

And, on its full, deep breast serene,
Like quiet isles my duties lie ;
It flows around them and between,
And makes them fresh and fair and
    green,
Sweet homes wherein to live and die.

SUMMER STORM

UNTREMULOUS in the river clear,
Toward the sky's image, hangs the imaged bridge ;
    So still the air that I can hear
The slender clarion of the unseen midge ;
    Out of the stillness, with a gathering creep,
Like rising wind in leaves, which now decreases,
Now lulls, now swells, and all the while increases,
    The huddling trample of a drove of sheep
Tilts the loose planks, and then as gradually ceases
    In dust on the other side ; life's emblem deep,   10
A confused noise between two silences,
Finding at last in dust precarious peace.
On the wide marsh the purple-blossomed grasses
    Soak up the sunshine ; sleeps the brimming tide,
Save when the wedge-shaped wake in silence passes
    Of some slow water-rat, whose sinuous glide
Wavers the long green sedge's shade from side to side ;
But up the west, like a rock-shivered surge,
    Climbs a great cloud edged with sun-whitened spray ;
Huge whirls of foam boil toppling o'er its verge,   20
    And falling still it seems, and yet it climbs alway.

Suddenly all the sky is hid
As with the shutting of a lid,
One by one great drops are falling
Doubtful and slow,

Down the pane they are crookedly crawling,
 And the wind breathes low ;
Slowly the circles widen on the river,
 Widen and mingle, one and all ;
Here and there the slenderer flowers shiver,   30
 Struck by an icy rain-drop's fall.

Now on the hills I hear the thunder mutter,
 The wind is gathering in the west ;
The upturned leaves first whiten and flutter,
 Then droop to a fitful rest ;
Up from the stream with sluggish flap
 Struggles the gull and floats away ;
Nearer and nearer rolls the thunder-clap,—
 We shall not see the sun go down to-day :
Now leaps the wind on the sleepy marsh,   40
 And tramples the grass with terrified feet,
The startled river turns leaden and harsh,
 You can hear the quick heart of the tempest beat.

 Look ! look ! that livid flash !
And instantly follows the rattling thunder,
As if some cloud-crag, split asunder,
 Fell, splintering with a ruinous crash,
On the Earth, which crouches in silence under ;
 And now a solid grey wall of rain
Shuts off the landscape, mile by mile ;   50
 For a breath's space I see the blue wood again,
And ere the next heart-beat, the wind-hurled pile,
 That seemed but now a league aloof,
 Bursts crackling o'er the sun-parched roof ;
Against the windows the storm comes dashing,
Through tattered foliage the hail tears crashing,
   The blue lightning flashes,
   The rapid hail clashes,
  The white waves are tumbling,
   And, in one baffled roar,   60
  Like the toothless sea mumbling
   A rock-bristled shore,
  The thunder is rumbling
  And crashing and crumbling,—
Will silence return nevermore ?

  Hush ! Still as death,
  The tempest holds his breath
  As from a sudden will ;
The rain stops short, but from the eaves
You see it drop, and hear it from the leaves,   70

All is so bodingly still ;
   Again, now, now, again
Plashes the rain in heavy gouts,
   The crinkled lightning
   Seems ever brightening,
    And loud and long
Again the thunder shouts
    His battle-song,—
    One quivering flash,
    One wildering crash,   80
Followed by silence dead and dull,
   As if the cloud, let go,
   Leapt bodily below
To whelm the earth in one mad overthrow,
   And then a total lull.

   Gone, gone, so soon !
No more my half-crazed fancy there,
Can shape a giant in the air,
No more I see his streaming hair,
The writhing portent of his form ;—   90
   The pale and quiet moon
Makes her calm forehead bare,
And the last fragments of the storm,
Like shattered rigging from a fight at sea,
Silent and few, are drifting over me.

LOVE

TRUE Love is but a humble, low-born thing,
And hath its food served up in earthen ware ;
It is a thing to walk with, hand in hand,
Through the every-dayness of this work-day world,
Baring its tender feet to every roughness,
Yet letting not one heart-beat go astray
From Beauty's law of plainness and content ;
A simple, fireside thing, whose quiet smile
Can warm earth's poorest hovel to a home ;
Which, when our autumn cometh, as it must,   10
And life in the chill wind shivers bare and leafless,
Shall still be blest with Indian-summer youth
In bleak November, and, with thankful heart,
Smile on its ample stores of garnered fruit,
As full of sunshine to our aged eyes
As when it nursed the blossoms of our spring.
Such is true Love, which steals into the heart
With feet as silent as the lightsome dawn
That kisses smooth the rough brows of the dark,

And hath its will through blissful gentleness,— 20
Not like a rocket, which, with savage glare,
Whirs suddenly up, then bursts, and leaves the night
Painfully quivering on the dazèd eyes ;
A love that gives and takes, that seëth faults,
Not with flaw-seeking eyes like needle points,
But loving-kindly ever looks them down
With the o'ercoming faith of meek forgiveness;
A love that shall be new and fresh each hour,
As is the golden mystery of sunset,
Or the sweet coming of the evening-star, 30
Alike, and yet most unlike, every day,
And seeming ever best and fairest *now* ;
A love that doth not kneel for what it seeks,
But faces Truth and Beauty as their peer,
Showing its worthiness of noble thoughts
By a clear sense of inward nobleness ;
A love that in its object findeth not
All grace and beauty, and enough to sate
Its thirst of blessing, but, in all of good
Found there, it sees but Heaven-granted types 40
Of good and beauty in the soul of man,
And traces, in the simplest heart that beats,
A family-likeness to its chosen one,
That claims of it the rights of brotherhood.
For love is blind but with the fleshly eye,
That so its inner sight may be more clear ;
And outward shows of beauty only so
Are needful at the first, as is a hand
To guide and to uphold an infant's steps :
Fine natures need them not : their earnest look 50
Pierces the body's mask of thin disguise,
And beauty ever is to them revealed,
Behind the unshapeliest, meanest lump of clay,
With arms outstretched and eager face ablaze,
Yearning to be but understood and loved.

TO PERDITA, SINGING

Thy voice is like a fountain,
  Leaping up in clear moonshine ;
Silver, silver, ever mounting,
    Ever sinking,
    Without thinking,
  To that brimful heart of thine.
Every sad and happy feeling,
Thou hast had in bygone years,
Through thy lips comes stealing,
    stealing,

  Clear and low ; 10
All thy smiles and all thy tears
  In thy voice awaken,
  And sweetness, wove of joy and woe,
    From their teaching it hath
      taken :
Feeling and music move together,
Like a swan and shadow ever
Floating on a sky-blue river
In a day of cloudless weather.

It hath caught a touch of sadness,
    Yet it is not sad ;   20
It hath tones of clearest gladness,
    Yet it is not glad ;
A dim, sweet twilight voice it is
    Where to-day's accustomed blue
Is over-greyed with memories,
    With starry feelings quivered
        through.

Thy voice is like a fountain
Leaping up in sunshine bright,
    And I never weary counting
Its clear droppings, lone and single,
Or when in one full gush they mingle,
    Shooting in melodious light.   32

Thine is music such as yields
Feelings of old brooks and fields,
And, around this pent-up room,
Sheds a woodland, free perfume ;
    O, thus forever sing to me !
    O, thus forever !
The green, bright grass of childhood
        bring to me,   39
    Flowing like an emerald river,
And the bright blue skies above !
O, sing them back, as fresh as ever,
Into the bosom of my love,—
    The sunshine and the merriment,
    The unsought, evergreen content,
    Of that never cold time,
The joy, that, like a clear breeze,
        went
    Through and through the old
        time !

Peace sits within thine eyes,
With white hands crossed in joyful
        rest,   50
While, through thy lips and face,
    arise
The melodies from out thy breast ;
    She sits and sings,
    With folded wings

    And white arms crost,
' Weep not for bygone things,
    They are not lost :
The beauty which the summer time
O'er thine opening spirit shed,
The forest oracles sublime   60
That filled thy soul with joyous
    dread,
The scent of every smallest flower
That made thy heart sweet for an
    hour,—
Yea, every holy influence,
Flowing to thee, thou knewest not
    whence,
In thine eyes to-day is seen,
Fresh as it hath ever been ;
Promptings of Nature, beckonings
    sweet,
Whatever led thy childish feet,
Still will linger unawares   70
The guiders of thy silver hairs ;
Every look and every word
Which thou givest forth to-day,
Tell of the singing of the bird
Whose music stilled thy boyish
    play.'

Thy voice is like a fountain,
Twinkling up in sharp starlight,
When the moon behind the mountain
Dims the low East with faintest
    white,
    Ever darkling,   80
    Ever sparkling,
We know not if 't is dark or bright ;
But, when the great moon hath rolled
    round,
And, sudden-slow, its solemn power
Grows from behind its black, clear-
    edgèd bound,
No spot of dark the fountain
    keepeth,
But, swift as opening eyelids,
    leapeth
Into a waving silver flower.

THE MOON

My soul was like the sea,
Before the moon was made,
Moaning in vague immensity,
  Of its own strength afraid,
  Unrestful and unstaid.
Through every rift it foamed in vain,
  About its earthly prison,
Seeking some unknown thing in pain,
And sinking restless back again,
  For yet no moon had risen :   10
Its only voice a vast dumb moan,
  Of utterless anguish speaking,
It lay unhopefully alone,
  And lived but in an aimless seeking.

So was my soul ; but when 't was full
  Of unrest to o'erloading,
A voice of something beautiful
Whispered a dim foreboding,
And yet so soft, so sweet, so low,
It had not more of joy than woe ;
And, as the sea doth oft lie still,
  Making its waters meet,   22
As if by an unconscious will,
  For the moon's silver feet,
So lay my soul within mine eyes
When thou, its guardian moon, didst
  rise.

And now, howe'er its waves above
  May toss and seem uneaseful,
One strong, eternal law of Love,
  With guidance sure and peaceful,
As calm and natural as breath,   31
Moves its great deeps through life and
  death.

REMEMBERED MUSIC

A FRAGMENT

THICK-RUSHING, like an ocean vast
  Of bisons the far prairie shaking,
The notes crowd heavily and fast
As surfs, one plunging while the last
  Draws seaward from its foamy
    breaking.

Or in low murmurs they began,
  Rising and rising momently,
As o'er a harp Aeolian
A fitful breeze, until they ran
  Up to a sudden ecstasy.

And then, like minute-drops of rain
  Ringing in water silverly,
They lingering dropped and dropped
  again,
Till it was almost like a pain
  To listen when the next would
    be.

SONG

TO M. L.

A LILY thou wast when I saw thee first,
    A lily-bud not opened quite,
    That hourly grew more pure and white,
By morning, and noontide, and evening nursed :
    In all of nature thou hadst thy share ;
        Thou wast waited on
        By the wind and sun ;
    The rain and the dew for thee took care ;
    It seemed thou never couldst be more fair.

A lily thou wast when I saw thee first,   10
  A lily-bud ; but O, how strange,
  How full of wonder was the change,
When, ripe with all sweetness, thy full bloom burst !
  How did the tears to my glad eyes start,
    When the woman-flower
    Reached its blossoming hour,
And I saw the warm deeps of thy golden heart !

Glad death may pluck thee, but never before
  The gold dust of thy bloom divine
  Hath dropped from thy heart into mine,   20
To quicken its faint germs of heavenly lore ;
  For no breeze comes nigh thee but carries away
    Some impulses bright
    Of fragrance and light,
  Which fall upon souls that are lone and astray,
To plant fruitful hopes of the flower of day.

ALLEGRA

I WOULD more natures were like thine,
  That never casts a glance before,—
Thou Hebe, who thy heart's bright wine
  So lavishly to all dost pour,
That we who drink forget to pine,
  And can but dream of bliss in store.

Thou canst not see a shade in life ;
  With sunward instinct thou dost rise,
And, leaving clouds below at strife,
  Gazest undazzled at the skies,
With all their blazing splendours rife,
  A songful lark with eagle's eyes.

Thou wast some foundling whom the Hours
  Nursed, laughing, with the milk of Mirth ;
Some influence more gay than ours
  Hath ruled thy nature from its birth,
As if thy natal stars were flowers
  That shook their seeds round thee on earth.

And thou, to lull thine infant rest,
  Wast cradled like an Indian child ;
All pleasant winds from south and west
  With lullabies thine ears beguiled,
Rocking thee in thine oriole's nest,
  Till Nature looked at thee and smiled.

Thine every fancy seems to borrow
  A sunlight from thy childish years,
Making a golden cloud of sorrow,
  A hope-lit rainbow out of tears,—
Thy heart is certain of to-morrow,
  Though 'yond to-day it never peers.

I would more natures were like thine,
  So innocently wild and free,
Whose sad thoughts, even, leap and shine,
  Like sunny wavelets in the sea,
Making us mindless of the brine,
  In gazing on the brilliancy.

THE FOUNTAIN

INTO the sunshine,
  Full of the light,
Leaping and flashing
  From morn till night !

Into the moonlight,
  Whiter than snow,
Waving so flower-like
  When the winds blow !

Into the starlight
  Rushing in spray,
Happy at midnight,
  Happy by day !

Ever in motion,
  Blithesome and cheery,
Still climbing heavenward,
  Never aweary ;—

Glad of all weathers,
  Still seeming best,
Upward or downward,
  Motion thy rest ;—

Full of a nature
  Nothing can tame,
Changed every moment,
  Ever the same ;—

Ceaseless aspiring,
  Ceaseless content,
Darkness or sunshine
  Thy element ;—

Glorious fountain !
  Let my heart be
Fresh, changeful, constant,
  Upward, like thee !

ODE

I

IN the old days of awe and keen-eyed wonder,
  The Poet's song with blood-warm truth was rife ;
He saw the mysteries which circle under
  The outward shell and skin of daily life.
Nothing to him were fleeting time and fashion,
  His soul was led by the eternal law ;
There was in him no hope of fame, no passion,
  But with calm, godlike eyes he only saw.
He did not sigh o'er heroes dead and buried,
  Chief-mourner at the Golden Age's hearse,   10
Nor deem that souls whom Charon grim had ferried
  Alone were fitting themes of epic verse :
He could believe the promise of to-morrow,
  And feel the wondrous meaning of to-day ;
He had a deeper faith in holy sorrow
  Than the world's seeming loss could take away.
To know the heart of all things was his duty,
  All things did sing to him to make him wise,
And, with a sorrowful and conquering beauty,
  The soul of all looked grandly from his eyes.   20
He gazed on all within him and without him,
  He watched the flowing of Time's steady tide,
And shapes of glory floated all about him
  And whispered to him, and he prophesied.

Than all men he more fearless was and freer,
   And all his brethren cried with one accord,—
' Behold the holy man !   Behold the Seer !
   Him who hath spoken with the unseen Lord ! '
He to his heart with large embrace had taken
   The universal sorrow of mankind,   30
And, from that root, a shelter never shaken,
   The tree of wisdom grew with sturdy rind.
He could interpret well the wondrous voices
   Which to the calm and silent spirit come ;
He knew that the One Soul no more rejoices
   In the star's anthem than the insect's hum.
He in his heart was ever meek and humble,
   And yet with kingly pomp his numbers ran,
As he foresaw how all things false should crumble
   Before the free, uplifted soul of man :   40
And, when he was made full to overflowing
   With all the loveliness of heaven and earth,
Out rushed his song, like molten iron glowing,
   To show God sitting by the humblest hearth.
With calmest courage he was ever ready
   To teach that action was the truth of thought,
And, with strong arm and purpose firm and steady,
   An anchor for the drifting world he wrought.
So did he make the meanest man partaker
   Of all his brother-gods unto him gave ;   50
All souls did reverence him and name him Maker,
   And when he died heaped temples on his grave.
And still his deathless words of light are swimming
   Serene throughout the great deep infinite
Of human soul, unwaning and undimming,
   To cheer and guide the mariner at night.

II

But now the Poet is an empty rhymer
   Who lies with idle elbow on the grass,
And fits his singing, like a cunning timer,
   To all men's prides and fancies as they pass.   60
Not his the song, which, in its metre holy,
   Chimes with the music of the eternal stars,
Humbling the tyrant, lifting up the lowly,
   And sending sun through the soul's prison-bars.
Maker no more,—O no ! unmaker rather,
   For he unmakes who doth not all put forth
The power given freely by our loving Father
   To show the body's dross, the spirit's worth.
Awake ! great spirit of the ages olden !
   Shiver the mists that hide thy starry lyre,   70
And let man's soul be yet again beholden

To thee for wings to soar to her desire.
O, prophesy no more to-morrow's splendour,
  Be no more shamefaced to speak out for Truth,
Lay on her altar all the gushings tender,
  The hope, the fire, the loving faith of youth !
O, prophesy no more the Maker's coming,
  Say not his onward footsteps thou canst hear
In the dim void, like to the awful humming
  Of the great wings of some new-lighted sphere ! 80
O, prophesy no more, but be the Poet !
  This longing was but granted unto thee
That, when all beauty thou couldst feel and know it,
  That beauty in its highest thou couldst be.
O thou who moanest tost with sealike longings,
  Who dimly hearest voices call on thee,
Whose soul is overfilled with mighty throngings
  Of love, and fear, and glorious agony,
Thou of the toil-strung hands and iron sinews
  And soul by Mother Earth with freedom fed, 90
In whom the hero-spirit yet continues,
  The old free nature is not chained or dead,
Arouse ! let thy soul break in music-thunder,
  Let loose the ocean that is in thee pent,
Pour forth thy hope, thy fear, thy love, thy wonder,
  And tell the age what all its signs have meant.
Where'er thy wildered crowd of brethren jostles,
  Where'er there lingers but a shadow of wrong,
There still is need of martyrs and apostles,
  There still are texts for never-dying song : 100
From age to age man's still aspiring spirit
  Finds wider scope and sees with clearer eyes,
And thou in larger measure dost inherit
  What made thy great forerunners free and wise.
Sit thou enthronèd where the Poet's mountain
  Above the thunder lifts its silent peak,
And roll thy songs down like a gathering fountain,
  They all may drink and find the rest they seek.
Sing ! there shall silence grow in earth and heaven,
  A silence of deep awe and wondering ; 110
For, listening gladly, bend the angels, even,
  To hear a mortal like an angel sing.

III

Among the toil-worn poor my soul is seeking
  For one to bring the Maker's name to light,
To be the voice of that almighty speaking
  Which every age demands to do it right.
Proprieties our silken bards environ ;
  He who would be the tongue of this wide land

Must string his harp with chords of sturdy iron
   And strike it with a toil-embrownèd hand;   120
One who hath dwelt with Nature well attended,
   Who hath learnt wisdom from her mystic books,
Whose soul with all her countless lives hath blended,
   So that all beauty awes us in his looks;
Who not with body's waste his soul hath pampered,
   Who as the clear northwestern wind is free,
Who walks with Form's observances unhampered,
   And follows the One Will obediently;
Whose eyes, like windows on a breezy summit,
   Control a lovely prospect every way;   130
Who doth not sound God's sea with earthly plummet,
   And find a bottom still of worthless clay;
Who heeds not how the lower gusts are working,
   Knowing that one sure wind blows on above,
And sees, beneath the foulest faces lurking,
   One God-built shrine of reverence and love;
Who sees all stars that wheel their shining marches
   Around the centre fixed of Destiny,
Where the encircling soul serene o'er-arches
   The moving globe of being like a sky;   140
Who feels that God and Heaven's great deeps are nearer
   Him to whose heart his fellow-man is nigh,
Who doth not hold his soul's own freedom dearer
   Than that of all his brethren, low or high;
Who to the Right can feel himself the truer
   For being gently patient with the wrong,
Who sees a brother in the evil-doer,
   And finds in Love the heart's-blood of his song;—
This, this is he for whom the world is waiting
   To sing the beatings of its mighty heart,   150
Too long hath it been patient with the grating
   Of scrannel-pipes, and heard it misnamed Art.
To him the smiling soul of man shall listen,
   Laying awhile its crown of thorns aside,
And once again in every eye shall glisten
   The glory of a nature satisfied.
His verse shall have a great commanding motion,
   Heaving and swelling with a melody
Learnt of the sky, the river, and the ocean,
   And all the pure, majestic things that be.   160
Awake, then, thou! we pine for thy great presence
   To make us feel the soul once more sublime,
We are of far too infinite an essence
   To rest contented with the lies of Time.
Speak out! and lo! a hush of deepest wonder
   Shall sink o'er all this many-voicèd scene,
As when a sudden burst of rattling thunder
   Shatters the blueness of a sky serene.

THE FATHERLAND

WHERE is the true man's fatherland?
　Is it where he by chance is born?
　Doth not the yearning spirit scorn
In such scant borders to be spanned?
O yes! his fatherland must be
As the blue heaven wide and free!

Is it alone where freedom is,
　Where God is God and man is man?
　Doth he not claim a broader span
For the soul's love of home than this?
O yes! his fatherland must be
As the blue heaven wide and free!

Where'er a human heart doth wear
　Joy's myrtle-wreath or sorrow's
　　gyves,

Where'er a human spirit strives
After a life more true and fair,
There is the true man's birthplace
　grand,
His is a world-wide fatherland!

Where'er a single slave doth pine,
　Where'er one man may help an-
　　other,—
　Thank God for such a birthright,
　　brother,—
That spot of earth is thine and
　mine!
There is the true man's birthplace
　grand,
His is a world-wide fatherland!

THE FORLORN

THE night is dark, the stinging sleet,
　Swept by the bitter gusts of air,
Drives whistling down the lonely
　street,
　And glazes on the pavement bare.

The street-lamps flare and struggle
　dim
　Through the grey sleet-clouds as
　　they pass,
Or, governed by a boisterous whim,
　Drop down and rustle on the glass.

One poor, heart-broken, outcast girl
　Faces the east-wind's searching
　　flaws,
And, as about her heart they whirl,
　Her tattered cloak more tightly
　　draws.

The flat brick walls look cold and
　bleak,
　Her bare feet to the sidewalk freeze;
Yet dares she not a shelter seek,
　Though faint with hunger and
　　disease.

The sharp storm cuts her forehead
　bare,
　And, piercing through her gar-
　　ments thin,
Beats on her shrunken breast, and
　there
　Makes colder the cold heart within.

She lingers where a ruddy glow
　Streams outward through an open
　　shutter,
Adding more bitterness to woe,
　More loneness to desertion utter.

One half the cold she had not felt
　Until she saw this gush of light
Spread warmly forth, and seem to
　melt
　Its slow way through the deadening
　　night.

She hears a woman's voice within,
　Singing sweet words her childhood
　　knew,
And years of misery and sin
　Furl off, and leave her heaven blue.

Her freezing heart, like one who sinks
  Outwearied in the drifting snow,
Drowses to deadly sleep and thinks
  No longer of its hopeless woe :

Old fields, and clear blue summer days,
  Old meadows, green with grass and
    trees
That shimmer through the trembling
    haze
  And whiten in the western breeze,

Old faces,—all the friendly past
  Rises within her heart again,
And sunshine from her childhood cast
  Makes summer of the icy rain.

Enhaloed by a mild, warm glow,
  From all humanity apart,
She hears old footsteps wandering
    slow
  Through the lone chambers of the
    heart.

Outside the porch before the door,
  Her cheek upon the cold, hard
    stone,
She lies, no longer foul and poor,
  No longer dreary and alone.

Next morning something heavily
  Against the opening door did
    weigh,
And there, from sin and sorrow free,
  A woman on the threshold lay.

A smile upon the wan lips told
  That she had found a calm release,
And that, from out the want and cold,
  The song had borne her soul in
    peace.

For, whom the heart of man shuts out,
  Sometimes the heart of God takes in,
And fences them all round about
  With silence mid the world's loud
    din ;

And one of his great charities
  Is Music, and it doth not scorn
To close the lids upon the eyes
  Of the polluted and forlorn ;

Far was she from her childhood's
    home,
  Farther in guilt had wandered
    thence,
Yet thither it had bid her come
  To die in maiden innocence.

MIDNIGHT

THE moon shines white and silent
  On the mist, which, like a tide
Of some enchanted ocean,
  O'er the wide marsh doth glide,
Spreading its ghost-like billows
  Silently far and wide.

A vague and starry magic
  Makes all things mysteries,
And lures the earth's dumb spirit
  Up to the longing skies,—
I seem to hear dim whispers,
  And tremulous replies.

The fireflies o'er the meadow
  In pulses come and go ;
The elm-trees' heavy shadow
  Weighs on the grass below ;
And faintly from the distance
  The dreaming cock doth crow.

All things look strange and mystic,
  The very bushes swell
And take wild shapes and motions,
  As if beneath a spell,—
They seem not the same lilacs
  From childhood known so well.

The snow of deepest silence
  O'er everything doth fall,
So beautiful and quiet,
  And yet so like a pall,—
As if all life were ended,
  And rest were come to all.

O wild and wondrous midnight,
  There is a might in thee
To make the charmèd body
  Almost like spirit be,
And give it some faint glimpses
  Of immortality !

A PRAYER

God ! do not let my loved one die,
But rather wait until the time
That I am grown in purity
Enough to enter thy pure clime,
Then take me, I will gladly go,
So that my love remain below !

O, let her stay ! She is by birth
What I through death must learn
to be ;
We need her more on our poor earth
Than thou canst need in heaven
with thee :

She hath her wings already, I
Must burst this earth-shell ere I fly.

Then, God, take me ! We shall be
near,
More near than ever, each to
each :
Her angel ears will find more clear
My heavenly than my earthly
speech ;
And still, as I draw nigh to thee,
Her soul and mine shall closer be.

THE HERITAGE

The rich man's son inherits lands,
And piles of brick, and stone, and
gold,
And he inherits soft white hands,
And tender flesh that fears the cold,
Nor dares to wear a garment old ;
A heritage, it seems to me,
One scarce would wish to hold in fee.

The rich man's son inherits cares ;
The bank may break, the factory
burn,
A breath may burst his bubble shares,
And soft white hands could hardly
earn
A living that would serve his turn ;
A heritage, it seems to me,
One scarce would wish to hold in fee.

The rich man's son inherits wants,
His stomach craves for dainty fare ;
With sated heart, he hears the pants
Of toiling hinds with brown arms
bare,
And wearies in his easy-chair ;
A heritage, it seems to me,
One scarce would wish to hold in fee.

What doth the poor man's son inherit ?
Stout muscles and a sinewy heart,
A hardy frame, a hardier spirit ;

King of two hands, he does his part
In every useful toil and art ;
A heritage, it seems to me,
A king might wish to hold in fee.

What doth the poor man's son inherit ?
Wishes o'erjoyed with humble
things,
A rank adjudged by toil-won merit,
Content that from employment
springs,
A heart that in his labour sings ;
A heritage, it seems to me,
A king might wish to hold in fee.

What doth the poor man's son inherit ?
A patience learned of being poor,
Courage, if sorrow come, to bear it,
A fellow-feeling that is sure
To make the outcast bless his door ;
A heritage, it seems to me,
A king might wish to hold in fee.

O rich man's son ! there is a toil
That with all others level stands ;—
Large charity doth never soil,
But only whiten, soft white hands ;
This is the best crop from thy
lands ;
A heritage, it seems to be,
Worth being rich to hold in fee.

O poor man's son! scorn not thy state;
  There is worse weariness than thine,
In merely being rich and great;
  Toil only gives the soul to shine,
And makes rest fragrant and benign;
A heritage, it seems to me,
Worth being poor to hold in fee.

Both, heirs to some six feet of sod,
  Are equal in the earth at last;
Both, children of the same dear God,
  Prove title to your heirship vast
By record of a well-filled past;
A heritage, it seems to me,
Well worth a life to hold in fee.

THE ROSE: A BALLAD

I

In his tower sat the poet
  Gazing on the roaring sea,
'Take this rose,' he sighed, 'and
    throw it
Where there's none that loveth me.
On the rock the billow bursteth
  And sinks back into the seas,
But in vain my spirit thirsteth
  So to burst and be at ease.
Take, O sea! the tender blossom
  That hath lain against my breast;
On thy black and angry bosom
  It will find a surer rest.
Life is vain, and love is hollow,
  Ugly death stands there behind,
Hate and scorn and hunger follow
  Him that toileth for his kind.'
Forth into the night he hurled it,
  And with bitter smile did mark
How the surly tempest whirled it
  Swift into the hungry dark.
Foam and spray drive back to leeward,
  And the gale, with dreary moan,
Drifts the helpless blossom seaward,
  Through the breakers all alone.

II

Stands a maiden, on the morrow,
  Musing by the wave-beat strand,
Half in hope and half in sorrow,
  Tracing words upon the sand:
'Shall I ever then behold him
  Who hath been my life so long,—
Ever to this sick heart fold him,—
  Be the spirit of his song?
Touch not, sea, the blessed letters
  I have traced upon thy shore,
Spare his name whose spirit fetters

Mine with love forevermore!'
Swells the tide and overflows it,
  But, with omen pure and meet,
Brings a little rose, and throws it
  Humbly at the maiden's feet.
Full of bliss she takes the token,
  And, upon her snowy breast,
Soothes the ruffled petals broken
  With the ocean's fierce unrest.
'Love is thine, O heart! and surely
  Peace shall also be thine own,
For the heart that trusteth purely
  Never long can pine alone.'

III

In his tower sits the poet,
  Blisses new and strange to him
Fill his heart and overflow it
  With a wonder sweet and dim.
Up the beach the ocean slideth
  With a whisper of delight,
And the moon in silence glideth
  Through the peaceful blue of night.
Rippling o'er the poet's shoulder
  Flows a maiden's golden hair,
Maiden lips, with love grown bolder,
  Kiss his moon-lit forehead bare.
'Life is joy, and love is power,
  Death all fetters doth unbind,
Strength and wisdom only flower
  When we toil for all our kind.
Hope is truth,—the future giveth
  More than present takes away,
And the soul forever liveth
  Nearer God from day to day.'
Not a word the maiden uttered,
  Fullest hearts are slow to speak,
But a withered rose-leaf fluttered
  Down upon the poet's cheek.

SONG

Violet! sweet violet!
Thine eyes are full of tears;
    Are they wet
    Even yet
With the thought of other years?
Or with gladness are they full,
For the night so beautiful,
And longing for those far-off spheres?

    Loved one of my youth thou wast,
    Of my merry youth,   10
      And I see,
      Tearfully,
All the fair and sunny past,
All its openness and truth,
Ever fresh and green in thee
As the moss is in the sea.

    Thy little heart, that hath with love
    Grown coloured like the sky above,
    On which thou lookest ever,—
      Can it know   20
      All the woe

Of hope for what returneth never,
All the sorrow and the longing
To these hearts of ours belonging?

    Out on it! no foolish pining
      For the sky
      Dims thine eye,
Or for the stars so calmly shining;
Like thee let this soul of mine
Take hue from that wherefor I long,
Self-stayed and high, serene and
    strong,   31
Not satisfied with hoping—but divine.

    Violet! dear violet!
    Thy blue eyes are only wet
With joy and love of Him who sent
    thee,
And for the fulfilling sense
Of that glad obedience
Which made thee all that Nature
    meant thee!

ROSALINE

Thou look'dst on me all yesternight,
Thine eyes were blue, thy hair was
    bright
As when we murmured our troth-
    plight
Beneath the thick stars, Rosaline!
Thy hair was braided on thy head,
As on the day we two were wed,
Mine eyes scarce knew if thou wert
    dead,—
But my shrunk heart knew, Rosaline!

The death-watch ticked behind the
    wall,
The blackness rustled like a pall,
The moaning wind did rise and fall
Among the bleak pines, Rosaline!
My heart beat thickly in mine ears:
The lids may shut out fleshly fears,
But still the spirit sees and hears,—
Its eyes are lidless, Rosaline!

A wildness rushing suddenly,
A knowing some ill shape is nigh,
A wish for death, a fear to die,—
Is not this vengeance, Rosaline?
A loneliness that is not lone,
A love quite withered up and
    gone,
A strong soul ousted from its throne,
What wouldst thou further, Rosaline?

'Tis drear such moonless nights as
    these,
Strange sounds are out upon the
    breeze,
And the leaves shiver in the trees,
And then thou comest, Rosaline!
I seem to hear the mourners go,
With long black garments trailing
    slow,
And plumes anodding to and fro,
As once I heard them, Rosaline!

Thy shroud is all of snowy white,
And, in the middle of the night,
Thou standest moveless and upright,
Gazing upon me, Rosaline !
There is no sorrow in thine eyes,
But evermore that meek surprise,—
O God ! thy gentle spirit tries
To deem me guiltless, Rosaline !

Above thy grave the robin sings,
And swarms of bright and happy
    things
Flit all about with sunlit wings,—
But I am cheerless, Rosaline !
The violets on the hillock toss,
The gravestone is o'ergrown with
    moss ;
For nature feels not any loss,—
But I am cheerless, Rosaline !

I did not know when thou wast dead ;
A blackbird whistling overhead
Thrilled through my brain ; I would
    have fled,
But dared not leave thee, Rosaline !
The sun rolled down, and very soon,
Like a great fire, the awful moon
Rose, stained with blood, and then
    a swoon
Crept chilly o'er me, Rosaline !

The stars came out ; and, one by
    one,
Each angel from his silver throne
Looked down and saw what I had
    done :
I dared not hide me, Rosaline !

I crouched ; I feared thy corpse
    would cry
Against me to God's quiet sky,
I thought I saw the blue lips try
To utter something, Rosaline !

I waited with a maddened grin
To hear that voice all icy thin
Slide forth and tell my deadly sin
To hell and heaven, Rosaline !
But no voice came, and then it
    seemed,
That, if the very corpse had screamed,
The sound like sunshine glad had
    streamed
Through that dark stillness, Rosaline !

And then, amid the silent night,
I screamed with horrible delight,
And in my brain an awful light
Did seem to crackle, Rosaline !
It is my curse ! sweet memories fall
From me like snow,—and only all
Of that one night, like cold worms,
    crawl
My doomed heart over, Rosaline !

Why wilt thou haunt me with thine
    eyes,
Wherein such blessed memories,
Such pitying forgiveness lies,
Than hate more bitter, Rosaline !
Woe 's me ! I know that love so high
As thine, true soul, could never die,
And with mean clay in churchyard
    lie,—
Would it might be so, Rosaline !

A REQUIEM

Aye, pale and silent maiden,
    Cold as thou liest there,
Thine was the sunniest nature
    That ever drew the air,
The wildest and most wayward,
    And yet so gently kind,
Thou seemedst but to body
    A breath of summer wind.

Into the eternal shadow
    That girds our life around,
Into the infinite silence
    Wherewith Death's shore is bound,
Thou hast gone forth, beloved !
    And I were mean to weep,
That thou hast left Life's shallows,
    And dost possess the Deep.

Thou liest low and silent,
　Thy heart is cold and still,
Thine eyes are shut forever,
　And Death hath had his will;
He loved and would have taken,
　I loved and would have kept,
We strove,—and he was stronger,
　And I have never wept.

Let him possess thy body,
　Thy soul is still with me,
More sunny and more gladsome
　Than it was wont to be:
Thy body was a fetter
　That bound me to the flesh,
Thank God that it is broken,
　And now I live afresh!

Now I can see thee clearly;
　The dusky cloud of clay,
That hid thy starry spirit,
　Is rent and blown away:
To earth I give thy body,
　Thy spirit to the sky,
I saw its bright wings growing,
　And knew that thou must fly.

Now I can love thee truly,
　For nothing comes between
The senses and the spirit,
　The seen and the unseen;
Lifts the eternal shadow,
　The silence bursts apart,
And the soul's boundless future
　Is present in my heart.

A PARABLE

WORN and footsore was the Prophet,
　When he gained the holy hill;
'God has left the earth,' he murmured,
　' Here his presence lingers still.

' God of all the olden prophets,
　Wilt thou speak with men no more?
Have I not as truly served thee
　As thy chosen ones of yore?

' Hear me, guider of my fathers,
　Lo! a humble heart is mine;
By thy mercy I beseech thee
　Grant thy servant but a sign!'

Bowing then his head, he listened
　For an answer to his prayer;
No loud burst of thunder followed,
　Not a murmur stirred the air:—

But the tuft of moss before him
　Opened while he waited yet,
And, from out the rock's hard bosom,
　Sprang a tender violet.

' God! I thank thee,' said the
　Prophet;
　' Hard of heart and blind was I,

Looking to the holy mountain
　For the gift of prophecy.

' Still thou speakest with thy children
　Freely as in eld sublime;
Humbleness, and love, and patience,
　Still give empire over time.

' Had I trusted in my nature,
　And had faith in lowly things,
Thou thyself wouldst then have
　　sought me,
　And set free my spirit's wings.

' But I looked for signs and wonders,
　That o'er men should give me sway;
Thirsting to be more than mortal,
　I was even less than clay.

' Ere I entered on my journey,
　As I girt my loins to start,
Ran to me my little daughter,
　The belovèd of my heart;—

' In her hand she held a flower,
　Like to this as like may be,
Which, beside my very threshold,
　She had plucked and brought to me.'

SONG

O MOONLIGHT deep and tender,
  A year and more agone,
Your mist of golden splendour
  Round my betrothal shone !

O elm-leaves dark and dewy,
  The very same ye seem,
The low wind trembles through ye,
  Ye murmur in my dream !

O river, dim with distance,
  Flow thus forever by,
A part of my existence
  Within your heart doth lie !

O stars, ye saw our meeting,
  Two beings and one soul,
Two hearts so madly beating
  To mingle and be whole !

O happy night, deliver
  Her kisses back to me,
Or keep them all, and give her
  A blissful dream of me !

SONNETS

I. TO A. C. L.

THROUGH suffering and sorrow thou hast passed
To show us what a woman true may be :
They have not taken sympathy from thee,
Nor made thee any other than thou wast,
Save as some tree, which, in a sudden blast,
Sheddeth those blossoms, that are weakly grown,
Upon the air, but keepeth every one
Whose strength gives warrant of good fruit at last :
So thou hast shed some blooms of gaiety,
But never one of steadfast cheerfulness ;
Nor hath thy knowledge of adversity
Robbed thee of any faith in happiness,
But rather cleared thine inner eyes to see
How many simple ways there are to bless.

II

WHAT were I, Love, if I were stripped of thee,
If thine eyes shut me out whereby I live,
Thou, who unto my calmer soul dost give
Knowledge, and Truth, and holy Mystery,
Wherein Truth mainly lies for those who see
Beyond the earthly and the fugitive,
Who in the grandeur of the soul believe,
And only in the Infinite are free ?
Without thee I were naked, bleak, and bare
As yon dead cedar on the sea-cliff's brow ;
And Nature's teachings, which come to me now,
Common and beautiful as light and air,
Would be as fruitless as a stream which still
Slips through the wheel of some old ruined mill.

III

I WOULD not have this perfect love of ours
Grow from a single root, a single stem,
Bearing no goodly fruit, but only flowers
That idly hide life's iron diadem :
It should grow alway like that Eastern tree
Whose limbs take root and spread forth constantly ;
That love for one, from which there doth not spring
Wide love for all, is but a worthless thing.
Not in another world, as poets prate,
Dwell we apart above the tide of things,
High floating o'er earth's clouds on faery wings ;
But our pure love doth ever elevate
Into a holy bond of brotherhood
All earthly things, making them pure and good.

IV

' FOR this true nobleness I seek in vain,
In woman and in man I find it not ;
I almost weary of my earthly lot,
My life-springs are dried up with burning pain.'
Thou find'st it not ? I pray thee look again,
Look *inward* through the depths of thine own soul.
How is it with thee ? Art thou sound and whole ?
Doth narrow search show thee no earthly stain ?
BE NOBLE ! and the nobleness that lies
In other men, sleeping, but never dead,
Will rise in majesty to meet thine own ;
Then wilt thou see it gleam in many eyes,
Then will pure light around thy path be shed,
And thou wilt nevermore be sad and lone.

V. TO THE SPIRIT OF KEATS

GREAT soul, thou sittest with me in my room,
Uplifting me with thy vast, quiet eyes,
On whose full orbs, with kindly lustre, lies
The twilight warmth of ruddy ember-gloom :
Thy clear, strong tones will oft bring sudden bloom
Of hope secure, to him who lonely cries,
Wrestling with the young poet's agonies,
Neglect and scorn, which seem a certain doom :
Yes ! the few words which, like great thunder-drops,
Thy large heart down to earth shook doubtfully,
Thrilled by the inward lightning of its might,
Serene and pure, like gushing joy of light,
Shall track the eternal chords of Destiny,
After the moon-led pulse of ocean stops.

VI

GREAT Truths are portions of the soul of man ;
Great souls are portions of Eternity ;
Each drop of blood that e'er through true heart ran
With lofty message, ran for thee and me ;
For God's law, since the starry song began,
Hath been, and still forevermore must be,
That every deed which shall outlast Time's span
Must goad the soul to be erect and free ;
Slave is no word of deathless lineage sprung,—
Too many noble souls have thought and died,
Too many mighty poets lived and sung,
And our good Saxon, from lips purified
With martyr-fire, throughout the world hath rung
Too long to have God's holy cause denied.

VII

I ASK not for those thoughts, that sudden leap
From being's sea, like the isle-seeming Kraken,
With whose great rise the ocean all is shaken
And a heart-tremble quivers through the deep ;
Give me that growth which some perchance deem sleep,
Wherewith the steadfast coral-stems uprise,
Which, by the toil of gathering energies,
Their upward way into clear sunshine keep,
Until, by Heaven's sweetest influences,
Slowly and slowly spreads a speck of green
Into a pleasant island in the seas,
Where, mid tall palms, the cane-roofed home is seen,
And wearied men shall sit at sunset's hour,
Hearing the leaves and loving God's dear power.

VIII. TO M. W., ON HER BIRTHDAY

MAIDEN, when such a soul as thine is born,
The morning-stars their ancient music make,
And, joyful, once again their song awake,
Long silent now with melancholy scorn ;
And thou, not mindless of so blest a morn,
By no least deed its harmony shalt break,
But shalt to that high chime thy footsteps take,
Through life's most darksome passes unforlorn ;
Therefore from thy pure faith thou shalt not fall,
Therefore shalt thou be ever fair and free,
And in thine every motion musical
As summer air, majestic as the sea,
A mystery to those who creep and crawl
Through Time, and part it from Eternity.

IX

My Love, I have no fear that thou shouldst die;
Albeit I ask no fairer life than this,
Whose numbering-clock is still thy gentle kiss,
While Time and Peace with hands enlockèd fly,—
Yet care I not where in Eternity
We live and love, well knowing that there is
No backward step for those who feel the bliss
Of Faith as their most lofty yearnings high:
Love hath so purified my being's core,
Meseems I scarcely should be startled, even,
To find, some morn, that thou hadst gone before;
Since, with thy love, this knowledge too was given,
Which each calm day doth strengthen more and more,
That they who love are but one step from Heaven.

X

I CANNOT think that thou shouldst pass away,
Whose life to mine is an eternal law,
A piece of nature that can have no flaw,
A new and certain sunrise every day;
But, if thou art to be another ray
About the Sun of Life, and art to live
Free from all of thee that was fugitive,
The debt of Love I will more fully pay,
Not downcast with the thought of thee so high,
But rather raised to be a nobler man,
And more divine in my humanity,
As knowing that the waiting eyes which scan
My life are lighted by a purer being,
And ask high, calm-browed deeds, with it agreeing.

XI

THERE never yet was flower fair in vain,
Let classic poets rhyme it as they will;
The seasons toil that it may blow again,
And summer's heart doth feel its every ill;
Nor is a true soul ever born for naught;
Wherever any such hath lived and died,
There hath been something for true freedom wrought,
Some bulwark levelled on the evil side:
Toil on, then, Greatness! thou art in the right,
However narrow souls may call thee wrong;
Be as thou wouldst be in thine own clear sight,
And so thou shalt be in the world's erelong;
For worldlings cannot, struggle as they may,
From man's great soul one great thought hide away.

XII. SUB PONDERE CRESCIT

THE hope of Truth grows stronger, day by day ;
I hear the soul of Man around me waking,
Like a great sea, its frozen fetters breaking,
And flinging up to heaven its sunlit spray,
Tossing huge continents in scornful play,
And crushing them, with din of grinding thunder,
That makes old emptinesses stare in wonder ;
The memory of a glory passed away
Lingers in every heart, as, in the shell,
Resounds the bygone freedom of the sea,
And every hour new signs of promise tell,
That the great soul shall once again be free,
For high, and yet more high, the murmurs swell
Of inward strife for truth and liberty.

XIII

BELOVED, in the noisy city here,
The thought of thee can make all turmoil cease ;
Around my spirit, folds thy spirit clear
Its still, soft arms, and circles it with peace ;
There is no room for any doubt or fear
In souls so overfilled with love's increase,
There is no memory of the bygone year
But growth in heart's and spirit's perfect ease :
How hath our love, half nebulous at first,
Rounded itself into a full-orbed sun !
How have our lives and wills (as haply erst
They were, ere this forgetfulness begun)
Through all their earthly distantness outburst,
And melted, like two rays of light in one !

XIV. ON READING WORDSWORTH'S SONNETS IN DEFENCE OF CAPITAL PUNISHMENT

As the broad ocean endlessly upheaveth,
With the majestic beating of his heart,
The mighty tides, whereof its rightful part
Each sea-wide bay and little weed receiveth,—
So, through his soul who earnestly believeth,
Life from the universal Heart doth flow,
Whereby some conquest of the eternal Woe,
By instinct of God's nature, he achieveth :
A fuller pulse of this all-powerful beauty
Into the poet's gulf-like heart doth tide,
And he more keenly feels the glorious duty
Of serving Truth, despised and crucified,—
Happy, unknowing sect or creed, to rest,
And feel God flow forever through his breast.

XV. THE SAME, CONTINUED

ONCE hardly in a cycle blossometh
A flower-like soul ripe with the seeds of song,
A spirit foreordained to cope with wrong,
Whose divine thoughts are natural as breath,
Who the old Darkness thickly scattereth
With starry words, that shoot prevailing light
Into the deeps, and wither, with the blight
Of serene Truth, the coward heart of Death :
Woe, if such spirit thwart its errand high,
And mock with lies the longing soul of man !
Yet one age longer must true Culture lie,
Soothing her bitter fetters as she can,
Until new messages of love outstart
At the next beating of the infinite Heart.

XVI. THE SAME, CONTINUED

THE love of all things springs from love of one ;
Wider the soul's horizon hourly grows,
And over it with fuller glory flows
The sky-like spirit of God ; a hope begun
In doubt and darkness 'neath a fairer sun
Cometh to fruitage, if it be of Truth ;
And to the law of meekness, faith, and ruth,
By inward sympathy, shall all be won :
This thou shouldst know, who, from the painted feature
Of shifting Fashion, couldst thy brethren turn
Unto the love of ever-youthful Nature,
And of a beauty fadeless and eterne ;
And always 't is the saddest sight to see
An old man faithless in Humanity.

XVII. THE SAME, CONTINUED

A POET cannot strive for despotism ;
His harp falls shattered ; for it still must be
The instinct of great spirits to be free,
And the sworn foes of cunning barbarism :
He who has deepest searched the wide abysm
Of that life-giving Soul which men call fate,
Knows that to put more faith in lies and hate
Than truth and love is the true atheism :
Upward the soul forever turns her eyes :
The next hour always shames the hour before ;
One beauty, at its highest, prophesies
That by whose side it shall seem mean and poor.
No Godlike thing knows aught of less and less,
But widens to the boundless Perfectness.

XVIII. THE SAME, CONTINUED

THEREFORE think not the Past is wise alone,
For Yesterday knows nothing of the Best,
And thou shalt love it only as the nest
Whence glory-wingèd things to Heaven have flown:
To the great Soul only are all things known;
Present and future are to her as past,
While she in glorious madness doth forecast
That perfect bud, which seems a flower full-blown
To each new Prophet, and yet always opes
Fuller and fuller with each day and hour,
Heartening the soul with odour of fresh hopes,
And longings high, and gushings of wide power,
Yet never is or shall be fully blown
Save in the forethought of the Eternal One.

XIX. THE SAME, CONCLUDED

FAR 'yond this narrow parapet of Time,
With eyes uplift, the poet's soul should look
Into the Endless Promise, nor should brook
One prying doubt to shake his faith sublime;
To him the earth is ever in her prime
And dewiness of morning; he can see
Good lying hid, from all eternity,
Within the teeming womb of sin and crime;
His soul should not be cramped by any bar,
His nobleness should be so Godlike high,
That his least deed is perfect as a star,
His common look majestic as the sky,
And all o'erflooded with a light from far,
Undimmed by clouds of weak mortality.

XX. TO M. O. S.

MARY, since first I knew thee, to this hour,
My love hath deepened, with my wiser sense
Of what in Woman is to reverence;
Thy clear heart, fresh as e'er was forest-flower,
Still opens more to me its beauteous dower;—
But let praise hush,—Love asks no evidence
To prove itself well-placed; we know not whence
It gleans the straws that thatch its humble bower:
We can but say we found it in the heart,
Spring of all sweetest thoughts, arch foe of blame,
Sower of flowers in the dusty mart,
Pure vestal of the poet's holy flame,—
This is enough, and we have done our part
If we but keep it spotless as it came.

XXI

Our love is not a fading, earthly flower:
Its wingèd seed dropped down from Paradise,
And, nursed by day and night, by sun and shower,
Doth momently to fresher beauty rise:
To us the leafless autumn is not bare,
Nor winter's rattling boughs lack lusty green.
Our summer hearts make summer's fullness, where
No leaf, or bud, or blossom may be seen:
For nature's life in love's deep life doth lie,
Love,—whose forgetfulness is beauty's death,
Whose mystic key these cells of Thou and I
Into the infinite freedom openeth,
And makes the body's dark and narrow grate
The wide-flung leaves of Heaven's palace-gate.

XXII. IN ABSENCE

These rugged, wintry days I scarce could bear,
Did I not know, that, in the early spring,
When wild March winds upon their errands sing,
Thou wouldst return, bursting on this still air,
Like those same winds, when, startled from their lair,
They hunt up violets, and free swift brooks
From icy cares, even as thy clear looks
Bid my heart bloom, and sing, and break all care:
When drops with welcome rain the April day,
My flowers shall find their April in thine eyes,
Save there the rain in dreamy clouds doth stay,
As loath to fall out of those happy skies;
Yet sure, my love, thou art most like to May,
That comes with steady sun when April dies.

XXIII. WENDELL PHILLIPS

He stood upon the world's broad threshold; wide
The din of battle and of slaughter rose;
He saw God stand upon the weaker side,
That sank in seeming loss before its foes:
Many there were who made great haste and sold
Unto the cunning enemy their swords,
He scorned their gifts of fame, and power, and gold,
And, underneath their soft and flowery words,
Heard the cold serpent hiss; therefore he went
And humbly joined him to the weaker part,
Fanatic named, and fool, yet well content
So he could be the nearer to God's heart,
And feel its solemn pulses sending blood
Through all the widespread veins of endless good.

XXIV. THE STREET

THEY pass me by like shadows, crowds on crowds,
Dim ghosts of men, that hover to and fro,
Hugging their bodies round them like thin shrouds
Wherein their souls were buried long ago :
They trampled on their youth, and faith, and love,
They cast their hope of human-kind away,
With Heaven's clear messages they madly strove,
And conquered,—and their spirits turned to clay :
Lo ! how they wander round the world, their grave,
Whose ever-gaping maw by such is fed,
Gibbering at living men, and idly rave,
' We, only, truly live, but ye are dead.'
Alas ! poor fools, the anointed eye may trace
A dead soul's epitaph in every face !

XXV

I GRIEVE not that ripe Knowledge takes away
The charm that Nature to my childhood wore,
For, with that insight, cometh, day by day,
A greater bliss than wonder was before ;
The real doth not clip the poet's wings,—
To win the secret of a weed's plain heart
Reveals some clue to spiritual things,
And stumbling guess becomes firm-footed art :
Flowers are not flowers unto the poet's eyes,
Their beauty thrills him by an inward sense ;
He knows that outward seemings are but lies,
Or, at the most, but earthly shadows, whence
The soul that looks within for truth may guess
The presence of some wondrous heavenliness.

XXVI. TO J. R. GIDDINGS

GIDDINGS, far rougher names than thine have grown
Smoother than honey on the lips of men ;
And thou shalt ay be honourably known,
As one who bravely used his tongue and pen,
As best befits a freeman,—even for those
To whom our Law's unblushing front denies
A right to plead against the lifelong woes
Which are the Negro's glimpse of Freedom's skies :
Fear nothing, and hope all things, as the Right
Alone may do securely ; every hour
The thrones of Ignorance and ancient Night
Lose somewhat of their long-usurpèd power,
And Freedom's lightest word can make them shiver
With a base dread that clings to them forever.

XXVII

I THOUGHT our love at full, but I did err ;
Joy's wreath drooped o'er mine eyes ; I could not see
That sorrow in our happy world must be
Love's deepest spokesman and interpreter :
But, as a mother feels her child first stir
Under her heart, so felt I instantly
Deep in my soul another bond to thee
Thrill with that life we saw depart from her ;
O mother of our angel child ! twice dear !
Death knits as well as parts, and still, I wis,
Her tender radiance shall infold us here,
Even as the light, borne up by inward bliss,
Threads the void glooms of space without a fear,
To print on farthest stars her pitying kiss.

L'ENVOI

WHETHER my heart hath wiser grown or not,
In these three years, since I to thee inscribed,
Mine own betrothed, the firstlings of my muse,—
Poor windfalls of unripe experience,
Young buds plucked hastily by childish hands
Not patient to await more full-blown flowers,—
⁕At least it hath seen more of life and men,
And pondered more, and grown a shade more sad ;
Yet with no loss of hope or settled trust
In the benignness of that Providence   10
Which shapes from out our elements awry
The grace and order that we wonder at,
The mystic harmony of right and wrong,
Both working out His wisdom and our good :
A trust, Beloved, chiefly learned of thee,
Who hast that gift of patient tenderness,
The instinctive wisdom of a woman's heart.
They tell us that our land was made for song,
With its huge rivers and sky-piercing peaks,
Its sealike lakes and mighty cataracts,   20
Its forests vast and hoar, and prairies wide,
And mounds that tell of wondrous tribes extinct.
But Poesy springs not from rocks and woods ;
Her womb and cradle are the human heart,
And she can find a nobler theme for song
In the most loathsome man that blasts the sight
Than in the broad expanse of sea and shore
Between the frozen deserts of the poles.
All nations have their message from on high,
Each the messiah of some central thought,   30

For the fulfilment and delight of Man :
One has to teach that labour is divine ;
Another Freedom ; and another Mind ;
And all, that God is open-eyed and just,
The happy centre and calm heart of all.

Are, then, our woods, our mountains, and our streams,
Needful to teach our poets how to sing ?
O maiden rare, far other thoughts were ours,
When we have sat by ocean's foaming marge,
And watched the waves leap roaring on the rocks,   40
Than young Leander and his Hero had,
Gazing from Sestos to the other shore.
The moon looks down and ocean worships her,
Stars rise and set, and seasons come and go
Even as they did in Homer's elder time,
But we behold them not with Grecian eyes :
Then they were types of beauty and of strength,
But now of freedom, unconfined and pure,
Subject alone to Order's higher law.
What cares the Russian serf or Southern slave   50
Though we should speak as man spake never yet
Of gleaming Hudson's broad magnificence,
Or green Niagara's never-ending roar ?
Our country hath a gospel of her own
To preach and practise before all the world,—
The freedom and divinity of man,
The glorious claims of human brotherhood,—
Which to pay nobly, as a freeman should,
Gains the sole wealth that will not fly away,—
And the soul's fealty to none but God.   60
These are realities, which make the shows
Of outward Nature, be they ne'er so grand,
Seem small, and worthless, and contemptible.
These are the mountain-summits for our bards,
Which stretch far upward into heaven itself,
And give such widespread and exulting view
Of hope, and faith, and onward destiny,
That shrunk Parnassus to a molehill dwindles.
Our new Atlantis, like a morning-star,
Silvers the mirk face of slow-yielding Night,   70
The herald of a fuller truth than yet
Hath gleamed upon the upraised face of Man
Since the earth glittered in her stainless prime,—
Of a more glorious sunrise than of old
Drew wondrous melodies from Memnon huge,
Yea, draws them still, though now he sit waist-deep
In the ingulfing flood of whirling sand,
And look across the wastes of endless grey,

Sole wreck, where once his hundred-gated Thebes
Pained with her mighty hum the calm, blue heaven :   80
Shall the dull stone pay grateful orisons,
And we till noonday bar the splendour out,
Lest it reproach and chide our sluggard hearts,
Warm-nestled in the down of Prejudice,
And be content, though clad with angel-wings,
Close-clipped, to hop about from perch to perch,
In paltry cages of dead men's dead thoughts ?
O, rather, like the skylark, soar and sing,
And let our gushing songs befit the dawn
And sunrise, and the yet unshaken dew   90
Brimming the chalice of each full-blown hope,
Whose blithe front turns to greet the growing day !
Never had poets such high call before,
Never can poets hope for higher one,
And, if they be but faithful to their trust,
Earth will remember them with love and joy,
And O, far better, God will not forget.
For he who settles Freedom's principles
Writes the death-warrant of all tyranny ;
Who speaks the truth stabs Falsehood to the heart,   100
And his mere word makes despots tremble more
Than ever Brutus with his dagger could.
Wait for no hints from waterfalls or woods,
Nor dream that tales of red men, brute and fierce,
Repay the finding of this Western World,
Or needed half the globe to give them birth :
Spirit supreme of Freedom ! not for this
Did great Columbus tame his eagle soul
To jostle with the daws that perch in courts ;
Not for this, friendless, on an unknown sea,   110
Coping with mad waves and more mutinous spirits,
Battled he with the dreadful ache at heart
Which tempts, with devilish subtleties of doubt,
The hermit of that loneliest solitude,
The silent desert of a great New Thought ;
Though loud Niagara were to-day struck dumb,
Yet would this cataract of boiling life
Rush plunging on and on to endless deeps,
And utter thunder till the world shall cease,—
A thunder worthy of the poet's song,   120
And which alone can fill it with true life.
The high evangel to our country granted
Could make apostles, yea, with tongues of fire,
Of hearts half-darkened back again to clay !
'Tis the soul only that is national,
And he who pays true loyalty to that
Alone can claim the wreath of patriotism.

Beloved! if I wander far and oft
From that which I believe, and feel, and know,
Thou wilt forgive, not with a sorrowing heart,   130
But with a strengthened hope of better things;
Knowing that I, though often blind and false
To those I love, and O, more false than all
Unto myself, have been most true to thee,
And that whoso in one thing hath been true
Can be as true in all. Therefore thy hope
May yet not prove unfruitful, and thy love
Meet, day by day, with less unworthy thanks,
Whether, as now, we journey hand in hand,
Or, parted in the body, yet are one   140
In spirit and the love of holy things.

MISCELLANEOUS POEMS

A LEGEND OF BRITTANY

PART FIRST

I

Fair as a summer dream was Margaret,—
   Such dream as in a poet's soul might start,
Musing of old loves while the moon doth set:
   Her hair was not more sunny than her heart,
Though like a natural golden coronet
   It circled her dear head with careless art,
Mocking the sunshine, that would fain have lent
To its frank grace a richer ornament.

II

His loved one's eyes could poet ever speak,
   So kind, so dewy, and so deep were hers,—
But, while he strives, the choicest phrase, too weak,
   Their glad reflection in his spirit blurs;
As one may see a dream dissolve and break
   Out of his grasp when he to tell it stirs,
Like that sad Dryad doomed no more to bless
The mortal who revealed her loveliness.

III

She dwelt forever in a region bright,
  Peopled with living fancies of her own,
Where naught could come but visions of delight,
  Far, far aloof from earth's eternal moan:
A summer cloud thrilled through with rosy light,
  Floating beneath the blue sky all alone,
Her spirit wandered by itself, and won
A golden edge from some unsetting sun.

IV

The heart grows richer that its lot is poor,—
  God blesses want with larger sympathies,—
Love enters gladliest at the humble door,
  And makes the cot a palace with his eyes;
So Margaret's heart a softer beauty wore,
  And grew in gentleness and patience wise,
For she was but a simple herdsman's child,
A lily chance-sown in the rugged wild.

V

There was no beauty of the wood or field
  But she its fragrant bosom-secret knew,
Nor any but to her would freely yield
  Some grace that in her soul took root and grew:
Nature to her glowed ever new-revealed,
  All rosy-fresh with innocent morning dew,
And looked into her heart with dim, sweet eyes
That left it full of sylvan memories.

VI

O, what a face was hers to brighten light,
  And give back sunshine with an added glow,
To wile each moment with a fresh delight,
  And part of memory's best contentment grow!
O, how her voice, as with an inmate's right,
  Into the strangest heart would welcome go,
And make it sweet, and ready to become
Of white and gracious thoughts the chosen home!

VII

None looked upon her but he straightway thought
  Of all the greenest depths of country cheer,
And into each one's heart was freshly brought
  What was to him the sweetest time of year,
So was her every look and motion fraught
  With out-of-door delights and forest lere;
Not the first violet on a woodland lea
Seemed a more visible gift of Spring than she.

VIII

Is love learned only out of poets' books ?
  Is there not somewhat in the dropping flood,
And in the nunneries of silent nooks,
  And in the murmured longing of the wood,
That could make Margaret dream of love-lorn looks,
  And stir a thrilling mystery in her blood
More trembly secret than Aurora's tear
Shed in the bosom of an eglatere ?

IX

Full many a sweet forewarning hath the mind,
  Full many a whispering of vague desire,
Ere comes the nature destined to unbind
  Its virgin zone, and all its deeps inspire,—
Low stirrings in the leaves, before the wind
  Wake all the green strings of the forest lyre,
Faint heatings in the calyx, ere the rose
Its warm voluptuous breast doth all unclose.

X

Long in its dim recesses pines the spirit,
  Wildered and dark, despairingly alone ;
Though many a shape of beauty wander near it,
  And many a wild and half-remembered tone
Tremble from the divine abyss to cheer it,
  Yet still it knows that there is only one
Before whom it can kneel and tribute bring,
At once a happy vassal and a king.

XI

To feel a want, yet scarce know what it is,
  To seek one nature that is always new,
Whose glance is warmer than another's kiss,
  Whom we can bare our inmost beauty to,
Nor feel deserted afterwards,—for this
  But with our destined co-mate we can do,—
Such longing instinct fills the mighty scope
Of the young soul with one mysterious hope.

XII

So Margaret's heart grew brimming with the lore
  Of love's enticing secrets ; and although
She had found none to cast it down before,
  Yet oft to Fancy's chapel she would go
To pay her vows, and count the rosary o'er
  Of her love's promised graces :—haply so
Miranda's hope had pictured Ferdinand
Long ere the gaunt wave tossed him on the strand.

XIII

A new-made star that swims the lonely gloom,
  Unwedded yet and longing for the sun,
Whose beams, the bride-gifts of the lavish groom,
  Blithely to crown the virgin planet run,
Her being was, watching to see the bloom
  Of love's fresh sunrise roofing one by one
Its clouds with gold, a triumph-arch to be
For him who came to hold her heart in fee.

XIV

Not far from Margaret's cottage dwelt a knight
  Of the proud Templars, a sworn celibate,
Whose heart in secret fed upon the light
  And dew of her ripe beauty, through the grate
Of his close vow catching what gleams he might
  Of the free heaven, and cursing all too late
The cruel faith whose black walls hemmed him in
And turned life's crowning bliss to deadly sin.

XV

For he had met her in the wood by chance,
  And, having drunk her beauty's wildering spell,
His heart shook like the pennon of a lance
  That quivers in a breeze's sudden swell,
And thenceforth, in a close-infolded trance,
  From mistily golden deep to deep he fell ;
Till earth did waver and fade far away
Beneath the hope in whose warm arms he lay.

XVI

A dark, proud man he was, whose half-blown youth
  Had shed its blossoms even in opening,
Leaving a few that with more winning ruth
  Trembling around grave manhood's stem might cling,
More sad than cheery, making, in good sooth,
  Like the fringed gentian, a late autumn spring :—
A twilight nature, braided light and gloom,
A youth half-smiling by an open tomb.

XVII

Fair as an angel, who yet inly wore
  A wrinkled heart foreboding his near fall ;
Who saw him alway wished to know him more,
  As if he were some fate's defiant thrall
And nursed a dreaded secret at his core ;
  Little he loved, but power the most of all,
And that he seemed to scorn, as one who knew
By what foul paths men choose to crawl thereto.

XVIII

He had been noble, but some great deceit
  Had turned his better instinct to a vice :
He strove to think the world was all a cheat,
  That power and fame were cheap at any price,
That the sure way of being shortly great
  Was even to play life's game with loaded dice,
Since he had tried the honest play and found
That vice and virtue differed but in sound.

XIX

Yet Margaret's sight redeemed him for a space
  From his own thraldom ; man could never be
A hypocrite when first such maiden grace
  Smiled in upon his heart ; the agony
Of wearing all day long a lying face
  Fell lightly from him, and, a moment free,
Erect with wakened faith his spirit stood
And scorned the weakness of his demon-mood.

XX

Like a sweet wind-harp to him was her thought,
  Which would not let the common air come near,
Till from its dim enchantment it had caught
  A musical tenderness that brimmed his ear
With sweetness more ethereal than aught
  Save silver-dropping snatches that whilere
Rained down from some sad angel's faithful harp
To cool her fallen lover's anguish sharp.

XXI

Deep in the forest was a little dell
  High overarchèd with the leafy sweep
Of a broad oak, through whose gnarled roots there fell
  A slender rill that sung itself asleep
Where its continuous toil had scooped a well
  To please the fairy folk ; breathlessly deep
The stillness was, save when the dreaming brook
From its small urn a drizzly murmur shook.

XXII

The wooded hills sloped upward all around
  With gradual rise, and made an even rim,
So that it seemed a mighty casque unbound
  From some huge Titan's brow to lighten him,
Ages ago, and left upon the ground,
  Where the slow soil had mossed it to the brim,
Till after countless centuries it grew
Into this dell, the haunt of noontide dew.

XXIII

Dim vistas, sprinkled o'er with sun-flecked green,
  Wound through the thickset trunks on every side,
And, toward the west, in fancy might be seen
  A Gothic window in its blazing pride,
When the low sun, two arching elms between,
  Lit up the leaves beyond, which, autumn-dyed
With lavish hues, would into splendour start,
Shaming the laboured panes of richest art.

XXIV

Here, leaning once against the old oak's trunk,
  Mordred, for such was the young Templar's name,
Saw Margaret come ; unseen, the falcon shrunk
  From the meek dove ; sharp thrills of tingling flame
Made him forget that he was vowed a monk,
  And all the outworks of his pride o'ercame :
Flooded he seemed with bright delicious pain,
As if a star had burst within his brain.

XXV

Such power hath beauty and frank innocence :
  A flower bloomed forth, that sunshine glad to bless,
Even from his love's long leafless stem ; the sense
  Of exile from Hope's happy realm grew less,
And thoughts of childish peace, he knew not whence,
  Thronged round his heart with many an old caress,
Melting the frost there into pearly dew
That mirrored back his nature's morning-blue.

XXVI

She turned and saw him, but she felt no dread,
  Her purity, like adamantine mail,
Did so encircle her ; and yet her head
  She drooped, and made her golden hair her veil,
Through which a glow of rosiest lustre spread,
  Then faded, and anon she stood all pale,
As snow o'er which a blush of northern-light
Suddenly reddens, and as soon grows white.

XXVII

She thought of Tristrem and of Lancilot,
  Of all her dreams, and of kind fairies' might,
And how that dell was deemed a haunted spot,
  Until there grew a mist before her sight,
And where the present was she half forgot,
  Borne backward through the realms of old delight,—
Then, starting up awake, she would have gone,
Yet almost wished it might not be alone.

XXVIII

How they went home together through the wood,
  And how all life seemed focussed into one
Thought-dazzling spot that set ablaze the blood,
  What need to tell ?   Fit language there is none
For the heart's deepest things. Who ever wooed
  As in his boyish hope he would have done ?
For, when the soul is fullest, the hushed tongue
Voicelessly trembles like a lute unstrung.

XXIX

But all things carry the heart's messages
  And know it not, nor doth the heart well know,
But Nature hath her will ; even as the bees,
  Blithe go-betweens, fly singing to and fro
With the fruit-quickening pollen ;—hard if these
  Found not some all unthought-of way to show
Their secret each to each ; and so they did,
And one heart's flower-dust into the other slid.

XXX

Young hearts are free ; the selfish world it is
  That turns them miserly and cold as stone,
And makes them clutch their fingers on the bliss
  Which but in giving truly is their own ;—
She had no dreams of barter, asked not his,
  But gave hers freely as she would have thrown
A rose to him, or as that rose gives forth
Its generous fragrance, thoughtless of its worth.

XXXI

Her summer nature felt a need to bless,
  And a like longing to be blest again ;
So, from her sky-like spirit, gentleness
  Dropt ever like a sunlit fall of rain,
And his beneath drank in the bright caress
  As thirstily as would a parchèd plain,
That long hath watched the showers of sloping grey
For ever, ever, falling far away.

XXXII

How should she dream of ill ? the heart filled quite
  With sunshine, like the shepherd's-clock at noon,
Closes its leaves around its warm delight ;
  Whate'er in life is harsh or out of tune
Is all shut out, no boding shade of blight
  Can pierce the opiate ether of its swoon :
Love is but blind as thoughtful justice is,
But naught can be so wanton-blind as bliss.

XXXIII

All beauty and all life he was to her ;
  She questioned not his love, she only knew
That she loved him, and not a pulse could stir
  In her whole frame but quivered through and through
With this glad thought, and was a minister
  To do him fealty and service true,
Like golden ripples hasting to the land
To wreck their freight of sunshine on the strand.

XXXIV

O dewy dawn of love ! O hopes that are
  Hung high, like the cliff-swallow's perilous nest,
Most like to fall when fullest, and that jar
  With every heavier billow ! O unrest
Than balmiest deeps of quiet sweeter far !
  How did ye triumph now in Margaret's breast,
Making it readier to shrink and start
Than quivering gold of the pond-lily's heart !

XXXV

Here let us pause : O, would the soul might ever
  Achieve its immortality in youth,
When nothing yet hath damped its high endeavour
  After the starry energy of truth !
Here let us pause, and for a moment sever
  This gleam of sunshine from the days unruth
That sometime come to all, for it is good
To lengthen to the last a sunny mood.

PART SECOND

I

As one who, from the sunshine and the green,
  Enters the solid darkness of a cave,
Nor knows what precipice or pit unseen
  May yawn before him with its sudden grave,
And, with hushed breath, doth often forward lean,
  Dreaming he hears the plashing of a wave
Dimly below, or feels a damper air
From out some dreary chasm, he knows not where ;

II

So, from the sunshine and the green of love,
  We enter on our story's darker part ;
And, though the horror of it well may move
  An impulse of repugnance in the heart,
Yet let us think, that, as there's naught above
  The all-embracing atmosphere of Art,
So also there is naught that falls below
Her generous reach, though grimed with guilt and woe.

III

Her fittest triumph is to show that good
    Lurks in the heart of evil evermore,
That love, though scorned, and outcast, and withstood,
    Can without end forgive, and yet have store ;
God's love and man's are of the selfsame blood,
    And He can see that always at the door
Of foulest hearts the angel-nature yet
Knocks to return and cancel all its debt.

IV

It ever is weak falsehood's destiny
    That her thick mask turns crystal to let through
The unsuspicious eyes of honesty ;
    But Margaret's heart was too sincere and true
Aught but plain truth and faithfulness to see,
    And Mordred's for a time a little grew
To be like hers, won by the mild reproof
Of those kind eyes that kept all doubt aloof.

V

Full oft they met, as dawn and twilight meet
    In northern climes ; she full of growing day
As he of darkness, which before her feet
    Shrank gradual, and faded quite away,
Soon to return ; for power had made love sweet
    To him, and, when his will had gained full sway,
The taste began to pall ; for never power
Can sate the hungry soul beyond an hour.

VI

He fell as doth the tempter ever fall,
    Even in the gaining of his loathsome end ;
God doth not work as man works, but makes all
    The crooked paths of ill to goodness tend ;
Let him judge Margaret ! If to be the thrall
    Of love, and faith too generous to defend
Its very life from him she loved, be sin,
What hope of grace may the seducer win ?

VII

Grim-hearted world, that look'st with Levite eyes
    On those poor fallen by too much faith in man,
She that upon thy freezing threshold lies,
    Starved to more sinning by thy savage ban,
Seeking that refuge because foulest vice
    More godlike than thy virtue is, whose span
Shuts out the wretched only, is more free
To enter Heaven than thou wilt ever be !

VIII

Thou wilt not let her wash thy dainty feet
   With such salt things as tears, or with rude hair
Dry them, soft Pharisee, that sitt'st at meat
   With him who made her such, and speak'st him fair,
Leaving God's wandering lamb the while to bleat
   Unheeded, shivering in the pitiless air:
Thou hast made prisoned virtue show more wan
And haggard than a vice to look upon.

IX

Now many months flew by, and weary grew
   To Margaret the sight of happy things;
Blight fell on all her flowers, instead of dew;
   Shut round her heart were now the joyous wings
Wherewith it wont to soar; yet not untrue,
   Though tempted much, her woman's nature clings
To its first pure belief, and with sad eyes
Looks backward o'er the gate of Paradise.

X

And so, though altered Mordred came less oft,
   And winter frowned where spring had laughed before
In his strange eyes, yet half her sadness doffed,
   And in her silent patience loved him more:
Sorrow had made her soft heart yet more soft,
   And a new life within her own she bore
Which made her tenderer, as she felt it move
Beneath her breast, a refuge for her love.

XI

This babe, she thought, would surely bring him back,
   And be a bond forever them between;
Before its eyes the sullen tempest-rack
   Would fade, and leave the face of heaven serene;
And love's return doth more than fill the lack,
   Which in his absence withered the heart's green:
And yet a dim foreboding still would flit
Between her and her hope to darken it.

XII

She could not figure forth a happy fate,
   Even for this life from heaven so newly come;
The earth must needs be doubly desolate
   To him scarce parted from a fairer home:
Such boding heavier on her bosom sate
   One night, as, standing in the twilight gloom,
She strained her eyes beyond that dizzy verge
At whose foot faintly breaks the future's surge.

XIII

Poor little spirit ! naught but shame and woe
   Nurse the sick heart whose lifeblood nurses thine :
Yet not those only ; love hath triumphed so,
   As for thy sake makes sorrow more divine :
And yet, though thou be pure, the world is foe
    To purity, if born in such a shrine ;
And, having trampled it for struggling thence,
Smiles to itself, and calls it Providence.

XIV

As thus she mused, a shadow seemed to rise
   From out her thought, and turn to dreariness
All blissful hopes and sunny memories,
   And the quick blood would curdle up and press
About her heart, which seemed to shut its eyes
   And hush itself, as who with shuddering guess
Harks through the gloom and dreads e'en now to feel
Through his hot breast the icy slide of steel.

XV

But, at that heart-beat, while in dread she was,
   In the low wind the honeysuckles gleam,
A dewy thrill flits through the heavy grass,
   And, looking forth, she saw, as in a dream,
Within the wood the moonlight's shadowy mass :
   Night's starry heart yearning to hers doth seem,
And the deep sky, full-hearted with the moon,
Folds round her all the happiness of June.

XVI

What fear could face a heaven and earth like this ?
   What silveriest cloud could hang 'neath such a sky ?
A tide of wondrous and unwonted bliss
   Rolls back through all her pulses suddenly,
As if some seraph, who had learned to kiss
   From the fair daughters of the world gone by,
Had wedded so his fallen light with hers,
Such sweet, strange joy through soul and body stirs.

XVII

Now seek we Mordred : he who did not fear
   The crime, yet fears the latent consequence :
If it should reach a brother Templar's ear,
   It haply might be made a good pretence
To cheat him of the hope he held most dear ;
   For he had spared no thought's or deed's expense,
That by and by might help his wish to clip
Its darling bride,—the high grandmastership.

XVIII

The apathy, ere a crime resolved is done,
  Is scarce less dreadful than remorse for crime ;
By no allurement can the soul be won
  From brooding o'er the weary creep of time ;
Mordred stole forth into the happy sun,
  Striving to hum a scrap of Breton rhyme,
But the sky struck him speechless, and he tried
In vain to summon up his callous pride.

XIX

In the courtyard a fountain leaped alway,
  A Triton blowing jewels through his shell
Into the sunshine ; Mordred turned away,
  Weary because the stone face did not tell
Of weariness, nor could he bear to-day,
  Heartsick, to hear the patient sink and swell
Of winds among the leaves, or golden bees
Drowsily humming in the orange-trees.

XX

All happy sights and sounds now came to him
  Like a reproach : he wandered far and wide,
Following the lead of his unquiet whim,
  But still there went a something at his side
That made the cool breeze hot, the sunshine dim ;
  It would not flee, it could not be defied,
He could not see it, but he felt it there,
By the damp chill that crept among his hair.

XXI

Day wore at last ; the evening-star arose,
  And throbbing in the sky grew red and set ;
Then with a guilty, wavering step he goes
  To the hid nook where they so oft had met
In happier season, for his heart well knows
  That he is sure to find poor Margaret
Watching and waiting there with lovelorn breast
Around her young dream's rudely scattered nest.

XXII

Why follow here that grim old chronicle
  Which counts the dagger-strokes and drops of blood ?
Enough that Margaret by his mad steel fell,
  Unmoved by murder from her trusting mood,
Smiling on him as Heaven smiles on Hell,
  With a sad love, remembering when he stood
Not fallen yet, the unsealer of her heart,
Of all her holy dreams the holiest part.

XXIII

His crime complete, scarce knowing what he did
   (So goes the tale), beneath the altar there
In the high church the stiffening corpse he hid,
   And then, to 'scape that suffocating air,
Like a scared ghoul out of the porch he slid ;
   But his strained eyes saw blood-spots everywhere,
And ghastly faces thrust themselves between
His soul and hopes of peace with blasting mien.

XXIV

His heart went out within him like a spark
   Dropt in the sea ; wherever he made bold
To turn his eyes, he saw, all stiff and stark,
   Pale Margaret lying dead ; the lavish gold
Of her loose hair seemed in the cloudy dark
   To spread a glory, and a thousandfold
More strangely pale and beautiful she grew :
Her silence stabbed his conscience through and through :

XXV

Or visions of past days,—a mother's eyes
   That smiled down on the fair boy at her knee,
Whose happy upturned face to hers replies,—
   He saw sometimes : or Margaret mournfully
Gazed on him full of doubt, as one who tries
   To crush belief that does love injury ;
Then she would wring her hands, but soon again
Love's patience glimmered out through cloudy pain.

XXVI

Meanwhile he dared not go and steal away
   The silent, dead-cold witness of his sin ;
He had not feared the life, but that dull clay,
   Those open eyes that showed the death within,
Would surely stare him mad ; yet all the day
   A dreadful impulse, whence his will could win
No refuge, made him linger in the aisle,
Freezing with his wan look each greeting smile.

XXVII

Now, on the second day there was to be
   A festival in church : from far and near
Came flocking in the sunburnt peasantry,
   And knights and dames with stately antique cheer,
Blazing with pomp, as if all faërie
   Had emptied her quaint halls, or, as it were,
The illuminated marge of some old book,
While we were gazing, life and motion took.

XXVIII

When all were entered, and the roving eyes
　Of all were stayed, some upon faces bright,
Some on the priests, some on the traceries
　That decked the slumber of a marble knight,
And all the rustlings over that arise
　From recognizing tokens of delight,
When friendly glances meet,—then silent ease
Spread o'er the multitude by slow degrees.

XXIX

Then swelled the organ : up through choir and nave
　The music trembled with an inward thrill
Of bliss at its own grandeur : wave on wave
　Its flood of mellow thunder rose, until
The hushed air shivered with the throb it gave,
　Then, poising for a moment, it stood still,
And sank and rose again, to burst in spray
That wandered into silence far away.

XXX

Like to a mighty heart the music seemed,
　That yearns with melodies it cannot speak,
Until, in grand despair of what it dreamed,
　In the agony of effort it doth break,
Yet triumphs breaking ; on it rushed and streamed
　And wantoned in its might, as when a lake,
Long pent among the mountains, bursts its walls
And in one crowding gush leaps forth and falls.

XXXI

Deeper and deeper shudders shook the air,
　As the huge bass kept gathering heavily,
Like thunder when it rouses in its lair,
　And with its hoarse growl shakes the low-hung sky,
It grew up like a darkness everywhere,
　Filling the vast cathedral ;—suddenly,
From the dense mass a boy's clear treble broke
Like lightning, and the full-toned choir awoke.

XXXII

Through gorgeous windows shone the sun aslant,
　Brimming the church with gold and purple mist,
Meet atmosphere to bosom that rich chant,
　Where fifty voices in one strand did twist
Their varicoloured tones, and left no want
　To the delighted soul, which sank abyssed
In the warm music cloud, while, far below,
The organ heaved its surges to and fro.

XXXIII

As if a lark should suddenly drop dead
  While the blue air yet trembled with its song,
So snapped at once that music's golden thread,
  Struck by a nameless fear that leapt along
From heart to heart, and like a shadow spread
  With instantaneous shiver through the throng,
So that some glanced behind, as half aware
A hideous shape of dread were standing there.

XXXIV

As when a crowd of pale men gather round,
  Watching an eddy in the leaden deep,
From which they deem the body of one drowned
  Will be cast forth, from face to face doth creep
An eager dread that holds all tongues fast bound
  Until the horror, with a ghastly leap,
Starts up, its dead blue arms stretched aimlessly,
Heaved with the swinging of the careless sea,—

XXXV

So in the faces of all these there grew,
  As by one impulse, a dark, freezing awe,
Which, with a fearful fascination drew
  All eyes toward the altar ; damp and raw
The air grew suddenly, and no man knew
  Whether perchance his silent neighbour saw
The dreadful thing which all were sure would rise
To scare the strained lids wider from their eyes.

XXXVI

The incense trembled as it upward sent
  Its slow, uncertain thread of wandering blue,
As 't were the only living element
  In all the church, so deep the stillness grew ;
It seemed one might have heard it, as it went,
  Give out an audible rustle, curling through
The midnight silence of that awestruck air,
More hushed than death, though so much life was there.

XXXVII

Nothing they saw, but a low voice was heard
  Threading the ominous silence of that fear,
Gentle and terrorless as if a bird,
  Wakened by some volcano's glare, should cheer
The murk air with his song ; yet every word
  In the cathedral's farthest arch seemed near,
As if it spoke to every one apart,
Like the clear voice of conscience in each heart.

XXXVIII

' O Rest, to weary hearts thou art most dear !
　O Silence, after life's bewildering din,
Thou art most welcome, whether in the sear
　Days of our age thou comest, or we win
Thy poppy-wreath in youth ! then wherefore here
　Linger I yet, once free to enter in
At that wished gate which gentle Death doth ope,
Into the boundless realm of strength and hope ?

XXXIX

' Think not in death my love could ever cease ;
　If thou wast false, more need there is for me
Still to be true ;　that slumber were not peace,
　If 't were unvisited with dreams of thee :
And thou hadst never heard such words as these,
　Save that in heaven I must forever be
Most comfortless and wretched, seeing this
Our unbaptizèd babe shut out from bliss.

XL

' This little spirit with imploring eyes
　Wanders alone the dreary wild of space ;
The shadow of his pain forever lies
　Upon my soul in this new dwelling-place ;
His loneliness makes me in Paradise
　More lonely, and, unless I see his face,
Even here for grief could I lie down and die,
Save for my curse of immortality.

XLI

' World after world he sees around him swim
　Crowded with happy souls, that take no heed
Of the sad eyes that from the night's faint rim
　Gaze sick with longing on them as they speed
With golden gates, that only shut on him ;
　And shapes sometimes from Hell's abysses freed
Flap darkly by him, with enormous sweep
Of wings that roughen wide the pitchy deep.

XLII

' I am a mother,—spirits do not shake
　This much of earth from them,—and I must pine
Till I can feel his little hands, and take
　His weary head upon this heart of mine ;
And, might it be, full gladly for his sake
　Would I this solitude of bliss resign,
And be shut out of Heaven to dwell with him
Forever in that silence drear and dim.

XLIII

' I strove to hush my soul, and would not speak
    At first, for thy dear sake ; a woman's love
Is mighty, but a mother's heart is weak,
    And by its weakness overcomes ; I strove
To smother bitter thoughts with patience meek,
    But still in the abyss my soul would rove,
Seeking my child, and drove me here to claim
The rite that gives him peace in Christ's dear name.

XLIV

' I sit and weep while blessed spirits sing ;
    I can but long and pine the while they praise,
And, leaning o'er the wall of Heaven, I fling
    My voice to where I deem my infant strays,
Like a robbed bird that cries in vain to bring
    Her nestlings back beneath her wings' embrace ;
But still he answers not, and I but know
That Heaven and earth are both alike in woe.'

XLV

Then the pale priests, with ceremony due,
    Baptized the child within its dreadful tomb
Beneath that mother's heart, whose instinct true
    Star-like had battled down the triple gloom
Of sorrow, love, and death : young maidens, too,
    Strewed the pale corpse with many a milkwhite bloom,
And parted the bright hair, and on the breast
Crossed the unconscious hands in sign of rest.

XLVI

Some said, that, when the priest had sprinkled o'er
    The consecrated drops, they seemed to hear
A sigh, as of some heart from travail sore
    Released, and then two voices singing clear,
Misereatur Deus, more and more
    Fading far upward, and their ghastly fear
Fell from them with that sound, as bodies fall
From souls upspringing to celestial hall.

PROMETHEUS

One after one the stars have risen and set,
Sparkling upon the hoarfrost on my chain :
The Bear, that prowled all night about the fold
Of the North-star, hath shrunk into his den,
Scared by the blithesome footsteps of the Dawn,
Whose blushing smile floods all the Orient ;

And now bright Lucifer grows less and less,
Into the heaven's blue quiet deep-withdrawn.
Sunless and starless all, the desert sky
Arches above me, empty as this heart 10
For ages hath been empty of all joy,
Except to brood upon its silent hope,
As o'er its hope of day the sky doth now.
All night have I heard voices: deeper yet
The deep low breathing of the silence grew,
While all about, muffled in awe, there stood
Shadows, or forms, or both, clear-felt at heart,
But, when I turned to front them, far along
Only a shudder through the midnight ran,
And the dense stillness walled me closer round. 20
But still I heard them wander up and down
That solitude, and flappings of dusk wings
Did mingle with them, whether of those hags
Let slip upon me once from Hades deep,
Or of yet direr torments, if such be,
I could but guess; and then toward me came
A shape as of a woman: very pale
It was, and calm; its cold eyes did not move,
And mine moved not, but only stared on them.
Their fixèd awe went through my brain like ice; 30
A skeleton hand seemed clutching at my heart,
And a sharp chill, as if a dank night fog
Suddenly closed me in, was all I felt:
And then, methought, I heard a freezing sigh,
A long, deep, shivering sigh, as from blue lips
Stiffening in death, close to mine ear. I thought
Some doom was close upon me, and I looked
And saw the red moon through the heavy mist,
Just setting, and it seemed as it were falling,
Or reeling to its fall, so dim and dead 40
And palsy-struck it looked. Then all sounds merged
Into the rising surges of the pines,
Which, leagues below me, clothing the gaunt loins
Of ancient Caucasus with hairy strength,
Sent up a murmur in the morning wind,
Sad as the wail that from the populous earth
All day and night to high Olympus soars,
Fit incense to thy wicked throne, O Jove!

Thy hated name is tossed once more in scorn
From off my lips, for I will tell thy doom. 50
And are these tears? Nay, do not triumph, Jove!
They are wrung from me but by the agonies
Of prophecy, like those sparse drops which fall
From clouds in travail of the lightning, when

The great wave of the storm high-curled and black
Rolls steadily onward to its thunderous break.
Why art thou made a god of, thou poor type
Of anger, and revenge, and cunning force ?
True Power was never born of brutish Strength,
Nor sweet Truth suckled at the shaggy dugs   60
Of that old she-wolf. Are thy thunderbolts,
That quell the darkness for a space, so strong
As the prevailing patience of meek Light,
Who, with the invincible tenderness of peace,
Wins it to be a portion of herself ?
Why art thou made a god of, thou, who hast
The never-sleeping terror at thy heart,
That birthright of all tyrants, worse to bear
Than this thy ravening bird on which I smile ?
Thou swear'st to free me, if I will unfold   70
What kind of doom it is whose omen flits
Across thy heart, as o'er a troop of doves
The fearful shadow of the kite. What need
To know that truth whose knowledge cannot save ?
Evil its errand hath, as well as Good ;
When thine is finished, thou art known no more :
There is a higher purity than thou,
And higher purity is greater strength ;
Thy nature is thy doom, at which thy heart
Trembles behind the thick wall of thy might.   80
Let man but hope, and thou art straightway chilled
With thought of that drear silence and deep night
Which, like a dream, shall swallow thee and thine :
Let man but will, and thou art god no more,
More capable of ruin than the gold
And ivory that image thee on earth.
He who hurled down the monstrous Titan-brood
Blinded with lightnings, with rough thunders stunned,
Is weaker than a simple human thought.
My slender voice can shake thee, as the breeze,   90
That seems but apt to stir a maiden's hair,
Sways huge Oceanus from pole to pole ;
For I am still Prometheus, and foreknow
In my wise heart the end and doom of all.

Yes, I am still Prometheus, wiser grown
By years of solitude,—that holds apart
The past and future, giving the soul room
To search into itself,—and long commune
With this eternal silence ;—more a god,
In my long-suffering and strength to meet   100
With equal front the direst shafts of fate,
Than thou in thy faint-hearted despotism,

Girt with thy baby-toys of force and wrath.
Yes, I am that Prometheus who brought down
The light to man, which thou, in selfish fear,
Hadst to thyself usurped,—his by sole right,
For Man hath right to all save Tyranny,—
And which shall free him yet from thy frail throne.
Tyrants are but the spawn of Ignorance,
Begotten by the slaves they trample on,   110
Who, could they win a glimmer of the light,
And see that Tyranny is always weakness,
Or Fear with its own bosom ill at ease,
Would laugh away in scorn the sand-wove chain
Which their own blindness feigned for adamant.
Wrong ever builds on quicksands, but the Right
To the firm centre lays its moveless base.
The tyrant trembles, if the air but stir
The innocent ringlets of a child's free hair,
And crouches, when the thought of some great spirit,   120
With world-wide murmur, like a rising gale,
Over men's hearts, as over standing corn,
Rushes, and bends them to its own strong will.
So shall some thought of mine yet circle earth,
And puff away thy crumbling altars, Jove !

And, wouldst thou know of my supreme revenge,
Poor tyrant, even now dethroned in heart,
Realmless in soul, as tyrants ever are,
Listen ! and tell me if this bitter peak,
This never-glutted vulture, and these chains   130
Shrink not before it ; for it shall befit
A sorrow-taught, unconquered Titan-heart.
Men, when their death is on them, seem to stand
On a precipitous crag that overhangs
The abyss of doom, and in that depth to see,
As in a glass, the features dim and vast
Of things to come, the shadows, as it seems,
Of what have been.   Death ever fronts the wise ;
Not fearfully, but with clear promises
Of larger life, on whose broad vans upborne,   140
Their outlook widens, and they see beyond
The horizon of the Present and the Past,
Even to the very source and end of things.
Such am I now : immortal woe hath made
My heart a seer, and my soul a judge
Between the substance and the shadow of Truth.
The sure supremeness of the Beautiful,
By all the martyrdoms made doubly sure
Of such as I am, this is my revenge,
Which of my wrongs builds a triumphal arch,   150

Through which I see a sceptre and a throne.
The pipings of glad shepherds on the hills,
Tending the flocks no more to bleed for thee,—
The songs of maidens pressing with white feet
The vintage on thine altars poured no more,—
The murmurous bliss of lovers, underneath
Dim grapevine bowers, whose rosy bunches press
Not half so closely their warm cheeks, unpaled
By thoughts of thy brute lust,—the hive-like hum
Of peaceful commonwealths, where sunburnt Toil   160
Reaps for itself the rich earth made its own
By its own labour, lightened with glad hymns
To an omnipotence which thy mad bolts
Would cope with as a spark with the vast sea,—
Even the spirit of free love and peace,
Duty's sure recompense through life and death,—
These are such harvests as all master-spirits
Reap, haply not on earth, but reap no less
Because the sheaves are bound by hands not theirs;
These are the bloodless daggers wherewithal   170
They stab fallen tyrants, this their high revenge:
For their best part of life on earth is when,
Long after death, prisoned and pent no more,
Their thoughts, their wild dreams even, have become
Part of the necessary air men breathe:
When, like the moon, herself behind a cloud,
They shed down light before us on life's sea,
That cheers us to steer onward still in hope.
Earth with her twining memories ivies o'er
Their holy sepulchres; the chainless sea,   180
In tempest or wide calm, repeats their thoughts;
The lightning and the thunder, all free things,
Have legends of them for the ears of men.
All other glories are as falling stars,
But universal Nature watches theirs:
Such strength is won by love of human kind.

　　Not that I feel that hunger after fame,
Which souls of a half-greatness are beset with;
But that the memory of noble deeds
Cries shame upon the idle and the vile,   190
And keeps the heart of Man forever up
To the heroic level of old time.
To be forgot at first is little pain
To a heart conscious of such high intent
As must be deathless on the lips of men;
But, having been a name, to sink and be
A something which the world can do without,
Which, having been or not, would never change

The lightest pulse of fate,—this is indeed
A cup of bitterness the worst to taste,   200
And this thy heart shall empty to the dregs.
Endless despair shall be thy Caucasus,
And memory thy vulture ; thou wilt find
Oblivion far lonelier than this peak.
Behold thy destiny ! Thou think'st it much
That I should brave thee, miserable god !
But I have braved a mightier than thou,
Even the tempting of this soaring heart,
Which might have made me, scarcely less than thou,
A god among my brethren weak and blind,—   210
Scarce less than thou, a pitiable thing
To be down-trodden into darkness soon.
But now I am above thee, for thou art
The bungling workmanship of fear, the block
That awes the swart Barbarian ; but I
Am what myself have made,—a nature wise
With finding in itself the types of all,—
With watching from the dim verge of the time
What things to be are visible in the gleams
Thrown forward on them from the luminous past,—   220
Wise with the history of its own frail heart,
With reverence and with sorrow, and with love,
Broad as the world, for freedom and for man.

Thou and all strength shall crumble, except Love,
By whom, and for whose glory, ye shall cease :
And, when thou art but a dim moaning heard
From out the pitiless gloom of Chaos, I
Shall be a power and a memory,
A name to fright all tyrants with, a light
Unsetting as the pole-star, a great voice   230
Heard in the breathless pauses of the fight
By truth and freedom ever waged with wrong,
Clear as a silver trumpet, to awake
Far echoes that from age to age live on
In kindred spirits, giving them a sense
Of boundless power from boundless suffering wrung :
And many a glazing eye shall smile to see
The memory of my triumph (for to meet
Wrong with endurance, and to overcome
The present with a heart that looks beyond,   240
Are triumph), like a prophet eagle, perch
Upon the sacred banner of the Right.
Evil springs up, and flowers, and bears no seed,
And feeds the green earth with its swift decay,
Leaving it richer for the growth of truth ;
But Good, once put in action or in thought,

Like a strong oak, doth from its boughs shed down
The ripe germs of a forest. Thou, weak god,
Shalt fade and be forgotten ! but this soul,
Fresh-living still in the serene abyss,　　　　　　　　250
In every heaving shall partake, that grows
From heart to heart among the sons of men,—
As the ominous hum before the earthquake runs
Far through the Aegean from roused isle to isle,—
Foreboding wreck to palaces and shrines,
And mighty rents in many a cavernous error
That darkens the free light to man :—This heart,
Unscarred by thy grim vulture, as the truth
Grows but more lovely 'neath the beaks and claws
Of Harpies blind that fain would soil it, shall　　　　260
In all the throbbing exultations share
That wait on freedom's triumphs, and in all
The glorious agonies of martyr-spirits,
Sharp lightning-throes to split the jagged clouds
That veil the future, showing them the end,—
Pain's thorny crown for constancy and truth,
Girding the temples like a wreath of stars.
This is a thought, that, like the fabled laurel,
Makes my faith thunder-proof ; and thy dread bolts
Fall on me like the silent flakes of snow　　　　　　270
On the hoar brows of agèd Caucasus :
But, O, thought far more blissful, they can rend
This cloud of flesh, and make my soul a star !

Unleash thy crouching thunders now, O Jove !
Free this high heart, which, a poor captive long,
Doth knock to be let forth, this heart which still,
In its invincible manhood, overtops
Thy puny godship, as this mountain doth
The pines that moss its roots. O, even now,
While from my peak of suffering I look down,　　　280
Beholding with a far-spread gush of hope
The sunrise of that Beauty, in whose face,
Shone all around with love, no man shall look
But straightway like a god he be uplift
Unto the throne long empty for his sake,
And clearly oft foreshadowed in brave dreams
By his free inward nature, which nor thou,
Nor any anarch after thee, can bind
From working its great doom,—now, now set free
This essence, not to die, but to become　　　　　　290
Part of that awful Presence which doth haunt
The palaces of tyrants, to scare off,
With its grim eyes and fearful whisperings
And hideous sense of utter loneliness,

All hope of safety, all desire of peace,
All but the loathed forefeeling of blank death,—
Part of that spirit which doth ever brood
In patient calm on the unpilfered nest
Of man's deep heart, till mighty thoughts grow fledged
To sail with darkening shadow o'er the world,   300
Filling with dread such souls as dare not trust
In the unfailing energy of Good,
Until they swoop, and their pale quarry make
Of some o'erbloated wrong,—that spirit which
Scatters great hopes in the seed-field of man,
Like acorns among grain, to grow and be
A roof for freedom in all coming time !

But no, this cannot be ; for ages yet,
In solitude unbroken, shall I hear
The angry Caspian to the Euxine shout,   310
And Euxine answer with a muffled roar,
On either side storming the giant walls
Of Caucasus with leagues of climbing foam
(Less, from my height, than flakes of downy snow),
That draw back baffled but to hurl again,
Snatched up in wrath and horrible turmoil,
Mountain on mountain, as the Titans erst,
My brethren, scaling the high seat of Jove,
Heaved Pelion upon Ossa's shoulders broad
In vain emprise. The moon will come and go   320
With her monotonous vicissitude ;
Once beautiful, when I was free to walk
Among my fellows, and to interchange
The influence benign of loving eyes,
But now by aged use grown wearisome ;—
False thought ! most false ! for how could I endure
These crawling centuries of lonely woe
Unshamed by weak complaining, but for thee,
Loneliest, save me, of all created things,
Mild-eyed Astarte, my best comforter,   330
With thy pale smile of sad benignity ?

Year after year will pass away and seem
To me, in mine eternal agony,
But as the shadows of dumb summer clouds,
Which I have watched so often darkening o'er
The vast Sarmatian plain, league-wide at first,
But, with still swiftness, lessening on and on
Till cloud and shadow meet and mingle where
The grey horizon fades into the sky,
Far, far to northward. Yes, for ages yet   340
Must I lie here upon my altar huge,

A sacrifice for man. Sorrow will be,
As it hath been, his portion ; endless doom,
While the immortal with the mortal linked
Dreams of its wings and pines for what it dreams,
With upward yearn unceasing. Better so :
For wisdom is meek sorrow's patient child,
And empire over self, and all the deep
Strong charities that make men seem like gods ;
And love, that makes them be gods, from her breasts   350
Sucks in the milk that makes mankind one blood.
Good never comes unmixed, or so it seems,
Having two faces, as some images
Are carved, of foolish gods ; one face is ill ;
But one heart lies beneath, and that is good,
As are all hearts, when we explore their depths.
Therefore, great heart, bear up ! thou art but type
Of what all lofty spirits endure, that fain
Would win men back to strength and peace through love :
Each hath his lonely peak, and on each heart   360
Envy, or scorn, or hatred, tears lifelong
With vulture beak ; yet the high soul is left ;
And faith, which is but hope grown wise ; and love
And patience, which at last shall overcome.

THE SHEPHERD OF KING ADMETUS

THERE came a youth upon the earth,
  Some thousand years ago,
Whose slender hands were nothing
    worth,
Whether to plough, or reap, or sow.

Upon an empty tortoise-shell
  He stretched some chords, and drew
Music that made men's bosoms swell
Fearless, or brimmed their eyes with
    dew.

Then King Admetus, one who had
  Pure taste by right divine,
Decreed his singing not too bad
To hear between the cups of wine :

And so, well pleased with being
    soothed
  Into a sweet half-sleep,
Three times his kingly beard he
    smoothed,
And made him viceroy o'er his sheep.

His words were simple words enough,
  And yet he used them so,
That what in other mouths was rough
In his seemed musical and low.

Men called him but a shiftless youth,
  In whom no good they saw ;
And yet, unwittingly, in truth,
They made his careless words their
    law.

They knew not how he learned at all,
  For idly, hour by hour,
He sat and watched the dead leaves
    fall,
Or mused upon a common flower.

It seemed the loveliness of things
  Did teach him all their use,
For, in mere weeds, and stones, and
    springs,
He found a healing power profuse.

Men granted that his speech was wise,
 But, when a glance they caught
Of his slim grace and woman's eyes,
They laughed, and called him good-
  for-naught.

Yet after he was dead and gone,
 And e'en his memory dim,

Earth seemed more sweet to live
  upon,
More full of love, because of him.

And day by day more holy grew
 Each spot where he had trod,
Till after-poets only knew
 Their first-born brother as a god.

THE TOKEN

It is a mere wild rosebud,
 Quite sallow now, and dry,
Yet there's something wondrous in it,
 Some gleams of days gone by,
Dear sights and sounds that are to me
The very moons of memory,
And stir my heart's blood far below
Its short-lived waves of joy and woe.

Lips must fade and roses wither,
 All sweet times be o'er ;
They only smile, and, murmuring
 ' Thither ! '
 Stay with us no more :
And yet ofttimes a look or smile,
Forgotten in a kiss's while,
Years after from the dark will start,
And flash across the trembling heart.

Thou hast given me many roses,
 But never one, like this,
O'erfloods both sense and spirit
 With such a deep, wild bliss ;
We must have instincts that glean
  up
Sparse drops of this life in the cup,
Whose taste shall give us all that we
Can prove of immortality.

Earth's stablest things are shadows,
 And, in the life to come,
Haply some chance-saved trifle
 May tell of this old home :
As now sometimes we seem to find,
In a dark crevice of the mind,
Some relic, which, long pondered o'er,
Hints faintly at a life before.

AN INCIDENT IN A RAILROAD CAR

He spoke of Burns : men rude and
  rough
Pressed round to hear the praise of
  one
Whose heart was made of manly,
  simple stuff,
 As homespun as their own.

And, when he read, they forward
  leaned,
Drinking, with thirsty hearts and
  ears,
His brook-like songs whom glory
  never weaned
 From humble smiles and tears.

Slowly there grew a tender awe,
 Sun-like, o'er faces brown and hard,
As if in him who read they felt and saw
 Some presence of the bard.

It was a sight for sin and wrong
And slavish tyranny to see,
A sight to make our faith more pure
  and strong
 In high humanity.

I thought, these men will carry hence
Promptings their former life above,
And something of a finer reverence
 For beauty, truth, and love.

God scatters love on every side
Freely among his children all,
And always hearts are lying open wide,
Wherein some grains may fall.

There is no wind but soweth seeds
Of a more true and open life,
Which burst, unlooked for, into high-
souled deeds,
With wayside beauty rife.

We find within these souls of ours
Some wild germs of a higher birth,
Which in the poet's tropic heart bear
flowers
Whose fragrance fills the earth.

Within the hearts of all men lie
These promises of wider bliss,
Which blossom into hopes that cannot
die,
In sunny hours like this.

All that hath been majestical
In life or death, since time began,
Is native in the simple heart of all,
The angel heart of man.

And thus, among the untaught
poor,
Great deeds and feelings find a
home,
That cast in shadow all the golden lore
Of classic Greece and Rome.

O, mighty brother-soul of man,
Where'er thou art, in low or high,
Thy skyey arches with exulting span
O'er-roof infinity !

All thoughts that mould the age
begin
Deep down within the primitive soul,
And from the many slowly upward
win
To one who grasps the whole :

In his wide brain the feeling deep
That struggled on the many's
tongue
Swells to a tide of thought, whose
surges leap
O'er the weak thrones of wrong.

All thought begins in feeling,—wide
In the great mass its base is hid,
And, narrowing up to thought, stands
glorified,
A moveless pyramid.

Nor is he far astray, who deems
That every hope, which rises and
grows broad
In the world's heart, by ordered
impulse streams
From the great heart of God.

God wills, man hopes : in common
souls
Hope is but vague and undefined,
Till from the poet's tongue the
message rolls
A blessing to his kind.

Never did Poesy appear
So full of heaven to me, as when
I saw how it would pierce through
pride and fear
To the lives of coarsest men.

It may be glorious to write
Thoughts that shall glad the two or
three
High souls, like those far stars that
come in sight
Once in a century ;—

But better far it is to speak
One simple word, which now and
then
Shall waken their free nature in the
weak
And friendless sons of men ;

To write some earnest verse or line,
Which, seeking not the praise of art,
Shall make a clearer faith and man-
hood shine
In the untutored heart.

He who doth this, in verse or prose,
May be forgotten in his day,
But surely shall be crowned at last
with those
Who live and speak for ay.

RHOECUS

God sends his teachers unto every age,
To every clime, and every race of men,
With revelations fitted to their growth
And shape of mind, nor gives the realm of Truth
Into the selfish rule of one sole race :
Therefore each form of worship that hath swayed
The life of man, and given it to grasp
The master-key of knowledge, reverence,
Infolds some germs of goodness and of right ;
Else never had the eager soul, which loathes   10
The slothful down of pampered ignorance,
Found in it even a moment's fitful rest.

There is an instinct in the human heart
Which makes that all the fables it hath coined,
To justify the reign of its belief
And strengthen it by beauty's right divine,
Veil in their inner cells a mystic gift,
Which, like the hazel twig, in faithful hands,
Points surely to the hidden springs of truth.
For, as in nature naught is made in vain,   20
But all things have within their hull of use
A wisdom and a meaning which may speak
Of spiritual secrets to the ear
Of spirit ; so, in whatsoe'er the heart
Hath fashioned for a solace to itself,
To make its inspirations suit its creed,
And from the niggard hands of falsehood wring
Its needful food of truth, there ever is
A sympathy with Nature, which reveals,
Not less than her own works, pure gleams of light   30
And earnest parables of inward lore.
Hear now this fairy legend of old Greece,
As full of freedom, youth, and beauty still
As the immortal freshness of that grace
Carved for all ages on some Attic frieze.

A youth named Rhoecus, wandering in the wood,
Saw an old oak just trembling to its fall,
And, feeling pity of so fair a tree,
He propped its grey trunk with admiring care,
And with a thoughtless footstep loitered on.   40
But, as he turned, he heard a voice behind
That murmured ' Rhoecus ! ' 'Twas as if the leaves,
Stirred by a passing breath, had murmured it,
And, while he paused bewildered, yet again
It murmured ' Rhoecus ! ' softer than a breeze.

LOWELL   D

He started and beheld with dizzy eyes
What seemed the substance of a happy dream
Stand there before him, spreading a warm glow
Within the green glooms of the shadowy oak.
It seemed a woman's shape, yet all too fair 50
To be a woman, and with eyes too meek
For any that were wont to mate with gods.
All naked like a goddess stood she there,
And like a goddess all too beautiful
To feel the guilt-born earthliness of shame.
' Rhoecus, I am the Dryad of this tree,'
Thus she began, dropping her low-toned words
Serene, and full, and clear, as drops of dew,
' And with it I am doomed to live and die ;
The rain and sunshine are my caterers, 60
Nor have I other bliss than simple life ;
Now ask me what thou wilt, that I can give,
And with a thankful joy it shall be thine.'

Then Rhoecus, with a flutter at the heart,
Yet, by the prompting of such beauty, bold,
Answered : ' What is there that can satisfy
The endless craving of the soul but love ?
Give me thy love, or but the hope of that
Which must be evermore my nature's goal.'
After a little pause she said again, 70
But with a glimpse of sadness in her tone,
' I give it, Rhoecus, though a perilous gift ;
An hour before the sunset meet me here.'
And straightway there was nothing he could see
But the green glooms beneath the shadowy oak,
And not a sound came to his straining ears
But the low trickling rustle of the leaves,
And far away upon an emerald slope
The falter of an idle shepherd's pipe.

Now, in those days of simpleness and faith, 80
Men did not think that happy things were dreams
Because they overstepped the narrow bourn
Of likelihood, but reverently deemed
Nothing too wondrous or too beautiful
To be the guerdon of a daring heart.
So Rhoecus made no doubt that he was blest,
And all along unto the city's gate
Earth seemed to spring beneath him as he walked,
The clear, broad sky looked bluer than its wont,
And he could scarce believe he had not wings, 90
Such sunshine seemed to glitter through his veins
Instead of blood, so light he felt and strange.

Young Rhoecus had a faithful heart enough,
But one that in the present dwelt too much,
And, taking with blithe welcome whatsoe'er
Chance gave of joy, was wholly bound in that,
Like the contented peasant of a vale,
Deemed it the world, and never looked beyond.
So, haply meeting in the afternoon
Some comrades who were playing at the dice, 100
He joined them, and forgot all else beside.

The dice were rattling at the merriest,
And Rhoecus, who had met but sorry luck,
Just laughed in triumph at a happy throw,
When through the room there hummed a yellow bee
That buzzed about his ear with down-dropped legs
As if to light. And Rhoecus laughed and said,
Feeling how red and flushed he was with loss,
' By Venus ! does he take me for a rose ? '
And brushed him off with rough, impatient hand. 110
But still the bee came back, and thrice again
Rhoecus did beat him off with growing wrath.
Then through the window flew the wounded bee,
And Rhoecus, tracking him with angry eyes,
Saw a sharp mountain-peak of Thessaly
Against the red disk of the setting sun,—
And instantly the blood sank from his heart,
As if its very walls had caved away.
Without a word he turned, and, rushing forth,
Ran madly through the city and the gate, 120
And o'er the plain, which now the wood's long shade,
By the low sun thrown forward broad and dim,
Darkened wellnigh unto the city's wall.

Quite spent and out of breath he reached the tree,
And, listening fearfully, he heard once more
The low voice murmur ' Rhoecus ! ' close at hand :
Whereat he looked around him, but could see
Naught but the deepening glooms beneath the oak.
Then sighed the voice, ' O Rhoecus ! nevermore
Shalt thou behold me or by day or night, 130
Me, who would fain have blessed thee with a love
More ripe and bounteous than ever yet
Filled up with nectar any mortal heart :
But thou didst scorn my humble messenger,
And sent'st him back to me with bruisèd wings.
We spirits only show to gentle eyes,
We ever ask an undivided love,
And he who scorns the least of Nature's works
Is thenceforth exiled and shut out from all.
Farewell ! for thou canst never see me more.' 140

Then Rhoecus beat his breast, and groaned aloud,
And cried, ' Be pitiful ! forgive me yet
This once, and I shall never need it more ! '
' Alas ! ' the voice returned, ' 't is thou art blind,
Not I unmerciful ; I can forgive,
But have no skill to heal thy spirit's eyes ;
Only the soul hath power o'er itself.'
With that again there murmured ' Nevermore ! '
And Rhoecus after heard no other sound,
Except the rattling of the oak's crisp leaves,   150
Like the long surf upon a distant shore,
Raking the sea-worn pebbles up and down.
The night had gathered round him : o'er the plain
The city sparkled with its thousand lights,
And sounds of revel fell upon his ear
Harshly and like a curse ; above, the sky,
With all its bright sublimity of stars,
Deepened, and on his forehead smote the breeze :
Beauty was all around him and delight,
But from that eve he was alone on earth.   160

THE FALCON

I KNOW a falcon swift and peerless
    As e'er was cradled in the pine ;
No bird had ever eye so fearless,
    Or wing so strong as this of mine.

The winds not better love to pilot
    A cloud with molten gold o'errun,
Than him, a little burning islet,
    A star above the coming sun.

For with a lark's heart he doth tower,
    By a glorious upward instinct drawn ;
No bee nestles deeper in the flower
    Than he in the bursting rose of dawn.

No harmless dove, no bird that singeth,
    Shudders to see him overhead ;
The rush of his fierce swooping bringeth
    To innocent hearts no thrill of dread.

Let fraud and wrong and baseness shiver,
    For still between them and the sky
The falcon Truth hangs poised forever
    And marks them with his vengeful eye.

TRIAL

I

WHETHER the idle prisoner through his grate
Watches the waving of the grass-tuft small,
Which, having colonized its rift i' th' wall,
Takes its free risk of good or evil fate,
And from the sky's just helmet draws its lot
Daily of shower or sunshine, cold or hot ;—
Whether the closer captive of a creed,
Cooped up from birth to grind out endless chaff,
Sees through his treadmill-bars the noonday laugh,
And feels in vain his crumpled pinions breed ;—   10
Whether the Georgian slave look up and mark,
With bellying sails puffed full, the tall cloud-bark
Sink northward slowly,—thou alone seem'st good,
Fair only thou, O Freedom, whose desire
Can light in muddiest souls quick seeds of fire,
And strain life's chords to the old heroic mood.

II

Yet are there other gifts more fair than thine,
Nor can I count him happiest who has never
Been forced with his own hand his chains to sever,
And for himself find out the way divine ;   20
He never knew the aspirer's glorious pains,
He never earned the struggle's priceless gains.
O, block by block, with sore and sharp endeavour,
Lifelong we build these human natures up
Into a temple fit for freedom's shrine,
And Trial ever consecrates the cup
Wherefrom we pour her sacrificial wine.

A GLANCE BEHIND THE CURTAIN

WE see but half the causes of our deeds,
Seeking them wholly in the outer life,
And heedless of the encircling spirit-world,
Which, though unseen, is felt, and sows in us
All germs of pure and world-wide purposes.
From one stage of our being to the next
We pass unconscious o'er a slender bridge,
The momentary work of unseen hands,
Which crumbles down behind us ; looking back,
We see the other shore, the gulf between,   10
And, marvelling how we won to where we stand,
Content ourselves to call the builder Chance.

We trace the wisdom to the apple's fall,
Not to the birth-throes of a mighty Truth
Which, for long ages in blank Chaos dumb,
Yet yearned to be incarnate, and had found
At last a spirit meet to be the womb
From which it might be born to bless mankind,—
Not to the soul of Newton, ripe with all
The hoarded thoughtfulness of earnest years,   20
And waiting but one ray of sunlight more
To blossom fully.

                              But whence came that ray ?
We call our sorrows Destiny, but ought
Rather to name our high successes so.
Only the instincts of great souls are Fate,
And have predestined sway : all other things,
Except by leave of us, could never be.
For Destiny is but the breath of God
Still moving in us, the last fragment left
Of our unfallen nature, waking oft   30
Within our thought, to beckon us beyond
The narrow circle of the seen and known,
And always tending to a noble end,
As all things must that overrule the soul,
And for a space unseat the helmsman, Will.
The fate of England and of freedom once
Seemed wavering in the heart of one plain man :
One step of his, and the great dial-hand,
That marks the destined progress of the world
In the eternal round from wisdom on   40
To higher wisdom, had been made to pause
A hundred years. That step he did not take,—
He knew not why, nor we, but only God,—
And lived to make his simple oaken chair
More terrible and grandly beautiful,
More full of majesty than any throne,
Before or after, of a British king.

Upon the pier stood two stern-visaged men,
Looking to where a little craft lay moored,
Swayed by the lazy current of the Thames,   50
Which weltered by in muddy listlessness.
Grave men they were, and battlings of fierce thought
Had trampled out all softness from their brows,
And ploughed rough furrows there before their time,
For other crop than such as homebred Peace
Sows broadcast in the willing soil of Youth.
Care, not of self, but of the commonweal,
Had robbed their eyes of youth, and left instead

A look of patient power and iron will,
And something fiercer, too, that gave broad hint 60
Of the plain weapons girded at their sides.
The younger had an aspect of command,—
Not such as trickles down, a slender stream,
In the shrunk channel of a great descent,
But such as lies entowered in heart and head,
And an arm prompt to do the 'hests of both.
His was a brow where gold were out of place,
And yet it seemed right worthy of a crown
(Though he despised such), were it only made
Of iron, or some serviceable stuff 70
That would have matched his sinewy brown face.
The elder, although such he hardly seemed
(Care makes so little of some five short years),
Had a clear, honest face, whose rough-hewn strength
Was mildened by the scholar's wiser heart
To sober courage, such as best befits
The unsullied temper of a well-taught mind,
Yet so remained that one could plainly guess
The hushed volcano smouldering underneath.
He spoke: the other, hearing, kept his gaze 80
Still fixed, as on some problem in the sky.

' O CROMWELL, we are fallen on evil times !
There was a day when England had wide room
For honest men as well as foolish kings :
But now the uneasy stomach of the time
Turns squeamish at them both. Therefore let us
Seek out that savage clime, where men as yet
Are free : there sleeps the vessel on the tide,
Her languid canvas drooping for the wind ;
Give us but that, and what need we to fear 90
This Order of the Council ? The free waves
Will not say, No, to please a wayward king,
Nor will the winds turn traitors at his beck :
All things are fitly cared for, and the Lord
Will watch as kindly o'er the exodus
Of us his servants now, as in old time.
We have no cloud or fire, and haply we
May not pass dry-shod through the ocean-stream ;
But, saved or lost, all things are in His hand.'
So spake he, and meantime the other stood 100
With wide grey eyes still reading the blank air,
As if upon the sky's blue wall he saw
Some mystic sentence, written by a hand,
Such as of old made pale the Assyrian king,
Girt with his satraps in the blazing feast.

'HAMPDEN ! a moment since, my purpose was
To fly with thee,—for I will call it flight,
Nor flatter it with any smoother name,—
But something in me bids me not to go ;
And I am one, thou knowest, who, unmoved   110
By what the weak deem omens, yet give heed
And reverence due to whatsoe'er my soul
Whispers of warning to the inner ear.
Moreover, as I know that God brings round
His purposes in ways undreamed by us,
And makes the wicked but his instruments
To hasten their own swift and sudden fall,
I see the beauty of his providence
In the King's order : blind, he will not let
His doom part from him, but must bid it stay   120
As 't were a cricket, whose enlivening chirp
He loved to hear beneath his very hearth.
Why should we fly ? Nay, why not rather stay
And rear again our Zion's crumbled walls,
Not, as of old the walls of Thebes were built,
By minstrel twanging, but, if need should be,
With the more potent music of our swords ?
Think'st thou that score of men beyond the sea
Claim more God's care than all of England here ?
No : when He moves His arm, it is to aid   130
Whole peoples, heedless if a few be crushed,
As some are ever, when the destiny
Of man takes one stride onward nearer home.
Believe it, 't is the mass of men He loves ;
And, where there is most sorrow and most want,
Where the high heart of man is trodden down
The most, 't is not because He hides His face
From them in wrath, as purblind teachers prate :
Not so : there most is He, for there is He
Most needed. Men who seek for Fate abroad   140
Are not so near His heart as they who dare
Frankly to face her where she faces them,
On their own threshold, where their souls are strong
To grapple with and throw her ; as I once,
Being yet a boy, did cast this puny king,
Who now has grown so dotard as to deem
That he can wrestle with an angry realm,
And throw the brawned Antaeus of men's rights.
No, Hampden ! they have half-way conquered Fate
Who go half-way to meet her,—as will I.   150
Freedom hath yet a work for me to do ;
So speaks that inward voice which never yet
Spake falsely, when it urged the spirit on
To noble deeds for country and mankind.

And, for success, I ask no more than this,—
To bear unflinching witness to the truth.
All true whole men succeed ; for what is worth
Success's name, unless it be the thought,
The inward surety, to have carried out
A noble purpose to a noble end,   160
Although it be the gallows or the block ?
'T is only Falsehood that doth ever need
These outward shows of gain to bolster her.
Be it we prove the weaker with our swords ;
Truth only needs to be for once spoke out,
And there 's such music in her, such strange rhythm,
As makes men's memories her joyous slaves,
And clings around the soul, as the sky clings
Round the mute earth, forever beautiful,
And, if o'erclouded, only to burst forth   170
More all-embracingly divine and clear :
Get but the truth once uttered, and 't is like
A star new-born, that drops into its place,
And which, once circling in its placid round,
Not all the tumult of the earth can shake.

  ' What should we do in that small colony
Of pinched fanatics, who would rather choose
Freedom to clip an inch more from their hair,
Than the great chance of setting England free ?
Not there, amid the stormy wilderness,   180
Should we learn wisdom ; or if learned, what room
To put it into act,—else worse than naught ?
We learn our souls more, tossing for an hour
Upon this huge and ever-vexèd sea
Of human thought, where kingdoms go to wreck
Like fragile bubbles yonder in the stream,
Than in a cycle of New England sloth,
Broke only by some petty Indian war,
Or quarrel for a letter more or less
In some hard word, which, spelt in either way,   190
Not their most learnèd clerks can understand.
New times demand new measures and new men ;
The world advances, and in time outgrows
The laws that in our fathers' day were best ;
And, doubtless, after us, some purer scheme
Will be shaped out by wiser men than we,
Made wiser by the steady growth of truth.
We cannot bring Utopia by force ;
But better, almost, be at work in sin,
Than in a brute inaction browse and sleep.   200
No man is born into the world, whose work
Is not born with him ; there is always work,

And tools to work withal, for those who will ;
And blessèd are the horny hands of toil !
The busy world shoves angrily aside
The man who stands with arms akimbo set,
Until occasion tells him what to do ;
And he who waits to have his task marked out
Shall die and leave his errand unfulfilled.
Our time is one that calls for earnest deeds :   210
Reason and Government, like two broad seas,
Yearn for each other with outstretchèd arms
Across this narrow isthmus of the throne,
And roll their white surf higher every day.
One age moves onward, and the next builds up
Cities and gorgeous palaces, where stood
The rude log huts of those who tamed the wild,
Rearing from out the forests they had felled
The goodly framework of a fairer state ;
The builder's trowel and the settler's axe   220
Are seldom wielded by the selfsame hand ;
Ours is the harder task, yet not the less
Shall we receive the blessing for our toil
From the choice spirits of the aftertime.
My soul is not a palace of the past,
Where outworn creeds, like Rome's grey senate, quake,
Hearing afar the Vandal's trumpet hoarse,
That shakes old systems with a thunder-fit.
The time is ripe, and rotten-ripe, for change ;
Then let it come : I have no dread of what   230
Is called for by the instinct of mankind ;
Nor think I that God's world will fall apart
Because we tear a parchment more or less.
Truth is eternal, but her effluence,
With endless change, is fitted to the hour ;
Her mirror is turned forward to reflect
The promise of the future, not the past.
He who would win the name of truly great
Must understand his own age and the next,
And make the present ready to fulfil   240
Its prophecy, and with the future merge
Gently and peacefully, as wave with wave.
The future works out great men's destinies ;
The present is enough for common souls,
Who, never looking forward, are indeed
Mere clay, wherein the footprints of their age
Are petrified forever : better those
Who lead the blind old giant by the hand
From out the pathless desert where he gropes,
And set him onward in his darksome way.   250
I do not fear to follow out the truth,

Albeit along the precipice's edge.
Let us speak plain : there is more force in names
Than most men dream of ; and a lie may keep
Its throne a whole age longer, if it skulk
Behind the shield of some fair-seeming name.
Let us call tyrants *tyrants*, and maintain
That only freedom comes by grace of God,
And all that comes not by his grace must fall ;
For men in earnest have no time to waste   260
In patching fig-leaves for the naked truth.

   ' I will have one more grapple with the man
Charles Stuart : whom the boy o'ercame,
The man stands not in awe of. I, perchance,
Am one raised up by the Almighty arm
To witness some great truth to all the world.
Souls destined to o'erleap the vulgar lot,
And mould the world unto the scheme of God,
Have a fore-consciousness of their high doom,
As men are known to shiver at the heart   270
When the cold shadow of some coming ill
Creeps slowly o'er their spirits unawares.
Hath Good less power of prophecy than Ill ?
How else could men whom God hath called to sway
Earth's rudder, and to steer the bark of Truth,
Beating against the tempest tow'rd her port,
Bear all the mean and buzzing grievances,
The petty martyrdoms, wherewith Sin strives
To weary out the tethered hope of Faith,
The sneers, the unrecognizing look of friends,   280
Who worship the dead corpse of old king Custom,
Where it doth lie in state within the Church,
Striving to cover up the mighty ocean
With a man's palm, and making even the truth
Lie for them, holding up the glass reversed,
To make the hope of man seem farther off ?
My God ! when I read o'er the bitter lives
Of men whose eager hearts were quite too great
To beat beneath the cramped mode of the day,
And see them mocked at by the world they love,   290
Haggling with prejudice for pennyworths
Of that reform which their hard toil will make
The common birthright of the age to come,—
When I see this, spite of my faith in God,
I marvel how their hearts bear up so long ;
Nor could they but for this same prophecy,
This inward feeling of the glorious end.

   ' Deem me not fond ; but in my warmer youth,
Ere my heart's bloom was soiled and brushed away,

I had great dreams of mighty things to come;   300
Of conquest, whether by the sword or pen
I knew not; but some conquest I would have,
Or else swift death: now wiser grown in years,
I find youth's dreams are but the flutterings
Of those strong wings whereon the soul shall soar
In after time to win a starry throne;
And so I cherish them, for they were lots,
Which I, a boy, cast in the helm of Fate.
Now will I draw them, since a man's right hand,
A right hand guided by an earnest soul,   310
With a true instinct, takes the golden prize
From out a thousand blanks.   What men call luck
Is the prerogative of valiant souls,
The fealty life pays its rightful kings.
The helm is shaking now, and I will stay
To pluck my lot forth; it were sin to flee!'

So they two turned together; one to die,
Fighting for freedom on the bloody field;
The other, far more happy, to become
A name earth wears forever next her heart;   320
One of the few that have a right to rank
With the true Makers: for his spirit wrought
Order from Chaos; proved that right divine
Dwelt only in the excellence of truth;
And far within old Darkness' hostile lines
Advanced and pitched the shining tents of Light.
Nor shall the grateful Muse forget to tell,
That—not the least among his many claims
To deathless honour—he was MILTON'S friend,
A man not second among those who lived   330
To show us that the poet's lyre demands
An arm of tougher sinew than the sword.

A CHIPPEWA LEGEND [1]

ἀλγεινὰ μέν μοι καὶ λέγειν ἐστὶν τάδε,
ἄλγος δὲ σιγᾶν.

AESCHYLUS, *Prom. Vinct.* **197, 198.**

THE old Chief, feeling now wellnigh his end,
Called his two eldest children to his side,
And gave them, in few words, his parting charge!
'My son and daughter, me ye see no more;
The happy hunting-grounds await me, green
With change of spring and summer through the year:

[1] For the leading incidents in this tale I am indebted to the very valuable 'Algic Researches' of Henry R. Schoolcraft, Esq.

But, for remembrance, after I am gone,
Be kind to little Sheemah for my sake :
Weakling he is and young, and knows not yet
To set the trap, or draw the seasoned bow ;   10
Therefore of both your loves he hath more need,
And he, who needeth love, to love hath right ;
It is not like our furs and stores of corn,
Whereto we claim sole title by our toil,
But the Great Spirit plants it in our hearts,
And waters it, and gives it sun, to be
The common stock and heritage of all :
Therefore be kind to Sheemah, that yourselves
May not be left deserted in your need.'

  Alone, beside a lake, their wigwam stood,   20
Far from the other dwellings of their tribe ;
And, after many moons, the loneliness
Wearied the elder brother, and he said,
' Why should I dwell here all alone, shut out
From the free, natural joys that fit my age ?
Lo, I am tall and strong, well skilled to hunt,
Patient of toil and hunger, and not yet
Have seen the danger which I dared not look
Full in the face ; what hinders me to be
A mighty Brave and Chief among my kin ? '   30
So, taking up his arrows and his bow,
As if to hunt, he journeyed swiftly on,
Until he gained the wigwams of his tribe,
Where, choosing out a bride, he soon forgot,
In all the fret and bustle of new life,
The little Sheemah and his father's charge.

  Now when the sister found her brother gone,
And that, for many days, he came not back,
She wept for Sheemah more than for herself ;
For Love bides longest in a woman's heart,   40
And flutters many times before he flies,
And then doth perch so nearly, that a word
May lure him back, as swift and glad as light :
And Duty lingers even when Love is gone,
Oft looking out in hope of his return ;
And, after Duty hath been driven forth,
Then Selfishness creeps in the last of all,
Warming her lean hands at the lonely hearth,
And crouching o'er the embers, to shut out
Whatever paltry warmth and light are left,   50
With avaricious greed, from all beside.
So, for long months, the sister hunted wide,
And cared for little Sheemah tenderly ;

But, daily more and more, the loneliness
Grew wearisome, and to herself she sighed,
' Am I not fair ? at least the glassy pool,
That hath no cause to flatter, tells me so ;
But, O, how flat and meaningless the tale,
Unless it tremble on a lover's tongue !
Beauty hath no true glass, except it be   60
In the sweet privacy of loving eyes.'
Thus deemed she idly, and forgot the lore
Which she had learned of nature and the woods,
That beauty's chief reward is to itself,
And that the eyes of Love reflect alone
The inward fairness, which is blurred and lost
Unless kept clear and white by Duty's care.
So she went forth and sought the haunts of men,
And, being wedded, in her household cares,
Soon, like the elder brother, quite forgot   70
The little Sheemah and her father's charge.

   But Sheemah, left alone within the lodge,
Waited and waited, with a shrinking heart,
Thinking each rustle was his sister's step,
Till hope grew less and less, and then went out,
And every sound was changed from hope to fear.
Few sounds there were :—the dropping of a nut,
The squirrel's chirrup, and the jay's harsh scream,
Autumn's sad remnants of blithe Summer's cheer,
Heard at long intervals, seemed but to make   80
The dreadful void of silence silenter.
Soon what small store his sister left was gone,
And, through the Autumn, he made shift to live
On roots and berries, gathered in much fear
Of wolves, whose ghastly howl he heard ofttimes,
Hollow and hungry, at the dead of night.
But Winter came at last, and, when the snow,
Thick-heaped for gleaming leagues o'er hill and plain,
Spread its unbroken silence over all,
Made bold by hunger, he was fain to glean   90
(More sick at heart than Ruth, and all alone)
After the harvest of the merciless wolf,
Grim Boaz, who, sharp-ribbed and gaunt, yet feared
A thing more wild and starving than himself :
Till, by degrees, the wolf and he grew friends,
And shared together all the winter through.

   Late in the Spring, when all the ice was gone,
The elder brother, fishing in the lake,
Upon whose edge his father's wigwam stood,
Heard a low moaning noise upon the shore :   100

Half like a child it seemed, half like a wolf,
And straightway there was something in his heart
That said, ' It is thy brother Sheemah's voice.'
So, paddling swiftly to the bank, he saw,
Within a little thicket close at hand,
A child that seemed fast changing to a wolf,
From the neck downward, grey with shaggy hair,
That still crept on and upward as he looked.
The face was turned away, but well he knew
That it was Sheemah's, even his brother's face.   110
Then with his trembling hands he hid his eyes,
And bowed his head, so that he might not see
The first look of his brother's eyes, and cried,
' O Sheemah ! O my brother, speak to me !
Dost thou not know me, that I am thy brother ?
Come to me, little Sheemah, thou shalt dwell
With me henceforth, and know no care or want ! '
Sheemah was silent for a space, as if
'T were hard to summon up a human voice,
And, when he spake, the sound was of a wolf's :   120
' I know thee not, nor art thou what thou say'st ;
I have none other brethren than the wolves,
And, till thy heart be changed from what it is,
Thou art not worthy to be called their kin.'
Then groaned the other, with a choking tongue,
' Alas ! my heart is changed right bitterly ;
'T is shrunk and parched within me even now ! '
And, looking upward fearfully, he saw
Only a wolf that shrank away and ran,
Ugly and fierce, to hide among the woods.   130

STANZAS ON FREEDOM

MEN ! whose boast it is that ye
Come of fathers brave and free,
If there breathe on earth a slave,
Are ye truly free and brave ?
If ye do not feel the chain,
When it works a brother's pain,
Are ye not base slaves indeed,
Slaves unworthy to be freed ?

Women ! who shall one day bear
Sons to breathe New England air,
If ye hear, without a blush,
Deeds to make the roused blood rush
Like red lava through your veins,
For your sisters now in chains,—
Answer ! are ye fit to be
Mothers of the brave and free ?

Is true Freedom but to break
Fetters for our own dear sake,
And, with leathern hearts, forget
That we owe mankind a debt ?
No ! true freedom is to share
All the chains our brothers wear,
And, with heart and hand, to be
Earnest to make others free !

They are slaves who fear to speak
For the fallen and the weak ;
They are slaves who will not choose
Hatred, scoffing, and abuse,
Rather than in silence shrink
From the truth they needs must think ;
They are slaves who dare not be
In the right with two or three.

COLUMBUS

THE cordage creaks and rattles in the wind,
With whims of sudden hush ; the reeling sea
Now thumps like solid rock beneath the stern,
Now leaps with clumsy wrath, strikes short, and, falling
Crumbled to whispery foam, slips rustling down
The broad backs of the waves, which jostle and crowd
To fling themselves upon that unknown shore,
Their used familiar since the dawn of time,
Whither this foredoomed life is guided on
To sway on triumph's hushed, aspiring poise   10
One glittering moment, then to break fulfilled.

How lonely is the sea's perpetual swing,
The melancholy wash of endless waves,
The sigh of some grim monster undescried,
Fear-painted on the canvas of the dark,
Shifting on his uneasy pillow of brine !
Yet night brings more companions than the day
To this drear waste ; new constellations burn,
And fairer stars, with whose calm height my soul
Finds nearer sympathy than with my herd   20
Of earthen souls, whose vision's scanty ring
Makes me its prisoner to beat my wings
Against the cold bars of their unbelief,
Knowing in vain my own free heaven beyond.
O God ! this world, so crammed with eager life,
That comes and goes and wanders back to silence
Like the idle wind, which yet man's shaping mind
Can make his drudge to swell the longing sails
Of highest endeavour,—this mad, unthrift world,
Which, every hour, throws life enough away   30
To make her deserts kind and hospitable,
Lets her great destinies be waved aside
By smooth, lip-reverent, formal infidels,
Who weigh the God they not believe with gold,
And find no spot in Judas, save that he,
Driving a duller bargain than he ought,
Saddled his guild with too cheap precedent.
O Faith ! if thou art strong, thine opposite
Is mighty also, and the dull fool's sneer
Hath ofttimes shot chill palsy through the arm   40
Just lifted to achieve its crowning deed,
And made the firm-based heart, that would have quailed
The rack or fagot, shudder like a leaf
Wrinkled with frost, and loose upon its stem.
The wicked and the weak, by some dark law,
Have a strange power to shut and rivet down

Their own horizon round us, to unwing
Our heaven-aspiring visions, and to blur
With surly clouds the Future's gleaming peaks,
Far seen across the brine of thankless years.   50
If the chosen soul could never be alone
In deep mid-silence, open-doored to God,
No greatness ever had been dreamed or done ;
Among dull hearts a prophet never grew ;
The nurse of full-grown souls is solitude.

The old world is effete ; there man with man
Jostles, and, in the brawl for means to live,
Life is trod underfoot,—Life, the one block
Of marble that 's vouchsafed wherefrom to carve
Our great thoughts, white and godlike, to shine down   60
The future, Life, the irredeemable block,
Which one o'er-hasty chisel-dint oft mars,
Scanting our room to cut the features out
Of our full hope, so forcing us to crown
With a mean head the perfect limbs, or leave
The god's face glowing o'er a satyr's trunk,
Failure's brief epitaph.

                Yes, Europe's world
Reels on to judgement ; there the common need,
Losing God's sacred use, to be a bond
'Twixt Me and Thee, sets each one scowlingly   70
O'er his own selfish hoard at bay ; no state,
Knit strongly with eternal fibres up
Of all men's separate and united weals,
Self-poised and sole as stars, yet one as light,
Holds up a shape of large Humanity
To which by natural instinct every man
Pays loyalty exulting, by which all
Mould their own lives, and feel their pulses filled
With the red, fiery blood of the general life,
Making them mighty in peace, as now in war   80
They are, even in the flush of victory, weak,
Conquering that manhood which should them subdue.
And what gift bring I to this untried world ?
Shall the same tragedy be played anew,
And the same lurid curtain drop at last
On one dread desolation, one fierce crash
Of that recoil which on its makers God
Lets Ignorance and Sin and Hunger make,
Early or late ? Or shall that commonwealth
Whose potent unity and concentric force   90
Can draw these scattered joints and parts of men
Into a whole ideal man once more,

Which sucks not from its limbs the life away,
But sends its flood-tide and creates itself
Over again in every citizen,
Be there built up ? For me, I have no choice ;
I might turn back to other destinies,
For one sincere key opes all Fortune's doors ;
But whoso answers not God's earliest call
Forfeits or dulls that faculty supreme   100
Of lying open to his genius
Which makes the wise heart certain of its ends.

Here am I ; for what end God knows, not I ;
Westward still points the inexorable soul :
Here am I, with no friend but the sad sea,
The beating heart of this great enterprise,
Which, without me, would stiffen in swift death ;
This have I mused on, since mine eye could first
Among the stars distinguish and with joy
Rest on that God-fed Pharos of the north,   110
On some blue promontory of heaven lighted
That juts far out into the upper sea ;
To this one hope my heart hath clung for years,
As would a foundling to the talisman
Hung round his neck by hands he knew not whose ;
A poor, vile thing and dross to all beside,
Yet he therein can feel a virtue left
By the sad pressure of a mother's hand,
And unto him it still is tremulous
With palpitating haste and wet with tears,   120
The key to him of hope and humanness,
The coarse shell of life's pearl, Expectancy.
This hope hath been to me for love and fame,
Hath made me wholly lonely on the earth,
Building me up as in a thick-ribbed tower,
Wherewith enwalled my watching spirit burned,
Conquering its little island from the Dark,
Sole as a scholar's lamp, and heard men's steps,
In the far hurry of the outward world,
Pass dimly forth and back, sounds heard in dream.   130
As Ganymede by the eagle was snatched up
From the gross sod to be Jove's cupbearer,
So was I lifted by my great design :
And who hath trod Olympus, from his eye
Fades not that broader outlook of the gods ;
His life's low valleys overbrow earth's clouds,
And that Olympian spectre of the past
Looms towering up in sovereign memory,
Beckoning his soul from meaner heights of doom.
Had but the shadow of the Thunderer's bird,   140

Flashing athwart my spirit, made of me
A swift-betraying vision's Ganymede,
Yet to have greatly dreamed precludes low ends ;
Great days have ever such a morning-red,
On such a base great futures are built up,
And aspiration, though not put in act,
Comes back to ask its plighted troth again,
Still watches round its grave the unlaid ghost
Of a dead virtue, and makes other hopes,
Save that implacable one, seem thin and bleak   150
As shadows of bare trees upon the snow,
Bound freezing there by the unpitying moon.

While other youths perplexed their mandolins,
Praying that Thetis would her fingers twine
In the loose glories of her lover's hair,
And wile another kiss to keep back day,
I, stretched beneath the many-centuried shade
Of some writhed oak, the wood's Laocoön,
Did of my hope a dryad mistress make,
Whom I would woo to meet me privily,   160
Or underneath the stars, or when the moon
Flecked all the forest floor with scattered pearls.
O days whose memory tames to fawning down
The surly fell of Ocean's bristled neck !

I know not when this hope enthralled me first,
But from my boyhood up I loved to hear
The tall pine-forests of the Apennine
Murmur their hoary legends of the sea,
Which hearing, I in vision clear beheld
The sudden dark of tropic night shut down   170
O'er the huge whisper of great watery wastes,
The while a pair of herons trailingly
Flapped inland, where some league-wide river hurled
The yellow spoil of unconjectured realms
Far through a gulf's green silence, never scarred
By any but the North-wind's hurrying keels.
And not the pines alone ; all sights and sounds
To my world-seeking heart paid fealty,
And catered for it as the Cretan bees
Brought honey to the baby Jupiter,   180
Who in his soft hand crushed a violet,
Godlike foremusing the rough thunder's gripe ;
Then did I entertain the poet's song,
My great Idea's guest, and, passing o'er
That iron bridge the Tuscan built to hell,
I heard Ulysses tell of mountain-chains
Whose adamantine links, his manacles,

The western main shook growling, and still gnawed.
I brooded on the wise Athenian's tale
Of happy Atlantis, and heard Björne's keel   190
Crunch the grey pebbles of the Vinland shore :
For I believed the poets ; it is they
Who utter wisdom from the central deep,
And, listening to the inner flow of things,
Speak to the age out of eternity.

Ah me ! old hermits sought for solitude
In caves and desert places of the earth,
Where their own heart-beat was the only stir
Of living thing that comforted the year ;
But the bald pillar-top of Simeon,   200
In midnight's blankest waste, were populous,
Matched with the isolation drear and deep
Of him who pines among the swarm of men,
At once a new thought's king and prisoner,
Feeling the truer life within his life,
The fountain of his spirit's prophecy,
Sinking away and wasting, drop by drop,
In the ungrateful sands of sceptic ears.
He in the palace-aisles of untrod woods
Doth walk a king ; for him the pent-up cell   210
Widens beyond the circles of the stars,
And all the sceptred spirits of the past
Come thronging in to greet him as their peer ;
But in the market-place's glare and throng
He sits apart, an exile, and his brow
Aches with the mocking memory of its crown.
Yet to the spirit select there is no choice ;
He cannot say, This will I do, or that,
For the cheap means putting Heaven's ends in pawn,
And bartering his bleak rocks, the freehold stern   220
Of destiny's first-born, for smoother fields
That yield no crop of self-denying will ;
A hand is stretched to him from out the dark,
Which grasping without question, he is led
Where there is work that he must do for God.
The trial still is the strength's complement,
And the uncertain, dizzy path that scales
The sheer heights of supremest purposes
Is steeper to the angel than the child.
Chances have laws as fixed as planets have,   230
And disappointment's dry and bitter root,
Envy's harsh berries, and the choking pool
Of the world's scorn, are the right mother-milk
To the tough hearts that pioneer their kind,
And break a pathway to those unknown realms

That in the earth's broad shadow lie enthralled ;
Endurance is the crowning quality,
And patience all the passion of great hearts ;
These are their stay, and when the leaden world
Sets its hard face against their fateful thought,   240
And brute strength, like a scornful conqueror,
Clangs his huge mace down in the other scale,
The inspired soul but flings his patience in,
And slowly that outweighs the ponderous globe,—
One faith against a whole earth's unbelief,
One soul against the flesh of all mankind.

Thus ever seems it when my soul can hear
The voice that errs not ; then my triumph gleams,
O'er the blank ocean beckoning, and all night
My heart flies on before me as I sail ;   250
Far on I see my lifelong enterprise,
Which rose like Ganges 'mid the freezing snows
Of a world's solitude, sweep broadening down,
And, gathering to itself a thousand streams,
Grow sacred ere it mingle with the sea ;
I see the ungated wall of chaos old,
With blocks Cyclopean hewn of solid night,
Fade like a wreath of unreturning mist
Before the irreversible feet of light ;—
And lo, with what clear omen in the east   260
On day's grey threshold stands the eager dawn,
Like young Leander rosy from the sea
Glowing at Hero's lattice !

             One day more
These muttering shoalbrains leave the helm to me :
God, let me not in their dull ooze be stranded ;
Let not this one frail bark, to hollow which
I have dug out the pith and sinewy heart
Of my aspiring life's fair trunk, be so
Cast up to warp and blacken in the sun,
Just as the opposing wind 'gins whistle off   270
His cheek-swollen pack, and from the leaning mast
Fortune's full sail strains forward !

              One poor day !—
Remember whose and not how short it is !
It is God's day, it is Columbus's.
A lavish day ! One day, with life and heart,
Is more than time enough to find a world.

    1844.

AN INCIDENT OF THE FIRE AT HAMBURG

THE tower of old Saint Nicholas soared upward to the skies,
Like some huge piece of Nature's make, the growth of centuries ;
You could not deem its crowding spires a work of human art,
They seemed to struggle lightward from a sturdy living heart.

Not Nature's self more freely speaks in crystal or in oak,
Than, through the pious builder's hand, in that grey pile she spoke ;
And as from acorn springs the oak, so, freely and alone,
Sprang from his heart this hymn to God, sung in obedient stone.

It seemed a wondrous freak of chance, so perfect, yet so rough,
A whim of Nature crystallized slowly in granite tough ;
The thick spires yearned towards the sky in quaint harmonious lines,
And in broad sunlight basked and slept, like a grove of blasted pines.

Never did rock or stream or tree lay claim with better right
To all the adorning sympathies of shadow and of light ;
And, in that forest petrified, as forester there dwells
Stout Herman, the old sacristan, sole lord of all its bells.

Surge leaping after surge, the fire roared onward red as blood,
Till half of Hamburg lay engulfed beneath the eddying flood ;
For miles away the fiery spray poured down its deadly rain,
And back and forth the billows sucked, and paused, and burst again.

From square to square with tiger leaps panted the lustful fire,
The air to leeward shuddered with the gasps of its desire ;
And church and palace, which even now stood whelmed but to the knee,
Lift their black roofs like breakers lone amid the whirling sea.

Up in his tower old Herman sat and watched with quiet look ;
His soul had trusted God too long to be at last forsook ;
He could not fear, for surely God a pathway would unfold
Through this red sea for faithful hearts, as once he did of old.

But scarcely can he cross himself, or on his good saint call,
Before the sacrilegious flood o'erleaped the churchyard wall ;
And, ere a *pater* half was said, 'mid smoke and crackling glare,
His island tower scarce juts its head above the wide despair.

Upon the peril's desperate peak his heart stood up sublime ;
His first thought was for God above, his next was for his chime ;
' Sing now and make your voices heard in hymns of praise,' cried he,
' As did the Israelites of old, safe walking through the sea !

' Through this red sea our God hath made the pathway safe to shore ;
Our promised land stands full in sight ; shout now as ne'er before ! '
And as the tower came crushing down, the bells, in clear accord,
Pealed forth the grand old German hymn,—' All good souls, praise the Lord!'

THE SOWER

I saw a Sower walking slow
Across the earth, from east to west ;
His hair was white as mountain snow,
His head drooped forward on his
    breast.

With shrivelled hands he flung his
    seed,
Nor ever turned to look behind ;
Of sight or sound he took no heed ;
It seemed he was both deaf and blind.

His dim face showed no soul beneath,
Yet in my heart I felt a stir,
As if I looked upon the sheath
That once had clasped Excalibur.

I heard, as still the seed he cast,
How, crooning to himself, he sung,
' I sow again the holy Past,
The happy days when I was young.

' Then all was wheat without a tare,
Then all was righteous, fair, and true ;
And I am he whose thoughtful care
Shall plant the Old World in the New.

' The fruitful germs I scatter free,
With busy hand, while all men sleep ;
In Europe now, from sea to sea,
The nations bless me as they reap.'

Then I looked back along his path,
And heard the clash of steel on steel,
Where man faced man, in deadly
    wrath,
While clanged the tocsin's hurrying
    peal.

The sky with burning towns flared red,
Nearer the noise of fighting rolled,
And brothers' blood, by brothers shed,
Crept, curdling, over pavements cold.

Then marked I how each germ of
    truth
Which through the dotard's fingers
    ran
Was mated with a dragon's tooth
Whence there sprang up an armèd
    man.

I shouted, but he could not hear ;
Made signs, but these he could not
    see ;
And still, without a doubt or fear,
Broadcast he scattered anarchy.

Long to my straining ears the blast
Brought faintly back the words he
    sung :
' I sow again the holy Past,
The happy days when I was young.'

HUNGER AND COLD

Sisters two, all praise to you,
With your faces pinched and blue ;
To the poor man you've been true
    From of old :
You can speak the keenest word,
You are sure of being heard,
From the point you're never stirred,
    Hunger and Cold !

Let sleek statesmen temporize ;
Palsied are their shifts and lies
When they meet your bloodshot eyes,
    Grim and bold ;

Policy you set at naught,
In their traps you'll not be caught,
You're too honest to be bought,
    Hunger and Cold !

Bolt and bar the palace door ;
While the mass of men are poor,
Naked truth grows more and more
    Uncontrolled ;
You had never yet, I guess,
Any praise for bashfulness,
You can visit sans court-dress,
    Hunger and Cold !

While the music fell and rose,
And the dance reeled to its close,
Where her round of costly woes
    Fashion strolled,
I beheld with shuddering fear
Wolves' eyes through the windows
    peer;
Little dream they you are near,
    Hunger and Cold!

When the toiler's heart you clutch,
Conscience is not valued much,
He recks not a bloody smutch
    On his gold:
Everything to you defers,
You are potent reasoners,
At your whisper Treason stirs,
    Hunger and Cold!

Rude comparisons you draw,
Words refuse to sate your maw,
Your gaunt limbs the cobweb law
    Cannot hold:
You're not clogged with foolish pride,
But can seize a right denied:
Somehow God is on your side,
    Hunger and Cold!

You respect no hoary wrong
More for having triumphed long;
Its past victims, haggard throng,
    From the mould

You unbury: swords and spears
Weaker are than poor men's tears,
Weaker than your silent years,
    Hunger and Cold!

Let them guard both hall and bower;
Through the window you will glower,
Patient till your reckoning hour
    Shall be tolled:
Cheeks are pale, but hands are red,
Guiltless blood may chance be shed,
But ye must and will be fed,
    Hunger and Cold!

God has plans man must not spoil,
Some were made to starve and toil,
Some to share the wine and oil,
    We are told:
Devil's theories are these,
Stifling hope and love and peace,
Framed your hideous lusts to please,
    Hunger and Cold!

Scatter ashes on thy head,
Tears of burning sorrow shed,
Earth! and be by Pity led
    To Love's fold;
Ere they block the very door
With lean corpses of the poor,
And will hush for naught but gore,
    Hunger and Cold!
1844.

THE LANDLORD

WHAT boot your houses and your
    lands?
    In spite of close-drawn deed and
        fence,
Like water, 'twixt your cheated hands,
They slip into the graveyard's sands,
    And mock your ownership's pre-
        tence.

How shall you speak to urge your
    right,
    Choked with that soil for which you
        lust?
The bit of clay, for whose delight
You grasp, is mortgaged, too; Death
    might
    Foreclose this very day in dust.

Fence as you please, this plain poor
    man,
    Whose only fields are in his wit,
Who shapes the world, as best he
    can,
According to God's higher plan,
    Owns you, and fences as is fit.

Though yours the rents, his incomes
    wax
    By right of eminent domain;
From factory tall to woodman's
    axe,
All things on earth must pay their
    tax,
    To feed his hungry heart and
        brain,

He takes you from your easy-chair,
  And what he plans that you must
      do ;
You sleep in down, eat dainty fare,—
He mounts his crazy garret-stair
  And starves, the landlord over you.

Feeding the clods your idlesse drains,
  You make more green six feet of
      soil ;

His fruitful word, like suns and rains,
Partakes the seasons' bounteous pains,
  And toils to lighten human toil.

Your lands, with force or cunning
      got,
  Shrink to the measure of the grave ;
But Death himself abridges not
The tenures of almighty thought,
  The titles of the wise and brave.

TO A PINE-TREE

FAR up on Katahdin thou towerest,
  Purple-blue with the distance and vast ;
Like a cloud o'er the lowlands thou lowerest,
  That hangs poised on a lull in the blast,
    To its fall leaning awful.

In the storm, like a prophet o'ermaddened,
  Thou singest and tossest thy branches ;
Thy heart with the terror is gladdened,
  Thou forebodest the dread avalanches,
    When whole mountains swoop valeward,

In the calm thou o'erstretchest the valleys
  With thine arms, as if blessings imploring,
Like an old king led forth from his palace,
  When his people to battle are pouring
    From the city beneath him.

To the lumberer asleep 'neath thy glooming
  Thou dost sing of wild billows in motion,
Till he longs to be swung 'mid their booming
  In the tents of the Arabs of ocean,
    Whose finned isles are their cattle.

For the gale snatches thee for his lyre,
  With mad hand crashing melody frantic,
While he pours forth his mighty desire
  To leap down on the eager Atlantic,
    Whose arms stretch to his playmate.

The wild storm makes his lair in thy branches,
  Preying thence on the continent under ;
Like a lion, crouched close on his haunches,
  There awaiteth his leap the fierce thunder,
    Growling low with impatience.

Spite of winter, thou keep'st thy green glory,
   Lusty father of Titans past number !
The snow-flakes alone make thee hoary,
    Nestling close to thy branches in slumber,
     And thee mantling with silence.

Thou alone know'st the splendour of winter,
   'Mid thy snow-silvered, hushed precipices,
Hearing crags of green ice groan and splinter,
    And then plunge down the muffled abysses
     In the quiet of midnight.

Thou alone know'st the glory of summer,
   Gazing down on thy broad seas of forest,
On thy subjects that send a proud murmur
    Up to thee, to their sachem, who towerest
     From thy bleak throne to heaven.

SI DESCENDERO IN INFERNUM, ADES

O, WANDERING dim on the extremest edge
   Of God's bright providence, whose spirits sigh
Drearily in you, like the winter sedge
    That shivers o'er the dead pool stiff and dry,
     A thin, sad voice, when the bold wind roars by
      From the clear North of Duty,—
Still by cracked arch and broken shaft I trace
That here was once a shrine and holy place
      Of the supernal Beauty,—
    A child's play-altar reared of stones and moss,
    With wilted flowers for offering laid across,
Mute recognition of the all-ruling Grace.

How far are ye from the innocent, from those
   Whose hearts are as a little lane serene,
Smooth-heaped from wall to wall with unbroke snows,
    Or in the summer blithe with lamb-cropped green,
    Save the one track, where naught more rude is seen
     Than the plump wain at even
Bringing home four months' sunshine bound in sheaves !—
How far are ye from those ! yet who believes
      That ye can shut out heaven ?
    Your souls partake its influence, not in vain
    Nor all unconscious, as that silent lane
Its drift of noiseless apple-blooms receives.

Looking within myself, I note how thin
   A plank of station, chance, or prosperous fate,
Doth fence me from the clutching waves of sin ;—
    In my own heart I find the worst man's mate,
    And see not dimly the smooth-hingèd gate
     That opes to those abysses

Where ye grope darkly,—ye who never knew
On your young hearts love's consecrating dew,
    Or felt a mother's kisses,
    Or home's restraining tendrils round you curled ;
    Ah, side by side with heart's-ease in this world
The fatal nightshade grows and bitter rue !

One band ye cannot break,—the force that clips
    And grasps your circles to the central light ;
Yours is the prodigal comet's long ellipse,
    Self-exiled to the farthest verge of night ;
    Yet strives with you no less that inward might
    No sin hath e'er imbruted ;—
The god in you the creed-dimmed eye eludes ;
The Law brooks not to have its solitudes
    By bigot feet polluted ;—
    Yet they who watch your God-compelled return
    May see your happy perihelion burn
Where the calm sun his unfledged planets broods.

TO THE PAST

WONDROUS and awful are thy silent halls,
    O kingdom of the past !
There lie the bygone ages in their palls,
    Guarded by shadows vast ;
    There all is hushed and breathless,
Save when some image of old error falls
    Earth worshipped once as deathless.

There sits drear Egypt, 'mid belea-
        guering sands,
    Half woman and half beast,
The burnt-out torch within her
        mouldering hands
    That once lit all the East ;
A dotard bleared and hoary,
There Asser crouches o'er the black-
        ened brands
    Of Asia's long-quenched glory.

Still as a city buried 'neath the sea
    Thy courts and temples stand ;
Idle as forms on wind-waved tapestry
    Of saints and heroes grand,
Thy phantasms grope and shiver,
Or watch the loose shores crumbling
        silently
    Into Time's gnawing river.

Titanic shapes with faces blank and
        dun,
    Of their old godhead lorn,
Gaze on the embers of the sunken sun,
    Which they misdeem for morn ;
    And yet the eternal sorrow
In their unmonarched eyes says day
        is done
    Without the hope of morrow.

O realm of silence and of swart eclipse,
    The shapes that haunt thy gloom
Make signs to us and move their
        withered lips
    Across the gulf of doom ;
    Yet all their sound and motion
Bring no more freight to us than
        wraiths of ships
    On the mirage's ocean.

And if sometimes a moaning wander-
        eth
    From out thy desolate halls,
If some grim shadow of thy living death
    Across our sunshine falls
    And scares the world to error,
The eternal life sends forth melodious
        breath
    To chase the misty terror.

Thy mighty clamours, wars, and
world-noised deeds
Are silent now in dust,
Gone like a tremble of the huddling
reeds
Beneath some sudden gust ;
Thy forms and creeds have van-
ished,
Tossed out to wither like unsightly
weeds
From the world's garden banished.

Whatever of true life there was in thee
Leaps in our age's veins ;
Wield still thy bent and wrinkled
empery,

And shake thine idle chains ;—
To thee thy dross is clinging,
For us thy martyrs die, thy prophets
see,
Thy poets still are singing.

Here, 'mid the bleak waves of our
strife and care,
Float the green Fortunate Isles
Where all thy hero-spirits dwell, and
share
Our martyrdoms and toils ;
The present moves attended
With all of brave and excellent and
fair
That made the old time splendid.

TO THE FUTURE

O LAND of Promise ! from what Pisgah's height
Can I behold thy stretch of peaceful bowers,
Thy golden harvests flowing out of sight,
Thy nestled homes and sun-illumined towers ?
Gazing upon the sunset's high-heaped gold,
Its crags of opal and of chrysolite,
Its deeps on deeps of glory, that unfold
Still brightening abysses,
And blazing precipices,
Whence but a scanty leap it seems to heaven,   10
Sometimes a glimpse is given
Of thy more gorgeous realm, thy more unstinted blisses.

O Land of Quiet ! to thy shore the surf
Of the perturbèd Present rolls and sleeps ;
Our storms breathe soft as June upon thy turf
And lure out blossoms ; to thy bosom leaps,
As to a mother's, the o'erwearied heart,
Hearing far off and dim the toiling mart,
The hurrying feet, the curses without number,
And, circled with the glow Elysian   20
Of thine exulting vision,
Out of its very cares wooes charms for peace and slumber.

To thee the earth lifts up her fettered hands
And cries for vengeance ; with a pitying smile
Thou blessest her, and she forgets her bands,
And her old woe-worn face a little while
Grows young and noble ; unto thee the Oppressor
Looks, and is dumb with awe ;
The eternal law,

Which makes the crime its own blindfold redresser,   30
Shadows his heart with perilous foreboding,
    And he can see the grim-eyed Doom
    From out the trembling gloom
Its silent-footed steeds towards his palace goading.

What promises hast thou for Poets' eyes,
    Aweary of the turmoil and the wrong !
To all their hopes what overjoyed replies !
    What undreamed ecstasies for blissful song !
Thy happy plains no war-trump's brawling clangor
    Disturbs, and fools the poor to hate the poor ;   40
The humble glares not on the high with anger ;
    Love leaves no grudge at less, no greed for more ;
In vain strives Self the godlike sense to smother ;
    From the soul's deeps
    It throbs and leaps ;
The noble 'neath foul rags beholds his long-lost brother.

To thee the Martyr looketh, and his fires
    Unlock their fangs and leave his spirit free ;
To thee the Poet 'mid his toil aspires,
    And grief and hunger climb about his knee,
Welcome as children ; thou upholdest   50
    The lone Inventor by his demon haunted ;
The Prophet cries to thee when hearts are coldest,
    And gazing o'er the midnight's bleak abyss,
    Sees the drowsed soul awaken at thy kiss,
And stretch its happy arms and leap up disenchanted.

Thou bringest vengeance, but so loving-kindly
    The guilty thinks it pity ; taught by thee,
Fierce tyrants drop the scourges wherewith blindly
    Their own souls they were scarring ; conquerors see   60
With horror in their hands the accursed spear
    That tore the meek One's side on Calvary,
And from their trophies shrink with ghastly fear ;
    Thou, too, art the Forgiver,
The beauty of man's soul to man revealing ;
    The arrows from thy quiver
Pierce Error's guilty heart, but only pierce for healing.

O, whither, whither, glory-wingèd dreams,
    From out Life's sweat and turmoil would ye bear me ?
Shut, gates of Fancy, on your golden gleams,—   70
    This agony of hopeless contrast spare me !
Fade, cheating glow, and leave me to my night !
    He is a coward, who would borrow
    A charm against the present sorrow

From the vague Future's promise of delight :
    As life's alarums nearer roll,
      The ancestral buckler calls,
      Self-clanging from the walls
    In the high temple of the soul ;
Where are most sorrows, there the poet's sphere is,   80
      To feed the soul with patience,
      To heal its desolations,
With words of unshorn truth, with love that never wearies.

HEBE

I saw the twinkle of white feet,
I saw the flash of robes descending ;
  Before her ran an influence fleet,
That bowed my heart like barley
    bending.

  As, in bare fields, the searching bees
Pilot to blooms beyond our finding,
  It led me on, by sweet degrees
Joy's simple honey-cells unbinding.

  Those Graces were that seemed
    grim Fates ;
With nearer love the sky leaned o'er
    me ;
  The long-sought Secret's golden
    gates
On musical hinges swung before me.

  I saw the brimmed bowl in her grasp
Thrilling with godhood ; like a lover
  I sprang the proffered life to clasp;—
The beaker fell ; the luck was over.

  The Earth has drunk the vintage
    up ;
What boots it patch the goblet's
    splinters ?
  Can Summer fill the icy cup,
Whose treacherous crystal is but
    Winter's ?

  O spendthrift haste ! await the
    Gods ;
Their nectar crowns the lips of
    Patience ;
  Haste scatters on unthankful sods
The immortal gift in vain libations.

  Coy Hebe flies from those that
    woo,
And shuns the hands would seize
    upon her ;
  Follow thy life, and she will sue
To pour for thee the cup of honour.

THE SEARCH

    I went to seek for Christ,
    And Nature seemed so fair
That first the woods and fields my youth enticed,
    And I was sure to find him there :
      The temple I forsook,
      And to the solitude
Allegiance paid ; but Winter came and shook
    The crown and purple from my wood ;
His snows, like desert sands, with scornful drift,
    Besieged the columned aisle and palace-gate ;

My Thebes, cut deep with many a solemn rift,
  But epitaphed her own sepulchred state :
Then I remembered whom I went to seek,
And blessed blunt Winter for his counsel bleak.

      Back to the world I turned,
        For Christ, I said, is King ;
So the cramped alley and the hut I spurned,
      As far beneath his sojourning :
        'Mid power and wealth I sought,
        But found no trace of him,
And all the costly offerings I had brought
      With sudden rust and mould grew dim :
I found his tomb, indeed, where, by their laws,
  All must on stated days themselves imprison,
Mocking with bread a dead creed's grinning jaws,
  Witless how long the life had thence arisen ;
Due sacrifice to this they set apart,
Prizing it more than Christ's own living heart.

      So from my feet the dust
        Of the proud World I shook ;
Then came dear Love and shared with me his crust,
      And half my sorrow's burden took.
        After the World's soft bed,
        Its rich and dainty fare,
Like down seemed Love's coarse pillow to my head,
  .   His cheap food seemed as manna rare ;
Fresh-trodden prints of bare and bleeding feet,
  Turned to the heedless city whence I came,
Hard by I saw, and springs of worship sweet
  Gushed from my cleft heart smitten by the same ;
Love looked me in the face and spake no words,
But straight I knew those footprints were the Lord's.

      I followed where they led,
        And in a hovel rude,
With naught to fence the weather from his head,
      The King I sought for meekly stood ;
        A naked, hungry child
        Clung round his gracious knee,
And a poor hunted slave looked up and smiled
  To bless the smile that set him free ;
New miracles I saw his presence do,—
  No more I knew the hovel bare and poor,
The gathered chips into a woodpile grew,
  The broken morsel swelled to goodly store ;
I knelt and wept : my Christ no more I seek,
His throne is with the outcast and the weak.

THE PRESENT CRISIS

WHEN a deed is done for Freedom, through the broad earth's aching breast
Runs a thrill of joy prophetic, trembling on from east to west,
And the slave, where'er he cowers, feels the soul within him climb
To the awful verge of manhood, as the energy sublime
Of a century bursts full-blossomed on the thorny stem of Time.

Through the walls of hut and palace shoots the instantaneous throe,
When the travail of the Ages wrings earth's systems to and fro ;
At the birth of each new Era, with a recognizing start,
Nation wildly looks at nation, standing with mute lips apart,
And glad Truth's yet mightier man-child leaps beneath the Future's heart.

So the Evil's triumph sendeth, with a terror and a chill,
Under continent to continent, the sense of coming ill,
And the slave, where'er he cowers, feels his sympathies with God
In hot tear-drops ebbing earthward, to be drunk up by the sod,
Till a corpse crawls round unburied, delving in the nobler clod.

For mankind are one in spirit, and an instinct bears along,
Round the earth's electric circle, the swift flash of right or wrong ;
Whether conscious or unconscious, yet Humanity's vast frame
Through its ocean-sundered fibres feels the gush of joy or shame ;—
In the gain or loss of one race all the rest have equal claim.

Once to every man and nation comes the moment to decide,
In the strife of Truth with Falsehood, for the good or evil side ;
Some great cause, God's new Messiah, offering each the bloom or blight,
Parts the goats upon the left hand, and the sheep upon the right,
And the choice goes by forever 'twixt that darkness and that light.

Hast thou chosen, O my people, on whose party thou shalt stand,
Ere the Doom from its worn sandals shakes the dust against our land ?
Though the cause of Evil prosper, yet 't is Truth alone is strong,
And, albeit she wander outcast now, I see around her throng
Troops of beautiful, tall angels, to enshield her from all wrong.

Backward look across the ages and the beacon-moments see,
That, like peaks of some sunk continent, jut through Oblivion's sea ;
Not an ear in court or market for the low foreboding cry
Of those Crises, God's stern winnowers, from whose feet earth's chaff must fly;
Never shows the choice momentous till the judgement hath passed by.

Careless seems the great Avenger ; history's pages but record
One death-grapple in the darkness 'twixt old systems and the Word ;
Truth forever on the scaffold, Wrong forever on the throne,—
Yet that scaffold sways the future, and, behind the dim unknown,
Standeth God within the shadow, keeping watch above his own.

We see dimly in the Present what is small and what is great,
Slow of faith, how weak an arm may turn the iron helm of fate,
But the soul is still oracular ; amid the market's din,
List the ominous stern whisper from the Delphic cave within,—
' They enslave their children's children who make compromise with sin.'

Slavery, the earth-born Cyclops, fellest of the giant brood,
Sons of brutish Force and Darkness, who have drenched the earth with blood,
Famished in his self-made desert, blinded by our purer day,
Gropes in yet unblasted regions for his miserable prey ;—
Shall we guide his gory fingers where our helpless children play ?

Then to side with Truth is noble when we share her wretched crust,
Ere her cause bring fame and profit, and 't is prosperous to be just ;
Then it is the brave man chooses, while the coward stands aside,
Doubting in his abject spirit, till his Lord is crucified,
And the multitude make virtue of the faith they had denied.

Count me o'er earth's chosen heroes,—they were souls that stood alone,
While the men they agonized for hurled the contumelious stone,
Stood serene, and down the future saw the golden beam incline
To the side of perfect justice, mastered by their faith divine,
By one man's plain truth to manhood and to God's supreme design.

By the light of burning heretics Christ's bleeding feet I track,
Toiling up new Calvaries ever with the cross that turns not back,
And these mounts of anguish number how each generation learned
One new word of that grand *Credo* which in prophet-hearts hath burned
Since the first man stood God-conquered with his face to heaven upturned.

For Humanity sweeps onward : where to-day the martyr stands,
On the morrow crouches Judas with the silver in his hands ;
Far in front the cross stands ready and the crackling fagots burn,
While the hooting mob of yesterday in silent awe return
To glean up the scattered ashes into History's golden urn.

'T is as easy to be heroes as to sit the idle slaves
Of a legendary virtue carved upon our fathers' graves,
Worshippers of light ancestral make the present light a crime ;—
Was the Mayflower launched by cowards, steered by men behind their time ?
Turn those tracks toward Past or Future, that make Plymouth Rock sublime?

They were men of present valour, stalwart old iconoclasts,
Unconvinced by axe or gibbet that all virtue was the Past's ;
But we make their truth our falsehood, thinking that hath made us free,
Hoarding it in mouldy parchments, while our tender spirits flee
The rude grasp of that great Impulse which drove them across the sea.

LOWELL   E

They have rights who dare maintain them; we are traitors to our sires,
Smothering in their holy ashes Freedom's new-lit altar-fires;
Shall we make their creed our jailer? Shall we, in our haste to slay,
From the tombs of the old prophets steal the funeral lamps away
To light up the martyr-fagots round the prophets of to-day?

New occasions teach new duties: Time makes ancient good uncouth;
They must upward still, and onward, who would keep abreast of Truth;
Lo, before us gleam her camp-fires! we ourselves must Pilgrims be,
Launch our Mayflower, and steer boldly through the desperate winter sea,
Nor attempt the Future's portal with the Past's blood-rusted key.

December, 1845.

AN INDIAN-SUMMER REVERIE

WHAT visionary tints the year puts on,
When falling leaves falter through motionless air
Or numbly cling and shiver to be gone!
How shimmer the low flats and pastures bare,
As with her nectar Hebe Autumn fills
The bowl between me and those distant hills,
And smiles and shakes abroad her misty, tremulous hair!

No more the landscape holds its wealth apart,
Making me poorer in my poverty,
But mingles with my senses and my heart;
My own projected spirit seems to me
In her own reverie the world to steep;
'T is she that waves to sympathetic sleep,
Moving, as she is moved, each field and hill and tree.

How fuse and mix, with what unfelt degrees,
Clasped by the faint horizon's languid arms,
Each into each, the hazy distances!
The softened season all the landscape charms;
Those hills, my native village that embay,
In waves of dreamier purple roll away,
And floating in mirage seem all the glimmering farms.

Far distant sounds the hidden chickadee
Close at my side; far distant sound the leaves;
The fields seem fields of dream, where Memory
Wanders like gleaning Ruth; and as the sheaves
Of wheat and barley wavered in the eye
Of Boaz as the maiden's glow went by,
So tremble and seem remote all things the sense receives.

The cock's shrill trump that tells of scattered corn,
Passed breezily on by all his flapping mates,
Faint and more faint, from barn to barn is borne,
Southward, perhaps to far Magellan's Straits;

Dimly I catch the throb of distant flails;
Silently overhead the hen-hawk sails,
With watchful, measuring eye, and for his quarry waits.

The sobered robin, hunger-silent now,
Seeks cedar-berries blue, his autumn cheer;
The squirrel, on the shingly shag-bark's bough,
Now saws, now lists with downward eye and ear,
Then drops his nut, and with a chipping bound
Whisks to his winding fastness underground;
The clouds like swans drift down the streaming atmosphere.

O'er yon bare knoll the pointed cedar shadows
Drowse on the crisp, grey moss; the ploughman's call
Creeps faint as smoke from black, fresh-furrowed meadows;
The single crow a single caw lets fall;
And all around me every bush and tree
Says Autumn's here, and Winter soon will be,
Who snows his soft, white sleep and silence over all.

The birch, most shy and ladylike of trees,
Her poverty, as best she may, retrieves,
And hints at her foregone gentilities
With some saved relics of her wealth of leaves;
The swamp-oak, with his royal purple on,
Glares red as blood across the sinking sun,
As one who proudlier to a falling fortune cleaves.

He looks a sachem, in red blanket wrapt,
Who, 'mid some council of the sad-garbed whites,
Erect and stern, in his own memories lapt,
With distant eye broods over other sights,
Sees the hushed wood the city's flare replace,
The wounded turf heal o'er the railway's trace,
And roams the savage Past of his undwindled rights.

The red-oak, softer-grained, yields all for lost,
And, with his crumpled foliage stiff and dry,
After the first betrayal of the frost,
Rebuffs the kiss of the relenting sky;
The chestnuts, lavish of their long-hid gold,
To the faint Summer, beggared now and old,
Pour back the sunshine hoarded 'neath her favouring eye.

The ash her purple drops forgivingly
And sadly, breaking not the general hush;
The maple-swamps glow like a sunset sea,
Each leaf a ripple with its separate flush;
All round the wood's edge creeps the skirting blaze
Of bushes low, as when, on cloudy days,
Ere the rain falls, the cautious farmer burns his brush.

O'er yon low wall, which guards one unkempt zone,
Where vines, and weeds, and scrub-oaks intertwine
  Safe from the plough, whose rough, discordant stone
Is massed to one soft grey by lichens fine,
    The tangled blackberry, crossed and recrossed, weaves
    A prickly network of ensanguined leaves ;
Hard by, with coral beads, the prim black-alders shine.

Pillaring with flame this crumbling boundary,
Whose loose blocks topple 'neath the ploughboy's foot,
  Who, with each sense shut fast except the eye,
Creeps close and scares the jay he hoped to shoot,
    The woodbine up the elm's straight stem aspires,
    Coiling it, harmless, with autumnal fires ;
In the ivy's paler blaze the martyr oak stands mute.

Below, the Charles—a stripe of nether sky,
Now hid by rounded apple-trees between,
  Whose gaps the misplaced sail sweeps bellying by,
Now flickering golden through a woodland screen,
    Then spreading out, at his next turn beyond,
    A silver circle like an inland pond—
Slips seaward silently through marshes purple and green.

Dear marshes ! vain to him the gift of sight
Who cannot in their various incomes share,
  From every season drawn, of shade and light,
Who sees in them but levels brown and bare ;
    Each change of storm or sunshine scatters free
    On them its largess of variety,
For Nature with cheap means still works her wonders rare.

In Spring they lie one broad expanse of green,
O'er which the light winds run with glimmering feet :
  Here, yellower stripes track out the creek unseen,
There, darker growths o'er hidden ditches meet ;
    And purpler stains show where the blossoms crowd,
    As if the silent shadow of a cloud
Hung there becalmed, with the next breath to fleet.

All round, upon the river's slippery edge,
Witching to deeper calm the drowsy tide,
  Whispers and leans the breeze-entangling sedge ;
Through emerald glooms the lingering waters slide,
    Or, sometimes wavering, throw back the sun,
    And the stiff banks in eddies melt and run
Of dimpling light, and with the current seem to glide.

In Summer 't is a blithesome sight to see,
As, step by step, with measured swing, they pass,
The wide-ranked mowers wading to the knee,
Their sharp scythes panting through the thick-set grass;
Then, stretched beneath a rick's shade in a ring,
Their nooning take, while one begins to sing
A stave that droops and dies 'neath the close sky of brass.

Meanwhile that devil-may-care, the bobolink,
Remembering duty, in mid-quaver stops
Just ere he sweeps o'er rapture's tremulous brink,
And 'twixt the winrows most demurely drops,
A decorous bird of business, who provides
For his brown mate and fledgelings six besides,
And looks from right to left, a farmer 'mid his crops.

Another change subdues them in the Fall,
But saddens not; they still show merrier tints,
Though sober russet seems to cover all;
When the first sunshine through their dew-drops glints,
Look how the yellow clearness, streamed across,
Redeems with rarer hues the season's loss,
As Dawn's feet there had touched and left their rosy prints.

Or come when sunset gives its freshened zest,
Lean o'er the bridge and let the ruddy thrill,
While the shorn sun swells down the hazy west,
Glow opposite;—the marshes drink their fill
And swoon with purple veins, then slowly fade
Through pink to brown, as eastward moves the shade,
Lengthening with stealthy creep, of Simond's darkening hill.

Later, and yet ere Winter wholly shuts,
Ere through the first dry snow the runner grates,
And the loath cart-wheel screams in slippery ruts,
While firmer ice the eager boy awaits,
Trying each buckle and strap beside the fire,
And until bedtime plays with his desire,
Twenty times putting on and off his new-bought skates;—

Then, every morn, the river's banks shine bright
With smooth plate-armour, treacherous and frail,
By the frost's clinking hammers forged at night,
'Gainst which the lances of the sun prevail,
Giving a pretty emblem of the day
When guiltier arms in light shall melt away,
And states shall move free-limbed, loosed from war's cramping mail.

And now those waterfalls the ebbing river
Twice every day creates on either side
   Tinkle, as through their fresh-sparred grots they shiver
In grass-arched channels to the sun denied ;
   High flaps in sparkling blue the far-heard crow,
   The silvered flats gleam frostily below,
Suddenly drops the gull and breaks the glassy tide.

But crowned in turn by vying seasons three,
Their winter halo hath a fuller ring ;
   This glory seems to rest immovably,—
The others were too fleet and vanishing ;
   When the hid tide is at its highest flow,
   O'er marsh and stream one breathless trance of snow
With brooding fullness awes and hushes everything.

The sunshine seems blown off by the bleak wind,
As pale as formal candles lit by day ;
   Gropes to the sea the river dumb and blind ;
The brown ricks, snow-thatched by the storm in play,
   Show pearly breakers combing o'er their lee,
   White crests as of some just enchanted sea,
Checked in their maddest leap and hanging poised midway.

But when the eastern blow, with rain aslant,
From mid-sea's prairies green and rolling plains
   Drives in his wallowing herds of billows gaunt,
And the roused Charles remembers in his veins
   Old Ocean's blood and snaps his gyves of frost,
   That tyrannous silence on the shores is tost
In dreary wreck, and crumbling desolation reigns.

Edgewise or flat, in Druid-like device,
With leaden pools between or gullies bare,
   The blocks lie strewn, a bleak Stonehenge of ice ;
No life, no sound, to break the grim despair,
   Save sullen plunge, as through the sedges stiff
   Down crackles riverward some thaw-sapped cliff,
Or when the close-wedged fields of ice crunch here and there.

But let me turn from fancy-pictured scenes
To that whose pastoral calm before me lies :
   Here nothing harsh or rugged intervenes ;
The early evening with her misty dyes
   Smooths off the ravelled edges of the nigh,
   Relieves the distant with her cooler sky,
And tones the landscape down, and soothes the wearied eyes.

There gleams my native village, dear to me,
Though higher change's waves each day are seen,
Whelming fields famed in boyhood's history,
Sanding with houses the diminished green ;
There, in red brick, which softening time defies,
Stand square and stiff the Muses' factories ;—
How with my life knit up is every well-known scene !

Flow on, dear river ! not alone you flow
To outward sight, and through your marshes wind ;
Fed from the mystic springs of long-ago,
Your twin flows silent through my world of mind :
Grow dim, dear marshes, in the evening's grey !
Before my inner sight ye stretch away,
And will forever, though these fleshly eyes grow blind.

Beyond the hillock's house-bespotted swell,
Where Gothic chapels house the horse and chaise,
Where quiet cits in Grecian temples dwell,
Where Coptic tombs resound with prayer and praise,
Where dust and mud the equal year divide,
There gentle Allston lived, and wrought, and died,
Transfiguring street and shop with his illumined gaze.

Virgilium vidi tantum,—I have seen
But as a boy, who looks alike on all,
That misty hair, that fine Undine-like mien,
Tremulous as down to feeling's faintest call ;—
Ah, dear old homestead ! count it to thy fame
That thither many times the Painter came ;—
One elm yet bears his name, a feathery tree and tall.

Swiftly the present fades in memory's glow,—
Our only sure possession is the past ;
The village blacksmith died a month ago,
And dim to me the forge's roaring blast ;
Soon fire-new mediaevals we shall see
Oust the black smithy from its chestnut-tree,
And that hewn down, perhaps, the beehive green and vast.

How many times, prouder than king on throne,
Loosed from the village school-dame's A's and B's,
Panting have I the creaky bellows blown,
And watched the pent volcano's red increase,
Then paused to see the ponderous sledge, brought down
By that hard arm voluminous and brown,
From the white iron swarm its golden vanishing bees.

Dear native town ! whose choking elms each year
With eddying dust before their time turn grey,
　　Pining for rain,—to me thy dust is dear ;
It glorifies the eve of summer day,
　　And when the westering sun half sunken burns,
　　The mote-thick air to deepest orange turns,
The westward horseman rides through clouds of gold away,

　　So palpable, I've seen those unshorn few,
The six old willows at the causey's end
　　(Such trees Paul Potter never dreamed nor drew),
Through this dry mist their chequering shadows send,
　　Striped, here and there, with many a long-drawn thread,
　　Where streamed through leafy chinks the trembling red,
Past which, in one bright trail, the hangbird's flashes blend.

　　Yes, dearer far thy dust than all that e'er,
Beneath the awarded crown of victory,
　　Gilded the blown Olympic charioteer ;
Though lightly prized the ribboned parchments three,
　　Yet *collegisse juvat*, I am glad
　　That here what colleging was mine I had,—
It linked another tie, dear native town, with thee !

　　Nearer art thou than simply native earth,
My dust with thine concedes a deeper tie ;
　　A closer claim thy soil may well put forth,
Something of kindred more than sympathy ;
　　For in thy bounds I reverently laid away
　　That blinding anguish of forsaken clay,
That title I seemed to have in earth and sea and sky,

　　That portion of my life more choice to me
(Though brief, yet in itself so round and whole)
　　Than all the imperfect residue can be ;—
The Artist saw his statue of the soul
　　Was perfect ; so, with one regretful stroke,
　　The earthen model into fragments broke,
And without her the impoverished seasons roll.

THE GROWTH OF THE LEGEND

A FRAGMENT

A LEGEND that grew in the forest's hush
Slowly as tear-drops gather and gush,
When a word some poet chanced to say
Ages ago, in his careless way,

Brings our youth back to us out of its shroud
Clearly as under yon thunder-cloud
I see that white sea-gull. It grew and grew,
From the pine-trees gathering a sombre hue,
Till it seems a mere murmur out of the vast
Norwegian forests of the past ;   10
And it grew itself like a true Northern pine,
First a little slender line,
Like a mermaid's green eyelash, and then anon
A stem that a tower might rest upon,
Standing spear-straight in the waist-deep moss,
Its bony roots clutching around and across,
As if they would tear up earth's heart in their grasp
Ere the storm should uproot them or make them unclasp ;
Its cloudy boughs singing, as suiteth the pine,
To shrunk snow-bearded sea-kings old songs of the brine,   20
Till they straightened and let their staves fall to the floor,
Hearing waves moan again on the perilous shore
Of Vinland, perhaps, while their prow groped its way
'Twixt the frothed gnashing tusks of some ship-crunching bay.

So, pine-like, the legend grew, strong-limbed and tall,
As the Gipsy child grows that eats crusts in the hall ;
It sucked the whole strength of the earth and the sky,
Spring, Summer, Fall, Winter, all brought it supply ;
'T was a natural growth, and stood fearlessly there,
True part of the landscape as sea, land, and air ;   30
For it grew in good times, ere the fashion it was
To force these wild births of the woods under glass,
And so, if 't is told as it should be told,
Though 't were sung under Venice's moonlight of gold,
You would hear the old voice of its mother, the pine,
Murmur sealike and northern through every line,
And the verses should grow, self-sustained and free,
Round the vibrating stem of the melody,
Like the lithe moonlit limbs of the parent tree.

Yes, the pine is the mother of legends ; what food   40
For their grim roots is left when the thousand-yeared wood,
The dim-aisled cathedral, whose tall arches spring
Light, sinewy, graceful, firm-set as the wing
From Michael's white shoulder, is hewn and defaced
By iconoclast axes in desperate waste,
And its wrecks seek the ocean it prophesied long,
Cassandra-like, crooning its mystical song ?
Then the legends go with them,—even yet on the sea
A wild virtue is left in the touch of the tree,
And the sailor's night-watches are thrilled to the core   50
With the lineal offspring of Odin and Thor.

Yes, wherever the pine-wood has never let in,
Since the day of creation, the light and the din
Of manifold life, but has safely conveyed
From the midnight primeval its armful of shade,
And has kept the weird Past with its sagas alive
'Mid the hum and the stir of To-day's busy hive,
There the legend takes root in the age-gathered gloom,
And its murmurous boughs for their sagas find room.

Where Aroostook, far-heard, seems to sob as he goes   60
Groping down to the sea 'neath his mountainous snows ;
Where the lake's frore Sahara of never-tracked white,
When the crack shoots across it, complains to the night
With a long, lonely moan, that leagues northward is lost,
As the ice shrinks away from the tread of the frost ;
Where the lumberers sit by the log-fires that throw
Their own threatening shadows far round o'er the snow,
When the wolf howls aloof, and the wavering glare
Flashes out from the blackness the eyes of the bear,
When the wood's huge recesses, half-lighted, supply   70
A canvas where Fancy her mad brush may try,
Blotting in giant Horrors that venture not down
Through the right-angled streets of the brisk, whitewashed town,
But skulk in the depths of the measureless wood
'Mid the Dark's creeping whispers that curdle the blood,
When the eye, glanced in dread o'er the shoulder, may dream,
Ere it shrinks to the camp-fire's companioning gleam,
That it saw the fierce ghost of the Red Man crouch back
To the shroud of the tree-trunk's invincible black ;—
There the old shapes crowd thick round the pine-shadowed camp,
Which shun the keen gleam of the scholarly lamp,   81
And the seed of the legend finds true Norland ground,
While the border-tale 's told and the canteen flits round.

A CONTRAST

Thy love thou sentest oft to me,
   And still as oft I thrust it back ;
Thy messengers I could not see
   In those who everything did lack,
   The poor, the outcast, and the
      black.

Pride held his hand before mine eyes,
   The world with flattery stuffed mine
      ears ;
I looked to see a monarch's guise,
   Nor dreamed thy love would knock
      for years,
   Poor, naked, fettered, full of tears.

Yet, when I sent my love to thee,
   Thou with a smile didst take it
      in,
And entertain'dst it royally,
   Though grimed with earth, with
      hunger thin,
   And leprous with the taint of sin.

Now every day thy love I meet,
   As o'er the earth it wanders wide,
With weary step and bleeding feet,
   Still knocking at the heart of pride
   And offering grace, though still
      denied.

EXTREME UNCTION

Go! leave me, Priest; my soul would be
  Alone with the consoler, Death;
Far sadder eyes than thine will see
  This crumbling clay yield up its breath;
These shrivelled hands have deeper stains
  Than holy oil can cleanse away,
Hands that have plucked the world's coarse gains
  As erst they plucked the flowers of May.

Call, if thou canst, to these grey eyes
  Some faith from youth's traditions wrung;
This fruitless husk which dustward dries
  Has been a heart once, has been young;
On this bowed head the awful Past
  Once laid its consecrating hands;
The Future in its purpose vast
  Paused, waiting my supreme commands.

But look! whose shadows block the door?
  Who are those two that stand aloof?
See! on my hands this freshening gore
  Writes o'er again its crimson proof!
My looked-for death-bed guests are met;
  There my dead Youth doth wring its hands,
And there, with eyes that goad me yet,
  The ghost of my Ideal stands!

God bends from out the deep and says,
  'I gave thee the great gift of life;
Wast thou not called in many ways?
  Are not my earth and heaven at strife?

I gave thee of my seed to sow,
  Bringest thou me my hundred-fold?'
Can I look up with face aglow,
  And answer, 'Father, here is gold'?

I have been innocent; God knows
  When first this wasted life began,
Not grape with grape more kindly grows,
  Than I with every brother-man:
Now here I gasp; what lose my kind,
  When this fast ebbing breath shall part?
What bands of love and service bind
  This being to the world's sad heart?

Christ still was wandering o'er the earth
  Without a place to lay his head;
He found free welcome at my hearth,
  He shared my cup and broke my bread:
Now, when I hear those steps sublime,
  That bring the other world to this,
My snake-turned nature, sunk in slime,
  Starts sideway with defiant hiss.

Upon the hour when I was born,
  God said, 'Another man shall be,'
And the great Maker did not scorn
  Out of himself to fashion me;
He sunned me with his ripening looks,
  And Heaven's rich instincts in me grew,
As effortless as woodland nooks
  Send violets up and paint them blue.

Yes, I who now, with angry tears,
  Am exiled back to brutish clod,
Have borne unquenched for fourscore years
  A spark of the eternal God;

And to what end ? How yield I back
　The trust for such high uses given ?
Heaven's light hath but revealed a
　　track
　Whereby to crawl away from
　　heaven.

Men think it is an awful sight
　To see a soul just set adrift
On that drear voyage from whose
　　night
　The ominous shadows never lift ;
But 't is more awful to behold
　A helpless infant newly born,
Whose little hands unconscious hold
　The keys of darkness and of morn.

Mine held them once ; I flung away
　Those keys that might have open set

The golden sluices of the day,
　But clutch the keys of darkness
　　yet ;
I hear the reapers singing go
　Into God's harvest ; I, that might
With them have chosen, here below
　Grope shuddering at the gates of
　　night.

O glorious Youth, that once wast
　　mine !
　O high Ideal ! all in vain
Ye enter at this ruined shrine
　Whence worship ne'er shall rise
　　again ;
The bat and owl inhabit here,
　The snake nests in the altar-stone,
The sacred vessels moulder near,
　The image of the God is gone.

THE OAK

WHAT gnarlèd stretch, what depth of shade, is his !
　There needs no crown to mark the forest's king ;
How in his leaves outshines full summer's bliss !
　Sun, storm, rain, dew, to him their tribute bring,
Which he with such benignant royalty
　Accepts, as overpayeth what is lent ;
All nature seems his vassal proud to be,
　And cunning only for his ornament.

How towers he, too, amid the billowed snows,
　An unquelled exile from the summer's throne,
Whose plain, uncinctured front more kingly shows,
　Now that the obscuring courtier leaves are flown.
His boughs make music of the winter air,
　Jewelled with sleet, like some cathedral front
Where clinging snow-flakes with quaint art repair
　The dints and furrows of time's envious brunt.

How doth his patient strength the rude March wind
　Persuade to seem glad breaths of summer breeze,
And win the soil that fain would be unkind,
　To swell his revenues with proud increase !
He is the gem ; and all the landscape wide
　(So doth his grandeur isolate the sense)
Seems but the setting, worthless all beside,
　An empty socket, were he fallen thence.

So, from oft converse with life's wintry gales,
   Should man learn how to clasp with tougher roots
The inspiring earth ; how otherwise avails
   The leaf-creating sap that sunward shoots ?
So every year that falls with noiseless flake
   Should fill old scars up on the stormward side,
And make hoar age revered for age's sake,
   Not for traditions of youth's leafy pride.

So, from the pinched soil of a churlish fate,
   True hearts compel the sap of sturdier growth,
So between earth and heaven stand simply great,
   That these shall seem but their attendants both ;
For nature's forces with obedient zeal
   Wait on the rooted faith and oaken will ;
As quickly the pretender's cheat they feel,
   And turn mad Pucks to flout and mock him still.

Lord ! all thy works are lessons ; each contains
   Some emblem of man's all-containing soul ;
Shall he make fruitless all thy glorious pains,
   Delving within thy grace an eyeless mole ?
Make me the least of thy Dodona-grove,
   Cause me some message of thy truth to bring,
Speak but a word through me, nor let thy love
   Among my boughs disdain to perch and sing.

AMBROSE

Never, surely, was holier man
Than Ambrose, since the world began ;
With diet spare and raiment thin
He shielded himself from the father of sin ;
With bed of iron and scourgings oft,
His heart to God's hand as wax made soft.

Through earnest prayer and watchings long
He sought to know 'tween right and wrong,
Much wrestling with the blessed Word
To make it yield the sense of the Lord,
That he might build a storm-proof creed
To fold the flock in at their need.

At last he builded a perfect faith,
Fenced round about with *The Lord thus saith ;*
To himself he fitted the doorway's size,
Meted the light to the need of his eyes,
And knew, by a sure and inward sign,
That the work of his fingers was divine.

Then Ambrose said, ' All those shall die
The eternal death who believe not as I ' ;
And some were boiled, some burned in fire,
Some sawn in twain, that his heart's desire,
For the good of men's souls, might be satisfied
By the drawing of all to the righteous side.

One day, as Ambrose was seeking the truth
In his lonely walk, he saw a youth
Resting himself in the shade of a tree ;
It had never been granted him to see
So shining a face, and the good man thought
'T were pity he should not believe as he ought.

So he set himself by the young man's side,
And the state of his soul with questions tried ;
But the heart of the stranger was hardened indeed,
Nor received the stamp of the one true creed ;
And the spirit of Ambrose waxed sore to find
Such face the porch of so narrow a mind.

' As each beholds in cloud and fire
The shape that answers his own desire,
So each,' said the youth, ' in the Law shall find
The figure and features of his mind ;
And to each in his mercy hath God allowed
His several pillar of fire and cloud.'

The soul of Ambrose burned with zeal
And holy wrath for the young man's weal :
' Believest thou then, most wretched youth,'
Cried he, ' a dividual essence in Truth ?
I fear me thy heart is too cramped with sin
To take the Lord in his glory in.'

Now there bubbled beside them where they stood
A fountain of waters sweet and good ;
The youth to the streamlet's brink drew near
Saying, ' Ambrose, thou maker of creeds, look here !
Six vases of crystal then he took,
And set them along the edge of the brook.

' As into these vessels the water I pour,
There shall one hold less, another more,
And the water unchanged, in every case,
Shall put on the figure of the vase ;
O thou, who wouldst unity make through strife,
Canst thou fit this sign to the Water of Life ? '

When Ambrose looked up, he stood alone,
The youth and the stream and the vases were gone ;
But he knew, by a sense of humbled grace,
He had talked with an angel face to face,
And felt his heart change inwardly,
As he fell on his knees beneath the tree.

ABOVE AND BELOW

I

O DWELLERS in the valley-land,
  Who in deep twilight grope and
    cower,
Till the slow mountain's dial-hand
  Shorten to noon's triumphal hour,
While ye sit idle, do ye think
  The Lord's great work sits idle too ?
That light dare not o'erleap the brink
Of morn, because 'tis dark with you?

Though yet your valleys skulk in night,
  In God's ripe fields the day is cried,
And reapers, with their sickles bright,
  Troop, singing, down the mountain-
    side :
Come up, and feel what health there is
  In the frank Dawn's delighted eyes,
As, bending with a pitying kiss,
  The night-shed tears of Earth she
    dries !

The Lord wants reapers: O, mount up,
  Before night comes, and says,
    ' Too late ! '
Stay not for taking scrip or cup,
  The Master hungers while ye wait ;
'T is from these heights alone your eyes
  The advancing spears of day can see,
That o'er the eastern hill-tops rise,
  To break your long captivity.

II

Lone watcher on the mountain-height,
  It is right precious to behold
The first long surf of climbing light
  Flood all the thirsty east with gold :
But we, who in the shadow sit,
  Know also when the day is nigh,
Seeing thy shining forehead lit
  With his inspiring prophecy.

Thou hast thine office ; we have ours;
  God lacks not early service here,
But what are thine eleventh hours
  He counts with us for morning
    cheer ;
Our day, for Him, is long enough,
  And when he giveth work to do,
The bruisèd reed is amply tough
  To pierce the shield of error through.

But not the less do thou aspire
  Light's earlier messages to preach ;
Keep back no syllable of fire,
  Plunge deep the rowels of thy
    speech.
Yet God deems not thine aeried sight
  More worthy than our twilight
    dim ;
For meek Obedience, too, is Light,
  And following that is finding Him.

THE CAPTIVE

IT was past the hour of trysting,
  But she lingered for him still ;
Like a child, the eager streamlet
  Leaped and laughed adown the hill,
Happy to be free at twilight
  From its toiling at the mill.

Then the great moon on a sudden
  Ominous, and red as blood,
Startling as a new creation,
  O'er the eastern hill-top stood,
Casting deep and deeper shadows
  Through the mystery of the wood.

Dread closed huge and vague about
    her,
And her thoughts turned fearfully
To her heart, if there some shelter
    From the silence there might be,
Like bare cedars leaning inland
    From the blighting of the sea.

Yet he came not, and the stillness
    Dampened round her like a tomb ;
She could feel cold eyes of spirits
    Looking on her through the gloom,
She could hear the groping footsteps
    Of some blind, gigantic doom.

Suddenly the silence wavered
    Like a light mist in the wind,
For a voice broke gently through it,
    Felt like sunshine by the blind,
And the dread, like mist in sunshine,
    Furled serenely from her mind.

' Once my love, my love forever,
    Flesh or spirit still the same,
If I missed the hour of trysting,
    Do not think my faith to blame ;
I, alas, was made a captive,
    As from Holy Land I came.

' On a green spot in the desert,
    Gleaming like an emerald star,
Where a palm-tree, in lone silence,
    Yearning for its mate afar,
Droops above a silver runnel,
    Slender as a scimitar,

' There thou 'lt find the humble
        postern
    To the castle of my foe ;
If thy love burn clear and faithful,
    Strike the gateway, green and low,
Ask to enter, and the warder
    Surely will not say thee no.'

Slept again the aspen silence,
    But her loneliness was o'er ;
Round her heart a motherly patience

Wrapt its arms forevermore ;
From her soul ebbed back the sorrow,
    Leaving smooth the golden shore.

Donned she now the pilgrim scallop,
    Took the pilgrim staff in hand ;
Like a cloud-shade, flitting eastward,
    Wandered she o'er sea and land ;
And her footsteps in the desert
    Fell like cool rain on the sand.

Soon, beneath the palm-tree's shadow,
    Knelt she at the postern low ;
And thereat she knocketh gently,
    Fearing much the warder's no ;
All her heart stood still and listened,
    As the door swung backward slow.

There she saw no surly warder
    With an eye like bolt and bar ;
Through her soul a sense of music
    Throbbed, and, like a guardian
        Lar,
On the threshold stood an angel,
    Bright and silent as a star.

Fairest seemed he of God's seraphs,
    And her spirit, lily-wise,
Blossomed when he turned upon her
    The deep welcome of his eyes,
Sending upward to that sunlight
    All its dew for sacrifice.

Then she heard a voice come onward
    Singing with a rapture new,
As Eve heard the songs in Eden,
    Dropping earthward with the dew ;
Well she knew the happy singer,
    Well the happy song she knew.

Forward leaped she o'er the threshold,
    Eager as a glancing surf ;
Fell from her the spirit's languor,
    Fell from her the body's scurf ;
'Neath the palm next day some
        Arabs
    Found a corpse upon the turf.

THE BIRCH-TREE

RIPPLING through thy branches goes the sunshine,
Among thy leaves that palpitate forever ;
Ovid in thee a pining Nymph had prisoned,
The soul once of some tremulous inland river,
Quivering to tell her woe, but, ah ! dumb, dumb, forever !

While all the forest, witched with slumberous moonshine,
Holds up its leaves in happy, happy silence,
Waiting the dew, with breath and pulse suspended,
I hear afar thy whispering, gleamy islands,
And track thee wakeful still amid the wide-hung silence.

Upon the brink of some wood-nestled lakelet,
Thy foliage, like the tresses of a Dryad,
Dripping about thy slim white stem, whose shadow
Slopes quivering down the water's dusky quiet,
Thou shrink'st as on her bath's edge would some startled Dryad.

Thou art the go-between of rustic lovers ;
Thy white bark has their secrets in its keeping ;
Reuben writes here the happy name of Patience,
And thy lithe boughs hang murmuring and weeping
Above her, as she steals the mystery from thy keeping.

Thou art to me like my belovèd maiden,
So frankly coy, so full of trembly confidences ;
Thy shadow scarce seems shade, thy pattering leaflets
Sprinkle their gathered sunshine o'er my senses,
And Nature gives me all her summer confidences.

Whether my heart with hope or sorrow tremble,
Thou sympathizest still ; wild and unquiet,
I fling me down ; thy ripple, like a river,
Flows valleyward, where calmness is, and by it
My heart is floated down into the land of quiet.

AN INTERVIEW WITH MILES STANDISH

I SAT one evening in my room,
  In that sweet hour of twilight
When blended thoughts, half light,
      half gloom,
  Throng through the spirit's skylight;
The flames by fits curled round the
      bars,
  Or up the chimney crinkled,
While embers dropped like falling stars,
  And in the ashes tinkled.

I sat and mused ; the fire burned
      low,
  And, o'er my senses stealing,
Crept something of the ruddy glow
  That bloomed on wall and ceiling ;
My pictures (they are very few,
  The heads of ancient wise men)
Smoothed down their knotted fronts,
      and grew
  As rosy as excisemen.

My antique high-backed Spanish chair
  Felt thrills through wood and
      leather,
That had been strangers since whilere,
  'Mid Andalusian heather,
The oak that made its sturdy frame
  His happy arms stretched over
The ox whose fortunate hide became
  The bottom's polished cover.

It came out in that famous bark,
  That brought our sires intrepid,
Capacious as another ark
  For furniture decrepit ;
For, as that saved of bird and beast
  A pair for propagation,
So has the seed of these increased
  And furnished half the nation.

Kings sit, they say, in slippery seats ;
  But those slant precipices
Of ice the northern voyager meets
  Less slippery are than this is ;
To cling therein would pass the wit
  Of royal man or woman,
And whatsoe'er can stay in it
  Is more or less than human.

I offer to all bores this perch,
  Dear well-intentioned people
With heads as void as week-day
    church,
  Tongues longer than the steeple ;
To folks with missions, whose gaunt
    eyes
  See golden ages rising,—
Salt of the earth ! in what queer Guys
  Thou'rt fond of crystallizing !

My wonder, then, was not unmixed
  With merciful suggestion,
When, as my roving eyes grew fixed
  Upon the chair in question,
I saw its trembling arms enclose
  A figure grim and rusty,
Whose doublet plain and plainer hose
  Were something worn and dusty.

Now even such men as Nature forms
  Merely to fill the street with,
Once turned to ghosts by hungry
    worms,
  Are serious things to meet with ;
Your penitent spirits are no jokes,
  And, though I'm not averse to
A quiet shade, even they are folks
  One cares not to speak first to.

Who knows, thought I, but he has
    come,
  By Charon kindly ferried,
To tell me of a mighty sum
  Behind my wainscot buried ?
There is a buccaneerish air
  About that garb outlandish—
Just then the ghost drew up his chair
  And said, ' My name is Standish.

' I come from Plymouth, deadly bored
  With toasts, and songs, and
    speeches,
As long and flat as my old sword,
  As threadbare as my breeches :
They understand us Pilgrims ! they,
  Smooth men with rosy faces,
Strength's knots and gnarls all pared
    away,
  And varnish in their places !

' We had some toughness in our
    grain,
  The eye to rightly see us is
Not just the one that lights the brain
  Of drawing-room Tyrtaeuses :
They talk about their Pilgrim blood,
  Their birthright high and holy !
A mountain-stream that ends in mud
  Methinks is melancholy.

' He had stiff knees, the Puritan,
  That were not good at bending ;
The homespun dignity of man
  He thought was worth defending ;
He did not, with his pinchbeck ore,
  His country's shame forgotten,
Gild Freedom's coffin o'er and o'er,
  When all within was rotten.

'These loud ancestral boasts of
    yours,
  How can they else than vex us ?
Where were your dinner orators
    When slavery grasped at Texas ?
Dumb on his knees was every one
    That now is bold as Caesar ;
Mere pegs to hang an office on
    Such stalwart men as these are.'

'Good sir,' I said, 'you seem much
    stirred ;
  The sacred compromises—'
'Now God confound the dastard
    word !
  My gall thereat arises :
Northward it hath this sense alone,
    That you, your conscience blinding,
Shall bow your fool's nose to the stone,
    When slavery feels like grinding.

''Tis shame to see such painted sticks
    In Vane's and Winthrop's places,
To see your spirit of Seventy-six
    Drag humbly in the traces,
With slavery's lash upon her back,
    And herds of office-holders
To shout applause, as, with a crack,
    It peels her patient shoulders.

'*We* forefathers to such a rout !—
    No, by my faith in God's word ! '
Half rose the ghost, and half drew out
    The ghost of his old broadsword,

Then thrust it slowly back again,
    And said, with reverent gesture,
'No, Freedom, no ! blood should not
    stain
  The hem of thy white vesture.

'I feel the soul in me draw near
    The mount of prophesying ;
In this bleak wilderness I hear
    A John the Baptist crying ;
Far in the east I see upleap
    The streaks of first forewarning,
And they who sowed the light shall reap
    The golden sheaves of morning.

'Child of our travail and our woe,
    Light in our day of sorrow,
Through my rapt spirit I foreknow
    The glory of thy morrow ;
I hear great steps, that through the
    shade
  Draw nigher still and nigher,
And voices call like that which bade
    The prophet come up higher.'

I looked, no form mine eyes could find,
    I heard the red cock crowing,
And through my window-chinks the
    wind
  A dismal tune was blowing ;
Thought I, My neighbour Buckingham
    Hath somewhat in him gritty,
Some Pilgrim-stuff that hates all sham,
    And he will print my ditty.

ON THE CAPTURE OF FUGITIVE SLAVES NEAR WASHINGTON

LOOK on who will in apathy, and stifle they who can,
The sympathies, the hopes, the words, that make man truly man ;
Let those whose hearts are dungeoned up with interest or with ease
Consent to hear with quiet pulse of loathsome deeds like these !

I first drew in New England's air, and from her hardy breast
Sucked in the tyrant-hating milk that will not let me rest ;
And if my words seem treason to the dullard and the tame,
'T is but my Bay-State dialect,—our fathers spake the same !

Shame on the costly mockery of piling stone on stone
To those who won our liberty, the heroes dead and gone,
While we look coldly on and see law-shielded ruffians slay
The men who fain would win their own, the heroes of to-day !

Are we pledged to craven silence ?   O, fling it to the wind,
The parchment wall that bars us from the least of human kind,
That makes us cringe and temporize, and dumbly stand at rest,
While Pity's burning flood of words is red-hot in the breast !

Though we break our fathers' promise, we have nobler duties first ;
The traitor to Humanity is the traitor most accursed ;
Man is more than Constitutions ; better rot beneath the sod,
Than be true to Church and State while we are doubly false to God !

We owe allegiance to the State ; but deeper, truer, more,
To the sympathies that God hath set within our spirit's core ;
Our country claims our fealty ; we grant it so, but then
Before Man made us citizens, great Nature made us men.

He's true to God who's true to man ; wherever wrong is done,
To the humblest and the weakest, 'neath the all-beholding sun,
That wrong is also done to us ; and they are slaves most base,
Whose love of right is for themselves, and not for all their race.

God works for all.   Ye cannot hem the hope of being free
With parallels of latitude, with mountain-range or sea.
Put golden padlocks on Truth's lips, be callous as ye will,
From soul to soul, o'er all the world, leaps one electric thrill.

Chain down your slaves with ignorance, ye cannot keep apart,
With all your craft of tyranny, the human heart from heart :
When first the Pilgrims landed on the Bay State's iron shore,
The word went forth that slavery should one day be no more.

Out from the land of bondage 't is decreed our slaves shall go,
And signs to us are offered, as erst to Pharaoh ;
If we are blind, their exodus, like Israel's of yore,
Through a Red Sea is doomed to be, whose surges are of gore.

'T is ours to save our brethren, with peace and love to win
Their darkened hearts from error, ere they harden it to sin ;
But if before his duty man with listless spirit stands,
Erelong the Great Avenger takes the work from out his hands.

TO THE DANDELION

Dear common flower, that grow'st beside the way,
Fringing the dusty road with harmless gold,
    First pledge of blithesome May,
Which children pluck, and, full of pride, uphold,
    High-hearted buccaneers, o'erjoyed that they
        Eldorado in the grass have found,
        Which not the rich earth's ample round
    May match in wealth, thou art more dear to me
    Than all the prouder summer-blooms may be.

Gold such as thine ne'er drew the Spanish prow
Through the primeval hush of Indian seas,
        Nor wrinkled the lean brow
Of age, to rob the lover's heart of ease ;
    'T is the Spring's largess, which she scatters now
To rich and poor alike, with lavish hand,
        Though most hearts never understand
    To take it at God's value, but pass by
    The offered wealth with unrewarded eye.

    Thou art my tropics and mine Italy ;
To look at thee unlocks a warmer clime ;
        The eyes thou givest me
Are in the heart, and heed not space or time :
    Not in mid June the golden-cuirassed bee
Feels a more summer-like warm ravishment
        In the white lily's breezy tent,
    His fragrant Sybaris, than I, when first
    From the dark green thy yellow circles burst.

    Then think I of deep shadows on the grass,
Of meadows where in sun the cattle graze,
        Where, as the breezes pass,
The gleaming rushes lean a thousand ways,
    Of leaves that slumber in a cloudy mass,
Or whiten in the wind, of waters blue
        That from the distance sparkle through
    Some woodland gap, and of a sky above,
    Where one white cloud like a stray lamb doth move.

    My childhood's earliest thoughts are linked with thee ;
The sight of thee calls back the robin's song,
        Who, from the dark old tree
Beside the door, sang clearly all day long,
    And I, secure in childish piety,
Listened as if I heard an angel sing
        With news from heaven, which he could bring
    Fresh every day to my untainted ears
    When birds and flowers and I were happy peers.

    How like a prodigal doth nature seem,
When thou, for all thy gold, so common art !
        Thou teachest me to deem
More sacredly of every human heart,
    Since each reflects in joy its scanty gleam
Of heaven, and could some wondrous secret show,
        Did we but pay the love we owe,
    And with a child's undoubting wisdom look
    On all these living pages of God's book.

THE GHOST-SEER

Ye who, passing graves by night,
Glance not to the left nor right,
Lest a spirit should arise,
Cold and white, to freeze your eyes,
Some weak phantom, which your doubt
Shapes upon the dark without
From the dark within, a guess
At the spirit's deathlessness,
Which ye entertain with fear
In your self-built dungeon here,   10
Where ye sell your God-given lives
Just for gold to buy you gyves,—
Ye without a shudder meet
In the city's noonday street,
Spirits sadder and more dread
Than from out the clay have fled,
Buried, beyond hope of light,
In the body's haunted night!

See ye not that woman pale?   19
There are bloodhounds on her trail!
Bloodhounds two, all gaunt and lean,
(For the soul their scent is keen,)
Want and Sin, and Sin is last,
They have followed far and fast;
Want gave tongue, and, at her howl,
Sin awakened with a growl.
Ah, poor girl! she had a right
To a blessing from the light;
Title-deeds to sky and earth
God gave to her at her birth;   30
But, before they were enjoyed,
Poverty had made them void,
And had drunk the sunshine up
From all nature's ample cup,
Leaving her a first-born's share
In the dregs of darkness there.
Often, on the sidewalk bleak,
Hungry, all alone, and weak,
She has seen, in night and storm,
Rooms o'erflow with firelight warm,
Which, outside the window-glass,
Doubled all the cold, alas!   42
Till each ray that on her fell
Stabbed her like an icicle,
And she almost loved the wail
Of the bloodhounds on her trail.
Till the floor becomes her bier,
She shall feel their pantings near,
Close upon her very heels,
Spite of all the din of wheels;   50
Shivering on her pallet poor,
She shall hear them at the door
Whine and scratch to be let in,
Sister bloodhounds, Want and Sin!

Hark: that rustle of a dress,
Stiff with lavish costliness!
Here comes one whose cheek would flush
But to have her garment brush
'Gainst the girl whose fingers thin
Wove the weary broidery in,   60
Bending backward from her toil,
Lest her tears the silk might soil,
And, in midnights chill and murk,
Stitched her life into the work,
Shaping from her bitter thought
Heart's-ease and forget-me-not,
Satirizing her despair
With the emblems woven there.
Little doth the wearer heed
Of the heart-break in the brede;   70
A hyena by her side
Skulks, down-looking,—it is Pride.
He digs for her in the earth,
Where lie all her claims of birth,
With his foul paws rooting o'er
Some long-buried ancestor,
Who, perhaps, a statue won
By the ill deeds he had done,
By the innocent blood he shed,
By the desolation spread   80
Over happy villages,
Blotting out the smile of peace.

There walks Judas, he who sold
Yesterday his Lord for gold,
Sold God's presence in his heart
For a proud step in the mart;
He hath dealt in flesh and blood;
At the bank his name is good;

At the bank, and only there,
'T is a marketable ware.   90
In his eyes that stealthy gleam
Was not learned of sky or stream,
But it has the cold, hard glint
Of new dollars from the mint.
Open now your spirit's eyes,
Look through that poor clay disguise
Which has thickened, day by day,
Till it keeps all light at bay,
And his soul in pitchy gloom
Gropes about its narrow tomb,   100
From whose dank and slimy walls
Drop by drop the horror falls.
Look ! a serpent lank and cold
Hugs his spirit fold on fold ;
From his heart, all day and night,
It doth suck God's blessed light.
Drink it will, and drink it must,
Till the cup holds naught but dust ;
All day long he hears it hiss,
Writhing in its fiendish bliss ;   110
All night long he sees its eyes
Flicker with foul ecstasies,
As the spirit ebbs away
Into the absorbing clay.

Who is he that skulks, afraid
Of the trust he has betrayed,
Shuddering if perchance a gleam
Of old nobleness should stream
Through the pent, unwholesome room,
Where his shrunk soul cowers in
        gloom,   120
Spirit sad beyond the rest
By more instinct for the best ?
'T is a poet who was sent
For a bad world's punishment,
By compelling it to see
Golden glimpses of To Be,
By compelling it to hear
Songs that prove the angels near ;
Who was sent to be the tongue
Of the weak and spirit-wrung,   130
Whence the fiery-winged Despair
In men's shrinking eyes might flare.
'T is our hope doth fashion us
To base use or glorious :
He who might have been a lark

Of Truth's morning, from the dark
Raining down melodious hope
Of a freer, broader scope,
Aspirations, prophecies,
Of the spirit's full sunrise,   140
Chose to be a bird of night,
That, with eyes refusing light,
Hooted from some hollow tree
Of the world's idolatry.
'T is his punishment to hear
Flutterings of pinions near,
And his own vain wings to feel
Drooping downward to his heel,
All their grace and import lost,
Burdening his weary ghost :   150
Ever walking by his side
He must see his angel guide,
Who at intervals doth turn
Looks on him so sadly stern,
With such ever-new surprise
Of hushed anguish in her eyes,
That it seems the light of day
From around him shrinks away,
Or drops blunted from the wall
Built around him by his fall.   160
Then the mountains, whose white
        peaks
Catch the morning's earliest streaks,
He must see, where prophets sit,
Turning east their faces lit,
Whence, with footsteps beautiful,
To the earth, yet dim and dull,
They the gladsome tidings bring
Of the sunlight's hastening :
Never can these hills of bliss
Be o'erclimbed by feet like his !

But enough ! O, do not dare   171
From the next the veil to tear,
Woven of station, trade, or dress,
More obscene than nakedness,
Wherewith plausible culture drapes
Fallen Nature's myriad shapes !
Let us rather love to mark
How the unextinguished spark
Will shine through the thin disguise
Of our customs, pomps, and lies,
And, not seldom blown to flame,
Vindicate its ancient claim.   182

STUDIES FOR TWO HEADS

I

Some sort of heart I know is hers,—
 I chanced to feel her pulse one night;
A brain she has that never errs,
 And yet is never nobly right ;
It does not leap to great results,
 But, in some corner out of sight,
 Suspects a spot of latent blight,
 And, o'er the impatient infinite,
She bargains, haggles, and consults.

Her eye,—it seems a chemic test 10
 And drops upon you like an acid ;
It bites you with unconscious zest,
 So clear and bright, so coldly placid;
It holds you quietly aloof,
 It holds,—and yet it does not win
  you ;
It merely puts you to the proof
 And sorts what qualities are in you;
It smiles, but never brings you nearer,
 It lights,—her nature draws not
  nigh ;   19
'T is but that yours is growing clearer
 To her assays ;—yes, try and try,
 You'll get no deeper than her eye.

There, you are classified : she 's gone
 Far, far away into herself ;
Each with its Latin label on,
Your poor components, one by one,
Are laid upon their proper shelf
In her compact and ordered mind,
And what of you is left behind   29
Is no more to her than the wind ;
In that clear brain, which, day and
  night,
  No movement of the heart e'er
   jostles,
Her friends are ranged on left and
  right,—
Here, silex, hornblende, syenite ;
 There, animal remains and fossils.

And yet, O subtile analyst,
 That canst each property detect
Of mood or grain, that canst untwist
 Each tangled skein of intellect,

And with thy scalpel eyes lay bare
Each mental nerve more fine than
  air,—   41
 O brain exact, that in thy scales
Canst weigh the sun and never err,
 For once thy patient science fails,
 One problem still defies thy art ;—
Thou never canst compute for her
 The distance and diameter
 Of any simple human heart.

II

Hear him but speak, and you will feel
 The shadows of the Portico
Over your tranquil spirit steal,
 To modulate all joy and woe
 To one subdued, subduing glow ;
Above our squabbling business-hours,
Like Phidian Jove's, his beauty lowers,
 His nature satirizes ours ;
 A form and front of Attic grace,
 He shames the higgling market-
  place,   10
And dwarfs our more mechanic powers.

What throbbing verse can fitly render
That face so pure, so trembling-tender?
 Sensation glimmers through its rest,
It speaks unmanacled by words,
 As full of motion as a nest
That palpitates with unfledged birds ;
 'Tis likest to Bethesda's stream,
Forewarned through all its thrilling
  springs,   19
 White with the angel's coming gleam,
And rippled with his fanning wings.

Hear him unfold his plots and plans,
And larger destinies seem man's ;
You conjure from his glowing face
The omen of a fairer race ;
With one grand trope he boldly spans
 The gulf wherein so many fall,
 'Twixt possible and actual ;
His first swift word, talaria-shod,
Exuberant with conscious God,   30
Out of the choir of planets blots
The present earth with all its spots.

Himself unshaken as the sky,
His words, like whirlwinds, spin on
high
  Systems and creeds pellmell to-
    gether ;
'T is strange as to a deaf man's eye,
While trees uprooted splinter by,
  The dumb turmoil of stormy
weather ;
  Less of iconoclast than shaper,
His spirit, safe behind the reach
Of the tornado of his speech,   41
  Burns calmly as a glowworm's
taper.

So great in speech, but, ah ! in act
  So overrun with vermin troubles,
The coarse, sharp-cornered, ugly fact
  Of life collapses all his bubbles :
Had he but lived in Plato's day,
  He might, unless my fancy errs,
Have shared that golden voice's sway
  O'er barefooted philosophers.
Our nipping climate hardly suits
The ripening of ideal fruits :   52
His theories vanquish us all summer,
But winter makes him dumb and
  dumber ;

To see him 'mid life's needful things
  Is something painfully bewildering;
He seems an angel with clipt wings
  Tied to a mortal wife and children,
And by a brother seraph taken   59
In the act of eating eggs and bacon.
Like a clear fountain, his desire
  Exults and leaps toward the light,
In every drop it says ' Aspire ! '
  Striving for more ideal height ;
And as the fountain, falling thence,
  Crawls baffled through the common
gutter,
So, from his speech's eminence,
He shrinks into the present tense,
  Unkinged by foolish bread and butter.

Yet smile not, worldling, for in deeds
  Not all of life that's brave and wise
is ;   71
He strews an ampler future's seeds,
  'T is your fault if no harvest rises ;
Smooth back the sneer ; for is it naught
  That all he is and has is Beauty's ?
By soul the soul's gains must be
  wrought,
The Actual claims our coarser thought,
  The Ideal hath its higher duties.

ON A PORTRAIT OF DANTE BY GIOTTO

Can this be thou who, lean and pale,
  With such immitigable eye
Didst look upon those writhing souls in bale,
  And note each vengeance, and pass by
Unmoved, save when thy heart by chance
Cast backward one forbidden glance,
  And saw Francesca, with child's glee,
  Subdue and mount thy wild-horse knee
And with proud hands control its fiery prance ?

With half-drooped lids, and smooth, round brow,
  And eye remote, that inly sees
Fair Beatrice's spirit wandering now
  In some sea-lulled Hesperides,
Thou movest through the jarring street,
Secluded from the noise of feet
  By her gift-blossom in thy hand,
  Thy branch of palm from Holy Land ;—
No trace is here of ruin's fiery sleet.

Yet there is something round thy lips
   That prophesies the coming doom,
The soft, grey herald-shadow ere the eclipse
   Notches the perfect disk with gloom ;
A something that would banish thee,
And thine untamed pursuer be,
   From men and their unworthy fates,
   Though Florence had not shut her gates,
And Grief had loosed her clutch and let thee free.

Ah ! he who follows fearlessly
   The beckonings of a poet-heart
Shall wander, and without the world's decree,
   A banished man in field and mart ;
Harder than Florence' walls the bar
Which with deaf sternness holds him far
   From home and friends, till death's release,
   And makes his only prayer for peace,
Like thine, scarred veteran of a lifelong war !

ON THE DEATH OF A FRIEND'S CHILD

DEATH never came so nigh to me before,
Nor showed me his mild face : oft had I mused
Of calm and peace and deep forgetfulness,
Of folded hands, closed eyes, and heart at rest,
And slumber sound beneath a flowery turf,
Of faults forgotten, and an inner place
Kept sacred for us in the heart of friends ;
But these were idle fancies, satisfied
With the mere husk of this great mystery,
And dwelling in the outward shows of things.   10
Heaven is not mounted to on wings of dreams,
Nor doth the unthankful happiness of youth
Aim thitherward, but floats from bloom to bloom,
With earth's warm patch of sunshine well content :
'T is sorrow builds the shining ladder up,
Whose golden rounds are our calamities,
Whereon our firm feet planting, nearer God
The spirit climbs, and hath its eyes unsealed.

True is it that Death's face seems stern and cold,
When he is sent to summon those we love,   20
But all God's angels come to us disguised ;
Sorrow and sickness, poverty and death,
One after other lift their frowning masks,
And we behold the seraph's face beneath,
All radiant with the glory and the calm

Of having looked upon the front of God.
With every anguish of our earthly part
The spirit's sight grows clearer ; this was meant
When Jesus touched the blind man's lids with clay.
Life is the jailer, Death the angel sent   30
To draw the unwilling bolts and set us free.
He flings not ope the ivory gate of Rest,—
Only the fallen spirit knocks at that,—
But to benigner regions beckons us,
To destinies of more rewarded toil.
In the hushed chamber, sitting by the dead,
It grates on us to hear the flood of life
Whirl rustling onward, senseless of our loss.
The bee hums on ; around the blossomed vine
Whirs the light humming-bird ; the cricket chirps ;   40
The locust's shrill alarum stings the ear ;
Hard by, the cock shouts lustily ; from farm to farm,
His cheery brothers, telling of the sun,
Answer, till far away the joyance dies :
We never knew before how God had filled
The summer air with happy living sounds ;
All round us seems an overplus of life,
And yet the one dear heart lies cold and still.
It is most strange, when the great miracle
Hath for our sakes been done, when we have had   50
Our inwardest experience of God,
When with his presence still the room expands,
And is awed after him, that naught is changed,
That Nature's face looks unacknowledging,
And the mad world still dances heedless on
After its butterflies, and gives no sign.
'T is hard at first to see it all aright :
In vain Faith blows her trump to summon back
Her scattered troop : yet, through the clouded glass
Of our own bitter tears, we learn to look   60
Undazzled on the kindness of God's face ;
Earth is too dark, and Heaven alone shines through.

It is no little thing, when a fresh soul
And a fresh heart, with their unmeasured scope
For good, not gravitating earthward yet,
But circling in diviner periods,
Are sent into the world,—no little thing,
When this unbounded possibility
Into the outer silence is withdrawn.
Ah, in this world, where every guiding thread   70
Ends suddenly in the one sure centre, death,
The visionary hand of Might-have-been
Alone can fill Desire's cup to the brim !

How changed, dear friend, are thy part and thy child's !
He bends above *thy* cradle now, or holds
His warning finger out to be thy guide ;
Thou art the nursling now ; he watches thee
Slow learning, one by one, the secret things
Which are to him used sights of every day ;
He smiles to see thy wondering glances con   80
The grass and pebbles of the spirit-world,
To thee miraculous ; and he will teach
Thy knees their due observances of prayer.
Children are God's apostles, day by day
Sent forth to preach of love, and hope, and peace ;
Nor hath thy babe his mission left undone.
To me, at least, his going hence hath given
Serener thoughts and nearer to the skies,
And opened a new fountain in my heart
For thee, my friend, and all : and O, if Death   90
More near approaches, meditates, and clasps
Even now some dearer, more reluctant hand,
God, strengthen thou my faith, that I may see
That 't is thine angel, who, with loving haste,
Unto the service of the inner shrine,
Doth waken thy belovèd with a kiss.

EURYDICE

HEAVEN's cup held down to me I
    drain,
The sunshine mounts and spurs my
    brain ;
Bathing in grass, with thirsty eye
I suck the last drop of the sky ;
With each hot sense I draw to the lees
The quickening out-door influences,
And empty to each radiant comer
A supernaculum of summer :
Not, Bacchus, all thy grosser juice
Could bring enchantment so profuse,
Though for its press each grape-bunch
    had   11
The white feet of an Oread.

Through our coarse art gleam, now
    and then,
The features of angelic men :
'Neath the lewd Satyr's veiling paint
Glows forth the Sibyl, Muse, or Saint ;
The dauber's botch no more obscures
The mighty master's portraitures.

And who can say what luckier beam
    The hidden glory shall redeem,   20
For what chance clod the soul may
    wait
To stumble on its nobler fate,
Or why, to his unwarned abode,
Still by surprises comes the God ?
Some moment, nailed on sorrow's
    cross,
May meditate a whole youth's loss,
Some windfall joy, we know not
    whence,
Redeem a lifetime's rash expense,
And, suddenly wise, the soul may mark,
Stripped of their simulated dark,
Mountains of gold that pierce the sky,
Girdling its valleyed poverty.   32

I feel ye, childhood's hopes, return,
With olden heats my pulses burn,—
Mine be the self-forgetting sweep,
The torrent impulse swift and wild,
Wherewith Taghkanic's rockborn child

Dares gloriously the dangerous leap,
And, in his sky-descended mood,
Transmutes each drop of sluggish
blood,   40
By touch of bravery's simple wand,
To amethyst and diamond,
Proving himself no bastard slip,
But the true granite-cradled one,
Nursed with the rock's primeval drip,
The cloud-embracing mountain's son

Prayer breathed in vain ! no wish's
sway
Rebuilds the vanished yesterday ;
For plated wares of Sheffield stamp
We gave the old Aladdin's lamp ;
'T is we are changed ; ah, whither
went   51
That undesigned abandonment,
That wise, unquestioning content,
Which could erect its microcosm
Out of a weed's neglected blossom,
Could call up Arthur and his peers
By a low moss's clump of spears,
Or, in its shingle trireme launched,
Where Charles in some green inlet
branched,

Could venture for the golden fleece
And dragon-watched Hesperides,
Or, from its ripple-shattered fate,
Ulysses' chances re-create ?   63

When, heralding life's every phase,
There glowed a goddess-veiling haze,
A plenteous, forewarning grace,
Like that more tender dawn that flies
Before the full moon's ample rise ?
Methinks thy parting glory shines
Through yonder grove of singing pines;
At that elm-vista's end I trace   71
Dimly thy sad leave-taking face,
Eurydice ! Eurydice !
The tremulous leaves repeat to me
Eurydice ! Eurydice !
No gloomier Orcus swallows thee
Than the unclouded sunset's glow ;
Thine is at least Elysian woe ;
Thou hast Good's natural decay,
And fadest like a star away   80
Into an atmosphere whose shine
With fuller day o'ermasters thine,
Entering defeat as 't were a shrine ;
For us,—we turn life's diary o'er
To find but one word,—Nevermore.

SHE CAME AND WENT

As a twig trembles, which a bird
    Lights on to sing, then leaves un-
    bent,
So is my memory thrilled and stirred;—
    I only know she came and went.

As clasps some lake, by gusts unriven,
    The blue dome's measureless con-
    tent,
So my soul held that moment's
    heaven ;—
    I only know she came and went.

As, at one bound, our swift spring heaps
    The orchards full of bloom and scent,
So clove her May my wintry sleeps ;—
    I only know she came and went.

An angel stood and met my gaze,
    Through the low doorway of my
    tent ;
The tent is struck, the vision stays ;—
    I only know she came and went.

O, when the room grows slowly
    dim,
    And life's last oil is nearly spent,
One gush of light these eyes will
    brim,
    Only to think she came and went.

THE CHANGELING

I HAD a little daughter,
  And she was given to me
To lead me gently backward
  To the Heavenly Father's knee,
That I, by the force of nature,
  Might in some dim wise divine
The depth of his infinite patience
  To this wayward soul of mine.

I know not how others saw her,
  But to me she was wholly fair,
And the light of the heaven she came
    from
  Still lingered and gleamed in her
    hair ;
For it was as wavy and golden,
  And as many changes took,
As the shadows of sun-gilt ripples
  On the yellow bed of a brook.

To what can I liken her smiling
  Upon me, her kneeling lover,
How it leaped from her lips to her eye-
    lids,
  And dimpled her wholly over,
Till her outstretched hands smiled also,
  And I almost seemed to see
The very heart of her mother
  Sending sun through her veins to me !

She had been with us scarce a twelve-
    month,
  And it hardly seemed a day,
When a troop of wandering angels
  Stole my little daughter away ;

Or perhaps those heavenly Zingari
  But loosed the hampering strings,
And when they had opened her cage-
    door,
  My little bird used her wings.

But they left in her stead a changeling,
  A little angel child,
That seems like her bud in full
    blossom,
  And smiles as she never smiled :
When I wake in the morning, I see it
  Where she always used to lie,
And I feel as weak as a violet
  Alone 'neath the awful sky.

As weak, yet as trustful also ;
  For the whole year long I see
All the wonders of faithful Nature
  Still worked for the love of me ;
Winds wander, and dews drip earth-
    ward,
  Rain falls, suns rise and set,
Earth whirls, and all but to prosper
  A poor little violet.

This child is not mine as the first was,
  I cannot sing it to rest,
I cannot lift it up fatherly
  And bliss it upon my breast ;
Yet it lies in my little one's cradle
  And sits in my little one's chair,
And the light of the heaven she's
    gone to
  Transfigures its golden hair.

THE PIONEER

WHAT man would live coffined with brick and stone,
  Imprisoned from the influences of air,
    And cramped with selfish landmarks everywhere,
When all before him stretches, furrowless and lone,
  The unmapped prairie none can fence or own ?

What man would read and read the selfsame faces,
  And, like the marbles which the windmill grinds,
    Rub smooth forever with the same smooth minds,
This year retracing last year's, every year's, dull traces,
  When there are woods and un-man-stifled spaces ?

What man o'er one old thought would pore and pore,
  Shut like a book between its covers thin
  For every fool to leave his dog's-ears in,
When solitude is his, and God forevermore,
  Just for the opening of a paltry door ?

What man would watch life's oozy element
  Creep Letheward forever, when he might
  Down some great river drift beyond men's sight,
To where the undethronèd forest's royal tent
  Broods with its hush o'er half a continent ?

What man with men would push and altercate,
  Piecing out crooked means for crooked ends,
  When he can have the skies and woods for friends,
Snatch back the rudder of his undismantled fate,
  And in himself be ruler, church, and state ?

Cast leaves and feathers rot in last year's nest,
  The wingèd brood, flown thence, new dwellings plan ;
  The serf of his own Past is not a man ;
To change and change is life, to move and never rest ;—
  Not what we are, but what we hope, is best.

The wild, free woods make no man halt or blind ;
  Cities rob men of eyes and hands and feet,
  Patching one whole of many incomplete ;
The general preys upon the individual mind,
  And each alone is helpless as the wind.

Each man is some man's servant ; every soul
  Is by some other's presence quite discrowned ;
  Each owes the next through all the imperfect round,
Yet not with mutual help ; each man is his own goal,
  And the whole earth must stop to pay his toll.

Here, life the undiminished man demands ;
  New faculties stretch out to meet new wants ;
  What Nature asks, that Nature also grants ;
Here man is lord, not drudge, of eyes and feet and hands,
  And to his life is knit with hourly bands.

Come out, then, from the old thoughts and old ways,
  Before you harden to a crystal cold
  Which the new life can shatter, but not mould ;
Freedom for you still waits, still, looking backward, stays,
  But widens still the irretrievable space.

LONGING

Of all the myriad moods of mind
  That through the soul come
    thronging,
Which one was e'er so dear, so kind,
  So beautiful as Longing ?
The thing we long for, that we are
  For one transcendent moment,
Before the Present poor and bare
  Can make its sneering comment.

Still, through our paltry stir and
  strife,
  Glows down the wished Ideal,
And Longing moulds in clay what Life
  Carves in the marble Real ;
To let the new life in, we know,
  Desire must ope the portal ;—
Perhaps the longing to be so
  Helps make the soul immortal.

Longing is God's fresh heavenward
  will
  With our poor earthward striving ;
We quench it that we may be still
  Content with merely living ;
But, would we learn that heart's full
  scope
  Which we are hourly wronging,
Our lives must climb from hope to hope
  And realize our longing.

Ah ! let us hope that to our praise
  Good God not only reckons
The moments when we tread his ways,
  But when the spirit beckons,—
That some slight good is also wrought
  Beyond self-satisfaction,
When we are simply good in thought,
  Howe'er we fail in action.

ODE TO FRANCE

FEBRUARY, 1848

I

As, flake by flake, the beetling avalanches
  Build up their imminent crags of noiseless snow,
Till some chance thrill the loosened ruin launches
  And the blind havoc leaps unwarned below,
So grew and gathered through the silent years
  The madness of a People, wrong by wrong.
There seemed no strength in the dumb toiler's tears,
  No strength in suffering ; but the Past was strong :
The brute despair of trampled centuries
  Leaped up with one hoarse yell and snapped its bands.   10
  Groped for its right with horny, callous hands,
And stared around for God with bloodshot eyes.
  What wonder if those palms were all too hard
For nice distinctions,—if that maenad throng—
  They whose thick atmosphere no bard
Had shivered with the lightning of his song,
  Brutes with the memories and desires of men,
  Whose chronicles were writ with iron pen,
    In the crooked shoulder and the forehead low,
      Set wrong to balance wrong,   20
      And physicked woe with woe ?

II

They did as they were taught ; not theirs the blame,
If men who scattered firebrands reaped the flame :
  They trampled Peace beneath their savage feet,
    And by her golden tresses drew
  Mercy along the pavement of the street.
O Freedom ! Freedom ! is thy morning-dew
    So gory red ?   Alas, thy light had ne'er
    Shone in upon the chaos of their lair !
They reared to thee such symbol as they knew,   30
    And worshipped it with flame and blood,
    A Vengeance, axe in hand, that stood
Holding a tyrant's head up by the clotted hair.

III

What wrongs the Oppressor suffered, these we know ;
  These have found piteous voice in song and prose ;
But for the Oppressed, their darkness and their woe,
  Their grinding centuries,—what Muse had those ?
Though hall and palace had nor eyes nor ears,
    Hardening a people's heart to senseless stone,
Thou knewest them, O Earth, that drank their tears,   40
    O Heaven, that heard their inarticulate moan !
They noted down their fetters, link by link ;
Coarse was the hand that scrawled, and red the ink ;
    Rude was their score, as suits unlettered men,
Notched with a headsman's axe upon a block :
What marvel if, when came the avenging shock,
    'T was Atë, not Urania, held the pen ?

IV

With eye averted, and an anguished frown,
  Loathingly glides the Muse through scenes of strife,
Where, like the heart of Vengeance up and down,   50
  Throbs in its framework the blood-muffled knife ;
Slow are the steps of Freedom, but her feet
  Turn never backward : hers no bloody glare ;
Her light is calm, and innocent, and sweet,
  And where it enters there is no despair :
Not first on palace and cathedral spire
Quivers and gleams that unconsuming fire ;
  While these stand black against her morning skies,
The peasant sees it leap from peak to peak
  Along his hills ; the craftsman's burning eyes   60
Own with cool tears its influence mother-meek ;
  It lights the poet's heart up like a star ;
  Ah ! while the tyrant deemed it still afar,

And twined with golden threads his futile snare,
  That swift, convicting glow all round him ran ;
   'T was close beside him there,
Sunrise whose Memnon is the soul of man.

v

O Broker-King, is this thy wisdom's fruit ?
  A dynasty plucked out as 't were a weed
  Grown rankly in a night, that leaves no seed !   70
Could eighteen years strike down no deeper root ?
  But now thy vulture eye was turned on Spain,—
A shout from Paris, and thy crown falls off,
  Thy race has ceased to reign,
And thou become a fugitive and scoff :
  Slippery the feet that mount by stairs of gold,
And weakest of all fences one of steel ;—
  Go and keep school again like him of old,
The Syracusan tyrant ;—thou mayst feel
Royal amid a birch-swayed commonweal !   80

VI

Not long can he be ruler who allows
  His time to run before him ; thou wast naught
Soon as the strip of gold about thy brows
  Was no more emblem of the People's thought :
Vain were thy bayonets against the foe
  Thou hadst to cope with ; thou didst wage
War not with Frenchmen merely ;—no,
  Thy strife was with the Spirit of the Age,
The invisible Spirit whose first breath divine
    Scattered thy frail endeavour,   90
And, like poor last year's leaves, whirled thee and thine
    Into the Dark forever !

VII

Is here no triumph ?   Nay, what though
The yellow blood of Trade meanwhile should pour
  Along its arteries a shrunken flow,
And the idle canvas droop around the shore ?
    These do not make a state,
    Nor keep it great ;
    I think God made
The earth for man, not trade ;   100
And where each humblest human creature
Can stand, no more suspicious or afraid,
Erect and kingly in his right of nature,
To heaven and earth knit with harmonious ties,—
  Where I behold the exultation

Of manhood glowing in those eyes
  That had been dark for ages,
  Or only lit with bestial loves and rages,
There I behold a Nation :
    The France which lies   110
  Between the Pyrenees and Rhine
    Is the least part of France ;
I see her rather in the soul whose shine
Burns through the craftsman's grimy countenance,
  In the new energy divine
    Of Toil's enfranchised glance.

VIII

    And if it be a dream,—
If the great Future be the little Past
'Neath a new mask, which drops and shows at last
The same weird, mocking face to balk and blast,—   120
Yet, Muse, a gladder measure suits the theme,
    And the Tyrtaean harp
    Loves notes more resolute and sharp,
Throbbing, as throbs the bosom, hot and fast :
    Such visions are of morning,
    Theirs is no vague forewarning,
The dreams which nations dream come true,
    And shape the world anew ;
      If this be a sleep,
      Make it long, make it deep,   130
O Father, who sendest the harvests men reap !
    While Labour so sleepeth,
    His sorrow is gone,
  No longer he weepeth,
  But smileth and steepeth
    His thoughts in the dawn ;
  He heareth Hope yonder
    Rain, lark-like, her fancies,
  His dreaming hands wander
    Mid heart's-ease and pansies ;   140
' 'T is a dream !   'T is a vision ! '
    Shrieks Mammon aghast ;
' The day's broad derision
    Will chase it at last ;
Ye are mad, ye have taken
A slumbering kraken
    For firm land of the Past ! '
Ah ! if he awaken,
    God shield us all then,
If this dream rudely shaken   150
    Shall cheat him again !

IX

Since first I heard our North-wind blow,
Since first I saw Atlantic throw
On our fierce rocks his thunderous snow,
I loved thee, Freedom ; as a boy
The rattle of thy shield at Marathon
    Did with a Grecian joy
    Through all my pulses run ;
But I have learned to love thee now ;
Without the helm upon thy gleaming brow,   160
    A maiden mild and undefiled
Like her who bore the world's redeeming child ;
    And surely never did thine altars glance
    With purer fires than now in France ;
    While, in their bright white flashes,
      Wrong's shadow, backward cast,
    Waves cowering o'er the ashes
      Of the dead, blaspheming Past,
    O'er the shapes of fallen giants,
      His own unburied brood,   170
Whose dead hands clench defiance
    At the overpowering Good :
And down the happy future runs a flood
    Of prophesying light ;
It shows an Earth no longer stained with blood,
Blossom and fruit where now we see the bud
    Of Brotherhood and Right.

ANTI-APIS

Praisest Law, friend ?   We, too, love it much as they that love it best ;
'T is the deep, august foundation, whereon Peace and Justice rest ;
On the rock primeval, hidden in the Past its bases be,
Block by block the endeavouring Ages built it up to what we see.

But dig down : the Old unbury ; thou shalt find on every stone
That each Age hath carved the symbol of what god to them was known.
Ugly shapes and brutish sometimes, but the fairest that they knew ;
If their sight were dim and earthward, yet their hope and aim were true.

Surely as the unconscious needle feels the far-off loadstar draw,
So strives every gracious nature to at-one itself with law ;
And the elder Saints and Sages laid their pious framework right
By a theocratic instinct covered from the people's sight.

As their gods were, so their laws were ; Thor the strong could reave and steal,
So through many a peaceful inlet tore the Norseman's eager keel ;
But a new law came when Christ came, and not blameless, as before,
Can we, paying him our lip-tithes, give our lives and faiths to Thor.

Law is holy: ay, but what law ? Is there nothing more divine
Than the patched-up broils of Congress,—venal, full of meat and wine ?
Is there, say you, nothing higher ? Naught, God save us ! that transcends
Laws of cotton texture, wove by vulgar men for vulgar ends ?

Did Jehovah ask their counsel, or submit to them a plan,
Ere he filled with loves, hopes, longings, this aspiring heart of man ?
For their edict does the soul wait, ere it swing round to the pole
Of the true, the free, the God-willed, all that makes it be a soul ?

Law is holy ; but not your law, ye who keep the tablets whole
While ye dash the Law to pieces, shatter it in life and soul ;
Bearing up the Ark is lightsome, golden Apis hid within,
While we Levites share the offerings, richer by the people's sin.

Give to Caesar what is Caesar's ? yes, but tell me, if you can,
Is this superscription Caesar's here upon our brother man ?
Is not here some other's image, dark and sullied though it be,
In this fellow-soul that worships, struggles Godward even as we ?

It was not to such a future that the Mayflower's prow was turned ;
Not to such a faith the martyrs clung, exulting as they burned ;
Not by such laws are men fashioned, earnest, simple, valiant, great
In the household virtues whereon rests the unconquerable state.

Ah ! there is a higher gospel, overhead the God-roof springs,
And each glad, obedient planet like a golden shuttle sings
Through the web which Time is weaving in his never-resting loom,—
Weaving seasons many-coloured, bringing prophecy to doom.

Think you Truth a farthing rushlight, to be pinched out when you will
With your deft official fingers, and your politicians' skill ?
Is your God a wooden fetish, to be hidden out of sight
That his block eyes may not see you do the thing that is not right ?

But the Destinies think not so ; to their judgement-chamber lone
Comes no noise of popular clamour, there Fame's trumpet is not blown ;
Your majorities they reck not ;—that you grant, but then you say
That you differ with them somewhat,—which is stronger, you or they ?

Patient are they as the insects that build islands in the deep ;
They hurl not the bolted thunder, but their silent way they keep ;
Where they have been that we know ; where empires towered that were not
    just ;
Lo ! the skulking wild fox scratches in a little heap of dust.
    1851.

A PARABLE

Said Christ our Lord, ' I will go and see
How the men, my brethren, believe in me.'
He passed not again through the gate of birth,
But made himself known to the children of earth.

Then said the chief priests, and rulers, and kings,
' Behold, now, the Giver of all good things ;
Go to, let us welcome with pomp and state
Him who alone is mighty and great.'

With carpets of gold the ground they spread
Wherever the Son of Man should tread,
And in palace-chambers lofty and rare
They lodged him, and served him with kingly fare.

Great organs surged through arches dim
Their jubilant floods in praise of him ;
And in church, and palace, and judgement-hall,
He saw his image high over all.

But still, wherever his steps they led,
The Lord in sorrow bent down his head,
And from under the heavy foundation-stones,
The son of Mary heard bitter groans.

And in church, and palace, and judgement-hall,
He marked great fissures that rent the wall,
And opened wider and yet more wide
As the living foundation heaved and sighed.

' Have ye founded your thrones and altars, then,
On the bodies and souls of living men ?
And think ye that building shall endure,
Which shelters the noble and crushes the poor ?

' With gates of silver and bars of gold
Ye have fenced my sheep from their Father's fold ;
I have heard the dropping of their tears
In heaven these eighteen hundred years.'

' O Lord and Master, not ours the guilt,
We build but as our fathers built,
Behold thine images, how they stand,
Sovereign and sole, through all our land.

' Our task is hard,—with sword and flame
To hold thine earth forever the same,
And with sharp crooks of steel to keep
Still, as thou leftest them, thy sheep.'

Then Christ sought out an artisan,
A low-browed, stunted, haggard man,
And a motherless girl, whose fingers thin
Pushed from her faintly want and sin.

These set he in the midst of them,
And as they drew back their garment-hem,
For fear of defilement, ' Lo, here,' said he,
' The images ye have made of me ! '

ODE

WRITTEN FOR THE CELEBRATION OF THE INTRODUCTION OF THE COCHITUATE WATER INTO THE CITY OF BOSTON

My name is Water : I have sped
  Through strange, dark ways, un-
    tried before,
By pure desire of friendship led,
  Cochituate's ambassador ;
He sends four royal gifts by me :
Long life, health, peace, and purity.

I'm Ceres' cup-bearer ; I pour,
  For flowers and fruits and all their
    kin,
Her crystal vintage, from of yore
  Stored in old Earth's selectest bin,
Flora's Falernian ripe, since God
The wine-press of the deluge trod.

In that far isle whence, iron-willed,
  The New World's sires their bark
    unmoored,
The fairies' acorn-cups I filled
  Upon the toadstool's silver board,
And, 'neath Herne's oak, for Shake-
    speare's sight,
Strewed moss and grass with diamonds
  bright.

No fairies in the Mayflower came,
  And, lightsome as I sparkle here,
For Mother Bay State, busy dame,
  I've toiled and drudged this many
    a year,
Throbbed in her engines' iron veins,
Twirled myriad spindles for her gains.

I, too, can weave : the warp I set
  Through which the sun his shuttle
    throws,
And, bright as Noah saw it, yet
  For you the arching rainbow glows,
A sight in Paradise denied
To unfallen Adam and his bride.

When Winter held me in his grip,
  You seized and sent me o'er the
    wave,
Ungrateful ! in a prison-ship ;
  But I forgive, not long a slave,
For, soon as summer south-winds
    blew,
Homeward I fled, disguised as dew.

For countless services I'm fit,
  Of use, of pleasure, and of gain,
But lightly from all bonds I flit,
  Nor lose my mirth, nor feel a stain ;
From mill and wash-tub I escape,
And take in heaven my proper shape.

So, free myself, to-day, elate
  I come from far o'er hill and
    mead,
And here, Cochituate's envoy, wait
  To be your blithesome Ganymede,
And brim your cups with nectar
    true
That never will make slaves of you.

LINES

SUGGESTED BY THE GRAVES OF TWO ENGLISH SOLDIERS ON CONCORD BATTLE-GROUND

THE same good blood that now refills
The dotard Orient's shrunken veins,
The same whose vigour westward thrills,
Bursting Nevada's silver chains,
Poured here upon the April grass,
Freckled with red the herbage new ;
On reeled the battle's trampling mass,
Back to the ash the bluebird flew.

Poured here in vain ;—that sturdy blood
Was meant to make the earth more green,
But in a higher, gentler mood
Than broke this April noon serene ;
Two graves are here : to mark the place,
At head and foot, an unhewn stone,
O'er which the herald lichens trace
The blazon of Oblivion.

These men were brave enough, and true
To the hired soldier's bull-dog creed ;
What brought them here they never knew,
They fought as suits the English breed :
They came three thousand miles, and died,
To keep the Past upon its throne ;
Unheard, beyond the ocean tide,
Their English mother made her moan.

The turf that covers them no thrill
Sends up to fire the heart and brain ;
No stronger purpose nerves the will,
No hope renews its youth again :

From farm to farm the Concord glides,
And trails my fancy with its flow ;
O'erhead the balanced hen-hawk slides,
Twinned in the river's heaven below.

But go, whose Bay State bosom stirs,
Proud of thy birth and neighbour's right,
Where sleep the heroic villagers
Borne red and stiff from Concord fight ;
Thought Reuben, snatching down his gun,
Or Seth, as ebbed the life away,
What earthquake rifts would shoot and run
World-wide from that short April fray ?

What then ? With heart and hand they wrought,
According to their village light ;
'Twas for the Future that they fought,
Their rustic faith in what was right :
Upon earth's tragic stage they burst
Unsummoned, in the humble sock ;
Theirs the fifth act ; the curtain first
Rose long ago on Charles's block.

Their graves have voices ; if they threw
Dice charged with fates beyond their ken,
Yet to their instincts they were true,
And had the genius to be men.
Fine privilege of Freedom's host,
Of even foot-soldiers for the Right !—
For centuries dead, ye are not lost,
Your graves send courage forth, and might.

TO ——

We, too, have autumns, when our leaves
  Drop loosely through the dampened air,
When all our good seems bound in sheaves,
  And we stand reaped and bare.

Our seasons have no fixed returns,
  Without our will they come and go ;
At noon our sudden summer burns,
  Ere sunset all is snow.

But each day brings less summer cheer,
  Crimps more our ineffectual spring,
And something earlier every year
  Our singing birds take wing.

As less the olden glow abides,
  And less the chillier heart aspires,
With drift-wood beached in past spring-tides
  We light our sullen fires.

By the pinched rushlight's starving beam
  We cower and strain our wasted sight,
To stitch youth's shroud up, seam by seam,
  In the long arctic night.

It was not so—we once were young—
  When Spring, to womanly Summer turning,
Her dew-drops on each grass-blade strung,
  In the red sunrise burning.

We trusted then, aspired, believed
  That earth could be remade to-morrow ;—
Ah, why be ever undeceived ?
  Why give up faith for sorrow ?

O thou, whose days are yet all spring,
  Faith, blighted once, is past retrieving ;
Experience is a dumb, dead thing ;
  The victory 's in believing.

FREEDOM

Are we, then, wholly fallen ?   Can it be
That thou, North wind, that from thy mountains bringest
Their spirit to our plains, and thou, blue sea,
Who on our rocks thy wreaths of freedom flingest,
As on an altar,—can it be that ye
Have wasted inspiration on dead ears,
Dulled with the too familiar clank of chains ?
The people's heart is like a harp for years
Hung where some petrifying torrent rains
Its slow-incrusting spray : the stiffened chords   10
Faint and more faint make answer to the tears
That drip upon them : idle are all words :
Only a silver plectrum wakes the tone
Deep buried 'neath that ever-thickening stone.

We are not free : Freedom doth not consist
In musing with our faces toward the Past,
While petty cares, and crawling interests, twist
Their spider-threads about us, which at last

Grow strong as iron chains, to cramp and bind
In formal narrowness heart, soul, and mind.   20
Freedom is recreated year by year,
In hearts wide open on the Godward side,
In souls calm-cadenced as the whirling sphere,
In minds that sway the future like a tide.
No broadest creeds can hold her, and no codes ;
She chooses men for her august abodes,
Building them fair and fronting to the dawn ;
Yet, when we seek her, we but find a few
Light footprints, leading morn-ward through the dew :
Before the day had risen, she was gone.   30

And we must follow : swiftly runs she on,
And, if our steps should slacken in despair,
Half turns her face, half smiles through golden hair,
Forever yielding, never wholly won :
That is not love which pauses in the race
Two close-linked names on fleeting sand to trace ;
Freedom gained yesterday is no more ours ;
Men gather but dry seeds of last year's flowers ;
Still there 's a charm ungranted, still a grace,
Still rosy Hope, the free, the unattained,   40
Makes us Possession's languid hand let fall ;
'T is but a fragment of ourselves is gained,—
The Future brings us more, but never all.

And, as the finder of some unknown realm,
Mounting a summit whence he thinks to see
On either side of him the imprisoning sea,
Beholds, above the clouds that overwhelm
The valley-land, peak after snowy peak
Stretch out of sight, each like a silver helm
Beneath its plume of smoke, sublime and bleak,   50
And what he thought an island finds to be
A continent to him first oped,—so we
Can from our height of Freedom look along
A boundless future, ours if we be strong ;
Or if we shrink, better remount our ships
And, fleeing God's express design, trace back
The hero-freighted Mayflower's prophet-track
To Europe, entering her blood-red eclipse.

 1848.

BIBLIOLATRES

Bowing thyself in dust before a Book,
And thinking the great God is thine alone,
O rash iconoclast, thou wilt not brook
What gods the heathen carves in wood and stone,
As if the Shepherd who from outer cold
Leads all his shivering lambs to one sure fold
Were careful for the fashion of his crook.

There is no broken reed so poor and base,
No rush, the bending tilt of swamp-fly blue,
But he therewith the ravening wolf can chase,
And guide his flock to springs and pastures new ;
Through ways unlooked for, and through many lands,
Far from the rich folds built with human hands,
The gracious footprints of his love I trace.

And what art thou, own brother of the clod,
That from his hand the crook would snatch away
And shake instead thy dry and sapless rod,
To scare the sheep out of the wholesome day ?
Yea, what art thou, blind, unconverted Jew,
That with thy idol-volume's covers two
Wouldst make a jail to coop the living God ?

Thou hear'st not well the mountain organ-tones
By prophet ears from Hor and Sinai caught,
Thinking the cisterns of those Hebrew brains
Drew dry the springs of the All-knower's thought,
Nor shall thy lips be touched with living fire,
Who blow'st old altar-coals with sole desire
To weld anew the spirit's broken chains.

God is not dumb, that he should speak no more ;
If thou hast wanderings in the wilderness
And find'st not Sinai, 't is thy soul is poor ;
There towers the mountain of the Voice no less,
Which whoso seeks shall find, but he who bends,
Intent on manna still and mortal ends,
Sees it not, neither hears its thundered lore.

Slowly the Bible of the race is writ,
And not on paper leaves nor leaves of stone ;
Each age, each kindred, adds a verse to it,
Texts of despair or hope, of joy or moan.
While swings the sea, while mists the mountains shroud,
While thunder's surges burst on cliffs of cloud,
Still at the prophets' feet the nations sit.

BEAVER BROOK

HUSHED with broad sunlight lies the hill,
And, minuting the long day's loss,
The cedar's shadow, slow and still,
Creeps o'er its dial of grey moss.

Warm noon brims full the valley's cup,
The aspen's leaves are scarce astir ;
Only the little mill sends up
Its busy, never-ceasing burr.

Climbing the loose-piled wall that hems
The road along the mill-pond's brink,
From 'neath the arching barberry-stems,
My footstep scares the shy chewink.

Beneath a bony buttonwood
The mill's red door lets forth the din ;
The whitened miller, dust-imbued,
Flits past the square of dark within.

No mountain torrent's strength is here;
Sweet Beaver, child of forest still,
Heaps its small pitcher to the ear,
And gently waits the miller's will.

Swift slips Undine along the race
Unheard, and then, with flashing bound,
Floods the dull wheel with light and grace,
And, laughing, hunts the loath drudge round.

The miller dreams not at what cost
The quivering millstones hum and whirl,
Nor how for every turn are tost
Armfuls of diamond and of pearl.

But Summer cleared my happier eyes
With drops of some celestial juice,
To see how Beauty underlies
Forevermore each form of use.

And more ; methought I saw that flood,
Which now so dull and darkling steals,
Thick, here and there, with human blood,
To turn the world's laborious wheels.

No more than doth the miller there,
Shut in our several cells, do we
Know with what waste of beauty rare
Moves every day's machinery.

Surely the wiser time shall come
When this fine overplus of might,
No longer sullen, slow, and dumb,
Shall leap to music and to light.

In that new childhood of the Earth
Life of itself shall dance and play,
Fresh blood in Time's shrunk veins make mirth,
And labour meet delight half-way.

MEMORIAL VERSES

KOSSUTH

A RACE of nobles may die out,
A royal line may leave no heir ;
Wise Nature sets no guards about
Her pewter plate and wooden ware.

But they fail not, the kinglier breed,
Who starry diadems attain ;
To dungeon, axe, and stake succeed
Heirs of the old heroic strain.

The zeal of Nature never cools,
Nor is she thwarted of her ends ;
When gapped and dulled her cheaper
tools,
Then she a saint and prophet spends.

Land of the Magyars ! though it
be
The tyrant may relink his chain,
Already thine the victory,
As the just Future measures gain.

Thou hast succeeded, thou hast won
The deathly travail's amplest worth ;
A nation's duty thou hast done,
Giving a hero to our earth.

And he, let come what will of woe,
Hath saved the land he strove to save;
No Cossack hordes, no traitor's blow,
Can quench the voice shall haunt his
grave.

' I Kossuth am : O Future, thou
That clear'st the just and blott'st the
vile,
O'er this small dust in reverence bow,
Remembering what I was erewhile.

' I was the chosen trump wherethrough
Our God sent forth awakening breath;
Came chains ? Came death ?   The
strain He blew
Sounds on, outliving chains and death.'

TO LAMARTINE
1848

I DID not praise thee when the crowd,
    'Witched with the moment's inspiration,
Vexed thy still ether with hosannas loud,
    And stamped their dusty adoration ;
    I but looked upward with the rest,
And, when they shouted Greatest, whispered Best.

They raised thee not, but rose to thee,
    Their fickle wreaths about thee flinging ;
So on some marble Phoebus the high sea
    Might leave his worthless seaweed clinging,
    But pious hands, with reverent care,
Make the pure limbs once more sublimely bare.

Now thou 'rt thy plain, grand self again,
    Thou art secure from panegyric,—
Thou who gav'st politics an epic strain,
    And actedst Freedom's noblest lyric ;
    This side the Blessed Isles, no tree
Grows green enough to make a wreath for thee.

Nor can blame cling to thee ; the snow
    From swinish footprints takes no staining,
But, leaving the gross soils of earth below,
    Its spirit mounts, the skies regaining,
  And unresentful falls again,
To beautify the world with dews and rain.

The highest duty to mere man vouchsafed
    Was laid on thee,—out of wild chaos,
When the roused popular ocean foamed and chafed,
    And vulture War from his Imaus
  Snuffed blood, to summon homely Peace,
And show that only order is release.

To carve thy fullest thought, what though
    Time was not granted ? Aye in history,
Like that Dawn's face which baffled Angelo
    Left shapeless, grander for its mystery,
  Thy great Design shall stand, and day
Flood its blind front from Orients far away.

Who says thy day is o'er ? Control,
    My heart, that bitter first emotion ;
While men shall reverence the steadfast soul,
    The heart in silent self-devotion
  Breaking, the mild, heroic mien,
Thou 'lt need no prop of marble, Lamartine.

If France reject thee, 't is not thine,
    But her own, exile that she utters ;
Ideal France, the deathless, the divine,
    Will be where thy white pennon flutters,
  As once the nobler Athens went
With Aristides into banishment.

No fitting metewand hath To-day
    For measuring spirits of thy stature ;
Only the Future can reach up to lay
    The laurel on that lofty nature,
  Bard, who with some diviner art
Hast touched the bard's true lyre, a nation's heart.

Swept by thy hand, the gladdened chords,
    Crashed now in discords fierce by others,
Gave forth one note beyond all skill of words,
    And chimed together, We are brothers.
  O poem unsurpassed ! it ran
All round the world, unlocking man to man.

France is too poor to pay alone
  The service of that ample spirit ;
Paltry seem low dictatorship and throne,
  If balanced with thy simple merit ;
  They had to thee been rust and loss ;
Thy aim was higher,—thou hast climbed a Cross !

TO JOHN G. PALFREY

THERE are who triumph in a losing cause,
Who can put on defeat, as 't were a wreath
Unwithering in the adverse popular breath,
  Safe from the blasting demagogue's applause ;
'T is they who stand for Freedom and God's laws.

And so stands Palfrey now, as Marvell stood,
Loyal to Truth dethroned, nor could be wooed
  To trust the playful tiger's velvet paws :
And if the second Charles brought in decay
  Of ancient virtue, if it well might wring   10
Souls that had broadened 'neath a nobler day,
  To see a losel, marketable king
Fearfully watering with his realm's best blood
  Cromwell's quenched bolts, that erst had cracked and flamed,
Scaring, through all their depths of courtier mud,
  Europe's crowned bloodsuckers,—how more ashamed
Ought we to be, who see Corruption's flood
  Still rise o'er last year's mark, to mine away
Our brazen idol's feet of treacherous clay !

O utter degradation ! Freedom turned   20
  Slavery's vile bawd, to cozen and betray
  To the old lecher's clutch a maiden prey,
If so a loathsome pander's fee be earned !
  And we are silent,—we who daily tread
A soil sublime, at least, with heroes' graves !—
  Beckon no more, shades of the noble dead !
Be dumb, ye heaven-touched lips of winds and waves !
  Or hope to rouse some Coptic dullard, hid
Ages ago, wrapt stiffly, fold on fold,
With cerements close, to wither in the cold,   30
  Forever hushed, and sunless pyramid !

  Beauty and Truth, and all that these contain,
Drop not like ripened fruit about our feet ;
  We climb to them through years of sweat and pain ;
  Without long struggle, none did e'er attain
The downward look from Quiet's blissful seat :

Though present loss may be the hero's part,
Yet none can rob him of the victor heart
Whereby the broad-realmed future is subdued,
And Wrong, which now insults from triumph's car, 40
Sending her vulture hope to raven far,
Is made unwilling tributary of Good.

O Mother State, how quenched thy Sinai fires !
Is there none left of thy stanch Mayflower breed ?
No spark among the ashes of thy sires,
Of Virtue's altar-flame the kindling seed ?
Are these thy great men, these that cringe and creep,
And writhe through slimy ways to place and power ?—
How long, O Lord, before thy wrath shall reap
Our frail-stemmed summer prosperings in their flower ? 50
O for one hour of that undaunted stock
That went with Vane and Sidney to the block !

O for a whiff of Naseby, that would sweep,
With its stern Puritan besom, all this chaff
From the Lord's threshing-floor ! Yet more than half
The victory is attained, when one or two,
Through the fool's laughter and the traitor's scorn,
Beside thy sepulchre can bide the morn,
Crucified Truth, when thou shalt rise anew.

TO W. L. GARRISON

'Some time afterward, it was reported to me by the city officers that they had
ferreted out the paper and its editor ; that his office was an obscure hole, his only
visible auxiliary a negro boy, and his supporters a few very insignificant persons of all
colours.'—*Letter of H. G. Otis.*

In a small chamber, friendless and unseen,
    Toiled o'er his types one poor, unlearned young man ;
The place was dark, unfurnitured, and mean ;—
    Yet there the freedom of a race began.

Help came but slowly ; surely no man yet
    Put lever to the heavy world with less :
What need of help ? He knew how types were set,
    He had a dauntless spirit, and a press.

Such earnest natures are the fiery pith,
    The compact nucleus, round which systems grow !
Mass after mass becomes inspired therewith,
    And whirls impregnate with the central glow.

O Truth ! O Freedom ! how are ye still born
    In the rude stable, in the manger nursed !
What humble hands unbar those gates of morn
    Through which the splendours of the New Day burst !

What ! shall one monk, scarce known beyond his cell,
    Front Rome's far-reaching bolts, and scorn her frown ?
Brave Luther answered YES ; that thunder's swell
    Rocked Europe, and discharmed the triple crown.

Whatever can be known of earth we know,
    Sneered Europe's wise men, in their snail-shells curled ;
No ! said one man in Genoa, and that No
    Out of the dark created this New World.

Who is it will not dare himself to trust ?
    Who is it hath not strength to stand alone ?
Who is it thwarts and bilks the inward MUST ?
    He and his works, like sand, from earth are blown.

Men of a thousand shifts and wiles, look here !
    See one straightforward conscience put in pawn
To win a world ; see the obedient sphere
    By bravery's simple gravitation drawn !

Shall we not heed the lesson taught of old,
    And by the Present's lips repeated still,
In our own single manhood to be bold,
    Fortressed in conscience and impregnable will ?

We stride the river daily at its spring,
    Nor, in our childish thoughtlessness, foresee,
What myriad vassal streams shall tribute bring,
    How like an equal it shall greet the sea.

O small beginnings, ye are great and strong,
    Based on a faithful heart and weariless brain !
Ye build the future fair, ye conquer wrong,
    Ye earn the crown, and wear it not in vain.

ON THE DEATH OF C. T. TORREY

WOE worth the hour when it is crime
    To plead the poor dumb bondman's cause,
When all that makes the heart sublime,
The glorious throbs that conquer time,
    Are traitors to our cruel laws !

He strove among God's suffering poor
   One gleam of brotherhood to send ;
The dungeon oped its hungry door
To give the truth one martyr more,
    Then shut,—and here behold the end !

O Mother State ! when this was done,
   No pitying throe thy bosom gave ;
Silent thou saw'st the death-shroud spun,
And now thou givest to thy son
   The stranger's charity,—a grave.

Must it be thus forever ? No !
   The hand of God sows not in vain ;
Long sleeps the darkling seed below,
The seasons come, and change, and go,
    And all the fields are deep with grain.

Although our brother lie asleep,
   Man's heart still struggles, still aspires ;
His grave shall quiver yet, while deep
Through the brave Bay State's pulses leap
    Her ancient energies and fires.

When hours like this the senses' gush
   Have stilled, and left the spirit room,
It hears amid the eternal hush
The swooping pinions' dreadful rush,
    That bring the vengeance and the doom ;—

Not man's brute vengeance, such as rends
   What rivets man to man apart,—
God doth not so bring round his ends,
But waits the ripened time, and sends
    His mercy to the oppressor's heart.

ELEGY ON THE DEATH OF DR. CHANNING

I DO not come to weep above thy pall,
   And mourn the dying-out of noble powers ;
The poet's clearer eye should see, in all
    Earth's seeming woe, the seed of Heaven's flowers.

Truth needs no champions : in the infinite deep
   Of everlasting Soul her strength abides,
From Nature's heart her mighty pulses leap,
    Through Nature's veins her strength, undying, tides.

Peace is more strong than war, and gentleness,
    Where force were vain, makes conquest o'er the wave ;
And love lives on and hath a power to bless,
    When they who loved are hidden in the grave.

The sculptured marble brags of death-strewn fields,
    And Glory's epitaph is writ in blood ;
But Alexander now to Plato yields,
    Clarkson will stand where Wellington hath stood.

I watch the circle of the eternal years,
    And read forever in the storied page
One lengthened roll of blood, and wrong, and tears,—
    One onward step of Truth from age to age.

The poor are crushed ; the tyrants link their chain ;
    The poet sings through narrow dungeon-grates ;
Man's hope lies quenched ;—and, lo ! with steadfast gain
    Freedom doth forge her mail of adverse fates.

Men slay the prophets ; fagot, rack, and cross
    Make up the groaning record of the past ;
But Evil's triumphs are her endless loss,
    And sovereign Beauty wins the soul at last.

No power can die that ever wrought for Truth ;
    Thereby a law of Nature it became,
And lives unwithered in its sinewy youth,
    When he who called it forth is but a name.

Therefore I cannot think thee wholly gone ;
    The better part of thee is with us still ;
Thy soul its hampering clay aside hath thrown,
    And only freer wrestles with the Ill.

Thou livest in the life of all good things ;
    What words thou spak'st for Freedom shall not die ;
Thou sleepest not, for now thy Love hath wings
    To soar where hence thy Hope could hardly fly.

And often, from that other world, on this
    Some gleams from great souls gone before may shine,
To shed on struggling hearts a clearer bliss,
    And clothe the Right with lustre more divine.

Thou art not idle : in thy higher sphere
    Thy spirit bends itself to loving tasks,
And strength to perfect what it dreamed of here
    Is all the crown and glory that it asks.

For sure, in Heaven's wide chambers, there is room
  For love and pity, and for helpful deeds ;
Else were our summons thither but a doom
  To life more vain than this in clayey weeds.

From off the starry mountain-peak of song,
  Thy spirit shows me, in the coming time,
An earth unwithered by the foot of wrong,
  A race revering its own soul sublime.

What wars, what martyrdoms, what crimes, may come,
  Thou knowest not, nor I ; but God will lead
The prodigal soul from want and sorrow home,
  And Eden ope her gates to Adam's seed.

Farewell ! good man, good angel now ! this hand
  Soon, like thine own, shall lose its cunning too ;
Soon shall this soul, like thine, bewildered stand,
  Then leap to thread the free, unfathomed blue :

When that day comes, O, may this hand grow cold,
  Busy, like thine, for Freedom and the Right ;
O, may this soul, like thine, be ever bold
  To face dark Slavery's encroaching blight !

This laurel-leaf I cast upon thy bier ;
  Let worthier hands than these thy wreath intwine ;
Upon thy hearse I shed no useless tear,—
  For us weep rather thou in calm divine !
    1842.

TO THE MEMORY OF HOOD

ANOTHER star 'neath Time's horizon dropped,
  To gleam o'er unknown lands and seas ;
Another heart that beat for freedom stopped,—
  What mournful words are these !

O Love Divine, that claspest our tired earth,
  And lullest it upon thy heart,
Thou knowest how much a gentle soul is worth
  To teach men what thou art !

His was a spirit that to all thy poor
  Was kind as slumber after pain :
Why ope so soon thy heaven-deep Quiet's door
  And call him home again ?

Freedom needs all her poets : it is they
  Who give her aspirations wings,
And to the wiser law of music sway
  Her wild imaginings.

Yet thou hast called him, nor art thou unkind,
  O Love Divine, for 't is thy will
That gracious natures leave their love behind
  To work for Freedom still.

Let laurelled marbles weigh on other tombs,
  Let anthems peal for other dead,
Rustling the bannered depth of minster-glooms
  With their exulting spread.

His epitaph shall mock the short-lived stone,
  No lichen shall its lines efface,
He needs these few and simple lines alone
  To mark his resting-place :—

' Here lies a Poet.   Stranger, if to thee
  His claim to memory be obscure,
If thou wouldst learn how truly great was he,
  Go, ask it of the poor.'

THE VISION OF SIR LAUNFAL

PRELUDE TO PART FIRST

OVER his keys the musing organist,
  Beginning doubtfully and far away,
First lets his fingers wander as they
    list,
  And builds a bridge from Dream-
    land for his lay :
Then, as the touch of his loved instru-
    ment
  Gives hope and fervour, nearer
    draws his theme,
First guessed by faint auroral flushes
    sent
  Along the wavering vista of his
    dream.

  Not only around our infancy
  Doth heaven with all its splendours
    lie ;   10
    Daily, with souls that cringe and
    plot,
  We Sinais climb and know it not.

Over our manhood bend the skies ;
  Against our fallen and traitor lives
The great winds utter prophecies ;
  With our faint hearts the mountain
    strives ;
Its arms outstretched, the druid wood
  Waits with its benedicite ;
And to our age's drowsy blood
  Still shouts the inspiring sea.   20

Earth gets its price for what Earth
    gives us ;
  The beggar is taxed for a corner to
    die in,
The priest hath his fee who comes and
    shrives us,
  We bargain for the graves we lie in ;
At the devil's booth are all things
    sold,
Each ounce of dross costs its ounce of
    gold ;

For a cap and bells our lives we pay,
Bubbles we buy with a whole soul's
    tasking :
  'T is heaven alone that is given
    away,
'T is only God may be had for the
    asking ;   30
No price is set on the lavish summer ;
June may be had by the poorest comer.

And what is so rare as a day in June ?
  Then, if ever, come perfect days ;
Then Heaven tries earth if it be in tune,
  And over it softly her warm ear
    lays :
Whether we look, or whether we
    listen,
We hear life murmur, or see it glisten ;
Every clod feels a stir of might,
  An instinct within it that reaches
    and towers,   40
And, groping blindly above it for light,
  Climbs to a soul in grass and flowers ;
The flush of life may well be seen
    Thrilling back over hills and
    valleys ;
The cowslip startles in meadows green,
    The buttercup catches the sun in
    its chalice,
And there's never a leaf nor a blade
    too mean
    To be some happy creature's palace ;
The little bird sits at his door in the
    sun,
    Atilt like a blossom among the
    leaves,   50
And lets his illumined being o'errun
  With the deluge of summer it
    receives ;
His mate feels the eggs beneath her
    wings,
And the heart in her dumb breast
    flutters and sings ;

He sings to the wide world, and she to
   her nest,—
In the nice ear of Nature which song
   is the best ?

Now is the high-tide of the year,
   And whatever of life hath ebbed
     away
Comes flooding back with a ripply
   cheer,
   Into every bare inlet and creek and
     bay ;   60
Now the heart is so full that a drop
   overfills it,
We are happy now because God wills
   it ;
No matter how barren the past may
   have been,
'T is enough for us now that the leaves
   are green ;
We sit in the warm shade and feel
   right well
How the sap creeps up and the blos-
   soms swell ;
We may shut our eyes, but we cannot
   help knowing
That skies are clear and grass is grow-
   ing ;
The breeze comes whispering in our ear,
That dandelions are blossoming near,
   That maize has sprouted, that
     streams are flowing,   71
That the river is bluer than the sky,
That the robin is plastering his house
   hard by ;
And if the breeze kept the good news
   back,
For other couriers we should not lack ;
   We could guess it all by yon heifer's
     lowing,—
And hark ! how clear bold chanticleer,
Warmed with the new wine of the
   year,
   Tells all in his lusty crowing !

Joy comes, grief goes, we know not
   how ;   80
Everything is happy now,
  Everything is upward striving ;

'T is as easy now for the heart to be
   true
As for grass to be green or skies to be
   blue,—
   'T is the natural way of living :
Who knows whither the clouds have
   fled ?
   In the unscarred heaven they leave
   no wake ;
And the eyes forget the tears they
   have shed,
   The heart forgets its sorrow and
   ache ;
The soul partakes the season's youth,
   And the sulphurous rifts of passion
     and woe   91
Lie deep 'neath a silence pure and
   smooth,
   Like burnt-out craters healed with
   snow.
What wonder if Sir Launfal now
Remembered the keeping of his vow ?

PART FIRST

I

' MY golden spurs now bring to me,
   And bring to me my richest mail,
For to-morrow I go over land and sea
   In search of the Holy Grail ;
Shall never a bed for me be spread,
Nor shall a pillow be under my head,
Till I begin my vow to keep ;
Here on the rushes will I sleep,
And perchance there may come a
   vision true
Ere day create the world anew.'
   Slowly Sir Launfal's eyes grew
   dim,   11
   Slumber fell like a cloud on him,
And into his soul the vision flew.

II

The crows flapped over by twos and
   threes,
In the pool drowsed the cattle up to
   their knees,

The little birds sang as if it were
The one day of summer in all the
    year,
And the very leaves seemed to sing on
    the trees :
The castle alone in the landscape lay
Like an outpost of winter, dull and
    grey :   20
'Twas the proudest hall in the North
    Countree,
And never its gates might opened be,
Save to lord or lady of high degree ;
Summer besieged it on every side,
But the churlish stone her assaults
    defied ;
She could not scale the chilly wall,
Though around it for leagues her
    pavilions tall
Stretched left and right,
Over the hills and out of sight ;
    Green and broad was every tent,
    And out of each a murmur went
Till the breeze fell off at night.   32

III

The drawbridge dropped with a surly
    clang,
And through the dark arch a charger
    sprang,
Bearing Sir Launfal, the maiden
    knight,
In his gilded mail, that flamed so
    bright
It seemed the dark castle had
    gathered all
Those shafts the fierce sun had shot
    over its wall
    In his siege of three hundred
    summers long,
And, binding them all in one blazing
    sheaf,   40
    Had cast them forth : so, young
    and strong,
And lightsome as a locust-leaf,
Sir Launfal flashed forth in his
    unscarred mail,
To seek in all climes for the Holy
    Grail.

IV

It was morning on hill and stream and
    tree,
    And morning in the young knight's
    heart ;
Only the castle moodily
Rebuffed the gifts of the sunshine free,
    And gloomed by itself apart ;
The season brimmed all other things up
Full as the rain fills the pitcher-plant's
    cup.   51

V

As Sir Launfal made morn through
    the darksome gate,
    He was 'ware of a leper, crouched
    by the same,
Who begged with his hand and
    moaned as he sate ;
    And a loathing over Sir Launfal
    came ;
The sunshine went out of his soul
    with a thrill,
    The flesh 'neath his armour 'gan
    shrink and crawl,
And midway its leap his heart stood
    still
    Like a frozen waterfall ;
For this man, so foul and bent of
    stature,   60
Rasped harshly against his dainty
    nature,
And seemed the one blot on the sum-
    mer morn,—
So he tossed him a piece of gold in scorn.

VI

The leper raised not the gold from the
    dust :
' Better to me the poor man's crust,
Better the blessing of the poor,
Though I turn me empty from his
    door ;
That is no true alms which the hand
    can hold ;
He gives nothing but worthless gold
    Who gives from a sense of duty ;
But he who gives but a slender mite,
And gives to that which is out of sight,

That thread of the all-sustaining
    Beauty   73
Which runs through all and doth all
    unite,—
The hand cannot clasp the whole of
    his alms,
The heart outstretches its eager palms,
For a god goes with it and makes it
    store
To the soul that was starving in dark-
    ness before.'

PRELUDE TO PART SECOND

DOWN swept the chill wind from the
    mountain peak,
    From the snow five thousand
        summers old ;
On open wold and hill-top bleak
    It had gathered all the cold,
And whirled it like sleet on the
    wanderer's cheek ;
It carried a shiver everywhere
From the unleafed boughs and
    pastures bare ;
The little brook heard it and built
    a roof
'Neath which he could house him,
    winter-proof ;
All night by the white stars' frosty
    gleams   10
He groined his arches and matched
    his beams ;
Slender and clear were his crystal spars
As the lashes of light that trim the
    stars :
He sculptured every summer delight
In his halls and chambers out of
    sight ;
Sometimes his tinkling waters slipt
Down through a frost-leaved forest-
    crypt,
Long, sparkling aisles of steel-
    stemmed trees
Bending to counterfeit a breeze ;
Sometimes the roof no fretwork knew
But silvery mosses that downward
    grew ;   21

Sometimes it was carved in sharp
    relief
With quaint arabesques of ice-fern leaf;
Sometimes it was simply smooth and
    clear
For the gladness of heaven to shine
    through, and here
He had caught the nodding bulrush-
    tops
And hung them thickly with diamond
    drops,
That crystalled the beams of moon
    and sun,
And made a star of every one :
No mortal builder's most rare device
Could match this winter-palace of ice ;
'Twas as if every image that mirrored
    lay   32
In his depths serene through the
    summer day,
Each fleeting shadow of earth and sky,
    Lest the happy model should be lost,
Had been mimicked in fairy masonry
    By the elfin builders of the frost.

Within the hall are song and laughter,
    The cheeks of Christmas glow red
        and jolly,
And sprouting is every corbel and
    rafter   40
    With lightsome green of ivy and
        holly ;
Through the deep gulf of the chimney
    wide
Wallows the Yule-log's roaring tide ;
The broad flame-pennons droop and
    flap
    And belly and tug as a flag in the
        wind ;
Like a locust shrills the imprisoned
    sap,
    Hunted to death in its galleries
        blind ;
And swift little troops of silent sparks,
    Now pausing, now scattering away
        as in fear,
Go threading the soot-forest's tangled
    darks   50
    Like herds of startled deer.

But the wind without was eager and
    sharp,
Of Sir Launfal's grey hair it makes
    a harp,
      And rattles and wrings
      The icy strings,
    Singing, in dreary monotone,
    A Christmas carol of its own,
    Whose burden still, as he might
      guess,
    Was—'Shelterless, shelterless, shel-
      terless ! '
The voice of the seneschal flared like
    a torch   60
As he shouted the wanderer away
    from the porch,
And he sat in the gateway and saw
    all night
    The great hall-fire, so cheery and
      bold,
    Through the window-slits of the
      castle old,
Build out its piers of ruddy light
Against the drift of the cold.

PART SECOND

I

THERE was never a leaf on bush or
    tree,
The bare boughs rattled shudder-
    ingly ;
The river was dumb and could not
    speak,
    For the weaver Winter its shroud
      had spun ;
A single crow on the tree-top bleak
    From his shining feathers shed off
      the cold sun ;
Again it was morning, but shrunk and
    cold,
As if her veins were sapless and old,
And she rose up decrepitly
For a last dim look at earth and sea.

II

Sir Launfal turned from his own hard
    gate,   11
For another heir in his earldom sate ;

An old, bent man, worn out and frail,
He came back from seeking the Holy
    Grail ;
Little he recked of his earldom's loss,
No more on his surcoat was blazoned
    the cross,
But deep in his soul the sign he wore,
The badge of the suffering and the
    poor.

III

Sir Launfal's raiment thin and spare
Was idle mail 'gainst the barbed air,
For it was just at the Christmas time;
So he mused, as he sat, of a sunnier
    clime,   22
And sought for a shelter from cold
    and snow
In the light and warmth of long-
    ago ;
He sees the snake-like caravan crawl
O'er the edge of the desert, black and
    small,
Then nearer and nearer, till, one by
    one,
He can count the camels in the sun,
As over the red-hot sands they pass
To where, in its slender necklace of
    grass,   30
The little spring laughed and leapt
    in the shade,
And with its own self like an infant
    played,
And waved its signal of palms.

IV

' For Christ's sweet sake, I beg an
    alms ' ;—
The happy camels may reach the
    spring,
But Sir Launfal sees only the grue-
    some thing,
The leper, lank as the rain-blanched
    bone,
That cowers beside him, a thing as
    lone
And white as the ice-isles of Northern
    seas
In the desolate horror of his disease.

v

And Sir Launfal said,—' I behold in
    thee   41
An image of Him who died on the tree;
Thou also hast had thy crown of
    thorns,—
Thou also hast had the world's buffets
    and scorns,—
And to thy life were not denied
The wounds in the hands and feet and
    side :
Mild Mary's Son, acknowledge me ;
Behold, through him, I give to thee !'

vi

Then the soul of the leper stood up in
    his eyes
    And looked at Sir Launfal, and
        straightway he   50
Remembered in what a haughtier guise
He had flung an alms to leprosie,
When he girt his young life up in
    gilded mail
And set forth in search of the Holy
    Grail.
The heart within him was ashes and
    dust ;
He parted in twain his single crust,
He broke the ice on the streamlet's
    brink,
And gave the leper to eat and drink,
'Twas a mouldy crust of coarse brown
    bread,
'T was water out of a wooden bowl,
Yet with fine wheaten bread was the
    leper fed,   61
    And 't was red wine he drank with
        his thirsty soul.

vii

As Sir Launfal mused with a downcast
    face,
A light shone round about the place ;
The leper no longer crouched at his side,
But stood before him glorified,
Shining and tall and fair and straight
As the pillar that stood by the
    Beautiful Gate,—
Himself the Gate whereby men can
Enter the temple of God in Man.

viii

His words were shed softer than
    leaves from the pine,   71
And they fell on Sir Launfal as snows
    on the brine,
That mingle their softness and quiet
    in one
With the shaggy unrest they float
    down upon ;
And the voice that was calmer than
    silence said,
' Lo it is I, be not afraid !
In many climes, without avail,
Thou hast spent thy life for the Holy
    Grail ;
Behold, it is here,—this cup which
    thou   ·
Didst fill at the streamlet for me but
    now ;   80
This crust is my body broken for thee,
This water His blood that died on the
    tree ;
The Holy Supper is kept, indeed,
In whatso we share with another's
    need ;
Not what we give, but what we share,—
For the gift without the giver is bare;
Who gives himself with his alms feeds
    three,—
Himself, his hungering neighbour,
    and Me.'   88

ix

Sir Launfal awoke as from a swound :
' The Grail in my castle here is found !
Hang my idle armour up on the wall,
Let it be the spider's banquet-hall ;
He must be fenced with stronger mail
Who would seek and find the Holy
    Grail.'

x

The castle gate stands open now,
    And the wanderer is welcome to the
        hall
As the hangbird is to the elm-tree
    bough ;
    No longer scowl the turrets tall,
The Summer's long siege at last is o'er ;
When the first poor outcast went in at
    the door,   100

She entered with him in disguise,
And mastered the fortress by surprise;
There is no spot she loves so well on ground,
She lingers and smiles there the whole year round ;
The meanest serf on Sir Launfal's land
Has hall and bower at his command ;
And there 's no poor man in the North Countrèe
But is lord of the earldom as much as he.   108

NOTE.—According to the mythology of the Romancers, the San Greal, or Holy Grail, was the cup out of which Jesus partook of the Last Supper with His disciples. It was brought into England by Joseph of Arimathea, and remained there, an object of pilgrimage and adoration, for many years in the keeping of his lineal descendants. It was incumbent upon those who had charge of it to be chaste in thought, word, and deed ; but one of the keepers having broken this condition, the Holy Grail disappeared. From that time it was a favourite enterprise of the knights of Arthur's court to go in search of it. Sir Galahad was at last successful in finding it, as may be read in the seventeenth book of the Romance of King Arthur. Tennyson has made Sir Galahad the subject of one of the most exquisite of his poems.

The plot (if I may give that name to anything so slight) of the foregoing poem is my own, and, to serve its purposes, I have enlarged the circle of competition in search of the miraculous cup in such a manner as to include, not only other persons than the heroes of the Round Table, but also a period of time subsequent to the date of King Arthur's reign !

READER ! *walk up at once (it will soon be too late)*
and buy at a perfectly ruinous rate

A

FABLE FOR CRITICS:

OR, BETTER,

(I like, as a thing that the reader's first fancy may strike,
an old-fashioned title-page,
such as presents a tabular view of the volume's contents,)

A GLANCE

AT A FEW OF OUR LITERARY PROGENIES

(Mrs. Malaprop's word)

FROM

THE TUB OF DIOGENES ;

A VOCAL AND MUSICAL MEDLEY

THAT IS,

A SERIES OF JOKES

By A Wonderful Quiz,

who accompanies himself with a rub-a-dub-dub, full of spirit and grace,
on the top of the tub.

Set forth in October, the 31st day,
In the year '48, G. P. Putnam, Broadway.

TO

CHARLES F. BRIGGS

THIS VOLUME IS AFFECTIONATELY INSCRIBED.

IT being the commonest mode of procedure, I premise a few candid remarks

TO THE READER :—

This trifle, begun to please only myself and my own private fancy, was laid on the shelf. But some friends, who had seen it, induced me, by dint of saying they liked it, to put it in print. That is, having come to that very conclusion, I consulted them when it could make no confusion. For (though in the gentlest of ways) they had hinted it was scarce worth the while, I should doubtless have printed it.

I began it, intending a Fable, a frail, slender thing, rhyme-ywinged, with a sting in its tail. But, by addings and alterings not previously planned,—digressions chance-hatched, like birds' eggs in the sand,—and dawdlings to suit every whimsey's demand (always freeing the bird which I held in my hand, for the two perched, perhaps out of reach, in the tree),—it grew by degrees to the size which you see. I was like the old woman that carried the calf, and my neighbours, like hers, no doubt, wonder and laugh, and when, my strained arms with their grown burthen full, I call it my Fable, they call it a bull.

Having scrawled at full gallop (as far as that goes) in a style that is neither good verse nor bad prose, and being a person whom nobody knows, some people will say I am rather more free with my readers than it is becoming to be, that I seem to expect them to wait on my leisure in following wherever I wander at pleasure, that, in short, I take more than a young author's lawful ease, and laugh in a queer way so

like Mephistopheles, that the public will doubt, as they grope through my rhythm, if in truth I am making fun *at* them or *with* them.

So the excellent Public is hereby assured that the sale of my book is already secured. For there is not a poet throughout the whole land but will purchase a copy or two out of hand, in the fond expectation of being amused in it, by seeing his betters cut up and abused in it. Now, I find, by a pretty exact calculation, there are something like ten thousand bards in the nation, of that special variety whom the Review and Magazine critics call *lofty* and *true*, and about thirty thousand (*this* tribe is increasing) of the kinds who are termed *full of promise* and *pleasing*. The Public will see by a glance at this schedule, that they cannot expect me to be over-sedulous about courting *them*, since it seems I have got enough fuel made sure of for boiling my pot.

As for such of our poets as find not their names mentioned once in my pages, with praises or blames, let them SEND IN THEIR CARDS, without further DELAY, to my friend G. P. PUTNAM, Esquire, in Broadway, where a LIST will be kept with the strictest regard to the day and the hour of receiving the card. Then, taking them up as I chance to have time (that is, if their names can be twisted in rhyme), I will honestly give each his PROPER POSITION, at the rate of ONE AUTHOR to each NEW EDITION. Thus a PREMIUM is offered sufficiently HIGH (as the magazines say when they tell their best lie) to induce bards to CLUB their resources and buy the balance of every edition, until they have all of them fairly been run through the mill.

One word to such readers (judicious and wise) as read books with something behind the mere eyes, of whom in the country, perhaps, there are two, including myself, gentle reader, and you. All the characters sketched in this slight *jeu d'esprit*, though, it may be, they seem, here and there, rather free, and drawn from a Mephistophelian standpoint, are *meant* to be faithful, and that is the grand point, and none but an owl would feel sore at a rub from a jester who tells you, without any subterfuge, that he sits in Diogenes' tub.

A PRELIMINARY NOTE TO THE SECOND EDITION,

though it well may be reckoned, of all composition, the species at once most delightful and healthy, is a thing which an author, unless he be wealthy and willing to pay for that kind of delight, is not, in all instances, called on to write. Though there are, it is said, who, their spirits to cheer, slip in a new title-page three times a year, and in his way snuff up an imaginary savour of that sweetest of dishes, the popular favour,—much as if a starved painter should fall to and treat the Ugolino inside to a picture of meat.

You remember (if not, pray turn over and look) that, in writing the preface which ushered my book, I treated you, excellent Public, not merely with a cool disregard, but downright cavalierly. Now I would not take back the least thing I then said, though I thereby could butter both sides of my bread, for I never could see that an author owed aught to the people he solaced, diverted, or taught; and, as for mere fame, I have long ago learned that the persons by whom it is finally earned are those with whom *your* verdict weighed not a pin, unsustained by the higher court sitting within.

But I wander from what I intended to say,—that you have, namely, shown such a liberal way of thinking, and so much æsthetic perception of anonymous worth in the handsome reception you gave to my book, spite of some private piques (having bought the first thousand in barely two weeks), that I think, past a doubt, if you measured the phiz of yours most devotedly, Wonderful Quiz, you would find that its vertical section was shorter, by an inch and two tenths, or 'twixt that and a quarter.

You have watched a child playing—in those wondrous years when belief is not bound to the eyes and the ears, and the vision divine is so clear and unmarred, that each baker of pies in the dirt is a bard ? Give a knife and a shingle, he fits out a fleet, and, on that little mud-puddle over the street, his fancy, in purest good faith, will make sail round the globe with a puff of his breath for a gale, will visit in barely ten minutes all climes, and find Northwestern passages hundreds of times. Or, suppose the young Poet fresh stored with delights from that Bible of childhood, the Arabian Nights, he will turn to a crony and cry, ' Jack, let 's play that I am a Genius ! ' Jacky straightway makes Aladdin's lamp out of a stone, and, for hours, they enjoy each his own supernatural powers. This is all very pretty and pleasant, but then suppose our two urchins have grown into men, and both have turned authors,—one says to his brother, ' Let 's play we're the American something or other,—say Homer or Sophocles, Goethe or Scott (only let them be big enough, no matter what). Come, you shall be Byron or Pope, which you choose : I 'll be Coleridge, and both shall write mutual reviews.' So they both (as mere strangers) before many days send each other a cord of anonymous bays. Each, piling his epithets, smiles in his sleeve to see what his friend can be made to believe ; each, reading the other's unbiased review, thinks—Here 's pretty high praise, but no more than is true. Well, we laugh at them both, and yet make no great fuss when the same farce is acted to benefit us. Even I, who, if asked, scarce a month since, what Fudge meant, should have answered, the dear

Public's critical judgement, begin to think sharp-witted Horace spoke sooth when he said, that the Public *sometimes* hit the truth.

In reading these lines, you perhaps have a vision of a person in pretty good health and condition; and yet, since I put forth my primary edition, I have been crushed, scorched, withered, used up and put down (by Smith with the cordial assistance of Brown), in all, if you put any faith in my rhymes, to the number of ninety-five several times, and, while I am writing,—I tremble to think of it, for I may at this moment be just on the brink of it,—Molybdostom, angry at being omitted, has begun a critique,—am I not to be pitied ? [1]

Now I shall not crush *them* since, indeed, for that matter, no pressure I know of could render them flatter; nor wither, nor scorch them,—no action of fire could make either them or their articles drier; nor waste time in putting them down—I am thinking not their own self-inflation will keep them from sinking; for there 's this contradiction about the whole bevy,—though without the least weight, they are awfully heavy. No, my dear honest bore, *surdo fabulam narras*, they are no more to me than a rat in the arras. I can walk with the Doctor, get facts from the Don, or draw out the Lambish quintessence of John, and feel nothing more than a half-comic sorrow, to think that they all will be lying to-morrow tossed carelessly up on the waste-paper shelves, and forgotten by all but their half-dozen selves. Once snug in my attic, my fire in a roar, I leave the whole pack of them outside the door. With Hakluyt or Purchas I wander away to the black northern seas or barbaric Cathay; get *jou* with O'Shanter, and sober me then with that builder of brick-kilnish dramas, rare Ben; snuff Herbert, as holy as a flower on a grave; with Fletcher wax tender, o'er Chapman grow brave; with Marlowe or Kyd take a fine poet-rave; in

Very, most Hebrew of Saxons, find peace; with Lycidas welter on vext Irish seas; with Webster grow wild, and climb earthward again, down by mystical Browne's Jacob's-ladder-like brain, to that spiritual Pepys (Cotton's version) Montaigne; find a new depth in Wordsworth, undreamed of before,—that divinely inspired, wise, deep, tender, grand—bore. Or, out of my study, the scholar thrown off, Nature holds up her shield 'gainst the sneer and the scoff; the landscape, forever consoling and kind, pours her wine and her oil on the smarts of the mind. The waterfall, scattering its vanishing gems; the tall grove of hemlocks, with moss on their stems, like plashes of sunlight; the pond in the woods, where no foot but mine and the bittern's intrudes; these are all my kind neighbours, and leave me no wish to say aught to you all, my poor critics, but—pish! I have buried the hatchet: I am twisting an allumette out of one of you now, and relighting my calumet. In your private capacities, come when you please, I will give you my hand and a fresh pipe apiece.

As I ran through the leaves of my poor little book, to take a fond author's first tremulous look, it was quite an excitement to hunt the *errata*, sprawled in as birds' tracks are in some kinds of strata (only these made things crookeder). Fancy an heir that a father had seen born well-featured and fair, turning suddenly wry-nosed, club-footed, squint-eyed, hair-lipped, wapper-jawed, carrot-haired, from a pride become an aversion,—my case was yet worse. A club-foot (by way of a change) in a verse, I might have forgiven, an *o*'s being wry, a limp in an *e*, or a cock in an *i*,—but to have the sweet babe of my brain served in *pi* ! I am not queasy-stomached, but such a Thyestean banquet as that was quite out of the question.

In the edition now issued, no pains

[1] The wise Scandinavians probably called their bards by the queer-looking title of Scald, in a delicate way, as it were, just to hint to the world the hot water they always get into.

are neglected, and my verses, as orators say, stand corrected. Yet some blunders remain of the Public's own make, which I wish to correct for my personal sake. For instance, a character drawn in pure fun and condensing the traits of a dozen in one, has been, as I hear, by some persons applied to a good friend of mine, whom to stab in the side, as we walked along chatting and joking together, would not be *my* way. I can hardly tell whether a question will ever arise in which he and I should by any strange fortune agree, but meanwhile my esteem for him grows as I know him, and, though not the best judge on earth of a poem, he knows what it is he is saying and why, and is honest and fearless, two good points which I have not found so rife I can easily smother my love for them, whether on my side or t'other.

For my other *anonymi*, you may be sure that I know what is meant by a caricature, and what by a portrait. There *are* those who think it is capital fun to be spattering their ink on quiet, unquarrelsome folk, but the minute the game changes sides and the others begin it, they see something savage and horrible in it. As for me I respect neither women nor men for their gender, nor own any sex in a pen. I choose just to hint to some causeless unfriends that, as far as I know, there are always two ends (and one of them heaviest, too) to a staff, and two parties also to every good laugh.

A FABLE FOR CRITICS

PHOEBUS, sitting one day in a laurel-tree's shade,
Was reminded of Daphne, of whom it was made,
For the god being one day too warm in his wooing,
She took to the tree to escape his pursuing;
Be the cause what it might, from his offers she shrunk,
And, Ginevra-like, shut herself up in a trunk;
And, though 'twas a step into which he had driven her,
He somehow or other had never forgiven her;
Her memory he nursed as a kind of a tonic,
Something bitter to chew when he'd play the Byronic,   10
And I can't count the obstinate nymphs that he brought over
By a strange kind of smile he put on when he thought of her.
' My case is like Dido's,' he sometimes remarked;
' When I last saw my love, she was fairly embarked
In a laurel, as *she* thought—but (ah, how Fate mocks !)
She has found it by this time a very bad box;
Let hunters from me take this saw when they need it,—
You're not always sure of your game when you've treed it.
Just conceive such a change taking place in one's mistress !
What romance would be left ?—who can flatter or kiss trees ?   20
And, for mercy's sake, how could one keep up a dialogue
With a dull wooden thing that will live and will die a log,—
Not to say that the thought would forever intrude
That you've less chance to win her the more she is wood ?
Ah ! it went to my heart, and the memory still grieves,
To see those loved graces all taking their leaves;

Those charms beyond speech, so enchanting but now,
As they left me forever, each making its bough !
If her tongue *had* a tang sometimes more than was right,
Her new bark is worse than ten times her old bite.'   30

Now, Daphne—before she was happily treeified—
Over all other blossoms the lily had deified,
And when she expected the god on a visit
('T was before he had made his intentions explicit),
Some buds she arranged with a vast deal of care,
To look as if artlessly twined in her hair,
Where they seemed, as he said, when he paid his addresses,
Like the day breaking through the long night of her tresses ;
So whenever he wished to be quite irresistible,
Like a man with eight trumps in his hand at a whist-table   40
(I feared me at first that the rhyme was untwistable,
Though I might have lugged in an allusion to Cristabel),—
He would take up a lily, and gloomily look in it,
As I shall at the ——, when they cut up my book in it.

Well, here, after all the bad rhyme I've been spinning,
I've got back at last to my story's beginning :
Sitting there, as I say, in the shade of his mistress,
As dull as a volume of old Chester mysteries,
Or as those puzzling specimens which, in old histories,
We read of his verses—the Oracles, namely,—   50
(I wonder the Greeks should have swallowed them tamely,
For one might bet safely whatever he has to risk,
They were laid at his door by some ancient Miss Asterisk,
And so dull that the men who retailed them out-doors
Got the ill name of augurs, because they were bores,—)
First, he mused what the animal substance or herb is
Would induce a moustache, for you know he's *imberbis* ;
Then he shuddered to think how his youthful position
Was assailed by the age of his son the physician ;
At some poems he glanced, had been sent to him lately,   60
And the metre and sentiment puzzled him greatly ;
' Mehercle ! I'd make such proceeding felonious,—
Have they all of them slept in the cave of Trophonius ?
Look well to your seat, ' tis like taking an airing
On a corduroy road, and that out of repairing ;
It leads one, 't is true, through the primitive forest,
Grand natural features, but then one has no rest ;
You just catch a glimpse of some ravishing distance,
When a jolt puts the whole of it out of existence,—
Why not use their ears, if they happen to have any ? '   70
—Here the laurel-leaves murmured the name of poor Daphne.

' O, weep with me, Daphne,' he sighed, ' for you know it's
A terrible thing to be pestered with poets !

But, alas, she is dumb, and the proverb holds good,
She never will cry till she 's out of the wood !
What would n't I give if I never had known of her ?
'T were a kind of relief had I something to groan over :
If I had but some letters of hers, now, to toss over,
I might turn for the nonce a Byronic philosopher,
And bewitch all the flats by bemoaning the loss of her.   80
One needs something tangible, though, to begin on,—
A loom, as it were, for the fancy to spin on ;
What boots all your grist ? it can never be ground
Till a breeze makes the arms of the windmill go round,
(Or, if 't is a water-mill, alter the metaphor,
And say it won't stir, save the wheel be well wet afore,
Or lug in some stuff about water ' so dreamily,'—
It is not a metaphor, though, 't is a simile) ;
A lily, perhaps, would set *my* mill a-going,
For just at this season, I think, they are blowing.   90
Here, somebody, fetch one ; not very far hence
They're in bloom by the score, 't is but climbing a fence ;
There's a poet hard by, who does nothing but fill his
Whole garden, from one end to t' other, with lilies ;
A very good plan, were it not for satiety,
One longs for a weed here and there, for variety ;
Though a weed is no more than a flower in disguise,
Which is seen through at once, if love give a man eyes.'

Now there happened to be among Phoebus's followers,
A gentleman, one of the omnivorous swallowers,   100
Who bolt every book that comes out of the press,
Without the least question of larger or less,
Whose stomachs are strong at the expense of their head,—
For reading new books is like eating new bread,
One can bear it at first, but by gradual steps he
Is brought to death's door of a mental dyspepsy.
On a previous stage of existence, our Hero
Had ridden outside, with the glass below zero ;
He had been, 't is a fact you may safely rely on,
Of a very old stock a most eminent scion,—   110
A stock all fresh quacks their fierce boluses ply on,
Who stretch the new boots Earth 's unwilling to try on,
Whom humbugs of all shapes and sorts keep their eye on,
Whose hair 's in the mortar of every new Zion,
Who, when whistles are dear, go directly and buy one,
Who think slavery a crime that we must not say fie on,
Who hunt, if they e'er hunt at all, with the lion
(Though they hunt lions also, whenever they spy one),
Who contrive to make every good fortune a wry one,
And at last choose the hard bed of honour to die on,   120

Whose pedigree, traced to earth's earliest years,
Is longer than anything else but their ears ;—
In short, he was sent into life with the wrong key,
He unlocked the door, and stept forth a poor donkey.
Though kicked and abused by his bipedal betters
Yet he filled no mean place in the kingdom of letters ;
Far happier than many a literary hack,
He bore only paper-mill rags on his back
(For it makes a vast difference which side the mill
One expends on the paper his labour and skill) ;   130
So, when his soul waited a new transmigration,
And Destiny balanced 'twixt this and that station,
Not having much time to expend upon bothers,
Remembering he 'd had some connexion with authors,
And considering his four legs had grown paralytic,—
She set him on two, and he came forth a critic.

Through his babyhood no kind of pleasure he took
In any amusement but tearing a book ;
For him there was no intermediate stage
From babyhood up to strait-laced middle age ;   140
There were years when he did n't wear coat-tails behind,
But a boy he could never be rightly defined ;
Like the Irish Good Folk, though in length scarce a span,
From the womb he came gravely, a little old man ;
While other boys' trousers demanded the toil
Of the motherly fingers on all kinds of soil,
Red, yellow, brown, black, clayey, gravelly, loamy,
He sat in the corner and read Viri Romae.
He never was known to unbend or to revel once
In base, marbles, hockey, or kick up the devil once ;   150
He was just one of those who excite the benevolence
Of your old prigs who sound the soul's depths with a ledger,
And are on the lookout for some young men to ' edger-
cate', as they call it, who won't be too costly,
And who'll afterward take to the ministry mostly ;
Who always wear spectacles, always look bilious,
Always keep on good terms with each *mater-familias*
Throughout the whole parish, and manage to rear
Ten boys like themselves, on four hundred a year :
Who, fulfilling in turn the same fearful conditions,   160
Either preach through their noses, or go upon missions.

In this way our hero got safely to college,
Where he bolted alike both his commons and knowledge ;
A reading-machine, always wound up and going,
He mastered whatever was not worth the knowing,
Appeared in a gown, and a vest of black satin,
To spout such a Gothic oration in Latin

That Tully could never have made out a word in it
(Though himself was the model the author preferred in it),
And grasping the parchment which gave him in fee   170
All the mystic and-so-forths contained in A. B.,
He was launched (life is always compared to a sea)
With just enough learning, and skill for the using it,
To prove he'd a brain, by forever confusing it.
So worthy St. Benedict, piously burning
With the holiest zeal against secular learning,
Nesciensque scienter, as writers express it,
Indoctusque sapienter a Roma recessit.

'T would be endless to tell you the things that he knew,
All separate facts, undeniably true,   180
But with him or each other they'd nothing to do ;
No power of combining, arranging, discerning,
Digested the masses he learned into learning ;
There was one thing in life he had practical knowledge for
(And this, you will think, he need scarce go to college for),—
Not a deed would he do, nor a word would he utter,
Till he'd weighed its relations to plain bread and butter.
When he left Alma Mater, he practised his wits
In compiling the journals' historical bits,—
Of shops broken open, men falling in fits,   190
Great fortunes in England bequeathed to poor printers,
And cold spells, the coldest for many past winters,—
Then, rising by industry, knack, and address,
Got notices up for an unbiased press,
With a mind so well poised, it seemed equally made for
Applause or abuse, just which chanced to be paid for :
From this point his progress was rapid and sure,
To the post of a regular heavy reviewer.

And here I must say he wrote excellent articles
On the Hebraic points, or the force of Greek particles,   200
They filled up the space nothing else was prepared for ;
And nobody read that which nobody cared for ;
If any old book reached a fiftieth edition,
He could fill forty pages with safe erudition :
He could gauge the old books by the old set of rules,
And his very old nothings pleased very old fools ;
But give him a new book, fresh out of the heart,
And you put him at sea without compass or chart,—
His blunders aspired to the rank of an art ;
For his lore was engraft, something foreign that grew in him,
Exhausting the sap of the native and true in him,   211
So that when a man came with a soul that was new in him,
Carving new forms of truth out of Nature's old granite,
New and old at their birth, like Le Verrier's planet,

Which, to get a true judgement, themselves must create
In the soul of their critic the measure and weight,
Being rather themselves a fresh standard of grace,
To compute their own judge, and assign him his place,
Our reviewer would crawl all about it and round it,
And, reporting each circumstance just as he found it,   220
Without the least malice,—his record would be
Profoundly aesthetic as that of a flea,
Which, supping on Wordsworth, should print, for our sakes,
Recollections of nights with the Bard of the Lakes,
Or, lodged by an Arab guide, ventured to render a
General view of the ruins at Denderah.

As I said, he was never precisely unkind,
The defect in his brain was just absence of mind ;
If he boasted, 't was simply that he was self-made,
A position which I, for one, never gainsaid,   230
My respect for my Maker supposing a skill
In His works which our Hero would answer but ill ;
And I trust that the mould which he used may be cracked, or he,
Made bold by success, may enlarge his phylactery,
And set up a kind of a man-manufactory,—
An event which I shudder to think about, seeing
That Man is a moral, accountable being.

He meant well enough, but was still in the way,
As a dunce always is, let him be where he may ;
Indeed, they appear to come into existence   240
To impede other folks with their awkward assistance ;
If you set up a dunce on the very North pole
All alone with himself, I believe, on my soul,
He 'd manage to get betwixt somebody's shins,
And pitch him down bodily, all in his sins,
To the grave polar bears sitting round on the ice,
All shortening their grace, to be in for a slice ;
Or, if he found nobody else there to pother,
Why, one of his legs would just trip up the other,
For there 's nothing we read of in torture's inventions,   250
Like a well-meaning dunce, with the best of intentions.

A terrible fellow to meet in society,
Not the toast that he buttered was ever so dry at tea ;
There he 'd sit at the table and stir in his sugar,
Crouching close for a spring, all the while, like a cougar ;
Be sure of your facts, of your measures and weights,
Of your time,—he 's as fond as an Arab of dates ;
You 'll be telling, perhaps, in your comical way,
Of something you 've seen in the course of the day ;
And, just as you 're tapering out the conclusion,   260
You venture an ill-fated classic allusion,—

The girls have all got their laughs ready, when, whack !
The cougar comes down on your thunderstruck back !
You had left out a comma,—your Greek's put in joint,
And pointed at cost of your story's whole point.
In the course of the evening you find chance for certain
Soft speeches to Anne, in the shade of the curtain :
You tell her your heart can be likened to *one* flower,
' And that, O most charming of women, 's the sunflower,
Which turns '—here a clear nasal voice, to your terror,   270
From outside the curtain, says, ' That 's all an error.'
As for him, he 's—no matter, he never grew tender,
Sitting after a ball, with his feet on the fender,
Shaping somebody's sweet features out of cigar smoke
(Though he 'd willingly grant you that such doings are smoke) ;
All women he damns with *mutabile semper*,
And if ever he felt something like love's distemper,
'T was towards a young lady who spoke ancient Mexican,
And assisted her father in making a lexicon ;
Though I recollect hearing him get quite ferocious   280
About Mary Clausum, the mistress of Grotius,
Or something of that sort,—but, no more to bore ye
With character-painting, I 'll turn to my story.

    Now, Apollo, who finds it convenient sometimes
To get his court clear of the makers of rhymes,
The *genus*, I think it is called, *irritabile*,
Every one of whom thinks himself treated most shabbily,
And nurses a—what is it ?—*immedicabile*,
Which keeps him at boiling-point, hot for a quarrel,
As bitter as wormwood, and sourer than sorrel,   290
If any poor devil but look at a laurel ;—
Apollo, I say, being sick of their rioting
(Though he sometimes acknowledged their verse had a quieting
Effect after dinner, and seemed to suggest a
Retreat to the shrine of a tranquil siesta),
Kept our Hero at hand, who, by means of a bray,
Which he gave to the life, drove the rabble away ;
And if that would n't do, he was sure to succeed,
If he took his review out and offered to read ;
Or, failing in plans of this milder description,   300
He would ask for their aid to get up a subscription,
Considering that authorship was n't a rich craft,
To print the ' American drama of Witchcraft '.
' Stay, I 'll read you a scene,'—but he hardly began,
Ere Apollo shrieked ' Help ' ! and the authors all ran :
And once, when these purgatives acted with less spirit,
And the desperate case asked a remedy desperate,
He drew from his pocket a foolscap epistle
As calmly as if 't were a nine-barrelled pistol,

And threatened them all with the judgement to come,   310
Of ' A wandering Star's first impressions of Rome '.
' Stop ! stop ! ' with their hands o'er their ears, screamed the Muses,
' He may go off and murder himself, if he chooses,
'T was a means self-defence only sanctioned his trying,
'T is mere massacre now that the enemy 's flying ;
If he 's forced to 't again, and we happen to be there,
Give us each a large handkerchief soaked in strong ether.'

    I called this a ' Fable for Critics ' ; you think it 's
More like a display of my rhythmical trinkets ;
My plot, like an icicle, 's slender and slippery,   320
Every moment more slender, and likely to slip awry,
And the reader unwilling *in loco desipere*
Is free to jump over as much of my frippery
As he fancies, and, if he 's a provident skipper, he
May have an Odyssean sway of the gales,
And get safe to port, ere his patience quite fails ;
Moreover, although 't is a slender return
For your toil and expense, yet my paper will burn,
And, if you have manfully struggled thus far with me,
You may e'en twist me up, and just light your cigar with me :
If too angry for that, you can tear me in pieces,   331
And my *membra disjecta* consign to the breezes,
A fate like great Ratzau's, whom one of those bores,
Who beflead with bad verses poor Louis Quatorze,
Describes (the first verse somehow ends with *victoire*),
As *dispersant partout et ses membres et sa gloire* ;
Or, if I were over-desirous of earning
A repute among noodles for classical learning,
I could pick you a score of allusions, I wis,
As new as the jests of *Didaskalos tis* ;   340
Better still, I could make out a good solid list
From recondite authors who do not exist,—
But that would be naughty : at least, I could twist
Something out of Absyrtus, or turn your inquiries
After Milton's prose metaphor, drawn from Osiris ;—
But, as Cicero says he won't say this or that
(A fetch, I must say, most transparent and flat),
After saying whate'er he could possibly think of,—
I simply will state that I pause on the brink of
A mire, ankle-deep, of deliberate confusion,   350
Made up of old jumbles of classic allusion,
So, when you were thinking yourselves to be pitied,
Just conceive how much harder your teeth you 'd have gritted,
An 't were not for the dullness I 've kindly omitted.

    I 'd apologize here for my many digressions,
Were it not that I 'm certain to trip into fresh ones

('T is so hard to escape if you get in their mesh once) ;
Just reflect, if you please, how 't is said by Horatius,
That Maeonides nods now and then, and, my gracious !
It certainly does look a little bit ominous   360
When he gets under way with *ton d' apameibomenos.*
(Here a something occurs which I 'll just clap a rhyme to,
And say it myself, ere a Zoilus have time to,—
Any author a nap like Van Winkle's may take,
If he only contrive to keep readers awake,
But he 'll very soon find himself laid on the shelf,
If *they* fall a-nodding when he nods himself.)

    Once for all, to return, and to stay, will I, nill I—
When Phoebus expressed his desire for a lily,
Our hero, whose homoeopathic sagacity   370
With an ocean of zeal mixed his drop of capacity,
Set off for the garden as fast as the wind
(Or, to take a comparison more to my mind,
As a sound politician leaves conscience behind),
And leaped the low fence, as a party hack jumps
O'er his principles, when something else turns up trumps.

    He was gone a long time, and Apollo, meanwhile,
Went over some sonnets of his with a file,
For, of all compositions, he thought that the sonnet
Best repaid all the toil you expended upon it ;   380
It should reach with one impulse the end of its course,
And for one final blow collect all of its force ;
Not a verse should be salient, but each one should tend
With a wave-like up-gathering to break at the end ;
So, condensing the strength here, there smoothing a wry kink,
He was killing the time, when up walked Mr. D——;
At a few steps behind him, a small man in glasses
Went dodging about, muttering, ' Murderers ! asses ! '
From out of his pocket a paper he 'd take,
With a proud look of martyrdom tied to its stake,   390
And, reading a squib at himself, he 'd say, ' Here I see
'Gainst American letters a bloody conspiracy,
They are all by my personal enemies written ;
I must post an anonymous letter to Britain,
And show that this gall is the merest suggestion
Of spite at my zeal on the Copyright question,
For, on this side the water, 't is prudent to pull
O'er the eyes of the public their national wool,
By accusing of slavish respect to John Bull
All American authors who have more or less   400
Of that anti-American humbug—success,
While in private we 're always embracing the knees
Of some twopenny editor over the seas,

And licking his critical shoes, for you know 't is
The whole aim of our lives to get one English notice ;
My American puffs I would willingly burn all
(They 're all from one source, monthly, weekly, diurnal)
To get but a kick from a transmarine journal ! '

So, culling the gibes of each critical scorner
As if they were plums, and himself were Jack Horner,   410
He came cautiously on, peeping round every corner,
And into each hole where a weasel might pass in,
Expecting the knife of some critic assassin,
Who stabs to the heart with a caricature,
Not so bad as those daubs of the Sun, to be sure,
Yet done with a dagger-o'-type, whose vile portraits
Disperse all one's good and condense all one's poor traits.

Apollo looked up, hearing footsteps approaching,
And slipped out of sight the new rhymes he was broaching,—
' Good day, Mr. D——, I 'm happy to meet,   420
With a scholar so ripe, and a critic so neat,
Who through Grub Street the soul of a gentleman carries ;
What news from that suburb of London and Paris
Which latterly makes such shrill claims to monopolize
The credit of being the New World's metropolis ? '

' Why, nothing of consequence, save this attack
On my friend there, behind, by some pitiful hack,
Who thinks every national author a poor one,
That is n't a copy of something that 's foreign,
And assaults the American Dick—'   430

' Nay, 't is clear
That your Damon there 's fond of a flea in his ear,
And, if no one else furnished them gratis, on tick
He would buy some himself, just to hear the old click ;
Why, I honestly think, if some fool in Japan
Should turn up his nose at the " Poems on Man ",
Your friend there by some inward instinct would know it,
Would get it translated, reprinted, and show it ;
As a man might take off a high stock to exhibit
The autograph round his own neck of the gibbet ;   440
Nor would let it rest so, but fire column after column,
Signed Cato, or Brutus, or something as solemn,
By way of displaying his critical crosses,
And tweaking that poor transatlantic proboscis,
His broadsides resulting (this last there 's no doubt of)
In successively sinking the craft they 're fired out of.
Now nobody knows when an author is hit,
If he don't have a public hysterical fit ;

Let him only keep close in his snug garret's dim ether,
And nobody 'd think of his foes—or him either ;   450
If an author have any least fibre of worth in him,
Abuse would but tickle the organ of mirth in him ;
All the critics on earth cannot crush with their ban
One word that 's in tune with the nature of man.'

  ' Well, perhaps so ; meanwhile I have brought you a book,
Into which if you 'll just have the goodness to look,
You may feel so delighted (when once you are through it)
As to deem it not unworth your while to review it,
And I think I can promise your thoughts, if you do,
A place in the next Democratic Review.'   460

  ' The most thankless of gods you must surely have thought me,
For this is the forty-fourth copy you 've brought me,
I have given them away, or at least I have tried,
But I 've forty-two left, standing all side by side
(The man who accepted that one copy died),—
From one end of a shelf to the other they reach,
" With the author's respects " neatly written in each.
The publisher, sure, will proclaim a Te Deum,
When he hears of that order the British Museum
Has sent for one set of what books were first printed   470
In America, little or big,—for 't is hinted
That this is the first truly tangible hope he
Has ever had raised for the sale of a copy.
I 've thought very often 't would be a good thing
In all public collections of books, if a wing
Were set off by itself, like the seas from the dry lands,
Marked *Literature suited to desolate islands*,
And filled with such books as could never be read
Save by readers of proofs, forced to do it for bread,—
Such books as one 's wrecked on in small country-taverns,   480
Such as hermits might mortify over in caverns,
Such as Satan, if printing had then been invented,
As the climax of woe, would to Job have presented,
Such as Crusoe might dip in, although there are few so
Outrageously cornered by fate as poor Crusoe ;
And since the philanthropists just now are banging
And gibbeting all who're in favour of hanging
(Though Cheever has proved that the Bible and Altar
Were let down from Heaven at the end of a halter,
And that vital religion would dull and grow callous,   490
Unrefreshed, now and then, with a sniff of the gallows),—
And folks are beginning to think it looks odd,
To choke a poor scamp for the glory of God ;
And that He who esteems the Virginia reel
A bait to draw saints from their spiritual weal,

And regards the quadrille as a far greater knavery
Than crushing His African children with slavery,—
Since all who take part in a waltz or cotillon
Are mounted for hell on the Devil's own pillion,
Who, as every true orthodox Christian well knows,   500
Approaches the heart through the door of the toes,—
That He, I was saying, whose judgements are stored
For such as take steps in despite of His word,
Should look with delight on the agonized prancing
Of a wretch who has not the least ground for his dancing,
While the State, standing by, sings a verse from the Psalter
About offering to God on His favourite halter,
And, when the legs droop from their twitching divergence,
Sells the clothes to a Jew, and the corpse to the surgeons ;—
Now, instead of all this, I think I can direct you all   510
To a criminal code both humane and effectual ;—
I propose to shut up every doer of wrong
With these desperate books, for such term, short or long,
As by statute in such cases made and provided,
Shall be by your wise legislators decided :
Thus :—Let murderers be shut, to grow wiser and cooler,
At hard labour for life on the works of Miss—— ;
Petty thieves, kept from flagranter crimes by their fears,
Shall peruse Yankee Doodle a blank term of years,—
That American Punch, like the English, no doubt,—   520
Just the sugar and lemons and spirit left out.

  ' But stay, here comes Tityrus Griswold, and leads on
The flocks whom he first plucks alive, and then feeds on,—
A loud-cackling swarm, in whose feathers warm-drest,
He goes for as perfect a—swan as the rest.

  ' There comes Emerson first, whose rich words, every one,
Are like gold nails in temples to hang trophies on,
Whose prose is grand verse, while his verse, the Lord knows,
Is some of it pr— No, 't is not even prose ;
I 'm speaking of metres ; some poems have welled   530
From those rare depths of soul that have ne'er been excelled ;
They 're not epics, but that does n't matter a pin,
In creating, the only hard thing 's to begin ;
A grass-blade 's no easier to make than an oak ;
If you 've once found the way, you 've achieved the grand stroke ;
In the worst of his poems are mines of rich matter,
But thrown in a heap with a crush and a clatter ;
Now it is not one thing nor another alone
Makes a poem, but rather the general tone,
The something pervading, uniting the whole,   540
The before unconceived, unconceivable soul,
So that just in removing this trifle or that, you
Take away, as it were, a chief limb of the statue ;

Roots, wood, bark, and leaves singly perfect may be,
But, clapt hodge-podge together, they don't make a tree.

  ' But, to come back to Emerson (whom, by the way,
I believe we left waiting),—his is, we may say,
A Greek head on right Yankee shoulders, whose range
Has Olympus for one pole, for t' other the Exchange;
He seems, to my thinking (although I'm afraid   550
The comparison must, long ere this, have been made),
A Plotinus-Montaigne, where the Egyptian's gold mist
And the Gascon's shrewd wit cheek-by-jowl coexist,
All admire, and yet scarcely six converts he's got
To I don't (nor they either) exactly know what;
For though he builds glorious temples, 't is odd
He leaves never a doorway to get in a god.
'T is refreshing to old-fashioned people like me
To meet such a primitive Pagan as he,
In whose mind all creation is duly respected   560
As parts of himself—just a little projected;
And who's willing to worship the stars and the sun,
A convert to—nothing but Emerson.
So perfect a balance there is in his head,
That he talks of things sometimes as if they were dead;
Life, nature, love, God, and affairs of that sort,
He looks at as merely ideas; in short,
As if they were fossils stuck round in a cabinet,
Of such vast extent that our earth's a mere dab in it;
Composed just as he is inclined to conjecture her,   570
Namely, one part pure earth, ninety-nine parts pure lecturer;
You are filled with delight at his clear demonstration,
Each figure, word, gesture, just fits the occasion,
With the quiet precision of science he'll sort 'em
But you can't help suspecting the whole a *post mortem*.

  ' There are persons, mole-blind to the soul's make and style,
Who insist on a likeness 'twixt him and Carlyle;
To compare him with Plato would be vastly fairer,
Carlyle's the more burly, but E. is the rarer;
He sees fewer objects, but clearlier, truelier,   580
If C.'s as original, E.'s more peculiar;
That he's more of a man you might say of the one,
Of the other he's more of an Emerson;
C.'s the Titan, as shaggy of mind as of limb,—
E. the clear-eyed Olympian, rapid and slim;
The one's two thirds Norseman, the other half Greek,
Where the one's most abounding, the other's to seek;
C.'s generals require to be seen in the mass,—
E.'s specialties gain if enlarged by the glass;
C. gives nature and God his own fits of the blues,   590
And rims common-sense things with mystical hues,—

E. sits in a mystery çalm and intense,
And looks coolly around him with sharp common-sense ;
C. shows you how every-day matters unite
With the dim transdiurnal recesses of night,—
While E., in a plain, preternatural way,
Makes mysteries matters of mere every day ;
C. draws all his characters quite *à la* Fuseli,—
He don't sketch their bundles of muscles and thews illy,
But he paints with a brush so untamed and profuse,   600
They seem nothing but bundles of muscles and thews ;
E. is rather like Flaxman, lines strait and severe,
And a colourless outline, but full, round, and clear ;—
To the men he thinks worthy he frankly accords
The design of a white marble statue in words.
C. labours to get at the centre, and then
Take a reckoning from there of his actions and men ;
E. calmly assumes the said centre as granted,
And, given himself, has whatever is wanted.

' He has imitators in scores, who omit   610
No part of the man but his wisdom and wit,—
Who go carefully o'er the sky-blue of his brain,
And when he has skimmed it once, skim it again ;
If at all they resemble him, you may be sure it is
Because their shoals mirror his mists and obscurities,
As a mud-puddle seems deep as heaven for a minute,
While a cloud that floats o'er is reflected within it.

' There comes——, for instance ; to see him 's rare sport,
Tread in Emerson's tracks with legs painfully short ;
How he jumps, how he strains, and gets red in the face,   620
To keep step with the mystagogue's natural pace !
He follows as close as a stick to a rocket,
His fingers exploring the prophet's each pocket.
Fie, for shame, brother bard ; with good fruit of your own,
Can't you let Neighbour Emerson's orchards alone ?
Besides, 't is no use, you 'll not find e'en a core,—
——has picked up all the windfalls before.
They might strip every tree, and E. never would catch 'em,
His Hesperides have no rude dragon to watch 'em ;
When they send him a dishful, and ask him to try 'em,   630
He never suspects how the sly rogues came by 'em ;
He wonders why 't is there are none such his trees on,
And thinks 'em the best he has tasted this season.

' Yonder, calm as a cloud, Alcott stalks in a dream,
And fancies himself in thy groves, Academe,
With the Parthenon nigh, and the olive-trees o'er him,
And never a fact to perplex him or bore him,

With a snug room at Plato's when night comes, to walk to,
And people from morning till midnight to talk to,
And from midnight till morning, nor snore in their listening ;—
So he muses, his face with the joy of it glistening,   641
For his highest conceit of a happiest state is
Where they'd live upon acorns, and hear him talk gratis ;
And indeed, I believe, no man ever talked better,—
Each sentence hangs perfectly poised to a letter ;
He seems piling words, but there 's royal dust hid
In the heart of each sky-piercing pyramid.
While he talks he is great, but goes out like a taper,
If you shut him up closely with pen, ink, and paper ;
Yet his fingers itch for 'em from morning till night,   650
And he thinks he does wrong if he don't always write ;
In this, as in all things, a lamb among men,
He goes to sure death when he goes to his pen.

  ' Close behind him is Brownson, his mouth very full
With attempting to gulp a Gregorian bull ;
Who contrives, spite of that, to pour out as he goes
A stream of transparent and forcible prose ;
He shifts quite about, then proceeds to expound
That 't is merely the earth, not himself, that turns round,
And wishes it clearly impressed on your mind   660
That the weathercock rules and not follows the wind ;
Proving first, then as deftly confuting each side,
With no doctrine pleased that 's not somewhere denied,
He lays the denier away on the shelf,
And then—down beside him lies gravely himself.
He 's the Salt River boatman, who always stands willing
To convey friend or foe without charging a shilling,
And so fond of the trip that, when leisure 's to spare,
He 'll row himself up, if he can't get a fare.
The worst of it is, that his logic 's so strong,   670
That of two sides he commonly chooses the wrong ;
If there *is* only one, why, he 'll split it in two,
And first pummel this half, then that, black and blue.
That white 's white needs no proof, but it takes a deep fellow
To prove it jet-black, and that jet-black is yellow.
He offers the true faith to drink in a sieve,—
When it reaches your lips there 's naught left to believe
But a few silly- (syllo-, I mean,) -gisms that squat 'em
Like tadpoles, o'erjoyed with the mud at the bottom.

  ' There is Willis, all *natty* and jaunty and gay,   680
Who says his best things in so foppish a way,
With conceits and pet phrases so thickly o'erlaying 'em,
That one hardly knows whether to thank him for saying 'em ;
Over-ornament ruins both poem and prose,
Just conceive of a Muse with a ring in her nose !

His prose had a natural grace of its own,
And enough of it, too, if he 'd let it alone ;
But he twitches and jerks so, one fairly gets tired,
And is forced to forgive where he might have admired ;
Yet whenever it slips away free and unlaced,   690
It runs like a stream with a musical waste,
And gurgles along with the liquidest sweep ;—
'T is not deep as a river, but who 'd have it deep ?
In a country where scarcely a village is found
That has not its author sublime and profound,
For some one to be slightly shoal is a duty,
And Willis's shallowness makes half his beauty.
His prose winds along with a blithe, gurgling error,
And reflects all of Heaven it can see in its mirror.
'T is a narrowish strip, but it is not an artifice,—   700
'T is the true out-of-doors with its genuine hearty phiz ;
It is Nature herself, and there 's something in that,
Since most brains reflect but the crown of a hat.
No volume I know to read under a tree,
More truly delicious than his A l'Abri,
With the shadows of leaves flowing over your book,
Like ripple-shades netting the bed of a brook ;
With June coming softly your shoulder to look over,
Breezes waiting to turn every leaf of your book over,
And Nature to criticize still as you read,—   710
The page that bears that is a rare one indeed.

' He 's so innate a cockney, that had he been born
Where plain bare-skin 's the only full-dress that is worn,
He 'd have given his own such an air that you 'd say
'T had been made by a tailor to lounge in Broadway.
His nature 's a glass of champagne with the foam on 't,
As tender as Fletcher, as witty as Beaumont ;
So his best things are done in the flush of the moment ;
If he wait, all is spoiled ; he may stir it and shake it,
But, the fixed air once gone, he can never remake it.   720
He might be a marvel of easy delightfulness,
If he would not sometimes leave the r out of sprightfulness ;
And he ought to let Scripture alone—'t is self-slaughter,
For nobody likes inspiration-and-water.
He 'd have been just the fellow to sup at the Mermaid,
Cracking jokes at rare Ben, with an eye to the barmaid,
His wit running up as Canary ran down,—
The topmost bright bubble on the wave of The Town.

' Here comes Parker, the Orson of parsons, a man
Whom the Church undertook to put under her ban   730
(The Church of Socinus, I mean),—his opinions
Being So- (ultra) -cinian, they shocked the Socinians ;

They believed—faith, I'm puzzled—I think I may call
Their belief a believing in nothing at all,
Or something of that sort ; I know they all went
For a general union of total dissent :
He went a step farther ; without cough or hem,
He frankly avowed he believed not in them ;
And, before he could be jumbled up or prevented,
From their orthodox kind of dissent he dissented.   740
There was heresy here, you perceive, for the right
Of privately judging means simply that light
Has been granted to *me*, for deciding on *you ;*
And in happier times, before Atheism grew,
The deed contained clauses for cooking you too,
Now at Xerxes and Knut we all laugh, yet our foot
With the same wave is wet that mocked Xerxes and Knut,
And we all entertain a sincere private notion,
That our *Thus far !* will have a great weight with the ocean.
'T was so with our liberal Christians : they bore   750
With sincerest conviction their chairs to the shore ;
They brandished their worn theological birches,
Bade natural progress keep out of the Churches,
And expected the lines they had drawn to prevail
With the fast-rising tide to keep out of their pale ;
They had formerly damned the Pontifical See,
And the same thing, they thought, would do nicely for P. ;
But he turned up his nose at their murmuring and shamming,
And cared (shall I say ?) not a d—— for their damming ;
So they first read him out of their church, and next minute 760
Turned round and declared he had never been in it.
But the ban was too small or the man was too big,
For he recks not their bells, books, and candles a fig
(He don't look like a man who would *stay* treated shabbily,
Sophroniscus' son's head o'er the features of Rabelais) ;—
He bangs and bethwacks them,—their backs he salutes
With the whole tree of knowledge torn up by the roots ;
His sermons with satire are plenteously verjuiced.
And he talks in one breath of Confutzee, Cass, Zerduscht,
Jack Robinson, Peter the Hermit, Strap, Dathan,   770
Cush, Pitt (not the bottomless, *that* he's no faith in),
Pan, Pillicock, Shakespeare, Paul, Toots, Monsieur Tonson,
Aldebaran, Alcander, Ben Khorat, Ben Jonson,
Thoth, Richter, Joe Smith, Father Paul, Judah Monis,
Musaeus, Muretus, *hem,*—μ Scorpionis,
Maccabee, Maccaboy, Mac—Mac—ah ! Machiavelli,
Condorcet, Count d'Orsay, Conder, Say, Ganganelli,
Orion, O'Connell, the Chevalier D'O,
(See the Memoirs of Sully,) το παν, the great toe
Of the statue of Jupiter, now made to pass   780
For that of Jew Peter by good Romish brass,

(You may add for yourselves, for I find it a bore,
All the names you have ever, or not, heard before,
And when you 've done that—why, invent a few more.)
His hearers can't tell you on Sunday beforehand,
If in that day's discourse they 'll be Bibled or Koraned,
For he' s seized the idea (by his martyrdom fired)
That all men (not orthodox) *may be* inspired ;
Yet though wisdom profane with his creed he may weave in,
He makes it quite clear what he *does n't* believe in,   790
While some, who decry him, think all Kingdom Come
Is a sort of a, kind of a, species of Hum,
Of which, as it were, so to speak, not a crumb
Would be left, if we did n't keep carefully mum,
And, to make a clean breast, that 't is perfectly plain
That *all* kinds of wisdom are somewhat profane ;
Now P.'s creed than this may be lighter or darker
But in one thing, 't is clear, he has faith, namely—Parker ;
And this is what makes him the crowd-drawing preacher,
There 's a background of god to each hard-working feature,   800
Every word that he speaks has been fierily furnaced
In the blast of a life that has struggled in earnest :
There he stands, looking more like a ploughman than priest,
If not dreadfully awkward, not graceful at least,
His gestures all downright and same, if you will,
As of brown-fisted Hobnail in hoeing a drill,
But his periods fall on you, stroke after stroke,
Like the blows of a lumberer felling an oak,
You forget the man wholly, you 're thankful to meet
With a preacher who smacks of the field and the street,   810
And to hear, you 're not over-particular whence,
Almost Taylor's profusion, quite Latimer's sense.

' There is Bryant, as quiet, as cool, and as dignified,
As a smooth, silent iceberg, that never is ignified,
Save when by reflection 't is kindled o' nights
With a semblance of flame by the chill Northern Lights.
He may rank (Griswold says so) first bard of your nation
(There 's no doubt that he stands in supreme ice-olation),
Your topmost Parnassus he may set his heel on,
But no warm applauses come, peal following peal on,—   820
He 's too smooth and too polished to hang any zeal on :
Unqualified merits, I 'll grant, if you choose, he has 'em,
But he lacks the one merit of kindling enthusiasm ;
If he stir you at all, it is just, on my soul,
Like being stirred up with the very North Pole.

' He is very nice reading in summer, but *inter
Nos*, we don't want *extra* freezing in winter ;
Take him up in the depth of July, my advice is,
When you feel an Egyptian devotion to ices.

But, deduct all you can, there 's enough that 's right good in him,
He has a true soul for field, river, and wood in him ;   831
And his heart, in the midst of brick walls, or where'er it is,
Glows, softens, and thrills with the tenderest charities—
To you mortals that delve in this trade-ridden planet ?
No, to old Berkshire's hills, with their limestone and granite.
If you 're one who *in loco* (add *foco* here) *desipis,*
You will get of his outermost heart (as I guess) a piece ;
But you 'd get deeper down if you came as a precipice,
And would break the last seal of its inwardest fountain,
If you only could palm yourself off for a mountain.   840
Mr. Quivis, or somebody quite as discerning,
Some scholar who 's hourly expecting his learning,
Calls B. the American Wordsworth ; but Wordsworth
Is worth near as much as your whole tuneful herd 's worth.
No, don't be absurd, he 's an excellent Bryant ;
But, my friends, you 'll endanger the life of your client,
By attempting to stretch him up into a giant :
If you choose to compare him, I think there are two per-
-sons fit for a parallel—Thompson and Cowper ; [1]
I don't mean exactly,—there 's something of each,   850
There 's T.'s love of nature, C.'s penchant to preach ;
Just mix up their minds so that C.'s spice of craziness
Shall balance and neutralize T.'s turn for laziness,
And it gives you a brain cool, quite frictionless, quiet,
Whose internal police nips the buds of all riot,—
A brain like a permanent strait-jacket put on
The heart that strives vainly to burst off a button,—
A brain which, without being slow or mechanic,
Does more than a larger less drilled, more volcanic ;
He 's a Cowper condensed, with no craziness bitten,   860
And the advantage that Wordsworth before him had written.

' But, my dear little bardlings, don't prick up your ears
Nor suppose I would rank you and Bryant as peers ;
If I call him an iceberg, I don't mean to say
There is nothing in that which is grand in its way ;
He is almost the one of your poets that knows
How much grace, strength, and dignity lie in Repose ;
If he sometimes fall short, he is too wise to mar
His thought's modest fullness by going too far ;
'T would be well if your authors should all make a trial   870
Of what virtue there is in severe self-denial,
And measure their writings by Hesiod's staff,
Which teaches that all has less value than half.

[1] To demonstrate quickly and easily how per-
versely absurd 'tis to sound this name *Cowper,*
As people in general call him named *super,*
I remark that he rhymes it himself with horse-trooper.

'There is Whittier, whose swelling and vehement heart
Strains the strait-breasted drab of the Quaker apart,
And reveals the live Man, still supreme and erect,
Underneath the bemummying wrappers of sect;
There was ne'er a man born who had more of the swing
Of the true lyric bard and all that kind of thing;
And his failures arise (though perhaps he don't know it)   880
From the very same cause that has made him a poet,—
A fervour of mind which knows no separation
'Twixt simple excitement and pure inspiration,
As my Pythoness erst sometimes erred from not knowing
If 't were I or mere wind through her tripod was blowing;
Let his mind once get head in its favourite direction
And the torrent of verse bursts the dams of reflection,
While, borne with the rush of the metre along,
The poet may chance to go right or go wrong,
Content with the whirl and delirium of song;   890
Then his grammar's not always correct, nor his rhymes,
And he's prone to repeat his own lyrics sometimes,
Not his best, though, for those are struck off at white-heats
When the heart in his breast like a trip-hammer beats,
And can ne'er be repeated again any more
Than they could have been carefully plotted before:
Like old what's-his-name there at the battle of Hastings
(Who, however, gave more than mere rhythmical bastings),
Our Quaker leads off metaphorical fights
For reform and whatever they call human rights,   900
Both singing and striking in front of the war,
And hitting his foes with the mallet of Thor;
Anne haec, one exclaims, on beholding his knocks,
Vestis filii tui, O leather-clad Fox?
Can that be thy son, in the battle's mid din,
Preaching brotherly love and then driving it in
To the brain of the tough old Goliah of sin,
With the smoothest of pebbles from Castaly's spring
Impressed on his hard moral sense with a sling?

'All honour and praise to the right-hearted bard   910
Who was true to The Voice when such service was hard,
Who himself was so free he dared sing for the slave
When to look but a protest in silence was brave;
All honour and praise to the women and men
Who spoke out for the dumb and the down-trodden then!
I need not to name them, already for each
I see History preparing the statue and niche;
They were harsh, but shall *you* be so shocked at hard words
Who have beaten your pruning-hooks up into swords,
Whose rewards and hurrahs men are surer to gain   920
By the reaping of men and of women than grain?

Why should *you* stand aghast at their fierce wordy war, if
You scalp one another for Bank or for Tariff ?
Your calling them cut-throats and knaves all day long
Doesn't prove that the use of hard language is wrong ;
While the World's heart beats quicker to think of such men
As signed Tyranny's doom with a bloody steel-pen,
While on Fourth-of-Julys beardless orators fright one
With hints at Harmodius and Aristogeiton,
You need not look shy at your sisters and brothers   930
Who stab with sharp words for the freedom of others ;—
No, a wreath, twine a wreath for the loyal and true
Who, for sake of the many, dared stand with the few,
Not of blood-spattered laurel for enemies braved,
But of broad, peaceful oak-leaves for citizens saved !

 ' Here comes Dana, abstractedly loitering along,
Involved in a paulo-post-future of song,
Who 'll be going to write what 'll never be written
Till the Muse, ere he think of it, gives him the mitten,—
Who is so well aware of how things should be done,   940
That his own works displease him before they 're begun,—
Who so well all that makes up good poetry knows,
That the best of his poems is written in prose ;
All saddled and bridled stood Pegasus waiting,
He was booted and spurred, but he loitered debating ;
In a very grave question his soul was immersed,—
Which foot in the stirrup he ought to put first ;
And, while this point and that he judicially dwelt on,
He, somehow or other, had written Paul Felton,
Whose beauties or faults, whichsoever you see there,   950
You 'll allow only genius could hit upon either.
That he once was the Idle Man none will deplore,
But I fear he will never be anything more ;
The ocean of song heaves and glitters before him,
The depth and the vastness and longing sweep o'er him,
He knows every breaker and shoal on the chart,
He has the Coast Pilot and so on by heart,
Yet he spends his whole life, like the man in the fable,
In learning to swim on his library-table.

 ' There swaggers John Neal, who has wasted in Maine   960
The sinews and cords of his pugilist brain,
Who might have been poet, but that, in its stead, he
Preferred to believe that he was so already ;
Too hasty to wait till Art's ripe fruit should drop,
He must pelt down an unripe and colicky crop ;
Who took to the law, and had this sterling plea for it,
It required him to quarrel, and paid him a fee for it ;
A man who 's made less than he might have, because
He always has thought himself more than he was,—

Who, with very good natural gifts as a bard,   970
Broke the strings of his lyre out by striking too hard,
And cracked half the notes of a truly fine voice,
Because song drew less instant attention than noise.
Ah, men do not know how much strength is in poise,
That he goes the farthest who goes far enough,
And that all beyond that is just bother and stuff.
No vain man matures, he makes too much new wood ;
His blooms are too thick for the fruit to be good ;
'T is the modest man ripens, 't is he that achieves
Just what 's needed of sunshine and shade he receives ;   980
Grapes, to mellow, require the cool dark of their leaves ;
Neal wants balance ; he throws his mind always too far,
Whisking out flocks of comets, but never a star ;
He has so much muscle, and loves so to show it,
That he strips himself naked to prove he 's a poet,
And, to show he could leap Art's wide ditch, if he tried,
Jumps clean o'er it, and into the hedge t' other side.
He has strength, but there 's nothing about him in keeping ;
One gets surelier onward by walking than leaping ;
He has used his own sinews himself to distress,   990
And had done vastly more had he done vastly less ;
In letters, too soon is as bad as too late ;
Could he only have waited he might have been great ;
But he plumped into Helicon up to the waist,
And muddied the stream ere he took his first taste.

    ' There is Hawthorne, with genius so shrinking and rare
That you hardly at first see the strength that is there ;
A frame so robust, with a nature so sweet,
So earnest, so graceful, so solid, so fleet,
Is worth a descent from Olympus to meet ;   1000
'T is as if a rough oak that for ages had stood,
With his gnarled bony branches like ribs of the wood,
Should bloom, after cycles of struggle and scathe,
With a single anemone trembly and rathe ;
His strength is so tender, his wildness so meek,
That a suitable parallel sets one to seek,—
He 's a John Bunyan Fouqué, a Puritan Tieck ;
When Nature was shaping him, clay was not granted
For making so full-sized a man as she wanted,
So, to fill out her model, a little she spared   1010
From some finer-grained stuff for a woman prepared,
And she could not have hit a more excellent plan
For making him fully and perfectly man.
The success of her scheme gave her so much delight,
That she tried it again, shortly after, in Dwight ;
Only, while she was kneading and shaping the clay,
She sang to her work in her sweet childish way,

And found, when she 'd put the last touch to his soul,
That the music had somehow got mixed with the whole.

' Here 's Cooper, who 's written six volumes to show   1020
He 's as good as a lord : well, let 's grant that he 's so ;
If a person prefer that description of praise,
Why, a coronet 's certainly cheaper than bays ;
But he need take no pains to convince us he 's not
(As his enemies say) the American Scott.
Choose any twelve men, and let C. read aloud
That one of his novels of which he 's most proud,
And I 'd lay any bet that, without ever quitting
Their box, they 'd be all, to a man, for acquitting.
He has drawn you one character, though, that is new,   1030
One wildflower he 's plucked that is wet with the dew
Of this fresh Western world, and, the thing not to mince,
He has done naught but copy it ill ever since ;
His Indians, with proper respect be it said,
Are just Natty Bumpo, daubed over with red,
And his very Long Toms are the same useful Nat,
Rigged up in duck pants and a sou'-wester hat
(Though once in a Coffin, a good chance was found
To have slipped the old fellow away underground).
All his other men-figures are clothes upon sticks,   1040
The *dernière chemise* of a man in a fix
(As a captain besieged, when his garrison 's small,
Sets up caps upon poles to be seen o'er the wall) ;
And the women he draws from one model don't vary,
All sappy as maples and flat as a prairie.
When a character 's wanted, he goes to the task
As a cooper would do in composing a cask ;
He picks out the staves, of their qualities heedful,
Just hoops them together as tight as is needful,
And, if the best fortune should crown the attempt, he   1050
Has made at the most something wooden and empty.

' Don't suppose I would underrate Cooper's abilities ;
If I thought you 'd do that, I should feel very ill at ease ;
The men who have given to *one* character life
And objective existence are not very rife ;
You may number them all, both prose-writers and singers,
Without overrunning the bounds of your fingers,
And Natty won't go to oblivion quicker
Than Adams the parson or Primrose the vicar.

' There is one thing in Cooper I like, too, and that is   1060
That on manners he lectures his countrymen gratis ;
Not precisely so either, because, for a rarity,
He is paid for his tickets in unpopularity.

Now he may overcharge his American pictures,
But you 'll grant there 's a good deal of truth in his strictures ;
And I honour the man who is willing to sink
Half his present repute for the freedom to think,
And, when he has thought, be his cause strong or weak,
Will risk t' other half for the freedom to speak,
Caring naught for what vengeance the mob has in store,   1070
Let that mob be the upper ten thousand or lower.

' There are truths you Americans need to be told,
And it never 'll refute them to swagger and scold ;
John Bull, looking o'er the Atlantic, in choler
At your aptness for trade, says you worship the dollar ;
But to scorn such eye-dollar-try 's what very few do,
And John goes to that church as often as you do.
No matter what John says, don't try to outcrow him,
'T is enough to go quietly on and outgrow him ;
Like most fathers, Bull hates to see Number One   1080
Displacing himself in the mind of his son,
And detests the same faults in himself he 'd neglected
When he sees them again in his child's glass reflected ;
To love one another you 're too like by half ;
If he is a bull, you 're a pretty stout calf,
And tear your own pasture for naught but to show
What a nice pair of horns you 're beginning to grow.

' There are one or two things I should just like to hint,
For you don't often get the truth told you in print ;
The most of you (this is what strikes all beholders)   1090
Have a mental and physical stoop in the shoulders ;
Though you ought to be free as the winds and the waves,
You 've the gait and the manners of runaway slaves ;
Though you brag of your New World, you don't half believe in it ;
And as much of the Old as is possible weave in it ;
Your goddess of freedom, a tight, buxom girl,
With lips like a cherry and teeth like a pearl,
With eyes bold as Herë's, and hair floating free,
And full of the sun as the spray of the sea,
Who can sing at a husking or romp at a shearing,   1100
Who can trip through the forests alone without fearing,
Who can drive home the cows with a song through the grass,
Keeps glancing aside into Europe's cracked glass,
Hides her red hands in gloves, pinches up her lithe waist,
And makes herself wretched with transmarine taste ;
She loses her fresh country charm when she takes
Any mirror except her own rivers and lakes.

' You steal Englishmen's books and think Englishmen's thought,
With their salt on her tail your wild eagle is caught ;

Your literature suits its each whisper and motion 1110
To what will be thought of it over the ocean ;
The cast clothes of Europe your statesmanship tries
And mumbles again the old blarneys and lies ;—
Forget Europe wholly, your veins throb with blood,
To which the dull current in hers is but mud ;
Let her sneer, let her say your experiment fails,
In her voice there 's a tremble e'en now while she rails,
And your shore will soon be in the nature of things
Covered thick with gilt drift-wood of runaway kings,
Where alone, as it were in a Longfellow's Waif, 1120
Her fugitive pieces will find themselves safe.
O my friends, thank your God, if you have one, that he
'Twixt the Old World and you set the gulf of a sea ;
Be strong-backed, brown-handed, upright as your pines,
By the scale of a hemisphere shape your designs,
Be true to yourselves and this new nineteenth age,
As a statue by Powers, or a picture by Page,
Plough, sail, forge, build, carve, paint, all things make new,
To your own New-World instincts contrive to be true,
Keep your ears open wide to the Future's first call, 1130
Be whatever you will, but yourselves first of all,
Stand fronting the dawn on Toil's heaven-scaling peaks,
And become my new race of more practical Greeks.—
Hem ! your likeness at present, I shudder to tell o't,
Is that you have your slaves, and the Greek had his helot.'

Here a gentleman present, who had in his attic
More pepper than brains, shrieked, 'The man 's a fanatic,
I 'm a capital tailor with warm tar and feathers,
And will make him a suit that 'll serve in all weathers ;
But we 'll argue the point first, I 'm willing to reason 't, 1140
Palaver before condemnation 's but decent ;
So, through my humble person, Humanity begs
Of the friends of true freedom a loan of bad eggs.'
But Apollo let one such a look of his show forth
As when ἤϊε νύκτι ἐοικώς, and so forth,
And the gentleman somehow slunk out of the way,
But, as he was going, gained courage to say,—
' At slavery in the abstract my whole soul rebels,
I am as strongly opposed to 't as any one else.'
' Ay, no doubt, but whenever I 've happened to meet 1150
With a wrong or a crime, it is always concrete ,'
Answered Phoebus severely ; then turning to us,
' The mistake of such fellows as just made the fuss
Is only in taking a great busy nation
For a part of their pitiful cotton-plantation.—
But there comes Miranda, Zeus ! where shall I flee to ?
She has such a penchant for bothering me too !

She always keeps asking if I don't observe a
Particular likeness 'twixt her and Minerva;
She tells me my efforts in verse are quite clever;—　1160
She 's been travelling now, and will be worse than ever;
One would think, though, a sharpsighted noter she 'd be
Of all that 's worth mentioning over the sea,
For a woman must surely see well, if she try,
The whole of whose being 's a capital I:
She will take an old notion, and make it her own,
By saying it o'er in her Sibylline tone,
Or persuade you 't is something tremendously deep,
By repeating it so as to put you to sleep;
And she well may defy any mortal to see through it,　1170
When once she has mixed up her infinite *me* through it.
There is one thing she owns in her own single right,
It is native and genuine—namely, her spite;
Though, when acting as censor, she privately blows
A censer of vanity 'neath her own nose.'

Here Miranda came up, and said, ' Phoebus! you know
That the infinite Soul has its infinite woe,
As I ought to know, having lived cheek by jowl,
Since the day I was born, with the Infinite Soul;
I myself introduced, I myself, I alone,　1180
To my Land's better life authors solely my own,
Who the sad heart of earth on their shoulders have taken,
Whose works sound a depth by Life's quiet unshaken,
Such as Shakespeare, for instance, the Bible, and Bacon,
Not to mention my own works; Time's nadir is fleet,
And, as for myself, I 'm quite out of conceit—'

' Quite out of conceit! I 'm enchanted to hear it,'
Cried Apollo aside. ' Who 'd have thought she was near it?
To be sure, one is apt to exhaust those commodities
One uses too fast, yet in this case as odd it is　1190
As if Neptune should say to his turbots and whitings,
" I 'm as much out of salt as Miranda's own writings "
(Which, as she in her own happy manner has said,
Sound a depth, for 't is one of the functions of lead).
She often has asked me if I could not find
A place somewhere near me that suited her mind;
I know but a single one vacant, which she,
With her rare talent that way, would fit to a T.
And it would not imply any pause or cessation
In the work she esteems her peculiar vocation,—　1200
She may enter on duty to-day, if she chooses,
And remain Tiring-woman for life to the Muses.'

Miranda meanwhile has succeeded in driving
Up into a corner, in spite of their striving,

A small flock of terrified victims, and there,
With an I-turn-the-crank-of-the-Universe air
And a tone which, at least to *my* fancy, appears
Not so much to be entering as boxing your ears,
Is unfolding a tale (of herself, I surmise,
For 't is dotted as thick as a peacock's with I's).   1210
Apropos of Miranda, I 'll rest on my oars
And drift through a trifling digression on bores,
For, though not wearing ear-rings *in more majorum*,
Our ears are kept bored just as if we still wore 'em.
There was one feudal custom worth keeping, at least,
Roasted bores made a part of each well-ordered feast,
And of all quiet pleasures the very *ne plus*
Was in hunting wild bores as the tame ones hunt us.
Archaeologians, I know, who have personal fears
Of this wise application of hounds and of spears,   1220
Have tried to make out, with a zeal more than wonted,
'T was a kind of wild swine that our ancestors hunted ;
But I 'll never believe that the age which has strewn
Europe o'er with cathedrals, and otherwise shown
That it knew what was what, could by chance not have known
(Spending, too, its chief time with its buff on, no doubt),
Which beast 't would improve the world most to thin out.
I divide bores myself, in the manner of rifles,
Into two great divisions, regardless of trifles ;—
There 's your smooth-bore and screw-bore, who do not much vary
In the weight of cold lead they respectively carry.   1231
The smooth-bore is one in whose essence the mind
Not a corner nor cranny to cling by can find ;
You feel as in nightmares sometimes, when you slip
Down a steep slated roof, where there 's nothing to grip ;
You slide and you slide, the blank horror increases,—
You had rather by far be at once smashed to pieces ;
You fancy a whirlpool below white and frothing,
And finally drop off and light upon—nothing.
The screw-bore has twists in him, faint predilections   1240
For going just wrong in the tritest directions ;
When he 's wrong he is flat, when he 's right he can't show it,
He 'll tell you what Snooks said about the new poet,[1]
Or how Fogrum was outraged by Tennyson's Princess ;
He has spent all his spare time and intellect since his
Birth in perusing, on each art and science,
Just the books in which no one puts any reliance,
And though *nemo*, we 're told, *horis omnibus sapit*,
The rule will not fit him, however you shape it,
For he has a perennial foison of sappiness ;   1250
He has just enough force to spoil half your day's happiness,

[1] (If you call Snooks an owl, he will show by his looks
     That he 's morally certain you're jealous of Snooks.)

And to make him a sort of mosquito to be with,
But just not enough to dispute or agree with.

These sketches I made (not to be too explicit)
From two honest fellows who made me a visit,
And broke, like the tale of the Bear and the Fiddle,
My reflections on Halleck short off by the middle ;
I sha' n't now go into the subject more deeply,
For I notice that some of my readers look sleep'ly ;
I will barely remark that, 'mongst civilized nations,   1260
There 's none that displays more exemplary patience
Under all sorts of boring, at all sorts of hours,
From all sorts of desperate persons, than ours.
Not to speak of our papers, our State legislatures,
And other such trials for sensitive natures,
Just look for a moment at Congress,—appalled,
My fancy shrinks back from the phantom it called ;
Why, there 's scarcely a member unworthy to frown
'Neath what Fourier nicknames the Boreal crown ;
Only think what that infinite bore-pow'r could do   1270
If applied with a utilitarian view ;
Suppose, for example, we shipped it with care
To Sahara's great desert and let it bore there ;
If they held one short session and did nothing else,
They 'd fill the whole waste with Artesian wells.
But 't is time now with pen phonographic to follow
Through some more of his sketches our laughing Apollo :—

' There comes Harry Franco, and, as he draws near,
You find that 's a smile which you took for a sneer ;
One half of him contradicts t' other ; his wont   1280
Is to say very sharp things and do very blunt ;
His manner 's as hard as his feelings are tender,
And a *sortie* he 'll make when he means to surrender ;
He 's in joke half the time when he seems to be sternest,
When he seems to be joking, be sure he 's in earnest ;
He has common sense in a way that 's uncommon,
Hates humbug and cant, loves his friends like a woman,
Builds his dislikes of cards and his friendships of oak,
Loves a prejudice better than aught but a joke,
Is half upright Quaker, half downright Come-outer,   1290
Loves Freedom too well to go stark mad about her,
Quite artless himself is a lover of Art,
Shuts you out of his secrets and into his heart,
And though not a poet, yet all must admire
In his letters of Pinto his skill on the liar.

' There comes Poe, with his raven, like Barnaby Rudge,
Three fifths of him genius and two fifths sheer fudge,
Who talks like a book of iambs and pentameters,
In a way to make people of common sense damn metres,

Who has written some things quite the best of their kind, 1300
But the heart somehow seems all squeezed out by the mind,
Who— But hey-day ! What 's this ? Messieurs Mathews and Poe,
You must n't fling mud-balls at Longfellow so,
Does it make a man worse that his character 's such
As to make his friends love him (as you think) too much ?
Why, there is not a bard at this moment alive
More willing than he that his fellows should thrive ;
While you are abusing him thus, even now
He would help either one of you out of a slough ;
You may say that he 's smooth and all that till you 're hoarse,
But remember that elegance also is force ; 1311
After polishing granite as much as you will,
The heart keeps its tough old persistency still ;
Deduct all you can, *that* still keeps you at bay ;
Why, he 'll live till men weary of Collins and Gray.
I 'm not over-fond of Greek metres in English,
To me rhyme 's a gain, so it be not too jinglish,
And your modern hexameter verses are no more
Like Greek ones than sleek Mr. Pope is like Homer ;
As the roar of the sea to the coo of a pigeon is, 1320
So, compared to your moderns, sounds old Melesigenes ;
I may be too partial, the reason, perhaps, o't is
That I 've heard the old blind man recite his own rhapsodies,
And my ear with that music impregnate may be,
Like the poor exiled shell with the soul of the sea,
Or as one can't bear Strauss when his nature is cloven
To its deeps within deeps by the stroke of Beethoven ;
But, set that aside, and 't is truth that I speak,
Had Theocritus written in English, not Greek,
I believe that his exquisite sense would scarce change a line 1330
In that rare, tender, virgin-like pastoral Evangeline.
That 's not ancient nor modern, its place is apart
Where time has no sway, in the realm of pure Art,
'T is a shrine of retreat from Earth's hubbub and strife
As quiet and chaste as the author's own life.

' There comes Philothea, her face all aglow,
She has just been dividing some poor creature's woe,
And can't tell which pleases her most, to relieve
His want, or his story to hear and believe ;
No doubt against many deep griefs she prevails, 1340
For her ear is the refuge of destitute tales ;
She knows well that silence is sorrow's best food,
And that talking draws off from the heart its black blood,
So she 'll listen with patience and let you unfold
Your bundle of rags as 't were pure cloth of gold,
Which, indeed, it all turns to as soon as she 's touched it,
And (to borrow a phrase from the nursery) *muched* it ;

She has such a musical taste, she will go
Any distance to hear one who draws a long bow ;
She will swallow a wonder by mere might and main,   1350
And thinks it Geometry's fault if she 's fain
To consider things flat, inasmuch as they 're plain ;
Facts with her are accomplished, as Frenchmen would say—
They will prove all she wishes them to either way,—
And, as fact lies on this side or that, we must try,
If we're seeking the truth, to find where it don't lie ;
I was telling her once of a marvellous aloe
That for thousands of years had looked spindling and sallow,
And, though nursed by the fruitfullest powers of mud,
Had never vouchsafed e'en so much as a bud,   1360
Till its owner remarked (as a sailor, you know,
Often will in a calm) that it never would blow,
For he wished to exhibit the plant, and designed
That its blowing should help him in raising the wind :
At last it was told him that if he should water
Its roots with the blood of his unmarried daughter
(Who was born, as her mother, a Calvinist, said,
With William Law's serious caul on her head),
It would blow as the obstinate breeze did when by a
Like decree of her father died Iphigenia ;   1370
At first he declared he himself would be blowed
Ere his conscience with such a foul crime he would load,
But the thought, coming oft, grew less dark than before,
And he mused, as each creditor knocked at his door,
If *this* were but done they would dun me no more ;
I told Philothea his struggles and doubts,
And how he considered the ins and the outs
Of the visions he had, and the dreadful dyspepsy,
How he went to the seër that lives at Po'keepsie,
How the seër advised him to sleep on it first,   1380
And to read his big volume in case of the worst,
And further advised he should pay him five dollars
For writing ℌum, ℌum, on his wristbands and collars ;
Three years and ten days these dark words he had studied
When the daughter was missed, and the aloe had budded ;
I told how he watched it grow large and more large,
And wondered how much for the show he should charge,—
She had listened with utter indifference to this, till
I told how it bloomed, and, discharging its pistil
With an aim the Eumenides dictated, shot   1390
The botanical filicide dead on the spot ;
It had blown, but he reaped not his horrible gains,
For it blew with such force as to blow out his brains,
And the crime was blown also, because on the wad,
Which was paper, was writ " Visitation of God ",
As well as a thrilling account of the deed
Which the coroner kindly allowed me to read.

'Well, my friend took this story up just, to be sure,
As one might a poor foundling that's laid at one's door;
She combed it and washed it and clothed it and fed it, 1400
And as if 't were her own child most tenderly bred it,
Laid the scene (of the legend, I mean) far away a-
mong the green vales underneath Himalaya,
And by artist-like touches, laid on here and there,
Made the whole thing so touching, I frankly declare
I have read it all thrice, and, perhaps I am weak,
But I found every time there were tears on my cheek.

'The pole, science tells us, the magnet controls,
But she is a magnet to emigrant Poles,
And folks with a mission that nobody knows, 1410
Throng thickly about her as bees round a rose;
She can fill up the *carets* in such, make their scope
Converge to some focus of rational hope,
And, with sympathies fresh as the morning, their gall
Can transmute into honey,—but this is not all;
Not only for those she has solace, O, say,
Vice's desperate nursling adrift in Broadway,
Who clingest, with all that is left of thee human,
To the last slender spar from the wreck of the woman,
Hast thou not found one shore where those tired drooping feet
Could reach firm mother-earth, one full heart on whose beat 1421
The soothed head in silence reposing could hear
The chimes of far childhood throb back on the ear?
Ah, there's many a beam from the fountain of day
That, to reach us unclouded, must pass, on its way,
Through the soul of a woman, and hers is wide ope
To the influence of Heaven as the blue eyes of Hope;
Yes, a great heart is hers, one that dares to go in
To the prison, the slave-hut, the alleys of sin,
And to bring into each, or to find there, some line 1430
Of the never completely out-trampled divine;
If her heart at high floods swamps her brain now and then,
'T is but richer for that when the tide ebbs agen,
As, after old Nile has subsided, his plain
Overflows with a second broad deluge of grain;
What a wealth would it bring to the narrow and sour
Could they be as a Child but for one little hour!

'What! Irving? thrice welcome, warm heart and fine brain,
You bring back the happiest spirit from Spain,
And the gravest sweet humour, that ever were there 1440
Since Cervantes met death in his gentle despair;
Nay, don't be embarrassed, nor look so beseeching,—
I sha'n't run directly against my own preaching,
And, having just laughed at their Raphaels and Dantes,
Go to setting you up beside matchless Cervantes;

But allow me to speak what I honestly feel,—
To a true poet-heart add the fun of Dick Steele,
Throw in all of Addison, *minus* the chill,
With the whole of that partnership's stock and good-will,
Mix well, and while stirring, hum o'er, as a spell,   1450
The fine *old* English Gentleman, simmer it well,
Sweeten just to your own private liking, then strain,
That only the finest and clearest remain,
Let it stand out of doors till a soul it receives
From the warm lazy sun loitering down through green leaves,
And you 'll find a choice nature, not wholly deserving
A name either English or Yankee,—just Irving.

  ' There goes,—but *stet nominis umbra*,—his name
You 'll be glad enough, some day or other, to claim,
And will all crowd about him and swear that you knew him   1460
If some English hack-critic should chance to review him.
The old *porcos ante ne projiciatis*
MARGARITAS, for him you have verified gratis ;
What matters his name ? Why, it may be Sylvester,
Judd, Junior, or Junius, Ulysses, or Nestor,
For aught *I* know or care ; 't is enough that I look
On the author of " Margaret ", the first Yankee book
With the *soul* of Down East in 't, and things farther East,
As far as the threshold of morning, at least,
Where awaits the fair dawn of the simple and true,   1470
Of the day that comes slowly to make all things new.
'T has a smack of pine woods, of bare field and bleak hill,
Such as only the breed of the Mayflower could till ;
The Puritan 's shown in it, tough to the core,
Such as prayed, smiting Agag on red Marston Moor :
With an unwilling humour, half choked by the drouth
In brown hollows about the inhospitable mouth ;
With a soul full of poetry, though it has qualms
About finding a happiness out of the Psalms ;
Full of tenderness, too, though it shrinks in the dark,   1480
Hamadryad-like, under the coarse, shaggy bark ;
That sees visions, knows wrestlings of God with the Will,
And has its own Sinais and thunderings still.'

  Here—' Forgive me, Apollo,' I cried, ' while I pour
My heart out to my birthplace : O loved more and more
Dear Baystate, from whose rocky bosom thy sons
Should suck milk, strong-will-giving, brave, such as runs
In the veins of old Graylock—who is it that dares
Call thee pedler, a soul wrapped in bank-books and shares ?
It is false ! She 's a Poet ! I see, as I write,   1490
Along the far railroad the steam-snake glide white,
The cataract-throb of her mill-hearts I hear,
The swift strokes of trip-hammers weary my ear,

Sledges ring upon anvils, through logs the saw screams,
Blocks swing to their place, beetles drive home the beams:—
It is songs such as these that she croons to the din
Of her fast-flying shuttles, year out and year in,
While from earth's farthest corner there comes not a breeze
But wafts her the buzz of her gold-gleaning bees:
What though those horn hands have as yet found small time
For painting and sculpture and music and rhyme?   1501
These will come in due order; the need that pressed sorest
Was to vanquish the seasons, the ocean, the forest,
To bridle and harness the rivers, the steam,
Making that whirl her mill-wheels, this tug in her team,
To vassalize old tyrant Winter, and make
Him delve surlily for her on river and lake;—
When this New World was parted, she strove not to shirk
Her lot in the heirdom, the tough, silent Work,
The hero-share ever, from Herakles down   1510
To Odin, the Earth's iron sceptre and crown:
Yes, thou dear, noble Mother! if ever men's praise
Could be claimed for creating heroical lays,
Thou hast won it; if ever the laurel divine
Crowned the Maker and Builder, that glory is thine!
Thy songs are right epic, they tell how this rude
Rock-rib of our earth here was tamed and subdued;
Thou hast written them plain on the face of the planet
In brave, deathless letters of iron and granite;
Thou hast printed them deep for all time; they are set   1520
From the same runic type-fount and alphabet
With thy stout Berkshire hills and the arms of thy Bay,—
They are staves from the burly old Mayflower lay.
If the drones of the Old World, in querulous ease,
Ask thy Art and thy Letters, point proudly to these,
Or, if they deny these are Letters and Art,
Toil on with the same old invincible heart;
Thou art rearing the pedestal broad-based and grand
Whereon the fair shapes of the Artist shall stand,
And creating, through labours undaunted and long,   1530
The theme for all Sculpture and Painting and Song!

' But my good mother Baystate wants no praise of mine,
She learned from *her* mother a precept divine
About something that butters no parsnips, her *forte*
In another direction lies, work is her sport
(Though she 'll courtesy and set her cap straight, that she will,
If you talk about Plymouth and red Bunker's hill).
Dear, notable goodwife! by this time of night,
Her hearth is swept clean, and her fire burning bright,
And she sits in a chair (of home plan and make) rocking,   1540
Musing much, all the while, as she darns on a stocking,

Whether turkeys will come pretty high next Thanksgiving,
Whether flour 'll be so dear, for, as sure as she 's living,
She will use rye-and-injun then, whether the pig
By this time ain't got pretty tolerable big,
And whether to sell it outright will be best,
Or to smoke hams and shoulders and salt down the rest,—
At this minute, she 'd swop all my verses, ah, cruel !
For the last patent stove that is saving of fuel ;
So I 'll just let Apollo go on, for his phiz   1550
Shows I 've kept him awaiting too long as it is.'

'If our friend, there, who seems a reporter, is done
With his burst of emotion, why, *I* will go on,'
Said Apollo ; some smiled, and, indeed, I must own
There was something sarcastic, perhaps, in his tone ;—

'There 's Holmes, who is matchless among you for wit ;
A Leyden-jar always full-charged, from which flit
The electrical tingles of hit after hit ;
In long poems 't is painful sometimes, and invites
A thought of the way the new Telegraph writes,   1560
Which pricks down its little sharp sentences spitefully
As if you got more than you 'd title to rightfully,
And you find yourself hoping its wild father Lightning
Would flame in for a second and give you a fright'ning.
He has perfect sway of what *I* call a sham metre,
But many admire it, the English pentameter,
And Campbell, I think, wrote most commonly worse,
With less nerve, swing, and fire in the same kind of verse,
Nor e'er achieved aught in 't so worthy of praise
As the tribute of Holmes to the grand *Marseillaise*.   1570
You went crazy last year over Bulwer's New Timon ;—
Why, if B., to the day of his dying, should rhyme on,
Heaping verses on verses and tomes upon tomes,
He could ne'er reach the best point and vigour of Holmes.
His are just the fine hands, too, to weave you a lyric
Full of fancy, fun, feeling, or spiced with satyric
In a measure so kindly, you doubt if the toes
That are trodden upon are your own or your foes'.

'There is Lowell, who 's striving Parnassus to climb
With a whole bale of *isms* tied together with rhyme,   1580
He might get on alone, spite of brambles and boulders,
But he can't with that bundle he has on his shoulders,
The top of the hill he will ne'er come nigh reaching
Till he learns the distinction 'twixt singing and preaching ;
His lyre has some chords that would ring pretty well,
But he 'd rather by half make a drum of the shell,
And rattle away till he 's old as Methusalem,
At the head of a march to the last new Jerusalem.

'There goes Halleck, whose Fanny's a pseudo Don Juan,
With the wickedness out that gave salt to the true one,   1590
He's a wit, though, I hear, of the very first order,
And once made a pun on the words soft Recorder;
More than this, he's a very great poet, I'm told,
And has had his works published in crimson and gold,
With something they call "Illustrations", to wit,
Like those with which Chapman obscured Holy Writ,[1]
Which are said to illustrate, because, as I view it,
Like *lucus a non*, they precisely don't do it;
Let a man who can write what himself understands
Keep clear, if he can, of designing men's hands,   1600
Who bury the sense, if there's any worth having,
And then very honestly call it engraving.
But, to quit *badinage*, which there is n't much wit in,
Halleck's better, I doubt not, than all he has written;
In his verse a clear glimpse you will frequently find,
If not of a great, of a fortunate mind,
Which contrives to be true to its natural loves
In a world of back-offices, ledgers, and stoves.
When his heart breaks away from the brokers and banks,
And kneels in his own private shrine to give thanks,   1610
There's a genial manliness in him that earns
Our sincerest respect (read, for instance, his "Burns"),
And we can't but regret (seek excuse where we may)
That so much of a man has been peddled away.

'But what's that? a mass-meeting? No, there come in lots,
The American Bulwers, Disraelis, and Scotts,
And in short the American everything-elses,
Each charging the others with envies and jealousies;—
By the way, 't is a fact that displays what profusions
Of all kinds of greatness bless free institutions,   1620
That while the Old World has produced barely eight
Of such poets as all men agree to call great,
And of other great characters hardly a score
(One might safely say less than that rather than more),
With you every year a whole crop is begotten,
They 're as much of a staple as corn is, or cotton;
Why, there's scarcely a huddle of log-huts and shanties
That has not brought forth its own Miltons and Dantes;
I myself know ten Byrons, one Coleridge, three Shelleys,
Two Raphaels, six Titians, (I think) one Apelles,   1630
Leonardos and Rubenses plenty as lichens,
One (but that one is plenty) American Dickens,
A whole flock of Lambs, any number of Tennysons,—
In short, if a man has the luck to have any sons,

---

[1] (Cuts rightly called wooden, as all must admit.)

He may feel pretty certain that one out of twain
Will be some very great person over again.
There is one inconvenience in all this, which lies
In the fact that by contrast we estimate size,[1]
And, where there are none except Titans, great stature
Is only a simple proceeding of nature.   1640
What puff the strained sails of your praise will you furl at, if
The calmest degree that you know is superlative ?
At Rome, all whom Charon took into his wherry must,
As a matter of course, be well *issimust* and *errimust*,
A Greek, too, could feel, while in that famous boat he tost,
That his friends would take care he was ιστοst and ωτατοst,
And formerly we, as through graveyards we past,
Thought the world went from bad to worst fearfully fast ;
Let us glance for a moment, 't is well worth the pains,
And note what an average graveyard contains ;   1650
There lie levellers levelled, duns done up themselves,
There are booksellers finally laid on their shelves,
Horizontally there lie upright politicians,
Dose-a-dose with their patients sleep faultless physicians,
There are slave-drivers quietly whipped underground,
There bookbinders, done up in boards, are fast bound,
There card-players wait till the last trump be played,
There all the choice spirits get finally laid,
There the babe that 's unborn is supplied with a berth,
There men without legs get their six feet of earth,   1660
There lawyers repose, each wrapped up in his case,
There seekers of office are sure of a place,
There defendant and plaintiff get equally cast,
There shoemakers quietly stick to the last,
There brokers at length become silent as stocks,
There stage-drivers sleep without quitting their box,
And so forth and so forth and so forth and so on,
With this kind of stuff one might endlessly go on ;
To come to the point, I may safely assert you
Will find in each yard every cardinal virtue ;[2]   1670
Each has six truest patriots : four discoverers of ether,
Who never had thought on 't nor mentioned it either ;
Ten poets, the greatest who ever wrote rhyme :
Two hundred and forty first men of their time :
One person whose portrait just gave the least hint
Its original had a most horrible squint :
One critic, most (what do they call it ?) reflective,

---

[1] That is in most cases we do, but not all,
      Past a doubt, there are men who are innately small,
      Such as Blank, who, without being 'minished a tittle,
      Might stand for a type of the Absolute Little.

[2] (And at this just conclusion will surely arrive,
      That the goodness of earth is more dead than alive.)

Who never had used the phrase ob- or subjective :
Forty fathers of Freedom, of whom twenty bred
Their sons for the rice-swamps, at so much a head,   1680
And their daughters for—faugh ! thirty mothers of Gracchi :
Non-resistants who gave many a spiritual black-eye :
Eight true friends of their kind, one of whom was a jailer :
Four captains almost as astounding as Taylor :
Two dozen of Italy's exiles who shoot us his
Kaisership daily, stern pen-and-ink Brutuses,
Who, in Yankee back-parlours, with crucified smile,[1]
Mount serenely their country's funereal pile :
Ninety-nine Irish heroes, ferocious rebellers
'Gainst the Saxon in cis-marine garrets and cellars,   1690
Who shake their dread fists o'er the sea and all that,—
As long as a copper drops into the hat :
Nine hundred Teutonic republicans stark
From Vaterland's battles just won—in the Park,
Who the happy profession of martyrdom take
Whenever it gives them a chance at a steak :
Sixty-two second Washingtons : two or three Jacksons
And so many everythings-else that it racks one's
Poor memory too much to continue the list,
Especially now they no longer exist ;—   1700
I would merely observe that you 've taken to giving
The puffs that belong to the dead to the living,
And that somehow your trump-of-contemporary-doom's tones
Is tuned after old dedications and tombstones.'

Here the critic came in and a thistle presented—[2]
From a frown to a smile the god's features relented,
As he stared at his envoy, who, swelling with pride,
To the god's asking look, nothing daunted, replied,—
' You 're surprised, I suppose, I was absent so long,
But your godship respecting the lilies was wrong ;   1710
I hunted the garden from one end to t' other,
And got no reward but vexation and bother,
Till, tossed out with weeds in a corner to wither,
This one lily I found and made haste to bring hither.'

' Did he think I had given him a book to review ?
I ought to have known what the fellow would do,'
Muttered Phoebus aside, ' for a thistle will pass
Beyond doubt for the queen of all flowers with an ass ;
He has chosen in just the same way as he 'd choose
His specimens out of the books he reviews ;   1720
And now, as this offers an excellent text,
I 'll give 'em some brief hints on criticism next.'

[1] Not forgetting their tea and their toast, though, the while.
[2] Turn back now to page—goodness only knows what,
And take a fresh hold on the thread of my plot.

So, musing a moment, he turned to the crowd,
And, clearing his voice, spoke as follows aloud :—

  ' My friends, in the happier days of the muse,
We were luckily free from such things as reviews ;
Then naught came between with its fog to make clearer
The heart of the poet to that of his hearer ;
Then the poet brought heaven to the people, and they
Felt that they, too, were poets in hearing his lay ;   1730
Then the poet was prophet, the past in his soul
Precreated the future, both parts of one whole ;
Then for him there was nothing too great or too small,
For one natural deity sanctified all ;
Then the bard owned no clipper and meter of moods
Save the spirit of silence that hovers and broods
O'er the seas and the mountains, the rivers and woods ;
He asked not earth's verdict, forgetting the clods,
His soul soared and sang to an audience of gods ;
'Twas for them that he measured the thought and the line,   1740
And shaped for their vision the perfect design,
With as glorious a foresight, a balance as true,
As swung out the worlds in the infinite blue ;
Then a glory and greatness invested man's heart,
The universal, which now stands estranged and apart,
In the free individual moulded, was Art ;
Then the forms of the Artist seemed thrilled with desire
For something as yet unattained, fuller, higher,
As once with her lips, lifted hands, and eyes listening,
And her whole upward soul in her countenance glistening,   1750
Eurydice stood—like a beacon unfired,
Which, once touched with flame, will leap heav'nward inspired—
And waited with answering kindle to mark
The first gleam of Orpheus that pained the red Dark.
Then painting, song, sculpture did more than relieve
The need that men feel to create and believe,
And as, in all beauty, who listens with love
Hears these words oft repeated—" beyond and above ",
So these seemed to be but the visible sign
Of the grasp of the soul after things more divine ;   1760
They were ladders the Artist erected to climb
O'er the narrow horizon of space and of time,
And we see there the footsteps by which men had gained
To the one rapturous glimpse of the never-attained,
As shepherds could erst sometimes trace in the sod
The last spurning print of a sky-cleaving god.

  ' But now, on the poet's dis-privacied moods
With *do this* and *do that* the pert critic intrudes ;
While he thinks he's been barely fulfilling his duty
To interpret 'twixt men and their own sense of beauty,   1770

And has striven, while others sought honour or pelf,
To make his kind happy as he was himself,
He finds he's been guilty of horrid offences
In all kinds of moods, numbers, genders, and tenses;
He's been *ob* and *sub*jective, what Kettle calls Pot,
Precisely, at all events, what he ought not,
You have done this, says one judge; *done that*, says another;
You should have done this, grumbles one; *that*, says 't other;
Never mind what he touches, one shrieks out *Taboo !*
And while he is wondering what he shall do,   1780
Since each suggests opposite topics for song,
They all shout together *you 're right !* and *you 're wrong !*

  ' Nature fits all her children with something to do,
He who would write and can't write, can surely review,
Can set up a small booth as critic and sell us his
Petty conceit and his pettier jealousies;
Thus a lawyer's apprentice, just out of his teens,
Will do for the Jeffrey of six magazines;
Having read Johnson's lives of the poets half through,
There's nothing on earth he's not competent to;   1790
He reviews with as much nonchalance as he whistles,—
He goes through a book and just picks out the thistles;
It matters not whether he blame or commend,
If he's bad as a foe, he's far worse as a friend:
Let an author but write what's above his poor scope,
He goes to work gravely and twists up a rope,
And, inviting the world to see punishment done,
Hangs himself up to bleach in the wind and the sun;
'T is delightful to see, when a man comes along
Who has anything in him peculiar and strong,   1800
Every cockboat that swims clear its fierce (pop) gundeck at him,
And make as he passes its ludicrous Peck at him—'

  Here Miranda came up and began, ' As to that—'
Apollo at once seized his gloves, cane, and hat,
And, seeing the place getting rapidly cleared,
I, too, snatched my notes and forthwith disappeared.

THE BIGLOW PAPERS

NOTICES OF AN INDEPENDENT PRESS

[I HAVE observed, reader (bene- or male-volent, as it may happen), that it is customary to append to the second editions of books, and to the second works of authors, short sentences commendatory of the first, under the title of *Notices of the Press*. These, I have been given to understand, are procurable at certain established rates, payment being made either in money or advertising patronage by the publisher, or by an adequate outlay of servility on the part of the author. Considering these things with myself, and also that such notices are neither intended, nor generally believed, to convey any real opinions, being a purely ceremonial accompaniment of literature, and resembling certificates to the virtues of various morbiferal panaceas, I conceived that it would be not only more economical to prepare a sufficient number of such myself, but also more immediately subservient to the end in view to prefix them to this our primary edition rather than await the contingency of a second, when they would seem to be of small utility. To delay attaching the *bobs* until the second attempt at flying the kite would indicate but a slender experience in that useful art. Neither has it escaped my notice, nor failed to afford me matter of reflection, that, when a circus or a caravan is about to visit Jaalam, the initial step is to send forward large and highly ornamented bills of performance to be hung in the bar-room and the post-office. These having been sufficiently gazed at, and beginning to lose their attractiveness except for the flies, and, truly, the boys also (in whom I find it impossible to repress, even during school-hours, certain oral and tele-graphic communications concerning the expected show), upon some fine morning the band enters in a gayly painted wagon, or triumphal chariot, and with noisy advertisement, by means of brass, wood, and sheepskin, makes the circuit of our startled village streets. Then as the exciting sounds draw nearer and nearer, do I desiderate those eyes of Aristarchus, 'whose looks were as a breeching to a boy.' Then do I perceive, with vain regret of wasted opportunities, the advantage of a pancratic or pantechnic education, since he is most reverenced by my little subjects who can throw the cleanest summerset or walk most securely upon the revolving cask. The story of the Pied Piper becomes for the first time credible to me (albeit confirmed by the Hameliners dating their legal instruments from the period of his exit), as I behold how those strains, without pretence of magical potency, bewitch the pupillary legs nor leave to the pedagogic an entire self-control. For these reasons, lest my kingly prerogative should suffer diminution, I prorogue my restless commons whom I follow into the street, chiefly lest some mischief may chance befall them. After the manner of such a band I send forward the following notices of domestic manufacture, to make brazen proclamation, not unconscious of the advantage which will accrue, if our little craft, *cymbula sutilis*, shall seem to leave port with a clipping breeze, and to carry, in nautical phrase, a bone in her mouth. Nevertheless, I have chosen, as being more equitable, to prepare some also sufficiently objurgatory, that readers of every taste may find a dish to their palate. I have modelled them upon actually existing specimens preserved in my own cabinet of natural curiosities. One, in particular, I had copied with tolerable exactness from a notice of one of my own discourses, which, from its superior tone and appearance of vast experience, I concluded to have been written by a man at least three hundred years of age, though I recollected no existing instance of such antediluvian longevity. Nevertheless, I afterwards discovered the author to be a young gentleman preparing for the ministry under the direction of one of my brethren in a neighboring town, and whom I have once instinctively corrected in a Latin quantity. But this I have been forced to omit, from its too great length.—H. W.]

From the *Universal Littery Universe*.

Full of passages which rivet the attention of the reader. . . . Under a rustic garb, sentiments are conveyed which should be committed to the memory and engraven on the heart of every moral and social being. . . . We consider this a *unique* performance. . . . We hope to see it soon introduced into our common schools. . . . Mr. Wilbur has performed his duties as editor with excellent taste and judgment. . . . This is a vein which we hope to see successfully prosecuted. . . . We hail the appearance of this work as a long stride toward the formation of a purely aboriginal, indigenous, native, and American literature. We rejoice to meet with an author national enough to break away from the slavish deference, too common among us, to English grammar and orthography. . . . Where all is so good, we are at a loss how to make extracts. . . . On the whole, we may call it a volume which no library, pretending to entire completeness, should fail to place upon its shelves.

From the *Higginbottomopolis Snapping-turtle*.

A collection of the merest balderdash and doggerel that it was ever our bad fortune to lay eyes on. The author is a vulgar buffoon, and the editor a talkative, tedious old fool. We use strong language, but should any of our readers peruse the book, (from which calamity Heaven preserve them!) they will find reasons for it thick as the leaves of Vallumbrozer, or, to use a still more expressive comparison, as the com-

bined heads of author and editor. The work is wretchedly got up. . . . We should like to know how much *British gold* was pocketed by this libeller of our country and her purest patriots.

From the *Oldfogrumville Mentor*.

We have not had time to do more than glance through this handsomely printed volume, but the name of its respectable editor, the Rev. Mr. Wilbur, of Jaalam, will afford a sufficient guaranty for the worth of its contents. . . . The paper is white, the type clear, and the volume of a convenient and attractive size. . . . In reading this elegantly executed work, it has seemed to us that a passage or two might have been retrenched with advantage, and that the general style of diction was susceptible of a higher polish. . . . On the whole, we may safely leave the ungrateful task of criticism to the reader. We will barely suggest, that in volumes intended, as this is, for the illustration of a provincial dialect and turns of expression, a dash of humor or satire might be thrown in with advantage. . . . The work is admirably got up. . . . This work will form an appropriate ornament to the centre-table. It is beautifully printed, on paper of an excellent quality.

From the *Dekay Bulwark*.

We should be wanting in our duty as the conductor of that tremendous engine, a public press, as an American, and as a man, did we allow such an opportunity as is presented to us by ' The Biglow Papers ' to pass by without entering our earnest protest against such attempts (now, alas ! too common) at demoralizing the public sentiment. Under a wretched mask of stupid drollery, slavery, war, the social glass, and, in short, all the valuable and time-honored institutions justly dear to our common humanity and especially to republicans, are made the butt of coarse and senseless ribaldry by this low-minded scribbler. It is time that the respectable and religious portion of our community should be aroused to the alarming inroads of foreign Jacobinism, sansculottism, and infidelity. It is a fearful proof of the wide-spread nature of this contagion, that these secret stabs at religion and virtue are given from under the cloak (*credite, posteri !*) of a clergyman. It is a mournful spectacle indeed to the patriot and Christian to see liberality and new ideas (falsely so called,—they are as old as Eden) invading the sacred precincts of the pulpit. . . . On the whole, we consider this volume as one of the first shocking results which we predicted would spring out of the late French ' Revolution ' (!).

From the Bungtown Copper and Comprehensive Tocsin (a try-weakly family journal).

Altogether an admirable work. . . . Full of humor, boisterous, but delicate,—of wit withering and scorching, yet combined with a pathos cool as morning dew,—of satire ponderous as the mace of Richard, yet keen as the scymitar of Saladin. . . . A work full of ' mountain-mirth ', mischievous as Puck, and lightsome as Ariel. . . . We know not whether to admire most the genial, fresh, and discursive concinnity of the author, or his playful fancy, weird imagination, and compass of style, at once both objective and subjective. . . . We might indulge in some criticisms, but, were the author other than he is, he would be a different being. As it is, he has a wonderful *pose*, which flits from flower to flower, and bears the reader irresistibly along on its eagle pinions (like Ganymede) to the ' highest heaven of invention '. . . . We love a book so purely objective. . . . Many of his pictures of natural scenery have an extraordinary subjective clearness and fidelity. . . . In fine, we consider this as one of the most extraordinary volumes of this or any age. We know of no English author who could have written it. It is a work to which the proud genius of our country, standing with one foot on the Aroostook and the other on the Rio Grande, and holding up the star-spangled banner amid the wreck of matter and the crush of worlds, may point with bewildering scorn of the punier efforts of enslaved Europe. . . . We hope soon to encounter our author among those higher walks of literature in which he is evidently capable of achieving enduring fame. Already we should be inclined to assign him a high position in the bright galaxy of our American bards.

From the Saltriver Pilot and Flag of Freedom.

A volume in bad grammar and worse taste. . . . While the pieces here collected were confined to their appropriate sphere in the corners of obscure newspapers, we considered them wholly beneath contempt, but, as the author has chosen to come forward in this public manner, he must expect the lash he so richly merits. . . . Contemptible slanders. . . . Vilest Billingsgate. . . .

Has raked all the gutters of our language. . . . The most pure, upright, and consistent politicians not safe from his malignant venom. . . . General Cushing comes in for a share of his vile calumnies. . . . The *Reverend* Homer Wilbur is a disgrace to his cloth. . . .

From the World-Harmonic-Æolian-Attachment.

Speech is silver : silence is golden. No utterance more Orphic than this. While, therefore, as highest author, we reverence him whose works continue heroically unwritten, we have also our hopeful word for those who with pen (from wing of goose loud-cackling, or seraph God-commissioned) record the thing that is revealed. . . . Under mask of quaintest irony, we detect here the deep, storm-tost (nigh ship-wracked) soul, thunder-scarred, semi-articulate, but ever climbing hopefully toward the peaceful summits of an Infinite Sorrow. . . . Yes, thou poor, forlorn Hosea, with Hebrew fire-flaming soul in thee, for thee also this life of ours has not been without its aspects of heavenliest pity and laughingest mirth. Conceivable enough ! Through coarse Thersites-cloak, we have revelation of the heart, wild-glowing, world-clasping, that is in him. Bravely he grapples with the life-problem as it presents itself to him, uncombed, shaggy, careless of the ' nicer proprieties ', inexpert of ' elegant diction ', yet with voice audible enough to whoso hath ears, up there on the gravelly side-hills, or down on the splashy, indiarubber-like salt-marshes of native Jaalam. To this soul also the *Necessity of Creating* somewhat has unveiled its awful front. If not Œdipuses and Electras and Alcestises, then in God's name Birdofredum Sawins ! These also shall get born into the world, and filch (if so need) a Zingali subsistence therein, these lank, omnivorous Yankees of his. He shall paint the Seen, since the Unseen will not sit to him. Yet in him also are Nibelungen-lays, and Iliads, and Ulysses-wanderings, and Divine Comedies,—if only once he could come at them ! Therein lies much, nay all ; for what truly is this which we name *All*, but that which we do *not* possess ? . . . Glimpses also are given us of an old father Ezekiel, not without paternal pride, as is the wont of such. A brown, parchment-hided old man of the geoponic or bucolic species, grey-eyed, we fancy, *queued* perhaps, with much weather-cunning and plentiful September-gale memories, bidding fair in good time to become the Oldest Inhabitant. After such hasty apparition, he vanishes and is seen no more. . . . Of ' Rev. Homer Wilbur, A.M., Pastor of the First Church in Jaalam ', we have small care to speak here. Spare touch in him of his Melesigenes namesake, save, haply, the—blindness ! A tolerably caliginose, nephelegeretous elderly gentleman, with infinite faculty of sermonizing, muscularized by long practice, and excellent digestive apparatus, and, for the rest, well-meaning enough, and with small private illuminations (somewhat tallowy, it is to be feared) of his own. To him, there, ' Pastor of the First Church in Jaalam,' our Hosea presents himself as a quite inexplicable Sphinx-riddle. A rich poverty of Latin and Greek,—so far is clear enough, even to eyes peering myopic through horn-lensed editorial spectacles,—but naught farther ? O purblind, well-meaning, altogether fuscous Melesigenes-Wilbur, there are things in him incommunicable by stroke of birch ! Did it ever enter that old bewildered head of thine that there was the *Possibility of the Infinite* in him ? To thee, quite wingless (and even featherless) biped, has not so much even as a dream of wings ever come ? ' Talented young parishioner ? ' Among the Arts whereof thou art *Magister*, does that of *seeing* happen to be one ? Unhappy *Artium Magister!* Somehow a Nemean lion, fulvous, torrid-eyed, dry-nursed in broad-howling sand-wildernesses of a sufficiently rare spirit-Libya (it may be supposed) has got whelped among the sheep. Already he stands wild-glaring, with feet clutching the ground as with oak-roots, gathering for a Remus-spring over the walls of thy little fold. In Heaven's name, go not near him with that flybite crook of thine ! In good time, thou painful preacher, thou wilt go to the appointed place of departed Artillery-Election Sermons, Right-Hands of Fellowship, and Results of Councils, gathered to thy spiritual fathers with much Latin of the Epitaphial sort ; thou, too, shalt have thy reward ; but on him the Eumenides have looked, not Xantippes of the pit, snake-tressed, finger-threatening, but radiantly calm as on antique gems ; for him paws impatient the winged courser of the gods, champing unwelcome bit ; him the starry deeps, the empyrean glooms, and far-dashing splendours await.

From the Onion Grove Phœnix.

A talented young townsman of ours, recently returned from a Continental tour, and who is already favourably known to our readers by his sprightly letters from abroad which have graced our columns, called at our office yesterday. We learn from him, that, having enjoyed the distinguished privilege, while in Germany, of an introduction to the celebrated Von Humbug, he took the opportunity to present that eminent man with a copy of the ' Biglow Papers '. The next morning he received the following note, which he has kindly furnished us for publication. We prefer to print it *verbatim*, knowing that our readers will readily forgive the few errors into which the illustrious writer has fallen, through ignorance of our language.

' HIGH-WORTHY MISTER !

' I shall also now especially happy starve, because I have more or less a work of one those aboriginal Red-Men seen in which have I so deaf an interest ever taken full-worthy on the self shelf with our Gottsched to be upset.

' Pardon my in the English-speech unpractice !

' VON HUMBUG.'

He also sent with the above note a copy of his famous work on ' Cosmetics ', to be presented to Mr. Biglow ; but this was taken from our friend by the English custom-house officers, probably through a petty national spite. No doubt, it has by this time found its way into the British Museum. We trust this outrage will be exposed in all our American papers. We shall do our best to bring it to the notice of the State Department. Our numerous readers will share in the pleasure we experience at seeing our young and vigorous national literature thus encouragingly patted on the head by this venerable and world-renowned German. We love to see these reciprocations of good-feeling between the different branches of the great Anglo-Saxon race.

[The following genuine ' notice ' having met my eye, I gladly insert a portion of it here, the more especially as it contains one of Mr. Biglow's poems not elsewhere printed.—H. W.]

From the Jaalam Independent Blunderbuss.

. . . But, while we lament to see our young townsman thus mingling in the heated contests of party politics, we think we detect in him the presence of talents which, if properly directed, might give an innocent pleasure to many. As a proof that he is competent to the production of other kinds of poetry, we copy for our readers a short fragment of a pastoral by him, the manuscript of which was loaned us by a friend. The title of it is ' The Courtin'.'

ZEKLE crep' up, quite unbeknown,
  An' peeked in thru the winder,
An' there sot Huldy all alone,
  'ith no one nigh to hender.

Agin' the chimbly crooknecks hung,
  An' in amongst 'em rusted
The ole queen's-arm thet gran'ther Young
  Fetched back frum Concord busted.

The wannut logs shot sparkles out
  Towards the pootiest, bless her !
An' leetle fires danced all about
  The chiny on the dresser.

The very room, coz she wuz in,
  Looked warm frum floor to ceilin',
An' she looked full ez rosy agin
  Ez th' apples she wuz peelin'.

She heerd a foot an' knowed it, tu,
  Araspin' on the scraper,—
All ways to once her feelins flew
  Like sparks in burnt-up paper.

He kin' o' l'itered on the mat,
  Some doubtfle o' the seekle ;
His heart kep' goin' pitypat,
  But hern went pity Zekle.

An' yet she gin her cheer a jerk
  Ez though she wished him furder
An' on her apples kep' to work
  Ez ef a wager spurred her.

' You want to see my Pa, I spose ? '
  ' Wal, no ; I come designin'—'
' To see my Ma ? She 's sprinklin' clo'es
  Agin to-morrow's i'nin'.'

He stood a spell on one foot fust
  Then stood a spell on tother,
An' on which one he felt the wust
  He could n't ha' told ye, nuther.

Sez he, ' I 'd better call agin ' ;
  Sez she, ' Think likely, *Mister* ' ;
The last word pricked him like a pin,
  An'—wal, he up and kist her.

When Ma bimeby upon 'em slips,
  Huldy sot pale ez ashes,
All kind o' smily round the lips
  An' teary round the lashes.

Her blood riz quick, though, like the tide
  Down to the Bay o' Fundy,
An' all I know is they wuz cried
  In meetin', come nex Sunday.

SATIS multis sese emptores futuros libri professis, Georgius Nichols, Cantabrigiensis, opus emittet de parte gravi sed adhuc neglecta historiæ naturalis, cum titulo sequenti, videlicet :

Conatus ad Delineationem naturalem nonnihil perfectiorem Scarabœi Bombilatoris, vulgo dicti HUMBUG, ab HOMERO WILBUR, Artium Magistro, Societatis historico-naturalis Jaalamensis Præside (Secretario, Socioque (eheu !) singulo), multarumque aliarum Societatum eruditarum (sive ineruditarum) tam domesticarum quam transmarinarum Socio—forsitan futuro.

PROEMIUM.

LECTORI BENEVOLO S.

Toga scholastica nondum deposita, quum systemata varia entomologica, a viris ejus scientiæ cultoribus studiosissimis summa diligentia ædificata, penitus indagâssem, non fuit quin luctuose omnibus in iis, quamvis aliter laude dignissimis, hiatum magni momenti perciperem. Tunc, nescio quo motu superiore impulsus, aut qua captus dulcedine operis, ad eum implendum (Curtius alter) me solemniter devovi. Nec ab isto labore, δαιμονίως imposito, abstinui antequam tractatulum sufficienter inconcinnum lingua vernacula perfeceram. Inde, juveniliter tumefactus, et barathro ineptiæ τῶν βιβλιοπωλῶν (necnon ' Publici Legentis ') nusquam explorato, me composuisse quod quasi placentas præfervidas (ut sic dicam) homines ingurgitarent credidi. Sed, quum huic et alio bibliopolæ MSS. mea submisissem et nihil solidius responsione valde negativa in Musæum meum retulissem, horror ingens atque misericordia, ob crassitudinem Lambertianam in cerebris homunculorum istius muneris cœlesti quadam ira infixam, me invasere. Extemplo mei solius impensis librum edere decrevi, nihil omnino dubitans quin ' Mundus Scientificus ' (ut aiunt) crumenam meam ampliter repleret. Nullam, attamen, ex agro illo meo parvulo segetem demessui, præter gaudium vacuum bene de Republica merendi. Iste panis meus pretiosus super aquas literarias fæculentas præfidenter jactus, quasi Harpyiarum quarundam (scilicet bibliopolarum istorum facinorosorum supradictorum) tactu rancidus, intra perpaucos dies mihi domum rediit. Et, quum ipse tali victu ali non tolerarem, primum in mentem venit pistori (typographo nempe) nihilominus solvendum esse. Animum non idcirco demisi, imo æque ac pueri naviculas suas penes se lino retinent (eo ut e recto cursu delapsas ad ripam retrahant), sic ego Argô meam chartaceam fluctibus laborantem a quæsitu velleris aurei, ipse potius tonsus pelleque exutus, mente solida revocavi. Metaphoram ut mutem, *boomarangam* meam a scopo aberrantem retraxi, dum majore vi, occasione ministrante, adversus Fortunam intorquerem. Ast mihi, talia volventi, et, sicut Saturnus ille παιδοβόρος, liberos intellectûs mei depascere fidenti, casus miserandus, nec antea inauditus, supervenit. Nam, ut ferunt Scythas pietatis causa et parsimoniæ, parentes suos mortuos devorâsse, sic filius hic meus primogenitus, Scythis ipsis minus mansuetus, patrem vivum totum et calcitrantem exsorbere enixus est. Nec tamen hac de causa sobolem meam esurientem exheredavi. Sed famem istam pro valido testimonio virilitatis roborisque potius habui, cibumque ad eam satiandam, salva paterna mea carne, petii. Et quia bilem illam scaturientem ad æs etiam concoquendum idoneam esse estimabam, unde æs alienum, ut minoris pretii, haberem, circumspexi. Rebus ita se habentibus, ab avunculo meo Johanne Doolittle, Armigero, impetravi ut pecunias necessarias suppeditaret, ne opus esset mihi universitatem relinquendi antequam ad gradum primum in artibus pervenissem. Tunc ego, salvum facere patronum meum munificum maxime cupiens, omnes libros primæ editionis operis mei non venditos una cum privilegio in omne ævum ejusdem imprimendi et edendi avunculo meo dicto pigneravi. Ex illo die, atro lapide notando, curæ vociferantes familiæ singulis annis cre-

scentis eo usque insultabant ut nunquam tam carum pignus e vinculis istis aheneis solvere possem.

Avunculo vero nuper mortuo, quum inter alios consanguineos testamenti ejus lectionem audiendi causa advenissem, erectis auribus verba talia sequentia accepi :—' Quoniam persuasum habeo meum dilectum nepotem Homerum, longa et intima rerum angustarum domi experientia, aptissimum esse qui divitias tueatur, beneficenterque ac prudenter iis divinis creditis utatur,—ergo, motus hisce cogitationibus, exque amore meo in illum magno, do, legoque nepoti caro meo supranominato omnes singularesque istas possessiones nec ponderabiles nec computabiles meas quæ sequuntur, scilicet : quingentos libros quos mihi pigneravit dictus Homerus, anno lucis 1792, cum privilegio edendi et repetendi opus istud " scientificum " (quod dicunt) suum, si sic elegerit. Tamen D. O. M. precor oculos Homeri nepotis mei ita aperiat eumque moveat, ut libros istos in bibliotheca unius e plurimis castellis suis Hispaniensibus tuto abscondat.'

His verbis (vix credibilibus) auditis, cor meum in pectore exsultavit. Deinde, quoniam tractatus Anglice scriptus spem auctoris fefellerat, quippe quum studium Historiæ Naturalis in Republica nostra inter factionis strepitum languescat, Latine versum edere statui, et eo potius quia nescio quomodo disciplina academica et duo diplomata proficiant, nisi quod peritos linguarum omnino mortuarum (et damnandarum, ut dicebat iste πανοῦργος Gulielmus Cobbett) nos faciant.

Et mihi adhuc superstes est tota illa editio prima, quam quasi crepitaculum per quod dentes caninos dentibam retineo.

OPERIS SPECIMEN.

(*Ad exemplum Johannis Physiophili speciminis Monachologiæ.*)

12. S. B. *Militaris*, WILBUR. *Carnifex*, JABLONSK. *Profanus*, DESFONT.

[Male hancce speciem *Cyclopem* Fabricius vocat, ut qui singulo oculo ad quod sui interest distinguitur. Melius vero Isaacus

Outis nullum inter S. milit. S. que Belzebul (Fabric. 152) discrimen esse defendit.]

Habitat civitat. Americ. austral.

Aureis lineis splendidus; plerumque tamen sordidus, utpote lanienas valde frequentans, fœtore sanguinis allectus. Amat quoque insuper septa apricari, neque inde, nisi maxima conatione detruditur. *Candidatus* ergo populariter vocatus. Caput cristam quasi pennarum ostendit. Pro cibo vaccam publicam callide mulget; abdomen enorme; facultas suctus haud facile estimanda. Otiosus, fatuus; ferox nihilominus, semperque dimicare paratus. Tortuose repit.

Capite sæpe maxima cum cura dissecto, ne illud rudimentum etiam cerebri commune omnibus prope insectis detegere poteram.

Unam de hoc S. milit. rem singularem notavi; nam S. Guineens. (Fabric. 143) servos facit, et idcirco a multis summa in reverentia habitus, quasi scintillas rationis pæne humanæ demonstrans.

24. S. B. *Criticus*, WILBUR. *Zoilus*, FABRIC. *Pygmæus*, CARLSEN.

[Stultissime Johannes Stryx cum S. punctato (Fabric. 64–109) confundit. Specimina quamplurima scrutationi microscopicæ subjeci, nunquam tamen unum ulla indicia puncti cujusvis prorsus ostendentem inveni.]

Præcipue formidolosus, insectatusque, in proxima rima anonyma sese abscondit, *we, we,* creberrime stridens. Ineptus, segnipes.

Habitat ubique gentium; in sicco; nidum suum terebratione indefessa ædificans. Cibus. Libros depascit; siccos præcipue.

MELIBŒUS-HIPPONAX.

THE

𝔅𝔦𝔤𝔩𝔬𝔴 𝔓𝔞𝔭𝔢𝔯𝔰,

EDITED,

WITH AN INTRODUCTION, NOTES, GLOSSARY, AND
COPIOUS INDEX,

BY

HOMER WILBUR, A. M.,

PASTOR OF THE FIRST CHURCH IN JAALAM, AND (PROSPECTIVE) MEMBER OF MANY
LITERARY, LEARNED, AND SCIENTIFIC SOCIETIES

(*for which see page* 209.)

The ploughman's whistle, or the trivial flute,
Finds more respect than great Apollo's lute.
Quarles's Emblems, B. ii. E. 8.

Margaritas, munde porcine, calcàsti : en, siliquas accipe.
Jac. Car. Fil. ad Pub. Leg. § 1.

NOTE TO TITLE-PAGE

It will not have escaped the attentive eye, that I have, on the title-page, omitted those honorary appendages to the editorial name which not only add greatly to the value of every book, but whet and exacerbate the appetite of the reader. For not only does he surmise that an honorary membership of literary and scientific societies implies a certain amount of necessary distinction on the part of the recipient of such decorations, but he is willing to trust himself more entirely to an author who writes under the fearful responsibility of involving the reputation of such bodies as the *S. Archæol. Dahom.* or the *Acad. Lit. et Scient. Kamtschat.* I cannot but think that the early editions of Shakespeare and Milton would have met with more rapid and general acceptance, but for the barrenness of their respective title-pages ; and I believe that, even now, a publisher of the works of either of those justly distinguished men would find his account in procuring their admission to the membership of learned bodies on the Continent,—a proceeding no whit more incongruous than the reversal of the judgment against Socrates, when he was already more than twenty centuries beyond the reach of antidotes, and when his memory had acquired a deserved respectability. I conceive that it was a feeling of the importance of this precaution which induced Mr. Locke to style himself ' Gent.' on the title-page of his Essay, as who should say to his readers that they could receive his metaphysics on the honour of a gentleman.

Nevertheless, finding that, without descending to a smaller size of type than would have been compatible with the dignity of the several societies to be named, I could not compress my intended list within the limits of a single page, and thinking, moreover, that the act would carry with it an air of decorous modesty, I have chosen to take the reader aside, as it were, into my private closet, and there not only exhibit to him the diplomas which I already possess, but also to furnish him with a prophetic vision of those which I may, without undue presumption, hope for, as not beyond the reach of human ambition and attainment. And I am the rather induced to this from the fact that my name has been unaccountably dropped from the last triennial catalogue of our beloved *Alma Mater*. Whether this is to be attributed to the difficulty of Latinizing any of those honorary adjuncts (with a complete list of which I took care to furnish the proper persons nearly a year beforehand), or whether it had its origin in any more culpable motives, I forbear to consider in this place, the matter being in course of painful investigation. But, however this may be, I felt the omission the more keenly, as I had, in expectation of the new catalogue, enriched the library of the Jaalam Athenæum with the old one then in my possession, by which means it has come about that my children will be deprived of a never-wearying winter-evening's amusement in looking out the name of their parent in that distinguished roll. Those harmless innocents had at least committed no——but I forbear, having intrusted my reflections and animadversions on this painful topic to the safe-keeping of my private diary, intended for posthumous publication. I state this fact here, in order that certain nameless individuals, who are, perhaps, overmuch congratulating themselves upon my silence, may know that a rod is in pickle which the vigorous hand of a justly incensed posterity will apply to their memories.

The careful reader will note that, in

the list which I have prepared, I have included the names of several Cisatlantic societies to which a place is not commonly assigned in processions of this nature. I have ventured to do this, not only to encourage native ambition and genius, but also because I have never been able to perceive in what way distance (unless we suppose them at the end of a lever) could increase the weight of learned bodies. As far as I have been able to extend my researches among such stuffed specimens as occasionally reach America, I have discovered no generic difference between the antipodal *Fogrum Japonicum* and the *F. Americanum* sufficiently common in our own immediate neighborhood. Yet, with a becoming deference to the popular belief that distinctions of this sort are enhanced in value by every additional mile they travel, I have intermixed the names of some tolerably distant literary and other associations with the rest.

I add here, also, an advertisement, which, that it may be the more readily understood by those persons especially interested therein, I have written in that curtailed and otherwise maltreated canine Latin, to the writing and reading of which they are accustomed.

OMNIB. PER TOT. ORB. TERRAR. CATALOG. ACADEM. EDD.

Minim. gent. diplom. ab inclytiss. acad. vest. orans, vir. honorand. operosiss., at sol. ut sciat. quant. glor. nom. meum (dipl. fort. concess.) catal. vest. temp. futur. affer., ill. subjec., addit. omnib. titul. honorar. qu. adh. non tant. opt. quam probab. put.

*** *Litt. Uncial. distinx. ut Præs. S. Hist. Nat. Jaal.*

HOMERUS WILBUR, Mr., Episc. Jaalam, S. T. D. 1850, et Yal. 1849, et Neo-Cæs. et Brun. et Gulielm. 1852, et Gul. et Mar. et Bowd. et Georgiop. et Viridimont. et Columb. Nov. Ebor. 1853, et Amherst. et Watervill. et S. Jarlath. Hib. et S. Mar. et S. Joseph. et S. And. Scot. 1854, et Nashvill. et Dart. et Dickins. et Concord. et Wash. et Columbian. et Charlest. et Jeff. et Dubl. et Oxon. et Cantab. et Cæt. 1855, P. U. N. C. H. et J. U. D. Gott. et Osnab. et Heidelb. 1860, et Acad. BORE US. Berolin. Soc., et SS. RR. Lugd. Bat. et Patav. et Lond. et Edinb. et Ins. Feejee. et Null. Terr. et Pekin. Soc. Hon. et S. H. S. et S. P. A. et A. A. S. et S. Humb. Univ. et S. Omn. Rer. Quarund. q. Aliar. Promov. Passamaquod. et H. P. C. et I. O. H. et A. Δ. Φ. et II. K. P. et Φ. B. K. et Peucin. et Erosoph. et Philadelph. et Frat. in Unit. et Σ. T. et S. Archæolog. Athen. et Acad. Scient. et Lit. Panorm. et SS. R. H. Matrit. et Beeloochist. et Caffrar. et Caribb. et M. S. Reg. Paris. et S. Am. Antiserv. Soc. Hon. et P. D. Gott. et LL. D. 1852, et D. C. L. et Mus. Doc. Oxon. 1860, et M. M. S. S. et M. D. 1854, et Med. Fac. Univ. Harv. Soc. et S. pro Convers. Pollywog. Soc. Hon. et Higgl. Piggl. et LL. B. 1853, et S. pro Christianiz. Moschet. Soc. et SS. Ante-Diluv. ubiq. Gent. Soc. Hon. et Civit. Cleric. Jaalam. et S. pro Diffus. General. Tenebr. Secret. Corr.

INTRODUCTION

WHEN, more than three years ago, my talented young parishioner, Mr. Biglow, came to me and submitted to my animadversions the first of his poems which he intended to commit to the more hazardous trial of a city newspaper, it never so much as entered my imagination to conceive that his productions would ever be gathered into a fair volume, and ushered into the august presence of the reading public by myself. So little are we short-sighted mortals able to predict the event! I confess that there is to me a quite new satisfaction in being associated (though only as sleeping partner) in a book which can stand by itself in an independent unity on the shelves of libraries. For there is always this drawback from the pleasure of printing a sermon, that, whereas the queasy stomach of this generation will not bear a discourse long enough to make a separate volume, those religious and godly-minded children (those Samuels, if I may call them so) of the brain must at first lie buried in an undistinguished heap, and then get such resurrection as is vouchsafed to them, mummy-wrapped with a score of others in a cheap binding, with no other mark of distinction than the word ' *Miscellaneous* ' printed upon the back. Far be it from me to claim any credit for the quite unexpected popularity which I am pleased to find these bucolic strains have attained unto. If I know myself, I am measurably free from the itch of vanity ; yet I may be allowed to say that I was not backward to recognize in them a certain wild, puckery, acidulous (sometimes even verging toward that point which, in our rustic phrase, is termed *shut-eye*) flavour, not wholly unpleasing, nor unwholesome, to palates cloyed with the sugariness of tamed and cultivated fruit. It may be, also, that some touches of my own, here and there, may have led to their wider acceptance, albeit solely from my larger experience of literature and authorship.[1]

I was, at first, inclined to discourage Mr. Biglow's attempts, as knowing that the desire to poetize is one of the diseases naturally incident to adolescence, which, if the fitting remedies be not at once and with a bold hand applied, may become chronic, and render one, who might else have become in due time an ornament of the social circle, a painful object even to nearest friends and relatives. But thinking, on a further experience, that there was a

germ of promise in him which required only culture and the pulling up of weeds from around it, I thought it best to set before him the acknowledged examples of English composition in verse, and leave the rest to natural emulation. With this view, I accordingly lent him some volumes of Pope and Goldsmith, to the assiduous study of which he promised to devote his evenings. Not long afterward, he brought me some verses written upon that model, a specimen of which I subjoin, having changed some phrases of less elegancy, and a few rhymes objectionable to the cultivated ear. The poem consisted of childish reminiscences, and the sketches which follow will not seem destitute of truth to those whose fortunate education began in a country village. And, first, let us hang up his charcoal portrait of the school-dame.

' Propped on the marsh, a dwelling now, I see
The humble school-house of my A, B, C,
Where well-drilled urchins, each behind his tire,
Waited in ranks the wished command to fire,
Then all together, when the signal came,
Discharged their *a-b abs* against the dame.
Daughter of Danaus, who could daily pour
In treacherous pipkins her Pierian store,
She, mid the volleyed learning firm and calm,   9
Patted the furloughed ferule on her palm,
And, to our wonder, could divine at once
Who flashed the pan, and who was downright dunce.

' There young Devotion learned to climb with ease
The gnarly limbs of Scripture family-trees,
And he was most commended and admired
Who soonest to the topmost twig perspired ;
Each name was called as many various ways
As pleased the reader's ear on different days,
So that the weather, or the ferule's stings,
Colds in the head, or fifty other things,

---

[1] The reader curious in such matters may refer (if he can find them) to ' A sermon preached on the Anniversary of the Dark Day,' ' An Artillery Election Sermon,' ' A Discourse on the Late Eclipse,' ' Dorcas, a Funeral Sermon on the Death of Madam Submit Tidd, Relict of the late Experience Tidd, Esq.,' &c., &c.

Transformed the helpless Hebrew thrice
   a week   21
To guttural Pequot or resounding Greek,
The vibrant accent skipping here and
   there,
Just as it pleased invention or despair ;
No controversial Hebraist was the Dame ;
With or without the points pleased her
   the same ;
If any tyro found a name too tough,
And looked at her, pride furnished skill
   enough ;
She nerved her larynx for the desperate
   thing,
And cleared the five-barred syllables at
   a spring.   30

Ah, dear old times ! there once it was my
   hap,
Perched on a stool, to wear the long-eared
   cap ;
From books degraded, there I sat at ease,
A drone, the envy of compulsory bees ;
Rewards of merit, too, full many a time,
Each with its woodcut and its moral
   rhyme,
And pierced half-dollars hung on ribbons
   gay
About my neck—to be restored next day,
I carried home, rewards as shining then
As those which deck the lifelong pains of
   men,   40
More solid than the redemanded praise
With which the world beribbons later days.

' Ah, dear old times ! how brightly ye re-
   turn !
How, rubbed afresh, your phosphor traces
   burn !
The ramble schoolward through dewspark-
   ling meads,
The willow-wands turned Cinderella steeds ;
The impromptu pinbent hook, the deep
   remorse
O'er the chance-captured minnow's inch-
   long corse ;   48
The pockets, plethoric with marbles round,
That still a space for ball and pegtop found,
Nor satiate yet, could manage to confine
Horsechestnuts, flagroot, and the kite's
   wound twine,
And, like the prophet's carpet could take in,
Enlarging still, the popgun's magazine ;
The dinner carried in the small tin pail,
Shared with some dog, whose most be-
   seeching tail
And dripping tongue and eager ears belied
The assumed indifference of canine pride ;
The caper homeward, shortened if the cart
Of Neighbor Pomeroy, trundling from the
   mart,   . 60

O'ertook me,—then, translated to the seat
I praised the steed, how stanch he was
   and fleet,
While the bluff farmer, with superior grin,
Explained where horses should be thick,
   where thin,
And warned me (joke he always had in
   store)
To shun a beast that four white stockings
   wore.
What a fine natural courtesy was his !
His nod was pleasure, and his full bow
   bliss ;
How did his well-thumbed hat, with ardor
   rapt,   69
Its curve decorous to each rank adapt !
How did it graduate with a courtly ease
The whole long scale of social differences,
Yet so gave each his measure running o'er,
None thought his own was less, his neigh-
   bor's more ;
The squire was flattered, and the pauper
   knew
Old times acknowledged 'neath the thread-
   bare blue !
Dropped at the corner of the embowered
   lane,
Whistling I wade the knee-deep leaves
   again,   78
While eager Argus, who has missed all day
The sharer of his condescending play,
Comes leaping onward with a bark elate
And boisterous tail to greet me at the gate ;
That I was true in absence to our love
Let the thick dog's-ears in my primer
   prove.'

I add only one further extract, which
will possess a melancholy interest to
all such as have endeavored to glean
the materials of revolutionary history
from the lips of aged persons, who took
a part in the actual making of it, and,
finding the manufacture profitable, continued the supply in an adequate proportion to the demand.

' Old Joe is gone, who saw hot Percy goad
   His slow artillery up the Concord road,
   A tale which grew in wonder, year by year,
   As, every time he told it, Joe drew near
   To the main fight, till, faded and grown
      gray,
   The original scene to bolder tints gave way ;
   Then Joe had heard the foe's scared
      double-quick
   Beat on stove drum with one uncaptured
      stick,

And, ere death came the lengthening tale
　　to lop,
Himself had fired, and seen a red-coat
　　drop ;　　　　　　　　　　　　　10
Had Joe lived long enough, that scramb-
　　ling fight
Had squared more nearly with his sense
　　of right,
And vanquished Percy, to complete the
　　tale,
Had hammered stone for life in Concord
　　jail.'

I do not know that the foregoing extracts ought not to be called my own rather than Mr. Biglow's, as, indeed, he maintained stoutly that my file had left nothing of his in them. I should not, perhaps, have felt entitled to take so great liberties with them, had I not more than suspected an hereditary vein of poetry in myself, a very near ancestor having written a Latin poem in the Harvard *Gratulatio* on the accession of George the Third. Suffice it to say, that, whether not satisfied with such limited approbation as I could conscientiously bestow, or from a sense of natural inaptitude, certain it is that my young friend could never be induced to any further essays in this kind. He affirmed that it was to him like writing in a foreign tongue,—that Mr. Pope's versification was like the regular ticking of one of Willard's clocks, in which one could fancy, after long listening, a certain kind of rhythm or tune, but which yet was only a poverty-stricken *tick, tick,* after all,—and that he had never seen a sweet-water on a trellis growing so fairly, or in forms so pleasing to his eye, as a fox-grape over a scrub-oak in a swamp. He added I know not what, to the effect that the sweet-water would only be the more disfigured by having its leaves starched and ironed out, and that Pegāsus (so he called him) hardly looked right with his mane and tail in curl-papers. These and other such opinions I did not long strive to eradicate, attributing them rather to a defective education and senses untuned by too long familiarity with purely natural objects, than to a perverted moral sense. I was the more inclined to this leniency since sufficient evidence was not to seek, that his verses, as wanting as they certainly were in classic polish and point, had somehow taken hold of the public ear in a surprising manner. So, only setting him right as to the quantity of the proper name Pegasus, I left him to follow the bent of his natural genius.

Yet could I not surrender him wholly to the tutelage of the pagan (which, literally interpreted, signifies village) muse without yet a further effort for his conversion, and to this end I resolved that whatever of poetic fire yet burned in myself, aided by the assiduous bellows of correct models, should be put in requisition. Accordingly, when my ingenious young parishioner brought to my study a copy of verses which he had written touching the acquisition of territory resulting from the Mexican war, and the folly of leaving the question of slavery or freedom to the adjudication of chance, I did myself indite a short fable or apologue after the manner of Gay and Prior, to the end that he might see how easily even such subjects as he treated of were capable of a more refined style and more elegant expression. Mr. Biglow's production was as follows :—

THE TWO GUNNERS

A FABLE

Two fellers, Isrel named and Joe,
One Sundy mornin' 'greed to go
Agunnin' soon'z the bells wuz done
And meetin' finally begun,
So'st no one would n't be about
Ther Sabbath-breakin' to spy out.

Joe did n't want to go a mite ;
He felt ez though 't warnt skeercely right,
But, when his doubts he went to speak on,
Isrel he up and called him Deacon,　　10
An' kep' apokin' fun like sin
An' then arubbin' on it in,
Till Joe, less skeered o' doin' wrong
Than bein' laughed at, went along.

Past noontime they went trampin' round
An' nary thing to pop at found,
Till, fairly tired o' their spree,
They leaned their guns agin a tree,

An' jest ez they wuz settin' down
To take their noonin', Joe looked roun'
And see (acrost lots in a pond   21
That warn't mor'n twenty rod beyond),
A goose that on the water sot
Ez ef awaitin' to be shot.

Isrel he ups and grabs his gun ;
Sez he, ' By ginger, here 's some fun ! '
' Don't fire,' sez Joe, ' it aint no use,
Thet 's Deacon Peleg's tame wil'-goose ' :
Sez Isrel, ' I don't care a cent,
I've sighted an' I'll let her went ' ;   30
Bang ! went queen's-arm, ole gander flopped
His wings a spell, an' quorked, an' dropped.

Sez Joe, ' I would n't ha' been hired
At that poor critter to ha' fired,
But sence it 's clean gin up the ghost,
We'll hev the tallest kind o' roast ;
I guess our waistbands'll be tight
'Fore it comes ten o'clock ternight.'

' I won't agree to no such bender,'
Sez Isrel ; ' keep it tell it 's tender ;   40
'Taint wuth a snap afore it 's ripe.'
Sez Joe, ' I'd jest ez lives eat tripe ;
You *air* a buster ter suppose
I 'd eat what makes me hol' my nose ! '

So they disputed to an' fro
Till cunnin' Isrel sez to Joe,
' Don't le's stay here an' play the fool,
Le 's wait till both on us git cool,
Jest for a day or two le's hide it
An' then toss up an' so decide it.'   50
' Agreed ! ' sez Joe, an' so they did,
An' the ole goose wuz safely hid.

Now 't wuz the hottest kind o' weather,
An' when at last they come together,
It did n't signify which won,
Fer all the mischief hed been done :
The goose wuz there, but, fer his soul,
Joe would n't ha' tetched it with a pole ;
But Isrel kind o' liked the smell on 't
An' made *his* dinner very well on 't.   60

My own humble attempt was in
manner and form following, and I print
it here, I sincerely trust, out of no vain-
glory, but solely with the hope of doing
good.

LEAVING THE MATTER OPEN
A TALE
BY HOMER WILBUR, A. M.

Two brothers once, an ill-matched pair,
Together dwelt (no matter where),
To whom an Uncle Sam, or some one,
Had left a house and farm in common.

The two in principles and habits
Were different as rats from rabbits ;
Stout Farmer North, with frugal care,
Laid up provision for his heir,
Not scorning with hard sun-browned hands
To scrape acquaintance with his lands :
Whatever thing he had to do   11
He did, and made it pay him, too ;
He sold his waste stone by the pound,
His drains made water-wheels spin round,
His ice in summer-time he sold,
His wood brought profit when 't was cold,
He dug and delved from morn till night,
Strove to make profit square with right,
Lived on his means, cut no great dash,
And paid his debts in honest cash.   20

On tother hand, his brother South
Lived very much from hand to mouth,
Played gentleman, nursed dainty hands,
Borrowed North's money on his lands,
And culled his morals and his graces
From cock-pits, bar-rooms, fights, and
     races ;
His sole work in the farming line
Was keeping droves of long-legged swine,
Which brought great bothers and expenses
To North in looking after fences,   30
And, when they happened to break through,
Cost him both time and temper too,
For South insisted it was plain
He ought to drive them home again,
And North consented to the work
Because he loved to buy cheap pork.

Meanwhile, South's swine increasing fast,
His farm became too small at last ;
So, having thought the matter over,
And feeling bound to live in clover   40
And never pay the clover's worth,
He said one day to Brother North :-

' Our families are both increasing,
And, though we labour without ceasing,
Our produce soon will be too scant
To keep our children out of want ;
They who wish fortune to be lasting
Must be both prudent and forecasting ;
We soon shall need more land ; a lot
I know, that cheaply can be bo't ;   50
You lend the cash, I'll buy the acres,
And we 'll be equally partakers.'

Poor North, whose Anglo-Saxon blood
Gave him a hankering after mud,
Wavered a moment, then consented,
And, when the cash was paid, repented ;
To make the new land worth a pin,
Thought he, it must be all fenced in.

For, if South's swine once get the run on 't
No kind of farming can be done on 't;
If that don't suit the other side,   61
'T is best we instantly divide.

But somehow South could ne'er incline
This way or that to run the line,
And always found some new pretence
'Gainst setting the division fence;
At last he said :—

      ' For peace's sake,
Liberal concessions I will make;
Though I believe, upon my soul,
I've a just title to the whole,   70
I'll make an offer which I call
Gen'rous,—we'll have no fence at all;
Then both of us, whene'er we choose,
Can take what part we want to use;
If you should chance to need it first,
Pick you the best, I'll take the worst.'

' Agreed !' cried North; thought he, This fall
With wheat and rye I'll sow it all;
In that way I shall get the start,   79
And South may whistle for his part.
So thought, so done, the field was sown,
And, winter having come and gone,
Sly North walked blithely forth to spy,
The progress of his wheat and rye;
Heavens, what a sight ! his brother's swine
Had asked themselves all out to dine;
Such grunting, munching, rooting, shoving,
The soil seemed all alive and moving,
As for his grain, such work they'd made on 't,
He couldn't spy a single blade on 't.

Off in a rage he rushed to South,   91
' My wheat and rye '—grief choked his mouth;
' Pray don't mind me,' said South, ' but plant
All of the new land that you want ';
' Yes, but your hogs,' cried North;
      ' The grain
Won't hurt them,' answered South again;
' But they destroy my crop ';
      ' No doubt;
'T is fortunate you 've found it out;
Misfortunes teach, and only they,
You must not sow it in their way ';
' Nay, you,' says North, ' must keep them out ';   101
' Did I create them with a snout ? '
Asked South demurely; ' as agreed,
The land is open to your seed,
And would you fain prevent my pigs
From running there their harmless rigs ?

God knows I view this compromise
With not the most approving eyes;
I gave up my unquestioned rights
For sake of quiet days and nights ;   110
I offered then, you know 't is true,
To cut the piece of land in two.'
' Then cut it now,' growls North;
      ' Abate
Your heat,' says South, ' 't is now too late;
I offered you the rocky corner,
But you, of your own good the scorner,
Refused to take it; I am sorry;
No doubt you might have found a quarry,
Perhaps a gold-mine, for aught I know,
Containing heaps of native rhino ;   120
You can't expect me to resign
My rights '—

      ' But where,' quoth North, ' are mine?'
' Your rights,' says tother, ' well, that 's funny,
I bought the land '—
      ' I paid the money ' ;
' That,' answered South, ' is from the point,
The ownership, you 'll grant, is joint;
I'm sure my only hope and trust is
Not law so much as abstract justice,
Though, you remember, 't was agreed
That so and so—consult the deed ;   130
Objections now are out of date,
They might have answered once, but Fate
Quashes them at the point we 've got to ;
Obsta principiis, that 's my motto.'
So saying, South began to whistle
And looked as obstinate as gristle,
While North went homeward, each brown paw
Clenched like a knot of natural law,
And all the while, in either ear,   139
Heard something clicking wondrous clear.

To turn now to other matters, there
are two things upon which it would
seem fitting to dilate somewhat more
largely in this place,—the Yankee
character and the Yankee dialect. And,
first, of the Yankee character, which
has wanted neither open maligners, nor
even more dangerous enemies in the
persons of those unskilful painters who
have given to it that hardness, angu-
larity, and want of proper perspective,
which, in truth, belonged, not to their
subject, but to their own niggard and
unskilful pencil.

New England was not so much the
colony of a mother country, as a Hagar
driven forth into the wilderness. The

little self-exiled band which came hither in 1620 came, not to seek gold, but to found a democracy. They came that they might have the privilege to work and pray, to sit upon hard benches and listen to painful preachers as long as they would, yea, even unto thirty-seventhly, if the spirit so willed it. And surely, if the Greek might boast his Thermopylæ, where three hundred men fell in resisting the Persian, we may well be proud of our Plymouth Rock, where a handful of men, women, and children not merely faced, but vanquished, winter, famine, the wilderness, and the yet more invincible *storge* that drew them back to the green island far away. These found no lotus growing upon the surly shore, the taste of which could make them forget their little native Ithaca ; nor were they so wanting to themselves in faith as to burn their ship, but could see the fair westwind belly the homeward sail, and then turn unrepining to grapple with the terrible Unknown.

As Want was the prime foe these hardy exodists had to fortress themselves against, so it is little wonder if that traditional feud is long in wearing out of the stock. The wounds of the old warfare were long a-healing, and an east-wind of hard times puts a new ache in every one of them. Thrift was the first lesson in their horn-book, pointed out, letter after letter, by the lean finger of the hard schoolmaster, Necessity. Neither were those plump, rosy-gilled Englishmen that came hither, but a hard-faced, atrabilious, earnest-eyed race, stiff from long wrestling with the Lord in prayer, and who had taught Satan to dread the new Puritan hug. Add two hundred years' influence of soil, climate, and exposure, with its necessary result of idiosyncrasies, and we have the present Yankee, full of expedients, half-master of all trades, inventive in all but the beautiful, full of shifts, not yet capable of comfort, armed at all points against the old enemy Hunger, longanimous, good at patching, not so careful for what is best

as for what will *do*, with a clasp to his purse and a button to his pocket, not skilled to build against Time, as in old countries, but against sore-pressing Need, accustomed to move the world with no πού στῶ but his own two feet, and no lever but his own long forecast. A strange hybrid, indeed, did circumstance beget, here in the New World, upon the old Puritan stock, and the earth never before saw such mystic-practicalism,such niggard-geniality,such calculating-fanaticism, such cast-iron-enthusiasm, such sour-faced-humour, such close-fisted-generosity. This new *Græculus esuriens* will make a living out of anything. He will invent new trades as well as tools. His brain is his capital, and he will get education at all risks. Put him on Juan Fernandez, and he would make a spelling-book first, and a salt-pan afterward. *In cœlum, jusseris, ibit,*—or the other way either,—it is all one, so anything is to be got by it. Yet, after all, thin, speculative Jonathan is more like the Englishman of two centuries ago than John Bull himself is. He has lost somewhat in solidity, has become fluent and adaptable, but more of the original groundwork of character remains. He feels more at home with Fulke Greville, Herbert of Cherbury, Quarles, George Herbert, and Browne, than with his modern English cousins. He is nearer than John, by at least a hundred years, to Naseby, Marston Moor, Worcester, and the time when, if ever, there were true Englishmen. John Bull has suffered the idea of the Invisible to be very much fattened out of him. Jonathan is conscious still that he lives in the world of the Unseen as well as of the Seen. To move John you must make your fulcrum of solid beef and pudding ; an abstract idea will do for Jonathan.

** TO THE INDULGENT READER

My friend, the Rev. Mr. Wilbur, having been seized with a dangerous fit of illness, before this Introduction had passed through the press, and being incapacitated for all literary exertion, sent to me his notes, memoranda, &c., and requested me to fashion them into some shape more fitting for the general eye. This, owing to the fragmentary and disjointed state of his manuscripts, I have felt wholly unable to do; yet, being unwilling that the reader should be deprived of such parts of his lucubrations as seemed more finished, and not well discerning how to segregate these from the rest, I have concluded to send them all to the press precisely as they are. COLUMBUS NYE,

Pastor of a Church in Bungtown Corner.

It remains to speak of the Yankee dialect. And, first, it may be premised, in a general way, that any one much read in the writings of the early colonists need not be told that the far greater share of the words and phrases now esteemed peculiar to New England, and local there, were brought from the mother country. A person familiar with the dialect of certain portions of Massachusetts will not fail to recognize, in ordinary discourse, many words now noted in English vocabularies as archaic, the greater part of which were in common use about the time of the King James translation of the Bible. Shakespeare stands less in need of a glossary to most New-Englanders than to many a native of the Old Country. The peculiarities of our speech, however, are rapidly wearing out. As there is no country where reading is so universal and newspapers are so multitudinous, so no phrase remains long local, but is transplanted in the mail-bags to every remotest corner of the land. Consequently our dialect approaches nearer to uniformity than that of any other nation.

The English have complained of us for coining new words. Many of those so stigmatized were old ones by them forgotten, and all make now an unquestioned part of the currency, wherever English is spoken. Undoubtedly, we have a right to make new words, as they are needed by the fresh aspects under which life presents itself here in the New World; and, indeed, wherever a language is alive, it grows. It might be questioned whether we could not establish a stronger title to the ownership of the English tongue than the mother-islanders themselves. Here, past all question, is to be its great home and centre. And not only is it already spoken here by greater numbers, but with a far higher popular average of correctness than in Britain. The great writers of it, too, we might claim as ours, were ownership to be settled by the number of readers and lovers.

As regards the provincialisms to be met with in this volume, I may say that the reader will not find one which is not (as I believe) either native or imported with the early settlers, nor one which I have not, with my own ears, heard in familiar use. In the metrical portion of the book, I have endeavoured to adapt the spelling as nearly as possible to the ordinary mode of pronunciation. Let the reader who deems me over-particular remember this caution of Martial :—

' *Quem recitas, meus est, O Fidentine, libellus;*
Sed male cum recitas, incipit esse tuus.'

A few further explanatory remarks will not be impertinent.

I shall barely lay down a few general rules for the reader's guidance.

1. The genuine Yankee never gives the rough sound to the *r* when he can help it, and often displays considerable ingenuity in avoiding it even before a vowel.

2. He seldom sounds the final *g*, a piece of self-denial, if we consider his partiality for nasals. The same of the final *d*, as *han'* and *stan'* for *hand* and *stand*.

3. The *h* in such words as *while, when, where,* he omits altogether.

4. In regard to *a*, he shows some inconsistency, sometimes giving a close and obscure sound, as *hev* for *have, hendy* for *handy, ez* for *as, thet* for *that,* and again giving it the broad sound it has in *father,* as *hânsome* for *handsome.*

5. To the sound *ou* he prefixes an *e* (hard to exemplify otherwise than orally).

The following passage in Shakespeare he would recite thus :—

' Neow is the winta uv eour discontent
Med glorious summa by this sun o' Yock,
An' all the cleouds thet leowered upun
    eour heouse
In the deep buzzum o' the oshin buried ;
Neow air eour breows beound 'ith vic-
    torious wreaths ;
Eour breused arms hung up fer moni-
    munce ;
Eour starn alarums changed to merry
    meetins,
Eour dreffle marches to delighfle masures.
Grim-visaged war heth smeuthed his
    wrinkled front,
An' neow, instid o' mountin' barebid
    steeds
To fright the souls o' ferfle edverseries,
He capers nimly in a lady's chämber,
To the lascivious pleasin' uv a loot.'

6. *Au,* in such words as *daughter* and *slaughter,* he pronounces *ah.*

7. To the dish thus seasoned add a drawl *ad libitum.*

[Mr. Wilbur's notes here become entirely fragmentary.—C. N.]

a. Unable to procure a likeness of Mr. Biglow, I thought the curious reader might be gratified with a sight of the editorial effigies. And here a choice between two was offered,—the one a profile (entirely black) cut by Doyle, the other a portrait painted by a native artist of much promise. The first of these seemed wanting in expression, and in the second a slight obliquity of the visual organs has been heightened (perhaps from an over-desire of force on the part of the artist) into too close an approach to actual *strabismus.* This slight divergence in my optical apparatus from the ordinary model—however I may have been taught to regard it in the light of a mercy rather than a cross, since it enabled me to give as much of directness and personal application to my discourses as met the wants of my congregation, without risk of offending any by being supposed to have him or her in my eye (as the saying is)—seemed yet to Mrs. Wilbur

a sufficient objection to the engraving of the aforesaid painting. We read of many who either absolutely refused to allow the copying of their features, as especially did Plotinus and Agesilaus among the ancients, not to mention the more modern instances of Scioppius, Palæottus, Pinellus, Velserus, Gataker, and others, or were indifferent thereto, as Cromwell.

β. Yet was Cæsar desirous of concealing his baldness. *Per contra,* my Lord Protector's carefulness in the matter of his wart might be cited. Men generally more desirous of being *improved* in their portraits than characters. Shall probably find very unflattered likenesses of ourselves in Recording Angel's gallery.

γ. Whether any of our national peculiarities may be traced to our use of stoves, as a certain closeness of the lips in pronunciation, and a smothered smoulderingness of disposition seldom roused to open flame ? An unrestrained intercourse with fire probably conducive to generosity and hospitality of soul. Ancient Mexicans used stoves, as the friar Augustin Ruiz reports, Hakluyt, III. 468,—but Popish priests not always reliable authority.

To-day picked my Isabella grapes. Crop injured by attacks of rose-bug in the spring. Whether Noah was justifiable in preserving this class of insects?

δ. Concerning Mr. Biglow's pedigree. Tolerably certain that there was never a poet among his ancestors. An ordination hymn attributed to a maternal uncle, but perhaps a sort of production not demanding the creative faculty.

His grandfather a painter of the grandiose or Michael Angelo school. Seldom painted objects smaller than houses or barns, and these with uncommon expression.

ε. Of the Wilburs no complete pedigree. The crest said to be a *wild boar,* whence, perhaps, the name (?). A connection with the Earls of Wilbraham (*quasi* wild boar ham) might be made out. This suggestion worth following up. In 1677, John W. m. Expect ——, had issue, 1. John, 2. Haggai, 3. Expect, 4. Ruhamah, 5. Desire.

' Hear lyes yᵉ bodye of Mrs Expect Wilber,
Yᵉ crewell salvages they kil'd her
Together wᵗʰ other Christian soles eleaven,
October yᵉ ix daye, 1707.
Yᵉ stream of Jordan sh' as crost ore
And now expeacts me on yᵉ other shore :
I live in hope her soon to join ;
Her earthlye yeeres were forty and nine.'
From Gravestone in Pekussett, North Parish.

This is unquestionably the same John who afterward (1711) married Tabitha Hagg or Ragg.

But if this were the case, she seems to have died early ; for only three years after, namely, 1714, we have evidence that he married Winifred, daughter of Lieutenant Tipping.

He seems to have been a man of substance, for we find him in 1696 conveying ' one undivided eightieth part of a salt-meadow ' in Yabbok, and he commanded a sloop in 1702.

Those who doubt the importance of genealogical studies *fuste potius quam argumento erudiendi.*

I trace him as far as 1723, and there lose him. In that year he was chosen selectman.

No gravestone. Perhaps overthrown when new hearse-house was built, 1802.

He was probably the son of John, who came from Bilham Comit. Salop. circa 1642.

This first John was a man of considerable importance, being twice mentioned with the honorable prefix of *Mr.* in the town records. Name spelt with two *l*-s.

' Hear lyeth yᵉ bod [*stone unhappily broken.*]
Mr. Ihon Willber [Esq.] [*I inclose this in brackets as doubtful. To me it seems clear.*]
Ob't die [*illegible ; looks like xvlll.*] . . . . .
    iii [*prob.* 1693.]
·   ·   ·   ·   ·   ·   paynt
·   ·   ·   ·   . deseased seinte :
A friend and [fath]er untoe all yᵉ opreast,
Hee gave yᵉ wicked familists noe reast,
When Sat[an bl]ewe his Antinomian blaste,
Wee clong to [Willber as a steadf]ast maste.
[A] gaynst yᵉ horrid Qua[kers] . . . . .'

It is greatly to be lamented that this curious epitaph is mutilated. It is said that the sacrilegious British soldiers made a target of this stone during the war of Independence. How odious an animosity which pauses not at the grave ! How brutal that which spares not the monuments of authentic history ! This is not improbably from the pen of Rev. Moody Pyram, who is mentioned by Hubbard as having been noted for a silver vein of poetry. If his papers be still extant, a copy might possibly be recovered.

THE BIGLOW PAPERS

No. I.

A LETTER

FROM MR. EZEKIEL BIGLOW OF JAALAM TO THE HON. JOSEPH T. BUCKINGHAM, EDITOR OF THE BOSTON COURIER, INCLOSING A POEM OF HIS SON, MR. HOSEA BIGLOW.

JAYLEM, june 1846.

MISTER EDDYTER :—Our Hosea wuz down to Boston last week, and he see a cruetin Sarjunt a struttin round as popler as a hen with 1 chicking, with 2 fellers a drummin and fifin arter him like all nater. the sarjunt he thout Hosea hed n't gut his i teeth cut cos he looked a kindo 's though he 'd jest com down, so he cal'lated to hook him in, but Hosy wood n't take none o' his sarse for all he hed much as 20 Rooster's tales stuck onto his hat and eenamost enuf brass a bobbin up and down on his shoulders and figureed onto his coat and trousis, let alone wut nater hed sot in his featers, to make a 6 pounder out on.

wal, Hosea he com home considerabal riled, and arter I 'd gone to bed I heern Him a thrashin round like a short-tailed Bull in fli-time. The old Woman ses she to me ses she, Zekle, ses she, our Hosee 's gut the cnollery or suthin anutner ses she, don't you Bee skeered, ses I, he 's oney amakin pottery [1] ses i, he 's ollers on hand at that ere busynes like Da & martin, and shure enuf, cum mornin, Hosy he cum down stares full chizzle, hare on eend and cote tales flyin, and sot rite of to go reed his varses to Parson Wilbur bein he haint aney grate shows o' book larnin himself, bimeby he cum back and sed the parson wuz dreffle tickled with 'em as i hoop you will Be, and said they wuz True grit.

Hosea ses taint hardly fair to call 'em hisn now, cos the parson kind o' slicked off sum o' the last varses, but he told Hosee he did n't want to put his ore in to tetch to the Rest on 'em, bein they wuz verry well As thay wuz, and then Hosy ses he sed suthin a nuther about Simplex Mundishes or sum sech feller, but I guess Hosea kind o' did n't hear him, for I never hearn o' nobody o' that name in this villadge, and I 've lived here man and boy 76 year cum next tater diggin, and thair aint no wheres a kitting spryer 'n I be.

If you print 'em I wish you 'd jest let folks know who hosy's father is, cos my ant Keziah used to say it 's nater to be curus ses she, she aint livin though and he 's a likely kind o' lad.

EZEKIEL BIGLOW.

THRASH away, you 'll *hev* to rattle
  On them kittle-drums o' yourn,—
'Taint a knowin' kind o' cattle
  Thet is ketched with mouldy corn ;
Put in stiff, you fifer feller,
  Let folks see how spry you be,—
Guess you 'll toot till you are yeller
  'Fore you git ahold o' me !

Thet air flag 's a leetle rotten,
  Hope it aint your Sunday's best ;—
Fact ! it takes a sight o' cotton
  To stuff out a soger's chest :
Sence we farmers hev to pay fer 't,
  Ef you must wear humps like these,
Sposin' you should try salt hay fer 't,
  It would du ez slick ez grease.

'Twould n't suit them Southun fellers,
  They 're a dreffle graspin' set,
We must ollers blow the bellers
  Wen they want their irons het ;

---

[1] *Aut insanit, aut versos facit.—H.W.*

May be it 's all right ez preachin',
　But *my* narves it kind o' grates,
Wen I see the overreachin'
　O' them nigger-drivin' States.

Them thet rule us, them slave-
　　traders,
　Haint they cut a thunderin' swarth
(Helped by Yankee renegaders),
　Thru the vartu o' the North !
We begin to think it 's nater
　To take sarse an' not be riled ;—
Who 'd expect to see a tater
　All on eend at bein' biled ?

Ez fer war, I call it murder,—
　There you hev it plain an' flat ;
I don't want to go no furder
　Than my Testyment fer that ;
God hez sed so plump an' fairly,
　It 's ez long ez it is broad,
An' you 've gut to git up airly
　Ef you want to take in God.

Taint your eppyletts an' feathers
　Make the thing a grain more right ;
'Taint afollerin' your bell-wethers
　Will excuse ye in His sight ;
Ef you take a sword an' dror it,
　An' go stick a feller thru,
Guv'ment aint to answer for it,
　God 'll send the bill to you.

Wut 's the use o' meetin'-goin'
　Every Sabbath, wet or dry,
Ef it 's right to go amowin'
　Feller-men like oats an' rye ?
I dunno but wut it 's pooty
　Trainin' round in bobtail coats,—
But it 's curus Christian dooty
　This 'ere cuttin' folks's throats.

They may talk o' Freedom's airy
　Tell they 're pupple in the face,—
It 's a grand gret cemetary
　Fer the barthrights of our race ;
They jest want this Californy
　So 's to lug new slave-states in
To abuse ye, an' to scorn ye,
　An' to plunder ye like sin.

Aint it cute to see a Yankee
　Take sech everlastin' pains,
All to git the Devil's thankee
　Helpin' on 'em weld their chains ?
Wy, it 's jest ez clear ez figgers,
　Clear ez one an' one make two,
Chaps thet make black slaves o'
　　niggers
　Want to make wite slaves o' you.

Tell ye jest the eend I 've come to
　Arter cipherin' plaguy smart,
An' it makes a handy sum, tu,
　Any gump could larn by heart ;
Laborin' man an' laborin' woman
　Hev one glory an' one shame.
Ev'y thin' thet 's done inhuman
　Injers all on 'em the same.

'Taint by turnin' out to hack folks
　You 're agoin' to git your right,
Nor by lookin' down on black folks
　Coz you 're put upon by wite ;
Slavery aint o' nary colour,
　'Taint the hide thet makes it wus,
All it keers fer in a feller
　'S jest to make him fill its pus.

Want to tackle *me* in, du ye ?
　I expect you 'll hev to wait ;
Wen cold lead puts daylight thru ye
　You 'll begin to kal'late ;
S'pose the crows wun't fall to pickin'
　All the carkiss from your bones,
Coz you helped to give a lickin'
　To them poor half-Spanish drones ?

Jest go home an' ask our Nancy
　Wether I 'd be sech a goose
Ez to jine ye,—guess you 'd fancy
　The etarnal bung wuz loose !
She wants me fer home consumption,
　Let alone the hay 's to mow,—
Ef you 're arter folks o' gumption,
　You 've a darned long row to hoe.

Take them editors thet 's crowin'
　Like a cockerel three months old,
Don't ketch any on 'em goin',
　Though they *be* so blasted bold ;

Aint they a prime lot o' fellers ?
  'Fore they think o' they will
    sprout
(Like a peach thet 's got the yellers),
  With the meanness bustin' out.

Wal, go 'long to help 'em stealin'
  Bigger pens to cram with slaves,
Help the men thet 's ollers dealin'
  Insults on your fathers' graves ;
Help the strong to grind the feeble,
  Help the many agin the few,
Help the men thet call your people
Witewashed slaves an' peddlin' crew !

Massachusetts, God forgive her,
  She 's akneelin' with the rest,
She, thet ough' to ha' clung ferever
  In her grand old eagle-nest ;
She thet ough' to stand so fearless
  Wile the wracks are round her
    hurled,
Holdin' up a beacon peerless
  To the oppressed of all the world !

Ha'n't they sold your coloured seamen?
  Ha'n't they made your env'ys wiz ?
Wut 'll make ye act like freemen ?
  Wut 'll git your dander riz ?
Come, I 'll tell ye wut I 'm thinkin'
  Is our dooty in this fix,
They 'd ha' done 't ez quick ez winkin'
  In the days o' seventy-six.

Clang the bells in every steeple,
  Call all true men to disown
The tradoocers of our people,
  The enslavers o' their own ;
Let our dear old Bay State proudly
  Put the trumpet to her mouth,
Let her ring this messidge loudly
  In the ears of all the South :—

' I 'll return ye good fer evil
  Much ez we frail mortils can,
But I wun't go help the Devil
  Makin' man the cus o' man ;
Call me coward, call me traiter,
  Jest ez suits your mean idees,—
Here I stand a tyrant-hater,
  An' the friend o' God an' Peace ! '

Ef I 'd *my* way I hed ruther
  We should go to work an' part,—
They take one way, we take t' other,
  Guess it would n't break my heart ;
Man hed ough' to put asunder
  Them thet God has noways jined ;
An' I should n't gretly wonder
  Ef there 's thousands o' my mind.

[The first recruiting sergeant on record
I conceive to have been that individual who
is mentioned in the Book of Job as *going to
and fro in the earth, and walking up and down
in it.* Bishop Latimer will have him to
have been a bishop, but to me that other
calling would appear more congenial. The
sect of Cainites is not yet extinct, who
esteemed the first-born of Adam to be the
most worthy, not only because of that privilege of primogeniture, but inasmuch as he
was able to overcome and slay his younger
brother. That was a wise saying of the
famous Marquis Pescara to the Papal Le-
gate, that *it was impossible for men to serve
Mars and Christ at the same time.* Yet in
time past the profession of arms was judged
to be *κατ' ἐξοχήν* that of a gentleman, nor
does this opinion want for strenuous up-
holders even in our day. Must we suppose,
then, that the profession of Christianity was
only intended for losels, or, at best, to afford
an opening for plebeian ambition ? Or shall
we hold with that nicely metaphysical Po-
meranian, Captain Vratz, who was Count
Königsmark's chief instrument in the murder of Mr. Thynne, that the Scheme of
Salvation has been arranged with an especial
eye to the necessities of the upper classes,
and that ' God would consider *a gentleman*
and deal with him suitably to the condition
and profession he had placed him in ' ? It
may be said of us all, *Exemplo plus quam
ratione vivimus.*—H. W.]

No. II.

A LETTER

FROM MR. HOSEA BIGLOW TO THE
HON. J. T. BUCKINGHAM, EDITOR
OF THE BOSTON COURIER, COVERING
A LETTER FROM MR. B. SAWIN,
PRIVATE IN THE MASSACHUSETTS
REGIMENT.

[This letter of Mr. Sawin's was not originally written in verse. Mr. Biglow, thinking
it peculiarly susceptible of metrical adorn-

ment, translated it, so to speak, into his own vernacular tongue. This is not the time to consider the question, whether rhyme be a mode of expression natural to the human race. If leisure from other and more important avocations be granted, I will handle the matter more at large in an appendix to the present volume. In this place I will barely remark, that I have sometimes noticed in the unlanguaged prattlings of infants a fondness for alliteration, assonance, and even rhyme, in which natural predisposition we may trace the three degrees through which our Anglo-Saxon verse rose to its culmination in the poetry of Pope. I would not be understood as questioning in these remarks that pious theory which supposes that children, if left entirely to themselves, would naturally discourse in Hebrew. For this the authority of one experiment is claimed, and I could, with Sir Thomas Browne, desire its establishment, inasmuch as the acquirement of that sacred tongue would thereby be facilitated. I am aware that Herodotus states the conclusion of Psammeticus to have been in favour of a dialect of the Phrygian. But, beside the chance that a trial of this importance would hardly be blessed to a Pagan monarch whose only motive was curiosity, we have on the Hebrew side the comparatively recent investigation of James the Fourth of Scotland. I will add to this prefatory remark, that Mr. Sawin, though a native of Jaalam, has never been a stated attendant on the religious exercises of my congregation. I consider my humble efforts prospered in that not one of my sheep hath ever indued the wolf's clothing of war, save for the comparatively innocent diversion of a militia training. Not that my flock are backward to undergo the hardships of *defensive* warfare. They serve cheerfully in the great army which fights even unto death

pro aris et focis, accoutred with the spade, the axe, the plane, the sledge, the spelling-book, and other such effectual weapons against want and ignorance and unthrift. I have taught them (under God) to esteem our human institutions as but tents of a night, to be stricken whenever Truth puts the bugle to her lips and sounds a march to the heights of wider-viewed intelligence and more perfect organization.—H. W.]

MISTER BUCKINUM, the follerin Billet was writ hum by a Yung feller of our town that wuz cussed fool enuff to goe atrottin inter Miss Chiff arter a Drum and fife. it ain't Nater for a feller to let on that he 's sick o' any bizness that He went intu off his own free will and a Cord, but I rather cal'late he 's middlin tired o' voluntearin By this Time. I bleeve u may put dependunts on his statemence. For I never heered nothin bad on him let Alone his havin what Parson Wilbur cals a *pong shong* for cocktales, and he ses it wuz a soshiashun of idees sot him agoin arter the Crootin Sargient cos he wore a cocktale onto his hat.

his Folks gin the letter to me and i shew it to parson Wilbur and he ses it oughter Bee printed. send It to mister Buckinum, ses he, i don't ollers agree with him, ses he, but by Time,[1] ses he, I *du* like a feller that aint a Feared.

I have intusspussed a Few refleck-shuns hear and thair. We 're kind o' prest with Hayin.

Ewers respecfly

HOSEA BIGLOW.

THIS kind o' sogerin' aint a mite like our October trainin',
A chap could clear right out from there ef 't only looked like rainin',
An' th' Cunnles, tu, could kiver up their shappoes with bandanners,
An' send the insines skootin' to the bar-room with their banners
(Fear o' gittin' on 'em spotted), an' a feller could cry quarter
Ef he fired away his ramrod arter tu much rum an' water.

---

[1] In relation to this expression, I cannot but think that Mr. Biglow has been too hasty in attributing it to me. Though Time be a comparatively innocent personage to swear by, and though Longinus in his discourse Περὶ Ὕψους have commended timely oaths as not only a useful but sublime figure of speech, yet I have always kept my lips free from that abomination. *Odi profanum vulgus*, I hate your swearing and hectoring fellows.—H. W.

Recollect wut fun we hed, you'n' I an' Ezry Hollis,
Up there to Waltham plain last fall, along o' the Cornwallis ? [1]
This sort o' thing aint *jest* like thet,—I wish thet I wuz furder,— [2]
Nimepunce a day fer killin' folks comes kind o' low fer murder,   10
(Wy I 've worked out to slarterin' some fer Deacon Cephas Billins,
An' in the hardest times there wuz I ollers tetched ten shillins,)
There 's sutthin' gits into my throat thet makes it hard to swaller,
It comes so nateral to think about a hempen collar ;
It 's glory,—but, in spite o' all my tryin' to git callous,
I feel a kind o' in a cart, aridin' to the gallus.
But wen it comes to *bein'* killed,—I tell ye I felt streaked
The fust time 't ever I found out wy baggonets wuz peaked ;
Here 's how it wuz : I started out to go to a fandango,
The sentinul he ups an' sez, ' Thet 's furder 'an you can go.'   20
' None o' your sarse,' sez I ; sez he, ' Stan' back ! ' ' Aint you a buster ? '
Sez I, ' I 'm up to all thet air, I guess I've ben to muster ;
I know wy sentinuls air sot ; you aint agoin' to eat us ;
Caleb haint no monopoly to court the seenoreetas ;
My folks to hum air full ez good ez hisn be, by golly ! '
An' so ez I wuz goin' by, not thinkin' wut would folly,
The everlastin' cus he stuck his one-pronged pitchfork in me
An' made a hole right thru my close ez ef I wuz an in'my.

Wal, it beats all how big I felt hoorawin' in ole Funnel
Wen Mister Bolles he gin the sword to our Leftenant Cunnle,   30
(It 's Mister Secondary Bolles,[3] thet writ the prize peace essay ;
Thet 's why he did n't list himself along o' us, I dessay,)
An' Rantoul, tu, talked pooty loud, but don't put *his* foot in it,
Coz human life 's so sacred thet he 's principled agin it,—
Though I myself can't rightly see it 's any wus achokin' on 'em,
Than puttin' bullets thru their lights, or with a bagnet pokin' on 'em ;
How dreffle slick he reeled it off (like Blitz at our lyceum
Ahaulin' ribbins from his chops so quick you skeercely see 'em),
About the Anglo-Saxon race (an' saxons would be handy
To du the buryin' down here upon the Rio Grandy),   40
About our patriotic pas an' our star-spangled banner,
Our country's bird alookin' on an' singin' out hosanner,
An' how he (Mister B. himself) wuz happy fer Ameriky,—
I felt, ez sister Patience sez, a leetle mite histericky.
I felt, I swon, ez though it wuz a dreffle kind o' privilege
Atrampin' round thru Boston streets among the gutter's drivelage ;
I act'lly thought it wuz a treat to hear a little drummin',
An' it did bonyfidy seem millanyum wuz acomin'

---

[1] i hait the Site of a feller with a muskit as I du pizn But their *is* fun to a cornwallis
I aint agoin' to deny it.—H. B.
[2] he means Not quite so fur I guess.—H. B.
[3] the ignerant creeter means Sekketary ; but he ollers stuck to his books like cobbler's
wax to an ile-stone.—H. B.

Wen all on us got suits (darned like them wore in the state prison)
An' every feller felt ez though all Mexico wuz hisn.[1]   50

This 'ere 's about the meanest place a skunk could wal diskiver
(Saltillo's Mexican, I b'lieve, fer wut we call Salt-river) ;
The sort o' trash a feller gits to eat doos beat all nater,
I 'd give a year's pay fer a smell o' one good blue-nose tater ;
The country here thet Mister Bolles declared to be so charmin'
Throughout is swarmin' with the most alarmin' kind o' varmin'.

He talked about delishis froots, but then it wuz a wopper all,
The holl on 't 's mud an' prickly pears, with here an' there a chapparal ;
You see a feller peekin' out, an', fust you know, a lariat
Is round your throat an' you a copse, 'fore you can say, 'Wut air ye at ?'[2]
You never see sech darned gret bugs (it may not be irrelevant   61
To say I 've seen a *scarabœus pilularius*[3] big ez a year old elephant),
The rigiment come up one day in time to stop a red bug
From runnin' off with Cunnle Wright,—'t wuz jest a common *cimex
    lectularius.*

One night I started up on eend an' thought I wuz to hum agin,
I heern a horn, thinks I it 's Sol the fisherman hez come agin,
His bellowses is sound enough,—ez I 'm a livin' creeter,
I felt a thing go thru my leg,—'t wuz nothin' more 'n a skeeter !
Then there 's the yaller fever, tu, they call it here el vomito,—
(Come, thet wun't du, you landcrab there, I tell ye to le' *go* my toe !
My gracious ! it 's a scorpion thet 's took a shine to play with 't,   71
I darsn't skeer the tarnal thing fer fear he 'd run away with 't.)
Afore I come away from hum I hed a strong persuasion
Thet Mexicans worn't human beans,[4]—an ourang outang nation,
A sort o' folks a chap could kill an' never dream on 't arter,
No more 'n a feller 'd dream o' pigs thet he hed hed to slarter ;
I 'd an idee thet they were built arter the darkie fashion all,
An' kickin' coloured folks about, you know, 's a kind o' national ;
But wen I jined I wornt so wise ez thet air queen o' Sheby,
Fer, come to look at 'em, they aint much diff'rent from wut we be,
An' here we air ascrougin' 'em out o' thir own dominions,   81
Ashelterin' 'em, ez Caleb sez, under our eagle's pinions,
Wich means to take a feller up jest by the slack o' 's trowsis
An' walk him Spanish clean right out o' all his homes an' houses ;

[1] it must be aloud that thare 's a streak of nater in lovin' sho, but it sartinly is 1 of the curusest things in nater to see a rispecktable dri goods dealer (deekon off a chutch mayby) a riggin' himself out in the Weigh they du and struttin' round in the Reign aspilin' his trowsis and making wet goods of himself. Ef any thin's foolisher and moor dicklus than militerry gloary it is milishy gloary.—H. B.
[2] these fellers are verry proppilly called Rank Heroes, and the more tha kill the ranker and more Herowick tha bekum.—H. B.
[3] it wuz 'tumblebug' as he Writ it, but the parson put the Latten instid. i sed tother maid better meeter, but he said tha was eddykated peepl to Boston and tha would n't stan' it no how. idnow as tha *wood* and idnow *as* tha wood.—H. B.
[4] he means human beins, that 's wut he means. i spose he kinder thought tha wuz human beans ware the Xisle Poles comes from.—H. B.

Wal, it doos seem a curus way, but then hooraw fer Jackson !
It must be right, fer Caleb sez it 's reg'lar Anglo-saxon.
The Mex'cans don't fight fair, they say, they piz'n all the water,
An' du amazin' lots o' things thet is n't wut they ough' to ;
Bein' they haint no lead, they make their bullets out o' copper
An' shoot the darned things at us, tu, wich Caleb sez aint proper ;
He sez they 'd ough' to stan' right up an' let us pop 'em fairly   91
(Guess wen he ketches 'em at thet he 'll hev to git up airly),
Thet our nation 's bigger 'n theirn an' so its rights air bigger,
An' thet it 's all to make 'em free thet we air pullin' trigger,
Thet Anglo Saxondom's idee 's abreakin' 'em to pieces,
An' thet idee 's thet every man doos jest wut he damn pleases ;
Ef I don't make his meanin' clear, perhaps in some respex I can,
I know thet ' every man ' don't mean a nigger or a Mexican ;
An' there 's another thing I know, an' thet is, ef these creeturs,
Thet stick an Anglosaxon mask onto State-prison feeturs,   100
Should come to Jaalam Centre fer to argify an' spout on 't,
The gals 'ould count the silver spoons the minnit they cleared out on 't.

This goin' ware glory waits ye haint one agreeable feetur,
An' ef it worn't fer wakin' snakes, I 'd home agin short meter ;
O, would n't I be off, quick time, ef 't worn't thet I wuz sartin
They 'd let the daylight into me to pay me fer desartin !
I don't approve o' tellin' tales, but jest to you I may state
Our ossifers aint wut they wuz afore they left the Bay-state ;
Then it wuz ' Mister Sawin, sir, you 're middlin' well now, be ye ?
Step up an' take a nipper, sir ; I 'm dreffle glad to see ye ' ;   110
But now it 's ' Ware 's my eppylet ? here, Sawin, step an' fetch it !
An' mind your eye, be thund' rin' spry, or, damn ye, you shall ketch it !'
Wal, ez the Doctor sez, some pork will bile so, but by mighty,
Ef I hed some on 'em to hum, I 'd give 'em linkum vity,
I 'd play the rogue's march on their hides an' other music follerin'—
But I must close my letter here, fer one on 'em 's ahollerin',
These Anglosaxon ossifers,—wall, taint no use ajawin ',
I 'm safe enlisted fer the war,
            Yourn,

BIRDOFREDOM SAWIN.

[Those have not been wanting (as, indeed, when hath Satan been to seek for attorneys ?) who have maintained that our late inroad upon Mexico was undertaken not so much for the avenging of any national quarrel, as for the spreading of free institutions and of Protestantism. *Capita vix duabus Anticyris medenda!* Verily I admire that no pious sergeant among these new Crusaders beheld Martin Luther riding at the front of the host upon a tamed pontifical bull, as, in that former invasion of Mexico, the zealous Gomara (spawn though he were of the Scarlet Woman) was favoured with a vision of St. James of Compostella, skewering the infidels upon his apostolical lance. We read, also, that Richard of the lion heart, having gone to Palestine on a similar errand of mercy, was divinely encouraged to cut the throats of such Paynims as refused to swallow the bread of life (doubtless that they might be thereafter incapacitated for swallowing the filthy gobbets of Mahound) by angels of heaven, who cried to the king and his knights,—*Seigneurs, tuez ! tuez !* providentially using the

French tongue, as being the only one understood by their auditors. This would argue for the pantoglottism of these celestial intelligences, while, on the other hand, the Devil, *teste* Cotton Mather, is unversed in certain of the Indian dialects. Yet must he be a semeiologist the most expert, making himself intelligible to every people and kindred by signs ; no other discourse, indeed, being needful, than such as the mackerel-fisher holds with his finned quarry, who, if other bait be wanting, can by a bare bit of white rag at the end of a string captivate those foolish fishes. Such piscatorial persuasion is Satan cunning in. Before one he trails a hat and feather, or a bare feather without a hat ; before another, a Presidential chair or a tide-waiter's stool, or a pulpit in the city, no matter what. To us, dangling there over our heads, they seem junkets dropped out of the seventh heaven, sops dipped in nectar, but, once in our mouths, they are all one, bits of fuzzy cotton.

This, however, by the way. It is time now *revocare gradum*. While so many miracles of this sort, vouched by eyewitnesses, have encouraged the arms of Papists, not to speak of Echetlaeus at Marathon and those *Dioscuri* (whom we must conclude imps of the pit) who sundry times captained the pagan Roman soldiery, it is strange that our first American crusade was not in some such wise also signalized. Yet it is said that the Lord hath manifestly prospered our armies. This opens the question, whether, when our hands are strengthened to make great slaughter of our enemies, it be absolutely and demonstratively certain that this might is added to us from above, or whether some Potentate from an opposite quarter may not have a finger in it, as there are few pies into which his meddling digits are not thrust. Would the Sanctifier and Setter-apart of the seventh day have assisted in a victory gained on the Sabbath, as was one in the late war ? Or has that day become less an object of his especial care since the year 1697, when so manifest a providence occurred to Mr. William Trowbridge, in answer to whose prayers, when he and all on shipboard with him were starving, a dolphin was sent daily, ' which was enough to serve 'em ; only on *Saturdays* they still catched a couple, and on the *Lord's Days* they could catch none at all ' ? Haply they might have been permitted, by way of mortification, to take some few sculpins (those banes of the salt-water angler), which un-

seemly fish would, moreover, have conveyed to them a symbolical reproof for their breach of the day, being known in the rude dialect of our mariners as *Cape Cod Clergymen.*

It has been a refreshment to many nice consciences to know that our Chief Magistrate would not regard with eyes of approval the (by many esteemed) sinful pastime of dancing, and I own myself to be so far of that mind, that I could not but set my face against this Mexican Polka, though danced to the Presidential piping with a Gubernatorial second. If ever the country should be seized with another such mania *de propaganda fide*, I think it would be wise to fill our bombshells with alternate copies of the Cambridge Platform and the Thirty-nine Articles, which would produce a mixture of the highest explosive power, and to wrap every one of our cannon-balls in a leaf of the New Testament, the reading of which is denied to those who sit in the darkness of Popery. Those iron evangelists would thus be able to disseminate vital religion and Gospel truth in quarters inaccessible to the ordinary missionary. I have seen lads, unimpregnate with the more sublimated punctiliousness of Walton, secure pickerel, taking their unwary *siesta* beneath the lily-pads too nigh the surface, with a gun and small shot. Why not, then, since gunpowder was unknown in the time of the Apostles (not to enter here upon the question whether it were discovered before that period by the Chinese), suit our metaphor to the age in which we live, and say *shooters* as well as *fishers* of men ?

I do much fear that we shall be seized now and then with a Protestant fervour, as long as we have neighbour Naboths whose wallowings in Papistical mire excite our horror in exact proportion to the size and desirableness of their vineyards. Yet I rejoice that some earnest Protestants have been made by this war,—I mean those who protested against it. Fewer they were than I could wish, for one might imagine America to have been colonized by a tribe of those nondescript African animals the Aye-Ayes, so difficult a word is *No* to us all. There is some malformation or defect of the vocal organs, which either prevents our uttering it at all, or gives it so thick a pronunciation as to be unintelligible. A mouth filled with the national pudding, or watering in expectation thereof, is wholly incompetent to this refractory monosyllable. An abject and herpetic Public Opinion is the Pope, the Anti-Christ, for us to protest against *e corde cordium.* And by what College of Cardinals is this our God's-vicar, our binder and looser, elected ? Very like, by the sacred conclave of Tag, Rag, and Bobtail, in the gracious atmosphere of the grog-shop. Yet it is of this that we must all be puppets. This thumps the pulpit-cushion, this guides the editor's pen, this wags the senator's tongue. This decides what Scriptures are canonical, and shuffles Christ away into the Apocrypha. According to that sentence fathered upon Solon, Οὕτω δημόσιον κακὸν ἔρχεται οἴκαδ' ἑκάστῳ. This unclean spirit is skilful to assume various shapes. I have known it to enter my own study and nudge my elbow of a Saturday, under the semblance of a wealthy member of my congregation. It were a great blessing, if every particular of what in the sum we call popular sentiment could carry about the name of its manufacturer stamped legibly upon it. I gave a stab under the fifth rib to that pestilent fallacy,—' Our country, right or wrong,'—by tracing its original to a speech of Ensign Cilley at a dinner of the Bungtown Fencibles.—H. W.]

No. III.

WHAT MR. ROBINSON THINKS

[A FEW remarks on the following verses will not be out of place. The satire in them was not meant to have any personal, but only a general, application. Of the gentleman upon whose letter they were intended as a commentary Mr. Biglow had never heard, till he saw the letter itself. The position of the satirist is oftentimes one which he would not have chosen, had the election been left to himself. In attacking bad principles, he is obliged to select some individual who has made himself their exponent, and in whom they are impersonate, to the end that what he says may not, through ambiguity, be dissipated *tenues in auras.* For what says Seneca ? *Longum iter per præcepta, breve et efficace per exempla.* A bad principle is comparatively harmless while it continues to be an abstraction, nor can the general mind comprehend it fully till it is printed in that large type which

all men can read at sight, namely, the life and character, the sayings and doings, of particular persons. It is one of the cunningest fetches of Satan, that he never exposes himself directly to our arrows, but, still dodging behind this neighbour or that acquaintance, compels us to wound him through them, if at all. He holds our affections as hostages, the while he patches up a truce with our conscience.

Meanwhile, let us not forget that the aim of the true satirist is not to be severe upon persons, but only upon falsehood, and, as Truth and Falsehood start from the same point, and sometimes even go along together for a little way, his business is to follow the path of the latter after it diverges, and to show her floundering in the bog at the end of it. Truth is quite beyond the reach of satire. There is so brave a simplicity in her, that she can no more be made ridiculous than an oak or a pine. The danger of the satirist is, that continual use may deaden his sensibility to the force of language. He becomes more and more liable to strike harder than he knows or intends. He may be careful to put on his boxing-gloves, and yet forget that, the older they grow, the more plainly may the knuckles inside be felt. Moreover, in the heat of contest, the eye is insensibly drawn to the crown of victory, whose tawdry tinsel glitters through that dust of the ring which obscures Truth's wreath of simple leaves. I have sometimes thought that my young friend, Mr. Biglow, needed a monitory hand laid on his arm,—*aliquid sufflaminandus erat.* I have never thought it good husbandry to water the tender plants of reform with *aqua fortis,* yet, where so much is to do in the beds, he were a sorry gardener who should wage a whole day's war with an iron scuffle on those ill weeds that make the garden-walks of life unsightly, when a sprinkle of Attic salt will wither them up. *Est ars etiam maledicendi,* says Scaliger, and truly it is a hard thing to say where the graceful gentleness of the lamb merges in downright sheepishness. We may conclude with worthy and wise Dr. Fuller, that ' one may be a lamb in private wrongs, but in hearing general affronts to goodness they are asses which are not lions.'—H. W.]

GUVENER B. is a sensible man ;
 He stays to his home an' looks arter his folks ;
He draws his furrer ez straight ez he can,
 An' into nobody's tater-patch pokes ;
   But John P.
   Robinson he
  Sez he wunt vote fer Guvener B.

My ! aint it terrible ?   Wut shall we du ?
 We can't never choose him o' course,—thet 's flat ;
Guess we shall hev to come round, (don't you ?)
 An' go in fer thunder an' guns, an' all that ;
   Fer John P.
   Robinson he
  Sez he wunt vote fer Guvener B.

Giner C. is a dreffle smart man :
 He 's ben on all sides thet give places or pelf ;
But consistency still wuz a part of his plan,—
 He 's ben true to *one* party,—an' thet is himself ;—
   So John P.
   Robinson he
  Sez he shall vote fer Giner C.

Giner C. he goes in fer the war ;
 He don't vally principle more 'n an old cud ;
Wut did God make us raytional creeturs fer,
 But glory an' gunpowder, plunder an' blood ?
   So John P.
   Robinson he
  Sez he shall vote fer Giner C.

We were gittin' on nicely up here to our village,
 With good old idees o' wut 's right an' wut aint,
We kind o' thought Christ went agin war an' pillage,
 An' thet eppyletts worn't the best mark of a saint ;
   But John P.
   Robinson he
  Sez this kind o' thing 's an exploded idee.

The side of our country must ollers be took,
 An' Presidunt Polk, you know, *he* is our country.
An' the angel thet writes all our sins in a book
 Puts the *debit* to him, an' to us the *per contry ;*
   An' John P.
   Robinson he
  Sez this is his view o' the thing to a T,

Parson Wilbur he calls all these argimunts lies ;
　　Sez they 're nothin' on airth but jest *fee, faw, fum :*
An' thet all this big talk of our destinies
　　Is half on it ign'ance, an' t' other half rum ;
　　　　But John P.
　　　　Robinson he
　　Sez it aint no sech thing ; an', of course, so must we.

Parson Wilbur sez *he* never heerd in his life
　　Thet th' Apostles rigged out in their swaller-tail coats,
An' marched round in front of a drum an' a fife,
　　To git some on 'em office, an' some on 'em votes ;
　　　　But John P.
　　　　Robinson he
　　Sez they did n't know everythin' down in Judee.

Wal, it 's a marcy we 've gut folks to tell us
　　The rights an' the wrongs o' these matters, I vow,—
God sends country lawyers, an' other wise fellers,
　　To start the world's team wen it gits in a slough ;
　　　　Fer John P.
　　　　Robinson he
　　Sez the world 'll go right, ef he hollers out Gee !

[The attentive reader will doubtless have perceived in the foregoing poem an allusion to that pernicious sentiment,—' Our country, right or wrong.' It is an abuse of language to call a certain portion of land, much more, certain personages, elevated for the time being to high station, our country. I would not sever nor loosen a single one of those ties by which we are united to the spot of our birth, nor minish by a tittle the respect due to the Magistrate. I love our own Bay State too well to do the one, and as for the other, I have myself for nigh forty years exercised, however unworthily, the function of Justice of the Peace, having been called thereto by the unsolicited kindness of that most excellent man and upright patriot, Caleb Strong. *Patriæ fumus igne alieno luculentior* is best qualified with this, —*Ubi libertas, ibi patria.* We are inhabitants of two worlds, and owe a double, but not a divided allegiance. In virtue of our clay, this little ball of earth exacts a certain loyalty of us, while, in our capacity as spirits, we are admitted citizens of an invisible and holier fatherland. There is a patriotism of the soul whose claim absolves us from our other and terrene fealty. Our true country is that ideal realm which we represent to ourselves under the names of religion, duty, and the like. Our terrestrial organizations are but far-off approaches to so fair a model, and all they are verily traitors who resist not any attempt to divert them from this their original intendment. When, therefore, one would have us to fling up our caps and shout with the multitude,— ' *Our country, however bounded !* ' he demands of us that we sacrifice the larger to the less, the higher to the lower, and that we yield to the imaginary claims of a few acres of soil our duty and privilege as liegemen of Truth. Our true country is bounded on the north and the south, on the east and the west, by Justice, and when she oversteps that invisible boundary-line by so much as a hair's-breadth, she ceases to be our mother, and chooses rather to be looked upon *quasi noverca.* That is a hard choice when our earthly love of country calls upon us to tread one path and our duty points us to another. We must make as noble and becoming an election as did Penelope between Icarius and Ulysses. Veiling our faces, we must take silently the hand of Duty to follow her.

Shortly after the publication of the foregoing poem, there appeared some comments upon it in one of the public prints which seemed to call for animadversion. I accordingly addressed to Mr. Buckingham, of the Boston Courier, the following letter.

' JAALAM, November 4, 1847.

' *To the Editor of the Courier :*

' RESPECTED SIR,—Calling at the post-office this morning, our worthy and efficient postmaster offered for my perusal a paragraph in the Boston Morning Post of the 3d instant, wherein certain effusions of the pastoral muse are attributed to the pen of Mr. James Russell Lowell. For aught I know or can affirm to the contrary, this Mr. Lowell may be a very deserving person and a youth of parts (though I have seen verses of his which I could never rightly understand) ; and if he be such, he, I am certain, as well as I, would be free from any proclivity to appropriate to himself whatever of credit (or discredit) may honestly belong to another. I am confident, that, in penning these few lines, I am only forestalling a disclaimer from that young gentleman, whose silence hitherto, when rumor pointed to himward, has excited in my bosom mingled emotions of sorrow and surprise. Well may my young parishioner, Mr. Biglow, exclaim with the poet,

" Sic vos non vobis," &c.

though, in saying this, I would not convey the impression that he is a proficient in the Latin tongue,—the tongue, I might add, of a Horace and a Tully.

' Mr. B. does not employ his pen, I can safely say, for any lucre of worldly gain, or to be exalted by the carnal plaudits of men, *digito monstrari*, &c. He does not wait upon Providence for mercies, and in his heart mean *merces*. But I should esteem myself as verily deficient in my duty (who am his friend and in some unworthy sort his spiritual *fidus Achates*, &c.), if I did not step forward to claim for him whatever measure of applause might be assigned to him by the judicious.

' If this were a fitting occasion, I might venture here a brief dissertation touching the manner and kind of my young friend's poetry. But I dubitate whether this abstruser sort of speculation (though enlivened by some apposite instances from Aristophanes) would sufficiently interest your oppidan readers. As regards their satirical tone, and their plainness of speech, I will only say, that, in my pastoral experience, I have found that the Arch-Enemy loves nothing better than to be treated as a religious, moral, and intellectual being, and that there is no *apage Sathanas !* so potent as ridicule. But it is a kind of weapon that

must have a button of good-nature on the point of it.

' The productions of Mr. B. have been stigmatized in some quarters as unpatriotic; but I can vouch that he loves his native soil with that hearty, though discriminating, attachment which springs from an intimate social intercourse of many years' standing. In the ploughing season, no one has a deeper share in the well-being of the country than he. If Dean Swift were right in saying that he who makes two blades of grass grow where one grew before confers a greater benefit on the state than he who taketh a city, Mr. B. might exhibit a fairer claim to the Presidency than General Scott himself. I think that some of those disinterested lovers of the hard-handed democracy, whose fingers have never touched anything rougher than the dollars of our common country, would hesitate to compare palms with him. It would do your heart good, respected Sir, to see that young man mow. He cuts a cleaner and wider swath than any in this town.

' But it is time for me to be at my Post. It is very clear that my young friend's shot has struck the lintel, for the Post is shaken (Amos ix. 1). The editor of that paper is a strenuous advocate of the Mexican war, and a colonel, as I am given to understand. I presume, that, being necessarily absent in Mexico, he has left his journal in some less judicious hands. At any rate, the Post has been too swift on this occasion. It could hardly have cited a more incontrovertible line from any poem than that which it has selected for animadversion, namely,—

" We kind o' thought Christ went agin war
    an' pillage."

' If the Post maintains the converse of this proposition, it can hardly be considered as a safe guide-post for the moral and religious portions of its party, however many other excellent qualities of a post it may be blessed with. There is a sign in London on which is painted,—" The Green Man." It would do very well as a portrait of any individual who would support so unscriptural a thesis. As regards the language of the line in question, I am bold to say that He who readeth the hearts of men will not account any dialect unseemly which conveys a sound and pious sentiment. I could wish that such sentiments were more common, however uncouthly expressed. Saint Ambrose affirms, that *veritas a quocunque* (why not, then, *quomodocunque ?*) *dicatur*, *a spiritu sancto est.* Digest also this of Baxter : " The plainest words are the most profitable oratory in the weightiest matters."

' When the paragraph in question was shown to Mr. Biglow, the only part of it which seemed to give him any dissatisfaction was that which classed him with the Whig party. He says, that, if resolutions are a nourishing kind of diet, that party must be in a very hearty and flourishing condition : for that they have quietly eaten more good ones of their own baking than he could have conceived to be possible without repletion. He has been for some years past (I regret to say) an ardent opponent of those sound doctrines of protective policy which form so prominent a portion of the creed of that party. I confess, that, in some discussions which I have had with him on this point in my study, he has displayed a vein of obstinacy which I had not hitherto detected in his composition. He is also (*horresco referens*) infected in no small measure with the peculiar notions of a print called the Liberator, whose heresies I take every proper opportunity of combating, and of which, I thank God, I have never read a single line.

' I did not see Mr. B.'s verses until they appeared in print, and there *is* certainly one thing in them which I consider highly improper. I allude to the personal references to myself by name. To confer notoriety on an humble individual who is labouring quietly in his vocation, and who keeps his cloth as free as he can from the dust of the political arena (though *væ mihi si non evangelizavero*), is no doubt an indecorum. The sentiments which he attributes to me I will not deny to be mine. They were embodied, though in a different form, in a discourse preached upon the last day of public fasting, and were acceptable to my entire people (of whatever political views), except the postmaster, who dissented *ex officio.* I observe that you sometimes devote a portion of your paper to a religious summary. I should be well pleased to furnish a copy of my discourse for insertion in this department of your instructive journal. By omitting the advertisements, it might easily be got within the limits of a single number, and I venture to insure you the sale of some scores of copies in this town. I will cheerfully render myself responsible for ten. It might possibly be advantageous to issue it as an *extra.* But perhaps you will not esteem it an object, and I will not press it. My offer does not spring from any weak desire of

seeing my name in print ; for I can enjoy this satisfaction at any time by turning to the Triennial Catalogue of the University, where it also possesses that added emphasis of Italics with which those of my calling are distinguished.

' I would simply add, that I continue to fit ingenuous youth for college, and that I have two spacious and airy sleeping apartments at this moment unoccupied. *Ingenuas didicisse,* &c. Terms, which vary according to the circumstances of the parents, may be known on application to me by letter, post-paid. In all cases the lad will be expected to fetch his own towels. This rule, Mrs. W. desires me to add, has no exceptions.

' Respectfully, your obedient servant,

' HOMER WILBUR, A. M.

' P. S. Perhaps the last paragraph may look like an attempt to obtain the insertion of my circular gratuitously. If it should appear to you in that light, I desire that you would erase it, or charge for it at the usual rates, and deduct the amount from the proceeds in your hands from the sale of my discourse, when it shall be printed. My circular is much longer and more explicit, and will be forwarded without charge to any who may desire it. It has been very neatly executed on a letter sheet, by a very deserving printer, who attends upon my ministry, and is a creditable specimen of the typographic art. I have one hung over my mantel-piece in a neat frame, where it makes a beautiful and appropriate ornament, and balances the profile of Mrs. W., cut with her toes by the young lady born without arms.

' H. W.

I have in the foregoing letter mentioned General Scott in connection with the Presidency, because I have been given to understand that he has blown to pieces and otherwise caused to be destroyed more Mexicans than any other commander. His claim would therefore be deservedly considered the strongest. Until accurate returns of the Mexicans killed, wounded, and maimed be obtained, it will be difficult to settle these nice points of precedence. Should it prove that any other officer has been more meritorious and destructive than General S., and has thereby rendered himself more worthy of the confidence and support of the conservative portion of our community, I shall cheerfully insert his name, instead of that of General S., in a future edition. It may be thought, likewise, that General S. has invalidated his claims by too much attention to the decencies of apparel, and the habits belonging to a gentleman. These abstruser points of statesmanship are beyond my scope. I wonder not that successful military achievement should attract the admiration of the multitude. Rather do I rejoice with wonder to behold how rapidly this sentiment is losing its hold upon the popular mind. It is related of Thomas Warton, the second of that honoured name who held the office of Poetry Professor at Oxford, that, when one wished to find him, being absconded, as was his wont, in some obscure alehouse, he was counselled to traverse the city with a drum and fife, the sound of which inspiring music would be sure to draw the Doctor from his retirement into the street. We are all more or less bitten with this martial insanity. *Nescio qua dulcedine* . . . . *cunctos ducit.* I confess to some infection of that itch myself. When I see a Brigadier-General maintaining his insecure elevation in the saddle under the severe fire of the training-field, and when I remember that some military enthusiasts, through haste, inexperience, or an over-desire to lend reality to those fictitious combats, will sometimes discharge their ramrods, I cannot but admire, while I deplore, the mistaken devotion of those heroic officers. *Semel insanivimus omnes.* I was myself, during the late war with Great Britain, chaplain of a regiment, which was fortunately never called to active military duty. I mention this circumstance with regret rather than pride. Had I been summoned to actual warfare, I trust that I might have been strengthened to bear myself after the manner of that reverend father in our New England Israel, Dr. Benjamin Colman, who, as we are told in Turell's life of him, when the vessel in which he had taken passage for England was attacked by a French privateer, ' fought like a philosopher and a Christian, ... and prayed all the while he charged and fired.' As this note is already long, I shall not here enter upon a discussion of the question, whether Christians may lawfully be soldiers. I think it sufficiently evident, that, during the first two centuries of the Christian era, at least, the two professions were esteemed incompatible. Consult Jortin on this head.— H. W.]

No. IV

REMARKS OF INCREASE D. O'PHACE, ESQUIRE, AT AN EXTRUMPERY CAUCUS IN STATE STREET, REPORTED BY MR. H. BIGLOW.

[THE ingenious reader will at once understand that no such speech as the following was ever *totidem verbis* pronounced. But there are simpler and less guarded wits, for the satisfying of which such an explanation may be needful. For there are certain invisible lines, which as Truth successively overpasses, she becomes Untruth to one and another of us, as a large river, flowing from one kingdom into another, sometimes takes a new name, albeit the waters undergo no change, how small soever. There is, moreover, a truth of fiction more veracious than the truth of fact, as that of the Poet, which represents to us things and events as they ought to be, rather than servilely copies them as they are imperfectly imaged in the crooked and smoky glass of our mundane affairs. It is this which makes the speech of Antonius, though originally spoken in no wider a forum than the brain of Shakespeare, more historically valuable than that other which Appian has reported, by as much as the understanding of the Englishman was more comprehensive than that of the Alexandrian. Mr. Biglow, in the present instance, has only made use of a license assumed by all the historians of antiquity, who put into the mouths of various characters such words as seem to them most fitting to the occasion and to the speaker. If it be objected that no such oration could ever have been delivered, I answer, that there are few assemblages for speech-making which do not better deserve the title of *Parliamentum Indoctorum* than did the sixth Parliament of Henry the Fourth, and that men still continue to have as much faith in the Oracle of Fools as ever Pantagruel had. Howell, in his letters, recounts a merry tale of a certain ambassador of Queen Elizabeth, who, having written two letters,—one to her Majesty, and the other to his wife,—directed them at cross-purposes, so that the Queen was beducked and bedeared and requested to send a change of hose, and the wife was beprincessed and otherwise unwontedly besuperlatived, till the one feared for the wits of her ambassador, and the other for those of her husband. In like manner it may be presumed that our speaker has misdirected some of his thoughts, and given to the whole theatre what he would have wished to confide only to a select auditory at the back of the curtain. For it is seldom that we can get any frank utterance from men, who address, for the most part, a Buncombe either in this world or the next. As for their audiences, it may be truly said of our people, that they enjoy one political institution in common with the ancient Athenians: I mean a certain profitless kind of *ostracism*, wherewith, nevertheless, they seem hitherto well enough content. For in Presidential elections, and other affairs of the sort, whereas I observe that the *oysters* fall to the lot of comparatively few, the *shells* (such as the privileges of voting as they are told to do by the *ostrivori* aforesaid, and of huzzaing at public meetings) are very liberally distributed among the people, as being their prescriptive and quite sufficient portion.

The occasion of the speech is supposed to be Mr. Palfrey's refusal to vote for the Whig candidate for the Speakership.—H. W.]

No ? Hez he ? He haint, though ? Wut ? Voted agin him ?
Ef the bird of our country could ketch him, she 'd skin him ;
I seem 's though I see her, with wrath in each quill,
Like a chancery lawyer, afilin' her bill,
An' grindin' her talents ez sharp ez all nater,
To pounce like a writ on the back o' the traitor.
Forgive me, my friends, ef I seem to be het,
But a crisis like this must with vigour be met ;
Wen an Arnold the star-spangled banner bestains,
Holl Fourth o' Julys seem to bile in my veins.   10

Who ever'd ha' thought sech a pisonous rig
Would be run by a chap thet wuz chose fer a Wig ?
' We knowed wut his principles wuz 'fore we sent him ? '
Wut wuz there in them from this vote to pervent him ?
A marciful Providunce fashioned us holler
O' purpose thet we might our principles swaller ;
It can hold any quantity on 'em, the belly can,
An' bring 'em up ready fer use like the pelican,
Or more like the kangaroo, who (wich is stranger)
Puts her family into her pouch wen there 's danger.   20
Aint principle precious ? then, who 's goin' to use it
Wen there 's resk o' some chap's gittin' up to abuse it ?
I can't tell the wy on 't, but nothin' is *so* sure
Ez thet principle kind o' gits spiled by exposure : [1]
A man thet lets all sorts o' folks git a sight on 't
Ough' to hev it all took right away, every mite on 't ;
Ef he can't keep it all to himself wen it 's wise to,
He aint one it 's fit to trust nothin' so nice to.

---

[1] The speaker is of a different mind from Tully, who, in his recently discovered tractate *De Republica*, tells us,—*Nec vero habere virtutem satis est, quasi artem aliquam, nisi utare*, and from our Milton, who says : ' I cannot praise a fugitive and cloistered virtue, unexercised and unbreathed, that never sallies out and sees her adversary, but slinks out of the race where that immortal garland is to be run for, *not without dust and heat.*'—*Areop.* He had taken the words out of the Roman's mouth, without knowing it, and might well exclaim with Austin (if a saint's name may stand sponsor for a curse), *Pereant qui ante nos nostra dixerint !*—H. W.

Besides, ther 's a wonderful power in latitude
To shift a man's morril relations an' attitude ;   30
Some flossifers think thet a fakkilty 's granted
The minnit it 's proved to be thoroughly wanted,
Thet a change o' demand makes a change o' condition,
An' thet everythin' 's nothin' except by position ;
Ez, fer instance, thet rubber-trees fust begun bearin'
Wen p'litikle conshunces come into wearin',—
Thet the fears of a monkey, whose holt chanced to fail,
Drawed the vertibry out to a prehensile tail ;
So, wen one's chose to Congriss, ez soon ez he 's in it,
A collar grows right round his neck in a minnit,   40
An' sartin it is thet a man cannot be strict
In bein' himself, wen he gits to the Deestrict,
Fer a coat thet sets wal here in ole Massachusetts,
Wen it gits on to Washinton, somehow askew sets.

Resolves, do you say, o' the Springfield Convention ?
Thet 's precisely the pint I was goin' to mention ;
Resolves air a thing we most gen'ally keep ill,
They're a cheap kind o' dust fer the eyes o' the people ;
A parcel o' delligits jest git together
An' chat fer a spell o' the crops an' the weather,   50
Then, comin' to order, they squabble awile
An' let off the speeches they 're ferful 'll spile ;
Then—Resolve,—Thet we wunt hev an inch o' slave territory ;
Thet Presidunt Polk's holl perceedins air very tory ;
Thet the war is a damned war, an' them thet enlist in it
Should hev a cravat with a dreffle tight twist in it ;
Thet the war is a war fer the spreadin' o' slavery ;
Thet our army desarves our best thanks fer their bravery ;
Thet we 're the original friends o' the nation,
All the rest air a paltry an' base fabrication ;   60
Thet we highly respect Messrs. A, B, an' C,
An' ez deeply despise Messrs. E, F, an' G.
In this way they go to the eend o' the chapter,
An' then they bust out in a kind of a raptur
About their own vartoo, an' folks's stone-blindness
To the men thet 'ould actilly do 'em a kindness,—
The American eagle,—the Pilgrims thet landed,—
Till on ole Plymouth Rock they git finally stranded.
Wal, the people they listen an' say, ' Thet 's the ticket ;
Ez fer Mexico, 't aint no great glory to lick it,   70
But 't would be a darned shame to go pullin' o' triggers
To extend the aree of abusin' the niggers.'

So they march in percessions, an' git up hooraws,
An' tramp thru the mud fer the good o' the cause,
An' think they 're a kind o' fulfillin' the prophecies,
Wen they 're on'y jest changin' the holders of offices ;

Ware A sot afore, B is comf'tably seated,
One humbug's victor'ous an' t' other defeated,
Each honnable doughface gits jest wut he axes,
An' the people,—their annooal soft-sodder an' taxes.   80

Now, to keep unimpaired all these glorious feeturs
Thet characterize morril an' reasonin' creeturs,
Thet give every paytriot all he can cram,
Thet oust the untrustworthy Presidunt Flam,
An' stick honest Presidunt Sham in his place,
To the manifest gain o' the holl human race,
An' to some indervidgewals on 't in partickler,
Who love Public Opinion an' know how to tickle her,—
I say thet a party with gret aims like these
Must stick jest ez close ez a hive full o' bees.   90

I 'm willin' a man should go tollable strong
Agin wrong in the abstract, fer thet kind o' wrong
Is ollers unpop'lar an' never gits pitied,
Because it 's a crime no one never committed ;
But he mus' n't be hard on partickler sins,
Coz then he'll be kickin' the people's own shins ;
On'y look at the Demmercrats, see wut they 've done
Jest simply by stickin' together like fun ;
They 've sucked us right into a mis'able war
Thet no one on airth aint responsible for ;   100
They 've run us a hundred cool millions in debt
(An' fer Demmercrat Horners ther 's good plums left yet) ;
They talk agin tayriffs, but act fer a high one,
An' so coax all parties to build up their Zion ;
To the people they 're ollers ez slick ez molasses,
An' butter their bread on both sides with The Masses,
Half o' whom they 've persuaded, by way of a joke,
Thet Washinton's mantelpiece fell upon Polk.

Now all o' these blessin's the Wigs might enjoy,
Ef they'd gumption enough the right means to imploy ; [1]   110
Fer the silver spoon born in Dermocracy's mouth
Is a kind of a scringe thet they hev to the South ;
Their masters can cuss 'em an' kick 'em an' wale 'em,
An' they notice it less 'an the ass did to Balaam ;
In this way they screw into second-rate offices
Wich the slaveholder thinks 'ould substract too much off his ease ;
The file-leaders, I mean, du, fer they, by their wiles,
Unlike the old viper, grow fat on their files.
Wal, the Wigs hev been tryin' to grab all this prey frum 'em
An' to hook this nice spoon o' good fortin' away frum 'em,   120
An' they might ha' succeeded, ez likely ez not,
In lickin' the Demmercrats all round the lot,

[1] That was a pithy saying of Persius, and fits our politicians without a wrinkle,—
Magister artis, ingeniique largitor ventar.—H. W.

Ef it warn't thet, wile all faithful Wigs were their knees on,
Some stuffy old codger would holler out, —' Treason !
You must keep a sharp eye on a dog thet hez bit you once,
An' *I* aint agoin' to cheat my constitoounts,'—
Wen every fool knows thet a man represents
Not the fellers thet sent him, but them on the fence,—
Impartially ready to jump either side
An' make the fust use of a turn o' the tide,—   130
The waiters on Providunce here in the city,
Who compose wut they call a State Centerl Committy.
Constitoounts air hendy to help a man in,
But arterwards don't weigh the heft of a pin.
Wy, the people can't all live on Uncle Sam's pus,
So they've nothin' to du with 't fer better or wus ;
It 's the folks thet air kind o' brought up to depend on 't
Thet hev any consarn in 't, an' thet is the end on 't.

Now here wuz New England ahevin' the honour
Of a chance at the Speakership showered upon her ;—   140
Do you say,—' She don't want no more Speakers, but fewer ;
She 's hed plenty o' them, wut she wants is a *doer* ' ?
Fer the matter o' thet, it 's notorous in town
Thet her own representatives du her quite brown.
But thet 's nothin' to du with it ; wut right hed Palfrey
To mix himself up with fanatical small fry ?
Warn't we gittin' on prime with our hot an' cold blowin',
Acondemnin' the war wilst we kep' it agoin' ?
We 'd assumed with gret skill a commandin' position,
On this side or thet, no one could n't tell wich one,   150
So, wutever side wipped, we 'd a chance at the plunder
An' could sue fer infringin' our paytented thunder ;
We were ready to vote fer whoever wuz eligible,
Ef on all pints at issoo he 'd stay unintelligible.
Wal, sposin' we hed to gulp down our perfessions,
We were ready to come out next mornin' with fresh ones ;
Besides, ef we did, 't was our business alone,
Fer could n't we du wut we would with our own ?
An' ef a man can, wen pervisions hev riz so,
Eat up his own words, it 's a marcy it is so.   160

Wy, these chaps frum the North, with back-bones to 'em, darn 'em,
'Ould be wuth more 'an Gennle Tom Thumb is to Barnum :
Ther 's enough thet to office on this very plan grow,
By exhibitin' how very small a man can grow ;
But an M. C. frum here ollers hastens to state he
Belongs to the order called invertebraty,
Wence some gret filologists judge primy fashy
Thet M. C. is M. T. by paronomashy ;
An' these few exceptions air *loosus naytury*
Folks 'ould put down their quarters to stare at, like fury.   170

It 's no use to open the door o' success,
Ef a member can bolt so fer nothin' or less;
Wy, all o' them grand constitootional pillers
Our fore-fathers fetched with 'em over the billers,
Them pillers the people so soundly hev slep' on,
Wile to slav'ry, invasion, an' debt they were swep' on,
Wile our Destiny higher an' higher kep' mountin'
(Though I guess folks 'll stare wen she hends her account in),
Ef members in this way go kicken' agin 'em,
They wunt hev so much ez a feather left in 'em.   180

An', ez fer this Palfrey,[1] we thought wen we 'd gut him in,
He 'd go kindly in wutever harness we put him in;
Supposin' we *did* know thet he wuz a peace man ?
Doos he think he can be Uncle Sammle's policeman,
An' wen Sam gits tipsy an' kicks up a riot,
Lead him off to the lockup to snooze till he 's quiet ?
Wy, the war is a war thet true paytriots can bear, ef
It leads to the fat promised land of a tayriff;
We don't go an' fight it, nor aint to be driv on,
Nor Demmercrats nuther, thet hev wut to live on;   190
Ef it aint jest the thing thet 's well pleasin' to God,
It makes us thought highly on elsewhere abroad;
The Rooshian black eagle looks blue in his eerie
An' shakes both his heads wen he hears o' Monteery;
In the Tower Victory sets, all of a fluster,
An' reads, with locked doors, how we won Cherry Buster;
An' old Philip Lewis—thet come an' kep' school here
Fer the mere sake o' scorin' his ryalist ruler
On the tenderest part of our kings *in futuro*—
Hides his crown underneath an old shut in his bureau,   200
Breaks off in his brags to a suckle o' merry kings,
How he often hed hided young native Amerrikins,
An' turnin' quite faint in the midst of his fooleries,
Sneaks down stairs to bolt the front door o' the Tooleries.[2]

[1] There is truth yet in this of Juvenal,—
      ' Dat veniam corvis, vexat censura columbas.'—H. W.

[2] Jortin is willing to allow of other miracles besides those recorded in Holy Writ, and why not of other prophecies ? It is granting too much to Satan to suppose him, as divers of the learned have done, the inspirer of the ancient oracles. Wiser, I esteem it, to give chance the credit of the successful ones. What is said here of Louis Philippe was verified in some of its minute particulars within a few months' time. Enough to have made the fortune of Delphi or Hammon, and no thanks to Beelzebub neither ! That of Seneca in Medea will suit here :—
      ' Rapida fortuna ac levis
    Præcepsque regno eripuit, exsilio dedit.'

Let us allow, even to richly deserved misfortune, our commiseration, and be not over-hasty meanwhile in our censure of the French people, left for the first time to govern themselves, remembering that wise sentence of Æschylus,—
      Ἅπας δὲ τραχὺς ὅστις ἂν νέον κρατῇ.   H. W.

You say,—' We 'd ha' scared 'em by growin' in peace,
A plaguy sight more then by bobberies like these ' ?
Who is it dares say thet our naytional eagle
Wun't much longer be classed with the birds thet air regal,
Coz theirn be hooked beaks, an' she, arter this slaughter,
'll bring back a bill ten times longer 'n she ough' to ' ?   210
Wut 's your name ? Come, I see ye, you up-country feller,
You 've put me out severil times with your beller ;
Out with it ! Wut ? Biglow ? I say nothin' furder,
Thet feller would like nothin' better 'n a murder ;
He 's a traiter, blasphemer, an' wut ruther worse is,
He puts all his ath'ism in dreffle bad verses ;
Socity aint safe till sech monsters air out on it,
Refer to the Post, ef you hev the least doubt on it ;
Wy, he goes agin war, agin indirect taxes,
Agin sellin' wild lands 'cept to settlers with axes,   220
Agin holdin' o' slaves, though he knows it 's the corner
Our libbaty rests on, the mis'able scorner !
In short, he would wholly upset with his ravages
All thet keeps us above the brute critters an' savages,
An' pitch into all kinds o' briles an' confusions
The holl of our civilized, free institutions ;
He writes fer thet ruther unsafe print, the Courier,
An' likely ez not hez a squintin' to Foorier ;
I 'll be——, thet is, I mean I 'll be blest,
Ef I hark to a word frum so noted a pest ;   230
I sha' n't talk with *him*, my religion 's too fervent.—
Good mornin', my friends, I 'm your most humble servant.

[Into the question, whether the ability to express ourselves in articulate language has been productive of more good or evil, I shall not here enter at large. The two faculties of speech and of speech-making are wholly diverse in their natures. By the first we make ourselves intelligible, by the last unintelligible, to our fellows. It has not seldom occurred to me (noting how in our national legislature everything runs to talk, as lettuces, if the season or the soil be unpropitious, shoot up lankly to seed, instead of forming handsome heads) that Babel was the first Congress, the earliest mill erected for the manufacture of gabble. In these days, what with Town Meetings, School Committees, Boards (lumber) of one kind and another, Congresses, Parliaments, Diets, Indian Councils, Palavers, and the like, there is scarce a village which has not its factories of this description driven by (milk-and-)water power. I cannot conceive the confusion of tongues to have been the curse of Babel, since I esteem my ignorance of other languages as a kind of Martello-tower, in which I am safe from the furious bombardments of foreign garrulity. For this reason I have ever preferred the study of the dead languages, those primitive formations being Ararats upon whose silent peaks I sit secure and watch this new deluge without fear, though it rain figures (*simulacra*, semblances) of speech forty days and nights together, as it not uncommonly happens. Thus is my coat, as it were, without buttons by which any but a vernacular wild bore can seize me. Is it not possible that the Shakers may intend to convey a quiet reproof and hint, in fastening their outer garments with hooks and eyes ?

This reflection concerning Babel, which I find in no Commentary, was first thrown upon my mind when an excellent deacon of my congregation (being infected with the Second Advent delusion) assured me that he had received a first instalment of the gift of tongues as a small earnest of larger possessions in the like kind to follow. For, of a truth, I could not reconcile it with my ideas of the Divine justice and mercy that the single wall which protected people of other languages from the incursions of this otherwise well-meaning propagandist should be broken down.

In reading Congressional debates, I have fancied, that, after the subsidence of those painful buzzings in the brain which result from such exercises, I detected a slender residuum of valuable information. I made the discovery that *nothing* takes longer in the saying than anything else, for as *ex nihilo nihil fit*, so from one polypus *nothing* any number of similar ones may be produced. I would recommend to the attention of *viva voce* debaters and controversialists the admirable example of the monk Copres, who, in the fourth century, stood for half an hour in the midst of a great fire, and thereby silenced a Manichæan antagonist who had less of the salamander in him. As for those who quarrel in print, I have no concern with them here, since the eyelids are a divinely granted shield against all such. Moreover, I have observed in many modern books that the printed portion is becoming gradually smaller, and the number of blank or fly-leaves (as they are called) greater. Should this fortunate tendency of literature continue, books will grow more valuable from year to year, and the whole Serbonian bog yield to the advances of firm arable land.

The sagacious Lacedæmonians hearing that Tesephone had bragged that he could talk all day long on any given subject, made no more ado, but forthwith banished him, whereby they supplied him a topic and at the same time took care that his experiment upon it should be tried out of ear-shot.

I have wondered, in the Representatives' Chamber of our own Commonwealth, to mark how little impression seemed to be produced by that emblematic fish suspended over the heads of the members. Our wiser ancestors, no doubt, hung it there as being the animal which the Pythagoreans reverenced for its silence, and which certainly in that particular does not so well merit the epithet *cold-blooded*, by which naturalists distinguish it, as certain bipeds, afflicted with ditch-water on the brain, who take occasion to tap themselves in Faneuil Halls, meeting-houses, and other places of public resort.—H. W.]

No. V.

THE DEBATE IN THE SENNIT

SOT TO A NUSEY RHYME

[THE incident which gave rise to the debate satirized in the following verses was the unsuccessful attempt of Drayton and Sayres to give freedom to seventy men and women, fellow-beings and fellow-Christians. Had Tripoli, instead of Washington, been the scene of this undertaking, the unhappy leaders in it would have been as secure of the theoretic as they now are of the practical part of martyrdom. I question whether the Dey of Tripoli is blessed with a District Attorney so benighted as ours at the seat of government. Very fitly is he named Key, who would allow himself to be made the instrument of locking the door of hope against sufferers in such a cause. Not all the waters of the ocean can cleanse the vile smutch of the jailer's fingers from off that little Key. *Ahenea clavis*, a brazen Key indeed !

Mr. Calhoun, who is made the chief speaker in this burlesque, seems to think that the light of the nineteenth century is to be put out as soon as he tinkles his little cow-bell curfew. Whenever slavery is touched, he sets up his scarecrow of dissolving the Union. This may do for the North, but I should conjecture that something more than a pumpkin-lantern is required to scare manifest and irretrievable Destiny out of her path. Mr. Calhoun cannot let go the apron-string of the Past. The Past is a good nurse, but we must be weaned from her sooner or later, even though, like Plotinus, we should run home from school to ask the breast, after we are tolerably well-grown youths. It will not do for us to hide our faces in her lap, whenever the strange Future holds out her arms and asks us to come to her.

But we are all alike. We have all heard it said, often enough, that little boys must not play with fire ; and yet, if the matches be taken away from us, and put out of reach upon the shelf, we must needs get into our little corner, and scowl and stamp and threaten the dire revenge of going to bed without our supper. The world shall stop till we get our dangerous plaything again. Dame Earth, meanwhile, who has more than enough household matters to mind, goes bustling hither and thither as a hiss or a sputter tells her that this or that kettle of hers is boiling over, and before bedtime we are glad to eat our porridge cold, and gulp down our dignity along with it.

Mr. Calhoun has somehow acquired the name of a great statesman, and, if it be great statesmanship to put lance in rest and run a tilt at the Spirit of the Age with the certainty of being next moment hurled neck and heels into the dust amid universal laughter, he deserves the title. He is the Sir Kay of our modern chivalry. He should remember the old Scandinavian mythus. Thor was the strongest of gods, but he could not wrestle with Time, nor so much as lift up a fold of the great snake which knit the universe together; and when he smote the Earth, though with his terrible mallet, it was but as if a leaf had fallen. Yet all the while it seemed to Thor that he had only been wrestling with an old woman, striving to lift a cat, and striking a stupid giant on the head.

And in old times, doubtless, the giants *were* stupid, and there was no better sport for the Sir Launcelots and Sir Gawains than to go about cutting off their great blundering heads with enchanted swords. But things have wonderfully changed. It is the giants, nowadays, that have the science and the intelligence, while the chivalrous Don Quixotes of Conservatism still cumber themselves with the clumsy armour of a bygone age. On whirls the restless globe through unsounded time, with its cities and its silences, its births and funerals, half light, half shade, but never wholly dark, and sure to swing round into the happy morning at last. With an involuntary smile, one sees Mr. Calhoun letting slip his pack-thread cable with a crooked pin at the end of it to anchor South Carolina upon the bank and shoal of the Past.—H. W.]

TO MR. BUCKENAM

MR. EDITER, As i wuz kinder prunin round, in a little nussry sot out a year or 2 a go, the Dbait in the sennit cum inter my mine An so i took & Sot it to wut I call a nussry rime. I hev made sum onnable Gentlemun speak that dident speak in a Kind uv Poetikul lie sense the seeson is dreffle backerd up This way

ewers as ushul

HOSEA BIGLOW.

' HERE we stan' on the Constitution, by thunder !
It 's a fact o' wich ther 's bushils o' proofs ;
Fer how could we trample on 't so, I wonder,
    Ef 't worn't thet it 's ollers under our hoofs ? '
        Sez John C. Calhoun, sez he ;
            ' Human rights haint no more
            Right to come on this floor,
        No more 'n the man in the moon,' sez he.

' The North haint no kind o' bisness with nothin',
An' you 've no idee how much bother it saves ;
We aint none riled by their frettin' an' frothin',
    We're *used* to layin' the string on our slaves,'
        Sez John C. Calhoun, sez he ;—
            Sez Mister Foote,
            ' I should like to shoot
        The holl gang, by the gret horn spoon ! ' sez he.

' Freedom's Keystone is Slavery, thet ther 's no doubt on,
It 's sutthin' thet 's—wha' d' ye call it ?—divine,—
An' the slaves thet we ollers *make* the most out on
    Air them north o' Mason an' Dixon's line,'
        Sez John C. Calhoun, sez he ;—
            ' Fer all thet,' sez Mangum,
            ' 'T would be better to hang 'em,
        An' so git red on 'em soon,' sez he.

''The mass ough' to labor an' we lay on soffies,
 Thet 's the reason I want to spread Freedom's aree ;
It puts all the cunninest on us in office,
 An' reelises our Maker's orig'nal idee,'
  Sez John C. Calhoun, sez he ;—
   ' Thet 's ez plain,' sez Cass,
   ' Ez thet some one 's an ass,
  It 's ez clear ez the sun is at noon,' sez he.

' Now don't go to say I 'm the friend of oppression,
 But keep all your spare breath fer coolin' your broth,
Fer I ollers hev strove (at least thet 's my impression)
 To make cussed free with the rights o' the North,'
  Sez John C. Calhoun, sez he ;—
   ' Yes,' sez Davis o' Miss.,
   ' The perfection o' bliss
  Is in skinnin' thet same old coon,' sez he.

' Slavery 's a thing thet depends on complexion,
 It 's God's law thet fetters on black skins don't chafe ;
Ef brains wuz to settle it (horrid reflection !)
 Wich of our onnable body 'd be safe ? '
  Sez John C. Calhoun, sez he ;—
   Sez Mister Hannegan,
   Afore he began agin,
  ' Thet exception is quite oppertoon,' sez he.

' Gen'nle Cass, Sir, you need n't be twitchin' your collar,
 Your merit 's quite clear by the dut on your knees,
At the North we don't make no distinctions o' color ;
 You can all take a lick at our shoes wen you please,'
  Sez John C. Calhoun, sez he ;—
   Sez Mister Jarnagin,
   ' They wunt hev to larn agin,
  They all on 'em know the old toon,' sez he.

' The slavery question aint no ways bewilderin'.
 North an' South hev one int'rest, it 's plain to a glance ;
No'thern men, like us patriarchs, don't sell their childrin,
 But they *du* sell themselves, ef they git a good chance,'
  Sez John C. Calhoun, sez he ;—
   Sez Atherton here,
   ' This is gittin' severe,
  I wish I could dive like a loon,' sez he.

' It 'll break up the Union, this talk about freedom,
 An' your fact'ry gals (soon ez we split) 'll make head,
An' gittin' some Miss chief or other to lead 'em,
 'll go to work raisin' promiscoous Ned,'

Sez John C. Calhoun, sez he ; —
    ' Yes, the North,' sez Colquitt,
    ' Ef we Southeners all quit,
Would go down like a busted balloon,' sez he.

' Jest look wut is doin', wut annyky's brewin'
    In the beautiful clime o' the olive an' vine,
All the wise aristoxy's a tumblin' to ruin,
    An' the sankylots drorin' an' drinkin' their wine,'
    Sez John C. Calhoun, sez he ; —
       ' Yes,' sez Johnson, ' in France
       They 're beginnin' to dance
Beëlzebub's own rigadoon,' sez he.

' The South 's safe enough, it don't feel a mite skeery,
    Our slaves in their darkness an' dut air tu blest
Not to welcome with proud hallylugers the cry
    Wen our eagle kicks yourn from the naytional nest,'
    Sez John C. Calhoun, sez he ; —
       ' O,' sez Westcott o' Florida,
       ' Wut treason is horrider
Then our priv'leges tryin' to proon ? ' sez he.

' It 's 'coz they 're so happy, thet, wen crazy sarpints
    Stick their nose in our bizness, we git so darned riled ;
We think it 's our dooty to give pooty sharp hints,
    Thet the last crumb of Edin on airth sha' n't be spiled,'
    Sez John C. Calhoun, sez he ; —
       ' Ah,' sez Dixon H. Lewis,
       ' It perfectly true is
Thet slavery 's airth 's grettest boon,' sez he.

[It was said of old time, that riches have wings ; and, though this be not applicable in a literal strictness to the wealth of our patriarchal brethren of the South, yet it is clear that their possessions have legs, and an unaccountable propensity for using them in a northerly direction. I marvel that the grand jury of Washington did not find a true bill against the North Star for aiding and abetting Drayton and Sayres. It would have been quite of a piece with the intelligence displayed by the South on other questions connected with slavery. I think that no ship of state was ever freighted with a more veritable Jonah than this same domestic institution of ours. Mephistopheles himself could not feign so bitterly, so satirically sad a sight as this of three millions of human beings crushed beyond help or hope by this one mighty argument,—*Our fathers knew no better !* Nevertheless, it is the unavoidable destiny of Jonahs to be cast overboard sooner or later. Or shall we try the experiment of hiding our Jonah in a safe place, that none may lay hands on him to make jetsam of him ? Let us, then, with equal forethought and wisdom, lash ourselves to the anchor, and await, in pious confidence, the certain result. Perhaps our suspicious passenger is no Jonah after all, being black. For it is well known that a superintending Providence made a kind of sandwich of Ham and his descendants, to be devoured by the Caucasian race.

In God's name, let all, who hear nearer and nearer the hungry moan of the storm and the growl of the breakers, speak out ! But, alas ! we have no right to interfere. If a man pluck an apple of mine, he shall be in danger of the justice ; but if he steal my brother, I must be silent. Who says this? Our Constitution, consecrated by the callous consuetude of sixty years, and grasped in triumphant argument by the left hand of him whose right hand clutches the clotted slave-whip. Justice, venerable with the undethronable majesty of countless æons, says,—SPEAK! The Past, wise with the sorrows and desolations of ages, from amid her shattered fanes and wolfhousing palaces, echoes,—SPEAK! Nature, through her thousand trumpets of freedom, her stars, her sunrises, her seas, her winds, her cataracts, her mountains blue with cloudy pines, blows jubilant encouragement, and cries,—SPEAK! From the soul's trembling abysses the still, small voice not vaguely murmurs,—SPEAK! But, alas! the Constitution and the Honourable Mr. Bagowind, M. C., say—BE DUMB!

It occurs to me to suggest, as a topic of inquiry in this connexion, whether, on that momentous occasion when the goats and the sheep shall be parted, the Constitution and the Honourable Mr. Bagowind, M. C., will be expected to take their places on the left as our hircine vicars.

> *Quid sum miser tunc dicturus?*
> *Quem patronum rogaturus?*

There is a point where toleration sinks into sheer baseness and poltroonery. The toleration of the worst leads us to look on what is barely better as good enough, and to worship what is only moderately good. Woe to that man, or that nation, to whom mediocrity has become an ideal!

Has our experiment of self-government succeeded, if it barely manage to *rub and go?* Here, now, is a piece of barbarism which Christ and the nineteenth century say shall cease, and which Messrs. Smith, Brown, and others say shall *not* cease. I would by no means deny the eminent respectability of these gentlemen, but I confess, that, in such a wrestling-match, I cannot help having my fears for them.

Discite justitiam, moniti, et non temnere divos.

H. W.]

No. VI.

THE PIOUS EDITOR'S CREED

[AT the special instance of Mr. Biglow, I preface the following satire with an extract from a sermon preached during the past summer, from Ezekiel xxxiv. 2 : ' Son of man, prophesy against the shepherds of Israel.' Since the Sabbath on which this discourse was delivered, the editor of the ' Jaalam Independent Blunderbuss' has unaccountably absented himself from our house of worship.

' I know of no so responsible position as that of the public journalist. The editor of our day bears the same relation to his time that the clerk bore to the age before the invention of printing. Indeed, the position which he holds is that which the clergyman should hold even now. But the clergyman chooses to walk off to the extreme edge of the world, and to throw such seed as he has clear over into that darkness which he calls the Next Life. As if *next* did not mean *nearest*, and as if any life were nearer than that immediately present one which boils and eddies all around him at the caucus, the ratification meeting, and the polls! Who taught him to exhort men to prepare for eternity, as for some future era of which the present forms no integral part? The furrow which Time is even now turning runs through the Everlasting, and in that must he plant, or nowhere. Yet he would fain believe and teach that we are *going* to have more of eternity than we have now. This *going* of his is like that of the auctioneer, on which *gone* follows before we have made up our minds to bid,—in which manner, not three months back, I lost an excellent copy of Chappelow on Job. So it has come to pass that the preacher, instead of being a living force, has faded into an emblematic figure at christenings, weddings, and funerals. Or, if he exercise any other function, it is as keeper and feeder of certain theologic dogmas, which, when occasion offers, he unkennels with a *staboy!* "to bark and bite as 't is their nature to," whence that reproach of *odium theologicum* has arisen.

' Meanwhile, see what a pulpit the editor mounts daily, sometimes with a congregation of fifty thousand within reach of his voice, and never so much as a nodder, even, among them! And from what a Bible can he choose his text,—a Bible which needs no translation, and which no priestcraft can shut and clasp from the laity,—the open volume of the world, upon which, with a pen of sunshine or destroying fire, the inspired Present is even now writing the annals of God! Methinks the editor who should understand his calling, and be equal thereto, would truly deserve that title of ποιμὴν λαῶν, which Homer bestows upon princes.

He would be the Moses of our nineteenth century ; and whereas the old Sinai, silent now, is but a common mountain stared at by the elegant tourist and crawled over by the hammering geologist, he must find his tables of the new law here among factories and cities in this Wilderness of Sin (Numbers xxxiii. 12) called Progress of Civilization, and be the captain of our Exodus into the Canaan of a truer social order.

‘ Nevertheless, our editor will not come so far within even the shadow of Sinai as Mahomet did, but chooses rather to construe Moses by Joe Smith. He takes up the crook, not that the sheep may be fed, but that he may never want a warm woollen suit and a joint of mutton.

Immemor, O, fidei, pecorumque oblite tuorum!

For which reason I would derive the name *editor* not so much from *edo*, to publish, as from *edo*, to eat, that being the peculiar profession to which he esteems himself called. He blows up the flames of political discord for no other occasion than that he may thereby handily boil his own pot. I believe there are two thousand of these mutton-loving shepherds in the United States, and of these, how many have even the dimmest perception of their immense power, and the duties consequent thereon ? Here and there, haply, one. Nine hundred and ninety-nine labour to impress upon the people the great principles of *Tweedledum*, and other nine hundred and ninety-nine preach with equal earnestness the gospel according to *Tweedledee.*’—H. W.]

I du believe in Freedom’s cause,
　Ez fur away ez Payris is ;
I love to see her stick her claws
　In them infarnal Phayrisees ;
It ’s wal enough agin a king
　To dror resolves an’ triggers,—
But libbaty ’s a kind o’ thing
　Thet don’t agree with niggers.

I du believe the people want
　A tax on teas an’ coffees,
Thet nothin’ aint extravygunt,—
　Purvidin’ I ’m in office ;
Fer I hev loved my country sence
　My eye-teeth filled their sockets,
An’ Uncle Sam I reverence,
　Partic’larly his pockets.

I du believe in *any* plan
　O’ levyin’ the taxes,
Ez long ez, like a lumberman,
　I git jest wut I axes ;
I go free-trade thru thick an’ thin,
　Because it kind o’ rouses
The folks to vote,—an’ keeps us in
　Our quiet custom-houses.

I du believe it ’s wise an’ good
　To sen’ out furrin missions,
Thet is, on sartin understood
　An’ orthydox conditions ;—
I mean nine thousan’ dolls. per ann.,
　Nine thousan’ more fer outfit,
An’ me to recommend a man
　The place ’ould jest about fit.

I du believe in special ways
　O’ prayin’ an’ convartin’ ;
The bread comes back in many days,
　An’ buttered, tu, fer sartin ;
I mean in preyin’ till one busts
　On wut the party chooses,
An’ in convartin’ public trusts
　To very privit uses.

I du believe hard coin the stuff
　Fer ’lectioneers to spout on ;
The people ’s ollers soft enough
　To make hard money out on ;
Dear Uncle Sam pervides fer his,
　An’ gives a good-sized junk to all,—
I don’t care *how* hard money is,
　Ez long ez mine ’s paid punctooal.

I du believe with all my soul
　In the gret Press’s freedom,
To pint the people to the goal
　An’ in the traces lead ’em ;
Palsied the arm thet forges yokes
　At my fat contracts squintin’,
An’ withered be the nose thet pokes
　Inter the gov’ment printin’ !

I du believe thet I should give
　Wut ’s his’n unto Cæsar,
Fer it ’s by him I move an’ live,
　Frum him my bread an’ cheese air ;

I du believe thet all o' me
Doth bear his superscription,—
Will, conscience, honour, honesty,
An' things o' thet description.

I du believe in prayer an' praise
To him thet hez the grantin'
O' jobs,—in every thin' thet pays,
But most of all in CANTIN';
This doth my cup with marcies fill,
This lays all thought o' sin to rest,
I *don't* believe in princerple,
But O, I *du* in interest.

I du believe in bein' this
Or thet, ez it may happen
One way or t' other hendiest is
To ketch the people nappin';
It aint by princerples nor men
My preudunt course is steadied,—
I scent wich pays the best, an' then
Go into it baldheaded,

I du believe thet holdin' slaves
Comes nat'ral to a Presidunt,
Let 'lone the rowdedow it saves
To hev a wal-broke precedunt;
Fer any office, small or gret,
I could n't ax with no face,
Without I 'd ben, thru dry an' wet,
Th' unrizzest kind o' doughface.

I du believe wutever trash
'll keep the people in blindness,—
Thet we the Mexicuns can thrash
Right inter brotherly kindness,
Thet bombshells, grape, an' powder
'n' ball
Air good-will's strongest magnets,
Thet peace, to make it stick at all,
Must be druv in with bagnets.

In short, I firmly du believe
In Humbug generally,
Fer it 's a thing thet I perceive
To hev a solid vally;
This heth my faithful shepherd ben,
In pasturs sweet heth led me,
An' this'll keep the people green
To feed ez they hev fed me.

[I subjoin here another passage from my
before-mentioned discourse.

' Wonderful, to him that has eyes to see
it rightly, is the newspaper. To me, for
example, sitting on the critical front bench
of the pit, in my study here in Jaalam, the
advent of my weekly journal is as that of
a strolling theatre, or rather of a puppet-
show, on whose stage, narrow as it is, the
tragedy, comedy, and farce of life are played
in little. Behold the whole huge earth sent
to me hebdomadally in a brown-paper
wrapper!

' Hither, to my obscure corner, by wind
or steam, on horseback or dromedary-back,
in the pouch of the Indian runner, or clicking over the magnetic wires, troop all the
famous performers from the four quarters
of the globe. Looked at from a point of
criticism, tiny puppets they seem all, as the
editor sets up his booth upon my desk and
officiates as showman. Now I can truly see
how little and transitory is life. The earth
appears almost as a drop of vinegar, on
which the solar microscope of the imagination must be brought to bear in order to
make out anything distinctly. That ani-
malcule there, in the pea-jacket, is Louis
Philippe, just landed on the coast of England. That other, in the grey surtout and
cocked hat, is Napoleon Bonaparte Smith,
assuring France that she need apprehend
no interference from him in the present
alarming juncture. At that spot, where you
seem to see a speck of something in motion,
is an immense mass-meeting. Look sharper,
and you will see a mite brandishing his
mandibles in an excited manner. That is
the great Mr. Soandso, defining his position
amid tumultuous and irrepressible cheers.
That infinitesimal creature, upon whom
some score of others, as minute as he, are
gazing in open-mouthed admiration, is a
famous philosopher, expounding to a select
audience their capacity for the Infinite.
That scarce discernible pufflet of smoke and
dust is a revolution. That speck there is
a reformer, just arranging the lever with
which he is to move the world. And lo, there
creeps forward the shadow of a skeleton
that blows one breath between its grinning
teeth, and all our distinguished actors are
whisked off the slippery stage into the dark
Beyond.

' Yes, the little show-box has its solemner
suggestions. Now and then we catch a
glimpse of a grim old man, who lays down
a scythe and hour-glass in the corner while
he shifts the scenes. There, too, in the dim

background, a weird shape is ever delving. Sometimes he leans upon his mattock, and gazes, as a coach whirls by, bearing the newly married on their wedding jaunt, or glances carelessly at a babe brought home from christening. Suddenly (for the scene grows larger and larger as we look) a bony hand snatches back a performer in the midst of his part, and him, whom yesterday two infinities (past and future) would not suffice, a handful of dust is enough to cover and silence forever. Nay, we see the same flesh-less fingers opening to clutch the showman himself, and guess, not without a shudder, that they are lying in wait for spectator also.

'Think of it: for three dollars a year I buy a season-ticket to this great Globe Theatre, for which God would write the dramas (only that we like farces, spectacles, and the tragedies of Apollyon better), whose scene-shifter is Time, and whose curtain is rung down by Death.

'Such thoughts will occur to me some-times as I am tearing off the wrapper of my newspaper. Then suddenly that other-wise too often vacant sheet becomes in-vested for me with a strange kind of awe. Look! deaths and marriages, notices of inventions, discoveries, and books, lists of promotions, of killed, wounded, and missing, news of fires, accidents, of sudden wealth and as sudden poverty;—I hold in my hand the ends of myriad invisible electric con-ductors, along which tremble the joys, sor-rows, wrongs, triumphs, hopes, and despairs of as many men and women everywhere. So that upon that mood of mind which seems to isolate me from mankind as a spectator of their puppet-pranks, another supervenes, in which I feel that I, too, un-known and unheard of, am yet of some import to my fellows. For, through my newspaper here, do not families take pains to send me, an entire stranger, news of a death among them? Are not here two who would have me know of their marriage? And, strangest of all, is not this singular person anxious to have me informed that he has received a fresh supply of Dimitry Bruisgins? But to none of us does the Present continue miraculous (even if for a moment discerned as such). We glance carelessly at the sunrise, and get used to Orion and the Pleiades. The wonder wears off, and to-morrow this sheet, in which a vision was let down to me from Heaven, shall be the wrappage to a bar of soap or the platter for a beggar's broken victuals.'—H. W.]

No. VII.

A LETTER

FROM A CANDIDATE FOR THE PRE-SIDENCY IN ANSWER TO SUTTIN QUESTIONS PROPOSED BY MR. HOSEA BIGLOW, INCLOSED IN A NOTE FROM MR. BIGLOW TO S. H. GAY, ESQ., EDITOR OF THE NATIONAL ANTI-SLAVERY STANDARD.

[CURIOSITY may be said to be the quality which pre-eminently distinguishes and se-gregates man from the lower animals. As we trace the scale of animated nature down-ward, we find this faculty (as it may truly be called) of the mind diminished in the savage, and quite extinct in the brute. The first object which civilized man pro-poses to himself I take to be the finding out whatsoever he can concerning his neigh-bours. *Nihil humanum a me alienum puto;* I am curious about even John Smith. The desire next in strength to this (an opposite pole, indeed, of the same magnet) is that of communicating the unintelligence we have carefully picked up.

Men in general may be divided into the inquisitive and the communicative. To the first class belong Peeping Toms, eaves-droppers, navel-contemplating Brahmins, metaphysicians, travellers, Empedocleses, spies, the various societies for promoting Rhinothism, Columbuses, Yankees, dis-coverers, and men of science, who present themselves to the mind as so many marks of interrogation wandering up and down the world, or sitting in studies and labora-tories. The second class I should again subdivide into four. In the first subdivision I would rank those who have an itch to tell us about themselves,—as keepers of diaries, insignificant persons generally, Montaignes, Horace Walpoles, autobiographers, poets. The second includes those who are anxious to impart information concerning other people,—as historians, barbers, and such. To the third belong those who labour to give us intelligence about nothing at all,—as novelists, political orators, the large ma-jority of authors, preachers, lecturers, and the like. In the fourth come those who are communicative from motives of public be-nevolence,—as finders of mares'-nests and bringers of ill news. Each of us two-legged fowls without feathers embraces all these subdivisions in himself to a greater or less degree, for none of us so much as lays an egg, or incubates a chalk one, but straightway the whole barnyard shall know it by our cackle or our cluck. *Omnibus hoc vitium est.* There are different grades in all these classes. One will turn his telescope toward a back-yard, another toward Uranus; one will tell you that he dined with Smith, another that he supped with Plato. In one particular, all men may be considered as belonging to the first grand division, inasmuch as they all seem equally desirous of discovering the mote in their neighbour's eye.

To one or another of these species every human being may safely be referred. I think it beyond a peradventure that Jonah prosecuted some inquiries into the digestive apparatus of whales, and that Noah sealed up a letter in an empty bottle, that news in regard to him might not be wanting in case of the worst. They had else been super or subter human. I conceive, also, that, as there are certain persons who continually peep and pry at the keyhole of that mysterious door through which, sooner or later, we all make our exits, so there are doubtless ghosts fidgeting and fretting on the other side of it, because they have no means of conveying back to this world the scraps of news they have picked up in that. For there is an answer ready somewhere to every question, the great law of *give and take* runs through all nature, and if we see a hook, we may be sure that an eye is waiting for it. I read in every face I meet a standing advertisement of information wanted in regard to A. B., or that the friends of C. D. can hear something to his disadvantage by application to such a one.

It was to gratify the two great passions of asking and answering that epistolary correspondence was first invented. Letters (for by this usurped title epistles are now commonly known) are of several kinds. First, there are those which are not letters at all,—as letters-patent, letters dimissory, letters enclosing bills, letters of administration, Pliny's letters, letters of diplomacy, of Cato, of Mentor, of Lords Lyttelton, Chesterfield, and Orrery, of Jacob Behmen, Seneca (whom St. Jerome includes in his list of sacred writers), letters from abroad, from sons in college to their fathers, letters of marque, and letters generally, which are in no wise letters of mark. Second, are real letters, such as those of Gray, Cowper, Walpole, Howell, Lamb, D. Y., the first letters from children (printed in staggering capitals), Letters from New York, letters of

credit, and others, interesting for the sake of the writer or the thing written. I have read also letters from Europe by a gentleman named Pinto, containing some curious gossip, and which I hope to see collected for the benefit of the curious. There are, besides, letters addressed to posterity,—as epitaphs, for example, written for their own monuments by monarchs, whereby we have lately become possessed of the names of several great conquerors and kings of kings, hitherto unheard of and still unpronounceable, but valuable to the student of the entirely dark ages. The letter which St. Peter sent to King Pepin in the year of grace 755, that of the Virgin to the magistrates of Messina, that of St. Gregory Thaumaturgus to the D—l, and that of this last-mentioned active police-magistrate to a nun of Girgenti, I would place in a class by themselves, as also the letters of candidates, concerning which I shall dilate more fully in a note at the end of the following poem. At present, *sat prata biberunt.* Only, concerning the shape of letters, they are all either square or oblong, to which general figures circular letters and round-robins also conform themselves.—H. W.]

DEER SIR its gut to be the fashun now to rite letters to the candid 8s and i wus chose at a publick Meetin in Jaalam to du wut wus nessary fur that town. i writ to 271 ginerals and gut ansers to 209. tha air called candid 8s but I don't see nothin candid about 'em. this here **1** wich I send wus thought satty's factory. I dunno as it's ushle to print Poscrips, but as all the ansers I got hed the saim, I sposed it wus best. times has gretly changed. Formaly to knock a man into a cocked hat wus to use him up, but now it ony gives him a chance fur the cheef madgustracy.—H. B.

DEAR SIR,—You wish to know my
notions
On sartin pints thet rile the land;
There's nothin' thet my natur so shuns
Ez bein' mum or underhand;
I 'm a straight-spoken kind o' creetur
Thet blurts right out wut's in his head,
An ef I 've one pecooler feetur,
It is a nose thet wunt be led.

So, to begin at the beginnin'
 An' come direcly to the pint,
I think the country 's underpinnin'
 Is some consid'ble out o' jint;
I aint agoin' to try your patience
 By tellin' who done this or thet,
I don't make no insinooations,
 I jest let on I smell a rat.

Thet is, I mean, it seems to me so,
 But, ef the public think I 'm wrong,
I wunt deny but wut I be so,—
 An', fact, it don't smell very strong;
My mind 's tu fair to lose its balance
 An' say wich party hez most sense;
There may be folks o' greater talence
 Thet can't set stiddier on the fence.

I 'm an eclectic; ez to choosin'
 'Twixt this an' thet, I 'm plaguy
  lawth;
I leave a side thet looks like losin',
 But (wile there 's doubt) I stick to
  both;
I stan' upon the Constitution,
 Ez preudunt statesmun say, who 've
  planned
A way to git the most profusion
 O' chances ez to *ware* they 'll stand.

Ez fer the war, I go agin it,—
 I mean to say I kind o' du,—
Thet is, I mean thet, bein' in it,
 The best way wuz to fight it thru;
Not but wut abstract war is horrid,
 I sign to thet with all my heart,—
But civlyzation *doos* git forrid
 Sometimes upon a powder-cart.

About thet darned Proviso matter
 I never hed a grain o' doubt,
Nor I aint one my sense to scatter
 So 'st no one could n't pick it
  out;
My love fer North an' South is equil,
 So I 'll jest answer plump an' frank,
No matter wut may be the sequil,—
 Yes, Sir, I *am* agin a Bank.

Ez to the answerin' o' questions,
 I 'm an off ox at bein' druv,
Though I aint one thet ary test shuns
 'll give our folks a helpin' shove;
Kind o' promiscoous I go it
 Fer the holl country, an' the ground
I take, ez nigh ez I can show it,
 Is pooty gen'ally all round.

I don't appruve o' givin' pledges;
 You 'd ough' to leave a feller free,
An' not go knockin' out the wedges
 To ketch his fingers in the tree;
Pledges air awfle breachy cattle
 Thet preudunt farmers don't turn
  out,—
Ez long 'z the people git their rattle,
 Wut is there fer 'm to grout about?

Ez to the slaves, there 's no confusion
 In *my* idees consarnin' them,—
I think they air an Institution,
 A sort of—yes, jest so,—ahem:
Do *I* own any? Of my merit
 On thet pint you yourself may
  jedge;
All is, I never drink no sperit,
 Nor I haint never signed no pledge.

Ez to my princerples, I glory
 In hevin' nothin' o' the sort;
I aint a Wig, I aint a Tory,
 I 'm jest a candidate, in short;
Thet 's fair an' square an' parpendicler,
 But, ef the Public cares a fig
To hev me an' thin' in particler,
 Wy, I 'm a kind o' peri-Wig.

P. S.

Ez we 're a sort o' privateerin',
 O' course, you know, it 's sheer an'
  sheer,
An' there is sutthin' wuth your
  hearin'
 I 'll mention in *your* privit ear;
Ef you git *me* inside the White House,
 Your head with ile I 'll kin' o' 'nint
By gittin' *you* inside the Light-house
 Down to the eend o' Jaalam Pint.

An' ez the North hez took to brustlin'
  At bein' scrouged frum off the roost,
I 'll tell ye wut 'll save all tusslin'
  An' give our side a harnsome
    boost,—
Tell 'em thet on the Slavery question
  I 'm RIGHT, although to speak I 'm
    lawth ;
This gives you a safe pint to rest on,
  An' leaves me frontin' South by
    North.

[And now of epistles candidatial, which are of two kinds,—namely, letters of acceptance, and letters definitive of position. Our republic, on the eve of an election, may safely enough be called a republic of letters. Epistolary composition becomes then an epidemic, which seizes one candidate after another, not seldom cutting short the thread of political life. It has come to such a pass, that a party dreads less the attacks of its opponents than a letter from its candidate. *Litera scripta manet*, and it will go hard if something bad cannot be made of it. General Harrison, it is well understood, was surrounded, during his candidacy, with the *cordon sanitaire* of a vigilance committee. No prisoner in Spielberg was ever more cautiously deprived of writing materials. The soot was scraped carefully from the chimney-places ; outposts of expert rifle-shooters rendered it sure death for any goose (who came clad in feathers) to approach within a certain limited distance of North Bend ; and all domestic fowls about the premises were reduced to the condition of Plato's original man. By these precautions the General was saved. *Parva componere magnis*, I remember, that, when party-spirit once ran high among my people, upon occasion of the choice of a new deacon, I, having my preferences, yet not caring too openly to express them, made use of an innocent fraud to bring about that result which I deemed most desirable. My stratagem was no other than the throwing a copy of the Complete Letter-Writer in the way of the candidate whom I wished to defeat. He caught the infection, and addressed a short note to his constituents, in which the opposite party detected so many and so grave improprieties (he had modelled it upon the letter of a young lady accepting a proposal of marriage), that he not only lost his election, but, falling under a suspicion of Sabellianism and I know not what (the widow Endive assured me that he was a Paralipomenon, to her certain knowledge), was forced to leave the town. Thus it is that the letter killeth.

The object which candidates propose to themselves in writing is to convey no meaning at all. And here is a quite unsuspected pitfall into which they successively plunge headlong. For it is precisely in such cryptographies that mankind are prone to seek for and find a wonderful amount and variety of significance. *Omne ignotum pro mirifico.* How do we admire at the antique world striving to crack those oracular nuts from Delphi, Hammon, and elsewhere, in only one of which can I so much as surmise that any kernel had ever lodged ; that, namely, wherein Apollo confessed that he was mortal. One Didymus is, moreover, related to have written six thousand books on the single subject of grammar, a topic rendered only more tenebrific by the labours of his successors, and which seems still to possess an attraction for authors in proportion as they can make nothing of it. A singular loadstone for theologians, also, is the Beast in the Apocalypse, whereof, in the course of my studies, I have noted two hundred and three several interpretations, each lethiferal to all the rest. *Non nostrum est tantas componere lites*, yet I have myself ventured upon a two hundred and fourth, which I embodied in a discourse preached on occasion of the demise of the late usurper, Napoleon Bonaparte, and which quieted, in a large measure, the minds of my people. It is true that my views on this important point were ardently controverted by Mr. Shearjashub Holden, the then preceptor of our academy, and in other particulars a very deserving and sensible young man, though possessing a somewhat limited knowledge of the Greek tongue. But his heresy struck down no deep root, and, he having been lately removed by the hand of Providence, I had the satisfaction of reaffirming my cherished sentiments in a sermon preached upon the Lord's day immediately succeeding his funeral. This might seem like taking an unfair advantage, did I not add that he had made provision in his last will (being celibate) for the publication of a posthumous tractate in support of his own dangerous opinions.

I know of nothing in our modern times which approaches so nearly to the ancient oracle as the letter of a Presidential candidate. Now, among the Greeks, the eating of beans was strictly forbidden to all such as had it in mind to consult those expert amphibologists, and this same prohibition on the part of Pythagoras to his disciples is understood to imply an abstinence from politics, beans having been used as ballots. That other explication, *quod videlicet sensus eo cibo obtundi existimaret*, though supported *pugnis et calcibus* by many of the learned, and not wanting the countenance of Cicero, is confuted by the larger experience of New England. On the whole, I think it safer to apply here the rule of interpretation which now generally obtains in regard to antique cosmogonies, myths, fables, proverbial expressions, and knotty points generally, which is, to find a common-sense meaning, and then select whatever can be imagined the most opposite thereto. In this way we arrive at the conclusion, that the Greeks objected to the questioning of candidates. And very properly, if, as I conceive, the chief point be not to discover what a person in that position is, or what he will do, but whether he can be elected. *Vos exemplaria Græca nocturna versate manu, versate diurna.*

But, since an imitation of the Greeks in this particular (the asking of questions being one chief privilege of freemen) is hardly to be hoped for, and our candidates will answer, whether they are questioned or not, I would recommend that these ante-electionary dialogues should be carried on by symbols, as were the diplomatic correspondences of the Scythians and Macrobii, or confined to the language of signs, like the famous interview of Panurge and Goatsnose. A candidate might then convey a suitable reply to all committees of inquiry by closing one eye, or by presenting them with a phial of Egyptian darkness to be speculated upon by their respective constituencies. These answers would be susceptible of whatever retrospective construction the exigencies of the political campaign might seem to demand, and the candidate could take his position on either side of the fence with entire consistency. Or, if letters must be written, profitable use might be made of the Dighton rock hieroglyphic or the cuneiform script, every fresh decipherer of which is enabled to educe a different meaning, whereby a sculptured stone or two supplies us, and will probably continue to supply posterity, with a very vast and various body of authentic history. For even the briefest epistle in the ordinary chirography is dangerous. There is scarce any style so compressed that superfluous words may not be detected in it. A severe critic might curtail that famous brevity of Cæsar's by two thirds, drawing his pen through the supererogatory *veni* and *vidi.* Perhaps, after all, the surest footing of hope is to be found in the rapidly increasing tendency to demand less and less of qualification in candidates. Already have statesmanship, experience, and the possession (nay, the profession, even) of principles been rejected as superfluous, and may not the patriot reasonably hope that the ability to write will follow? At present, there may be death in pot-hooks as well as pots, the loop of a letter may suffice for a bow-string, and all the dreadful heresies of Antislavery may lurk in a flourish.—H. W.]

No. VIII.

A SECOND LETTER FROM
B. SAWIN, ESQ.

[IN the following epistle, we behold Mr. Sawin returning, a *miles emeritus*, to the bosom of his family. *Quantum mutatus!* The good Father of us all had doubtless intrusted to the keeping of this child of his certain faculties of a constructive kind. He had put in him a share of that vital force, the nicest economy of every minute atom of which is necessary to the perfect development of Humanity. He had given him a brain and heart, and so had equipped his soul with the two strong wings of knowledge and love, whereby it can mount to hang its nest under the eaves of heaven. And this child, so dowered, he had intrusted to the keeping of his vicar, the State. How stands the account of that stewardship? The State, or Society (call her by what name you will), had taken no manner of thought of him till she saw him swept out into the street, the pitiful leavings of last night's debauch, with cigar-ends, lemon-parings, tobacco-quids, slops, vile stenches, and the whole loathsome next-morning of the bar-room,—an own child of the Almighty God! I remember him as he was brought to be christened, a ruddy, rugged babe; and now there he wallows, reeking, seething,—the dead corpse, not of a man, but of a soul,—a putrefying lump, horrible for the life that is in it. Comes the wind of heaven, that good Samaritan, and parts the hair upon his forehead, nor is too nice to kiss those parched, cracked lips; the morning opens upon him her eyes full of pitying sunshine, the sky yearns down to him,—and there he lies fermenting. O sleep! let me not profane thy holy name by calling that stertorous unconsciousness a slumber! By and by comes along the State, God's vicar. Does she say,—' My poor, forlorn foster-child! Behold here a force which I will make dig and plant and build for me'? Not so, but,—' Here is a recruit ready-made to my hand, a piece of destroying energy lying unprofitably idle.' So she claps an ugly grey suit on him, puts a musket in his grasp, and sends him off, with Gubernatorial and other god-speeds, to do duty as a destroyer.

I made one of the crowd at the last Mechanics' Fair, and, with the rest, stood gazing in wonder at a perfect machine, with its soul of fire, its boiler-heart that sent the hot blood pulsing along the iron arteries, and its thews of steel. And while I was admiring the adaptation of means to end, the harmonious involutions of contrivance, and the never-bewildered complexity, I saw a grimed and greasy fellow, the imperious engine's lackey and drudge, whose sole office was to let fall, at intervals, a drop or two of oil upon a certain joint. Then my soul said within me, See there a piece of mechanism to which that other you marvel at is but as the rude first effort of a child,—a force which not merely suffices to set a few wheels in motion, but which can send an impulse all through the infinite future,—a contrivance, not for turning out pins, or stitching buttonholes, but for making Hamlets and Lears. And yet this thing of iron shall be housed, waited on, guarded from rust and dust, and it shall be a crime but so much as to scratch it with a pin; while the other, with its fire of God in it, shall be buffeted hither and thither, and finally sent carefully a thousand miles to be the target for a Mexican cannon-ball. Unthrifty Mother State! My heart burned within me for pity and indignation, and I renewed this covenant with my own soul,—*In aliis mansuetus ero, at, in blasphemiis contra Christum, non ita.*—H. W.]

I SPOSE you wonder ware I be; I can't tell, fer the soul o' me,
Exacly ware I be myself,—meanin' by thet the holl o' me.
Wen I left hum, I hed two legs, an' they worn't bad ones neither
(The scaliest trick they ever played wuz bringin' on me hither),
Now one on 'em 's I dunno ware; —they thought I wuz adyin',
An' sawed it off, because they said 't wuz kin' o' mortifyin';
I 'm willin' to believe it wuz, an' yit I don't see, nuther,
Wy one shoud take to feelin' cheap a minnit sooner 'n t' other,
Sence both wuz equilly to blame; but things is ez they be;
It took on so they took it off, an' thet 's enough fer me: 10
There 's one good thing, though, to be said about my wooden new one,—
The liquor can't git into it ez 't used to in the true one;
So it saves drink; an' then, besides, a feller can't beg
A gretter blessin' then to hev one ollers sober peg;
It 's true a chap 's in want o' two fer follerin' a drum,
But all the march I' m up to now is jest to Kingdom Come.

I 've lost one eye, but thet 's a loss it 's easy to supply
Out o' the glory that I 've gut, fer thet is all my eye;
An' one is big enough, I guess, by diligently usin' it,
To see all I shall ever git by way o' pay fer losin' it;   20
Off'cers I notice, who git paid fer all our thumps an' kickins,
Du wal by keepin' single eyes arter the fattest pickins;
So, ez the eye 's put fairly out, I 'll larn to go without it,
An' not allow *myself* to be no gret put out about it.
Now, le' me see, thet is n't all; I used, 'fore leavin' Jaalam,
To count things on my finger-eends, but sutthin' seems to ail 'em:
Ware 's my left hand? O, darn it, yes, I recollect wut 's come on 't;
I haint no left arm but my right, an' thet 's gut jest a thumb on 't;

It aint so hendy ez it wuz to cal'late a sum on 't.
I've hed some ribs broke,—six (I b'lieve),—I haint kep' no account on 'em ;
Wen pensions git to be the talk, I'll settle the amount on 'em.   31
An' now I'm speakin' about ribs, it kin' o' brings to mind
One thet I could n't never break,—the one I lef' behind ;
Ef you should see her, jest clear out the spout o' your invention
An' pour the longest sweetnin' in about an annooal pension,
An' kin' o' hint (in case, you know, the critter should refuse to be
Consoled) I aint so 'xpensive now to keep ez wut I used to be ;
There 's one arm less, ditto one eye, an' then the leg thet 's wooden
Can be took off an' sot away wenever ther 's a puddin'.

I spose you think I'm comin' back ez opperlunt ez thunder,   40
With shiploads o' gold images an' varus sorts o' plunder ;
Wal, 'fore I vullinteered, I thought this country wuz a sort o'
Canaan, a reg'lar Promised Land flowin' with rum an' water
Ware propaty growed up like time, without no cultivation,
An' gold wuz dug ez taters be among our Yankee nation,
Ware nateral advantages were pufficly amazin',
Ware every rock there wuz about with precious stuns wuz blazin',
Ware mill-sites filled the country up ez thick ez you could cram em'
An' desput rivers run about a beggin' folks to dam 'em ;
Then there were meetinhouses, tu, chockful o' gold an' silver   50
Thet you could take, an' no one could n't hand ye in no bill fer ;—
Thet 's wut I thought afore I went, thet 's wut them fellers told us
Thet stayed to hum an' speechified an' to the buzzards sold us ;
I thought thet gold-mines could be gut cheaper than Chiny asters,
An' see myself acomin' back like sixty Jacob Astors ;
But sech idees soon melted down an' did n't leave a grease-spot ;
I vow my holl sheer o' the spiles would n't come nigh a V spot ;
Although, most anywares we 've ben, you need n't break no locks,
Nor run no kin' o' risks, to fill your pocket full o' rocks.
I 'xpect I mentioned in my last some o' the nateral feeturs   60
O' this all-fiered buggy hole in th' way o' awfle creeturs,
But I fergut to name (new things to speak on so abounded)
How one day you 'll most die o' thust, an' 'fore the next git drownded.
The clymit seems to me jest like a teapot made o' pewter
Our Prudence hed, thet would n't pour (all she could du) to suit her ;
Fust place the leaves 'ould choke the spout, so 's not a drop 'ould dreen out,
Then Prude 'ould tip an' tip an' tip, till the holl kit bust clean out,
The kiver-hinge-pin bein' lost, tea-leaves an' tea an' kiver
'ould all come down *kerswosh !* ez though the dam broke in a river.
Jest so 't is here ; holl months there aint a day o' rainy weather,   70
An' jest ez th' officers 'ould be a layin' heads together
Ez t' how they 'd mix their drink at sech a milingtary deepot,—
'T would pour ez though the lid wuz off the everlastin' teapot.
The cons'quence is, thet I shall take, wen I 'm allowed to leave here,
One piece o' propaty along, an' thet 's the shakin' fever ;

It 's reggilar employment, though, an' thet aint thought to harm one,
Nor 't aint so tiresome ez it wuz with t' other leg an' arm on ;
An' it 's a consolation, tu, although it doos n't pay,
To hev it said you 're some gret shakes in any kin' o' way.
'T worn't very long, I tell ye wut, I thought o' fortin-makin',—   80
One day a reg'lar shiver-de-freeze, an' next ez good ez bakin',—
One day abrilin' in the sand, then smoth'rin' in the mashes,—
Git up all sound, be put to bed a mess o' hacks an' smashes,
But then, thinks I, at any rate there 's glory to be hed,—
Thet 's an investment, arter all, thet may n't turn out so bad ;
But somehow, wen we 'd fit an' licked, I ollers found the thanks
Gut kin' o' lodged afore they come ez low down ez the ranks ;
The Gin'rals gut the biggest sheer, the Cunnles next, an' so on,—
We never gut a blasted mite o' glory ez I know on ;
An' spose we hed, I wonder how you 're goin' to contrive its   90
Division so 's to give a piece to twenty thousand privits ;
Ef you should multiply by ten the portion o' the brav'st one,
You would n't git more 'n half enough to speak of on a grave-stun ;
We git the licks,—we 're jest the grist thet 's put into War's hoppers ;
Leftenants is the lowest grade thet helps pick up the coppers.
It may suit folks thet go agin a body with a soul in 't,
An' aint contented with a hide without a bagnet hole in 't ;
But glory is a kin' o' thing *I* sha' n't pursue no furder,
Coz thet 's the off'cers parquisite,—yourn 's on'y jest the murder.

Wal, arter I gin glory up, thinks I at least there 's one   100
Thing in the bills we aint hed yit, an' thet's the GLORIOUS FUN ;
Ef once we git to Mexico, we fairly may persume we
All day an' night shall revel in the halls o' Montezumy.
I 'll tell ye wut *my* revels wuz, an' see how you would like 'em ;
We never gut inside the hall : the nighest ever *I* come
Wuz stan'in' sentry in the sun (an', fact, it *seemed* a cent'ry)
A ketchin' smells o' biled an' roast thet come out thru the entry,
An' hearin' ez I sweltered thru my passes an' repasses,
A rat-tat-too o' knives an' forks, a clinkty-clink o' glasses :
I can't tell off the bill o' fare the Ginrals hed inside ;   110
All I know is, thet out o' doors a pair o' soles wuz fried,
An' not a hunderd miles away frum ware this child wuz posted,
A Massachusetts citizen wuz baked an' biled an' roasted ;
The on'y thing like revellin' thet ever come to me
Wuz bein' routed out o' sleep by thet darned revelee.

They say the quarrel 's settled now ; fer my part I 've some doubt on 't,
't 'll take more fish-skin than folks think to take the rile clean out on 't ;
At any rate I 'm so used up I can't do no more fightin',
The on'y chance thet 's left to me is politics or writin' ;
Now, ez the people 's gut to hev a milingtary man,   120
An' I aint nothin' else jest now, I 've hit upon a plan ;

The can'idatin' line, you know, 'ould suit me to a T,
An' ef I lose, 't wunt hurt my ears to lodge another flea ;
So I 'll set up ez can'idate fer any kin' o' office,
(I mean fer any thet includes good easy-cheers an' soffies ;
Fer ez tu runnin' fer a place ware work 's the time o' day,
You know thet 's wut I never did,—except the other way) ;
Ef it 's the Presidential cheer fer wich I 'd better run,
Wut two legs anywares about could keep up with my one ?
There aint no kin' o' quality in can'idates, it 's said,   130
So useful ez a wooden leg,—except a wooden head ;
There 's nothin' aint so poppylar—(wy, it 's a parfect sin
To think wut Mexico hez paid fer Santy Anny's pin ;)—
Then I haint gut no princerples, an', sence I wuz knee-high,
I never *did* hev any gret, ez you can testify ;
I 'm a decided peace-man, tu, an' go agin the war,—
Fer now the holl on 't 's gone an' past, wut is there to go *for ?*
Ef, wile you 're 'lectioneerin' round, some curus chaps should beg
To know my views o' state affairs, jest answer WOODEN LEG !
Ef they aint settisfied with thet, an' kin' o' pry an' doubt   140
An' ax fer sutthin' deffynit, jest say ONE EYE PUT OUT !
Thet kin' o' talk I guess you 'll find 'll answer to a charm,
An, wen you 're druv tu nigh the wall, hol' up my missin' arm ;
Ef they should nose round fer a pledge, put on a vartuous look
An' tell 'em thet 's precisely wut I never gin nor—took !

Then you can call me ' Timbertoes ',— thet 's wut the people likes ;
Sutthin' combinin' morril truth with phrases sech ez strikes ;
Some say the people 's fond 'o this, or thet, or wut you please,—
I tell ye wut the people want is jest correct idees ;
' Old Timbertoes,' you see, 's a creed it 's safe to be quite bold on,   150
There 's nothin' in 't the other side can any ways git hold on ;
It 's a good tangible idee, a sutthin' to embody
Thet valooable class o' men who look thru brandy-toddy ;
It gives a Party Platform, tu, jest level with the mind
Of all right-thinkin', honest folks thet mean to go it blind ;
Then there air other good hooraws to dror on ez you need 'em,
Sech ez the ONE-EYED SLARTERER, the BLOODY BIRDOFREDUM :
Them's wut takes hold o' folks thet think, ez well ez o' the masses,
An' makes you sartin o' the aid o' good men of all classes.

There 's one thing I 'm in doubt about ; in order to be Presidunt,   160
It 's absolutely ne'ssary to be a Southern residunt ;
The Constitution settles thet, an' also thet a feller
Must own a nigger o' some sort, jet black, or brown, or yeller.
Now I haint no objections agin particklar climes,
Nor agin ownin' anythin' (except the truth sometimes),
But, ez I haint no capital, up there among ye, maybe,
You might raise funds enough fer me to buy a low-priced baby,

An' then to suit the No'thern folks, who feel obleeged to say
They hate an' cuss the very thing they vote fer every day,
Say you 're assured I go full butt for Libbaty's diffusion   170
An' made the purchis on'y jest to spite the Institootion ;—
But, golly ! there 's the currier's hoss upon the pavement pawin' !
I 'll be more 'xplicit in my next.

                    Yourn,
                                BIRDOFREDUM SAWIN.

[We have now a tolerably fair chance of estimating how the balance-sheet stands between our returned volunteer and glory. Supposing the entries to be set down on both sides of the account in fractional parts of one hundred, we shall arrive at something like the following result :—

B. Sawin, Esq., in account with (Blank)
                    Glory.

Cr.			*Dr.*
By loss of one leg,	20	To one 675th	
„ do. one arm,	15	three cheers	
„ do. four fin-		in Faneuil	
gers, . . .	5	Hall, . . .	30
„ do. one eye	10	„ do. do. on oc-	
„ the breaking		casion of pre-	
of six ribs, .	6	sentation of	
„ having served		sword to Co-	
underColonel		lonel Wright,	25
Cushing one		„ one suit of	
month, . .	44	grey clothes	
		(ingeniously	
		unbecoming)	15
		To musical enter-	
		t a i n m e n t s	
		(drum and fife	
		six months), .	5
		„ one dinner af-	
		ter return .	1
		„ chance of pen-	
		sion, . . .	1
		„ privilege of	
		drawing long-	
		bow during	
		rest of natural	
		life, ...	23
E. E. 100			100

It would appear that Mr. Sawin found the actual feast curiously the reverse of the bill of fare advertised in Faneuil Hall and other places. His primary object seems to have been the making of his fortune. *Quæ-renda pecunia primum, virtus post nummos.* He hoisted sail for Eldorado, and ship-wrecked on Point Tribulation. *Quid non mortalia pectora cogis, auri sacra fames?* The speculation has sometimes crossed my mind, in that dreary interval of drought which intervenes between quarterly stipendiary showers, that Providence, by the creation of a money-tree, might have simplified wonderfully the sometimes perplexing problem of human life. We read of bread-trees, the butter for which lies ready-churned in Irish bogs. Milk-trees we are assured of in South America, and stout Sir John Hawkins testifies to water-trees in the Canaries. Boot-trees bear abundantly in Lynn and elsewhere ; and I have seen, in the entries of the wealthy, hat-trees with a fair show of fruit. A family-tree I once cultivated myself, and found therefrom but a scanty yield, and that quite tasteless and innutritious. Of trees bearing men we are not without examples ; as those in the park of Louis the Eleventh of France. Who has forgotten, moreover, that olive-tree, growing in the Athenian's back-garden, with its strange uxorious crop, for the general propagation of which, as of a new and precious variety, the philosopher Diogenes, hitherto uninterested in arboriculture, was so zealous ? In the *sylva* of our own Southern States, the females of my family have called my attention to the china-tree. Not to multiply examples, I will barely add to my list the birch-tree, in the smaller branches of which has been implanted so miraculous a virtue for communicating the Latin and Greek languages, and which may well, therefore, be classed among the trees producing necessaries of life,—*venerabile donum fatalis virgæ.* That money-trees existed in the golden age there want not prevalent reasons for our believing. For does not the old proverb, when it asserts that money does not grow on *every* bush, imply *a fortiori* that there were certain bushes which did produce it ? Again, there is another ancient saw to the effect that money is the *root* of all evil. From which two adages it may be safe to infer that the aforesaid species of tree first degenerated into a shrub, then absconded underground, and finally, in our iron age, vanished altogether. In favourable exposures it may be conjectured that a specimen or two survived to a great age, as in the garden of the Hesperides; and, indeed, what else could that tree in the Sixth Æneid have been, with a branch whereof the Trojan hero procured admission to a territory, for the entering of which money is a surer passport than to a certain other more profitable (too) foreign kingdom? Whether these speculations of mine have any force in them, or whether they will not rather, by most readers, be deemed impertinent to the matter in hand, is a question which I leave to the determination of an indulgent posterity. That there were, in more primitive and happier times, shops where money was sold,—and that, too, on credit and at a bargain,—I take to be matter of demonstration. For what but a dealer in this article was that Æolus who supplied Ulysses with motive-power for his fleet in bags? What that Ericus, King of Sweden, who is said to have kept the winds in his cap? what, in more recent times, those Lapland Nornas who traded in favourable breezes? All which will appear the more clearly when we consider, that, even to this day, *raising the wind* is proverbial for raising money, and that brokers and banks were invented by the Venetians at a later period.

And now for the improvement of this digression. I find a parallel to Mr. Sawin's fortune in an adventure of my own. For, shortly after I had first broached to myself the before-stated natural-historical and archæological theories, as I was passing, *hæc negotia penitus mecum revolvens*, through one of the obscure suburbs of our New England metropolis, my eye was attracted by these words upon a sign-board,—CHEAP CASH-STORE. Here was at once the confirmation of my speculations, and the substance of my hopes. Here lingered the fragment of a happier past, or stretched out the first tremulous organic filament of a more fortunate future. Thus glowed the distant Mexico to the eyes of Sawin, as he looked through the dirty pane of the recruiting-office window, or speculated from the summit of that mirage-Pisgah which the imps of the bottle are so cunning in raising up. Already had my Alnaschar-fancy (even during that first half-believing glance) expended in various useful directions the funds to be obtained by pledging the manu-

script of a proposed volume of discourses. Already did a clock ornament the tower of the Jaalam meeting-house, a gift appropriately, but modestly, commemorated in the parish and town records, both, for now many years, kept by myself. Already had my son Seneca completed his course at the University. Whether, for the moment, we may not be considered as actually lording it over those Baratarias with the viceroyalty of which Hope invests us, and whether we are ever so warmly housed as in our Spanish castles, would afford matter of argument. Enough that I found that sign-board to be no other than a bait to the trap of a decayed grocer. Nevertheless, I bought a pound of dates (getting short weight by reason of immense flights of harpy flies who pursued and lighted upon their prey even in the very scales), which purchase I made, not only with an eye to the little ones at home, but also as a figurative reproof of that too frequent habit of my mind, which, forgetting the due order of chronology, will often persuade me that the happy sceptre of Saturn is stretched over this Astræa-forsaken nineteenth century.

Having glanced at the ledger of Glory under the title *Sawin, B.*, let us extend our investigations, and discover if that instructive volume does not contain some charges more personally interesting to ourselves. I think we should be more economical of our resources, did we thoroughly appreciate the fact, that, whenever Brother Jonathan seems to be thrusting his hand into his own pocket, he is, in fact, picking ours. I confess that the late *muck* which the country has been running has materially changed my views as to the best method of raising revenue. If, by means of direct taxation, the bills for every extraordinary outlay were brought under our immediate eye, so that, like thrifty housekeepers, we could see where and how fast the money was going, we should be less likely to commit extravagances. At present, these things are managed in such a hugger-mugger way, that we know not what we pay for; the poor man is charged as much as the rich; and, while we are saving and scrimping at the spigot, the government is drawing off at the bung. If we could know that a part of the money we expend for tea and coffee goes to buy powder and balls, and that it is Mexican blood which makes the clothes on our backs more costly, it would set some of us athinking. During the present fall, I have often pictured to myself a government official entering my study and handing me the following bill :—

WASHINGTON, Sept. 30, 1848.

REV. HOMER WILBUR to **Uncle Samuel**,

Dr.

To his share of work done in Mexico
on partnership account, sundry
jobs, as below.

,, killing, maiming, and wounding about 5,000 Mexicans, . .	$ 2.00
,, slaughtering one woman carrying water to wounded, . . .	.10
,, extra work on two different Sabbaths (one bombardment and one assault), whereby the Mexicans were prevented from defiling themselves with the idolatries of high mass, . .	3.50
,, throwing an especially fortunate and Protestant bombshell into the Cathedral at Vera Cruz, whereby several female Papists were slain at the altar, . .	.50
,, his proportion of cash paid for conquered territory, . .	1.75
,, do. do. for conquering do. .	1.50
,, manuring do. with new superior compost called ' American Citizen,'	.50
,, extending the area of freedom and Protestantism, . . .	.01
,, glory, ...	.01
	$ 9.87

Immediate payment is requested.

N. B.   Thankful for former favours, U. S. requests a continuance of patronage.   Orders executed with neatness and dispatch. Terms as low as those of any other contractor for the same kind and style of work.

I can fancy the official answering my look of horror with,—' Yes, Sir, it looks like a high charge, Sir ; but in these days slaughtering is slaughtering.'   Verily, I would that every one understood that it was ; for it goes about obtaining money under the false pretence of being glory. For me, I have an imagination which plays me uncomfortable tricks.   It happens to me sometimes to see a slaughterer on his way home from his day's work, and forthwith my imagination puts a cocked-hat upon his head, and epaulettes upon his shoulders, and sets him up as a candidate for the Presidency.   So, also, on a recent public occasion, as the place assigned to

the ' Reverend Clergy ' is just behind that of ' Officers of the Army and Navy ' in processions, it was my fortune to be seated at the dinner-table over against one of these respectable persons.   He was arrayed as (out of his own profession) only kings, court-officers, and footmen are in Europe, and Indians in America.   Now what does my over-officious imagination but set to work upon him, strip him of his gay livery, and present him to me coatless, his trousers thrust into the tops of a pair of boots thick with clotted blood, and a basket on his arm out of which lolled a gore-smeared axe, thereby destroying my relish for the temporal mercies upon the board before me !— H. W.]

No. IX.

A THIRD LETTER FROM

B. SAWIN, ESQ.

[UPON the following letter slender comment will be needful.   In what river Selemnus has Mr. Sawin bathed, that he has become so swiftly oblivious of his former loves ?   From an ardent and (as befits a soldier) confident wooer of that coy bride, the popular favour, we see him subside of a sudden into the (I trust not jilted) Cincinnatus, returning to his plough with a goodly sized branch of willow in his hand ; figuratively returning, however, to a figurative plough, and from no profound affection for that honoured implement of husbandry (for which, indeed, Mr. Sawin never displayed any decided predilection), but in order to be gracefully summoned therefrom to more congenial labors.   It would seem that the character of the ancient Dictator had become part of the recognized stock of our modern political comedy, though, as our term of office extends to a quadrennial length, the parallel is not so minutely exact as could be desired.   It is sufficiently so, however, for purposes of scenic representation.   An humble cottage (if built of logs, the better) forms the Arcadian background of the stage.   This rustic paradise is labelled Ashland, Jaalam, North Bend, Marshfield, Kinderhook, or Bâton Rouge, as occasion demands.   Before the door stands a something with one handle (the other painted in proper perspective), which represents, in happy ideal vagueness, the plough.   To this the defeated candidate rushes with delirious joy, welcomed as a father by appropriate groups of happy labourers, or from it the successful one is torn with difficulty, sustained alone by a noble sense of public duty. Only I have observed, that, if the scene be laid at Baton Rouge or Ashland, the labourers are kept carefully in the background, and are heard to shout from behind the scenes in a singular tone resembling ululation, and accompanied by a sound not unlike vigorous clapping. This, however, may be artistically in keeping with the habits of the rustic population of those localities. The precise connexion between agricultural pursuits and statesmanship, I have not been able, after diligent inquiry, to discover. But, that my investigations may not be barren of all fruit, I will mention one curious statistical fact, which I consider thoroughly established, namely, that no real farmer ever attains practically beyond a seat in General Court, however theoretically qualified for more exalted station.

It is probable that some other prospec has been opened to Mr. Sawin, and that h has not made this great sacrifice withou some definite understanding in regard t a seat in the cabinet or a foreign mission It may be supposed that we of Jaalam wer not untouched by a feeling of villatic prid in beholding our townsman occupying s large a space in the public eye. And t me, deeply revolving the qualifications ne cessary to a candidate in these frugal times those of Mr. S. seemed peculiarly adapte to a successful campaign. The loss of a leg an arm, an eye, and four fingers reduce him so nearly to the condition of a *vox e prœterea nihil*, that I could think of nothing but the loss of his head by which his chanc could have been bettered. But since h has chosen to balk our suffrages, we mus content ourselves with what we can get remembering *lactucas non esse dandas, dun cardui sufficiant.*—H. W.]

I SPOSE you recollect thet I explained my gennle views
In the last billet thet I writ, 'way down frum Veery Cruze,
Jest arter I 'd a kind o' ben spontanously sot up
To run unannermously fer the Presidential cup ;
O' course it worn't no wish o' mine, 't wuz ferflely distressin',
But poppiler enthusiasm gut so almighty pressin'
Thet, though like sixty all along I fumed an' fussed an' sorrered,
There did n't seem no ways to stop their bringin' on me forrerd :
Fact is, they udged the matter so, I could n't help admittin'
The Father o' his Country's shoes no feet but mine 'ould fit in.   10
Besides the savin' o' the soles fer ages to succeed,
Seein' thet with one wannut foot, a pair 'd be more 'n I need ;
An', tell ye wut, them shoes 'll want a thund'rin sight o' patchin',
Ef this ere fashion is to last we 've gut into o' hatchin'
A pair o' second Washintons fer every new election,—
Though, fer ez number one 's consarned, I don't make no objection.

I wuz agoin' on to say thet wen at fust I saw
The masses would stick to 't I wuz the Country's father-'n-law
(They would ha' hed it *Father*, but I told 'em 't would n't du,
Coz thet wuz sutthin' of a sort they could n't split in tu,   20
An' Washinton hed hed the thing laid fairly to his door,
Nor dars n't say 't worn't his'n, much ez sixty year afore),
But 't aint no matter ez to thet ; wen I wuz nomernated,
'T worn't natur but wut I should feel consid'able elated,
An' wile the hooraw o' the thing wuz kind o' noo an' fresh,
I thought our ticket would ha' caird the country with a resh.

Sence I 've come hum, though, an' looked round, I think I seem to find
Strong argimunts ez thick ez fleas to make me change my mind ;

It 's clear to any one whose brain aint fur gone in a phthisis,
Thet hail Columby's happy land is goin' thru a crisis,   30
An' 't would n't noways du to hev the people's mind distracted
By bein' all to once by sev'ral pop'lar names attackted ;
'T would save holl haycartloads o' fuss an' three four months o' jaw,
Ef some illustrous paytriot should back out an' withdraw ;
So, ez I aint a crooked stick, jest like—like ole (I swow,
I dunno ez I know his name)—I 'll go back to my plough.

Wenever an Amerikin distinguished politishin
Begins to try et wut they call definin' his posishin,
Wal, I, fer one, feel sure he aint gut nothin' to define ;
It 's so nine cases out o' ten, but jest that tenth is mine ;   40
And 't aint no more 'n is proper 'n' right in sech a sitooation
To hint the course you think 'll be the savin' o' the nation ;
To funk right out o' p'lit'cal strife aint thought to be the thing,
Without you deacon off the toon you want your folks should sing ;
So I edvise the noomrous friends thet 's in one boat with me
To jest up killock, jam right down their hellum hard a lee,
Haul the sheets taut, an', laying out upon the Suthun tack,
Make fer the safest port they can, wich, *I* think, is Ole Zack.

Next thing you 'll want to know, I spose, wut argimunts I seem
To see thet makes me think this ere 'll be the strongest team ;   50
Fust place, I 've ben consid'ble round in bar-rooms an' saloons
Agetherin' public sentiment, 'mongst Demmercrats and Coons,
An' 't aint ve'y offen thet I meet a chap but wut goes in
Fer Rough an' Ready, fair an' square, hufs, taller, horns, an' skin ;
I don't deny but wut, fer one, ez fur ez I could see,
I did n't like at fust the Pheladelphy nomernee :
I could ha' pinted to a man thet wuz, I guess, a peg
Higher than him,—a soger, tu, an' with a wooden leg ;
But every day with more an' more o' Taylor zeal I'm burnin',
Seein' wich way the tide thet sets to office is aturnin' ;   60
Wy, into Bellers's we notched the votes down on three sticks,—
'T wuz Birdofredum *one*, Cass *aught*, an' Taylor *twenty-six*,
An' bein' the on'y canderdate thet wuz upon the ground,
They said 't wuz no more 'n right thet I should pay the drinks all round ;
Ef I 'd expected sech a trick, I would n't ha' cut my foot
By goin' an' votin' fer myself like a consumed coot ;
It did n't make no diff'rence, though ; I wish I may be cust,
Ef Bellers wuz n't slim enough to say he would n't trust !

Another pint thet influences the minds o' sober jedges
Is thet the Gin'ral hez n't gut tied hand an' foot with pledges ;   70
He hez n't told ye wut he is, an' so there aint no knowin'
But wut he may turn out to be the best there is agoin' ;
This, at the on'y spot thet pinched, the shoe directly eases,
Coz every one is free to 'xpect percisely wut he pleases :
I want free-trade ; you don't ; the Gin'ral is n't bound to neither ;—
I vote my way ; you, yourn ; an' both air sooted to a T there.

Ole Rough an' Ready, tu, 's a Wig, but without bein' ultry
(He 's like a holsome hayin' day, thet 's warm, but is n't sultry);
He 's jest wut I should call myself, a kin' o' *scratch* ez 't ware,
Thet aint exactly all a wig nor wholly your own hair;   80
I 've ben a Wig three weeks myself, jest o' this mod'rate sort,
An' don't find them an' Demmercrats so different ez I thought;
They both act pooty much alike, an' push an' scrouge an' cus;
They 're like two pickpockets in league fer Uncle Samwell's pus;
Each takes a side, an' then they squeeze the ole man in between 'em,
Turn all his pockets wrong side out an' quick ez lightnin' clean 'em;
To nary one on 'em I 'd trust a secon'-handed rail
No furder off 'an I could sling a bullock by the tail.

Webster sot matters right in thet air Mashfiel' speech o' his 'n;—
'Taylor,' sez he, ' aint nary ways the one thet I 'd a chizzen,   90
Nor he aint fittin' fer the place, an' like ez not he aint
No more 'n a tough ole bullethead, an' no gret of a saint;
But then,' sez he, ' obsarve my pint, he 's jest ez good to vote fer
Ez though the greasin' on him worn't a thing to hire Choate fer;
Aint it ez easy done to drop a ballot in a box
Fer one ez 't is fer t' other, fer the bulldog ez the fox ? '
It takes a mind like Dannel's, fact, ez big ez all ou' doors,
To find out thet it looks like rain arter it fairly pours;
I 'gree with him, it aint so dreffle troublesome to vote
Fer Taylor arter all,—it 's jest to go an' change your coat;   100
Wen he 's once greased, you 'll swaller him an' never know on 't, scurce,
Unless he scratches, goin' down, with them 'ere Gin'ral's spurs.
I 've ben a votin' Demmercrat, ez reg'lar as a clock,
But don't find goin' Taylor gives my narves no gret 'f a shock;
Truth is, the cutest leadin' Wigs, ever sence fust they found
Wich side the bread gut buttered on, hev kep' a edgin' round;
They kin' o' slipt the planks frum out th' ole platform one by one
An' made it gradooally noo, 'fore folks know'd wut wuz done,
Till, fur 'z I know, there aint an inch thet I could lay my han' on,
But I, or any Demmercrat, feels comf'tble to stan' on,   110
An' ole Wig doctrines act'lly look, their occ'pants bein' gone,
Lonesome ez staddles on a mash without no hayricks on.

I spose it 's time now I should give my thoughts upon the plan,
Thet chipped the shell at Buffalo, o' settin' up ole Van.
I used to vote fer Martin, but, I swan, I 'm clean disgusted,—
He aint the man thet I can say is fittin' to be trusted;
He aint half antislav'ry 'nough, nor I aint sure, ez some be,
He 'd go in fer abolishin' the Deestrick o' Columby;
An', now I come to recollec, it kin' o' makes me sick 'z
A horse, to think o' wut he wuz in eighteen thirty-six.   120
An' then, another thing;—I guess, though mebby I am wrong,
This Buff'lo plaster aint agoin' to dror almighty strong;

Some folks, I know, hev gut th' idee thet No'thun dough'll **rise,**
Though, 'fore I see it riz an' baked, I would n't trust my eyes ;
'T will take more emptins, a long chalk, than this noo party 's gut,
To give sech heavy cakes ez them a start, I tell ye wut.
But even ef they caird the day, there would n't be no endurin'
To stan' upon a platform with sech critters ez Van Buren ;—
An' his son John, tu, I can't think how thet 'ere chap should dare
To speak ez he doos ; wy, they say he used to cuss an' swear !   130
I spose he never read the hymn thet tells how down the stairs
A feller with long legs wuz throwed thet would n't say his prayers.
This brings me to another pint : the leaders o' the party
Aint jest sech men ez I can act along with free an' hearty ;
They aint not quite respectable, an' wen a feller's morrils
Don't toe the straightest kin' o' mark, wy, him an' me jest quarrils.
I went to a free soil meetin' once, an' wut d' ye think I see ?
A feller was aspoutin' there thet act'lly come to me,
About two year ago last spring, ez nigh ez I can jedge,
An' axed me ef I did n't want to sign the Temprunce pledge !   140
He's one o' them that goes about an' sez you hed n't ough' ter
Drink nothin', mornin', noon, or night, stronger 'an Taunton water.
There 's one rule I 've ben guided by, in settlin' how to vote, ollers,—
I take the side thet *is n't* took by them consarned teetotallers.

Ez fer the niggers, I 've ben South, an' thet hez changed my min' ;
A lazier ; more ongrateful set you could n't nowers fin'.
You know I mentioned in my last thet I should buy a nigger,
Ef I could make a purchase at a pooty mod'rate figger ;
So, ez there 's nothin' in the world I 'm fonder of 'an gunnin',
I closed a bargain finally to take a feller runnin'.   150
I shou'dered queen's-arm an' stumped out, an' wen I come t' th' swamp,
'T worn't very long aforc I gut upon the nest o' Pomp ;
I come acrost a kin' o' hut, an', playin' round the door,
Some little woolly-headed cubs, ez many 'z six or more.
At fust I thought o' firin', but *think twice* is safest ollers ;
There aint, thinks I, not one on 'em but 's wuth his twenty dollars,
Or would be, ef I hed 'em back into a Christian land,—
How temptin' all on 'em would look upon an auction-stand !
(Not but wut *I* hate Slavery, in th' abstract, stem to starn,—
I leave it ware our fathers did, a privit State consarn.)   160
Soon 'z they see me, they yelled an' run, but Pomp wuz out ahoein'
A leetle patch o' corn he hed, or else there aint no knowin'
He would n't ha' took a pop at me ; but I hed gut the start,
An' wen he looked, I vow he groaned ez though he 'd broke his heart ;
He done it like a wite man, tu, ez nat'ral ez a pictur,
The imp'dunt, pis'nous hypocrite ! wus 'an a boy constrictur.
' You can't gum *me*, I tell ye now, an' so you need n't try,
I 'xpect my eye-teeth every mail, so jest shet up,' sez I.
' Don't go to actin' ugly now, or else I 'll let her strip,
You 'd best draw kindly, seein' 'z how I 've gut ye on the hip ;   170

Besides, you darned ole fool, it aint no gret of a disaster
To be benev'lently druv back to a contented master,
Ware you hed Christian priv'ledges you don't seem quite aware on,
Or you'd ha' never run away from bein' well took care on ;
Ez fer kin' treatment, wy, he wuz so fond on ye, he said
He'd give a fifty spot right out, to git ye, 'live or dead ;
Wite folks aint sot by half ez much ; 'member I run away,
Wen I wuz bound to Cap'n Jakes, to Mattysqumscot Bay ;
Don' know him, likely ? Spose not ; wal, the mean ole codger went
An' offered—wut reward, think ? Wal, it worn't no *less* 'n a cent.'   180

Wal, I jest gut 'em into line, an' druv 'em on afore me,
The pis'nous brutes, I'd no idee o' the ill-will they bore me ;
We walked till som'ers about noon, an' then it grew so hot
I thought it best to camp awile, so I chose out a spot
Jest under a magnoly tree, an' there right down I sot ;
Then I unstrapped my wooden leg, coz it begun to chafe,
An' laid it down 'long side o' me, supposin' all wuz safe ;
I made my darkies all set down around me in a ring,
An' sot an kin' o' ciphered up how much the lot would bring ;
But, wile I drinked the peaceful cup of a pure heart an' min'   190
(Mixed with some wiskey, now an' then), Pomp he snaked up behin',
An creepin' grad'lly close tu, ez quiet ez a mink,
Jest grabbed my leg, and then pulled foot, quicker 'an you could wink,
An', come to look, they each on 'em hed gut behin' a tree,
An' Pomp poked out the leg a piece, jest so ez I could see,
An' yelled to me to throw away my pistils an' my gun,
Or else thet they'd cair off the leg, an' fairly cut an' run.
I vow I did n't b'lieve there wuz a decent alligatur
Thet hed a heart so destitoot o' common human natur ;
However, ez there worn't no help, I finally give in   200
An' heft my arms away to git my leg safe back agin.
Pomp gethered all the weapins up, an' then he come an' grinned,
He showed his ivory some, I guess, an' sez, ' You 're fairly pinned ;
Jest buckle on your leg agin, an' git right up an' come,
'T wun't du fer fammerly men like me to be so long frum hum.'
At fust I put my foot right down an' swore I would n't budge.
' Jest ez you choose,' sez he, quite cool, ' either be shot or trudge.'
So this black-hearted monster took an' act'lly druv me back
Along the very feetmarks o' my happy mornin' track,
An' kep' me pris'ner 'bout six months, an' worked me, tu, like sin,   210
Till I hed gut his corn an' his Carliny taters in ;
He made me larn him readin', tu (although the crittur saw
How much it hut my morril sense to act agin the law),
So'st he could read a Bible he'd gut ; an' axed ef I could pint
The North Star out ; but there I put his nose some out o' jint,
Fer I weeled roun' about sou'west, an', lookin' up a bit,
Picked out a middlin' shiny one an' tole him thet wuz it.
Fin'lly, he took me to the door, an', givin' me a kick,

Sez,—' Ef you know wut 's best fer ye, be off, now, double-quick ;
The winter-time 's a comin' on, an', though I gut ye cheap,   220
You 're so darned lazy, I don't think you 're hardly wuth your keep ;
Besides, the childrin 's growin' up, an' you aint jest the model
I 'd like to hev 'em immertate, an' so you 'd better toddle ! '

Now is there anythin' on airth 'll ever prove to me
Thet renegader slaves like him air fit fer bein' free ?
D'you think they 'll suck me in to jine the Buff'lo chaps, an' them
Rank infidels thet go agin the Scriptur'l cus o' Shem ?
Not by a jugfull ! sooner 'n thet, I 'd go thru fire an' water ;
Wen I hev once made up my mind, a meet'nhus aint sotter ;
No, not though all the crows thet flies to pick my bones wuz cawin',—   230
I guess we 're in a Christian land,—

Yourn,

BIRDOFREDUM SAWIN.

[Here, patient reader, we take leave of each other, I trust with some mutual satisfaction. I say *patient*, for I love not that kind which skims dippingly over the surface of the page, as swallows over a pool before rain. By such no pearls shall be gathered. But if no pearls there be (as, indeed, the world is not without example of books wherefrom the longest-winded diver shall bring up no more than his proper handful of mud), yet let us hope that an oyster or two may reward adequate perseverance. If neither pearls nor oysters, yet is patience itself a gem worth diving deeply for.

It may seem to some that too much space has been usurped by my own private lucubrations, and some may be fain to bring against me that old jest of him who preached all his hearers out of the meeting-house save only the sexton, who, remaining for yet a little space, from a sense of official duty, at last gave out also, and, presenting the keys, humbly requested our preacher to lock the doors, when he should have wholly relieved himself of his testimony. I confess to a satisfaction in the self act of preaching, nor do I esteem a discourse to be wholly thrown away even upon a sleeping or unintelligent auditory. I cannot easily believe that the Gospel of Saint John, which Jacques Cartier ordered to be read in the Latin tongue to the Canadian savages, upon his first meeting with them, fell altogether upon stony ground. For the earnestness of the preacher is a sermon appreciable by dullest intellects and most alien ears. In this wise did Episcopius convert many to his opinions, who yet understood not the language in which he discoursed. The chief thing is that the messenger believe that he has an authentic message to deliver. For counterfeit messengers that mode of treatment which Father John de Plano Carpini relates to have prevailed among the Tartars would seem effectual, and, perhaps, deserved enough. For my own part, I may lay claim to so much of the spirit of martyrdom as would have led me to go into banishment with those clergymen whom Alphonso the Sixth of Portugal drave out of his kingdom for refusing to shorten their pulpit eloquence. It is possible, that, having been invited into my brother Biglow's desk, I may have been too little scrupulous in using it for the venting of my own peculiar doctrines to a congregation drawn together in the expectation and with the desire of hearing him.

I am not wholly unconscious of a peculiarity of mental organization which impels me, like the railroad-engine with its train of cars, to run backward for a short distance in order to obtain a fairer start. I may compare myself to one fishing from the rocks when the sea runs high, who, misinterpreting the suction of the undertow for the biting of some large fish, jerks suddenly, and finds that he has *caught bottom*, hauling in upon the end of his line a trail of various *algæ*, among which, nevertheless, the naturalist may haply find somewhat to repay the disappointment of the angler. Yet have I conscientiously endeavoured to adapt myself to the impatient temper of the age, daily degenerating more and more from the high standard of our pristine New England. To the catalogue of lost arts I would mournfully add also that of listening to two-hour sermons. Surely we have been abridged into a race of pygmies. For, truly, in those of the old discourses yet subsisting to us in print, the endless spinal column of divisions and subdivisions can be likened to nothing so exactly as to the vertebræ of the saurians, whence the theorist may conjecture a race of Anakim proportionate to the withstanding of these other monsters. I say Anakim rather than Nephelim, because there seem reasons for supposing that the race of those whose heads (though no giants) are constantly enveloped in clouds (which that name imports) will never become extinct. The attempt to vanquish the innumerable *heads* of one of those aforementioned discourses may supply us with a plausible interpretation of the second labour of Hercules, and his successful experiment with fire affords us a useful precedent.

But while I lament the degeneracy of the age in this regard, I cannot refuse to succumb to its influence. Looking out through my study-window, I see Mr. Biglow at a distance busy in gathering his Baldwins, of which, to judge by the number of barrels lying about under the trees, his crop is more abundant than my own,—by which sight I am admonished to turn to those orchards of the mind wherein my labours may be more prospered, and apply myself diligently to the preparation of my next Sabbath's discourse.—H. W.]

MELIBOEUS-HIPPONAX.

THE

𝕭𝖎𝖌𝖑𝖔𝖜 𝕻𝖆𝖕𝖊𝖗𝖘

SECOND SERIES

῎Εστιν ἄρ' ὁ ἰδιωτισμὸς ἐνίοτε τοῦ κόσμου παραπολὺ ἐμφανιστικώτερον.

LONGINUS.

' J'aimerois mieulx que mon fils apprinst aux tavernes à parler, qu'aux escholes de la parlerie.'

MONTAIGNE.

‚Unſer Sprach iſt auch ein Sprach und kan ſo wohl ein Sack nennen als die Latiner saccus.'

FISCHART.

' Vim rebus aliquando ipsa verborum humilitas affert.'

QUINTILIANUS.

' O ma lengo,
Plantarèy une estèlo à toun froun encrumit ! '

JASMIN.

TO

E. R. HOAR.

' Multos enim, quibus loquendi ratio non desit, invenias, quos curiose potius loqui dixeris quam Latine ; quomodo et illa Attica anus Theophrastum, hominem alioqui disertissimum, annotata unius affectatione verbi, hospitem dixit, nec alio se id deprehendisse interrogata respondit, quam quod nimium Attice loqueretur.'—QUINTILIANUS.

' Et Anglice sermonicari solebat populo, sed secundum linguam Norfolchie ubi natus et nutritus erat.'—CRONICA JOCELINI.

' La politique est une pierre attachée au cou de la littérature, et qui en moins de six mois la submerge. . . . Cette politique va offenser mortellement une moitié des lecteurs, et ennuyer l'autre qui l'a trouvée bien autrement spéciale et énergique dans le journal du matin.'—HENRI BEYLE.

INTRODUCTION

THOUGH prefaces seem of late to have fallen under some reproach, they have at least this advantage, that they set us again on the feet of our personal consciousness and rescue us from the gregarious mock-modesty or cowardice of that *we* which shrills feebly throughout modern literature like the shrieking of mice in the walls of a house that has passed its prime. Having a few words to say to the many friends whom the ' Biglow Papers ' have won me, I shall accordingly take the freedom of the first person singular of the personal pronoun. Let each of the good-natured unknown who have cheered me by the written communication of their sympathy look upon this Introduction as a private letter to himself.

When, more than twenty years ago, I wrote the first of the series, I had no definite plan and no intention of ever writing another. Thinking the Mexican war, as I think it still, a national crime committed in behoof of Slavery, our common sin, and wishing to put the feeling of those who thought as I did in a way that would tell, I imagined to myself such an upcountry man as I had often seen at antislavery gatherings, capable of district-school English, but always instinctively falling back into the natural stronghold of his homely dialect when heated to the point of self-forgetfulness. When I began to carry out my conception and to write in my assumed character, I found myself in a strait between two perils. On the one hand, I was in danger of being carried beyond the limit of my own opinions, or at least of that temper with which every man should speak his mind in print, and on the other I feared the risk of seeming to vulgarize a deep and sacred conviction. I needed on occasion to rise above the level of mere *patois*, and for this purpose conceived the Rev. Mr. Wilbur, who should express the more cautious element of the New England character and its pedantry, as Mr. Biglow should serve for its homely common-sense vivified and heated by conscience. The parson was to be the complement rather than the antithesis of his parishioner, and I felt or fancied a certain humorous element in the real identity of the two under a seeming incongruity. Mr. Wilbur's fondness for scraps of Latin, though drawn from the life, I adopted deliberately to heighten the contrast. Finding soon after that I needed some one as a mouthpiece of the mere drollery, for I conceive that true humour is never divorced from moral conviction, I invented Mr. Sawin for the clown of my little puppet-show. I meant to embody in him that half-conscious *un*-morality which I had noticed as the recoil in gross natures from a puritanism that still strove to keep in its creed the intense savour which had long gone out of its faith and life. In the three I thought I should find room enough to express, as it was my plan to do, the popular feeling and opinion of the time. For the names of two of my characters, since I have received some remonstrances from very worthy persons who happen to bear them, I would say that they were purely fortuitous, probably mere unconscious memories of signboards or directories. Mr. Sawin's sprang from the accident of a rhyme at the end of his first epistle, and I purposely christened him by the impossible surname of Birdofredum not more to stigmatize him as the incarnation of ' Manifest Destiny,' in other words, of national recklessness as to right and wrong, than to avoid the chance of wounding any private sensitiveness.

The success of my experiment soon began not only to astonish me, but to make me feel the responsibility of knowing that I held in my hand a weapon instead of the mere fencing-stick I had supposed. Very far from being a popular author under my own name, so far, indeed, as to be almost unread, I found the verses of my pseudonym copied everywhere; I saw them pinned up in workshops; I heard them quoted and their authorship debated; I once even, when rumour had at length caught up my name in one of its eddies, had the satisfaction of overhearing it demonstrated, in the pauses of a concert, that *I* was utterly incompetent to have written anything of the kind. I had read too much not to know the utter worthlessness of contemporary reputation, especially as regards satire, but I knew also that by giving a certain amount of influence it also had its worth, if that influence were used on the right side. I had learned, too, that the first requisite of good writing is to have an earnest and definite purpose, whether æsthetic or moral, and that even good writing, to please long, must have more than an average amount either of imagination or common-sense. The first of these falls to the lot of scarcely one in several generations; the last is within the reach of many in every one that passes; and of this an author may fairly hope to become in part the mouthpiece. If I put on the cap and bells and made myself one of the court-fools of King Demos, it was less to make his majesty laugh than to win a passage to his royal ears for certain serious things which had deeply at heart. I say this because there is no imputation that could be more galling to any man's self-respect than that of being a mere jester. I endeavoured, by generalizing my satire, to give it what value I could beyond the passing moment and the immediate application. How far I have succeeded I cannot tell, but I have had better luck than I ever looked for in seeing my verses survive to pass beyond their nonage.

In choosing the Yankee dialect, I did not act without forethought. It had

long seemed to me that the great vice of American writing and speaking was a studied want of simplicity, that we were in danger of coming to look on our mother-tongue as a dead language, to be sought in the grammar and dictionary rather than in the heart, and that our only chance of escape was by seeking it at its living sources among those who were, as Scottowe says of Major-General Gibbons, 'divinely illiterate.' President Lincoln, the only really great public man whom these latter days have seen, was great also in this, that he was master—witness his speech at Gettysburg—of a truly masculine English, classic because it was of no special period, and level at once to the highest and lowest of his countrymen. But whoever should read the debates in Congress might fancy himself present at a meeting of the city council of some city of Southern Gaul in the decline of the Empire, where barbarians with a Latin varnish emulated each other by being more than Ciceronian. Whether it be want of culture, for the highest outcome of that is simplicity, or for whatever reason, it is certain that very few American writers or speakers wield their native language with the directness, precision, and force that are common as the day in the mother country. We use it like Scotsmen, not as if it belonged to us, but as if we wished to prove that we belonged to it, by showing our intimacy with its written rather than with its spoken dialect. And yet all the while our popular idiom is racy with life and vigour and originality, bucksome (as Milton used the word) to our new occasions, and proves itself no mere graft by sending up new suckers from the old root in spite of us. It is only from its roots in the living generations of men that a language can be reinforced with fresh vigour for its needs; what may be called a literate dialect grows ever more and more pedantic and foreign, till it becomes at last as unfitting a vehicle for living thought as monkish Latin. That we should all be made to talk like books is the danger with which we are threatened by the Universal Schoolmaster, who does his best to enslave the minds and memories of his victims to what he esteems the best models of English composition, that is to say, to the writers whose style is faultily correct and has no blood-warmth in it. No language after it has faded into *diction*, none that cannot suck up the feeding juices secreted for it in the rich mother-earth of common folk, can bring forth a sound and lusty book. True vigour and heartiness of phrase do not pass from page to page, but from man to man, where the brain is kindled and the lips suppled by downright living interests and by passion in its very throe. Language is the soil of thought, and our own especially is a rich leaf-mould, the slow deposit of ages, the shed foliage of feeling, fancy, and imagination, which has suffered an earth-change, that the vocal forest, as Howell called it, may clothe itself anew with living green. There is death in the dictionary; and, where language is too strictly limited by convention, the ground for expression to grow in is limited also; and we get a *potted* literature, Chinese dwarfs instead of healthy trees.

But while the schoolmaster has been busy starching our language and smoothing it flat with the mangle of a supposed classical authority, the newspaper reporter has been doing ever more harm by stretching and swelling it to suit his occasions. A dozen years ago I began a list, which I have added to from time to time, of some of the changes which may be fairly laid at his door. I give a few of them as showing their tendency, all the more dangerous that their effect, like that of some poisons, is insensibly cumulative, and that they are sure at last of effect among a people whose chief reading is the daily paper. I give in two columns the old style and its modern equivalent.

Old Style.	New Style.
Was hanged.	Was launched into eternity.
When the halter was put round his neck.	When the fatal noose was adjusted about the neck of the unfortunate victim of his own unbridled passions.
A great crowd came to see.	A vast concourse was assembled to witness
Great fire.	Disastrous conflagration.
The fire spread.	The conflagration extended its devastating career.
House burned.	Edifice consumed.
The fire was got under.	The progress of the devouring element was arrested.
Man fell.	Individual was precipitated.
A horse and wagon ran against.	A valuable horse attached to a vehicle driven by J. S., in the employment of J. B., collided with.
The frightened horse.	The infuriated animal.
Sent for the doctor.	Called into requisition the services of the family physician.
The mayor of the city in a short speech welcomed.	The chief magistrate of the metropolis, in well-chosen and eloquent language, frequently interrupted by the plaudits of the surging multitude, officially tendered the hospitalities.
I shall say a few words.	I shall, with your permission, beg leave to offer some brief observations.
Began his answer.	Commenced his rejoinder.

A bystander advised.

One of those omnipresent characters who, as if in pursuance of some previous arrangement, are certain to be encountered in the vicinity when an accident occurs, ventured the suggestion.

He died.

He deceased, he passed out of existence, his spirit quitted its earthly habitation, winged its way to eternity, shook off its burden, etc.

In one sense this is nothing new. The school of Pope in verse ended by wire-drawing its phrase to such thinness that it could bear no weight of meaning whatever. Nor is fine writing by any means confined to America. All writers without imagination fall into it of necessity whenever they attempt the figurative. I take two examples from Mr. Merivale's ' History of the Romans under the Empire', which, indeed, is full of such. ' The last years of the age familiarly styled the Augustan were singularly barren of the literary glories from which its celebrity was chiefly derived. One by one the stars in its firmament had been lost to the world ; Virgil and Horace, etc., had long since died ; the charm which the imagination of Livy had thrown over the earlier annals of Rome had ceased to shine on the details of almost contemporary history ; and if the flood of his eloquence still continued flowing, we can hardly suppose that the stream was as rapid, as fresh, and as clear as ever.' I will not waste time in criticizing the bad English or the mixture of metaphor in these sentences, but will simply cite another from the same author which is even worse. ' The shadowy phantom of the Republic continued to flit before the eyes of the Cæsar. There was still, he apprehended, a germ of sentiment existing, on which a scion of his own house, or even a stranger, might boldly throw himself and raise the standard of patrician independence.' Now a ghost may haunt a murderer, but hardly, I should think, to scare him with the threat of taking a new lease of its old tenement. And fancy the *scion* of a *house* in the act of *throwing itself* upon *a germ of sentiment* to *raise a standard !*

I am glad, since we have so much in the same kind to answer for, that this bit of horticultural rhetoric is from beyond sea. I would not be supposed to condemn truly imaginative prose. There is a simplicity of splendour, no less than of plainness, and prose would be poor indeed if it could not find a tongue for that meaning of the mind which is behind the meaning of the words. It has sometimes seemed to me that in England there was a growing tendency to curtail language into a mere convenience, and to defecate it of all emotion as thoroughly as algebraic signs. This has arisen, no doubt, in part from that healthy national contempt of humbug which is characteristic of Englishmen, in part from that sensitiveness to the ludicrous which makes them so shy of expressing feeling, but in part also, it is to be feared, from a growing distrust, one might almost say hatred, of whatever is supermaterial. There is something sad in the scorn with which their journalists treat the notion of there being such a thing as a national ideal, seeming utterly to have forgotten that even in the affairs of this world the imagination is as much matter-of-fact as the understanding. If we were to trust the impression made on us by some of the cleverest and most characteristic of their periodical literature, we should think England hopelessly stranded on the good-humoured cynicism of well-to-do middle-age, and should fancy it an enchanted nation, doomed to sit forever with its feet under the mahogany in that after-dinner mood which follows conscientious repletion, and which it is ill-manners to disturb with any topics more exciting than the quality of the wines. But there are already symptoms that a large class of Englishmen are getting weary of the dominion of consols and divine common-sense, and to believe that eternal three *per cent* is not the chief end of man, nor the highest and only kind of interest to which the powers and opportunities of England are entitled.

The quality of exaggeration has often been remarked on as typical of American character, and especially of American humour. In Dr. Petri's *Gedrängtes Handbuch der Fremdwörter*, we are told that the word *humbug* is commonly used for the exaggerations of the North-Americans. To be sure, one would be tempted to think the dream of Columbus half fulfilled, and that Europe had found in the West a nearer way to Orientalism, at least in diction. But it seems to me that a great deal of what is set down as mere extravagance is more fitly to be called intensity and picturesqueness, symptoms of the imaginative faculty in full health and strength, though producing, as yet, only the raw and formless material in which poetry is to work. By and by, perhaps, the world will see it fashioned into poem and picture, and Europe, which will be hard pushed for originality erelong, may have to thank us for a new sensation. The French continue to find Shakespeare exaggerated because he treated English just as our country-folk do when they speak of a ' steep price,' or say that they ' freeze to ' a thing. The first postulate of an original literature is that a people should use their language instinctively and unconsciously, as if it were a lively part of their growth and personality, not as the mere torpid boon of education or inheritance. Even Burns contrived to write very poor verse and prose in English. Vulgarisms are often only poetry in the egg. The late Mr. Horace Mann, in one of his public addresses, commented at some length on the beauty and moral significance of the French phrase *s'orienter*, and called on his young friends to practise upon it in life. There was not a Yankee in his audience whose problem had not always been to find out what was *about east,* and to shape his course accordingly. This charm which a familiar expression gains by being commented, as it were, and set in a new light by a foreign language, is curious and instructive. I cannot help thinking that Mr. Matthew Arnold forgets this a little too much sometimes when he writes of the beauties of French style. It would not be hard to find in the works of French Academicians phrases as coarse as those he cites from Burke, only they are veiled by the unfamiliarity of the language. But, however this may be, it is certain that poets and peasants please us in the same way by translating words back again to their primal freshness, and infusing them with a delightful strangeness which is anything but alienation. What, for example, is Milton's ' *edge* of battle ' but a doing into English of the Latin *acies ?* *Was die Gans gedacht das der Schwan vollbracht*, what the goose but thought, that the swan full brought (or, to de-Saxonize it a little, what the goose conceived, that the swan achieved), and it may well be that the life, invention, and vigour shown by our popular speech, and the freedom with which it is shaped to the instant want of those who use it, are of the best omen for our having a swan at last. The part I have taken on myself is that of the humbler bird.

But it is affirmed that there is something innately vulgar in the Yankee dialect. M. Sainte-Beuve says, with his usual neatness : ' *Je définis un patois une ancienne langue qui a eu des malheurs, ou encore une langue toute jeune et qui n'a pas fait fortune.*' The first part of his definition applies to a dialect like the Provençal, the last to the Tuscan before Dante had lifted it into a classic, and neither, it seems to me, will quite fit a *patois*, which is not properly a dialect, but rather certain archaisms, proverbial phrases, and modes of pronunciation, which maintain themselves among the uneducated side by side with the finished and universally accepted language. Norman French, for example, or Scotch down to the time of James VI, could hardly be called *patois*, while I should be half inclined to name the Yankee a *lingo* rather than a dialect. It has retained a few words now fallen into disuse in the mother country, like *to tarry, to progress, fleshy, fall*, and some others ; it has changed the meaning of some, as in *freshet* ; and it has clung to what I suspect to have been the broad Norman pronunciation of *e* (which Molière puts into the mouth of his rustics) in such words as *sarvant, parfect, vartoo*, and the like. It maintains something of the French sound of *a* also in words like *chămber, dănger* (though the latter had certainly begun to take its present sound so early as 1636, when I find it sometimes spelt *dainger*). But in general it may be said that nothing can be found in it which does not still survive in some one or other of the English provincial dialects. I am not speaking now of Americanisms properly so called, that is, of words or phrases which have grown into use here either through necessity, invention, or accident, such as a *carry*, a *one-horse affair*, a *prairie*, to *vamose*. Even these are fewer than is sometimes taken for granted. But I think some fair defence may be made against the charge of vulgarity. Properly speaking, vulgarity is in the thought, and not in the word or the way of pronouncing it. Modern French, the most polite of languages, is barbarously vulgar if compared with the Latin out of which it has been corrupted, or even with Italian. There is a wider gap, and one implying greater boorishness, between *ministerium* and *métier*, or *sapiens* and *sachant*, than between *druv* and *drove* or *agin* and *against*, which last is plainly an arrant superlative. Our rustic *cover-lid* is nearer its French original than the diminutive *coverlet*, into which it has been ignorantly corrupted in politer speech. I obtained from three cultivated Englishmen at different times three diverse pronunciations of a single word,—*cowcumber, coocumber*, and *cucumber*. Of these the first, which is Yankee also, comes nearest to the nasality of *concombre*. Lord Ossory assures us that Voltaire saw the best society in England, and Voltaire tells his countrymen that *handkerchief* was pronounced *hankercher*. I find it so spelt in Hakluyt and elsewhere. This enormity the Yankee still persists in, and as there is always a reason for such deviations from the sound as represented by the spelling, may we not suspect two sources of derivation, and find an ancestor for *kercher* in *couverture* rather than in *couvrechef* ? And what greater phonetic vagary (which Dryden, by the way, called *fegary*) in our *lingua rustica* than this *ker* for *couvre* ? I copy from the fly-leaves of my books where I have noted them from time to time a few examples of pronunciation and phrase which will show that the Yankee often has antiquity and very respectable literary authority on his side. My list might be largely increased by referring to glossaries, but to them every one can go for himself, and I have gathered enough for my purpose.

I will take first those cases in which something like the French sound has been preserved in certain single letters and diphthongs. And this opens a curious question as to how long this Gallicism maintained itself in England. Sometimes a divergence in pronunciation has given us two words with different meanings, as in *genteel* and *jaunty*, which I find coming in toward the close of the seventeenth century, and wavering between *genteel* and *jantee*. It is usual in America to drop the *u* in words ending in *our*,—a very proper change recommended by Howell two centuries ago, and carried out by him so far as his printers would allow. This and the corresponding changes in *musique, musick*, and the like, which he also advocated, show that in his time the French accent indicated by the superfluous letters (for French had once nearly as strong an accent as Italian) had gone out of use. There is plenty of French accent down to the end of Elizabeth's reign. In Daniel we have *riches'* and *counsel'*, in Bishop Hall *comet'*, *chapëlain'*, in Donne *pictures'*, *virtue'*, *presence'*, *mortal'*, *merit'*, *hainous'*, *giant'*, with many more, and Marston's satires are full of them. The two latter, however, are not to be relied on, as they may be suspected of Chaucerizing. Herrick writes *baptime*. The tendency to throw the accent backward began early. But the incongruities are perplexing, and perhaps mark the period of transition. In Warner's 'Albion's England' we have *creator'* and *crëature'* side by side with the modern *creator* and *creature*. *E'nvy* and *e'nvying* occur in Campion (1602), and yet *envy'* survived Milton. In some cases we have gone back again nearer to the French, as in *rev'enue* for *reven'ue*. I had been so used to hearing *imbecile* pronounced with the accent on the first syllable, which is in accordance with the general tendency in such matters, that I was surprised to find *imbec'ile* in a verse of Wordsworth. The dictionaries all give it so. I asked a highly cultivated Englishman, and he declared for *imbeceel'*. In general it may be assumed that accent will finally settle on the syllable dictated by greater ease and therefore quickness of utterance. *Blas'phemous*, for example, is more rapidly pronounced than *blasphem'ous*, to which our Yankee clings, following in this the usage of many of the older poets. *Amer'ican* is easier than *Ameri'-can*, and therefore the false quantity has carried the day, though the true one may be found in George Herbert, and even so late as Cowley.

To come back to the matter in hand. Our 'uplandish man' retains the soft or thin sound of the *u* in some words, such as *rule*, *truth* (sometimes also pronounced *trüth*, not *trooth*), while he says *noo* for *new*, and gives to *view* and *few* so indescribable a mixture of the two sounds with a slight nasal tincture that it may be called the Yankee shibboleth. Spenser writes *deow* (*dew*) which can only be pronounced with the Yankee

nasality. In *rule* the least sound of *a* precedes the *u*. I find *reule* in Pecock's 'Repressor.' He probably pronounced it *rayoolë*, as the old French word from which it is derived was very likely to be sounded at first, with a reminiscence of its original *regula*. Tindal has *rueler*, and the Coventry Plays have *preudent*. As for *noo*, may it not claim some sanction in its derivation, whether from *nouveau* or *neuf*, the ancient sound of which may very well have been *noof*, as nearer *novus*? *Beef* would seem more like to have come from *buffe* than from *bœuf*, unless the two were mere varieties of spelling. The Saxon *few* may have caught enough from its French cousin *peu* to claim the benefit of the same doubt as to sound; and our slang phrase *a few* (as 'I licked him a few') may well appeal to *un peu* for sense and authority. Nay, might not *lick* itself turn out to be the good old word *lam* in an English disguise, if the latter should claim descent as, perhaps, he fairly might, from the Latin *lambere*? The New England *ferce* for *fierce*, and *perce* for *pierce* (sometimes heard as *fairce* and *pairce*), are also Norman. For its antiquity I cite the rhyme of *verse* and *pierce* in Chapman and Donne, and in some commendatory verses by a Mr. Berkenhead before the poems of Francis Beaumont. Our *pairlous* for *perilous* is of the same kind, and is nearer Shakespeare's *parlous* than the modern pronunciation. One other Gallicism survives in our pronunciation. Perhaps I should rather call it a semi-Gallicism, for it is the result of a futile effort to reproduce a French sound with English lips. Thus for *joint*, *employ*, *royal*, we have *jynt*, *emply*, *ryle*, the last differing only from *rile* (*roil*) in a prolongation of the *y* sound. In Walter de Biblesworth I find *solives* Englished by *gistes*. This, it is true, may have been pronounced *jeests*, but the pronunciation *jystes* must have preceded the present spelling, which was no doubt adopted after the radical meaning was forgotten, as analogical with other words in *oi*. In the same way after

Norman-French influence had softened the *l* out of *would* (we already find *woud* for *veut* in N. F. poems), *should* followed the example, and then an *l* was put into *could*, where it does not belong, to satisfy the logic of the eye, which has affected the pronunciation and even the spelling of English more than is commonly supposed. I meet with *eyster* for *oyster* as early as the fourteenth century. I find *dystrye* for *destroy* in the Coventry Plays, *viage* in Bishop Hall and Middleton the dramatist, *bile* for *boil* in Donne and Chrononhotontholomos, *line* for *loin* in Hall, *ryall* and *chyse* (for *choice*) in the Coventry Plays. In Chapman's 'All Fools' is the misprint of *employ* for *imply*, fairly inferring an identity of sound in the last syllable. Indeed, this pronunciation was habitual till after Pope, and Rogers tells us that the elegant Gray said *naise* for *noise* just as our rustics still do. Our *cornish* (which I find also in Herrick) remembers the French better than *cornice* does. While, clinging more closely to the Anglo-Saxon in dropping the *g* from the end of the present participle, the Yankee now and then pleases himself with an experiment in French nasality in words ending in *n*. It is not, so far as my experience goes, very common, though it may formerly have been more so. *Capting*, for instance, I never heard save in jest, the habitual form being *kepp'n*. But at any rate it is no invention of ours. In that delightful old volume, 'Ane Compendious Buke of Godly and Spirituall Songs,' in which I know not whether the piety itself or the simplicity of its expression be more charming, I find *burding*, *garding*, and *cousing*, and in the State Trials *uncerting* used by a gentleman. I confess that I like the *n* better than the *ng*.

Of Yankee preterites I find *risse* and *rize* for *rose* in Middleton and Dryden, *clim* in Spenser, *chees* (*chose*) in Sir John Mandevil, *give* (*gave*) in the Coventry Plays, *shet* (*shut*) in Golding's Ovid,[1] *het* in Chapman and in Weever's Epitaphs,

thriv and *smit* in Drayton, *quit* in Ben Jonson and Henry More, and *pled* in the Paston Letters, nay, even in the fastidious Landor. *Rid* for *rode* was anciently common. So likewise was *see* for *saw*, but I find it in no writer of authority (except Golding), unless Chaucer's *seie* was so sounded. *Shew* is used by Hector Boece, Giles Fletcher, Drummond of Hawthornden, and in the Paston Letters. Similar strong preterites, like *snew*, *thew*, and even *mew*, are not without example. I find *sew* for *sewed* in Piers Ploughman. Indeed, the anomalies in English preterites are perplexing. We have probably transferred *flew* from *flow* (as the preterite of which I have heard it) to *fly* because we had another preterite in *fled*. Of weak preterites the Yankee retains *growed*, *blowed*, for which he has good authority, and less often *knowed*. His *sot* is merely a broad sounding of *sat*, no more inelegant than the common *got* for *gat*, which he further degrades into *gut*. When he says *darst*, he uses a form as old as Chaucer.

The Yankee has retained something of the long sound of the *a* in such words as *axe*, *wax*, pronouncing them *exe*, *wex* (shortened from *aix*, *waix*). He also says *hev* and *hed* (*hăve*, *hăd*) for *have* and *had*. In most cases he follows an Anglo-Saxon usage. In *aix* for *axle* he certainly does. I find *wex* and *aisches* (*ashes*) in Pecock, and *exe* in the Paston Letters. Golding rhymes *wax* with *wexe* and spells *challenge chelenge*. Chaucer wrote *hendy*. Dryden rhymes *can* with *men*, as Mr. Biglow would. Alexander Gill, Milton's teacher, in his 'Logonomia' cites *hez* for *hath* as peculiar to Lincolnshire. I find *hayth* in Collier's 'Bibliographical Account of Early English Literature' under the date 1584, and Lord Cromwell so wrote it. Sir Christopher Wren wrote *belcony*. Our *fect* is only the O. F. *faict*. *Thaim* for *them* was common in the sixteenth century. We have an example of the same thing in the double form of the

---

[1] Cited in Warton's 'Obs. Faery Queen.'

verb *thrash, thresh.* While the New-Englander cannot be brought to say *instead* for *instid* (commonly *'stid* where not the last word in a sentence), he changes the *i* into *e* in *red* for *rid, tell* for *till, hender* for *hinder, rense* for *rinse.* I find *red* in the old interlude of ' Ther-sytes,' *tell* in a letter of Daborne to Henslowe, and also, I shudder to mention it, in a letter of the great Duchess of Marlborough, Atossa herself ! It occurs twice in a single verse of the Chester Plays,

' *Tell* the day of dome, *tell* the beames blow.'

From the word *blow* is formed *blowth,* which I heard again this summer after a long interval. Mr. Wright [1] explains it as meaning ' a blossom.' With us a single blossom is a *blow,* while *blowth* means the blossoming in general. A farmer would say that there was a good blowth on his fruit-trees. The word retreats farther inland and away from the railways, year by year. Wither rhymes *hinder* with *slender,* and Shakespeare and Lovelace have *renched* for *rinsed.* In ' Gammer Gurton ' is *sence* for *since* ; Marlborough's Duchess so writes it, and Donne rhymes *since* with *Amiens* and *patience,* Bishop Hall and Otway with *pretence,* Chapman with *citizens,* Dryden with *providence.* Indeed, why should not *sithence* take that form ? Dryden's wife (an earl's daughter) has *tell* for *till,* Margaret, mother of Henry VII, writes *seche* for *such,* and our *ef* finds authority in the old form *yeffe.*

E sometimes takes the place of *u,* as *jedge, tredge, bresh.* I find *tredge* in the interlude of ' Jack Jugler,' *bresh* in a citation by Collier from ' London Cries ' of the middle of the seventeenth century, and *resche* for *rush* (fifteenth century) in the very valuable ' Volume of Vocabularies ' edited by Mr. Wright. *Resce* is one of the Anglo-Saxon forms of the word in Bosworth's A. S. Dictionary. Golding has *shet.* The Yankee always shortens the *u* in the ending

ture, making *ventur, natur, pictur,* and so on. This was common, also, among the educated of the last generation. I am inclined to think it may have been once universal, and I certainly think it more elegant than the vile *vencher, naycher, pickcher,* that have taken its place, sounding like the invention of a lexicographer with his mouth full of hot pudding. Nash in his ' Pierce Penniless ' has *ventur,* and so spells it, and I meet it also in Spenser, Drayton, Ben Jonson, Herrick, and Prior. Spenser has *tort'rest,* which can be contracted only from *tortur* and not from *torcher.* Quarles rhymes *nature* with *creator,* and Dryden with *satire,* which he doubtless pronounced according to its older form of *satyr.* Quarles has also *torture* and *mortar.* Mary Boleyn writes *kreatur.*

I shall now give some examples which cannot so easily be ranked under any special head. Gill charges the Eastern counties with *kiver* for *cover,* and *ta* for *to.* The Yankee pronounces both *too* and *to* like *ta* (like the *tou* in *touch*) where they are not emphatic. When they are, both become *tu.* In old spelling, *to* is the common (and indeed correct) form of *too,* which is only *to* with the sense of *in addition.* I suspect that the sound of our *too* has caught something from the French *tout,* and it is possible that the old *too too* is not a reduplication, but a reminiscence of the feminine form of the same word (*toute*) as anciently pronounced, with the *e* not yet silenced. Gill gives a Northern origin to *geaun* for *gown* and *waund* for *wound* (*vulnus*). Lovelace has *waund,* but there is something too dreadful in suspecting Spenser (who *borealized* in his pastorals) of having ever been guilty of *geaun !* And yet some delicate mouths even now are careful to observe the Hibernicism of *ge-ard* for *guard,* and *ge-url* for *girl.* Sir Philip Sidney (*credite posteri !*) wrote *furr* for *far.* I would hardly have believed it had I not seen it in *fac-simile.*

[1] Dictionary of Obsolete and Provincial English.

As some consolation, I find *furder* in Lord Bacon and Donne, and Wither rhymes *far* with *cur*. The Yankee, who omits the final *d* in many words, as do the Scotch, makes up for it by adding one in *geound*. The purist does not feel the loss of the *d* sensibly in *lawn* and *yon*, from the former of which it has dropped again after a wrongful adoption (retained in *laundry*), while it properly belongs to the latter. But what shall we make of *git*, *yit*, and *yis*? I find *yis* and *git* in Warner's 'Albion's England,' yet rhyming with *wit*, *admit*, and *fit* in Donne, with *wit* in the 'Revenger's Tragedy,' Beaumont, and Suckling, with *writ* in Dryden, and latest of all with *wit* in Sir Hanbury Williams. Prior rhymes *fitting* and *begetting*. Worse is to come. Among others, Donne rhymes *again* with *sin*, and Quarles repeatedly with *in*. *Ben* for *been*, of which our dear Whittier is so fond, has the authority of Sackville, 'Gammer Gurton' (the work of a bishop), Chapman, Dryden, and many more, though *bin* seems to have been the common form. Whittier's accenting the first syllable of *rom'ance* finds an accomplice in Drayton among others, and though manifestly wrong, is analogous with *Rom'ans*. Of other Yankeeisms, whether of form or pronunciation, which I have met with I add a few at random. Pecock writes *sowdiers* (*sogers*, *soudoyers*), and Chapman and Gill *sodder*. This absorption of the *l* is common in various dialects, especially in the Scottish. Pecock writes also *biyende*, and the authors of 'Jack Jugler' and 'Gammer Gurton' *yender*. The Yankee includes '*yon*' in the same category, and says 'hither an' yen,' for 'to and fro.' (Cf. German *jenseits*.) Pecock and plenty more have *wrastle*. Tindal has *agynste*, *gretter*, *shett*, *ondone*, *debytë*, and *scace*. 'Jack Jugler' has *scacely* (which I have often heard, though *skurce* is the common form), and Donne and Dryden make *great* rhyme with *set*. In the inscription on Caxton's tomb

I find *ynd* for *end*, which the Yankee more often makes *eend*, still using familiarly the old phrase 'right anend' for 'continuously.' His 'stret (straight) along' in the same sense, which I thought peculiar to him, I find in Pecock. Tindal's *debytë* for *deputy* is so perfectly Yankee that I could almost fancy the brave martyr to have been deacon of the First Parish at Jaalam Centre. 'Jack Jugler' further gives us *playsent* and *sartayne*. Dryden rhymes *certain* with *parting*, and Chapman and Ben Jonson use *certain*, as the Yankee always does, for *certainly*. The 'Coventry Mysteries' have *occapied*, *massage*, *nateralle*, *materal* (*material*), and *meracles*,—all excellent Yankeeisms. In the 'Quatre fils, Aymon' (1504),[1] is *vertus* for *virtuous*. Thomas Fuller called *volume vollum*, I suspect, for he spells it *volumne*. However, *per contra*, Yankees habitually say *colume* for *column*. Indeed, to prove that our ancestors brought their pronunciation with them from the Old Country, and have not wantonly debased their mother tongue, I need only to cite the words *scriptur*, *Israll*, *athists*, and *cherfulness* from Governor Bradford's 'History.' So the good man wrote them, and so the good descendants of his fellow-exiles still pronounce them. Brampton Gurdon writes *shet* in a letter to Winthrop. *Purtend* (*pretend*) has crept like a serpent into the 'Paradise of Dainty Devices'; *purvide*, which is not so bad, is in Chaucer. These, of course, are universal vulgarisms, and not peculiar to the Yankee. Butler has a Yankee phrase, and pronunciation too, in 'To which these *carr'ings-on* did tend.' Langham or Laneham, who wrote an account of the festivities at Kenilworth in honour of Queen Bess, and who evidently tried to spell phonetically, makes *sorrows* into *sororz*. Herrick writes *hollow* for *halloo*, and perhaps pronounced it (*horresco suggerens!*) *holla*, as Yankees do. Why not, when it comes from *holà*? I find

---

[1] Cited in Collier. (I give my authority where I do not quote from the original book.)

ffelaschyppe (fellowship) in the Coventry Plays. Spenser and his queen neither of them scrupled to write *afore*, and the former feels no inelegance even in *chaw* and *idee*. *'Fore* was common till after Herrick. Dryden has *do's* for *does*, and his wife spells *worse wosce*. *Afeared* was once universal. Warner has *ery* for *ever a ;* nay, he also has *illy*, with which we were once ignorantly reproached by persons more familiar with Murray's Grammar than with English literature. And why not *illy ?* Mr. Bartlett says it is 'a word used by writers of an inferior class, who do not seem to perceive that *ill* is itself an adverb, without the termination *ly*,' and quotes Dr. Messer, President of Brown University, as asking triumphantly, 'Why don't you say *welly ?'* I should like to have had Dr. Messer answer his own question. It would be truer to say that it was used by people who still remembered that *ill* was an adjective, the shortened form of *evil*, out of which Shakespeare ventured to make *evilly*. I find *illy* in Warner. The objection to *illy* is not an etymological one, but simply that it is contrary to good usage, —a very sufficient reason. *Ill* as an adverb was at first a vulgarism, precisely like the rustic's when he says, 'I was treated *bad*.' May not the reason of this exceptional form be looked for in that tendency to dodge what is hard to pronounce, to which I have already alluded ? If the letters were distinctly uttered, as they should be, it would take too much time to say *ill-ly, well-ly*, and it is to be observed that we have avoided *smally* [1] and *tally* in the same way, though we add *ish* to them without hesitation in *smallish* and *tallish*. We have, to be sure, *dully* and *fully*, but for the one we prefer *stupidly*, and the other (though this may have come from eliding the *y* before *as*) is giving way to *full*. The uneducated, whose utterance is slower, still make adverbs when they will by adding *like* to all manner of adjectives.

We have had *big* charged upon us, because we use it where an Englishman would now use *great*. I fully admit that it were better to distinguish between them, allowing to *big* a certain contemptuous quality ; but as for authority, I want none better than that of Jeremy Taylor, who, in his noble sermon 'On the Return of Prayer,' speaks of ' Jesus, whose spirit was meek and gentle up to the greatness of the *biggest* example.' As for our double negative, I shall waste no time in quoting instances of it, because it was once as universal in English as it still is in the neo-Latin languages, where it does not strike us as vulgar. I am not sure that the loss of it is not to be regretted. But surely I shall admit the vulgarity of slurring or altogether eliding certain terminal consonants ? I admit that a clear and sharp-cut enunciation is one of the crowning charms and elegancies of speech. Words so uttered are like coins fresh from the mint, compared with the worn and dingy drudges of long service,—I do not mean American coins, for those look less badly the more they lose of their original ugliness. No one is more painfully conscious than I of the contrast between the rifle-crack of an Englishman's *yes* and *no*, and the wet-fuse drawl of the same monosyllables in the mouths of my countrymen. But I do not find the dropping of final consonants disagreeable in Allan Ramsay or Burns, nor do I believe that our literary ancestors were sensible of that inelegance in the fusing them together of which we are conscious. How many educated men pronounce the *t* in *chestnut ?* how many say *pentise* for *penthouse*, as they should ? When a Yankee skipper says that he is 'boun' for Gloster' (not Gloucëster, with the leave of the Universal Schoolmaster), he but speaks like Chaucer or an old balladsinger, though they would have pronounced it *boon*. This is one of the cases where the *d* is surreptitious, and

---

[1] The word occurs in a letter of Mary Boleyn, in Golding, and Warner.

has been added in compliment to the verb *bind*, with which it has nothing to do. If we consider the root of the word (though of course I grant that every race has a right to do what it will with what is so peculiarly its own as its speech), the *d* has no more right there than at the end of *gone*, where it is often put by children, who are our best guides to the sources of linguistic corruption, and the best teachers of its processes. Cromwell, minister of Henry VIII, writes *worle* for *world*. Chapman has *wan* for *wand*, and *lawn* has rightfully displaced *laund*, though with no thought, I suspect, of etymology. Rogers tells us that Lady Bathurst sent him some letters written to William III by Queen Mary, in which she addresses him as '*Dear Husban*'. The old form *expoun*', which our farmers use, is more correct than the form with a barbarous *d* tacked on which has taken its place. Of the kind opposite to this, like our *gownd* for *gown*, and the London cockney's *wind* for *wine*, I find *drownd* for *drown* in the 'Misfortunes of Arthur' (1584), and in Swift. And, by the way, whence came the long sound of *wind* which our poets still retain, and which survives in 'winding' a horn, a totally different word from 'winding' a kite-string? We say *behind* and *hinder* (comparative), and yet *to hinder*. Shakespeare pronounced *kind kind*, or what becomes of his play on that word and *kin* in Hamlet? Nay, did he not even (shall I dare to hint it?) drop the final *d* as the Yankee still does? John Lilly plays in the same way on *kindred* and *kindness*. But to come to some other ancient instances. Warner rhymes *bounds* with *crowns*, *grounds* with *towns*, *text* with *sex*, *worst* with *crust*, *interrupts* with *cups*; Drayton, *defects* with *sex*; Chapman, *amends* with *cleanse*; Webster, *defects* with *checks*; Ben Jonson, *minds* with *combines*; Marston, *trust* and *obsequious*, *clothes* and *shows*; Dryden gives the same sound to *clothes*, and has also *minds*

with *designs*. Of course, I do not affirm that their ears may not have told them that these were imperfect rhymes (though I am by no means sure even of that), but they surely would never have tolerated any such had they suspected the least vulgarity in them. Prior has the rhyme *first* and *trust*, but puts it into the mouth of a landlady. Swift has *stunted* and *burnt it*, an intentionally imperfect rhyme, no doubt, but which I cite as giving precisely the Yankee pronunciation of *burned*. Donne couples in unhallowed wedlock *after* and *matter*, thus seeming to give to both the true Yankee sound; and it is not uncommon to find *after* and *daughter*. Worse than all, in one of Dodsley's Old Plays we have *onions* rhyming with *minions*,—I have tears in my eyes while I record it. And yet what is viler than the universal *Misses* (*Mrs.*) for *Mistress*? This was once a vulgarism, and in 'The Miseries of Inforced Marriage' the rhyme (printed as prose in Dodsley's Old Plays by Collier),

'To make my young *mistress*,
Delighting in *kisses*,'

is put into the mouth of the clown. Our people say *Injun* for *Indian*. The tendency to make this change where *i* follows *d* is common. The Italian *giorno* and French *jour* from *diurnus* are familiar examples. And yet *Injun* is one of those depravations which the taste challenges peremptorily, though it have the authority of Charles Cotton —who rhymes '*Indies*' with '*cringes*' —and four English lexicographers, beginning with Dr. Sheridan, bid us say *invidgeous*. Yet after all it is no worse than the debasement which all our terminations in *tion* and *tience* have undergone, which yet we hear with *resignashun* and *payshunce*, though it might have aroused both *impat-i-ence* and *indigna-ti-on* in Shakespeare's time. When George Herbert tells us that if the sermon be dull,

'God takes a text and preacheth pati-ence,'

the prolongation of the word seems to

convey some hint at the longanimity of the virtue. Consider what a poor curtal we have made of Ocean. There was something of his heave and expanse in *o-ce-an*, and Fletcher knew how to use it when he wrote so fine a verse as the second of these, the best deep-sea verse I know,—

'In desperate storms stem with a little rudder
The tumbling ruins of the oceän.'

Oceanus was not then wholly shorn of his divine proportions, and our modern *oshun* sounds like the gush of small-beer in comparison. Some other contractions of ours have a vulgar air about them. *More 'n* for *more than*, as one of the worst, may stand for a type of such. Yet our old dramatists are full of such obscurations (elisions they can hardly be called) of the *th*, making *whe'r* of *whether*, *bro'r* of *brother*, *smo'r* of *smother*, *mo'r* of *mother*, and so on. Indeed, it is this that explains the word *rare* (which has Dryden's support), and which we say of meat where an Englishman would use *underdone*. I do not believe, with the dictionaries, that it had ever anything to do with the Icelandic *hrar* (*raw*), as it plainly has not in *rareripe*, which means earlier ripe. And I do not believe it, for this reason, that the earlier form of the word with us was, and the commoner now in the inland parts still is, so far as I can discover, *raredone*. Golding has 'egs reere-rosted.' I find *rather* as a monosyllable in Donne, and still better, as giving the sound, rhyming with *fair* in Warner. There is an epigram of Sir Thomas Browne in which the words *rather than* make a monosyllable:

'What furie is 't to take Death's part
And rather than by Nature, die by Art!'

The contraction *more 'n* I find in the old play 'Fuimus Troes,' in a verse where the measure is so strongly accented as to leave it beyond doubt,—

'A golden crown whose heirs
More than half the world subdue.'

It may be, however, that the contraction is in 'th' orld.' It is unmistakable in the 'Second Maiden's Tragedy':—

'It were but folly,
Dear soul, to boast of *more than* I can perform.'

Is our *gin* for *given* more violent than *mar'l* for *marvel*, which was once common, and which I find as late as Herrick? Nay, Herrick has *gin* (spelling it *g'en*), too, as do the Scotch, who agree with us likewise in preferring *chimly* to *chimney*.

I will now leave pronunciation and turn to words or phrases which have been supposed peculiar to us, only pausing to pick up a single dropped stitch, in the pronunciation of the word *sup'reme*, which I had thought native till I found it in the well-languaged Daniel. I will begin with a word of which I have never met with any example in print. We express the first stage of withering in a green plant suddenly cut down by the verb *to wilt*. It is, of course, own cousin of the German *welken*, but I have never come upon it in print, and my own books of reference give me faint help. Graff gives *welhèn*, *marcescere*, and refers to *weih* (*weak*), and conjecturally to A. S. *hvelan*. The A. S. *wealwian* (*to wither*) is nearer, but not so near as two words in the Icelandic, which perhaps put us on the track of its ancestry,—*velgi*, *tepefacere* (and *velki*, with the derivative) meaning *contaminare*. *Wilt*, at any rate, is a good word, filling, as it does, a sensible gap between drooping and withering, and the imaginative phrase 'he wilted right down,' like 'he caved right in,' is a true Americanism. *Wilt* occurs in English provincial glossaries, but is explained by *wither*, which with us it does not mean. We have a few words such as *cache*, *cohog*, *carry* (*portage*), *shoot* (*chute*), *timber* (*forest*), *bushwhack* (to pull a boat along by the bushes on the edge of a stream), *buckeye* (a picturesque word for the horse-chestnut); but how many can we be said to have fairly brought into the language, as Alexander Gill, who first mentions Americanisms, meant it when he said,

'*Sed et ab Americanis nonnulla mutu-amur ut* MAIZ *et* CANOA'? Very few, I suspect, and those mostly by borrowing from the French, German, Spanish, or Indian. 'The Dipper' for the 'Great Bear' strikes me as having a native air. *Bogus*, in the sense of *worthless*, is undoubtedly ours, but is, I more than suspect, a corruption of the French *bagasse* (from low Latin *bagasea*), which travelled up the Mississippi from New Orleans, where it was used for the refuse of the sugar-cane. It is true, we have modified the meaning of some words. We use *freshet* in the sense of *flood*, for which I have not chanced upon any authority. Our New England cross between Ancient Pistol and Dugald Dalgetty, Captain Underhill, uses the word (1638) to mean a *current*, and I do not recollect it elsewhere in that sense. I therefore leave it with a ? for future explorers. *Crick* for *creek* I find in Captain John Smith in the dedication of Fuller's 'Holy Warre,' and *run*, meaning a *small stream*, in Waymouth's 'Voyage' (1605). *Humans* for *men*, which Mr. Bartlett includes in his 'Dictionary of Americanisms,' is Chapman's habitual phrase in his translation of Homer. I find it also in the old play of 'The Hog hath lost his Pearl.' *Dogs* for *andirons* is still current in New England, and in Walter de Biblesworth I find *chiens* glossed in the margin by *andirons*. *Gunning* for *shooting* is in Drayton. We once got credit for the poetical word *fall* for autumn, but Mr. Bartlett and the last edition of Webster's Dictionary refer us to Dryden. It is even older, for I find it in Drayton, and Bishop Hall has *autumn fall*. Middleton plays upon the word: 'May'st thou have a reasonable good *spring*, for thou art like to have many dangerous foul *falls*.' Daniel does the same, and Coleridge uses it as we do. Gray uses the archaism *picked* for *peaked*, and the word *smudge* (as our backwoodsmen do) for a smothered fire. Lord Herbert of Cherbury (more properly perhaps than even Sidney, the last *preux*

chevalier) has 'the Emperor's folks' just as a Yankee would say it. *Loan* for *lend*, with which we have hitherto been blackened, I must retort upon the mother island, for it appears so long ago as in 'Albion's England.' *Fleshy*, in the sense of *stout*, may claim Ben Jonson's warrant. *Chore* is also Jonson's word, and I am inclined to prefer it to *chare* and *char*, because I think that I see a more natural origin in it for the French *jour*—whence it might come to mean a day's work, and thence a job—than anywhere else. *At onst* for *at once* I thought a corruption of our own, till I found it in the Chester Plays. I am now inclined to suspect it no corruption at all, but only an erratic and obsolete superlative *at onest*. To '*progress*' was flung in our teeth till Mr. Pickering retorted with Shakespeare's 'doth pro'gress down thy cheeks.' I confess that I was never satisfied with this answer, because the accent was different, and because the word might here be reckoned a substantive quite as well as a verb. Mr. Bartlett (in his dictionary above cited) adds a surrebutter in a verse from Ford's 'Broken Heart.' Here the word is clearly a verb, but with the accent unhappily still on the first syllable. Mr. Bartlett says that he 'cannot say whether the word was used in Bacon's time or not.' It certainly was, and with the accent we give to it. Ben Jonson, in the 'Alchemist,' has this verse,

'Progress' so from extreme unto extreme,'

and Sir Philip Sidney,

'Progressing then from fair Turias' golden place.'

Surely we may now sleep in peace, and our English cousins will forgive us, since we have cleared ourselves from any suspicion of originality in the matter! *Poor* for *lean*, *thirds* for *dower*, and *dry* for *thirsty* I find in Middleton's plays. *Dry* is also in Skelton and in the 'World' (1754). In a note on Middleton, Mr. Dyce thinks it needful to explain the phrase *I can't tell* (universal in America) by the gloss *I could not say*. Middleton also uses *snecked*, which I had believed an Americanism till I saw it there. It is, of course, only another form of *snatch*, analogous to *theek* and *thatch* (cf. the proper names Dekker and Thacher), *break* (*brack*) and *breach*, *make* (still common with us) and *match*. '*Long on* for *occasioned by* ('who is this 'long on?') occurs likewise in Middleton. '*Cause why* is in Chaucer. *Raising* (an English version of the French *leaven*) for *yeast* is employed by Gayton in his 'Festivous Notes on Don Quixote.' I have never seen an instance of our New England word *emptins* in the same sense, nor can I divine its original. Gayton has *limekill ;* also *shuts* for *shutters*, and the latter is used by Mrs. Hutchinson in her 'Life of Colonel Hutchinson.' Bishop Hall, and Purchas in his 'Pilgrims,' have *chist* for *chest*, and it is certainly nearer *cista*, as well as to its form in the Teutonic languages, whence probably we got it. We retain the old sound in *cist*, but *chest* is as old as Chaucer. Lovelace says *wropt* for *wrapt*. '*Musicianer*' I had always associated with the militia-musters of my boyhood, and too hastily concluded it an abomination of our own, but Mr. Wright calls it a Norfolk word, and I find it to be as old as 1642 by an extract in Collier. 'Not worth the time of day' had passed with me for native till I saw it in Shakespeare's 'Pericles.' For *slick* (which is only a shorter sound of *sleek*, like *crick* and the now universal *britches* for *breeches*) I will only call Chapman and Jonson. 'That's a sure card!' and 'That's a stinger!' both sound like modern slang, but you will find the one in the old interlude of 'Thersytes' (1537), and the other in Middleton. 'Right here' a favourite phrase with our orators and with a certain class of our editors, turns up *passim* in the Chester and Coventry plays. Mr. Dickens found something very ludicrous in what he considered our neologism *right away*. But I find a phrase very

like it, and which I would gladly suspect to be a misprint for it, in 'Gammer Gurton' :—

'Lyght it and bring it *tite away*.'

After all, what is it but another form of *straightway ? Cussedness*, meaning *wickedness*, *malignity*, and *cuss*, a sneaking, ill-natured fellow, in such phrases as 'He done it out o' pure cussedness,' and 'He is a nateral cuss,' have been commonly thought Yankeeisms. To vent certain contemptuously indignant moods they are admirable in their rough-and-ready way. But neither is our own. *Cursydnesse*, in the same sense of malignant wickedness, occurs in the Coventry Plays, and *cuss* may perhaps claim to have come in with the Conqueror. At least the term is also French. Saint Simon uses it and confesses its usefulness. Speaking of the Abbé Dubois, he says, 'Qui étoit en plein ce qu'un mauvais françois appelle un *sacre*, mais qui ne se peut guère exprimer autrement.' 'Not worth a cuss,' though supported by 'not worth a damn,' may be a mere corruption, since 'not worth a *cress*' is in 'Piers Ploughman.' 'I don't see it' was the popular slang a year or two ago, and seemed to spring from the soil ; but no, it is in Cibber's 'Careless Husband.' *Green sauce* for *vegetables* I meet in Beaumont and Fletcher, Gayton, and elsewhere. Our rustic pronunciation *sahce* (for either the diphthong *au* was anciently pronounced *ah*, or else we have followed abundant analogy in changing it to the latter sound, as we have in *chance, dance*, and so many more) may be the older one, and at least gives some hint at its ancestor *salsa*. *Warn*, in the sense of *notify*, is, I believe, now peculiar to us, but Pecock so employs it. *To cotton to* is, I rather think, an Americanism. The nearest approach to it I have found is *cotton together*, in Congreve's 'Love for Love.' To *cotton* or *cotten*, in another sense, is old and common. Our word means to *cling*, and its origin, possibly, is to be sought in another direction, perhaps in A. S. *cvead*, which means *mud, clay* (both proverbially clinging), or better yet, in the Icelandic *qvoda* (otherwise *kód*), meaning *resin* and *glue*, which are κατ᾽ ἐξοχήν sticky substances. To *spit cotton* is, I think, American, and also, perhaps, *to flax* for *to beat*. *To the halves* still survives among us, though apparently obsolete in England. It means either to let or to hire a piece of land, receiving half the profit in money or in kind (*partibus locare*). I mention it because in a note by some English editor, to which I have lost my reference, I have seen it wrongly explained. The editors of Nares cite Burton. *To put*, in the sense of *to go*, as *Put!* for *Begone!* would seem our own, and yet it is strictly analogous to the French *se mettre à la voie*, and the Italian *mettersi in via*. Indeed, Dante has a verse,

' *Io sarei* [for *mi sarei*] *già messo per lo sentiero*,'

which, but for the indignity, might be translated,

' I should, ere this, have *put* along the way.'

I deprecate in advance any share in General Banks's notions of international law, but we may all take a just pride in his exuberant eloquence as something distinctively American. When he spoke a few years ago of 'letting the Union slide,' even those who, for political purposes, reproached him with the sentiment, admired the indigenous virtue of his phrase. Yet I find 'let the world slide ' in Heywood's 'Edward IV '; and in Beaumont and Fletcher's ' Wit without Money ' Valentine says,

' Will you drink,
And let the world slide ? '

So also in Sidney's *Arcadia*,

' Let his dominion slide.'

In the one case it is put into the mouth of a clown, in the other, of a gentleman, and was evidently proverbial. It has even higher sanction, for Chaucer writes,

' Well nigh all other curës *let he slide*.'

Mr. Bartlett gives ' above one's bend ' as an Americanism ; but compare Hamlet's ' to the top of my bent.' *In his tracks* for *immediately* has acquired an American accent, and passes where he can for a native, but is an importation nevertheless ; for what is he but the Latin *e vestigio*, or at best the Norman French *eneslespas*, both which have the same meaning ? *Hotfoot* (provincial also in England), I find in the old romance of ' Tristan,'

' *Si s'en parti* CHAUT PAS.'

Like for *as* is never used in New England, but is universal in the South and West. It has on its side the authority of two kings (*ego sum rex Romanorum et supra grammaticam*), Henry VIII and Charles I. This were ample, without throwing into the scale the scholar and poet Daniel. *Them* was used as a nominative by the majesty of Edward VI, by Sir P. Hoby, and by Lord Paget (in Froude's ' History '). I have never seen any passage adduced where *guess* was used as the Yankee uses it. The word was familiar in the mouths of our ancestors, but with a different shade of meaning from that we have given it, which is something like *rather think*, though the Yankee implies a confident certainty by it when he says, ' I guess I *du!* ' There are two examples in Otway, one of which (' So in the struggle, I guess the note was lost ') perhaps might serve our purpose, and Coleridge's

' I guess 't was fearful there to see '

certainly comes very near. But I have a higher authority than either in Selden, who, in one of his notes to the ' Polyolbion,' writes, ' The first inventor of them (I *guess* you dislike not the addition) was one Berthold Swartz.' Here he must mean by it, ' I take it for granted.' Another peculiarity almost as prominent is the beginning sentences, especially in answer to questions, with ' well.' Put before such a phrase as ' How d'e do ? ' it is commonly short, and has the sound of *wul*, but in reply it is deliberative, and the various shades of meaning which can be conveyed by difference of intonation, and by prolonging or abbreviating, I should vainly attempt to describe. I have heard *ooaahl, wahl, ahl, wăl*, and something nearly approaching the sound of the *le* in *able*. Sometimes before ' I ' it dwindles to a mere *l*, as " 'l *I* dunno.' A friend of mine (why should I not please myself, though I displease him, by brightening my page with the initials of the most exquisite of humorists, J. H. ?) told me that he once heard five ' wells,' like pioneers, precede the answer to an inquiry about the price of land. The first was the ordinary *wul*, in deference to custom ; the second, the long, perpending *ooahl*, with a falling inflection of the voice ; the third, the same, but with the voice rising, as if in despair of a conclusion, into a plaintively nasal whine ; the fourth, *wulh*, ending in the aspirate of a sigh ; and then, fifth, came a short, sharp *wal*, showing that a conclusion had been reached. I have used this latter form in the ' Biglow Papers,' because, if enough nasality be added, it represents most nearly the average sound of what I may call the interjection.

A locution prevails in the Southern and Middle States which is so curious that, though never heard in New England, I will give a few lines to its discussion, the more readily because it is extinct elsewhere. I mean the use of *allow* in the sense of *affirm*, as ' I allow that 's a good horse.' I find the word so used in 1558 by Anthony Jenkinson in Hakluyt : ' Corne they sowe not, neither doe eate any bread, mocking the Christians for the same, and disabling our strengthe, saying we live by eating the toppe of a weede, and drinke a drinke made of the same, *allowing* theyr great devouring of flesh and drinking of milke to be the increase of theyr strength.' That is, they undervalued our strength, and affirmed their own to be the result of a certain diet. In another passage of the same narrative the word has its more common meaning of approving or praising :

' The said king, much *allowing* this declaration, said.' Ducange quotes Bracton *sub voce* ADLOCARE for the meaning ' to admit as proved,' and the transition from this to ' affirm ' is by no means violent. At the same time, when we consider some of the meanings of *allow* in old English, and of *allouer* in old French, and also remember that the verbs *prize* and *praise* are from one root, I think we must admit *allaudare* to a share in the paternity of *allow*. The sentence from Hakluyt would read equally well, ' contemning our strengthe, . . . and praising (or valuing) their great eating of flesh as the cause of their increase in strength.' After all, if we confine ourselves to *allocare*, it may turn out that the word was somewhere and somewhen used for *to bet*, analogously to *put up, put down, post* (cf. Spanish *apostar*), and the like. I hear boys in the street continually saying, ' I bet that 's a good horse,' or what not, meaning by no means to risk anything beyond their opinion in the matter.

The word *improve*, in the sense of ' to occupy, make use of, employ,' as Dr. Pickering defines it, he long ago proved to be no neologism. He would have done better, I think, had he substituted *profit by* for *employ*. He cites Dr. Franklin as saying that the word had never, so far as he knew, been used in New England before he left it in 1723, except in Dr. Mather's ' Remarkable Providences,' which he oddly calls a ' very old book.' Franklin, as Dr. Pickering goes on to show, was mistaken. Mr. Bartlett in his ' Dictionary ' merely abridges Pickering. Both of them should have confined the application of the word to material things, its extension to which is all that is peculiar in the supposed American use of it. For surely ' Complete Letter-Writers ' have been ' *improving* this opportunity ' time out of mind. I will illustrate the word a little further, because Pickering cites no English authorities ; Skelton has a passage in his ' Phyllyp Sparowe,' which I quote he rather as it contains also the word *llowed*, and as it distinguishes *improve* from *employ* :—

> 'His [Chaucer's] Englysh well alowed,
> So as it is *enprowed*,
> For as it is enployd,
> There is no English voyd.'

Here the meaning is *to profit by*. In Fuller's 'Holy Warre' (1647), we have 'The Egyptians standing on the firm ground, were thereby enabled to *improve* and enforce their darts to the utmost.' Here the word might certainly mean *to make use of*. Mrs. Hutchinson (Life of Colonel H.) uses the word in the same way : 'And therefore did not *emproove* his interest to engage the country in the quarrell.' Swift in one of his letters says : 'There is not an acre of land in Ireland turned to half its advantage ; yet it is better *improved* than the people.' I find it also in, Strength out of Weakness' (1652), and Plutarch's 'Morals' (1714), but I know of only one example of its use in the purely American sense, and that is, a very good *improvement* for a mill' in the 'State Trials' (Speech of the Attorney-General in the Lady Ivy's case, 1684). In the sense of *employ*, I could cite a dozen old English authorities.

In running over the fly-leaves of those delightful folios for this reference, I find a note which reminds me of another word, for our abuse of which we have been deservedly ridiculed. I mean *lady*. It is true I might cite the example of the Italian *donna* [1] (*domina*), which has been treated in the same way by a whole nation, and not, as *lady* among us, by the uncultivated only. It perhaps grew into use in the half-democratic republics of Italy in the same way and for the same reasons as with us. But I admit that our abuse of the word is villanous. I know of an orator who once said in a public meeting where sonnets preponderated, that ' the ladies were last at the cross and first at the tomb ' ! But similar sins were committed before our day and in the mother

country. In the 'State Trials' I learn of ' a *gentlewoman* that lives cook with ' such a one, and I hear the Lord High Steward speaking of the wife of a waiter at a bagnio as a *gentlewoman* ! From the same authority, by the way, I can state that our vile habit of chewing tobacco had the somewhat unsavoury example of Titus Oates, and I know by tradition from an eyewitness that the elegant General Burgoyne partook of the same vice. Howell, in one of his letters (dated 26 August, 1623), speaks thus of another ' institution ' which many have thought American : ' They speak much of that boisterous Bishop of Halverstadt (for so they term him here), that, having taken a place wher ther were two Monasteries of Nuns and Friers, he caus'd divers feather-beds to be rip'd, and all the feathers to be thrown in a great Hall, whither the Nuns and Friers were thrust naked with their bodies oil'd and pitch'd, and to tumble among the feathers.' Howell speaks as if the thing were new to him, and I know not if the ' boisterous ' Bishop was the inventor of it, but I find it practised in England before our Revolution.

Before leaving the subject, I will add a few comments made from time to time on the margin of Mr. Bartlett's excellent ' Dictionary,' to which I am glad thus publicly to acknowledge my many obligations. ' Avails ' is good old English, and the *vails* of Sir Joshua Reynolds's porter are famous. Averse *from*, averse *to*, and in connection with them the English vulgarism ' different *to*.' The corrupt use of *to* in these cases, as well as in the Yankee ' he lives to Salem,' ' to home,' and others, must be a very old one, for in the one case it plainly arose from confounding the two French prepositions *à* (from Latin *ad* and *ab*), and in the other from translating the first of them. I once thought ' different to ' a modern vulgarism, and Mr. Thackeray, on my pointing it out to him in ' Henry Esmond,' confessed it to be an anachronism. Mr. Bartlett refers to ' the old writers quoted in

---

[1] *Dame*, in English, is a decayed gentlewoman of the same family.

Richardson's Dictionary' for 'different to,' though in my edition of that work all the examples are with *from*. But I find *to* used invariably by Sir R. Hawkins in Hakluyt. *Banjo* is a negro corruption of O. E. *bandore*. *Bind-weed* can hardly be modern, for *wood-bind* is old and radically right, intertwining itself through *bindan* and *windan* with classic stems. *Bobolink :* is this a contraction for Bob o' Lincoln ? I find *bobolynes*, in one of the poems attributed to Skelton, where it may be rendered *giddy-pate*, a term very fit for the bird in his ecstasies. *Cruel* for *great* is in Hakluyt. *Bowling-alley* is in Nash's 'Pierce Pennilesse.' *Curious*, meaning *nice*, occurs continually in old writers, and is as old as Pecock's 'Repressor.' *Droger* is O. E. *drugger*. *Educational* is in Burke. *Feeze* is only a form of *fizz*. To *fix*, in the American sense, I find used by the Commissioners of the United Colonies so early as 1675, 'their arms well *fixed* and fit for service.' To *take the foot in the hand* is German ; so is to *go under*. *Gundalow* is old : I find *gundelo* in Hakluyt, and *gundello* in Booth's reprint of the folio Shakespeare of 1623. *Gonoff* is O. E. *gnoffe*. *Heap* is in 'Piers Ploughman' ('and other names *an heep*'), and in Hakluyt ('seeing such a *heap* of their enemies ready to devour them'). To *liquor* is in the 'Puritan' ('call 'em in, and liquor 'em a little'). To *loaf :* this, I think, is unquestionably German. *Laufen* is pronounced *lofen* in some parts of Germany, and I once heard one German student say to another, *Ich lauf* (lofe) *hier bis du wiederkehrest*, and he began accordingly to saunter up and down, in short, to *loaf*. To *mull*, Mr. Bartlett says, means 'to soften, to dispirit,' and quotes from 'Margaret,' —'There has been a pretty considerable *mullin* going on among the doctors,'—where it surely cannot mean what he says it does. We have always heard *mulling* used for *stirring, bustling*, sometimes in an underhand way. It is a metaphor derived probably from *mulling* ⁅wine, and the word itself must

be a corruption of *mell*, from O. F. *mesler*. *Pair* of stairs is in Hakluyt. To *pull up stakes* is in Curwen's Journal, and therefore pre-Revolutionary. I think I have met with it earlier. *Raise :* under this word Mr. Bartlett omits 'to raise a house,' that is, the frame of a wooden one, and also the substantive formed from it, a *raisin*'. *Retire* for *go to bed* is in Fielding's 'Amelia.' *Setting-poles* cannot be new, for I find 'some *set* [the boats] with long *poles*' in Hakluyt. *Shoulder-hitters :* I find that *shoulder-striker* is old, though I have lost the reference to my authority. *Snag* is no new word, though perhaps the Western application of it is so ; but I find in Gill the proverb, 'A bird in the bag is worth two on the snag.' Dryden has *swop* and *to rights*. *Trail*. Hakluyt has 'many wayes *traled* by the wilde beastes.'

I subjoin a few phrases not in Mr Bartlett's book which I have heard. *Bald-headed :* 'to go it bald-headed' in great haste, as where one rushes out without his hat. *Bogue :* 'I don't gi' much done 'thout I *bogue* right in along 'th my men.' *Carry :* a *portage*. *Cat-nap* a short doze. *Cat-stick :* a small stick. *Chowder-head :* a muddle-brain. *Cling john :* a soft cake of rye. *Cocoa-nut* the head. *Cohees' :* applied to the people of certain settlements in Western Pennsylvania, from their use of the archaic form *Quo' he*. *Dunnow'z know :* the nearest your true Yankee ever comes to acknowledging ignorance. *Essence-pedler :* a skunk. *First rate and a half. Fish-flakes*, for drying fish : O. E. *fleck* (*cratis*). *Gander party :* a social gathering of men only. *Gawnicus :* a dolt. *Hawkins's whet stone :* rum ; in derision of one Hawkins, a well-known temperance-lecturer. *Hyper :* to bustle : 'I mus' *hype* about an' git tea.' *Keeler-tub :* one in which dishes are washed. ('An Greasy Joan doth *keel* the pot.') *Lap tea :* where the guests are too many to sit at table. *Last of pea-time :* to be hard-up. *Lōse-laid* (loose-laid) a weaver's term, and probably English weak-willed. *Malahack :* to cut up hastily or awkwardly. *Moonglade :* a beautiful word : for the track of moonlight on the water. *Off-ox :* an unmanageable, cross-grained fellow. *Old Driver, Old Splitfoot ;* the Devil. *Onhitch :* to pull trigger (cf. Spanish *disparar*). *Popular :* conceited. *Rote :* sound of surf before a storm. *Rot-gut :* cheap whisky ; the word occurs in Heywood's 'English Traveller' and Addison's 'Drummer,' for a poor kind of drink. *Seem :* it is habitual with the New-Englander to put this verb to strange uses, as, 'I can't *seem* to be suited,' 'I could n't *seem* to know him.' *Sidehill*, for *hillside*. *State-house :* this seems an Americanism, whether invented or derived from the Dutch *Stadhuys*, I know not. *Strike* and *string :* from the game of ninepins ; to make a *strike* is to knock down all the pins with one ball, hence it has come to mean fortunate, successful. *Swampers :* men who break out roads for lumberers. *Tormented :* euphemism for damned, as, 'not a tormented cent.' *Virginia fence, to make a :* to walk like a drunken man.

It is always worth while to note down the erratic words or phrases which one meets with in any dialect. They may throw light on the meaning of other words, on the relationship of languages, or even on history itself. In so composite a language as ours they often supply a different form to express a different shade of meaning, as in *viol* and *fiddle, thrid* and *thread, smother* and *smoulder*, where the *l* has crept in by a false analogy with *would*. We have given back to England the excellent adjective *lengthy*, formed honestly like *earthy, drouthy*, and others, thus enabling their journalists to characterize our President's messages by a word civilly compromising between *long* and *tedious*, so as not to endanger the peace of the two countries by wounding our national sensitiveness to British criticism. Let me give two curious examples

of the antiseptic property of dialects at which I have already glanced. Dante has *dindi* as a childish or low word for *danari* (money), and in Shropshire small Roman coins are still dug up which the peasants call *dinders*. This can hardly be a chance coincidence, but seems rather to carry the word back to the Roman soldiery. So our farmers say *chuk, chuk*, to their pigs, and *ciacco* is one of the Italian words for *hog*. When a countryman tells us that he 'fell *all of a heap*,' I cannot help thinking that he unconsciously points to an affinity between our word *tumble*, and the Latin *tumulus*, that is older than most others. I believe that words, or even the mere intonation of them, have an astonishing vitality and power of propagation by the root, like the gardener's pest, quitch-grass,[1] while the application or combination of them may be new. It is in these last that my countrymen seem to me full of humour, invention, quickness of wit, and that sense of subtle analogy which needs only refining to become fancy and imagination. Prosaic as American life seems in many of its aspects to a European, bleak and bare as it is on the side of tradition, and utterly orphaned of the solemn inspiration of antiquity, I cannot help thinking that the ordinary talk of unlettered men among us is fuller of metaphor and of phrases that suggest lively images than that of any other people I have seen. Very many such will be found in Mr. Bartlett's book, though his short list of proverbs at the end seem to me, with one or two exceptions, as un-American as possible. Most of them have no character at all but coarseness, and are quite too long-skirted for working proverbs, in which language always 'takes off its coat to it,' as a Yankee would say. There are plenty that have a more native and puckery flavour, seedlings from the old stock often, and yet new varieties. One hears such not seldom among us Easterners, and the

[1] Which, whether in that form, or under its aliases *witch*-grass and *cooch*-grass, points us back to its original Saxon *quick*.

West would yield many more. ' Mean enough to steal acorns from a blind hog'; ' Cold as the north side of a Jenooary gravestone by starlight'; ' Hungry as a graven image'; ' Pop'lar as a hen with one chicken'; ' A hen's time ain't much'; ' Quicker 'n greased lightnin''; ' Ther 's sech a thing ez bein' *tu*' (our Yankee paraphrase of μηδὲν ἄγαν); hence the phrase *tooin' round*, meaning a supererogatory activity like that of flies; ' Stingy enough to skim his milk at both eends'; ' Hot as the Devil's kitchen'; ' Handy as a pocket in a shirt'; ' He 's a whole team and the dog under the wagon'; ' All deacons are good, but there 's odds in deacons' (to *deacon* berries is to put the largest atop); ' So thievish they hev to take in their stone walls nights'; [1] may serve as specimens. ' I take my tea *barfoot*,' said a backwoodsman when asked if he would have cream and sugar. (I find *barfoot*, by the way, in the Coventry Plays.) A man speaking to me once of a very rocky clearing said, ' Stone 's got a pretty heavy mortgage on that land,' and I overheard a guide in the woods say to his companions who were urging him to sing, ' Wal, I *did* sing once, but toons gut invented, an' thet spilt my trade.' Whoever has driven over a stream by a bridge made of *slabs* will feel the picturesque force of the epithet *slab-bridged* applied to a fellow of shaky character. Almost every county has some good die-sinker in phrase, whose mintage passes into the currency of the whole neighbourhood. Such a one described the county jail (the one stone building where all the dwellings are of wood) as ' the house whose underpinnin' come up to the eaves,' and called hell ' the place where they did n't rake up their fires nights.' I once asked a stage-driver if the other side of a hill were as steep as the one we were climbing : ' Steep ? chain lightnin' could n' go down it 'thout puttin' the shoe on ! ' And this brings me back to the exaggeration of which I

spoke before. To me there is something very taking in the negro ' so black tha charcoal made a chalk-mark on him, and the wooden shingle ' painted s like marble that it sank in water,' a if its very consciousness or its vanity had been over-persuaded by the cunning of the painter. I heard a man, in orde to give a notion of some very cold weather, say to another that a certain Joe, who had been taking mercury found a lump of quicksilver in each boot, when he went home to dinner This power of rapidly dramatizing a dry fact into flesh and blood, and the vivid conception of Joe as a human thermometer, strike me as showing a poetic sense that may be refined into faculty. At any rate there is humou here, and not mere quickness of wit —the deeper and not the shallowe quality. The *tendency* of humour i always towards overplus of expres sion, while the very essence of wh is its logical precision. Captain Bass Hall denied that our people had an humour, deceived, perhaps, by the gravity of manner. But this ver seriousness is often the outward sig of that humorous quality of the min which delights in finding an elemen of identity in things seemingly the mos incongruous, and then again in forcin an incongruity upon things identica Perhaps Captain Hall had no humou himself, and if so he would never fin it. Did he always feel the point what was said to himself ? I doubt i because I happen to know a chance h once had given him in vain. The Captai was walking up and down the verand of a country tavern in Massachusett while the coach changed horses. thunder-storm was going on, an with that pleasant European air of in direct self-compliment in condescenc ing to be surprised by American meri which we find so conciliating, he sai to a countryman lounging agains the door, ' Pretty heavy thunder yo have here.' The other, who had divine

---

[1] And, by the way, the Yankee never says ' o' nights,' but uses the older adverbi form, analogous to the German *nachts*.

at a glance his feeling of generous concession to a new country, drawled gravely, 'Waal, we *du*, considerin' the number of inhabitants.' This, the more I analyze it, the more humorous does it seem. The same man was capable of wit also, when he would. He was a cabinet-maker, and was once employed to make some commandment-tables for the parish meetinghouse. The parson, a very old man, annoyed him by looking into his workshop every morning, and cautioning him to be very sure to pick out 'clear mahogany without any *knots* in it.' At last, wearied out, he retorted one day : 'Wal, Dr. B., I guess ef I was to leave the *nots* out o' some o' the c'man'ments, 't 'ould soot you full ez wal !'

If I had taken the pains to write down the proverbial or pithy phrases I have heard, or if I had sooner thought of noting the Yankeeisms I met with in my reading, I might have been able to do more justice to my theme. But I have done all I wished in respect to pronunciation, if I have proved that where we are vulgar, we have the countenance of very good company. For, as to the *jus et norma loquendi*, I agree with Horace and those who have paraphrased or commented him, from Boileau to Gray. I think that a good rule for style is Galiani's definition of sublime oratory,—'l'art de tout dire sans être mis à la Bastille dans un pays où il est défendu de rien dire.' I profess myself a fanatical purist, but with a hearty contempt for the speech-gilders who affect purism without any thorough, or even pedagogic, knowledge of the engendure, growth, and affinities of the noble language about whose *mésalliances* they profess (like Dean Alford) to be so solicitous. If *they* had their way—! "Doch es sey,' says Lessing, 'dass jene gothische Höflichkeit eine unentbehrliche Tugend des heutigen Umganges ist. Soll sie darum unsere Schriften eben so schaal und falsch machen als unsern Umgang ?' And Drayton was not far wrong in affirming that

' 'T is possible to climb,
To kindle, or to slake,
   Although in Skelton's rhyme.'

Cumberland in his Memoirs tells us that when, in the midst of Admiral Rodney's great sea-fight, Sir Charles Douglas said to him, 'Behold, Sir George, the Greeks and Trojans contending for the body of Patroclus !' the Admiral answered, peevishly, 'Damn the Greeks and damn the Trojans ! I have other things to think of.' After the battle was won, Rodney thus to Sir Charles, 'Now, my dear friend, I am at the service of your Greeks and Trojans, and the whole of Homer's Iliad, or as much of it as you please !' I had some such feeling of the impertinence of our pseudo-classicality when I chose our homely dialect to work in. Should we be nothing, because somebody had contrived to be something (and that perhaps in a provincial dialect) ages ago ? and to be nothing by our very attempt to be that something, which they had already been, and which therefore nobody could be again without being a bore ? Is there no way left, then, I thought, of being natural, of being *naïf*, which means nothing more than native, of belonging to the age and country in which you are born ? The Yankee, at least, is a new phenomenon ; let us try to be *that*. It is perhaps a *pis aller*, but is not *No Thoroughfare* written up everywhere else ? In the literary world, things seemed to me very much at they were in the latter half of the last century. Pope, skimming the cream of good sense and expression wherever he could find it, had made, not exactly poetry, but an honest, saleable butter of worldly wisdom which pleasantly lubricated some of the drier morsels of life's daily bread, and, seeing this, scores of harmlessly insane people went on for the next fifty years coaxing his buttermilk with the regular up and down of the pentameter churn. And in our day do we not scent everywhere, and even carry away in our clothes against our will, that faint perfume of musk which Mr. Tennyson has left behind him, or worse, of Heine's *patchouli?* And might it not be possible to escape them by turning into one of our narrow New England lanes, shut in though it were by bleak stone walls on either hand, and where no better flowers were to be gathered than golden-rod and hardhack?

Beside the advantage of getting out of the beaten track, our dialect offered others hardly inferior. As I was about to make an endeavour to state them, I remembered something that the clear-sighted Goethe had said about Hebel's *Allemannische Gedichte*, which, making proper deduction for special reference to the book under review, expresses what I would have said far better than I could hope to do: ' Allen diesen innern guten Eigenschaften kommt die behagliche naive Sprache sehr zu statten. Man findet mehrere sinnlich bedeutende und wohlklingende Worte . . . . von einem, zwei Buchstaben, Abbreviationen, Contractionen, viele kurze, leichte Sylben, neue Reime, welches, mehr als man glaubt, ein Vortheil für den Dichter ist.' Diese Elemente werden durch glückliche Constructionen und lebhafte Formen zu einem Styl zusammengedrängt der zu diesem Zwecke vor unserer Bücher-sprache grosse Vorzüge hat.' Of course I do not mean to imply that *I* have come near achieving any such success as the great critic here indicates, but I think the success is *there*, and to be plucked by some more fortunate hand.

Nevertheless, I was encouraged by the approval of many whose opinions I valued. With a feeling too tender and grateful to be mixed with any vanity, I mention as one of these the late A. H. Clough, who more than any one of those I have known (no longer living), except Hawthorne, impressed me with the constant presence of that indefinable thing we call genius. He often suggested that I should try my hand at some Yankee Pastorals, which would admit of more sentiment and a higher tone without foregoing the advantage offered by the dialect. I have never completed anything of the kind, but, in this Second Series, both my remembrance of his counsel and the deeper feeling called up by the great interests at stake, led me to venture some passages nearer to what is called poetical than could have been admitted without incongruity into the former series. The time seemed calling to me, with the old poet,—

' Leave, then, your wonted prattle,
   The oaten reed forbear ;
For I hear a sound of battle,
   And trumpets rend the air ! '

The only attempt I had ever made at anything like a pastoral (if that may be called an attempt which was the result almost of pure accident) was in ' The Courtin'.' While the introduction to the First Series was going through the press, I received word from the printer that there was a blank page left which must be filled. I sat down at once and improvised another fictitious ' notice of the press,' in which, because verse would fill up space more cheaply than prose, I inserted an extract from a supposed ballad of Mr. Biglow. I kept no copy of it, and the printer, as directed, cut it off when the gap was filled. Presently I began to receive letters asking for the rest of it, sometimes for the *balance* of it. I had none, but to answer such demands, I patched a conclusion upon it in a later edition. Those who had only the first continued to importune me. Afterward, being asked to write it out as an autograph for the Baltimore Sanitary Commission Fair, I added other verses, into some of which I infused a little more sentiment in a homely way, and after a fashion completed it by sketching in the characters and making a connected story. Most likely I have spoiled it, but I shall put it at the end of this Introduction to answer once for all those kindly importunings.

As I have seen extracts from what

purported to be writings of Mr. Biglow, which were not genuine, I may properly take this opportunity to say, that the two volumes now published contain every line I ever printed under that pseudonym, and that I have never, so far as I can remember, written an anonymous article (elsewhere than in the *North American Review* and the *Atlantic Monthly*, during my editorship of it) except a review of Mrs. Stowe's 'Minister's Wooing,' and, some twenty years ago, a sketch of the antislavery movement in America for an English journal.

A word more on pronunciation. I have endeavoured to express this so far as I could by the types, taking such pains as, I fear, may sometimes make the reading harder than need be. At the same time, by studying uniformity I have sometimes been obliged to sacrifice minute exactness. The emphasis often modifies the habitual sound. For example, *for* is commonly *'er* (a shorter sound than *fur* for *far*), but when emphatic it always becomes *for*, as 'wut *for!*' So *too* is pronounced like *to* (as it was anciently spelt), and *to* like *ta* (the sound as in the *ou* of *touch*), but, *too*, when emphatic, changes into *tue*, and *to*, sometimes, in similar cases, into *toe*, as, 'I did n' hardly know wut *toe* du!' Where vowels come together, or one precedes another following an aspirate, the two melt together, as was common with the older poets who formed their versification on French or Italian models. Drayton is thoroughly Yankee when he says 'I 'xpect,' and Pope when he says 't' inspire.' *With* becomes sometimes *'ith*, *'ŭth*, or *'th*, or even disappears wholly where it comes before *he*, as, 'I went along th' Square' (along with the Squire), the *are* sound being an archaism which I have noticed also in *choir*, like the old Scottish *quhair*. Herrick has, 'Of flowers ne'er sucked by th' theeving bee.') *Without* becomes *athout* and *'thout*. *Afterwards* always retains its locative *s*, and is pronounced always *ahterwurds'*, with

a strong accent on the last syllable. This oddity has some support in the erratic *towards'* instead of *to'wards*, which we find in the poets and sometimes hear. The sound given to the first syllable of *to'wards*, I may remark, sustains the Yankee lengthening of the *o* in *to*. At the beginning of a sentence, *ahterwurds* has the accent on the first syllable; at the end of one, on the last; as, '*ah'terwurds* he tol' me,' 'he tol' me *ahterwurds'*.' The Yankee never makes a mistake in his aspirates. *U* changes in many words to *e*, always in *such, brush, tush, hush, rush, blush*, seldom in *much*, oftener in *trust* and *crust*, never in *mush, gust, bust, tumble*, or (?) *flush*, in the latter case probably to avoid confusion with *flesh*. I have heard *flush* with the *ĕ* sound, however. For the same reason, I suspect, never in *gush* (at least, I never heard it), because we have already one *gesh* for *gash*. *A* and *i* short frequently become *e* short. *U* always becomes *o* in the prefix *un* (except *unto*), and *o* in return changes to *u* short in *uv* for *of*, and in some words beginning with *om*. *T* and *d*, *b* and *p*, *v* and *w*, remain intact. So much occurs to me in addition to what I said on this head in the preface to the former volume.

Of course in what I have said I wish to be understood as keeping in mind the difference between provincialisms properly so called and *slang*. *Slang* is always vulgar, because it is not a natural but an affected way of talking, and all mere tricks of speech or writing are offensive. I do not think that Mr. Biglow can be fairly charged with vulgarity, and I should have entirely failed in my design, if I had not made it appear that high and even refined sentiment may coexist with the shrewder and more comic elements of the Yankee character. I believe that what is essentially vulgar and mean-spirited in politics seldom has its source in the body of the people, but much rather among those who are made timid by their wealth or selfish by their love of power. A democracy can *afford* much better than an aristocracy to follow out its convictions, and is perhaps better qualified to build those convictions on plain principles of right and wrong, rather than on the shifting sands of expediency. I had always thought ' Sam Slick ' a libel on the Yankee character, and a complete falsification of Yankee modes of speech, though, for aught I know, it may be true in both respects so far as the British provinces are concerned. To me the dialect was native, was spoken all about me when a boy, at a time when an Irish day-labourer was as rare as an American one now. Since then I have made a study of it so far as opportunity allowed. But when I write in it, it is as in a mother tongue, and I am carried back far beyond any studies of it to long-ago noonings in my father's hay-fields, and to the talk of Sam and Job over their jug of *blackstrap* under the shadow of the ash-tree which still dapples the grass whence they have been gone so long.

But life is short, and prefaces should be. And so, my good friends, to whom this introductory epistle is addressed, farewell. Though some of you have remonstrated with me, I shall never write any more ' Biglow Papers,' however great the temptation,—great especially at the present time,—unless it be to complete the original plan of this Series by bringing out Mr. Sawin as an ' original Union man.' The very favour with which they have been received is a hindrance to me, by forcing on me a self-consciousness from which I was entirely free when I wrote the First Series. Moreover, I am no longer the same careless youth, with nothing to do but live to myself, my books, and my friends, that I was then. I always hated politics, in the ordinary sense of the word, and I am not likely to grow fonder of them, now that I have learned how rare it is to find a man who can keep principle clear from party and personal prejudice, or can conceive the possibility of

another's doing so. I feel as if I coul in some sort claim to be an *emeritu* and I am sure that political sati will have full justice done it by tha genuine and delightful humorist, th Rev. Petroleum V. Nasby. I regre that I killed off Mr. Wilbur so soon, f he would have enabled me to bring int this preface a number of learne quotations, which must now go begging, and also enabled me t dispersonalize myself into a vicariou egotism. He would have helped m likewise in clearing myself from a charg which I shall briefly touch on, becaus my friend Mr. Hughes has found needful to defend me in his prefac to one of the English editions of th ' Biglow Papers.' I thank Mr. Hughe heartily for his friendly care of my goo name, and were his Preface accessib to my readers here (as I am glad it not, for its partiality makes me blush I should leave the matter where h left it. The charge is of profanity brought in by persons who proclaime African slavery of Divine institutio and is based (so far as I have hear on two passages in the First Series—

' An' you 've gut to git up airly,
    Ef you want to take in God,'

and,

' God 'll send the bill to you,'

and on some Scriptural illustrations b Mr. Sawin.

Now, in the first place, I was writin under an assumed character, and mus talk as the person would whose mout piece I made myself. Will an one familiar with the New Englan countryman venture to tell me tha he does *not* speak of sacred thing familiarly ? that Biblical allusion (allusions, that is, to the single boo with whose language, from his church going habits, he is intimate) are n frequent on his lips ? If so, he cann have pursued his studies of the charac ter on so many long-ago muster-field and at so many cattle-shows as I. Bu I scorn any such line of defence, an will confess at once that one of the things I am proud of in my countrymen is (I am not speaking now of such persons as I have assumed Mr. Sawin to be) that they do not put their Maker away far from them, or interpret the fear of God into being afraid of Him. The Talmudists had conceived a deep truth when they said, that 'all things were in the power of God, save the fear of God'; and when people stand in great dread of an invisible power, I suspect they mistake quite another personage for the Deity. I might justify myself for the passages criticized by many parallel ones from Scripture, but I need not. The Reverend Homer Wilbur's note-books supply me with three apposite quotations. The first is from a Father of the Roman Church, the second from a Father of the Anglican, and the third from a Father of Modern English poetry. The Puritan divines would furnish me with many more such. St. Bernard says, *Sapiens nummularius est Deus: nummum fictum non recipiet;* 'A cunning money-changer is God: he will take in no base coin.' Latimer says, 'You shall perceive that God, by this example, shaketh us by the noses and taketh us by the ears.' Familiar enough, both of them, one would say! But I should think Mr. Biglow had verily stolen the last of the two maligned passages from Dryden's 'Don Sebastian,' where I find

And beg of Heaven to charge the bill on me!'

And there I leave the matter, being willing to believe that the Saint, the Martyr, and even the Poet, were as careful of God's honour as my critics are ever likely to be.

J. R. L.

THE COURTIN'.

God makes sech nights, all white an' still
  Fur 'z you can look or listen,
Moonshine an' snow on field an' hill,
  All silence an' all glisten.

Zekle crep' up quite unbeknown
  An' peeked in thru' the winder,
An' there sot Huldy all alone,
  'ith no one nigh to hender.

A fireplace filled the room's one side
  With half a cord o' wood in—
There warn't no stoves (tell comfort died)
  To bake ye to a puddin'.

The wa'nut logs shot sparkles out
  Towards the pootiest, bless her,
An' leetle flames danced all about
  The chiny on the dresser.

Agin the chimbley crook-necks hung,
  An' in amongst 'em rusted
The ole queen's-arm thet gran'ther Young
  Fetched back from Concord busted.

The very room, coz she was in,
  Seemed warm from floor to ceilin',
An' she looked full ez rosy agin
  Ez the apples she was peelin'.

'T was kin' o' kingdom-come to look
  On sech a blessed cretur,
A dogrose blushin' to a brook
  Ain't modester nor sweeter.

He was six foot o' man, A 1,
  Clear grit an' human natur';
None could n't quicker pitch a ton
  Nor dror a furrer straighter.

He 'd sparked it with full twenty gals,
  Hed squired 'em, danced 'em, druv 'em,
Fust this one, an' then thet, by spells—
  All is, he could n't love 'em.

But long o' her his veins 'ould run
    All crinkly like curled maple,
The side she breshed felt full o' sun
    Ez a south slope in Ap'il.

She thought no v'ice hed sech a swing
    Ez hisn in the choir ;
My ! when he made Ole Hunderd
    ring,
    She *knowed* the Lord was nigher.

An' she 'd blush scarlit, right in prayer,
    When her new meetin'-bunnet
Felt somehow thru' its crown a pair
    O' blue eyes sot upon it.

Thet night, I tell ye, she looked *some* !
    She seemed to 've gut a new soul,
For she felt sartin-sure he 'd come,
    Down to her very shoe-sole.

She heered a foot, an' knowed it
    tu,
    A-raspin' on the scraper,—
All ways to once her feelins flew
    Like sparks in burnt-up paper.

He kin' o' l'itered on the mat,
    Some doubtfle o' the sekle,
His heart kep' goin' pity-pat,
    But hern went pity Zekle.

An' yit she gin her cheer a jerk
    Ez though she wished him furder,
An' on her apples kep' to work,
    Parin' away like murder.

' You want to see my Pa, I s'pose ? '
    ' Wal . . . no . . . I come dasignin' '—

' To see my Ma ? She 's sprinklin'
    clo'es
    Agin to-morrer's i'nin'.'

To say why gals acts so or so,
    Or don't, 'ould be presumin' ;
Mebby to mean *yes* an' say *no*
    Comes nateral to women.

He stood a spell on one foot fust,
    Then stood a spell on t' other,
An' on which one he felt the wust
    He could n't ha' told ye nuther.

Says he, ' I 'd better call agin ' ;
    Says she, ' Think likely, Mister ' :
Thet last word pricked him like a pin,
    An' . . . Wal, he up an' kist her.

When Ma bimeby upon 'em slips,
    Huldy sot pale ez ashes,
All kin' o' smily roun' the lips
    An' teary roun' the lashes.

For she was jes' the quiet kind
    Whose naturs never vary,
Like streams that keep a summer mind
    Snowhid in Jenooary.

The blood clost roun' her heart felt
    glued
Too tight for all expressin',
Tell mother see how metters stood,
    An' gin 'em both her blessin'.

Then her red come back like the tide
    Down to the Bay o' Fundy,
An' all I know is they was cried
    In meetin' come nex' Sunday.

THE BIGLOW PAPERS, SECOND SERIES

No. I

BIRDOFREDUM SAWIN, ESQ., TO MR. HOSEA BIGLOW

ETTER FROM THE REVEREND HOMER WILBUR, M. A., ENCLOSING THE EPISTLE AFORESAID

JAALAM, 15th Nov., 1861.

* * * * *

IT is not from any idle wish to obtrude my humble person with undue prominence upon the publick view that resume my pen upon the present occasion. *Juniores ad labores.* But having been a main instrument in escuing the talent of my young parishioner from being buried in the ground, by giving it such warrant with the world as could be derived from name already widely known by several printed discourses (all of which I may be permitted without immodesty to state have been deemed worthy of preservation in the Library of Harvard College by my esteemed friend Mr. Sibley), it seemed becoming that I should not only testify to the genuineness of the following production, but call attention to it, the more as Mr. Biglow had so long been silent as to be in danger of absolute oblivion. I insinuate no claim to any share in the authorship (*vix ea nostra voco*) of the works already published by Mr. Biglow, but merely take to myself the credit of having fulfilled toward them the office of taster (*experto crede*), who, having first tried, could afterward bear witness (*credenzen* it was aptly named by the Germans), an office always arduous, and sometimes even dangerous, as in the case of those devoted persons who venture their lives in the deglutition of patent medicines (*dolus latet in generalibus,*

there is deceit in the most of them) and thereafter are wonderfully preserved long enough to append their signatures to testimonials in the diurnal and hebdomadal prints. I say not this as covertly glancing at the authors of certain manuscripts which have been submitted to my literary judgement (though an epick in twenty-four books on the ' Taking of Jericho ' might, save for the prudent forethought of Mrs. Wilbur in secreting the same just as I had arrived beneath the walls and was beginning a catalogue of the various horns and their blowers, too ambitiously emulous in longanimity of Homer's list of ships, might, I say, have rendered frustrate any hope I could entertain *vacare Musis* for the small remainder of my days), but only the further to secure myself against any imputation of unseemly forth-putting. I will barely subjoin, in this connexion, that, whereas Job was left to desire, in the soreness of his heart, that his adversary had written a book, as perchance misanthropically wishing to indite a review thereof, yet was not Satan allowed so far to tempt him as to send Bildad, Eliphaz, and Zophar each with an unprinted work in his wallet to be submitted to his censure. But of this enough. Were I in need of other excuse, I might add that I write by the express desire of Mr. Biglow himself, whose entire winter leisure is occupied, as he assures me, in answering demands for autographs, a labour exacting enough in itself, and egregiously so to him, who, being no ready penman, cannot sign so much as his name without strange contortions of the face (his nose, even, being essential to complete success) and painfully suppressed Saint-Vitus-dance of every muscle in his body. This, with his having been put in the Commission of the Peace by our excellent Governor (*O, si sic omnes!*) immediately on his accession to office, keeps him continually employed. *Haud inexpertus loquor*, having for many years written myself J. P., and being not seldom applied to for specimens of my chirography, a request to which I have sometimes over weakly assented, believing as I do that nothing written of set purpose can properly be called an autograph, but only those unpremeditated sallies and lively runnings which betray the fireside Man instead of the hunted Notoriety doubling on his pursuers. But it is time that I should bethink me of St. Austin's prayer, *libera me a meipso*, if I would arrive at the matter in hand.

Moreover, I had yet another reason for taking up the pen myself. I am informed that the *Atlantic Monthly* is mainly indebted for its success to the contributions and editorial supervision of Dr. Holmes, whose excellent 'Annals of America' occupy an honoured place upon my shelves. The journal itself I have never seen; but if this be so, it might seem that the recommendation of a brother-clergyman (though *par magis quam similis*) should carry a greater weight. I suppose that you have a department for historical lucubrations, and should be glad, if deemed desirable, to forward for publication my 'Collections for the Antiquities of Jaalam,' and my (now happily complete) pedigree of the Wilbur family from its *fons et origo*, the Wild Boar of Ardennes. Withdrawn from the active duties of my profession by the settlement of a colleague-pastor, the Reverend Jeduthun Hitchcock, formerly of Brutus Four-Corners, I might find time for further contributions to general literature on similar topicks. I have made large advances towards a completer genealogy of Mrs. Wilbur's family, the Pilcoxes, not, if I know myself, from any idle vanity, but with the sole desire of rendering myself useful in my day and generation. *Nulla dies*

sine lineâ. I inclose a meteorological register, a list of the births, deaths, and marriages, and a few *memorabilia* of longevity, in Jaalam East Parish for the last half-century. Though spared to the unusual period of more than eighty years, I find no diminution of my faculties or abatement of my natural vigour, except a scarcely sensible decay of memory and a necessity of recurring to younger eyesight or spectacles for the finer print in Cruden. It would gratify me to make some further provision for declining years from the emoluments of my literary labours. I had intended to effect an insurance on my life, but was deterred therefrom by a circular from one of the offices, in which the sudden death of so large a proportion of the insured was set forth as an inducement, that it seemed to me little less than a tempting of Providence. *Neque in summâ inopiâ levis esse senectus potest, ne sapienti quidem.*

Thus far concerning Mr. Biglow; and so much seemed needful (*brevis esse laboro*) by way of preliminary, after a silence of fourteen years. He greatly fears lest he may in this essay have fallen below himself, well knowing that, if exercise be dangerous on a full stomach, no less so is writing on a full reputation. Beset as he has been on all sides, he could not refrain, and would only imprecate patience till he shall again have 'got the hang' (as he calls it) of an accomplishment long disused. The letter of Mr. Sawin was received some time in last June and others have followed which will in due season be submitted to the publick. How largely his statements are to be depended on, I more than merely dubitate. He was always distinguished for a tendency to exaggeration,—it might almost be qualified by a stronger term. *Fortiter mentire aliquid hœret*, seemed to be his favourite rule of rhetorick. That he is actually where he says he is the postmark would seem to confirm; that he was received with the publick demonstra tions he describes would appear consonant with what we know of the habits of those regions ; but further than this I venture not to decide. I have sometimes suspected a vein of humour in him which leads him to speak by contraries ; but since, in the unrestrained intercourse of private life, I have never observed in him any striking powers of invention, I am the more willing to put a certain qualified faith in the incidents and the details of life and manners which give to his narratives some portion of the interest and entertainment which characterizes a Century Sermon.

It may be expected of me that I should say something to justify myself with the world for a seeming inconsistency with my well-known principles in allowing my youngest son to raise a company for the war, a fact known to all through the medium of the publick prints. I did reason with the young man, but *expellas naturam furcâ, lamenusque recurrit.* Having myself been a chaplain in 1812, I could the less wonder that a man of war had sprung from my loins. It was, indeed, grievous to send my Benjamin, the child of my old age ; but after the discomfiture of Manassas, I with my own hands did buckle on his armour, trusting in the great Comforter and Commander for strength according to my need. For truly the memory of a brave son dead in his shroud were a greater staff of my declining years than a living coward (if those may be said to have lived who carry all of themselves into the grave with them), though his days might be long in the land, and he should get much goods. It is not till our earthen vessels are broken that we find and truly possess the treasure that was laid up in them. *Migravi in animam meam,* I have sought refuge in my own soul ; nor would I be shamed by the heathen comedian with his *Nequam illud verbum, bene vult, nisi bene facit.* During our dark days, I read constantly in the inspired book of Job, which I believe to contain more food to maintain the fibre of the soul for right living and high thinking than all pagan literature together, though I would by no means vilipend the study of the classicks. There I read that Job said in his despair, even as the fool saith in his heart there is no God,—' The tabernacles of robbers prosper, and they that provoke God are secure.' (*Job* xii. 6.) But I sought farther till I found this Scripture also, which I would have those perpend who have striven to turn our Israel aside to the worship of strange gods :—' If I did despise the cause of my man-servant or of my maid-servant when they contended with me, what then shall I do when God riseth up ? and when he visiteth, what shall I answer him ? ' (*Job* xxxi. 13, 14.) On this text I preached a discourse on the last day of Fasting and Humiliation with general acceptance, though there were not wanting one or two Laodiceans who said that I should have waited till the President announced his policy. But let us hope and pray, remembering this of Saint Gregory, *Vult Deus rogari, vult cogi, vult quâdam importunitate vinci.*

We had our first fall of snow on Friday last. Frosts have been unusually backward this fall. A singular circumstance occurred in this town on the 20th October, in the family of Deacon Pelatiah Tinkham. On the previous evening, a few moments before family prayers,

.   .   .   .   .

[The editors of the *Atlantic* find it necessary here to cut short the letter of their valued correspondent, which seemed calculated rather on the rates of longevity in Jaalam than for less favoured localities. They have every encouragement to hope that he will write again.]

With esteem and respect,
Your obedient servant,
HOMER WILBUR, A. M.

It 's some consid'ble of a spell sence I hain't writ no letters,
An' ther' 's gret changes hez took place in all polit'cle metters ;
Some canderdates air dead an' gone, an' some hez ben defeated,
Which 'mounts to pooty much the same ; fer it 's ben proved repeated
A betch o' bread thet hain't riz once ain't goin' to rise agin,
An' it 's jest money throwed away to put the emptins in :
But thet 's wut folks wun't never larn ; they dunno how to go,
Arter you want their room, no more 'n a bullet-headed beau ;
Ther' 's ollers chaps a-hangin' roun' thet can't see peatime 's past,
Mis'ble as roosters in a rain, heads down an' tails half-mast :   10
It ain't disgraceful bein' beat, when a holl nation doos it,
But Chance is like an amberill,—it don't take twice to lose it.

I spose you 're kin' o' cur'ous, now, to know why I hain't writ.
Wal, I 've ben where a litt'ry taste don't somehow seem to git
Th' encouragement a feller 'd think, thet 's used to public schools,
An' where sech things ez paper 'n' ink air clean agin the rules :
A kind o' vicyvarsy house, built dreffle strong an' stout,
So 's 't honest people can't get in, ner t' other sort git out,
An' with the winders so contrived, you 'd prob'ly like the view
Better alookin' in than out, though it seems sing'lar, tu ;   20
But then the landlord sets by ye, can't bear ye out o' sight,
And locks ye up ez reg'lar ez an outside door at night.

This world is awfle contrary : the rope may stretch your neck
Thet mebby kep' another chap frum washin' off a wreck ;
An' you may see the taters grow in one poor feller's patch,
So small no self-respectin' hen thet vallied time 'ould scratch,
So small the rot can't find 'em out, an' then agin, nex' door,
Ez big ez wut hogs dream on when they 're 'most too fat to snore.
But groutin' ain't no kin' o' use ; an' ef the fust throw fails,
Why, up an' try agin, thet 's all,—the coppers ain't all tails ;   30
Though I *hev* seen 'em when I thought they hed n't no more head
Than 'd sarve a nussin' Brigadier thet gits some ink to shed.

When I writ last, I 'd ben turned loose by thet blamed nigger, Pomp,
Ferlorner than a musquash, ef you 'd took an' dreened his swamp :
But I ain't o' the meechin' kind, thet sets an' thinks fer weeks
The bottom 's out o' th' univarse coz their own gillpot leaks.
I hed to cross bayous an' criks, (wal, it did beat all natur',)
Upon a kin' o' corderoy, fust log, then alligator ;
Luck'ly, the critters warn't sharp-sot ; I guess 't wuz overruled
They 'd done their mornin's marketin' an' gut their hunger cooled ;   40
Fer missionaries to the Creeks an' runaways are viewed
By them an' folks ez sent express to be their reg'lar food ;
Wutever 't wuz, they laid an' snoozed ez peacefully ez sinners,
Meek ez disgestin' deacons be at ordination dinners ;
Ef any on 'em turned an' snapped, I let 'em kin' o' taste
My live-oak leg, an' so, ye see, ther' warn't no gret o' waste ;

Fer they found out in quicker time than ef they 'd ben to college
'T warn't heartier food than though 't wuz made out o' the tree o' knowledge.
But *I* tell *you* my other leg hed larned wut pizon-nettle meant,
An' var'ous other usefle things, afore I reached a settlement,   50
An' all o' me thet wuz n't sore an' sendin' prickles thru me
Wuz jest the leg I parted with in lickin' Montezumy :
A useful limb it 's ben to me, an' more of a support
Than wut the other hez ben,—coz I dror my pension for 't.

Wal, I gut in at last where folks wuz civerlized an' white,
Ez I diskivered to my cost afore 't warn't hardly night ;
Fer 'z I wuz settin' in the bar a-takin' sunthin' hot,
An' feelin' like a man agin, all over in one spot,
A feller thet sot oppersite, arter a squint at me,
Lep up an' drawed his peacemaker, an', ' Dash it, Sir,' suz he,   60
' I 'm doubledashed ef you ain't him thet stole my yaller chettle,
(You 're all the stranger thet 's around,) so now you 've gut to settle ;
It ain't no use to argerfy ner try to cut up frisky,
I know ye ez I know the smell of ole chain-lightnin' whisky ;
We 're lor-abidin' folks down here, we 'll fix ye so 's 't a bar
Would n' tech ye with a ten-foot pole ; (Jedge, you jest warm the tar ;)
You 'll think you 'd better ha' gut among a tribe o' Mongrel Tartars,
'fore we 've done showin' how we raise our Southun prize tar-martyrs ;
A moultin' fallen cherubim, ef he should see ye, 'd snicker,
Thinkin' he warn't a suckemstance. Come, genlemun, le' 's liquor ;   70
An', Gin'ral, when you 've mixed the drinks an' chalked 'em up, tote roun'
An' see ef ther' 's a feather-bed (thet 's borryable) in town.
We 'll try ye fair, ole Grafted-leg, an' ef the tar wun't stick,
Th' ain't not a juror here but wut 'll 'quit ye double-quick.'
To cut it short, I wun't say sweet, they gi' me a good dip,
(They ain't *perfessin'* Bahptists here,) then give the bed a rip,—
The jury 'd sot, an' quicker 'n a flash they hetched me out, a livin'
Extemp'ry mammoth turkey-chick fer a Fejee Thanksgivin'.
Thet I felt some stuck up is wut it 's nat'ral to suppose,
When poppylar enthusiasm hed funnished me sech clo'es ;   80
(Ner 't ain't without edvantiges, this kin' o' suit, ye see,
It 's water-proof, an' water 's wut I like kep' out o' me ;)
But nut content with thet, they took a kerridge from the fence
An' rid me roun' to see the place, entirely free 'f expense,
With forty-'leven new kines o' sarse without no charge acquaintcd me,
Gi' me three cheers, an' vowed thet I wuz all their fahncy painted me ;
They treated me to all their eggs ; (they keep 'em I should think,
Fer sech ovations, pooty long, for they wuz mos' distinc' ;)
They starred me thick 'z the Milky-Way with indiscrim'nit cherity,
Fer wut we call reception eggs air sunthin' of a rerity ;   90
Green ones is plentifle anough, skurce wuth a nigger's getherin',
But your dead-ripe ones ranges high fer treatin' Nothun bretherin ;
A spotteder, ringstreakeder child the' warn't in Uncle Sam's
Holl farm,—a cross of striped pig an' one o' Jacob's lambs ;

'T wuz Dannil in the lions' den, new an' enlarged edition,
An' everythin' fust-rate o' 'ts kind ; the' warn't no impersition.
People 's impulsiver down here than wut our folks to home be,
An' kin' o' go it 'ith a resh in raisin' Hail Columby :
Thet 's *so* : an' they swarmed out like bees, for your real Southun men's
Time is n't o' much more account than an ole settin' hen's ;   100
(They jest work semioccashnally, or else don't work at all,
An' so their time an' 'tention both air at saci'ty's call.)
Talk about hospatality ! wut Nothun town d' ye know
Would take a totle stranger up an' treat him gratis so ?
You 'd better b'lieve ther' 's nothin' like this spendin' days an' nights
Along 'ith a dependent race fer civerlizin' whites.

But this wuz all prelim'nary ; it 's so Gran' Jurors here
Fin' a true bill, a hendier way than ourn, an' nut so dear ;
So arter this they sentenced me, to make all tight 'n' snug,
Afore a reg'lar court o' law, to ten years in the Jug.   110
I did n't make no gret defence : you don't feel much like speakin',
When, ef you let your clamshells gape, a quart o' tar will leak in :
I *hev* hearn tell o' wingèd words, but pint o' fact it tethers
The spoutin' gift to hev your words *tu* thick sot on with feathers,
An' Choate ner Webster would n't ha' made an A 1 kin' o' speech
Astride a Southun chestnut horse sharper 'n a baby's screech.
Two year ago they ketched the thief, 'n' seein' I wuz innercent,
They jest uncorked an' le' me run, an' in my stid the sinner sent
To see how *he* liked pork 'n' pone flavoured with wa'nut saplin',
An' nary social priv'ledge but a one-hoss, starn-wheel chaplin.   120
When I come out, the folks behaved mos' gen'manly an' harnsome ;
They 'lowed it would n't be more 'n right, ef I should cuss 'n' darn some :
The Cunnle he apolergized ; suz he, ' I 'll du wut 's right,
I 'll give ye settisfection now by shootin' ye at sight,
An' give the nigger (when he 's caught), to pay him fer his trickin'
In gittin' the wrong man took up, a most H fired lickin',—
It 's jest the way with all on 'em, the inconsistent critters,
They 're 'most enough to make a man blaspheme his mornin' bitters ;
I 'll be your frien' thru thick an' thin an' in all kines o' weathers,
An' all you 'll hev to pay fer 's jest the waste o' tar an' feathers :   130
A lady owned the bed, ye see, a widder, tu, Miss Shennon ;
It wuz her mite ; we would ha' took another, ef ther 'd ben one :
We don't make *no* charge for the ride an' all the other fixins.
Le' 's liquor ; Gin'ral, you can chalk our friend for all the mixins.'
A meetin' then wuz called, where they ' RESOLVED, Thet we respec'
B. S. Esquire for quallerties o' heart an' intellec'
Peculiar to Columby's sile, an' not to no one else's,
Thet makes Európean tyrans scringe in all their gilded pel'ces,
An' doos gret honour to our race an' Southun institootions ' :
(I give ye jest the substance o' the leadin' resolootions :)   140
' RESOLVED, Thet we revere in him a soger 'thout a flor,
A martyr to the princerples o' libbaty an' lor :

Resolved, Thet other nations all, ef sot 'longside o' us,
For vartoo, larnin', chivverlry, ain't noways wuth a cuss.'
They gut up a subscription, tu, but no gret come o' *thet ;*
I 'xpect in cairin' of it roun' they took a leaky hat ;
Though Southun genelmun ain't slow at puttin' down their name,
When they can write,) fer in the eend it comes to jes' the same,
Because, ye see, 't 's the fashion here to sign an' not to think
A critter 'd be so sordid ez to ax 'em for the chink :   150
I did n't call but jest on one, an' *he* drawed toothpick on me,
An' reckoned he warn't goin' to stan' no sech doggauned econ'my ;
So nothin' more wuz realized, 'ceptin' the good-will shown,
Than ef 't had ben from fust to last a reg'lar Cotton Loan.
It 's a good way, though, come to think, coz ye enjy the sense
O' lendin' lib'rally to the Lord, an' nary red o' 'xpense :
Sence then I 've gut my name up for a gin'rous-hearted man
By jes' subscribin' right an' left on this high-minded plan ;
've gin away my thousans so to every Southun sort
O' missions, colleges, an' sech, ner ain't no poorer for 't.   160

' warn't so bad off, arter all ; I need n't hardly mention
That Guv'ment owed me quite a pile for my arrears o' pension,—
  mean the poor, weak thing we *hed :* we run a new one now,
Thet strings a feller with a claim up ta the nighes' bough,
An' *prectises* the rights o' man, purtects down-trodden debtors,
Ner wun't hev creditors about ascrougin' o' their betters :
Jeff 's gut the last idees ther' is, poscrip', fourteenth edition,
He knows it takes some enterprise to run an oppersition ;
Ourn 's the fust thru-by-daylight train, with all ou'doors for deepot ;
Yourn goes so slow you 'd think 't wuz drawed by a las' cent'ry teapot ;—
Wal, I gut all on 't paid in gold afore our State seceded,   171
An' done wal, for Confed'rit bonds warn't jest the cheese I needed :
Nut but wut they 're ez *good* ez gold, but then it 's hard a-breakin' on 'em,
An' ignorant folks is ollers sot an' wun't git used to takin' on 'em ;
They 're wuth ez much ez wut they wuz afore ole Mem'nger signed 'em,
An' go off middlin' wal for drinks, when ther' 's a knife behind 'em ;
We *du* miss silver, jes' fer thet an' ridin' in a bus,
Now we 've shook off the desputs thet wuz suckin' at our pus ;
An' it 's *because* the South 's so rich ; 't wuz nat'ral to expec'
Supplies o' change wuz jes' the things we should n't recollec' ;   180
We 'd ough' to ha' thought aforehan', though, o' thet good rule o' Crockett's,
For 't 's tiresome cairin' cotton-bales an' niggers in your pockets,
Ner 't ain't quite hendy to pass off one o' your six-foot Guineas
An' git your halves an' quarters back in gals an' pickaninnies :
Wal, 't ain't quite all a feller 'd ax, but then ther' 's this to say,
t 's on'y jest among ourselves thet we expec' to pay ;
Our system would ha' caird us thru in any Bible cent'ry,
fore this onscripterl plan come up o' books by double entry ;
We go the patriarkle here out o' all sight an' hearin',
For Jacob warn't a suckemstance to Jeff at financierin' ;   190

He never 'd thought o' borryin' from Esau like all nater
An' then cornfiscatin' all debts to sech a small pertater ;
There 's p'litickle econ'my, now, combined 'ith morril beauty
Thet saycrifices privit eends (your in'my's, tu) to dooty !
Wy, Jeff 'd ha' gin him five an' won his eye-teeth 'fore he knowed it,
An', stid o' wastin' pottage, he 'd ha' eat it up an' owed it.
But I wuz goin' on to say how I come here to dwall ;—
'Nough said, thet, arter lookin' roun', I liked the place so wal,
Where niggers doos a double good, with us atop to stiddy 'em,
By bein' proofs o' prophecy an' suckleatin' medium,   200
Where a man 's sunthin' coz he 's white, an' whisky 's cheap ez fleas,
An' the financial pollercy jes' sooted my idees,
Thet I friz down right where I wuz, married the Widder Shennon,
(Her thirds wuz part in cotton-land, part in the curse o' Canaan,)
An' here I be ez lively ez a chipmunk on a wall,
With nothin' to feel riled about much later 'n Eddam's fall.

Ez fur ez human foresight goes, we made an even trade :
She gut an overseer, an' I a fem'ly ready-made,
The youngest on 'em 's 'mos' growed up, rugged an' spry ez weazles,
So 's 't ther' 's no resk o' doctors' bills fer hoopin'-cough an' measles.
Our farm 's at Turkey-Buzzard Roost, Little Big Boosy River,   211
Wal located in all respex,—fer 't ain't the chills 'n' fever
Thet makes my writin' seem to squirm ; a Southuner 'd allow I'd
Some call to shake, for I 've jest hed to meller a new cowhide.
Miss S. is all 'f a lady ; th' ain't no better on Big Boosy
Ner one with more accomplishmunts 'twixt here an' Tuscaloosy ;
She 's an F. F., the tallest kind, an' prouder 'n the Gran' Turk,
An' never hed a relative thet done a stroke o' work ;
Hern ain't a scrimpin' fem'ly sech ez *you* git up Down East,
Th' ain't a growed member on 't but owes his thousuns et the least :
She *is* some old ; but then agin ther' 's drawbacks in my sheer :   221
Wut 's left o' me ain't more 'n enough to make a Brigadier :
Wust is, thet she hez tantrums ; she 's like Seth Moody's gun
(Him thet wuz nicknamed frum his limp Ole Dot an' Kerry One) ;
He 'd left her loaded up a spell, an' hed to git her clear,
So he onhitched,—Jeerusalem ! the middle o' last year
Wuz right nex' door compared to where she kicked the critter tu
(Though *jest* where he brought up wuz wut no human never knew) ;
His brother Asaph picked her up an' tied her to a tree,
An' then she kicked an hour 'n' a half afore she 'd let it be :   230
Wal, Miss S. *doos* hev cuttins-up an' pourins-out o' vials,
But then she hez her widder's thirds, an' all on us hez trials.
My objec', though, in writin' now warn't to allude to sech,
But to another suckemstance more dellykit to tech,—
I want thet you should grad'lly break my merriage to Jerushy,
An' there 's a heap of argymunts thet 's emple to indooce ye :
Fust place, State's Prison,—wal, it 's true it warn't fer crime, o' course,
But then it 's jest the same fer her in gittin' a disvorce ;

Nex' place, my State 's secedin' out hez leg'lly lef' me free
To merry any one I please, pervidin' it 's a she ;   240
Fin'lly, I never wun't come back, she need n't hev no fear on 't,
But then it 's wal to fix things right fer fear Miss S. should hear on 't ;
Lastly, I 've gut religion South, an' Rushy she 's a pagan
Thet sets by th' graven imiges o' the gret Nothun Dagon ;
(Now I hain't seen one in six munts, for, sence our Treashry Loan,
Though yaller boys is thick anough, eagles hez kind o' flown ;)
An' ef J wants a stronger pint than them thet I hev stated,
Wy, she 's an aliun in'my now, an' I 've been cornfiscated,—
For sence we 've entered on th' estate o' the late nayshnul eagle,
She hain't no kin' o' right but jes' wut I allow ez legle :   250
Wut *doos* Secedin' mean, ef 't ain't thet nat'rul rights hez riz, 'n'
Thet wut is mine 's my own, but wut 's another man's ain't his'n ?

Besides, I could n't do no else ; Miss S. suz she to me,
' You 've sheered my bed,' [thet's when I paid my interduction fee
To Southun rites,] ' an' kep' your sheer,' [wal, I allow it sticked
So 's 't I wuz most six weeks in jail afore I gut me picked,]
' Ner never paid no demmiges ; but thet wun't do no harm,
Pervidin' thet you 'll ondertake to oversee the farm ;
(My eldes' boy 's so took up, wut with the Ringtail Rangers
An' settin' in the Jestice-Court for welcomin' o' strangers ' ;)   260
[He sot on *me* ;] ' an' so, ef you 'll jest ondertake the care
Upon a mod'rit sellery, we 'll up an' call it square ;
But ef you *can't* conclude,' suz she, an' give a kin' o' grin,
' Wy, the Gran' Jurymen, I 'xpect, 'll hev to set agin.'
That 's the way metters stood at fust ; now wut wuz I to du,
But jes' to make the best on 't an' off coat an' buckle tu ?
Ther' ain't a livin' man thet finds an income necessarier
Than me,—bimeby I 'll tell ye how I fin'lly come to merry her.

She hed another motive, tu : I mention of it here
T" encourage lads thet 's growin' up to study 'n' persevere,   270
An' show 'em how much better 't pays to mind their winter-schoolin'
Than to go off on benders 'n' sech, an' waste their time in foolin' ;
Ef 't warn't for studyin' evenins, why, I never 'd ha' ben here
An orn'ment o' saciety, in my approprut spear :
She wanted somebody, ye see, o' taste an' cultivation,
To talk along o' preachers when they stopt to the plantation ;
For folks in Dixie th't read an' rite, onless it is by jarks,
Is skurce ez wut they wuz among th' oridgenle patriarchs ;
To fit a feller f' wut they call the soshle higherarchy,
All thet you 've gut to know is jes' beyund an evrage darky ;   280
Schoolin' 's wut they can't seem to stan', they 're tu consarned high-pressure,
An' knowin' t' much might spile a boy for bein' a Secesher.
We hain't no settled preachin' here, ner ministeril taxes ;
The min'ster's only settlement 's the carpet-bag he packs his
Razor an' soap-brush intu, with his hymbook an' his Bible,—
But they *du* preach, I swan to man, it 's puf'kly indescrib'le !

They go it like an Ericsson's ten-hoss-power coleric ingine,
An' make Ole Split-Foot winch an' squirm, for all he 's used to singein' ;
Hawkins's whetstone ain't a pinch o' primin' to the innards
To hearin' on 'em put free grace t' a lot o' tough old sinhards !   290
But I must eend this letter now : 'fore long I 'll send a fresh un ;
I 've lots o' things to write about, perticklerly Seceshun :
I 'm called off now to mission-work, to let a leetle law in
To Cynthy's hide : an' so, till death, Yourn,

                    BIRDOFREDUM SAWIN.

No. II
MASON AND SLIDELL: A YANKEE IDYLL

TO THE EDITORS OF THE ATLANTIC
MONTHLY

JAALAM, 6th Jan., 1862.

GENTLEMEN,—I was highly gratified
by the insertion of a portion of my letter
in the last number of your valuable and
entertaining Miscellany, though in
a type which rendered its substance
inaccessible even to the beautiful
new spectacles presented to me by
a Committee of the Parish on New
Year's Day. I trust that I was able to
bear your very considerable abridge-
ment of my lucubrations with a spirit
becoming a Christian. My third
granddaughter, Rebekah, aged fourteen
years, and whom I have trained to read
slowly and with proper emphasis
(a practice too much neglected in our
modern systems of education), read
aloud to me the excellent essay upon
' Old Age,' the authour of which I
cannot help suspecting to be a young
man who has never yet known what it
was to have snow (*canities morosa*)
upon his own roof. *Dissolve frigus,
large super foco ligna reponens,* is a rule
for the young, whose wood-pile is yet
abundant for such cheerful lenitives.
A good life behind him is the best
thing to keep an old man's shoulders
from shivering at every breath of
sorrow or ill-fortune. But methinks it
were easier for an old man to feel the
disadvantages of youth than the

advantages of age. Of these latter I
reckon one of the chiefest to be this :
that we attach a less inordinate value
to our own productions, and, dis-
trusting daily more and more our own
wisdom (with the conceit whereof at
twenty we wrap ourselves away from
knowledge as with a garment), do
reconcile ourselves with the wisdom
of God. I could have wished, indeed,
that room might have been made for the
residue of the anecdote relating to
Deacon Tinkham, which would not
only have gratified a natural curiosity
on the part of the publick (as I have
reason to know from several letters of
inquiry already received), but would
also, as I think, have largely increased
the circulation of your Magazine in
this town. *Nihil humani alienum*
there is a curiosity about the affair
of our neighbours which is not only
pardonable, but even commendable.
But I shall abide a more fitting season.

As touching the following literary
effort of Esquire Biglow, much might
be profitably said on the topick of
Idyllick and Pastoral Poetry, and
concerning the proper distinctions to
be made between them, from Theocritus, the inventor of the former, to
Collins, the latest authour I know of
who has emulated the classicks in the
latter style. But in the time of a Civil
War worthy a Milton to defend and
a Lucan to sing, it may be reasonably
doubted whether the publick, never too
studious of serious instruction, might
not consider other objects more
deserving of present attention. Con

cerning the title of Idyll, which Mr. Biglow has adopted at my suggestion, it may not be improper to animadvert, that the name properly signifies a poem somewhat rustick in phrase (for, though the learned are not agreed as to the particular dialect employed by Theocritus, they are universanimous both as to its rusticity and its capacity of rising now and then to the level of more elevated sentiments and expressions), while it is also descriptive of real scenery and manners. Yet it must be admitted that the production now in question (which here and there bears perhaps too plainly the marks of my correcting hand) does partake of the nature of a Pastoral, inasmuch as the interlocutors therein are purely imaginary beings, and the whole is little better than κapnoῦ σκιᾶς ὄναρ. The plot was, as I believe, suggested by the 'Twa Briggs' of Robert Burns, a Scottish poet of the last century, as that found its prototype in the 'Mutual Complaint of Plainstanes and Causey' by Fergusson, though the metre of this latter be different by a foot in each verse. I reminded my talented young parishioner and friend that Concord Bridge had long since yielded to the edacious tooth of Time. But he answered me to this effect: that there was no greater mistake of an authour than to suppose the reader had no fancy of his own; that, if once that faculty was to be called into activity, it were *better* to be in for the whole sheep than the shoulder; and that he knew Concord like a book, —an expression questionable in propriety, since there are few things with which he is not more familiar than with the printed page. In proof of what he affirmed, he showed me some verses which with others he had stricken out as too much delaying the action, but which I communicate in this place because they rightly define 'punkinseed' (which Mr. Bartlett would have a kind of perch,—a creature to which I have found a rod or pole not to be so easily equivalent in our inland

waters as in the books of arithmetic), and because it conveys an eulogium on the worthy son of an excellent father, with whose acquaintance (*eheu, fugaces anni !*) I was formerly honoured.

' But nowadays the Bridge ain't wut they show,
So much ez Em'son, Hawthorne, an' Thoreau.
I know the village, though ; was sent there once
A-schoolin', 'cause to home I played the dunce ;
An' I 've ben sence a-visitin' the Jedge,
Whose garding whispers with the river's edge,
Where I 've sot mornin's lazy as the bream,
Whose on'y business is to head up-stream,
(We call 'em punkin-seed,) or else in chat
Along 'th the Jedge, who covers with his hat
More wit an' gumption an' shrewd Yankee sense
Than there is mosses on an ole stone fence.'

Concerning the subject-matter of the verses, I have not the leisure at present to write so fully as I could wish, my time being occupied with the preparation of a discourse for the forthcoming bi-centenary celebration of the first settlement of Jaalam East Parish. It may gratify the publick interest to mention the circumstance, that my investigations to this end have enabled me to verify the fact (of much historick importance, and hitherto hotly debated) that Shearjashub Tarbox was the first child of white parentage born in this town, being named in his father's will under date August 7th, or 9th, 1662. It is well known that those who advocate the claims of Mehetable Goings are unable to find any trace of her existence prior to October of that year. As respects the settlement of the Mason and Slidell question, Mr. Biglow has not incorrectly stated the popular sentiment, so far as I can judge by its expression in this locality. For myself, I feel more sorrow than resentment : for I am old enough to have heard those talk of England who still, even after the unhappy estrangement, could not unschool their lips from calling her the Mother-Country. But England has insisted on ripping up old wounds, and has undone the healing work of fifty years ; for nations do not reason, they only feel, and the *spretæ injuria formæ* rankles in their minds as bitterly as in that of a woman. And because this is so, I feel the more satisfaction that our Government has acted (as all Goverments should, standing as they do between the people and their passions) as if it had arrived at years of discretion. There are three short and simple words, the hardest of all to pronounce in any language (and I suspect they were no easier before the confusion of tongues), but which no man or nation that cannot utter can claim to have arrived at manhood. Those words are, *I was wrong ;* and I am proud that, while England played the boy, our rulers had strength enough from the People below and wisdom enough from God above to quit themselves like men.

The sore points on both sides have been skilfully exasperated by interested and unscrupulous persons, who saw in a war between the two countries the only hope of profitable return for their investment in Confederate stock, whether political or financial. The always supercilious, often insulting, and sometimes even brutal tone of British journals and publick men has certainly not tended to soothe whatever resentment might exist in America.

' Perhaps it was right to dissemble your love,
But why did you kick me down stairs ? '

We have no reason to complain that England, as a necessary consequence of her clubs, has become a great society for the minding of other people's business, and we can smile good-naturedly when she lectures other nations on the sins of arrogance and conceit ; but we may justly consider it a breach of the political *convenances* which are expected to regulate the intercourse of one well-bred government with another, when men holding places in the ministry allow themselves to dictate our domestic policy, to instruct us in our duty, and to stigmatize as unholy a war for the rescue of whatever a high-minded people should hold most vital and most sacred. Was it in good taste, that I may use the mildest term, for Earl Russell to expound our own Constitution to President Lincoln, or to make a new and fallacious application of an old phrase for our benefit, and tell us that the Rebels were fighting for independence and we for empire ? As if all wars for independence were by nature just and deserving of sympathy, and all wars for empire ignoble and worthy only of reprobation, or as if these easy phrases in any way characterized this terrible struggle,—terrible not so truly in any superficial sense, as from the essential and deadly enmity of the principles that underlie it. His Lordship's bit of borrowed rhetoric would justify Smith O'Brien, Nana Sahib, and the Maori chieftains, while it would condemn nearly every war in which England has ever been engaged. Was it so very presumptuous in us to think that it would be decorous in English statesmen if they spared time enough to acquire some kind of knowledge, though of the most elementary kind, in regard to this country and the questions at issue here, before they pronounced so off-hand a judgement ? Or is political information expected to come Dogberry-fashion in England, like reading and writing, by nature ?

And now all respectable England is wondering at our irritability, and sees a quite satisfactory explanation of it in our national vanity. *Suave mari magno*, it is pleasant, sitting in the easy-chairs of Downing Street, to sprinkle pepper on the raw wounds of a kindred people struggling for life, and philosophical to find in self-conceit the cause of our instinctive resentment. Surely we were of all nations the least liable to any temptation of vanity at a time when the gravest anxiety and the keenest sorrow were never absent from our hearts. Nor is conceit the exclusive attribute of any one nation. The earliest of English travellers, Sir John Mandeville, took a less provincial view of the matter when he said, ' For fro what partie of the erthe that men duellen, other aboven or beneathen, it semethe alweys to hem that duellen that thei gon more righte than any other folke.' The English have always had their fair share of this amiable quality. We may say of them still, as the authour of the *Lettres Cabalistiques* said of them more than a century ago, ' *Ces derniers disent naturellement qu'il n'y a qu'eux qui soient estimables.*' And, as he also says, ' *J'aimerois presque autant tomber entre les mains d'un Inquisiteur que d'un Anglois qui me fait sentir sans cesse combien il s'estime plus que moi, et qui ne daigne me parler que pour injurier ma Nation et pour m'ennuyer du récit des grandes qualités de la sienne.*' Of *this* Bull we may safely say with Horace, *habet fœnum in cornu.* What we felt to be especially insulting was the quiet assumption that the descendants of men who left the Old World for the sake of principle, and who had made the wilderness into a New World patterned after an Idea, could not possibly be susceptible of a generous or lofty sentiment, could have no feeling of nationality deeper than that of a tradesman for his shop. One would have thought, in listening to England, that we were presumptuous in fancying that we were a nation at all, or had any other principle of union than that of booths at a fair, where there is no higher notion of government than the constable, or better image of God than that stamped upon the current coin.

It is time for Englishmen to consider whether there was nothing in the spirit of their press and of their leading public men calculated to rouse a just indignation, and to cause a permanent estrangement on the part of any nation capable of self-respect, and sensitively jealous, as ours then was, of foreign interference. Was there nothing in the indecent haste with which belligerent rights were conceded to the Rebels, nothing in the abrupt tone assumed in the Trent case, nothing in the fitting out of Confederate privateers, that might stir the blood of a people already overcharged with doubt, suspicion, and terrible responsibility ? The laity in any country do not stop to consider points of law, but they have an instinctive appreciation of the *animus* that actuates the policy of a foreign nation ; and in our own case they remembered that the British authorities in Canada did not wait till diplomacy could send home to England for her slow official tinder-box to fire the ' Caroline.' Add to this, what every sensible American knew, that the moral support of England was equal to an army of two hundred thousand men to the Rebels, while it insured us another year or two of exhausting war. It was not so much the spite of her words (though the time might have been more tastefully chosen) as the actual power for evil in them that we felt as a deadly wrong. Perhaps the most immediate and efficient cause of mere irritation was the sudden and unaccountable change of manner on the other side of the water. Only six months before, the Prince of Wales had come over to call us cousins ; and everywhere it was nothing but ' our American brethren,' that great offshoot of British institutions in the New World, so almost identical with them in laws, language, and literature,—this last of the alliterative compliments being so bitterly true, that perhaps it will not be retracted even now. To this outburst of long-repressed affection we responded with genuine warmth, if with something of the awkwardness of a poor relation bewildered with the sudden tightening of the ties of consanguinity when it is rumored that he has come into a large estate. Then came the Rebellion, and, *presto !* a flaw in our titles was discovered, the plate we were promised at the family table is flung at our head, and we were again the scum of creation, intolerably vulgar, at once cowardly and overbearing,—no relations of theirs, after all, but a dreggy hybrid of the basest bloods of Europe. Panurge was not quicker to call Friar John his *former* friend. I cannot help thinking of Walter Mapes's jingling paraphrase of Petronius,—

' Dummodo sim splendidis vestibus ornatus,
Et multa familia sim circumvallatus,
Prudens sum et sapiens et morigeratus,
Et tuus nepos sum et tu meus cognatus,'—

which I may freely render thus :—

So long as I was prosperous, I'd dinners by the dozen,
Was well-bred, witty, virtuous, and everybody's cousin ;
If luck should turn, as well she may, her fancy is so flexile,
Will virtue, cousinship, and all return with her from exile ?

There was nothing in all this to exasperate a philosopher, much to make him smile rather ; but the earth's surface is not chiefly inhabited by philosophers, and I revive the recollection of it now in perfect good-humour, merely by way of suggesting to our *ci-devant* British cousins, that it would have been easier for them to hold their tongues than for us to keep our tempers under the circumstances.

The English Cabinet made a blunder, unquestionably, in taking it so hastily for granted that the United States had fallen forever from their position as a first-rate power, and it was natural that they should vent a little of their vexation on the people whose inexplicable obstinacy in maintaining freedom and order, and in resisting degradation, was likely to convict them of their mistake. But if bearing a grudge be the sure mark of a small mind in the individual, can it be a proof of high spirit in a nation ? If the result of the present estrangement between the two countries shall be to make us more independent of British twaddle (*Indomito nec dira ferens stipendia Tauro*), so much the better ; but if it

is to make us insensible to the value of British opinion in matters where it gives us the judgment of an impartial and cultivated outsider, if we are to shut ourselves out from the advantages of English culture, the loss will be ours, and not theirs. Because the door of the old homestead has been once slammed in our faces, shall we in a huff reject all future advances of conciliation, and cut ourselves foolishly off from any share in the humanizing influences of the place, with its ineffable riches of association, its heirlooms of immemorial culture, its historic monuments, ours no less than theirs, its noble gallery of ancestral portraits ? We have only to succeed, and England will not only respect, but, for the first time, begin to understand us. And let us not, in our justifiable indignation at wanton insult, forget that England is not the England only of snobs who dread the democracy they do not comprehend, but the England of history, of heroes, statesmen, and poets, whose names are dear, and their influence as salutary to us as to her.

Let us strengthen the hands of those in authority over us, and curb our own tongues, remembering that General Wait commonly proves in the end more than a match for General Headlong, and that the Good Book ascribes safety to a multitude, indeed, but not to a mob, of counsellours. Let us remember and perpend the words of Paulus Emilius to the people of Rome ; that, ' if they judged they could manage the war to more advantage by any other, he would willing yield up his charge ; but if they confided in him, *they were not to make themselves his colleagues in his office, or raise reports, or criticise his actions, but, without talking, supply him with means and assistance necessary to the carrying on of the war ; for, if they proposed to command their own commander, they would render this expedition more ridiculous than the former.*' (*Vide Plutarchum in Vitâ P. E.*) Let us also not forget what the same excellent authour says concerning Perseus's fear of spending money, and not permit the covetousness of Brother Jonathan to be the good fortune of Jefferson Davis. For my own part, till I am ready to admit the Commander-in-Chief to my pulpit, I shall abstain from planning his battles. If courage be the sword, yet is patience the armour of a nation; and in our desire for peace, let us never be willing to surrender the Constitution bequeathed us by fathers at least as wise as ourselves (even with Jefferson Davis to help us), and, with those degenerate Romans, *tuta et presentia quam vetera et periculosa malle.*

And not only should we bridle our own tongues, but the pens of others, which are swift to convey useful intelligence to the enemy. This is no new inconvenience ; for, under date, 3d June, 1745, General Pepperell wrote thus to Governor Shirley from Louisbourg : ' What your Excellency observes of the *army's being made acquainted with any plans proposed, until ready to be put in execution,* has always been disagreeable to me, and I have given many cautions relating to it. But when your Excellency considers that *our Council of War consists of more than twenty members,* I am persuaded you will think it *impossible for me to hinder it,* if any of them will persist in communicating to inferior officers and soldiers what ought to be kept secret. I am informed that the Boston newspapers are filled with paragraphs from private letters relating to the expedition. Will your Excellency permit me to say I think it may be of ill consequence ? Would it not be convenient, if your Excellency should forbid the Printers' inserting such news ? ' Verily, if *tempora mutantur,* we may question the *et nos mutamur in illis ;* and if tongues be leaky, it will need all hands at the pumps to save the Ship of State. Our history dotes and repeats itself. If Sassycus (rather than Alcibiades) find a parallel in Beauregard, so Weakwash, as he is called by the brave Lieutenant Lion Gardiner, need not seek far among our own Sachems for his antitype.

With respect,
> Your ob^t humble serv^t,
> HOMER WILBUR, A. M.

I LOVE to start out arter night 's begun,
An' all the chores about the farm are done,
The critters milked an' foddered, gates shet fast,
Tools cleaned aginst to-morrer, supper past,
An' Nancy darnin' by her ker'sene lamp,—
I love, I say, to start upon a tramp,
To shake the kinkles out o' back an' legs,
An' kind o' rack my life off from the dregs
Thet 's apt to settle in the buttery-hutch
Of folks thet foller in one rut too much :   10
Hard work is good an' wholesome, past all doubt ;
But 't ain't so, ef the mind gits tuckered out.
Now, bein' born in Middlesex, you know,
There 's certin spots where I like best to go :
The Concord road, for instance, (I, for one,
Most gin'lly ollers call it *John Bull's Run,*)
The field o' Lexin'ton where England tried
The fastest colours thet she ever dyed,
An' Concord Bridge, thet Davis, when he came,
Found was the bee-line track to heaven an' fame,   20

Ez all roads be by natur', ef your soul
Don't sneak thru shun-pikes so 's to save the toll.

They 're 'most too fur away, take too much time
To visit of'en, ef it ain't in rhyme ;
But the' 's a walk thet 's hendier, a sight,
An' suits me fust-rate of a winter's night,—
I mean the round whale's-back o' Prospect Hill.
I love to l'iter there while night grows still,
An' in the twinklin' villages about,
Fust here, then there, the well-saved lights goes out,   30
An' nary sound but watch-dogs' false alarms,
Or muffled cock-crows from the drowsy farms,
Where some wise rooster (men act jest thet way)
Stands to 't thet moon-rise is the break o' day :
(So Mister Seward sticks a three-months' pin
Where the war 'd oughto eend, then tries agin ;
My gran'ther's rule was safer 'n 't is to crow :
Don't never prophesy—onless ye know.)
I love to muse there till it kind o' seems
Ez ef the world went eddyin' off in dreams ;   40
The northwest wind thet twitches at my baird
Blows out o' sturdier days not easy scared,
An' the same moon thet this December shines
Starts out the tents an' booths o' Putnam's lines ;
The rail-fence posts, acrost the hill thet runs,
Turn ghosts o' sogers should'rin' ghosts o' guns ;
Ez wheels the sentry, glints a flash o' light,
Along the firelock won at Concord Fight,
An', 'twixt the silences, now fur, now nigh,
Rings the sharp chellenge, hums the low reply.   50

Ez I was settin' so, it warn't long sence,
Mixin' the puffict with the present tense,
I heerd two voices som'ers in the air,
Though, ef I was to die, I can't tell where :
Voices I call 'em : 't was a kind o' sough
Like pine-trees thet the wind 's ageth'rin' through ;
An', fact, I thought it *was* the wind a spell,
Then some misdoubted, could n't fairly tell,
Fust sure, then not, jest as you hold an eel,
I knowed, an' did n't,—fin'lly seemed to feel   60
'T was Concord Bridge a talkin' off to kill
With the Stone Spike thet 's druv thru Bunker Hill ;
Whether 't was so, or ef I on'y dreamed,
I could n't say ; I tell it ez it seemed.

THE BRIDGE

Wal, neighbor, tell us wut 's turned up thet 's new ?
You 're younger 'n I be,—nigher Boston, tu :

An' down to Boston, ef you take their showin',
Wut they don't know ain't hardly wuth the knowin'.
Ther 's *sunthin'* goin' on, I know : las' night
The British sogers killed in our gret fight   70
(Nigh fifty year they hed n't stirred nor spoke)
Made sech a coil you 'd thought a dam hed broke :
Why, one he up an' beat a revellee
With his own crossbones on a holler tree,
Till all the graveyards swarmed out like a hive
With faces I hain't seen sence Seventy-five.
Wut *is* the news ?   'T ain't good, or they 'd be cheerin'.
Speak slow an' clear, for I 'm some hard o' hearin'.

THE MONIMENT

I don't know hardly ef it 's good or bad,—

THE BRIDGE

At wust, it can't be wus than wut we 've had.   80

THE MONIMENT

You know them envys thet the Rebbles sent,
An' Cap'n Wilkes he borried o' the Trent ?

THE BRIDGE

Wut ! they ha'n't hanged 'em ?   Then their wits is gone !
Thet 's the sure way to make a goose a swan !

THE MONIMENT

No : England she *would* hev 'em, *Fee, Faw, Fum !*
(Ez though she hed n't fools enough to home,)
So they 've returned 'em—

THE BRIDGE

                  Hev they ?   Wal, by heaven,
Thet 's the wust news I 've heerd sence Seventy-seven !
By George, I meant to say, though I declare
It 's 'most enough to make a deacon swear.   90

THE MONIMENT

Now don't go off half-cock : folks never gains
By usin' pepper-sarse instid o' brains.
Come, neighbor, you don't understand—

THE BRIDGE

                           How ?   Hey ?
Not understand ?   Why, wut 's to hender, pray ?
Must I go huntin' round to find a chap
To tell me when my face hez hed a slap ?

THE MONIMENT

See here : the British they found out a flaw
In Cap'n Wilkes's readin' o' the law :
(They *make* all laws, you know, an' so, o' course,
It 's nateral they should understan' their force :)   100
He 'd oughto ha' took the vessel into port,
An' hed her sot on by a reg'lar court ;
She was a mail-ship, an' a steamer, tu,
An' thet, they say, hez changed the pint o' view,
Coz the old practice, bein' meant for sails,
Ef tried upon a steamer, kind o' fails ;
You *may* take out despatches, but you mus' n't
Take nary man—

THE BRIDGE

You mean to say, you dus' n't !
Changed pint o' view ! No, no,—it 's overboard
With law an' gospel, when their ox is gored !   110
I tell ye, England's law, on sea an' land,
Hez ollers ben, ' *I 've gut the heaviest hand.*'
Take nary man ? Fine preachin' from *her* lips !
Why, she hez taken hunderds from our ships,
An' would agin, an' swear she had a right to,
Ef we warn't strong enough to be perlite to.
Of all the sarse thet I can call to mind,
England *doos* make the most onpleasant kind :
It 's you 're the sinner ollers, she 's the saint ;
Wut 's good 's all English, all thet is n't ain't ;   120
Wut profits her is ollers right an' just,
An' ef you don't read Scriptur so, you must ;
She 's praised herself ontil she fairly thinks
There ain't no light in Natur when she winks ;
Hain't she the Ten Comman'ments in her pus ?
Could the world stir 'thout she went, tu, ez nus ?
She ain't like other mortals, thet 's a fact :
She never stopped the habus-corpus act,
Nor specie payments, nor she never yet
Cut down the int'rest on her public debt ;   130
She don't put down rebellions, lets 'em breed,
An' 's ollers willin' Ireland should secede ;
She 's all thet 's honest, honnable, an' fair,
An' when the vartoos died they made her heir.

THE MONIMENT

Wal, wal, two wrongs don't never make a right ;
Ef we 're mistaken, own up, an' don't fight :
For gracious' sake, ha' n't we enough to du
'thout gettin' up a fight with England, tu ?
She thinks we 're rabble-rid—

THE BRIDGE

An' so we càn't
Distinguish 'twixt *You ought n't* an' *You sha' n't !*   140
She jedges by herself ; she 's no idear
How 't stiddies folks to give 'em their fair sheer :
The odds 'twixt her an' us is plain 's a steeple,—
Her People 's turned to Mob, our Mob 's turned People.

THE MONIMENT

She 's riled jes' now—

THE BRIDGE

Plain proof her cause ain't strong,—
The one thet fust gits mad 's 'most ollers wrong.
Why, sence she helped in lickin' Nap the Fust,
An' pricked a bubble jest agoin' to bust,
With Rooshy, Prooshy, Austry, all assistin',
Th' ain't nut a face but wut she 's shook her fist in,   150
Ez though she done it all, an' ten times more,
An' nothin' never hed gut done afore,
Nor never could agin', 'thout she wuz spliced
On to one eend an' gin th' old airth a hoist.
She *is* some punkins, thet I wun't deny,
(For ain't she some related to you 'n' I ?)
But there 's a few small intrists here below
Outside the counter o' John Bull an' Co,
An', though they can't conceit how 't should be so,
I guess the Lord druv down Creation's spiles   160
'thout no *gret* helpin' from the British Isles,
An' could contrive to keep things pooty stiff
Ef they withdrawed from business in a miff ;
I ha' n't no patience with sech swellin' fellers ez
Think God can't forge 'thout them to blow the bellerses.

THE MONIMENT

You 're ollers quick to set your back aridge,
Though 't suits a tom-cat more 'n a sober bridge :
Don't you git het : they thought the thing was planned ;
They 'll cool off when they come to understand.

THE BRIDGE

Ef *thet* 's wut you expect, you 'll hev to wait: 170
Folks never understand the folks they hate :
She 'll fin' some other grievance jest ez good,
'fore the month 's out, to git misunderstood.
England cool off ! She 'll do it, ef she sees
She 's run her head into a swarm o' bees.

I ain't so prejudiced ez wut you spose:
I hev thought England was the best thet goes;
Remember (no, you can't), when *I* was reared,
God save the King was all the tune you heerd:
But it 's enough to turn Wachuset roun'   180
This stumpin' fellers when you think they 're down.

THE MONIMENT

But, neighbour, ef they prove their claim at law,
The best way is to settle, an' not jaw.
An' don't le' 's mutter 'bout the awfle bricks
We 'll give 'em, ef we ketch 'em in a fix:
That 'ere 's most frequently the kin' o' talk
Of critters can't be kicked to toe the chalk;
Your ' You 'll see *nex*' time ! ' an' ' Look out bumby ! '
'Most ollers ends in eatin' umble-pie.
'T wun't pay to scringe to England: will it pay   190
To fear that meaner bully, old ' They 'll say ' ?
Suppose they *du* say: words are dreffle bores,
But they ain't quite so bad ez seventy-fours.
Wut England wants is jest a wedge to fit
Where it 'll help to widen out our split:
She 's found her wedge, an' 't ain't for us to come
An' lend the beetle thet 's to drive it home.
For growed-up folks like us 't would be a scandle,
When we git sarsed, to fly right off the handle.
England ain't *all* bad, coz she thinks us blind: 200
Ef she can't change her skin, she can her mind;
An' we shall see her change it double-quick,
Soon ez we 've proved thet we 're a-goin' to lick.
She an' Columby's gut to be fas' friends:
For the world prospers by their privit ends:
'T would put the clock back all o' fifty years
Ef they should fall together by the ears.

THE BRIDGE

I 'gree to thet; she 's nigh us to wut France is;
But then she 'll hev to make the fust advances;
We 've gut pride, tu, an' gut it by good rights,   210
An' ketch *me* stoopin' to pick up the mites
O' condescension she 'll be lettin' fall
When she finds out we ain't dead arter all !
I tell ye wut, it takes more 'n one good week
Afore *my* nose forgits it 's hed a tweak.

THE MONIMENT

She 'll come out right bumby, thet I 'll engage,
Soon ez she gits to seein' we 're of age;
This talkin' down o' hers ain't wuth a fuss;
It 's nat'ral ez nut likin' 't is to us;

Ef we 're agoin' to prove we *be* growed-up,   220
'T wunt be by barkin' like a tarrier pup,
But turnin' to an' makin' things ez good
Ez wut we 're ollers braggin' that we could ;
We 're bound to be good friends, an' so we 'd oughto,
In spite of all the fools both sides the water.

THE BRIDGE

I b'lieve thet 's so ; but hearken in your ear,—
I 'm older 'n you,—Peace wun't keep house with Fear :
Ef you want peace, the thing you 've gut to du
Is jes' to show you 're up to fightin', tu.
I recollect how sailors' rights was won,   230
Yard locked in yard, hot gun-lip kissin' gun :
Why, afore thet, John Bull sot up thet he
Hed gut a kind o' mortgage on the sea ;
You 'd thought he held by Gran'ther Adam's will,
An' ef you knuckle down, *he* 'll think so still.
Better thet all our ships an' all their crews
Should sink to rot in ocean's dreamless ooze,
Each torn flag wavin' chellenge ez it went,
An' each dumb gun a brave man's moniment,
Than seek sech peace ez only cowards crave :   240
Give *me* the peace of dead men or of brave !

THE MONIMENT

I say, ole boy, it ain't the Glorious Fourth :
You 'd oughto larned 'fore this wut talk wuz worth.
It ain't *our* nose thet gits put out o' jint ;
It 's England thet gives up her dearest pint.
We 've gut, I tell ye now, enough to du
In our own fem'ly fight, afore we 're thru.
I hoped, las' spring, jest arter Sumter's shame,
When every flag-staff flapped its tethered flame,
An' all the people, startled from their doubt,   250
Come must'rin' to the flag with sech a shout,—
I hoped to see things settled 'fore this fall,
The Rebbles licked, Jeff Davis hanged, an' all ;
Then come Bull Run, an' *sence* then I 've ben waitin'
Like boys in Jennooary thaw for skatin',
Nothin' to du but watch my shadder's trace
Swing, like a ship at anchor, roun' my base,
With daylight's flood an' ebb : it 's gittin' slow,
An' I 'most think we 'd better let 'em go.
I tell ye wut, this war 's a-goin' to cost—   260

THE BRIDGE

An' I tell *you* it wun't be money lost ;
Taxes milks dry, but, neighbour, you 'll allow
Thet havin' things onsettled kills the cow :

We 've gut to fix this thing for good an' all ;
It 's no use buildin' wut 's a-goin' to fall.
I 'm older 'n you, an' I 've seen things an' men,
An' *my* experunce,—tell ye wut it 's ben :
Folks thet worked thorough was the ones thet thriv,
But bad work follers ye ez long 's ye live ;
You can't git red on 't ; jest ez sure ez sin,   270
It 's ollers askin' to be done agin :
Ef we should part, it would n't be a week
'Fore your soft-soddered peace would spring aleak.
We 've turned our cuffs up, but, to put her thru,
We must git mad an' off with jackets, tu ;
'T wun't du to think thet killin' ain't perlite,—
You 've gut to be in airnest, ef you fight ;
Why, two-thirds o' the Rebbles 'ould cut dirt,
Ef they once thought thet Guv'ment meant to hurt ;
An' I *du* wish our Gin'rals hed in mind   280
The folks in front more than the folks behind ;
You wun't do much ontil you think it 's God,
An' not constitoounts, thet holds the rod ;
We want some more o' Gideon's sword, I jedge,
For proclamations ha'n't no gret of edge ;
There 's nothin' for a cancer but the knife,
Onless you set by 't more than by your life.
I 've seen hard times ; I see a war begun
Thet folks thet love their bellies never 'd won ;
Pharo's lean kine hung on for seven long year ;   290
But when 't was done, we did n't count it dear.
Why, law an' order, honor, civil right,
Ef they *ain't* wuth it, wut *is* wuth a fight ?
I 'm older 'n you : the plough, the axe, the mill,
All kin's o' labour an' all kin's o' skill,
Would be a rabbit in a wile-cat's claw,
Ef 't warn't for thet slow critter, 'stablished law ;
Onsettle *thet,* an' all the world goes whiz,
A screw 's gut loose in everythin' there is :
Good buttresses once settled, don't you fret   300
An' stir 'em ; take a bridge's word for thet !
Young folks are smart, but all ain't good thet 's new
I guess the gran'thers they knowed sunthin', tu.

THE MONIMENT

Amen to thet ! build sure in the beginnin' :
An' then don't never tech the underpinnin' :
Th' older a guv'ment is, the better 't suits ;
New ones hunt folks's corns out like new boots :
Change jes' for change, is like them big hotels
Where they shift plates, an' let ye live on smells.

THE BRIDGE

Wal, don't give up afore the ship goes down: 310
It's a stiff gale, but Providence wun't drown;
An' God wun't leave us yit to sink or swim,
Ef we don't fail to du wut's right by Him.
This land o' ourn, I tell ye, 's gut to be
A better country than man ever see.
I feel my sperit swellin' with a cry
Thet seems to say, ' Break forth an' prophesy ! '
O strange New World, thet yit wast never young,
Whose youth from thee by gripin' need was wrung,
Brown foundlin' o' the woods, whose baby-bed   320
Was prowled roun' by the Injun's cracklin' tread,
An' who grew'st strong thru shifts an' wants an' pains,
Nussed by stern men with empires in their brains,
Who saw in vision their young Ishmel strain
With each hard hand a vassal ocean's mane,
Thou, skilled by Freedom an' by gret events
To pitch new States ez Old-World men pitch tents,
Thou, taught by Fate to know Jehovah's plan
Thet man's devices can't unmake a man,
An' whose free latch-string never was drawed in   330
Against the poorest child of Adam's kin,—
The grave's not dug where traitor hands shall lay
In fearful haste thy murdered corse away !
I see—
            Jest here some dogs begun to bark,
So thet I lost old Concord's last remark :
I listened long, but all I seemed to hear
Was dead leaves gossipin' on some birch-trees near ;
But ez they hed n't no gret things to say,
An' sed 'em often, I come right away,
An', walkin' home'ards, jest to pass the time,   340
I put some thoughts thet bothered me in rhyme ;
I hain't hed time to fairly try 'em on,
But here they be—it 's

JONATHAN TO JOHN

It don't seem hardly right, John,
    When both my hands was full,
To stump me to a fight, John,—
    Your cousin, tu, John Bull !
        Ole Uncle S. sez he, ' I guess
        We know it now,' sez he,
' The lion's paw is all the law,
        Accordin' to J. B.,
        Thet 's fit for you an' me ! '

You wonder why we're hot, John ?
    Your mark wuz on the guns,
The neutral guns, thet shot, John,
    Our brothers an' our sons :
        Ole Uncle S. sez he, ' I guess
        There 's human blood,' sez he,
' By fits an' starts, in Yankee hearts,
        Though 't may surprise J. B.
        More 'n it would you an' me.'

Ef *I* turned mad dogs loose, John,
  On *your* front-parlor stairs,
Would it jest meet your views, John,
  To wait an' sue their heirs ?
    Ole Uncle S. sez he, ' I guess,
    I on'y guess,' sez he,
' Thet ef Vattel on *his* toes fell,
  'T would kind o' rile J. B.,
  Ez wal ez you an' me ! '

Who made the law thet hurts, John,
  Heads I win,—ditto tails ?
' *J. B.*' was on his shirts, John,
  Onless my memory fails,
    Ole Uncle S. sez he, ' I guess
    (I 'm good at thet),' sez he,
' Thet sauce for goose ain't *jest* the juice
    For ganders with J. B.,
    No more 'n with you or me ! '

When your rights was our wrongs, John,
  You did n't stop for fuss,—
Britanny's trident prongs, John,
  Was good 'nough law for us.
    Ole Uncle S. sez he, ' I guess,
    Though physic 's good,' sez he,
' It does n't foller thet he can swaller
    Prescriptions signed ' *J. B.*,'
    Put up by you an' me ! '

We own the ocean, tu, John :
  You mus' n' take it hard,
Ef we can't think with you, John.
  It 's jest your own back-yard.
    Ole Uncle S. sez he, ' I guess,
    Ef *thet* 's his claim,' sez he,
' The fencin'-stuff 'll cost enough
    To bust up friend J. B.,
    Ez wal ez you an' me ! '

Why talk so dreffle big, John,
  Of honor when it meant
You did n't care a fig, John,
  But jest for *ten per cent ?*
    Ole Uncle S. sez he, ' I guess
    He 's like the rest,' sez he :
' When all is done, it 's number one
    Thet 's nearest to J. B.,
    Ez wal ez t' you an' me ! '

We give the critters back, John,
  Cos Abram thought 't was right ;
It warn't your bullyin' clack, John,
  Provokin' us to fight.
    Ole Uncle S. sez he, ' I guess
    We 've a hard row,' sez he,
' To hoe jest now ; but thet somehow,
    May happen to J. B.,
    Ez wal ez you an' me ! '

We ain't so weak an' poor, John,
  With twenty million people,
An' close to every door, John,
  A school-house an' a steeple.
    Ole Uncle S. sez he, ' I guess,
    It is a fact,' sez he,
' The surest plan to make a Man
    Is, think him so, J. B.,
    Ez much ez you or me ! '

Our folks believe in Law, John ;
  An' it 's for her sake, now,
They 've left the axe an' saw, John,
  The anvil an' the plough.
    Ole Uncle S. sez he, ' I guess,
    Ef 't warnt for law,' sez he,
' There 'd be one shindy from here to Indy ;
    An' thet don't suit J. B.
    (When 't ain't 'twixt you an' me !) '

We know we 've got a cause, John,
  Thet 's honest, just, an' true ;
We thought 't would win applause, John,
  Ef nowheres else, from you.
    Ole Uncle S. sez he, ' I guess
    His love of right,' sez he,
' Hangs by a rotten fibre o' cotton :
    There 's natur' in J. B.,
    Ez wal ez you an' me ! '

The South says, ' *Poor folks down !*' John,
  An' ' *All men up !*' say we,—
White, yaller, black, an' brown, John :
  Now which is your idee ?

Ole Uncle S. sez he, ' I guess,
  John preaches wal,' sez he ;
' But, sermon thru, an' come to *du*,
  Why, there 's the old J. B.
    A crowdin' you an' me ! '

Shall it be love, or hate, John ?
  It 's you thet 's to decide ;
Ain't *your* bonds held by Fate, John,
  Like all the world's beside ?
    Ole Uncle S. sez he, ' I guess
    Wise men forgive,' sez he,
' But not forget ; an' some time yet
    Thet truth may strike J. B.,
    Ez wal ez you an' me ! '

God means to make this land, John,
  Clear thru, from sea to sea,
Believe an' understand, John,
  The *wuth* o' bein' free.
    Ole Uncle S. sez he, ' I guess,
    God's price is high,' sez he ;
' But nothin' else than wut He sells
    Wears long, an' thet J. B.
    May larn, like you an' me ! '

No. III

BIRDOFREDUM SAWIN, ESQ., TO MR. HOSEA BIGLOW

With the following Letter from the REVEREND HOMER WILBUR, A. M.

TO THE EDITORS OF THE ATLANTIC MONTHLY

JAALAM, 7th Feb., 1862.

RESPECTED FRIENDS,—If I know myself,—and surely a man can hardly be supposed to have overpassed the limit of fourscore years without attaining to some proficiency in that most useful branch of learning (*e cœlo descendit*, says the pagan poet),—I have no great smack of that weakness which would press upon the publick attention any matter pertaining to my private affairs. But since the following letter of Mr. Sawin contains not only a direct allusion to myself, but that in connection with a topick of interest to all those engaged in the publick ministrations of the sanctuary, I may be pardoned for touching briefly thereupon. Mr. Sawin was never a stated attendant upon my preaching, —never, as I believe, even an occasional one, since the erection of the new house (where we now worship) in 1845. He did, indeed, for a time, supply a not unacceptable bass in the choir ; but, whether on some umbrage (*omnibus hoc vitium est cantoribus*) taken against the bass-viol, then, and till his decease in 1850 (*æt.* 77,) under the charge of Mr. Asaph Perley, or, as was reported by others, on account of an imminent subscription for a new bell, he thenceforth absented himself from all outward and visible communion. Yet he seems to have preserved (*altâ mente repostum*), as it were, in the pickle of a mind soured by prejudice, a lasting *scunner*, as he would call it, against our staid and decent form of worship ; for I would rather in that wise interpret his fling, than suppose that any chance tares sown by my pulpit discourses should survive so long, while good seed too often fails to root itself. I humbly trust that I have no personal feeling in the matter ; though I know that, if we sound any man deep enough, our lead shall bring up the mud of human nature at last. The Bretons believe in an evil spirit which they call *ar c'houskezik*, whose office it is to make the congregation drowsy ; and though I have never had reason to think that he was specially busy among my flock, yet have I seen enough to make me sometimes regret the hinged seats of the ancient meeting-house, whose lively clatter, not unwillingly intensified by boys beyond eyeshot of the tithing-man, served at intervals as a wholesome *réveil*. It is true, I have numbered among my parishioners some who are proof against the prophylactick fennel, nay, whose gift of somnolence rivalled that of the Cretan Rip Van Winkle, Epimenides, and who, nevertheless, complained not so much of the substance as of the length of my (by them unheard) discourses. Some ingenious persons of a philosophick turn have assured us that our pulpits were set too high, and that the soporifick tendency increased with the ratio of the angle in which the hearer's eye was constrained to seek the preacher. This were a curious topick for investigation. There can be no doubt that some sermons are pitched too high, and I remember many struggles with the drowsy fiend in my youth. Happy Saint Anthony of Padua, whose finny acolytes, however they might profit, could never murmur ! *Quare fremuerunt gentes ?* Who is he that can twice a week be inspired, or has eloquence (*ut ita dicam*) always on tap ? A good man, and, next to David, a sacred poet (himself, haply, not inexpert of evil in this particular), has said,—

' The worst speak something good : if all want sense,
God takes a text and preacheth patience.'

There are one or two other points in Mr. Sawin's letter which I would also briefly animadvert upon. And first, concerning the claim he sets up to a certain superiority of blood and lineage in the people of our Southern States, now unhappily in rebellion against lawful authority and their own better interests. There is a sort of opinions, anachronisms at once and anachorisms, foreign both to the age and the country, that maintain a feeble and buzzing existence, scarce to be called life, like winter flies, which in mild weather crawl out from obscure nooks and crannies to expatiate in the sun, and sometimes acquire vigor enough to disturb with their enforced familiarity the studious hours of the scholar. One of the most stupid and pertinacious of these is the theory that the Southern States were settled by a class of emigrants from the Old World socially superior to those who founded the institutions of New England. The Virginians especially lay claim to this

generosity of lineage, which were of no possible account, were it not for the fact that such superstitions are sometimes not without their effect on the course of human affairs. The early adventurers to Massachusetts at least paid their passages ; no felons were ever shipped thither ; and though it be true that many deboshed younger brothers of what are called good families may have sought refuge in Virginia, it is equally certain that a great part of the early deportations thither were the sweepings of the London streets and the leavings of the London stews. It was this my Lord Bacon had in mind when he wrote : ' It is a shameful and unblessed thing to take the scum of people and wicked condemned men to be the people with whom you plant.' That certain names are found there is nothing to the purpose, for, even had an *alias* been beyond the invention of the knaves of that generation, it is known that servants were often called by their masters' names, as slaves are now. On what the heralds call the spindle side, some, at least, of the oldest Virginian families are descended from matrons who were exported and sold for so many hogsheads of tobacco the head. So notorious was this, that it became one of the jokes of contemporary playwrights, not only that men bankrupt in purse and character were ' food for the Plantations ' (and this before the settlement of New England), but also that any drab would suffice to wive such pitiful adventurers. ' Never choose a wife as if you were going to Virginia,' says Middleton in one of his comedies. The mule is apt to forget all but the equine side of his pedigree. How early the counterfeit nobility of the Old Dominion became a topick of ridicule in the Mother Country may be learned from a play of Mrs. Behn's, founded on the Rebellion of Bacon : for even these kennels of literature may yield a fact or two to pay the raking. Mrs. Flirt, the keeper of a Virginia ordinary, calls herself the daughter of a baronet ' undone in the late rebellion,'—her father having in truth been a tailor,—and three of the Council, assuming to themselves an equal splendor of origin, are shown to have been, one 'a broken exciseman who came over a poor servant,' another a tinker transported for theft, and the third 'a common pickpocket often flogged at the cart's tail.' The ancestry of South Carolina will as little pass muster at the Herald's Visitation, though I hold them to have been more reputable, inasmuch as many of them were honest tradesmen and artisans, in some measure exiles for conscience' sake, who would have smiled at the high-flying nonsense of their descendants. Some of the more respectable were Jews. The absurdity of supposing a population of eight millions all sprung from gentle loins in the course of a century and a half is too manifest for confutation. But of what use to discuss the matter? An expert genealogist will provide any solvent man with a *genus et proavos* to order. My Lord Burleigh said (and the Emperor Frederick II before him), that 'nobility was ancient riches,' whence also the Spanish were wont to call their nobles *ricos hombres,* and the aristocracy of America are the descendants of those who first became wealthy, by whatever means. Petroleum will in this wise be the source of much good blood among our posterity. The aristocracy of the South, such as it is, has the shallowest of all foundations, for it is only skin-deep,—the most odious of all, for, while affecting to despise trade, it traces its origin to a successful traffick in men, women, and children, and still draws its chief revenues thence. And though, as Doctor Chamberlayne consolingly says in his *Present State of England,* 'to become a Merchant of Foreign Commerce, without serving any Apprentisage, hath been allowed no disparagement to a Gentleman born, especially to a younger Brother,' yet I conceive that he would hardly have made a like exception in favour of the particular trade in question. Oddly enough this trade reverses the ordinary standards of social respectability no less than of morals, for the retail and domestick is as creditable as the wholesale and foreign is degrading to him who follows it. Are our morals, then, no better than *mores* after all? I do not believe that such aristocracy as exists at the South (for I hold with Marius, *fortissimum quemque generosissimum*) will be found an element of anything like persistent strength in war,—thinking the saying of Lord Bacon (whom one quaintly called *inductionis dominus et Verulamii*) as true as it is pithy, that 'the more gentlemen, ever the more books of subsidies.' It is odd enough as an historical precedent, that, while the fathers of New England were laying deep in religion, education, and freedom the basis of a polity which has substantially outlasted any then existing, the first work of the founders of Virginia, as may be seen in Wingfield's *Memorial,* was conspiracy and rebellion, —odder yet, as showing the changes which are wrought by circumstance, that the first insurrection in South Carolina was against the aristocratical scheme of the Proprietary Government. I do not find that the cuticular aristocracy of the South has added anything to the refinements of civilization except the carrying of bowie-knives and the chewing of tobacco,—a high-toned Southern gentleman being commonly not only *quadrumanous* but *quidruminant.*

I confess that the present letter of Mr. Sawin increases my doubts as to the sincerity of the convictions which he professes, and I am inclined to think that the triumph of the legitimate Government, sure sooner or later to take place, will find him and a large majority of his newly adopted fellow-citizens (who hold with Dædalus, the primal sitter-on-the-fence, that *medium tenere tutissimum*) original Union men. The criticisms towards the close of his letter on certain of our failings are worthy to be seriously perpended; for he is not, as I think, without a spice of vulgar shrewdness. *Fas est et ab hoste doceri :* there is no reckoning without your host. As to the good-nature in us which he seems to gird at, while I would not consecrate a chapel, as they have not scrupled to do in France, to *Nôtre Dame de la Haine* (Our Lady of Hate), yet I cannot forget that the corruption of good-nature is the generation of laxity of principle. Good-nature is our national character-istick; and though it be, perhaps, nothing more than a culpable weakness or cowardice, when it leads us to put up tamely with manifold impositions and breaches of implied contracts, (as too frequently in our publick conveyances,) it becomes a positive crime, when it leads us to look unresent-fully on peculation, and to regard treason to the best Government that ever existed as something with which a gentleman may shake hands without soiling his fingers. I do not think the gallows-tree the most profitable member of our *Sylva ;* but, since it continues to be planted, I would fain see a Northern limb ingrafted on it, that it may bear some other fruit than loyal Ten-nesseeans.

A relick has recently been discovered on the east bank of Bushy Brook in North Jaalam, which I conceive to be an inscription in Runick characters relating to the early expedition of the Northmen to this continent. I shall make fuller investigations, and com-municate the result in due season.

Respectfully,

Your obedient servant,

HOMER WILBUR, A. M.

P.S.—I inclose a year's subscription from Deacon Tinkham.

I HED it on my min' las' time, when I to write ye started,
To tech the leadin' featurs o' my gittin' me converted ;
But, ez my letters hez to go clearn roun' by way o' Cuby,
'T wun't seem no staler now than then, by th' time it gits where you be.
You know up North, though secs an' things air plenty ez you please,
Ther' warn't nut one on 'em thet come jes' square with my idees :
They all on 'em wuz too much mixed with Covenants o' Works,
An' would hev answered jest ez wal for Afrikins an' Turks,
Fer where 's a Christian's privilege an' his rewards ensuin',
Ef 't ain't perfessin' right an eend 'thout nary need o' doin' ?   10
I dessay they suit workin'-folks thet ain't noways pertic'lar,
But nut your Southun gen'leman thet keeps his parpendic'lar ;
I don't blame nary man thet casts his lot along o' *his* folks,
But ef you cal'late to save *me*, 't must be with folks thet *is* folks ;
Cov'nants o' works go 'ginst my grain, but down here I 've found out
The true fus'-fem'ly A 1 plan,—here 's how it come about.
When I fus' sot up with Miss S., sez she to me, sez she,
' Without you git religion, Sir, the thing can't never be ;
Nut but wut I respeck,' sez she, ' your intellectle part,
But you wun't noways du for me athout a change o' heart :   20
Nothun religion works wal North, but it 's ez soft ez spruce,
Compared to ourn, for keepin' sound,' sez she, ' upon the goose ;
A day's experunce 'd prove to ye, ez easy 'z pull a trigger,
It takes the Southun pint o' view to raise ten bales a nigger ;
You 'll fin' thet human natur', South, ain't wholesome more 'n skin-deep,
An' once 't a darkie 's took with it, he wun't be wuth his keep.'

How *shell* I git it, Ma'am ? ' sez I.   ' Attend the nex' camp-meetin','
Sez she, ' an' it 'll come to ye ez cheap ez onbleached sheetin'.'

Wal, so I went along an' hearn most an impressive sarmon
About besprinklin' Afriky with fourth-proof dew o' Harmon :   30
He did n't put no weaknin' in, but gin it tu us hot,
Z ef he an' Satan 'd ben two bulls in one five-acre lot :
I don't purtend to foller him, but give ye jes' the heads ;
For pulpit ellerkence, you know, 'most ollers kin' o' spreads.
Ham's seed wuz gin to us in chairge, an' should n't we be li'ble
In Kingdom Come, ef we kep' back their priv'lege in the Bible ?
The cusses an' the promerses make one gret chain, an' ef
You snake one link out here, one there, how much on 't ud be lef' ?
All things wuz gin to man for 's use, his sarvice, an' delight ;
An' don't the Greek an' Hebrew words thet mean a Man mean White ?
Ain't it belittlin' the Good Book in all its proudes' featurs   41
To think 't wuz wrote for black an' brown an' 'lasses-coloured creaturs,
Thet could n' read it, ef they would, nor ain't by lor allowed to,
But ough' to take wut we think suits their naturs, an' be proud to ?
Warn't it more prof'table to bring your raw materil thru
Where you can work it inta grace an' inta cotton, tu,
Than sendin' missionaries out where fevers might defeat 'em,
An' ef the butcher did n' call, their p'rishioners might eat 'em ?
An' then, agin, wut airthly use ?   Nor 't warn't our fault, in so fur
Ez Yankee skippers would keep on a-totin' on 'em over.   50
'T improved the whites by savin' 'em from ary need o' wurkin',
An' kep' the blacks from bein' lost thru idleness an' shirkin' ;
We took to 'em ez nat'ral ez a barn-owl doos to mice,
An' hed our hull time on our hands to keep us out o' vice ;
'T made us feel ez pop'lar ez a hen doos with one chicken,
An' fill our place in Natur's scale by givin' 'em a lickin' :
For why should Cæsar git his dues more 'n Juno, Pomp, an' Cuffy ?
't 's justifyin' Ham to spare a nigger when he 's stuffy.
Where 'd their soles go tu, like to know, ef we should let 'em ketch
Freeknowledgism an' Fourierism an' Speritoolism an' sech ?   60
When Satan sets himself to work to raise his very bes' muss,
He scatters roun' onscriptur'l views relatin' to Ones'mus.
You 'd ough' to seen, though, how his facs an' argymunce an' figgers
Drawed tears o' real conviction from a lot o' pen'tent niggers !
't warn't like Wilbur's meetin', where you 're shet up in a pew,
Your dickeys sorrin' off your ears, an' bilin' to be thru ;
ther' wuz a tent clost by thet hed a kag o' sunthin' in it,
Where you could go, ef you wuz dry, an' damp ye in a minute ;
An' ef you did dror off a spell, ther' wuz n't no occasion
To lose the thread, because, ye see, he bellered like all Bashan.   70
't 's dry work follerin' argymunce an' so, 'twix' this an' thet,
felt conviction weighin' down somehow inside my hat ;
't growed an' growed like Jonah's gourd, a kin' o' whirlin' ketched me,
Until I fin'lly clean gin out an' owned up thet he d' fetched me ;

LOWELL   M

An' when nine tenths o' th' perrish took to tumblin' roun' an' hollerin',
I did n' fin' no gret in th' way o' turnin' tu an' follerin'.
Soon ez Miss S. see thet, sez she, ' *Thet* 's wut I call wuth seein' ' !
Thet 's actin' like a reas'nable an' intellectle bein' ! '
An' so we fin'lly made it up, concluded to hitch hosses,
An' here I be 'n my ellermunt among creation's bosses ;   8c
Arter I 'd drawed sech heaps o' blanks, Fortin at last hez sent a prize,
An' chose me for a shinin' light o' missionary entaprise.

This leads me to another pint on which I 've changed my plan
O' thinkin' so 's 't I might become a straight-out Southun man.
Miss S. (her maiden name wuz Higgs, o' the fus' fem'ly here)
On her Ma's side 's all Juggernot, on Pa's all Cavileer,
An' sence I 've merried into her an' stept into her shoes,
It ain't more 'n nateral thet I should modderfy my views :
I 've ben a-readin' in Debow ontil I 've fairly gut
So 'nlightened thet I 'd full ez lives ha' ben a Dook ez nut ;   9c
An' when we 've laid ye all out stiff, an' Jeff hez gut his crown,
An' comes to pick his nobles out, *wun't* this child be in town !
We 'll hev an Age o' Chivverlry surpassin' Mister Burke's,
Where every fem'ly is fus'-best an' nary white man works :
Our system 's sech, the thing 'll root ez easy ez a tater ;
For while your lords in furrin parts ain't noways marked by natur',
Nor sot apart from ornery folks in featurs nor in figgers,
Ef ourn 'll keep their faces washed, you 'll know 'em from their niggers.
Ain't *sech* things wuth secedin' for, an' gittin' red o' you
Thet waller in your low idees, an' will till all is blue ?   10c
Fact is, we *air* a diff'rent race, an' I, for one, don't see,
Sech havin' ollers ben the case, how w' ever *did* agree.
It 's sunthin' thet you lab'rin'-folks up North hed ough' to think on,
Thet Higgses can't bemean themselves to rulin' by a Lincoln,—
Thet men, (an' guv'nors, tu,) thet hez sech Normal names ez Pickens,
Accustomed to no kin' o' work, 'thout 't is to givin' lickins,
Can't masure votes with folks thet get their livins from their farms,
An' prob'ly think thet Law 's ez good ez hevin' coats o' arms.
Sence I 've ben here, I 've hired a chap to look about for me
To git me a transplantable an' thrifty fem'ly-tree,   11c
An' he tells *me* the Sawins is ez much o' Normal blood
Ez Pickens an' the rest on 'em, an' older 'n Noah's flood.
Your Normal schools wun't turn ye into Normals, for it 's clear,
Ef eddykatin' done the thing, they 'd be some skurcer here.
Pickenses, Boggses, Pettuses, Magoffins, Letchers, Polks,—
Where can you scare up names like them among your mudsill folks ?
Ther 's nothin' to compare with em', you 'd fin', ef you should glance,
Among the tip-top femerlies in Englan', nor in France :
I 've hearn from 'sponsible men whose word wuz full ez good 's their note
Men thet can run their face for drinks, an' keep a Sunday coat,   12c
That they wuz all on 'em come down, an' come down pooty fur,
From folks thet, 'thout their crowns wuz on, ou' doors would n' never stir

Nor thet ther' warn't a Southun man but wut wuz *primy fashy*
O' the bes' blood in Europe, yis, an' Afriky an' Ashy:
Sech bein' the case, is 't likely we should bend like cotton wickin',
Or set down under anythin' so low-lived ez a lickin' ?
More 'n this,—hain't we the literatoor an science, tu, by gorry ?
Hain't we them intellectle twins, them giants, Simms an' Maury,
Each with full twice the ushle brains, like nothin' thet I know,
'thout 't wuz a double-headed calf I see once to a show ?   130

For all thet, I warn't jest at fust in favour o' secedin';
I wuz for layin' low a spell to find out where 't wuz leadin',
For hevin' South-Carliny try her hand at sepritnationin',
She takin' resks an' findin' funds, an' we co-operationin',—
I mean a kin' o' hangin' roun' an' settin' on the fence,
Till Prov'dunce pinted how to jump an' save the most expense ;
I recollected thet 'ere mine o' lead to Shiraz Centre
Thet bust up Jabez Pettibone, an' didn't want to ventur'
'Fore I wuz sartin wut come out ud pay for wut went in,
For swappin' silver off for lead ain't the sure way to win ;   140
(An', fact, it *doos* look now ez though—but folks must live an' larn—
We should git lead, an' more 'n we want, out o' the Old Consarn ;)
But when I see a man so wise an' honest ez Buchanan
A-lettin' us hev all the forts an' all the arms an' cannon,
Admittin' we wuz nat'lly right an' you wuz nat'lly wrong,
Coz you wuz lab'rin'-folks an' we wuz wut they call *bong-tong*,
An' coz there warn't no fight in ye more 'n in a mashed potater,
While two o' *us* can't skurcely meet but wut we fight by natur',
An' th' ain't a bar-room here would pay for openin' on 't a night,
Without it giv the priverlege o' bein' shot at sight,   150
Which proves we 're Natur's noblemen, with whom it don't surprise
The British aristoxy should feel boun' to sympathize,—
Seein' all this, an' seein', tu, the thing wuz strikin' roots
While Uncle Sam sot still in hopes thet some one 'd bring his boots,
I thought th' ole Union's hoops wuz off, an' let myself be sucked in
To rise a peg an' jine the crowd thet went for reconstructin',—
Thet is to hev the pardnership under th' ole name continner
Jest ez it wuz, we drorrin' pay, you findin' bone an' sinner,—
On'y to put it in the bond, an' enter 't in the journals,
Thet you 're the nat'ral rank an' file, an' we the nat'ral kurnels.   160

Now this I thought a fees'ble plan, thet 'ud work smooth ez grease,
Suitin' the Nineteenth Century an' Upper Ten idees,
An' there I meant to stick, an' so did most o' th' leaders, tu,
Coz we all thought the chance wuz good o' puttin' on it thru ;
But Jeff he hit upon a way o' helpin' on us forrard
By bein' unannermous,—a trick you ain't quite up to, Norrard.
A Baldin hain't no more 'f a chance with them new apple-corers
Than folks's oppersition views aginst the Ringtail Roarers ;
They 'll take 'em out on him 'bout east,—one canter on a rail
Makes a man feel unannermous ez Jonah in the whale ;   170

Or ef he 's a slow-moulded cuss thet can't seem quite t' 'gree,
He gits the noose by tellergraph upon the nighes' tree :
Their mission-work with Afrikins hez put 'em up, thet 's sartin,
To all the mos' across-lot ways o' preachin' an' convartin' ;
I 'll bet my hat th' ain't nary priest, nor all on em together,
Thet cairs conviction to the min' like Reveren' Taranfeather ;
Why, he sot up with me one night, an' laboured to sech purpose,
Thet (ez an owl by daylight 'mongst a flock o' teazin' chirpers
Sees clearer 'n mud the wickedness o' eatin' little birds)
I see my error an' agreed to shen it arterwurds ;   180
An' I should say, (to jedge our folks by facs in my possession,)
Thet three 's Unannermous where one 's a 'Riginal Secession ;
So it 's a thing you fellers North may safely bet your chink on,
Thet we 're all water-proofed agin th' usurpin' reign o' Lincoln.

Jeff 's *some*.   He 's gut another plan thet hez pertic'lar merits,
In givin' things a cheerfle look an' stiffnin' loose-hung sperits ;
For while your million papers, wut with lyin' an' discussin',
Keep folks's tempers all on eend a-fumin' an a-fussin',
A-wondrin' this an' guessin' thet, an' dreadin' every night
The breechin' o' the Univarse 'll break afore it 's light,   190
Our papers don't purtend to print on'y wut Guv'ment choose,
An' thet insures us all to git the very best o' noose :
Jeff hez it of all sorts an' kines, an' sarves it out ez wanted,
So 's 't every man gits wut he likes an' nobody ain't scanted ;
Sometimes it 's vict'ries (they 're 'bout all ther' is that 's cheap down here,)
Sometimes it 's France an' England on the jump to interfere.
Fact is, the less the people know o' wut ther' is a-doin',
The hendier 't is for Guv'ment, sence it henders trouble brewin' ;
An' nooze is like a shinplaster,—it 's good, ef you believe it,
Or, wut 's all same, the other man thet 's goin' to receive it :   200
Ef you 've a son in th' army, wy, it 's comfortin' to hear
He 'll hev no gretter resk to run than seein' th' in'my's rear,
Coz, ef an F. F. looks at 'em, they ollers break an' run,
Or wilt right down ez debtors will thet stumble on a dun,
(An' this, ef an'thin', proves the wuth o' proper fem'ly pride,
Fer sech mean shucks ez creditors are all on Lincoln's side) ;
Ef I hev scrip thet wun't go off no more 'n a Belgin rifle,
An' read thet it 's at par on 'Change, it makes me feel deli'fle ;
It 's cheerin', tu, where every man mus' fortify his bed,
To hear thet Freedom 's the one thing our darkies mos'ly dread,   210
An' thet experunce, time 'n' agin, to Dixie's Land hez shown
Ther' 's nothin' like a powder-cask fer a stiddy corner-stone ;
Ain't it ez good ez nuts, when salt is sellin' by the ounce
For its own weight in Treash'ry-bons, (ef bought in small amounts,)
When even whiskey 's gittin' skurce an' sugar can't be found,
To know thet all the ellerments o' luxury abound ?
An' don't it glorify sal'-pork, to come to understand
It 's wut the Richmon' editors call fatness o' the land !

Nex' thing to knowin' you 're well off is *nut* to know when y' ain't ;
An' ef Jeff says all 's goin' wal, who 'll ventur' t' say it ain't ?   220

This cairn the Constitooshun roun' ez Jeff doos in his hat
Is hendier a dreffle sight, an' comes more kin' o' pat.
I tell ye wut, my jedgement is you 're pooty sure to fail,
Ez long 'z the head keeps turnin' back for counsel to the tail :
Th' advantiges of our consarn for bein' prompt air gret,
While, 'long o' Congress, you can't strike, 'f you git an iron het ;
They bother roun' with argooin', an' var'ous sorts o' foolin',
To make sure ef it 's leg'lly het, an' all the while it 's coolin',
So 's 't when you come to strike, it ain't no gret to wish ye j'y on,
An' hurts the hammer 'z much or more ez wut it doos the iron,   230
Jeff don't allow no jawin'-sprees for three months at a stretch,
Knowin' the ears long speeches suits air mostly made to metch ;
He jes' ropes in your tonguey chaps an' reg'lar ten-inch bores
An' lets 'em play at Congress, ef they 'll du it with closed doors ;
So they ain't no more bothersome than ef we' d took an' sunk 'em,
An' yit enj'y th' exclusive right to one another's Buncombe
'thout doin' nobody no hurt, an' 'thout its costin' nothin,'
Their pay bein' jes' Confedrit funds, they findin' keep an' clothin' ;
They taste the sweets o' public life, an' plan their little jobs,
An' suck the Treash'ry, (no gret harm, for it 's ez dry ez cobs,)   240
An' go thru all the motions jest ez safe ez in a prison,
An' hev their business to themselves, while Buregard hez hisn :
Ez long 'z he gives the Hessians fits, committees can't make bother
'bout whether 't 's done the legle way or whether 't 's done the t'other.
An' *I* tell *you* you 've gut to larn thet War ain't one long teeter
Betwixt *I wan' to* an' *'T wun't du*, debatin' like a skeetur
Afore he lights,—all is, to give the other side a millin',
An' arter thet 's done, th' ain't no resk but wut the lor 'll be willin' ;
No metter wut the guv'ment is, ez nigh ez I can hit it,
A lickin' 's constitooshunal, pervidin' *We* don't git it.   250
Jeff don't stan' dilly-dallyin', afore he takes a fort,
(With no one in,) to git the leave o' the nex' Soopreme Court,
Nor don't want forty-'leven weeks o' jawin' an' expoundin',
To prove a nigger hez a right to save him, ef he 's drowndin' ;
Whereas ole Abram 'd sink afore he 'd let a darkie boost him,
Ef Taney should n't come along an' hed n't interdooced him.
It ain't your twenty millions thet 'll ever block Jeff's game,
But one Man thet wun't let 'em jog jest ez he 's takin' aim :
Your numbers they may strengthen ye or weaken ye, ez 't heppens
They 're willin' to be helpin' hands or wuss'n-nothin' cap'ns.   260

I 've chose my side, an' 't ain't no odds ef I wuz drawed with magnets.
Or ef I thought it prudenter to jine the nighes' bagnets ;
I 've made my ch'ice, an' ciphered out, from all I see an' heard,
Th' ole Constitooshun never 'd git her decks for action cleared,
Long 'z you elect for Congressmen poor shotes thet want to go
Coz they can't seem to git their grub no otherways than so,

An' let your bes' men stay to home coz they wun't show ez talkers,
Nor can't be hired to fool ye an' sof'-soap ye at a caucus,—
Long 'z ye set by Rotashun more 'n ye do by folks's merits,
Ez though experunce thriv by change o' sile, like corn an' kerrits,—   270
Long 'z you allow a critter's ' claims ' coz, spite o' shoves an' tippins,
He 's kep' his private pan jest where 't would ketch mos' public drippins',—
Long 'z A. 'll turn tu an' grin' B.'s exe, ef B. 'll help him grin' hisn,
(An' thet 's the main idee by which your leadin' men hev risen,)—
Long 'z you let *ary* exe be groun', 'less 't is to cut the weasan'
O' sneaks thet dunno till they 're told wut is an' wut ain't Treason,—
Long 'z ye give out commissions to a lot o' peddlin' drones
Thet trade in whiskey with their men an' skin 'em to their bones,—
Long 'z ye sift out ' safe ' canderdates thet no one ain't afeard on
Coz they 're so thund'rin' eminent for bein' never heard on,   280
An' hain't no record, ez it 's called, for folks to pick a hole in,
Ez ef it hurt a man to hev a body with a soul in,
An' it wuz ostentashun to be showin' on 't about,
When half his feller-citizens contrive to du without,—
Long 'z you suppose your votes can turn biled kebbage into brain,
An' ary man thet 's pop'lar 's fit to drive a lightnin'-train,—
Long 'z you believe democracy means *I'm ez good ez you be*,
An' that a feller from the ranks can't be a knave or booby,—
Long 'z Congress seems purvided, like yer street-cars an' yer 'busses,
With ollers room for jes' one more o' your spiled-in-bakin' cusses,   290
Dough 'thout the emptins of a soul, an' yit with means about 'em
(Like essence-peddlers [1]) thet 'll make folks long to be without 'em,
Jest heavy 'nough to turn a scale thet 's doubtfle the wrong way,
An' make their nat'ral arsenal o' bein' nasty pay,—
Long 'z them things last, (an' *I* don't see no gret signs of improvin',)
I sha' n't up stakes, not hardly yit, nor 't would n't pay for movin' ;
For, 'fore you lick us, it 'll be the long'st day ever *you* see.
Yourn, (ez I 'xpec' to be nex' spring,)

B., Markiss o' Big Boosy.

No. IV.

A MESSAGE OF JEFF DAVIS
IN SECRET SESSION.

Conjecturally reported by H. Biglow.

TO THE EDITORS OF THE ATLANTIC
MONTHLY.

Jaalam, 10th March, 1862.

Gentlemen,—My leisure has been so entirely occupied with the hitherto fruitless endeavour to decypher the Runick inscription whose fortunate discovery I mentioned in my last communication, that I have not found time to discuss, as I had intended, the great problem of what we are to do with slavery,—a topick on which the publick mind in this place is at present more than ever agitated. What my wishes and hopes are I need not say, but for safe conclusions I do not conceive that we are yet in possession of facts enough on which to bottom them with certainty. Acknowledging the hand of Providence, as I do, in all events, I am sometimes inclined to

[1] A rustic euphemism for the American variety of the *Mephitis.*—H. W.

think that they are wiser than we, and am willing to wait till we have made this continent once more a place where freemen can live in security and honour, before assuming any further responsibility. This is the view taken by my neighbour Habakkuk Sloansure, Esq., the president of our bank, whose opinion in the practical affairs of life has great weight with me, as I have generally found it to be justified by the event, and whose counsel, had I followed it, would have saved me from an unfortunate investment of a considerable part of the painful economies of half a century in the North-west-Passage Tunnel. After a somewhat animated discussion with this gentleman, a few days since, I expanded, on the *audi alteram partem* principle, something which he happened to say by way of illustration, into the following fable.

FESTINA LENTE.

Once on a time there was a pool
Fringed all about with flag-leaves cool
And spotted with cow-lilies garish,
Of frogs and pouts the ancient parish.
Alders the creaking redwings sink on,
Tussocks that house blithe Bob o' Lincoln
Hedged round the unassailed seclusion,
Where muskrats piled their cells Carthusian;
And many a moss-embroidered log,
The watering-place of summer frog,   10
Slept and decayed with patient skill,
As watering-places sometimes will.

Now in this Abbey of Theleme,
Which realized the fairest dream
That ever dozing bull-frog had,
Sunned on a half-sunk lily-pad,
There rose a party with a mission
To mend the polliwogs' condition,
Who notified the sélectmen
To call a meeting there and then.   20
'Some kind of steps,' they said, ' are needed ;
They don't come on so fast as we did :
Let 's dock their tails ; if that don't make
   'em
Frogs by brevet, the Old One take 'em !
That boy, that came the other day
To dig some flag-root down this way,
His jack-knife left, and 't is a sign
That Heaven approves of our design :
'T were wicked not to urge the step on,
When Providence has sent the weapon.'

Old croakers, deacons of the mire,   31
That led the deep batrachian choir,
Uk! Uk! Caronk! with bass that might
Have left Lablache's out of sight,
Shook nobby heads, and said, ' No go !
You 'd better let 'em try to grow :
Old Doctor Time is slow, but still
He does know how to make a pill.'

But vain was all their hoarsest bass,
Their old experience out of place,   40
And spite of croaking and entreating,
The vote was carried in marsh-meeting.

' Lord knows,' protest the polliwogs,
' We 're anxious to be grown-up frogs ;
But do not undertake the work
Of Nature till she prove a shirk ;
'T is not by jumps that she advances,
But wins her way by circumstances :
Pray, wait awhile, until you know
We 're so contrived as not to grow ;   50
Let Nature take her own direction,
And she 'll absorb our imperfection ;
You might n't like 'em to appear with,
But we must have the things to steer with.'

' No,' piped the party of reform,
' All great results are ta'en by storm :
Fate holds her best gifts till we show
We 've strength to make her let them go ;
The Providence that works in history,
And seems to some folks such a mystery,   61
Does not creep slowly on *incog.*,
But moves by jumps, a mighty frog ;
No more reject the Age's chrism,
Your queues are an anachronism ;
No more the Future's promise mock,
But lay your tails upon the block,
Thankful that we the means have voted
To have you thus to frogs promoted.'

The thing was done, the tails were cropped,
And home each philotadpole hopped,   70
In faith rewarded to exult,
And wait the beautiful result.
Too soon it came ; our pool, so long
The theme of patriot bull-frog's song,
Next day was reeking, fit to smother,
With heads and tails that missed each
   other,—
Here snoutless tails, there tailless snouts ;
The only gainers were the pouts.

MORAL.

From lower to the higher next,
Not to the top, is Nature's text ;   80
And embryo Good, to reach full stature,
Absorbs the Evil in its nature.

I think that nothing will ever give permanent peace and security to this continent but the extirpation of Slavery therefrom, and that the occasion is· nigh ; but I would do nothing hastily or vindictively, nor presume to jog the elbow of Providence. No desperate measures for me till we are sure that all others are hopeless, —*flectere si nequeo* SUPEROS, *Acheronta movebo*. To make Emancipation a reform instead of a revolution is worth a little patience, that we may have the Border States first, and then the non-slaveholders of the Cotton States, with us in principle,—a consummation that seems to be nearer than many imagine. *Fiat justitia, ruat cœlum*, is not to be taken in a literal sense by statesmen, whose problem is to get justice done with as little jar as possible to existing order, which has at least so much of heaven in it that it is not chaos. Our first duty toward our enslaved brother is to educate him, whether he be white or black. The first need of the free black is to elevate himself according to the standard of this material generation. So soon as the Ethiopian goes in his chariot, he will find not only Apostles, but Chief Priests and Scribes and Pharisees willing to ride with him.

Nil habet infelix paupertas durius in se
Quam quod ridiculos homines facit.

I rejoice in the President's late Message, which at last proclaims the Government on the side of freedom, justice, and sound policy.

As I write, comes the news of our disaster at Hampton Roads. I do not understand the supineness which, after fair warning, leaves wood to an unequal conflict with iron. It is not enough merely to have the right on our side, if we stick to the old flint-lock of tradition. I have observed in my parochial experience (*haud ignarus mali*) that the Devil is prompt to adopt the latest inventions of destructive warfare, and may thus take even such a three-decker as Bishop Butler at an advantage. It is curious, that, as gunpowder made armour useless on shore, so armour is having its revenge by baffling its old enemy at sea,—and that, while gunpowder robbed land warfare of nearly all its picturesqueness to give even greater stateliness and sublimity to a sea-fight, armour bids fair to degrade the latter into a squabble between two iron-shelled turtles.

Yours, with esteem and respect,
HOMER WILBUR, A. M.

P. S.—I had wellnigh forgotten to say that the object of this letter is to enclose a communication from the gifted pen of Mr. Biglow.

I SENT you a messige, my friens, t' other day,
To tell you I 'd nothin' pertickler to say :
't wuz the day our new nation gut kin' o' stillborn,
So 't wuz my pleasant dooty t' acknowledge the corn,
An' I see clearly then, ef I did n't before,
Thet the *augur* in inauguration means *bore*.
I need n't tell *you* thet my messige wuz written
To diffuse correc' notions in France an' Gret Britten,
An' agin to impress on the poppylar mind
The comfort an' wisdom o' goin' it blind,—
To say thet I did n't abate not a hooter
O' my faith in a happy an' glorious futur',
Ez rich in each soshle an' p'litickle blessin'
Ez them thet we now hed the joy o' possessin',
With a people united, an' longin' to die
For wut *we* call their country, without askin' why,

10

An' all the gret things we concluded to slope for
Ez much within reach now ez ever—to hope for.
We 've gut all the ellerments, this very hour,
Thet make up a fus'-class, self-governin' power :   20
We 've a war, an' a debt, an' a flag ; an' ef this
Ain't to be inderpendunt, why, wut on airth is ?
An' nothin' now henders our takin' our station
Ez the freest, enlightenedest, civerlized nation,
Built up on our bran'-new politickle thesis
Thet a Gov'ment's fust right is to tumble to pieces,—
I say nothin' henders our takin' our place
Ez the very fus'-best o' the whole human race,
A spittin' tobacker ez proud ez you please
On Victory's bes' carpets, or loafin' at ease   30
In the Tool'ries front-parlour, discussin' affairs
With our heels on the backs o' Napoleon's new chairs,
An' princes a-mixin' our cocktails an' slings,—
Excep', wal, excep' jest a very few things,
Sech ez navies an' armies an' wherewith to pay,
An' gittin' our sogers to run t' other way,
An' not be too over-pertickler in tryin'
To hunt up the very las' ditches to die in.

Ther' are critters so base thet they want it explained
Jes' wut is the totle amount thet we 've gained,   40
Ez ef we could maysure stupenjious events
By the low Yankee stan'ard o' dollars an' cents :
They seem to forgit, thet, sence last year revolved,
We 've succeeded in gittin' seceshed an' dissolved,
An' thet no one can't hope to git thru dissolootion
'thout some kin' o' strain on the best Constitootion.
Who asks for a prospec' more flettrin' an' bright,
When from here clean to Texas it 's all one free fight ?
Hain't we rescued from Seward the gret leadin' featurs
Thet makes it wuth while to be reasonin' creaturs ?   50
Hain't we saved Habus Coppers, improved it in fact,
By suspendin' the Unionists 'stid o' the Act ?
Ain't the laws free to all ? Where on airth else d' ye see
Every freeman improvin' his own rope an' tree ?
Ain't our piety sech (in our speeches an' messiges)
Ez t' astonish ourselves in the bes'-composed pessiges,
An' to make folks thet knowed us in th' ole state o' things
Think convarsion ez easy ez drinkin' gin-slings ?

It 's ne'ssary to take a good confident tone
With the public ; but here, jest amongst us, I own   60
Things look blacker 'n thunder. Ther' 's no use denyin'
We 're clean out o' money, an' 'most out o' lyin' ;

Two things a young nation can't mennage without,
Ef she wants to look wal at her fust comin' out;
For the fust supplies physickle strength, while the second
Gives a morril edvantage thet's hard to be reckoned:
For this latter I'm willin' to du wut I can;
For the former you'll hev to consult on a plan,—
Though our *fust* want (an' this pint I want your best views on)
Is plausible paper to print I. O. U.s on.   70
Some gennlemen think it would cure all our cankers
In the way o' finance, ef we jes' hanged the bankers;
An' I own the proposle 'ud square with my views,
Ef their lives wuz n't all thet we 'd left 'em to lose.
Some say thet more confidence might be inspired,
Ef we voted our cities an' towns to be fired,—
A plan thet 'ud suttenly tax our endurance,
Coz 't would be our own bills we should git for th' insurance;
But cinders, no metter how sacred we think 'em,
Might n't strike furrin minds ez good sources of income,   80
Nor the people, perhaps, would n't like the eclaw
O' bein' all turned into paytriots by law.
Some want we should buy all the cotton an' burn it,
On a pledge, when we 've gut thru the war, to return it,—
Then to take the proceeds an' hold *them* ez security
For an issue o' bonds to be met at maturity
With an issue o' notes to be paid in hard cash
On the fus' Monday follerin' the 'tarnal Allsmash:
This hez a safe air, an', once hold o' the gold,
'ud leave our vile plunderers out in the cold,   90
An' *might* temp' John Bull, ef it warn't for the dip he
Once gut from the banks o' my own Mississippi.
Some think we could make, by arrangin' the figgers,
A hendy home-currency out of our niggers;
But it wun't du to lean much on ary sech staff,
For they 're gittin' tu current a'ready, by half.

One gennleman says, ef we lef' our loan out
Where Floyd could git hold on 't *he* 'd take it, no doubt;
But 't ain't jes' the takin, though 't hez a good look,
We mus' git sunthin' out on it arter it 's took,   100
An' we need now more 'n ever, with sorrer I own,
Thet some one another should let us a loan,
Sence a soger wun't fight, on'y jes' while he draws his
Pay down on the nail, for the best of all causes,
'thout askin' to know wut the quarrel 's about,—
An' once come to thet, why, our game is played out.
It 's ez true ez though I should n't never hev said it,
Thet a hitch hez took place in our system o' credit;
I swear it 's all right in my speeches an' messiges,
But ther' 's idees afloat, ez ther' is about sessiges: 110

Folks wun't take a bond ez a basis to trade on,
Without nosin' round to find out wut it 's made on,
An' the thought more an' more thru the public min' crosses
Thet our Treshry hez gut 'mos' too many dead hosses.
Wut 's called credit, you see, is some like a balloon,
Thet looks while it 's up 'most ez harnsome 'z a moon,
But once git a leak in 't an' wut looked so grand
Caves righ' down in a jiffy ez flat ez your hand.
Now the world is a dreffle mean place, for our sins,
Where ther' ollus is critters about with long pins   120
A-prickin' the bubbles we 've blowed with sech care,
An' provin' ther' 's nothin' inside but bad air:
They 're all Stuart Millses, poor-white trash, an' sneaks,
Without no more chivverlry 'n Choctaws or Creeks,
Who think a real gennleman's promise to pay
Is meant to be took in trade's ornery way:
Them fellers an' I could n' never agree;
They 're the nateral foes o' the Southun Idee;
I 'd gladly take all of our other resks on me
To be red o' this low-lived politikle 'con'my!   130

Now a dastardly notion is gittin' about
Thet our bladder is bust an' the gas oozin' out,
An' onless we can mennage in some way to stop it,
Why, the thing 's a gone coon, an' we might ez wal drop it.
Brag works wal at fust, but it ain't jes' the thing
For a stiddy inves'ment the shiners to bring,
An' votin' we 're prosp'rous a hundred times over
Wun't change bein' starved into livin' on clover.
Manassas done sunthin' tow'rds drawin' the wool
O'er the green, antislavery eyes o' John Bull: 140
Oh, *warn't* it a godsend, jes' when sech tight fixes
Wuz crowdin' us mourners, to throw double-sixes!
I wuz tempted to think, an' it wuz n't no wonder,
Ther' wuz reelly a Providence,—over or under,—
When, all packed for Nashville, I fust ascertained
From the papers up North wut a victory we 'd gained.
't wuz the time for diffusin' correc' views abroad
Of our union an' strength an' relyin' on God;
An', fact, when I 'd gut thru my fust big surprise,
I much ez half b'lieved in my own tallest lies,   150
An' conveyed the idee thet the whole Southun popperlace
Wuz Spartans all on the keen jump for Thermopperlies,
Thet set on the Lincolnites' bombs till they bust,
An' fight for the priv'lege o' dyin' the fust;
But Roanoke, Bufort, Millspring, an' the rest
Of our recent starn-foremost successes out West,
Hain't left us a foot for our swellin' to stand on,—
We 've showed *too* much o' wut Buregard calls *abandon*,

For all our Thermopperlies (an' it's a marcy
We hain't hed no more) hev ben clean vicy-varsy,   160
An' wut Spartans wuz lef' when the battle wuz done
Wuz them thet wuz too unambitious to run.

Oh, ef we hed on'y jes' gut Reecognition,
Things now would ha' ben in a different position !
You 'd ha' hed all you wanted : the paper blockade
Smashed up into toothpicks ; unlimited trade
In the one thing thet's needfle, till niggers, I swow,
Hed ben thicker 'n provisional shin-plasters now ;
Quinine by the ton 'ginst the shakes when they seize ye ;
Nice paper to coin into C. S. A. specie ;   170
The voice of the driver 'd be heerd in our land,
An' the univarse scringe, ef we lifted our hand :
Would n't *thet* be some like a fulfillin' the prophecies,
With all the fus' fem'lies in all the fust offices ?
't wuz a beautiful dream, an' all sorrer is idle,—
But *ef* Lincoln *would* ha' hanged Mason an' Slidell !
For would n't the Yankees hev found they 'd ketched Tartars,
Ef they 'd raised two sech critters as them into martyrs
Mason *wuz* F. F. V., though a cheap card to win on,
But t' other was jes' New York trash to begin on ;   180
They ain't o' no good in Európean pellices,
But think wut a help they 'd ha' ben on their gallowses !
They 'd ha' felt they wuz truly fulfillin' their mission,
An', oh, how dog-cheap we 'd ha' gut Reecognition !

But somehow another, wutever we 've tried,
Though the the'ry 's fust-rate, the facs *wun't* coincide :
Facs are contrary 'z mules, an' ez hard in the mouth,
An' they allus hev showed a mean spite to the South.
Sech bein' the case, we hed best look about
For some kin' o' way to slip *our* necks out :   190
Le' 's vote our las' dollar, ef one can be found,
(An', at any rate, votin' it hez a good sound,)—
Le' 's swear thet to arms all our people is flyin',
(The critters can't read, an' wun't know how wer 're lyin',)–
Thet Toombs is advancin' to sack Cincinnater,
With a rovin' commission to pillage an' slahter,—
Thet we 've throwed to the winds all regard for wut 's lawfle,
An' gone in for sunthin' promiscu'sly awfle.
Ye see, hitherto, it 's our own knaves an' fools
Thet we 've used, (those for whetstones, an' t' others ez tools,) 200
An' now our las' chance is in puttin' to test
The same kin' o' cattle up North an' out West,—
Your Belmonts, Vallandighams, Woodses, an' sech,
Poor shotes thet ye could n't persuade us to tech,
Not in ornery times, though we 're willin' to feed 'em
With a nod now an' then, when we happen to need 'em ;

Why, for my part, I'd ruther shake hands with a nigger
Than with cusses that load an' don't darst dror a trigger;
They're the wust wooden nutmegs the Yankees produce,
Shaky everywheres else, an' jes' sound on the goose;   210
They ain't wuth a cuss, an' I set nothin' by 'em,
But we're in sech a fix thet I s'pose we mus' try 'em.
I —   But, Gennlemen, here's a despatch jes' come in
Which shows thet the tide's begun turnin' agin',—
Gret Cornfedrit success!   C'lumbus eevacooated!
I mus' run down an' hev the thing properly stated,
An' show wut a triumph it is, an' how lucky
To fin'lly git red o' thet cussed Kentucky,—
An' how, sence Fort Donelson, winnin' the day
Consists in triumphantly gittin' away.   220

No. V.

SPEECH OF HONOURABLE PRESERVED DOE IN SECRET CAUCUS.

TO THE EDITORS OF THE ATLANTIC MONTHLY.

JAALAM, 12th April, 1862.

GENTLEMEN,—As I cannot but hope that the ultimate, if not speedy, success of the national arms is now sufficiently ascertained, sure as I am of the righteousness of our cause and its consequent claim on the blessing of God, (for I would not show a faith inferior to that of the Pagan historian with his *Facile evenit quod Dis cordi est,*) it seems to me a suitable occasion to withdraw our minds a moment from the confusing din of battle to objects of peaceful and permanent interest.   Let us not neglect the monuments of preterite history because what shall be history is so diligently making under our eyes.   *Cras ingens iterabimus œquor;* to-morrow will be time enough for that stormy sea; to-day let me engage the attention of your readers with the Runick inscription to whose fortunate discovery I have heretofore alluded.   Well may we say with the poet, *Multa renascuntur quæ jam cecidere.*   And I would premise, that, although I can no longer resist the evidence of my own senses from the stone before me to the ante-Columbian discovery of this continent by the Northmen, *gens inclytissima,* as they are called in a Palermitan inscription, written fortunately in a less debatable character than that which I am about to decipher, yet I would by no means be understood as wishing to vilipend the merits of the great Genoese, whose name will never be forgotten so long as the inspiring strains of ' Hail Columbia ' shall continue to be heard.   Though he must be stripped also of whatever praise may belong to the experiment of the egg, which I find proverbially attributed by Castilian authors to a certain Juanito or Jack, (perhaps an offshoot of our giant-killing mythus,) his name will still remain one of the most illustrious of modern times.   But the impartial historian owes a duty likewise to obscure merit, and my solicitude to render a tardy justice is perhaps quickened by my having known those who, had their own field of labour been less secluded, might have found a readier acceptance with the reading publick.   I could give an example, but I forbear: *forsitan nostris ex ossibus oritur ultor.*

Touching Runick inscriptions, I find that they may be classed under three general heads: 1°.   Those which are understood by the Danish Royal

Society of Northern Antiquaries, and Professor Rafn, their Secretary; 2°. Those which are comprehensible only by Mr. Rafn; and 3°. Those which neither the Society, Mr. Rafn, nor anybody else can be said in any definite sense to understand, and which accordingly offer peculiar temptations to enucleating sagacity. These last are naturally deemed the most valuable by intelligent antiquaries, and to this class the stone now in my possession fortunately belongs. Such give a picturesque variety to ancient events, because susceptible oftentimes of as many interpretations as there are individual archæologists; and since facts are only the pulp in which the Idea or event-seed is softly imbedded till it ripen, it is of little consequence what colour or flavour we attribute to them, provided it be agreeable. Availing myself of the obliging assistance of Mr. Arphaxad Bowers, an ingenious photographick artist, whose house-on-wheels has now stood for three years on our Meeting-House Green, with the somewhat contradictory inscription, —' our motto is onward,'—I have sent accurate copies of my treasure to many learned men and societies, both native and European. I may hereafter communicate their different and (*me judice*) equally erroneous solutions. I solicit also, Messrs. Editors, your own acceptance of the copy herewith enclosed. I need only premise further, that the stone itself is a goodly block of metamorphick sandstone, and that the Runes resemble very nearly the ornithichnites or fossil bird-tracks of Dr. Hitchcock, but with less regularity or apparent design than is displayed by those remarkable geological monuments. These are rather the *non bene junctarum discordia semina rerum.* Resolved to leave no door open to cavil, I first of all attempted the elucidation of this remarkable example of lithick literature by the ordinary modes, but with no adequate return for my labour. I then considered myself amply justified in resorting to that heroick treatment the

felicity of which, as applied by the great Bentley to Milton, had long ago enlisted my admiration. Indeed, I had already made up my mind, that, in case good fortune should throw any such invaluable record in my way, I would proceed with it in the following simple and satisfactory method. After a cursory examination, merely sufficing for an approximative estimate of its length, I would write down a hypothetical inscription based upon antecedent probabilities, and then proceed to extract from the characters engraven on the stone a meaning as nearly as possible conformed to this *a priori* product of my own ingenuity. The result more than justified my hopes, inasmuch as the two inscriptions were made without any great violence to tally in all essential particulars. I then proceeded, not without some anxiety, to my second test, which was, to read the Runick letters diagonally, and again with the same success. With an excitement pardonable under the circumstances, yet tempered with thankful humility, I now applied my last and severest trial, my *experimentum crucis.* I turned the stone, now doubly precious in my eyes, with scrupulous exactness upside down. The physical exertion so far displaced my spectacles as to derange for a moment the focus of vision. I confess that it was with some tremulousness that I readjusted them upon my nose, and prepared my mind to bear with calmness any disappointment that might ensue. But, *O albo dies notanda lapillo !* what was my delight to find that the change of position had effected none in the sense of the writing, even by so much as a single letter ! I was now, and justly, as I think, satisfied of the conscientious exactness of my interpretation. It is as follows :—

HERE

BJARNA GRIMOLFSSON

FIRST DRANK CLOUD-BROTHER

THROUGH CHILD-OF-LAND-AND-

WATER :

that is, drew smoke through a reed stem. In order words, we have here a record of the first smoking of the herb *Nicotiana Tabacum* by an European on this continent. The probable results of this discovery are so vast as to baffle conjecture. If it be objected, that the smoking of a pipe would hardly justify the setting up of a memorial stone, I answer, that even now the Moquis Indian, ere he takes his first whiff, bows reverently toward the four quarters of the sky in succession, and that the loftiest monuments have been reared to perpetuate fame, which is the dream of the shadow of smoke. The *Saga*, it will be remembered, leaves this Bjarna to a fate something like that of Sir Humphrey Gilbert, on board a sinking ship in the ' wormy sea,' having generously given up his place in the boat to a certain Icelander. It is doubly pleasant, therefore, to meet with this proof that the brave old man arrived safely in Vinland, and that his declining years were cheered by the respectful attentions of the dusky denizens of our then uninvaded forests. Most of all was I gratified, however, in thus linking forever the name of my native town with one of the most momentous occurrences of modern times. Hitherto Jaalam, though in soil, climate, and geographical position as highly qualified to be the theatre of remarkable historical incidents as any spot on the earth's surface, has been, if I may say it without seeming to question the wisdom of Providence, almost maliciously neglected, as it might appear, by occurrences of world-wide interest in want of a situation. And in matters of this nature it must be confessed that adequate events are as necessary as the *vates sacer* to record them. Jaalam stood always modestly ready, but circumstances made no fitting response to her generous intentions. Now, however, she assumes her place on the historick roll. I have hitherto been a zealous opponent of the Circean herb, but I shall now re-examine the question without bias.

I am aware that the Rev. Jonas Tutchel, in a recent communication to the Bogus Four Corners Weekly Meridian, has endeavoured to show that this is the sepulchral inscription of Thorwald Eriksson, who, as is well known, was slain in Vinland by the natives. But I think he has been misled by a preconceived theory, and cannot but feel that he has thus made an ungracious return for my allowing him to inspect the stone with the aid of my own glasses (he having by accident left his at home) and in my own study. The heathen ancients might have instructed this Christian minister in the rites of hospitality; but much is to be pardoned to the spirit of self-love. He must indeed be ingenious who can make out the words *hër hvilir* from any characters in the inscription in question, which, whatever else it may be, is certainly not mortuary. And even should the reverend gentleman succeed in persuading some fantastical wits of the soundness of his views, I do not see what useful end he will have gained. For if the English Courts of Law hold the testimony of gravestones from the burial-grounds of Protestant dissenters to be questionable, even where it is essential in proving a descent, I cannot conceive that the epitaphial assertions of heathens should be esteemed of more authority by any man of orthodox sentiments.

At this moment, happening to cast my eyes upon the stone, whose characters a transverse light from my southern window brings out with singular distinctness, another interpretation has occurred to me, promising even more interesting results. I hasten to close my letter in order to follow at once the clue thus providentially suggested.

I enclose, as usual, a contribution from Mr. Biglow, and remain,

Gentlemen, with esteem and respect,

Your Obedient Humble Servant,

HOMER WILBUR, A. M.

I THANK ye, my friens, for the warmth o' your greetin' :
Ther' 's few airthly blessins but wut 's vain an' fleetin' ;
But ef ther' is one thet hain't *no* cracks an' flaws,
An' is wuth goin' in for, it 's pop'lar applause ;
It sends up the sperits ez lively ez rockets,
An' I feel it—wal, down to the eend o' my pockets.
Jes' lovin' the people is Canaan in view,
But it 's Canaan paid quarterly t' hev 'em love you ;
It 's a blessin' thet 's breakin' out ollus in fresh spots ;
It 's a-follerin' Moses 'thout losin' the flesh-pots.   10
But, Gennlemen, 'scuse me, I ain't sech a raw cus
Ez to go luggin' ellerkence into a caucus,—
Thet is, into one where the call comprehends
Nut the People in person, but on'y their friends ;
I 'm so kin' o' used to convincin' the masses
Of th' edvantage o' bein' self-governin' asses,
I forgot thet *we* 're all o' the sort thet pull wires
An' arrange for the public their wants an' desires,
An' thet wut we hed met for wuz jes' to agree
Wut the People's opinions in futur' should be.   20

Now, to come to the nub, we 've ben all disappinted,
An' our leadin' ideas are a kind o' disjinted,—
Though, fur ez the nateral man could discern,
Things ough' to ha' took most an oppersite turn.
But The'ry is jes' like a train on the rail,
Thet, weather or no, puts her thru without fail,
While Fac' 's the ole stage thet gits sloughed in the ruts,
An' hez to allow for your darned efs an' buts,
An' so, nut intendin' no pers'nal reflections,
They don't—don't nut allus, thet is,—make connections :   30
Sometimes, when it really doos seem thet they 'd oughter
Combine jest ez kindly ez new rum an' water,
Both 'll be jest ez sot in their ways ez a bagnet,
Ez otherwise-minded ez th' eends of a magnet,
An' folks like you 'n' me, thet ain't ept to be sold,
Git somehow or 'nother left out in the cold.

I expected 'fore this, 'thout no gret of a row,
Jeff D. would ha' ben where A. Lincoln is now,
With Taney to say 't wuz all legle an' fair,
An' a jury o' Deemocrats ready to swear   40
Thet the ingin o' State gut throwed into the ditch
By the fault o' the North in misplacin' the switch.
Things wuz ripenin' fust-rate with Buchanan to nuss 'em ;
But the People they would n't be Mexicans, cuss 'em !
Ain't the safeguards o' freedom upsot, 'z you may say,
Ef the right o' rev'lution is took clean away ?
An' doos n't the right primy-fashy include
The bein' entitled to nut be subdued ?

The fact is, we 'd gone for the Union so strong,
When Union meant South ollus right an' North wrong,   50
Thet the people gut fooled into thinkin' it might
Worry on middlin' wal with the North in the right.
We might ha' ben now jest ez prosp'rous ez France,
Where p'litikle enterprise hez a fair chance,
An' the people is heppy an' proud et this hour,
Long ez they hev the votes, to let Nap hev the power ;
But *our* folks they went an' believed wut we 'd told 'em,
An', the flag once insulted, no mortle could hold 'em.
'T wuz pervokin' jest when we wuz cert'in to win,—
An' I, for one, wun't trust the masses agin :   60
For a people thet knows much ain't fit to be free
In the self-cockin', back-action style o' J. D.

I can't believe now but wut half on 't is lies ;
For who 'd thought the North wuz a-goin' to rise,
Or take the pervokin'est kin' of a stump,
'thout 't wuz sunthin' ez pressin' ez Gabr'el's las' trump ?
Or who 'd ha' supposed, arter *sech* swell an' bluster
'bout the lick-ary-ten-on-ye fighters they 'd muster,
Raised by hand on briled lightnin', ez op'lent 'z you please
In a primitive furrest o' femmily-trees,—   70
Who 'd ha' thought thet them Southuners ever 'ud show
Starns with pedigrees to 'em like theirn to the foe,
Or, when the vamosin' come, ever to find
Nat'ral masters in front an' mean white folks behind ?
By ginger, ef I 'd ha' known half I know now,
When I wuz to Congress, I would n't, I swow,
Hev let 'em cair on so high-minded an' sarsy,
'thout *some* show o' wut you may call vicy-varsy.
To be sure, we wuz under a contrac' jes' then
To be dreffle forbearin' towards Southun men ;   80
We hed to go sheers in preservin' the bellance :
An' ez they seemed to feel they wuz wastin' their tellents
'thout some un to kick, 't warn't more 'n proper, you know,
Each should funnish his part ; an' sence they found the toe
An' we wuz n't cherubs—wal, we found the buffer,
For fear thet the Compromise System should suffer.

I wun't say the plan hed n't onpleasant featurs,—
For men are perverse an' onreasonin' creaturs,
An' forgit thet in this life 't ain't likely to heppen
Their own privit fancy should ollus be cappen,—   90
But it worked jest ez smooth ez the key of a safe,
An' the gret Union bearins played free from all chafe.
They warn't hard to suit, ef they hed their own way,
An' we (thet is, some on us) made the thing pay :
't wuz a fair give-an'-take out of Uncle Sam's heap ;
Ef they took wut warn't theirn, wut we give come ez cheap ;

The elect gut the offices down to tide-waiter,
The people took skinnin' ez mild ez a tater,
Seemed to choose who they wanted tu, footed the bills,
An' felt kind o' 'z though they wuz havin' their wills,   100
Which kep' 'em ez harmless an' cherfle ez crickets,
While all we invested wuz names on the tickets:
Wal, ther' 's nothin', for folks fond o' lib'ral consumption
Free o' charge, like democ'acy tempered with gumption !

Now warn't thet a system wuth pains in presarvin',
Where the people found jints an' their frien's done the carvin',—
Where the many done all o' their thinkin' by proxy,
An' were proud on 't ez long ez 't wuz christened Democ'cy,—
Where the few let us sap all o' Freedom's foundations,
Ef you call it reformin' with prudence an' patience,   110
An' were willin' Jeff's snake-egg should hetch with the rest,
Ef you writ ' Constitootional ' over the nest ?
But it 's all out o' kilter, ('t wuz too good to last,)
An' all jes' by J. D.'s perceedin' too fast ;
Ef he 'd on'y hung on for a month or two more,
We 'd ha' gut things fixed nicer 'n they hed ben before :
Afore he drawed off an' lef' all in confusion,
We wuz safely entrenched in the ole Constitootion,
With an outlyin', heavy-gun, casemated fort
To rake all assailants,—I mean th' S. J. Court.   120
Now I never 'll acknowledge (nut ef you should skin me)
't wuz wise to abandon sech works to the in'my,
An' let him fin' out thet wut scared him so long,
Our whole line of argyments, lookin' so strong,
All our Scriptur' an' law, every the'ry an' fac',
Wuz Quaker-guns daubed with Pro-slavery black.
Why, ef the Republicans ever should git
Andy Johnson or some one to lend 'em the wit
An' the spunk jes' to mount Constitootion an' Court
With Columbiad guns, your real ekle-rights sort,   130
Or drill out the spike from the ole Declaration
Thet can kerry a solid shot clearn roun' creation,
We 'd better take maysures for shettin' up shop,
An' put off our stock by a vendoo or swop.

But they wun't never dare tu ; you 'll see 'em in Edom
'fore they ventur' to go where their doctrines 'ud lead 'em :
They 've ben takin' our princerples up ez we dropt 'em,
An' thought it wuz terrible 'cute to adopt 'em ;
But they 'll fin' out 'fore long thet their hope 's ben deceivin' 'em,
An' thet princerples ain't o' no good, ef you b'lieve in 'em ·   140
It makes 'em tu stiff for a party to use,
Where they 'd ough' to be easy 'z an ole pair o' shoes.
If *we* say 'n our pletform thet all men are brothers,
We don't mean thet some folks ain't more so 'n some others ;

An' it 's wal understood thet we make a selection,
An' thet brotherhood kin' o' subsides arter 'lection.
The fust thing for sound politicians to larn is,
Thet Truth, to dror kindly in all sorts o' harness,
Mus' be kep' in the abstract,—for, come to apply it,
You 're ept to hurt some folks's interists by it.   150
Wal, these 'ere Republicans (some on 'em) ects
Ez though gineral mexims 'ud suit speshle facts ;
An' there 's where we 'll nick 'em, there 's where they 'll be lost :
For applyin' your princerple 's wut makes it cost,
An' folks don't want Fourth o' July t' interfere
With the business-consarns o' the rest o' the year,
No more 'n they want Sunday to pry an' to peek
Into wut they are doin' the rest o' the week.

A ginooine statesman should be on his guard,
Ef he *must* hev beliefs, nut to b'lieve 'em tu hard ;   160
For, ez sure ez he does, he 'll be blartin' 'em out
'thout regardin' the natur' o' man more 'n a spout,
Nor it don't ask much gumption to pick out a flaw
In a party whose leaders are loose in the jaw :
An' so in our own case I ventur' to hint
Thet we 'd better nut air our perceedin's in print,
Nor pass resserlootions ez long ez your arm
Thet may, ez things heppen to turn, do us harm ;
For when you 've done all your real meanin' to smother,
The darned things 'll up an' mean sunthin' or 'nother.   170
Jeff'son prob'ly meant wal with his ' born free an' ekle,'
But it 's turned out a real crooked stick in the sekle ;
It 's taken full eighty-odd year—don't you see ?—
From the pop'lar belief to root out thet idee,
An', arter all, suckers on 't keep buddin' forth
In the nat'lly onprincipled mind o' the North.
No, never say nothin' without you 're compelled tu,
An' then don't say nothin' thet you can be held tu,
Nor don't leave no friction-idees layin' loose
For the ign'ant to put to incend'ary use.   180

You know I 'm a feller thet keeps a skinned eye
On the leetle events thet go skurryin' by,
Coz it 's of'ner by them than by gret ones you 'll see
Wut the p'litickle weather is likely to be.
Now I don't think the South 's more 'n begun to be licked,
But I *du* think, ez Jeff says, the windbag 's gut pricked ;
It 'll blow for a spell an' keep puffin' an' wheezin',
The tighter our army an' navy keep squeezin',—
For they can't help spread-eaglein' long 'z ther' 's a mouth
To blow Enfield's Speaker thru lef' at the South.   190
But it 's high time for us to be settin' our faces
Towards reconstructin' the national basis,

With an eye to beginnin' agin on the jolly ticks
We used to chalk up 'hind the back-door o' politics;
An' the fus' thing 's to save wut of Slav'ry ther' 's lef'
Arter this (I mus' call it) imprudence o' Jeff:
For a real good Abuse, with its roots fur an' wide,
Is the kin' o' thing I like to hev on my side;
A Scriptur' name makes it ez sweet ez a rose,
An' it 's tougher the older an' uglier it grows—   200
(I ain't speakin' now o' the righteousness of it,
But the p'litickle purchase it gives an' the profit).

Things look pooty squally, it must be allowed,
An' I don't see much signs of a bow in the cloud:
Ther' 's too many Deemocrats—leaders wut 's wuss—
Thet go for the Union 'thout carin' a cuss
Ef it helps ary party thet ever wuz heard on,
So our eagle ain't made a split Austrian bird on.
But ther' 's still some consarvative signs to be found
Thet shows the gret heart o' the People is sound: 210
(Excuse me for usin' a stump-phrase agin,
But, once in the way on 't, they *will* stick like sin:)
There 's Phillips, for instance, hez jes' ketched a Tartar
In the Law-'n'-Order Party of ole Cincinnater;
An' the Compromise System ain't gone out o' reach,
Long 'z you keep the right limits on freedom o' speech.
'T warn't none too late, neither, to put on the gag,
For he 's dangerous now he goes in for the flag.
Nut thet I altogether approve o' bad eggs,
They 're mos' gin'lly argymunt on its las' legs,—   220
An' their logic is ept to be tu indiscriminate,
Nor don't ollus wait the right objecs to 'liminate;
But there is a variety on 'em, you 'll find,
Jest ez usefle an' more, besides bein' refined,—
I mean o' the sort thet are laid by the dictionary,
Sech ez sophisms an' cant, thet 'll kerry conviction ary
Way thet you want to the right class o' men,
An' are staler than all 't ever come from a hen:
'Disunion' done wal till our resh Southun friends
Took the savor all out on 't for national ends;   230
But I guess 'Abolition' 'll work a spell yit,
When the war 's done, an' so will 'Forgive-an'-forgit.'
Times mus' be pooty thoroughly out o' all jint,
Ef we can't make a good constitootional pint;
An' the good time 'll come to be grindin' our exes,
When the war goes to seed in the nettle o' texes:
Ef Jon'than don't squirm, with sech helps to assist him,
I give up my faith in the free-suffrage system;
Democ'cy wun't be nut a mite interestin',
Nor p'litikle capital much wuth investin';   240

An' my notion is, to keep dark an' lay low
Till we see the right minute to put in our blow.—

But I 've talked longer now 'n I hed any idee,
An' ther' 's others you want to hear more 'n you du me ;
So I 'll set down an' give thet 'ere bottle a skrimmage,
For I 've spoke till I 'm dry ez a real graven image.

No. VI.

SUNTHIN' IN THE PASTORAL LINE.

TO THE EDITORS OF THE ATLANTIC MONTHLY.

JAALAM, 17th May, 1862.

GENTLEMEN,—At the special request of Mr. Biglow, I intended to inclose, together with my own contribution, (into which, at my suggestion, he has thrown a little more of pastoral sentiment than usual,) some passages from my sermon on the day of the National Fast, from the text, ' Remember them that are in bonds, as bound with them,' *Heb.* xiii. 3. But I have not leisure sufficient at present for the copying of them, even were I altogether satisfied with the production as it stands. I should prefer, I confess, to contribute the entire discourse to the pages of your respectable miscellany, if it should be found acceptable upon perusal, especially as I find the difficulty in selection of greater magnitude than I had anticipated. What passes without challenge in the fervour of oral delivery, cannot always stand the colder criticism of the closet. I am not so great an enemy of Eloquence as my friend Mr. Biglow would appear to be from some passages in his contribution for the current month. I would not, indeed, hastily suspect him of covertly glancing at myself in his somewhat caustick animadversions, albeit some of the phrases he girds at are not entire strangers to my lips. I am a more hearty admirer of the Puritans than seems now to be the fashion, and believe, that, if they Hebraized a little too much in their speech, they showed remarkable practical sagacity as statesmen and founders. But such phenomena as Puritanism are the results rather of great religious than merely social convulsions, and do not long survive them. So soon as an earnest conviction has cooled into a phrase, its work is over, and the best that can be done with it is to bury it. *Ite, missa est.* I am inclined to agree with Mr. Biglow that we cannot settle the great political questions which are now presenting themselves to the nation by the opinions of Jeremiah or Ezekiel as to the wants and duties of the Jews in their time, nor do I believe that an entire community with their feelings and views would be practicable or even agreeable at the present day. At the same time I could wish that their habit of subordinating the actual to the moral, the flesh to the spirit, and this world to the other, were more common. They had found out, at least, the great military secret that soul weighs more than body.—But I am suddenly called to a sick-bed in the household of a valued parishioner.

With esteem and respect,

Your obedient servant,

HOMER WILBUR.

Once git a smell o' musk into a draw,
An' it clings hold like precerdents in law :
Your gra'ma'am put it there,—when, goodness knows,—
To jes' this-worldify her Sunday-clo'es ;

But the old chist wun't sarve her gran'son's wife,
(For, 'thout new funnitoor, wut good in life ?)
An' so ole clawfoot, from the precinks dread
O' the spare chamber, slinks into the shed,
Where, dim with dust, it fust or last subsides
To holdin' seeds an' fifty things besides ;   10
But better days stick fast in heart an' husk,
An' all you keep in 't gits a scent o' musk.

Jes' so with poets : wut they 've airly read
Gits kind o' worked into their heart an' head,
So 's 't they can't seem to write but jest on sheers
With furrin countries or played-out ideers,
Nor hev a feelin', ef it doos n't smack
O' wut some critter chose to feel 'way back :
This makes 'em talk o' daisies, larks, an' things,
Ez though we 'd nothin' here that blows an' sings,—   20
(Why, I 'd give more for one live bobolink
Than a square mile o' larks in printer's ink,)—
This makes 'em think our fust o' May is May,
Which 't ain't, for all the almanicks can say.

O little city-gals, don't never go it
Blind on the word o' noospaper or poet !
They 're apt to puff, an' May-day seldom looks
Up in the country ez it doos in books ;
They 're no more like than hornets'-nests an' hives,
Or printed sarmons be to holy lives.   30
I, with my trouses perched on cowhide boots,
Tuggin' my foundered feet out by the roots,
Hev seen ye come to fling on April's hearse
Your muslin nosegays from the milliner's,
Puzzlin' to find dry ground your queen to choose,
An' dance your throats sore in morocker shoes :
I 've seen ye an' felt proud, thet, come wut would,
Our Pilgrim stock wuz pithed with hardihood.
Pleasure doos make us Yankees kind o' winch,
Ez though 't wuz sunthin' paid for by the inch ;   40
But yit we du contrive to worry thru,
Ef Dooty tells us thet the thing 's to du,
An' kerry a hollerday, ef we set out,
Ez stiddily ez though 't wuz a redoubt.

I, country-born an' bred, know where to find
Some blooms thet make the season suit the mind,
An' seem to metch the doubtin' blue-bird's notes,—
Half-vent'rin' liverworts in furry coats,
Bloodroots, whose rolled-up leaves ef you oncurl,
Each on 'em 's cradle to a baby-pearl,—   50

But these are jes' Spring's pickets; sure ez sin,
The rebble frosts 'll try to drive 'em in;
For half our May 's so awfully like May n't,
't would rile a Shaker or an evrige saint;
Though I own up I like our back'ard springs
Thet kind o' haggle with their greens an' things,
An' when you 'most give up, 'ithout more words
Toss the fields full o' blossoms, leaves, an' birds:
Thet 's Northun natur', slow an' apt to doubt,
But when it *doos* git stirred, ther' 's no gin-out!   60

Fust come the blackbirds clatt'rin' in tall trees,
An' settlin' things in windy Congresses,—
Queer politicians, though, for I 'll be skinned
Ef all on 'em don't head aginst the wind.
'fore long the trees begin to show belief,—
The maple crimsons to a coral-reef,
Then saffern swarms swing off from all the willers
So plump they look like yaller caterpillars,
Then gray hossches'nuts leetle hands unfold
Softer 'n a baby's be at three days old: 70
Thet 's robin-redbreast's almanick; he knows
Thet arter this ther' 's only blossom-snows;
So, choosin' out a handy crotch an' spouse,
He goes to plast'rin' his adobë house.

Then seems to come a hitch,—things lag behind,
Till some fine mornin' Spring makes up her mind,
An' ez, when snow-swelled rivers cresh their dams
Heaped-up with ice thet dovetails in an' jams,
A leak comes spirtin' thru some pin-hole cleft,
Grows stronger, fercer, tears out right an' left,   80
Then all the waters bow themselves an' come,
Suddin, in one gret slope o' shedderin' foam,
Jes' so our Spring gits everythin' in tune
An' gives one leap from April into June:
Then all comes crowdin' in; afore you think,
Young oak-leaves mist the side-hill woods with pink;
The catbird in the laylock-bush is loud;
The orchards turn to heaps o' rosy cloud;
Red-cedars blossom tu, though few folks know it,
An' look all dipt in sunshine like a poet;   90
The lime-trees pile their solid stacks o' shade
An' drows'ly simmer with the bees' sweet trade;
In ellum-shrouds the flashin' hangbird clings
An' for the summer vy'ge his hammock slings;
All down the loose-walled lanes in archin' bowers
The barb'ry droops its strings o' golden flowers,
Whose shrinkin' hearts the school-gals love to try
With pins,—they 'll worry yourn so, boys, bimeby!

But I don't love your cat'logue style,—do you ?—
Ez ef to sell off Natur' by vendoo ;   100
One word with blood in 't 's twice ez good ez two :
'nuff sed, June's bridesman, poet o' the year,
Gladness on wings, the bobolink, is here ;
Half-hid in tip-top apple-blooms he swings,
Or climbs aginst the breeze with quiverin' wings,
Or, givin' way to 't in a mock despair,
Runs down, a brook o' laughter, thru the air.

I ollus feel the sap start in my veins
In Spring, with curus heats an' prickly pains,
Thet drive me, when I git a chance, to walk   110
Off by myself to hev a privit talk
With a queer critter thet can't seem to 'gree
Along o' me like most folks,—Mister Me.
Ther' 's times when I 'm unsoshle ez a stone,
An' sort o' suffocate to be alone,—
I 'm crowded jes' to think thet folks are nigh,
An' can't bear nothin' closer than the sky ;
Now the wind 's full ez shifty in the mind
Ez wut it is ou'-doors, ef I ain't blind,
An' sometimes, in the fairest sou'west weather,   120
My innard vane pints east for weeks together,
My natur' gits all goose-flesh, an' my sins
Come drizzlin' on my conscience sharp ez pins :
Wal, et sech times I jes' slip out o' sight
An' take it out in a fair stan'-up fight
With the one cuss I can't lay on the shelf,
The crook'dest stick in all the heap,—Myself.

'T wuz so las' Sabbath arter meetin'-time :
Findin' my feelin's would n't noways rhyme
With nobody's, but off the hendle flew   130
An' took things from an east-wind pint o' view,
I started off to lose me in the hills
Where the pines be, up back o' 'Siah's Mills :
Pines, ef you 're blue, are the best friends I know,
They mope an' sigh an' sheer your feelin's so,—
They hesh the ground beneath so, tu, I swan,
You half-forgit you 've gut a body on.
Ther' 's a small school'us' there where four roads meet,
The door-steps hollered out by little feet,
An' side-posts carved with names whose owners grew   140
To gret men, some on 'em, an' deacons, tu ;
't ain't used no longer, coz the town hez gut
A high-school, where they teach the Lord knows wut :
Three-story larnin' 's pop'lar now ; I guess
We thriv' ez wal on jes' two stories less,

For it strikes me ther' 's sech a thing ez sinnin'
By overloadin' children's underpinnin' :
Wal, here it wuz I larned my A B C,
An' it 's a kind o' favourite spot with me.

We 're curus critters : Now ain't jes' the minute   150
Thet ever fits us easy while we 're in it ;
Long ez 't wuz futur', 't would be perfect bliss,—
Soon ez it 's past, *thet* time 's wuth ten o' this ;
An' yit there ain't a man thet need be told
Thet Now 's the only bird lays eggs o' gold.
A knee-high lad, I used to plot an' plan
An' think 't wuz life's cap-sheaf to be a man ;
Now, gittin' grey, there's nothin' I enjoy
Like dreamin' back along into a boy :
So the ole school'us' is a place I choose   160
Afore all others, ef I want to muse ;
I set down where I used to set, an' git
My boyhood back, an' better things with it,—
Faith, Hope, an' sunthin', ef it is n't Cherrity,
It 's want o' guile, an' thet 's ez gret a rerrity,—
While Fancy's cushin', free to Prince and Clown,
Makes the hard bench ez soft ez milkweed-down.

Now, 'fore I knowed, thet Sabbath arternoon
Thet I sot out to tramp myself in tune,
I found me in the school'us' on my seat,   170
Drummin' the march to No-wheres with my feet.
Thinkin' o' nothin', I 've heerd ole folks say
Is a hard kind o' dooty in its way :
It 's thinkin' everythin' you ever knew,
Or ever hearn, to make your feelin's blue.
I sot there tryin' thet on for a spell :
I thought o' the Rebellion, then o' Hell,
Which some folks tell ye now is jest a metterfor
(A the'ry, p'raps, it wun't *feel* none the better for) ;
I thought o' Reconstruction, wut we 'd win   180
Patchin' our patent self-blow-up agin :
I thought ef this 'ere milkin' o' the wits,
So much a month, warn't givin' Natur' fits,—
Ef folks warn't druv, findin' their own milk fail,
To work the cow thet hez an iron tail,
An' ef idees 'thout ripenin' in the pan
Would send up cream to humour ary man :
From this to thet I let my worryin' creep,
Till finally I must ha' fell asleep.

Our lives in sleep are some like streams thet glide   190
'twixt flesh an' sperrit boundin' on each side,
Where both shores' shadders kind o' mix an' mingle
In sunthin' thet ain't jes' like either single ;

An' when you cast off moorin's from To-day
An' down towards To-morrer drift away,
The imiges thet tengle on the stream
Make a new upside-down'ard world o' dream:
Sometimes they seem like sunrise-streaks an' warnin's
O' wut 'll be in Heaven on Sabbath-mornin's,
An', mixed right in ez ef jest out o' spite,   200
Sunthin' thet says your supper ain't gone right.
I 'm gret on dreams, an' often when I wake,
I 've lived so much it makes my mem'ry ache,
An' can't skurce take a cat-nap in my cheer
'thout hevin' 'em, some good, some bad, all queer.

Now I wuz settin' where I 'd ben, it seemed,
An' ain't sure yit whether I r'ally dreamed,
Nor, ef I did, how long I might ha' slep',
When I hearn some un stompin' up the step,
An' lookin' round, ef two an' two make four,   210
I see a Pilgrim Father in the door.
He wore a steeple-hat, tall boots, an' spurs
With rowels to 'em big ez ches'nut-burrs,
An' his gret sword behind him sloped away
Long 'z a man's speech thet dunno wut to say.—
' Ef your name 's Biglow, an' your given-name
Hosee,' sez he, ' it 's arter you I came ;
I 'm your gret-gran'ther multiplied by three.'—
' My *wut ?* ' sez I.—' Your gret-gret-gret,' sez he :
' You would n't ha' never ben here but for me.   220
Two hundred an' three year ago this May
The ship I come in sailed up Boston Bay ;
I 'd been a cunnle in our Civil War,—
But wut on airth hev *you* gut up one for ?
Coz we du things in England, 't ain't for you
To git a notion you can du 'em tu :
I 'm told you write in public prints : ef true,
It 's nateral you should know a thing or two.'—
' Thet air 's an argymunt I can't endorse,—
't would prove, coz you wear spurs, you kep' a horse. 230
For brains,' sez I, ' wutever you may think,
Ain't boun' to cash the drafs o' pen-an'-ink,—
Though mos' folks write ez ef they hoped jes' quickenin'
The churn would argoo skim-milk into thickenin' ;
But skim-milk ain't a thing to change its view
O' wut it 's meant for more 'n a smoky flue.
But du pray tell me, 'fore we furder go,
How in all Natur' did you come to know
'bout our affairs,' sez I, ' in Kingdom-Come ? '—
' Wal, I worked round at sperrit-rappin' some,   240
An' danced the tables till their legs wuz gone,

In hopes o' larnin' wut wuz goin' on,'
Sez he, ' but mejums lie so like all-split
Thet I concluded it wuz best to quit.
But, come now, ef you wun't confess to knowin',
You 've some conjectures how the thing 's a-goin'.'—
' Gran'ther,' sez I, ' a vane warn't never known
Nor asked to hev a jedgment of its own ;
An' yit, ef 't ain't gut rusty in the jints,
It 's safe to trust its say on certin pints :   250
It knows the wind's opinions to a T,
An' the wind settles wut the weather 'll be.'
' I never thought a scion of our stock
Could grow the wood to make a weathercock ;
When I wuz younger 'n you, skurce more 'n a shaver,
No airthly wind,' sez he, ' could make me waver ! '
(Ez he said this, he clinched his jaw an' forehead,
Hitchin' his belt to bring his sword-hilt forrard.)—
' Jes so it wuz with me,' sez I, ' I swow,
When I wuz younger 'n wut you see me now,—   260
Nothin' from Adam's fall to Huldy's bonnet,
Thet I warn't full-cocked with my jedgment on it ;
But now I 'm gittin' on in life, I find
It 's a sight harder to make up my mind,—
Nor I don't often try tu, when events
Will du it for me free of all expense.
The moral question 's ollus plain enough,—
It 's jes' the human-natur' side thet 's tough ;
Wut 's best to think may n't puzzle me nor you,—
The pinch comes in decidin' wut to *du ;*   270
Ef you *read* History, all runs smooth ez grease,
Coz there the men ain't nothin' more 'n ideas,—
But come to *make* it, ez we must to-day,
Th' ideas hev arms an' legs an' stop the way :
It 's easy fixin' things in facts an' figgers,—
They can't resist, nor warn't brought up with niggers ;
But come to try your the'ry on,—why, then
Your facts an' figgers change to ign'ant men
Actin' ez ugly—' —' Smite 'em hip an' thigh ! '
Sez gran'ther, ' and let every man-child die !   280
Oh for three weeks o' Crommle an' the Lord !
Up, Isr'el, to your tents an' grind the sword ! '
' Thet kind o' thing worked wal in ole Judee,
But you forgit how long it 's ben A. D. ;
You think thet 's ellerkence,—I call it shoddy,
A thing,' sez I, ' wun't cover soul nor body ;
I like the plain all-wool o' commonsense,
Thet warms ye now, an' will a twelvemonth hence.
You took to follerin' where the Prophets beckoned,
An', fust you knowed on, back come Charles the Second ;

Now wut I want 's to hev all *we* gain stick,   291
An' not to start Millennium too quick ;
We hain't to punish only, but to keep,
  An' the cure 's gut to go a cent'ry deep.'
' Wal, milk-an'-water ain't the best o' glue,'
Sez he, ' an' so you 'll find before you 're thru ;
Ef reshness venters sunthin', shilly-shally
Loses ez often wut 's ten times the vally.
Thet exe of ourn, when Charles's neck gut split,
Opened a gap thet ain't bridged over yit :   300
Slav'ry 's your Charles, the Lord hez gin the exe—
  'Our Charles,' sez I, ' hez gut eight million necks.
The hardest question ain't the black man's right,
The trouble is to 'mancipate the white ;
One 's chained in body an' can be sot free,
But t' other 's chained in soul to an idee :
It 's a long job, but we shall worry thru it ;
Ef bagnets fail, the spellin'-book must du it.'
' Hosee,' sez he, ' I think you 're goin' to fail :
The rettlesnake ain't dangerous in the tail ;   310
This 'ere rebellion 's nothin but the rettle,—
You 'll stomp on thet an' think you 've won the bettle ;
It 's Slavery thet 's the fangs an' thinkin' head,
An' ef you want selvation, cresh it dead,—
An' cresh it suddin, or you 'll larn by waitin'
Thet Chance wun't stop to listen to debatin' ! '—
' God's truth ! ' sez I,—' an' ef *I* held the club,
An' knowed jes' where to strike,—but there 's the rub ! ' —
' Strike soon,' sez he, ' or you 'll be deadly ailin',—
Folks thet 's afeared to fail are sure o' failin' ;   320
God hates your sneakin' creturs thet believe
He 'll settle things they run away an' leave ! '
He brought his foot down fercely, ez he spoke,
An' give me sech a startle thet I woke.

No. VII.
LATEST VIEWS OF MR. BIGLOW.

PRELIMINARY NOTE.

[IT is with feelings of the liveliest pain that we inform our readers of the death of the Reverend Homer Wilbur, A. M., which took place suddenly, by an apoplectic stroke, on the afternoon of Christmas day, 1862. Our venerable friend (for so we may venture to call him, though we never enjoyed the high privilege of his personal acquaintance) was in his eighty-fourth year, having been born June 12, 1779, at Pigsgusset Precinct (now West Jerusha) in the then District of Maine. Graduated with distinction at Hubville College in 1805, he pursued his theological studies with the late Reverend Preserved Thacker, D. D., and was called to the charge of the First Society in Jaalam in 1809, where he remained till his death.

' As an antiquary he has probably left no superior, if, indeed, an equal,' writes his friend and colleague, the Reverend Jeduthun Hitchcock, to whom we are indebted for the above facts ; ' in proof of which I need only allude to his "History of Jaalam, Genealogical, Topographical, and Ecclesiastical," 1849, which has won him an eminent and enduring place in our more solid and useful literature. It is only to be regretted that his intense application to historical studies should have so entirely withdrawn him from the pursuit of poetical composition, for which he was endowed by Nature with a remarkable aptitude. His well-known hymn, beginning "With clouds of care encompassed round," has been attributed in some collections to the late President Dwight, and it is hardly presumptuous to affirm that the simile of the rainbow in the eighth stanza would do no discredit to that polished pen.'

We regret that we have not room at present for the whole of Mr. Hitchcock's exceedingly valuable communication. We hope to lay more liberal extracts from it before our readers at an early day. A summary of its contents will give some notion of its importance and interest. It contains : 1st, A biographical sketch of Mr. Wilbur, with notices of his predecessors in the pastoral office, and of eminent clerical contemporaries ; 2d, An obituary of deceased, from the Punkin-Falls 'Weekly Parallel' ; 3d, A list of his printed and manuscript productions and of projected works ; 4th, Personal anecdotes and recollections, with specimens of table-talk ; 5th, A tribute to his relict, Mrs. Dorcas (Pilcox) Wilbur ; 6th, A list of graduates fitted for different colleges by Mr. Wilbur, with biographical memoranda touching the more distinguished ; 7th, Concerning learned, charitable, and other societies, of which Mr. Wilbur was a member, and of those with which, had his life been prolonged, he would doubtless have been associated, with a complete catalogue of such Americans as have been Fellows of the Royal Society ; 8th, A brief summary of Mr. Wilbur's latest conclusions concerning the Tenth Horn of the Beast in its special application to recent events for which the public, as Mr. Hitchcock assures us, have been waiting with feelings of lively anticipation ; 9th, Mr. Hitchcock's own views on the same topic ; and, 10th, A brief essay on the importance of local histories. It will be apparent that the duty of preparing Mr. Wilbur's biography could not have fallen into more sympathetic hands.

In a private letter with which the reverend gentleman has since favoured us, he expresses the opinion that Mr. Wilbur's life was shortened by our unhappy civil war. It disturbed his studies, dislocated all his habitual associations and trains of thought, and unsettled the foundations of a faith, rather the result of habit than conviction, in the capacity of man for self-government. 'Such has been the felicity of my life,' he said to Mr. Hitchcock, on the very morning of the day he died, ' that, through the divine mercy, I could always say, *Summum nec metuo diem, nec opto.* It has been my habit, as you know, on every recurrence of this blessed anniversary, to read Milton's "Hymn of the Nativity" till its sublime harmonies so dilated my soul and quickened its spiritual sense that I seemed to hear that other song which gave assurance to the shepherds that there was One who would lead them also in green pastures and beside the still waters. But to-day I have been unable to think of anything but that mournful text, " I came not to send peace, but a sword," and, did it not smack of pagan presumptuousness, could almost wish I had never lived to see this day.'

Mr. Hitchcock also informs us that his friend ' lies buried in the Jaalam graveyard, under a large red-cedar which he specially admired. A neat and substantial monument is to be erected over his remains, with a Latin epitaph written by himself ; for he was accustomed to say, pleasantly, " that there was at least one occasion in a scholar's life when he might show the advantages of a classical training." '

The following fragment of a letter addressed to us, and apparently intended to accompany Mr. Biglow's contribution to the present number, was found upon his table after his decease.— EDITORS ATLANTIC MONTHLY.]

TO THE EDITORS OF THE ATLANTIC MONTHLY.

JAALAM, 24th Dec., 1862.

RESPECTED SIRS,—The infirm state of my bodily health would be a sufficient apology for not taking up the pen at this time, wholesome as I deem it for the mind to apricate in the shelter of epistolary confidence, were it not that a considerable, I might even say a large, number of individuals in this parish expect from their pastor some publick expression of sentiment at this crisis. Moreover, *Qui tacitus ardet magis uritur.* In trying times like these, the besetting sin of undisciplined minds is to seek refuge from inexplicable realities in the dangerous stimulant of angry partisanship or the indolent narcotick of vague and hopeful vaticination : *fortunamque suo temperat arbitrio.* Both by reason of my age and my natural temperament, I am unfitted for either. Unable to penetrate the inscrutable judgements of God, I am more than ever thankful that my life has been prolonged till I could in some small measure comprehend His mercy. As there is no man who does not at some time render himself amenable to the one,—*quum vix justus sit securus,*— so there is none that does not feel himself in daily need of the other.

I confess I cannot feel, as some do, a personal consolation for the manifest evils of this war in any remote or contingent advantages that may spring from it. I am old and weak, I can bear little, and can scarce hope to see better days ; nor is it any adequate compensation to know that Nature is old and strong and can bear much. Old men philosophize over the past, but the present is only a burthen and a weariness. The one lies before them like a placid evening landscape ; the other is full of the vexations and anxieties of housekeeping. It may be true enough that *miscet hæc illis, prohibetque Clotho fortunam stare,* but he who said it was fain at last to call in Atropos with her shears before her time ; and I cannot help selfishly mourning that the fortune of our Republick could not at least stand till my days were numbered.

Tibullus would find the origin of wars in the great exaggeration of riches, and does not stick to say that in the days of the beechen trencher there was peace. But averse as I am by nature from all wars, the more as they have been especially fatal to libraries, I would have this one go on till we are reduced to wooden platters again, rather than surrender the principle to defend which it was undertaken. Though I believe Slavery to have been the cause of it, by so thoroughly demoralizing Northern politicks for its own purposes as to give opportunity and hope to treason, yet I would not have our thought and purpose diverted from their true object,—the maintenance of the idea of Government. We are not merely suppressing an enormous riot, but contending for the possibility of permanent order coexisting with democratical fickleness ; and while I would not superstitiously venerate form to the sacrifice of substance, neither would I forget that an adherence to precedent and prescription can alone give that continuity and coherence under a democratical constitution which are inherent in the person of a despotick monarch and the selfishness of an aristocratical class. *Stet pro ratione voluntas* is as dangerous in a majority as in a tyrant.

I cannot allow the present production of my young friend to go out without a protest from me against a certain extremeness in his views, more pardonable in the poet than in the philosopher. While I agree with him, that the only cure for rebellion is suppression by force, yet I must animadvert upon certain phrases where I seem to see a coincidence with a popular fallacy on the subject of compromise. On the one hand there are those who do not see that the vital principle of Government and the seminal principle of Law cannot properly be made a subject of compromise at all, and on the other those who are equally blind to the truth that without a compromise of individual opinions, interests, and even rights, no society would be possible. *In medio tutissimus.* For my own part, I would gladly——

Ef I a song or two could make
  Like rockets druv by their own burnin',
All leap an' light, to leave a wake
  Men's hearts an' faces skyward turnin' !—
But, it strikes me, 't ain't jest the time
  Fer stringin' words with settisfaction :
Wut 's wanted now 's the silent rhyme
  'Twixt upright Will an' downright Action.

Words, ef you keep 'em, pay their keep,
  But gabble 's the short cut to ruin ;
It 's gratis, (gals half-price,) but cheap
  At no rate, ef it henders doin' ;
Ther' 's nothin' wuss, 'less 't is to set
  A martyr-prem'um upon jawrin' :
Teapots git dangerous, ef you shet
  Their lids down on 'em with Fort Warren.

'Bout long enough it 's ben discussed
  Who sot the magazine afire,
An' whether, ef Bob Wickliffe bust,
  'T would scare us more or blow us higher.
D' ye s'pose the Gret Foreseer's plan
  Wuz settled fer him in town-meetin' ?
Or thet ther' 'd ben no Fall o' Man,
  Ef Adam 'd on'y bit a sweetin' ?

Oh, Jon'than, ef you want tu be
  A rugged chap agin an' hearty,
Go fer wutever 'll hurt Jeff D.,
  Nut wut 'll boost up ary party.
Here 's hell broke loose, an' we lay flat
  With half the univarse a-singein',
Till Sen'tor This an' Gov'nor Thet
  Stop squabblin' fer the garding-ingin.

It 's war we 're in, not politics ;
  It 's systems wrastlin' now, not parties ;
An' victory in the eend 'll fix
  Where longest will an' truest heart is.
An' wut 's the Guv'ment folks about ?
  Tryin' to hope ther' 's nothin' doin',
An' look ez though they did n't doubt
  Sunthin' pertickler wuz a-brewin'.

Ther' 's critters yit thet talk an' act
  Fer wut they call Conciliation ;
They 'd hand a buff'lo-drove a tract
  When they wuz madder than all Bashan.
Conciliate ? it jest means *be kicked,*
  No metter how they phrase an' tone it ;
It means thet we 're to set down licked,
  Thet we 're poor shotes an' glad to own it !

A war on tick 's ez dear 'z the deuce,
  But it wun't leave no lastin' traces,
Ez 't would to make a sneakin' truce
  Without no moral specie-basis :
Ef green-backs ain't nut jest the cheese,
  I guess ther' 's evils thet 's extremer,—
Fer instance,—shinplaster idees
  Like them put out by Gov'nor Seymour.

Last year, the Nation, at a word,
  When tremblin' Freedom cried to shield her,

Flamed weldin' into one keen sword
   Waitin' an' longin' fer a wielder:
A splendid flash!—but how 'd the
    grasp
   With sech a chance ez thet wuz
    tally?
Ther' warn't no meanin' in our clasp,—
   Half this, half thet, all shilly-shally.

More men? More Man! It 's there
   we fail;
   Weak plans grow weaker yit by
    lengthenin';
Wut use in addin' to the tail,
   When it 's the head 's in need o'
    strengthenin'?
We wanted one thet felt all Chief
   From roots o' hair to sole o' stockin',
Square-sot with thousan'-ton belief
   In him an' us, ef earth went rockin'!

Ole Hick'ry would n't ha' stood see-
    saw
   'Bout doin' things till they wuz
    done with,—
He 'd smashed the tables o' the Law
   In time o' need to load his gun
    with;
He could n't see but jest one side,—
   Ef his, 't wuz God's, an' thet wuz
    plenty;
An' so his ' *Forrards!* ' multiplied
   An army's fightin' weight by
    twenty.

But this 'ere histin', creak, creak,
    creak,
   Your cappen's heart up with a
    derrick,
This tryin' to coax a lightnin'-streak
   Out of a half-discouraged hay-rick,
This hangin' on mont' arter mont'
   Fer one sharp purpose 'mongst the
    twitter,—
I tell ye, it doos kind o' stunt
   The peth and sperit of a critter.

In six months where 'll the People be,
   Ef leaders look on revolution
Ez though it wuz a cup o' tea,—
   Jest social el'ments in solution?

This weighin' things doos wal enough
   When war cools down, an' comes
    to writin';
But while it 's makin', the true stuff
   Is pison-mad, pig-headed fightin'.

Democ'acy gives every man
   The right to be his own oppressor;
But a loose Gov'ment ain't the plan,
   Helpless ez spilled beans on a
    dresser:
I tell ye one thing we might larn
   From them smart critters, the
    Seceders,—
Ef bein' right 's the fust consarn,
   The 'fore-the-fust 's cast-iron
    leaders.

But 'pears to me I see some signs
   Thet we 're a-goin' to use our
    senses:
Jeff druv us into these hard lines,
   An' ough' to bear his half th'
    expenses;
Slavery 's Secession's heart an' will,
   South, North, East, West, where'er
    you find it,
An' ef it drors into War's mill,
   D' ye say them thunder-stones sha'
    n't grind it?

D' ye s'pose, ef Jeff giv *him* a lick,
   Ole Hick'ry 'd tried his head to
    sof'n
So 's 't would n't hurt thet ebony
    stick
   Thet 's made our side see stars so
    of'n?
' No! ' he 'd ha' thundered, ' On your
    knees,
   An' own one flag, one road to glory!
Soft-heartedness, in times like these,
   Shows sof'ness in the upper story!'

An' why should we kick up a muss
   About the Pres'dunt's proclama-
    tion?
It ain't a-goin' to lib'rate us,
   Ef we don't like emancipation:

The right to be a cussed fool
  Is safe from all devices human,
It 's common (ez a gin'l rule)
  To every critter born o' woman.

So *we* 're all right, an' I, fer one,
  Don't think our cause 'll lose in
    vally
By rammin' Scriptur' in our gun,
  An' gittin' Natur' fer an ally :
Thank God, say I, fer even a plan
  To lift one human bein's level,
Give one more chance to make a man,
  Or, anyhow, to spile a devil !

Not thet I 'm one thet much expec'
  Millennium by express to-morrer ;
They *will* miscarry,—I rec'lec'
  Tu many on 'em, to my sorrer :
Men ain't made angels in a day,
  No matter how you mould an'
    labour 'em,—
Nor 'riginal ones, I guess, don't stay
  With Abe so of'n ez with Abraham.

The'ry thinks Fact a pooty thing,
  An' wants the banns read right
    ensuin' ;
But fact wun't noways wear the ring,
  'Thout years o' settin' up an'
    wooin' :
Though, arter all, Time's dial-plate
  Marks cent'ries with the minute-
    finger,
An' Good can't never come tu late,
  Though it doos seem to try an'
    linger.

An' come wut will, I think it 's grand
  Abe 's gut his will et last bloom-
    furnaced
In trial-flames till it 'll stand
  The strain o' bein' in deadly
    earnest :
Thet 's wut we want,—we want to
    know
  The folks on our side hez the
    bravery
To b'lieve ez hard, come weal, come
    woe,
  In Freedom ez Jeff doos in Slavery.

Set the two forces foot to foot,
  An' every man knows who 'll be
    winner,
Whose faith in God hez ary root
  Thet goes down deeper than his
    dinner :
Then 't will be felt from pole to pole,
  Without no need o' proclamation,
Earth's biggest Country 's gut her
    soul
  An' risen up Earth's Greatest
    Nation !

No. VIII

KETTELOPOTOMACHIA

PRELIMINARY NOTE

In the month of February, 1866, the editors of the ' Atlantic Monthly ' received from the Rev. Mr. Hitchcock of Jaalam a letter enclosing the macaronic verses which follow, and promising to send more, if more should be communicated. ' They were rapped out on the evening of Thursday last past,' he says, ' by what claimed to be the spirit of my late predecessor in the ministry here, the Rev. Dr. Wilbur, through the medium of a young man at present domiciled in my family. As to the possibility of such spiritual manifestations, or whether they be properly so entitled, I express no opinion, as there is a division of sentiment on that subject in the parish, and many persons of the highest respectability in social standing entertain opposing views. The young man who was improved as a medium submitted himself to the experiment with manifest reluctance, and is still unprepared to believe in the authenticity of the manifestations. During his residence with me his deportment has always been exemplary ; he has been constant in his attendance upon our family devotions and the public ministrations of the Word, and has more than once privately stated to me, that the latter had often brought him under deep concern of mind. The table is an ordinary quadrupedal one, weighing about thirty pounds, three feet seven inches and a half in height, four feet square on the top, and of beech or maple, I am not definitely prepared to say which. It had once belonged to my respected predecessor, and had been, so far as I can learn upon careful inquiry, of perfectly regular and correct habits up to the evening in question. On that occasion the young man previously alluded to had been sitting with his hands resting carelessly upon it, while I read over to him at his request certain portions of my last Sabbath's discourse. On a sudden the rappings, as they are called, commenced to render themselves audible, at first faintly, but in process of time more distinctly and with violent agitation of the table. The young man expressed himself both surprised and pained by the wholly unexpected, and, so far as he was concerned, unprecedented occurrence. At the earnest solicitation, however, of several who happened to be present, he consented to go on with the experiment, and with the assistance of the alphabet commonly employed in similar emergencies, the following communication was obtained and written down immediately by myself. Whether any, and if so, how much weight should be attached to it, I venture no decision. That Dr. Wilbur had sometimes employed his leisure in Latin versification I have ascertained to be the case, though all that has been discovered of that nature among his papers consists of some fragmentary passages of a version into hexameters of portions of the Song of Solomon. These I had communicated about a week or ten days previous[ly] to the young gentleman who officiated as medium in the communication afterwards received. I have thus, I believe, stated all the material facts that have any elucidative bearing upon this mysterious occurrence.'

So far Mr. Hitchcock, who seems perfectly master of Webster's unabridged quarto, and whose flowing style leads him into certain further expatiations for which we have not room. We have since learned that the young man he speaks of was a sophomore, put under his care during a sentence of rustication from —— College, where he had distinguished himself rather by physical experiments on the comparative power of resistance in window-glass to various solid substances, than in the more regular studies of the place. In answer to a letter of inquiry, the professor of Latin says, ' There was no harm in the boy that I know of beyond his loving mischief more than Latin, nor can I think of any spirits likely to possess him except those commonly called animal. He was certainly not remarkable for his Latinity, but I see nothing in the verses you enclose that would lead me to think them beyond his capacity, or the result of any special inspiration whether of beech or maple. Had that of *birch* been tried upon him earlier and more faithfully, the verses would perhaps have been better in quality and certainly in quantity.' This exact and thorough scholar then goes on to point out many false quantities and barbarisms. It is but fair to say, however, that the author, whoever he was, seems not to have been unaware of some of them himself, as is shown by a great many notes appended to the verses as we received them, and purporting to be by Scaliger, Bentley and others,— among them the *Esprit de Voltaire*. These we have omitted as clearly meant to be humorous and altogether failing therein.

Though entirely satisfied that the verses are altogether unworthy of Mr Wilbur, who seems to have been a tolerable Latin scholar after the fashion of his day, yet we have determined to print them here partly as belonging to the *res gestæ* of this collection, and partly as a warning to their putative author which may keep him from such indecorous pranks for the future.

KETTELOPOTOMACHIA

P. Ovidii Nasonis carmen heroicum macaronicum perplexametrum, inter Getas getico more compostum, denuo per medium ardentispiritualem, adjuvante mensâ diabolice obsessâ, recuperatum, curâque Jo. Conradi Schwarzii umbræ, aliis necnon plurimis adjuvantibus, restitutum.

LIBER I

PUNCTORUM garretos colens et cellara Quinque,
Gutteribus quæ et gaudes sundayam abstingere frontem,
Plerumque insidos solita fluitare liquore
Tanglepedem quem homines appellant Di quoque rotgut,
Pimpliidis, rubicundaque, Musa, O, bourbonolensque,   5
Fenianas rixas procul, alma, brogipotentis
Patricii cyathos iterantis et horrida bella,
Backos dum virides viridis Brigitta remittit,
Linquens, eximios celebrem, da, Virginienses
Rowdes, præcipue et TE, heros alte, Polarde !   10
Insignes juvenesque, illo certamine lictos,
Colemane, Tylere, nec vos oblivione relinquam.

Ampla aquilæ invictæ fausto est sub tegmine terra,
Backyfer, ooiskeo pollens, ebenoque bipede,
Socors præsidum et altrix (denique quidruminantium),   15
Duplefveorum uberrima ; illis et integre cordi est
Deplere assidue et sine proprio incommodo fiscum ;
Nunc etiam placidum hoc opus invictique secuti,
Goosam aureos ni eggos voluissent immo necare
Quæ peperit, saltem ac de illis meliora merentem.   20
  Condidit hanc Smithius Dux, Captinus inclytus ille
Regis Ulyssæ instar, docti arcum intendere longum ;
Condidit ille Johnsmith, Virginiamque vocavit,
Settledit autem Jacobus rex, nomine primus,
Rascalis implens ruptis, blagardisque deboshtis,   25
Militibusque ex Falstaffi legione fugatis
Wenchisque illi quas poterant seducere nuptas ;
Virgineum, ah, littus matronis talibus impar !
Progeniem stirpe ex hoc non sine stigmate ducunt
Multi sese qui jactant regum esse nepotes :   30
Haud omnes, Mater, genitos quæ nuper habebas
Bello fortes, consilio cautos, virtute decoros,
Jamque et habes, sparso si patrio in sanguine virtus,
Mostrabisque iterum, antiquis sub astris reducta !
De illis qui upkikitant, dicebam, rumpora tanta,   35
Letcheris et Floydis magnisque Extra ordine Billis ;
Est his prisca fides jurare et breakere wordum ;
Poppere fellerum a tergo, aut stickere clam bowiknifo,
Haud sane facinus, dignum sed victrice lauro ;
Larrupere et nigerum, factum præstantius ullo :   40

Ast chlamydem piciplumatam, Icariam, flito et ineptam,
Yanko gratis induere, illum et valido railo
Insuper acri equitare docere est hospitio uti.
  Nescio an ille Polardus duplefveoribus ortus,
Sed reputo potius de radice poorwitemanorum ;   45
Fortuiti proles, ni fallor, Tylerus erat
Præsidis, omnibus ab Whiggis nominatus a poor cuss ;
Et nobilem tertium evincit venerabile nomen.
Ast animosi omnes bellique ad tympana ha ! ha !
Vociferant læti, procul et si prœlia, sive   50
Hostem incautum atsito possunt shootere salvi ;
Imperiique capaces, esset si stylus agmen,
Pro dulci spoliabant et sine dangere fito.
Præ ceterisque Polardus : si Secessia licta,
Se nunquam licturum jurat, res et unheardof,   55
Verbo hæsit, similisque audaci roosteri invicto,
Dunghilli solitus rex pullos whoppere molles,
Grantum, hirelingos stripes quique et splendida tollunt
Sidera, et Yankos, territum et omnem sarsuit orbem.
  Usque dabant operam isti omnes, noctesque diesque,   60
Samuelem demulgere avunculum, id vero siccum ;
Uberibus sed ejus, et horum est culpa, remotis,
Parvam domi vaccam, nec mora minima, quærunt,
Lacticarentem autem et droppam vix in die dantem ;
Reddite avunculi, et exclamabant, reddite pappam !   65
Polko ut consule, gemens, Billy immurmurat Extra ;
Echo respondit, thesauro ex vacuo, pappam !
Frustra explorant pocketa, ruber nare repertum ;
Officia expulsi aspiciunt rapta, et Paradisum
Occlusum, viridesque haud illis nascere backos ;   70
Stupent tunc oculis madidis spittantque silenter.
Adhibere usu ast longo vires prorsus inepti,
Si non ut qui grindeat axve trabemve reuolvat,
Virginiam excruciant totis nunc mightibu' matrem ;
Non melius, puta, nono panis dimidiumne est ?   75
  Readere ibi non posse est casus commoner ullo ·
Tanto intentius imprimere est opus ergo statuta ·
Nemo propterea pejor, melior, sine doubto,
Obtineat qui contractum, si et postea rhino ;
Ergo Polardus, si quis, inexsuperabilis heros,   80
Colemanus impavidus nondum, atque in purpure natus
Tylerus Iohanides celerisque in flito Nathaniel,
Quisque optans digitos in tantum stickere pium,
Adstant accincti imprimere aut perrumpere leges :
Quales os miserum rabidi tres ægre molossi,   85
Quales aut dubium textum atra in veste ministri,
Tales circumstabant nunc nostri inopes hoc job.
  Hisque Polardus voce canoro talia fatus :
Primum autem, veluti est mos, præceps quisque liquorat,

Quisque et Nicotianum ingens quid inserit atrum,   90
Heroûm nitidum decus et solamen avitum,
Masticat ac simul altisonans, spittatque profuse :
Quis de Virginia meruit præstantius unquam ?
Quis se pro patria curavit impigre tutum ?
Speechisque articulisque hominum quis fortior ullus,   95
Ingeminans pennæ lickos et vulnera vocis ?
Quisnam putidius (hic) sarsuit Yankinimicos,
Sæpius aut dedit ultro datam et broke his parolam ?
Mente inquassatus solidâque, tyranno minante,
Horrisonis (hic) bombis mœnia et alta quatente,   100
Sese promptum (hic) jactans Yankos lickere centum,
Atque ad lastum invictus non surrendidit unquam ?
Ergo haud meddlite, posco, mique relinquite (hic) hoc job,
Si non—knifumque enormem mostrat spittatque tremendus.
    Dixerat : ast alii reliquorant et sine pauso   105
Pluggos incumbunt maxillis, uterque vicissim
Certamine innocuo valde madidam inquinat assem :
Tylerus autem, dumque liquorat aridus hostis,
Mirum aspicit duplumque bibentem, astante Lyæo ;
Ardens impavidusque edidit tamen impia verba ;   110
Duplum quamvis te aspicio, esses atque viginti,
Mendacem dicerem totumque (hic) thrasherem acervum ;
Nempe et thrasham, doggonatus (hic) sim nisi faxem ;
Lambastabo omnes catawompositer-(hic) que chawam
Dixit et impulsus Ryeo ruitur bene titus,   115
Illi nam gravidum caput et laterem habet in hatto.
    Hunc inhiat titubansque Polardus, optat et illum
Stickere inermem, protegit autem rite Lyæus,
Et pronos geminos, oculis dubitantibus, heros
Cernit et irritus hostes, dumque excogitat utrum   120
Primum inpitchere, corruit, inter utrosque recumbit,
Magno asino similis nimio sub pondere quassus :
Colemanus hos mœstus, triste ruminansque solamen,
Inspicit hiccans, circumspittat terque cubantes ;
Funereisque his ritibus humidis inde solutis,   125
Sternitur, invalidusque illis superincidit infans ;
Hos sepelit somnus et snorunt cornisonantes,
Watchmanus inscios ast calybooso deinde reponit.

No. IX

[The Editors of the ' Atlantic ' have received so many letters of inquiry concerning the literary remains of the late Mr. Wilbur, mentioned by his colleague and successor, Rev. Jeduthan Hitchcock, in a communication from which we made some extracts in our number for February, 1863, and have been so repeatedly urged to print some part of them for the gratification of the public, that they felt it their duty at least to make some effort to satisfy so urgent a demand. They have accordingly carefully examined the papers intrusted to them, but find most of the productions of Mr. Wilbur's pen so fragmentary, and even chaotic, written as they are on the backs of letters in an exceedingly cramped chirography, — here a memorandum for a sermon; there an observation of the weather; now the measurement of an extraordinary head of cabbage, and then of the cerebral capacity of some reverend brother deceased; a calm inquiry into the state of modern literature, ending in a method of detecting if milk be impoverished with water, and the amount thereof; one leaf beginning with a genealogy, to be interrupted half-way down with an entry that the brindle cow had calved,—that any attempts at selection seemed desperate. His only complete work, 'An Enquiry concerning the Tenth Horn of the Beast,' even in the abstract of it given by Mr. Hitchcock, would, by a rough computation of the printers, fill five entire numbers of our journal, and as he attempts, by a new application of decimal fractions, to identify it with the Emperor Julian, seems hardly of immediate concern to the general reader. Even the Table-Talk, though doubtless originally highly interesting in the domestic circle, is so largely made up of theological discussion and matters of local or preterite interest, that we have found it hard to extract anything that would at all satisfy expectation. But, in order to silence further inquiry, we subjoin a few passages as illustrations of its general character.]

I think I could go near to be a perfect Christian if I were always a visitor, as I have sometimes been, at the house of some hospitable friend. I can show a great deal of self-denial where the best of everything is urged upon me with kindly importunity. It is not so very hard to turn the other cheek for a kiss. And when I meditate upon the pains taken for our entertainment in this life, on the endless variety of seasons, of human character and fortune, on the costliness of the hangings and furniture of our dwelling here, I sometimes feel a singular joy in looking upon myself as God's guest, and cannot but believe that we should all be wiser and happier, because more grateful, if we were always mindful of our privilege in this regard. And should we not rate more cheaply any honour that men could pay us, if we remembered that every day we sat at the table of the Great King? Yet must we not forget that we are in strictest bonds His servants also; for there is no impiety so abject as that which expects to be *dead-headed* (*ut ita dicam*) through life, and which, calling itself trust in Providence, is in reality asking Providence to trust us and taking up all our goods on false pretences. It is a wise rule to take the world as we find it, not always to leave it so.

It has often set me thinking when I find that I can always pick up plenty of empty nuts under my shagbark-tree. The squirrels know them by their lightness, and I have seldom seen one with the marks of their teeth in it. What a school-house is the world, if our wits would only not play truant! For I observe that men set most store by forms and symbols in proportion as they are mere shells. It is the outside they want and not the kernel. What stores of such do not many who in material things are as shrewd as the squirrels, lay up for the spiritual winter-supply of themselves and their children! I have seen churches that seemed to me garners of these withered nuts, for it is wonderful how prosaic is the apprehension of symbols by the minds of most men. It is not one sect nor another, but all, who, like the dog of the fable, have let drop the spiritual substance of symbols for their material shadow. If one attribute miraculous virtues to mere holy water that beautiful emblem of inward purification at the door of God's house, another cannot comprehend the significance of baptism without being ducked over head and ears in the liquid vehicle thereof.

[Perhaps a word of historical comment may be permitted here. My late revered predecessor was, I would humbly affirm, as free from prejudice as falls to the lot of the most highly favoured individuals of our species. To be sure, I have heard him say that, 'what were called strong prejudices, were in fact only the repulsion of sensitive organizations from that moral and even physical effluvium through which some natures by providential appointment, like certain unsavoury quadrupeds, gave warning of their neighbourhood. Better ten mistaken suspicions of this kind than one close encounter.' This he said somewhat in heat, on being questioned as to his motives for always refusing his pulpit to those itinerant professors of vicarious benevolence who end their discourses by taking up a collection. But at another time I remember his saying, 'that there was one large thing which small minds always found room for, and that was great prejudices.' This, however, by the way. The statement which I purposed to make was simply this. Down to A. D. 1830, Jaalam had consisted of a single parish, with one house set apart for religious services. In that year the foundations of a Baptist Society were laid by the labours of Elder Joash Q. Balcom, 2d. As the members of the new body were drawn from the First Parish, Mr. Wilbur was for a time considerably exercised in mind. He even went so far as on one occasion to follow the reprehensible practice of the earlier Puritan divines in choosing a punning text, and preached from Hebrews xiii. 9 : 'Be not carried about with *divers* and strange doctrines.' He afterwards, in accordance with one of his own maxims, —' to get a dead injury out of the mind as soon as is decent, bury it, and then ventilate,'—in accordance with this maxim, I say, he lived on very friendly terms with Rev. Shearjashub Scrimgour,

present pastor of the Baptist Society in Jaalam. Yet I think it was never unpleasing to him that the church edifice of that society (though otherwise a creditable specimen of architecture) remained without a bell, as indeed it does to this day. So much seemed necessary to do away with any appearance of acerbity toward a respectable community of professing Christians, which might be suspected in the conclusion of the above paragraph.—J. H.]

In lighter moods he was not averse from an innocent play upon words. Looking up from his newspaper one morning as I entered his study he said, ' When I read a debate in Congress, I feel as if I were sitting at the feet of Zeno in the shadow of the Portico.' On my expressing a natural surprise, he added, smiling, ' Why, at such times the only view which honourable members give me of what goes on in the world is through their intercalumniations.' I smiled at this after a moment's reflection, and he added gravely, ' The most punctilious refinement of manners is the only salt that will keep a democracy from stinking ; and what are we to expect from the people, if their representatives set them such lessons ? Mr. Everett's whole life has been a sermon from this text. There was, at least, this advantage in duelling, that it set a certain limit on the tongue.' In this connexion, I may be permitted to recall a playful remark of his upon another occasion. The painful divisions in the First Parish, A. D. 1844, occasioned by the wild notions in respect to the rights of (what Mr. Wilbur, so far as concerned the reasoning faculty, always called) the unfairer part of creation, put forth by Miss Parthenia Almira Fitz, are too well known to need more than a passing allusion. It was during these heats, long since happily allayed, that Mr. Wilbur remarked that ' the Church had more trouble in dealing with one *she*resiarch than with twenty *he*resiarchs,' and that the men's *conscia recti*, or certainty of being right, was nothing to the women's.

When I once asked his opinion of a poetical composition on which I had expended no little pains, he read it attentively, and then remarked, ' Unless one's thought pack more neatly in verse than in prose, it is wiser to refrain. Commonplace gains nothing by being translated into rhyme, for it is something which no hocus-pocus can transubstantiate with the real presence of living thought. You entitle your piece, " My Mother's Grave," and expend four pages of useful paper in detailing your emotions there. But, my dear sir, watering does not improve the quality of ink, even though you should do it with tears. To publish a sorrow to Tom, Dick, and Harry is in some sort to advertise its unreality, for I have observed in my intercourse with the afflicted that the deepest grief instinctively hides its face with its hands and is silent. If your piece were printed, I have no doubt it would be popular, for people like to fancy that they feel much better than the trouble of feeling. I would put all poets on oath whether they have striven to say everything they possibly could think of, or to leave out all they could not help saying. In your own case, my worthy young friend, what you have written is merely a deliberate exercise, the gymnastic of sentiment. For your excellent maternal relative is still alive, and is to take tea with me this evening, D.V. Beware of simulated feeling; it is hypocrisy's first cousin; it is especially dangerous to a preacher; for he who says one day, " Go to, let me seem to be pathetic," may be nearer than he thinks to saying, " Go to, let me seem to be virtuous, or earnest, or under sorrow for sin." Depend upon it, Sappho loved her verses more sincerely than she did Phaon, and Petrarch his sonnets better than Laura, who was indeed but his poetical stalking-horse. After you shall have once heard that muffled rattle of the clods on the coffin-lid of an irreparable loss, you will grow acquainted with a pathos that will make all elegies hateful. When I was of your age, I also for a time mistook my desire to write verses for an authentic call of my nature in that direction. But one day as I was going forth for a walk, with my head full of an " Elegy on the Death of Flirtilla," and vainly groping after a rhyme for *lily* that should not be *silly* or *chilly*, I saw my eldest boy Homer busy over the rain-water hogshead, in that childish experiment at parthenogenesis, the changing a horse-hair into a water-snake. An immersion of six weeks showed no change in the obstinate filament. Here was a stroke of unintended sarcasm. Had I not been doing in my study precisely what my boy was doing out of doors ? Had my thoughts any more chance of coming to life by being submerged in rhyme than his hair by soaking in water ? I burned my elegy and took a course of Edwards on the Will. People do not make poetry; it is made out of *them* by a process for which I do not find myself fitted. Nevertheless, the writing of verses is a good rhetorical exercitation, as teaching us what to shun most carefully in prose. For prose bewitched is like window-glass with bubbles in it, distorting what it should show with pellucid veracity.'

It is unwise to insist on doctrinal points as vital to religion. The Bread of Life is wholesome and sufficing in itself, but gulped down with these kick-shaws cooked up by theologians, it is apt to produce an indigestion, nay, even at last an incurable dyspepsia of scepticism.

One of the more inexcusable weaknesses of Americans is in signing their names to what are called credentials. But for my interposition, a person who shall be nameless would have taken from this town a recommendation for an office of trust subscribed by the selectmen and all the voters of both parties, ascribing to him as many good qualities as if it had been his tombstone. The excuse was that it would be well for the town to be rid of him, as it would erelong be obliged to maintain him. I would not refuse my name to modest merit, but I would be as cautious as in signing a bond. [I trust I shall be subjected to no imputation of unbecoming vanity, if I mention the fact that Mr. W. indorsed my own qualifications as teacher of the highschool at Pequash Junction. J. H.] When I see a certificate of character with everybody's name to it, I regard it as a letter of introduction from the Devil. Never give a man your name unless you are willing to trust him with your reputation.

There seem nowadays to be two sources of literary inspiration,—fullness of mind and emptiness of pocket.

I am often struck, especially in reading Montaigne, with the obviousness and familiarity of a great writer's thoughts, and the freshness they gain because said by him. The truth is, we mix their greatness with all they say and give it our best attention. Johannes Faber sic cogitavit, would be no enticing preface to a book, but an accredited name gives credit like the signature of a note of hand. It is the advantage of fame that it is always privileged to take the world by the button, and a thing is weightier for Shakespeare's uttering it by the whole amount of his personality.

It is singular how impatient men are with overpraise of others, how patient with overpraise of themselves ; and yet the one does them no injury, while the other may be their ruin.

People are apt to confound mere alertness of mind with attention. The one is but the flying abroad of all the faculties to the open doors and windows at every passing rumour ; the other is the concentration of every one of them in a single focus, as in the alchemist over his alembic at the moment of expected projection. Attention is the stuff that memory is made of, and memory is accumulated genius.

Do not look for the Millennium as imminent. One generation is apt to get all the wear it can out of the cast clothes of the last, and is always sure to use up every paling of the old fence that will hold a nail in building the new.

You suspect a kind of vanity in my genealogical enthusiasm. Perhaps you are right ; but it is a universal foible. Where it does not show itself in a personal and private way, it becomes public and gregarious. We flatter ourselves in the Pilgrim Fathers, and the Virginian offshoot of a transported convict swells with the fancy of a cavalier ancestry. Pride of birth, I have noticed, takes two forms. One complacently traces himself up to a coronet ; another, defiantly, to a lapstone. The sentiment is precisely the same in both cases, only that one is the positive and the other the negative pole of it.

Seeing a goat the other day kneeling in order to graze with less trouble, it seemed to me a type of the common notion of prayer. Most people are ready enough to go down on their knees for material blessings, but how few for those spiritual gifts which alone are an answer to our orisons, if we but knew it !

Some people, nowadays, seem to have hit upon a new moralization of the moth and the candle. They would lock up the light of Truth, lest poor Psyche should put it out in her effort to draw nigh to it.

No. X

MR. HOSEA BIGLOW TO THE EDITOR OF THE ATLANTIC MONTHLY

DEAR SIR,—Your letter come to han'
    Requestin' me to please be funny ;
But I ain't made upon a plan
    Thet knows wut 's comin', gall or
      honey :
Ther' 's times the world doos look so
      queer,
    Odd fancies come afore I call 'em ;
An' then agin, for half a year,
    No preacher 'thout a call 's more
      solemn.

You 're 'n want o' sunthin' light an'
      cute,
    Rattlin' an' shrewd an' kin' o'
      jingleish,
An' wish, pervidin' it 'ould suit,
    I 'd take an' citify my English.
I *ken* write long-tailed, ef I please,—
    But when I 'm jokin', no, I
      thankee ;
Then, 'fore I know it, my idees
    Run helter-skelter into Yankee.

Sence I begun to scribble rhyme,
    I tell ye wut, I hain't ben foolin' ;
The parson's books, life, death, an'
      time
    Hev took some trouble with my
      schoolin' ;
Nor th' airth don't git put out with
      me,
    Thet love her 'z though she wuz
      a woman ;
Why, th' ain't a bird upon the tree
    But half forgives my bein' human.

An' yit I love th' unhighschooled way
    Ol' farmers hed when I wuz
      younger ;
Their talk wuz meatier, an' 'ould stay,
    While book-froth seems to whet
      your hunger ;

For puttin' in a downright lick
    'twixt Humbug's eyes, ther' 's few
      can metch it,
An' then it helves my thoughts ez
      slick
    Ez stret-grained hickory doos a
      hetchet.

But when I can't, I can't, thet 's
      all,
    For Natur' won't put up with
      gullin' ;
Idees you hev to shove an' haul
    Like a druv pig ain't wuth a
      mullein :
Live thoughts ain't sent for ; thru
      all rifts
    O' sense they pour an' resh ye on-
      wards,
Like rivers when south-lyin' drifts
    Feel thet th' old airth 's a-wheelin'
      sunwards.

Time wuz, the rhymes come crowdin'
      thick
    Ez office-seekers arter 'lection,
An' into ary place 'ould stick
    Without no bother nor objection ;
But sence the war my thoughts hang
      back
    Ez though I wanted to enlist 'em,
An' subs'tutes,—*they* don't never
      lack,
    But then they 'll slope afore you 've
      mist 'em.

Nothin' don't seem like wut it wuz ;
    I can't see wut there is to hender,
An' yit my brains jes' go buzz,
      buzz,
    Like bumblebees agin a winder ;
'fore these times come, in all airth's
      row,
    Ther' wuz one quiet place, my
      head in,
Where I could hide an' think,—but
      now
    It 's all one teeter, hopin', dreadin'.

Where's Peace? I start, some
  clear-blown night,
  When gaunt stone walls grow numb
  an' number,
An', creakin' 'cross the snow-crus'
  white,
  Walk the col' starlight into summer;
Up grows the moon, an' swell by swell
  Thru the pale pasturs silvers dim-
  mer
Than the last smile thet strives to tell
  O' love gone heavenward in its
  shimmer.

I hev ben gladder o' sech things
  Than cocks o' spring or bees o'
  clover,
They filled my heart with livin'
  springs,
  But now they seem to freeze 'em
  over ;
Sights innercent ez babes on knee,
  Peaceful ez eyes o' pastur'd cattle,
Jes' coz they be so, seem to me
  To rile me more with thoughts o'
  battle.

In-doors an' out by spells I try ;
  Ma'am Natur' keeps her spin-wheel
  goin',
But leaves my natur' stiff and dry
  Ez fiel's o' clover arter mowin' ;
An' her jes' keepin' on the same,
  Calmer 'n a clock, an' never carin',
An' findin' nary thing to blame,
  Is wus than ef she took to swearin'.

Snow-flakes come whisperin' on the
  pane
  The charm makes blazin' logs so
  pleasant,
But I can't hark to wut they're say'n',
  With Grant or Sherman ollers
  present ;
The chimbleys shudder in the gale,
  Thet lulls, then suddin takes to
  flappin'
Like a shot hawk, but all 's ez stale
  To me ez so much sperit-rappin'.

Under the yaller-pines I house,
  When sunshine makes 'em all
  sweet-scented,
An' hear among their furry boughs
  The baskin' west-wind purr con-
  tented,
While 'way o'erhead, ez sweet an'
  low
  Ez distant bells thet ring for meetin'
The wedged wil' geese their bugles
  blow,
  Further an' further South re-
  treatin'.

Or up the slippery knob I strain
  An' see a hundred hills like islan's
Lift their blue woods in broken chain
  Out o' the sea o' snowy silence ;
The farm-smokes, sweetes' sight on
  airth,
  Slow thru the winter air a-shrinkin'
Seem kin' o' sad, an' roun' the hearth
  Of empty places set me thinkin'.

Beaver roars hoarse with meltin'
  snows,
  An' rattles di'mon's from his
  granite ;
Time wuz, he snatched away my
  prose,
  An' into psalms or satires ran it ;
But he, not all the rest thet once
  Started my blood to country-
  dances,
Can't set me goin' more 'n a dunce
  Thet hain't no use for dreams an'
  fancies.

Rat-tat-tat-tattle thru the street
  I hear the drummers makin' riot,
An' I set thinkin' o' the feet
  Thet follered once an' now are
  quiet,—
White feet ez snowdrops innercent,
  Thet never knowed the paths o'
  Satan,
Whose comin' step ther' 's ears thet
  won't,
  No, not lifelong, leave off awaitin'.

Why, hain't I held 'em on my knee ?
 Did n't I love to see 'em growin',
Three likely lads ez wal could be,
 Hahnsome an' brave an' not tu
  knowin' ?
I set an' look into the blaze
 Whose natur', jes' like theirn,
  keeps climbin',
Ez long 'z it lives, in shinin' ways,
 An' half despise myself for rhymin'.

Wut 's words to them whose faith
  an' truth
 On War's red techstone rang true
  metal,
Who ventered life an' love an' youth
 For the gret prize o' death in battle ?
To him who, deadly hurt, agen
 Flashed on afore the charge's
  thunder,
Tippin' with fire the bolt of men
 Thet rived the Rebel line asunder ?
'T ain't right to hev the young go fust,
 All throbbin' full o' gifts an' graces,
Leavin' life's paupers dry ez dust
 To try an' make b'lieve fill their
  places :
Nothin' but tells us wut we miss,
 Ther' 's gaps our lives can't never
  fay in,
An' thet world seems so fur from this
 Lef' for us loafers to grow grey in !

My eyes cloud up for rain ; my mouth
 Will take to twitchin' roun' the
  corners ;
I pity mothers, tu, down South,
 For all they sot among the scorners:
I 'd sooner take my chance to stan'
 At Jedgement where your meanest
  slave is,
Than at God's bar hol' up a han'
 Ez drippin' red ez yourn, Jeff
  Davis !

Come, Peace ! not like a mourner
  bowed
 For honour lost an' dear ones wasted,
But proud, to meet a people proud,
 With eyes thet tell o' triumph
  tasted !

Come, with han' grippin' on the hilt,
 An' step thet proves ye Victory's
  daughter !
Longin' for you, our sperits wilt
 Like shipwrecked men's on raf's
  for water.

Come, while our country feels the lift
 Of a gret instinct shoutin' forwards,
An' knows thet freedom ain't a gift
 Thet tarries long in han's o'
  cowards !
Come, sech ez mothers prayed for,
  when
 They kissed their cross with lips
  thet quivered,
An' bring fair wages for brave men,
 A nation saved, a race delivered !

No. XI

MR. HOSEA BIGLOW'S SPEECH IN MARCH MEETING

TO THE EDITOR OF THE ATLANTIC MONTHLY

JAALAM, April 5, 1866.

MY DEAR SIR,—

(an' noticin' by your kiver thet you 're some dearer than wut you wuz, I enclose the deffrence) I dunno ez I know jest how to interdooce this las' perduction of my mews, ez Parson Willber allus called 'em, which is goin' to be the last an' stay the last onless sunthin' pertikler sh'd interfear which I don't expec' ner I wun't yield tu ef it wuz ez pressin' ez a deppity Shiriff. Sence Mr. Wilbur's disease I hev n't hed no one that could dror out my talons. He ust to kind o' wine me up an' set the penderlum agoin' an' then somehow I seemed to go on tick as it wear tell I run down, but the noo minister ain't of the same brewin' nor I can't seem to git ahold of no kine of huming nater in him but sort of slide rite off as you du on the eedge of a mow. Minnysteeril natur is wal enough an' a site better 'n most other kines I know on, but the other sort sech as Welbor hed wuz of the Lord's makin' an' naterally more wonderfle an' sweet tastin' leastways to me so fur as heerd from. He used to interdooce 'em smooth ez ile athout sayin' nothin' in pertickler an' I misdoubt he did n't set so much by the sec'nd Ceres as wut he done by the Fust, fact, he let on onct thet his mine misgive him of a sort of fallin' off in spots. He wuz as outspoken as a norwester *he* wuz, but I tole him I hoped the fall wuz from so high up thet a feller could ketch a good many times fust afore comin' bunt onto the ground as I see Jethro C. Swett from the meetin' house steeple up to th' old perrish, an' took up for dead but he's alive now an' spry as wut you be. Turnin' of it over I recclected how they ust to put wut they called Argymunce onto the frunts of poymns, like poorches afore housen whare you could rest ye a spell whilst you wuz concludin' whether you'd go in or not espeshully ware tha wuz darters, though I most allus found it the best plen to go in fust an' think afterwards an' the gals likes it best tu. I dno as speechis ever hez any argimunts to 'em, I never see none thet hed an' I guess they never du but tha must allus be a B'ginnin' to everythin' athout it is Eternity so I'll begin rite away an' anybody may put it afore any of his speeches ef it soots an' welcome. I don't claim no paytent.

THE ARGYMUNT

Interducshin, w'ich may be skipt. Begins by talkin' about himself : thet's jest natur an' most gin'ally allus pleasin', I b'leeve I've notist, to *one* of the cumpany, an' thet's more than wut you can say of most speshes of talkin'. Nex' comes the gittin' the goodwill of the orjunce by lettin' 'em gether from wut you kind of ex'dentally let drop thet they air about East, A one, an' no mistaik, skare 'em up an' take 'em as they rise. Spring interdooced with a fiew approput flours. Speech finally begins witch nobuddy need n't

feel obolygated to read as I never read 'em an' never shell this one ag'in. Subjick staited ; expanded; delayted ; extended. Pump lively. Subjick staited ag'in so 's to avide all mistaiks. Ginnle remarks ; continooed ; kerried on ; pushed furder ; kind o' gin out. Subjick *re*-staited ; dielooted ; stirred up permiscoous. Pump ag'in. Gits back to where he sot out. Can't seem to stay thair. Ketches into Mr. Seaward's hair. Breaks loose ag'in an' staits his subjick ; stretches it ; turns it ; folds it ; onfolds it ; folds it ag'in so 's 't no one can't find it. Argoos with an imedginary bean thet ain't aloud to say nothin' in repleye. Gives him a real good dressin' an' is settysfide he's rite. Gits into Johnson's hair. No use tryin' to git into his head. Gives it up. Hez to stait his subjick ag'in ; doos it back'ards, sideways, eendways, criss-cross, bevellin', noways. Gits finally red on it. Concloods. Concloods more. Reads some xtrax. Sees his subjick a-nosin' round arter him ag'in. Tries to avide it. Wun't du. *Mis*states it. Can't conjectur' no other plawsable way of staytin' on it. Tries pump. No fx. Finely concloods to conclood. Yeels the flore.

You kin spall an' punctooate thet as you please. I allus do, it kind of puts a noo soot of close onto a word, thisere funattick spellin' doos an' takes 'em out of the prissen dress they wair in the Dixonary. Ef I squeeze the cents out of 'em it's the main thing, an' wut they wuz made for ; wut's left's jest pummis.

Mistur Wilbur sez he to me onct, sez he, ' Hosee,' sez he, ' in litterytoor the only good thing is Natur. It's amazin' hard to come at,' sez he, ' but onct git it an' you've gut everythin'. Wut's the sweetest small on airth ? ' sez he. ' Noomone hay,' sez I, pooty bresk, for he wuz allus hankerin' round in hayin'. ' Nawthin' of the kine,' sez he. ' My leetle Huldy's breath,' sez I ag'in. ' You're a good lad,' sez he, his eyes sort of ripplin' like, for he lost a babe onct nigh about her age,—' you're a good lad; but 't ain't thet nuther,' sez he. 'Ef you want to know,' sez he, ' open your winder of a mornin' et ary season, and you 'll larn thet the best of perfooms is jest fresh air, *fresh air,*' sez he, emphysizin', 'athout no mixtur. Thet 's wut *I* call natur in writin', and it bathes my lungs and washes 'em sweet whenever I git a whiff on 't,' sez he. I offen think o' thet when I set down to write, but the winders air *so* ept to git stuck, an' breakin' a pane costs sunthin'.

Yourn for the last time,

Nut to be continooed,

HOSEA BIGLOW.

I DON'T much s'pose, hows'ever I should plen it,
I could git boosted into th' House or Sennit,—
Nut while the twolegged gab-machine 's so plenty,
'nablin' one man to du the talk o' twenty;
I 'm one o' them thet finds it ruther hard
To mannyfactur' wisdom by the yard,
An' maysure off, accordin' to demand,
The piece-goods el'kence that I keep on hand,
The same ole pattern runnin' thru an' thru,
An' nothin' but the customer thet 's new.   10
I sometimes think, the furder on I go,
Thet it gits harder to feel sure I know,
An' when I 've settled my idees, I find
't warn't I sheered most in makin' up my mind;
't wuz this an' thet an' t' other thing thet done it,
Sunthin' in th' air, I could n' seek nor shun it.
Mos' folks go off so quick now in discussion,
All th' ole flint locks seems altered to percussion,
Whilst I in agin' sometimes git a hint,
Thet I 'm percussion changin' back to flint;   20
Wal, ef it 's so, I ain't agoin' to werrit,
For th' ole Queen's-arm hez this pertickler merit,—
It gives the mind a hahnsome wedth o' margin
To kin' o' make its will afore dischargin':
I can't make out but jest one ginnle rule,—
No man need go an' *make* himself a fool,
Nor jedgement ain't like mutton, thet can't bear
Cookin' tu long, nor be took up tu rare.

Ez I wuz say'n', I hain't no chance to speak
So 's 't all the country dreads me onct a week,   30
But I 've consid'ble o' thet sort o' head
Thet sets to home an' thinks wut *might* be said,
The sense thet grows an' werrits underneath,
Comin' belated like your wisdom-teeth,
An' git so el'kent, sometimes, to my gardin
Thet I don' vally public life a fardin'.
Our Parson Wilbur (blessin's on his head!)
'mongst other stories of ole times he hed,
Talked of a feller thet rehearsed his spreads
Beforehan' to his rows o' kebbige-heads,   40

(Ef 't war n't Demossenes, I guess 't wuz Sisro,)
Appealin' fust to thet an' then to this row,
Accordin' ez he thought thet his idees
Their diff'runt ev'riges o' brains 'ould please ;
' An',' sez the Parson, ' to hit right, you must
Git used to maysurin' your hearers fust ;
For, take my word for 't, when all 's come an' past,
The kebbige-heads 'll cair the day et last ;
Th' ain't ben a meetin' sence the worl' begun
But they made (raw or biled ones) ten to one.'   50

I 've allus foun' 'em, I allow, sence then
About ez good for talkin' to ez men ;
They 'll take edvice, like other folks, to keep,
(To use it 'ould be holdin' on 't tu cheap,)
They listen wal, don' kick up when you scold 'em,
An' ef they 've tongues, hev sense enough to hold 'em ;
Though th' ain't no denger we shall lose the breed,
I gin'lly keep a score or so for seed,
An' when my sappiness gits spry in spring,
So 's 't my tongue itches to run on full swing,   60
I fin' 'em ready-planted in March-meetin',
Warm ez a lyceum-audience in their greetin',
An' pleased to hear my spoutin' frum the fence,—
Comin', ez 't doos, entirely free 'f expense.
This year I made the follerin' observations
Extrump'ry, like most other tri'ls o' patience,
An', no reporters bein' sent express
To work their abstrac's up into a mess
Ez like th' oridg'nal ez a woodcut pictur'
Thet chokes the life out like a boy-constrictor,   70
I 've writ 'em out, an' so avide all jeal'sies
'twixt nonsense o' my own an' some one's else's.

(N. B. Reporters gin'lly git a hint
To make dull orjunces seem 'live in print,
An', ez I hev t' report myself, I vum,
I 'll put th' applauses where they 'd *ough' to* come !)

MY FELLER KEBBIGE-HEADS, who look so green,
I vow to gracious thet ef I could dreen
The world of all its hearers but jest you,
't would leave 'bout all tha' is wuth talkin' to,   80
An' you, my ven'able ol' frien's, thet show
Upon your crowns a sprinklin' o' March snow,
Ez ef mild Time had christened every sense
For wisdom's church o' second innocence,
Nut Age's winter, no, no sech a thing,
But jest a kin' o' slippin'-back o' spring,—
                                        [Sev'ril noses blowed.]

We' ve gathered here, ez ushle, to decide
Which is the Lord's an' which is Satan's side,
Coz all the good or evil thet can heppen
Is 'long o' which on 'em you choose for Cappen.   90
[Cries o' ' Thet 's so ! ']

Aprul 's come back ; the swellin' buds of oak
Dim the fur hillsides with a purplish smoke ;
The brooks are loose an', singing to be seen,
(Like gals,) make all the hollers soft an' green ;
The birds are here, for all the season 's late ;
They take the sun's height an' don' never wait ;
Soon 'z he officially declares it 's spring
Their light hearts lift 'em on a north'ard wing,
An' th' ain't an acre, fur ez you can hear,
Can't by the music tell the time o' year ;   100
But thet white dove Carliny scared away,
Five year ago, jes' sech an Aprul day ;
Peace, that we hoped 'ould come an' build last year
An' coo by every housedoor, is n't here,—
No, nor wun't never be, for all our jaw,
Till we 're ez brave in pol'tics ez in war !
O Lord, ef folks wuz made so 's 't they could see
The begnet-pint there is to an idee !   [Sensation.]
Ten times the danger in 'em th' is in steel ;
They run your soul thru an' you never feel,   110
But crawl about an' seem to think you 're livin',
Poor shells o' men, nut wuth the Lord's forgivin',
Tell you come bunt ag'in a real live fect,
An' go to pieces when you 'd ough' to ect !
Thet kin' o' begnet 's wut we 're crossin' now,
An' no man, fit to nevvigate a scow,
'ould stan' expectin' help from Kingdom Come,
While t' other side druv their cold iron home.

My frien's, you never gethered from my mouth,
No, nut one word ag'in the South ez South,   120
Nor th' ain't a livin' man, white, brown, nor black,
Gladder 'n wut I should be to take 'em back ;
But all I ask of Uncle Sam is fust
To write up on his door, ' No goods on trust ' ;
[Cries of ' Thet 's the ticket ! ']
Give us cash down in ekle laws for all,
An' they 'll be snug inside afore nex' fall.
Give wut they ask, an' we shell hev Jamaker,
Wuth minus some consid'able an acre ;
Give wut they need, an' we shell git 'fore long
A nation all one piece, rich, peacefle, strong ;   130
Make 'em Amerikin, an' they 'll begin
To love their country ez they loved their sin ;

Let 'em stay Southun, an' you 've kep' a sore
Ready to fester ez it done afore.
No mortle man can boast of perfic' vision,
But the one moleblin' thing is Indecision,
An' th' ain't no futur' for the man nor state
Thet out of j-u-s-t can't spell great.
Some folks 'ould call thet reddikle ; do you ?
'T was commonsense afore the war wuz thru ;   140
Thet loaded all our guns an' made 'em speak
So 's 't Europe heared 'em clearn acrost the creek ;
' They 're drivin' o' their spiles down now,' sez she,
' To the hard grennit o' God's fust idee ;
Ef they reach thet, Democ'cy need n't fear
The tallest airthquakes *we* can git up here.'
Some call 't insultin' to ask *ary* pledge,
An' say 't will only set their teeth on edge,
But folks you 've jest licked, fur 'z I ever see,
Are 'bout ez mad 'z they wal know how to be ;   150
It 's better than the Rebs themselves expected
'fore they see Uncle Sam wilt down henpected ;
Be kind 'z you please, but fustly make things fast,
For plain Truth 's all the kindness thet 'll last ;
Ef treason is a crime, ez *some* folks say,
How could we punish it a milder way
Than sayin' to 'em, ' Brethren, lookee here,
We 'll jes' divide things with ye, sheer an' sheer,
An sence both come o' pooty strong-backed daddies,
You take the Darkies, ez we 've took the Paddies ;   160
Ign'ant an' poor we took 'em by the hand,
An' they 're the bones an' sinners o' the land.'
I ain't o' them thet fancy there 's a loss on
Every inves'ment thet don't start from Bos'on ;
But I know this : our money 's safest trusted
In sunthin', come wut will, thet *can't* be busted,
An' thet 's the old Amerikin idee,
To make a man a Man an' let him be.

[Gret applause.]

Ez for their l'yalty, don't take a goad to 't,
But I do' want to block their only road to 't   170
By lettin' 'em believe thet they can git
Mor 'n wut they lost, out of our little wit :
I tell ye wut, I 'm 'fraid we 'll drif' to leeward
'thout we can put more stiffenin' into Seward ;
He seems to think Columby 'd better ect
Like a scared widder with a boy stiff-necked
Thet stomps an' swears he wun't come in to supper ;
She mus' set up for him, ez weak ez Tupper,
Keepin' the Constitootion on to warm,
Tell he 'll eccept her 'pologies in form :   180

The neighbours tell her he 's a cross-grained cuss
Thet needs a hidin' 'fore he comes to wus ;
' No,' sez Ma Seward, ' he 's ez good 'z the best,
All he wants now is sugar-plums an' rest ' ;
' He sarsed my Pa,' sez one ; ' He stoned my son,'
Another edds. ' O, wal, 't wuz jest his fun.'
' He tried to shoot our Uncle Samwell dead.'
' 'T wuz only tryin' a noo gun he hed.'
' Wal, all we ask 's to hev it understood
You 'll take his gun away from him for good ;   190
We don't, wal, nut exac'ly, like his play,
Seein' he allus kin' o' shoots our way.
You kill your fatted calves to no good eend,
'thout his fust sayin', " Mother, I hev sinned ! " '
                    [' Amen ! ' frum Deac'n Greenleaf.]

The Pres'dunt *he* thinks thet the slickest plan
'ould be t' allow thet he 's our on'y man,
An' thet we fit thru all thet dreffle war
Jes' for his private glory an' eclor ;
' Nobody ain't a Union man,' sez he,
' 'thout he agrees, thru thick an' thin, with me ;   200
War n't Andrew Jackson's 'nitials jes' like mine ?
An' ain't thet sunthin' like a right divine
To cut up ez kentenkerous ez I please,
An' treat your Congress like a nest o' fleas ? '
Wal, I expec' the People would n' care, if
The question now wuz techin' bank or tariff,
But I conclude they 've 'bout made up their mind
This ain't the fittest time to go it blind,
Nor these ain't metters thet with pol'tics swings,
But goes 'way down amongst the roots o' things ;   210
Coz Sumner talked o' whitewashin' one day
They wun't let four years' war be throwed away.
' Let the South hev her rights ? ' They say, ' Thet 's you !
But nut greb hold of other folks's tu.'
Who owns this country, is it they or Andy ?
Leastways it ough' to be the People *and* he ;
Let him be senior pardner, ef he 's so,
But let them kin' o' smuggle in ez Co ;   [Laughter.]
Did he diskiver it ?   Consid'ble numbers
Think thet the job wuz taken by Columbus.   220
Did he set tu an' make it wut it is ?
Ef so, I guess the One-Man-power *hez* riz.
Did he put thru the rebbles, clear the docket,
An' pay th' expenses out of his own pocket ?
Ef thet 's the case, then everythin' I exes
Is t' hev him come an' pay my ennooal texes.
                    [Profound sensation.]

Was 't he thet shou'dered all them million guns ?
Did he lose all the fathers, brothers, sons ?
Is this ere pop'lar gov'ment thet we run
A kin' o' sulky, made to kerry one ?   230
An' is the country goin' to knuckle down
To hev Smith sort their letters 'stid o' Brown ?
Who wuz the 'Nited States 'fore Richmon' fell ?
Wuz the South needfle their full name to spell ?
An' can't we spell it in thet short-han' way
Till th' underpinnin' 's settled so 's to stay ?
Who cares for the Resolves of '61,
Thet tried to coax an airthquake with a bun ?
Hez act'ly nothin' taken place sence then
To larn folks they must hendle fects like men ?   240
Ain't *this* the true p'int ? Did the Rebs accep' 'em ?
Ef nut, whose fault is 't thet we hev n't kep 'em ?
War n't there *two* sides ? an' don't it stend to reason
Thet this week's 'Nited States ain't las' week's treason ?
When all these sums is done, with nothin' missed,
An' nut afore, this school 'll be dismissed.

I knowed ez wal ez though I 'd seen 't with eyes
Thet when the war wuz over copper 'd rise,
An' thet we 'd hev a rile-up in our kettle
't would need Leviathan's whole skin to settle :   250
I thought 't would take about a generation
'fore we could wal begin to be a nation,
But I allow I never did imegine
't would be our Pres'dunt thet 'ould drive a wedge in
To keep the split from closin' ef it could,
An' healin' over with new wholesome wood ;
For th' ain't no chance o' healin' while they think
Thet law an' gov'ment 's only printer's ink ;
I mus' confess I thank him for discoverin'
The curus way in which the States are sovereign ;   260
They ain't nut *quite* enough so to rebel,
But, when they fin' it 's costly to raise h—,
                          [A groan from Deac'n G.]
Why, then, for jes' the same superl'tive reason,
They 're 'most too much so to be tetched for treason ;
They *can't* go out, but ef they somehow *du*,
Their sovereignty don't noways go out tu ;
The State goes out, the sovereignty don't stir,
But stays to keep the door ajar for her.
He thinks secession never took 'em out,
An' mebby he 's correc', but I misdoubt ;   270
Ef they war n't out, then why, 'n the name o' sin,
Make all this row 'bout lettin' of 'em in ?

In law, p'r'aps nut; but there's a diffurence, ruther,
Betwixt your mother-'n-law an' real mother, [Derisive cheers.]
An' I, for one, shall wish they 'd all been *som'eres,*
Long 'z U. S. Texes are sech reg'lar comers.
But, O my patience ! must we wriggle back
Into th' ole crooked, pettyfoggin' track,
When our artil'ry-wheels a road hev cut
Stret to our purpose ef we keep the rut ?   280
War 's jes' dead waste excep' to wipe the slate
Clean for the cyph'rin' of some nobler fate.   [Applause.]

Ez for dependin' on their oaths an' thet,
't wun't bind 'em mor 'n the ribbin roun' my het ;
I heared a fable once from Othniel Starns,
That pints it slick ez weathercocks do barns :
Onct on a time the wolves hed certing rights
Inside the fold ; they used to sleep there nights.
An', bein' cousins o' the dogs, they took
Their turns et watchin', reg'lar ez a book ;   290
But somehow, when the dogs hed gut asleep,
Their love o' mutton beat their love o' sheep,
Till gradilly the shepherds come to see
Things war n't agoin' ez they 'd ough' to be ;
So they sent off a deacon to remonstrate
Along 'th wolves an' urge 'em to go on straight ;
They did n' seem to set much by the deacon,
Nor preachin' did n' cow 'em, nut to speak on ;
Fin'ly they swore thet they 'd go out an' stay,
An' hev their fill o' mutton every day ;   300
Then dogs an' shepherds, after much hard dammin',
                                          [Groan from Deac'n G.]
Turned tu an' give 'em a tormented lammin',
An' sez, ' Ye sha' n't go out, the murrain rot ye,
To keep us wastin' half our time to watch ye ! '
But then the question come, How live together
'thout losin' sleep, nor nary yew nor wether ?
Now there wuz some dogs (noways wuth their keep)
That sheered their cousins' tastes an' sheered the sheep ;
They sez, ' Be gin'rous, let 'em swear right in,
An', ef they backslide, let 'em swear ag'in ;   310
Jes' let 'em put on sheep-skins whilst they 're swearin' ;
To ask for more 'ould be beyond all bearin'.'
' Be gin'rous for yourselves, where *you* 're to pay,
Thet 's the best prectice,' sez a shepherd grey ;
' Ez for their oaths they wun't be wuth a button,
Long 'z you don't cure 'em o' their taste for mutton ;
Th' ain't but one solid way, howe'er you puzzle :
Tell they 're convarted, let 'em wear a muzzle.'
                                    [Cries of ' Bully for you ! ']

I 've noticed thet each half-baked scheme's abetters
Are in the hebbit o' producin' letters   320
Writ by all sorts o' never-heard-on fellers,
'bout ez oridge'nal ez the wind in bellers ;
I 've noticed, tu, it 's the quack med'cine gits
(An' needs) the grettest heaps o' stiffykits ;
                    [Two apothekeries goes out.]
Now, sence I lef' off creepin' on all fours,
I hain't ast no man to endorse my course ;
It 's full ez cheap to be your own endorser,
An' ef I 've made a cup, I 'll fin' the saucer ;
But I 've some letters here from t' other side,
An' them 's the sort thet helps me to decide ;   330
Tell me for wut the copper-comp'nies hanker,
An' I 'll tell you jest where it 's safe to anchor.   [Faint hiss.]
Fus'ly the Hon'ble B. O. Sawin writes
Thet for a spell he could n' sleep o' nights,
Puzzlin' which side wus preudentest to pin to,
Which wuz th' ole homestead, which the temp'ry leanto ;
Et fust he jedged 't would right-side-up his pan
To come out ez a 'ridge'nal Union man,
' But now,' he sez, ' I ain't nut quite so fresh ;
The winnin' horse is goin' to be Secesh ;   340
You might, las' spring, hev eas'ly walked the course,
'fore we contrived to doctor th' Union horse ;
Now *we* 're the ones to walk aroun' the nex' track:
Jest you take hold an' read the follerin' extrac',
Out of a letter I received last week
From an ole frien' thet never sprung a leak,
A Nothun Dem'crat o' th' ole Jarsey blue,
Born copper-sheathed an' copper-fastened tu.'

' These four years past it hez been tough
To say which side a feller went for ;   350
Guideposts all gone, roads muddy 'n' rough,
An' nothin' duin' wut 't wuz meant for ;
Pickets a-firin' left an' right,
Both sides a lettin' rip et sight,—
Life war n't wuth hardly payin' rent for.

' Columby gut her back up so,
It war n't no use a-tryin' to stop her,—
War's emptin's riled her very dough
An' made it rise an' act improper ;
't wuz full ez much ez I could du   360
To jes' lay low an' worry thru,
'thout hevin' to sell out my copper.

' Afore the war your mod'rit men
Could set an' sun 'em on the fences,

Cyph'rin' the chances up, an' then
Jump off which way bes' paid expenses ;
Sence, 't wus so resky ary way,
I did n't hardly darst to say
I 'greed with Paley's Evidences.   [Groan from **Deac'n G.**]

' Ask Mac ef tryin' to set the fence   370
War n't like bein' rid upon a rail on 't,
Headin' your party with a sense
O' bein' tipjint in the tail on 't,
An' tryin' to think thet, on the whole,
You kin' o' quasi own your soul
When Belmont 's gut a bill o' sale on 't ?
                              [Three cheers for **Grant and Sherman.**]

' Come peace, I sposed thet folks 'ould like
Their pol'tics done ag'in by proxy
Give their noo loves the bag an' strike
A fresh trade with their reg'lar doxy ;   380
But the drag 's broke, now slavery 's gone,
An' there 's gret resk they 'll blunder on,
Ef they ain't stopped, to real Democ'cy.

' We 've gut an awful row to hoe
In this 'ere job o' reconstructin' ;
Folks dunno skurce which way to go,
Where th' ain't some boghole to be ducked in ;
But one thing 's clear ; there *is* a crack,
Ef we pry hard, 'twixt white an' black,
Where the ole makebate can be tucked in.   390

' No white man sets in airth's broad aisle
Thet I ain't willin' t' own ez brother,
An' ef he 's heppened to strike ile,
I dunno, fin'ly, but I 'd ruther ;
An' Paddies, long 'z they vote all right,
Though they ain't jest a nat'ral white,
I hold one on 'em good 'z another.   [Applause.]

' Wut *is* there lef' I 'd like to know,
Ef 't ain't the difference o' colour,
To keep up self-respec' an' show   400
The human natur' of a fullah ?
Wut good in bein' white, onless
It 's fixed by law, nut lef' to guess,
That we are smarter an' they duller ?

' Ef we 're to hev our ekle rights,
't wun't du to 'low no competition ;
Th' ole debt doo us for bein' whites
Ain't safe onless we stop th' emission

O' these noo notes, whose specie base
Is human natur', 'thout no trace   410
O' shape, nor colour, nor condition.   [Continood applause.]

' So fur I 'd writ an' could n' jedge
Aboard wut boat I 'd best take pessige,
My brains all mincemeat, 'thout no edge
Upon 'em more than tu a sessige,
But now it seems ez though I see
Sunthin' resemblin' an idee,
Sence Johnson's speech an' veto message.

' I like the speech best, I confess,
The logic, preudence, an' good taste on 't,   420
An' it 's so mad, I ruther guess
There 's some dependence to be placed on 't ;   [Laughter.]
It 's narrer, but 'twixt you an' me,
Out o' the allies o' J. D.
A temp'ry party can be based on 't.

' Jes' to hold on till Johnson 's thru
An' dug his Presidential grave is,
An' *then !*—who knows but we could slew
The country roun' to put in—— ?
Wun't some folks rare up when we pull   430
Out o' their eyes our Union wool
An' larn 'em wut a p'lit'cle shave is !

' Oh, did it seem 'z ef Providunce
Could ever send a second Tyler ?
To see the South all back to once,
Reapin' the spiles o' the Freesiler,
Is cute ez though an ingineer
Should claim th' old iron for his sheer
Coz 't was himself that bust the biler ! '   [Gret laughter.]

Thet tells the story ! Thet 's wut we shall git   440
By tryin' squirtguns on the burnin' Pit ;
For the day never comes when it 'll du
To kick off Dooty like a worn-out shoe.
I seem to hear a whisperin' in the air,
A sighin' like, of unconsoled despair,
Thet comes from nowhere an' from everywhere,
An' seems to say, ' Why died we ? war n't it, then,
To settle, once for all, thet men wuz men ?
Oh, airth's sweet cup snetched from us barely tasted,
The grave's real chill is feelin' life wuz wasted ?   450
O, you we lef', long-lingerin' et the door,
Lovin' you best, coz we loved Her the more,

Thet Death, not we, had conquered, we should feel
Ef she upon our memory turned her heel,
An' unregretful throwed us all away
To flaunt it in a Blind Man's Holiday ! '

My frien's, I 've talked nigh on to long enough.
I hain't no call to bore ye coz ye 're tough ;
My lungs are sound, an' our own v'ice delights
Our ears, but even kebbige-heads hez rights.   460
It 's the las' time thet I shell e'er address ye,
But you 'll soon fin' some new tormentor: bless ye !
   [Tumult'ous applause and cries of ' Go on !' ' Don't stop ! ']

GLOSSARY

(The entries marked ' (Eng. ed.) ' were added in the authorized English
edition of 1859 by Thomas Hughes: ' I have added some half-dozen words
to the glossary, at which I thought that English readers might perhaps
stumble.')

A

Act'lly, *actually.*
Air, *are.*
Airth, *earth.*
Airy, *area.*
Aree, *area.*
Arter, *after.*
Ax, *ask.*

B

Beller, *bellow.*
Bellowses, *lungs.*
Ben, *been.*
Bile, *boil.*
Bimeby, *by and by.*
Blurt out, *to speak bluntly.*
Bust, *burst.*
Buster, *a roistering blade* ; used also as
 a general superlative.

C

Caird, *carried.*
Cairn, *carrying.*
Caleb, *a turncoat.*
Cal'late, *calculate.*
Cass, *a person with two lives.*
Close, *clothes.*
Cockerel, *a young cock.*
Cocktail, *a kind of drink* ; also, *an ornament
 peculiar to soldiers.*
Convention, *a place where people are imposed
 on* ; *a juggler's show.*

Coons, *a cant term for a now defunct party* ;
 derived, perhaps, from the fact of their
 being commonly *up a tree.*
Cornwallis, *a sort of muster in masquerade* ;
 supposed to have had its origin soon after
 the Revolution, and to commemorate the
 surrender of Lord Cornwallis. It took the
 place of the old Guy Fawkes procession.
Crooked stick, *a perverse, froward person.*
Cunnle, *a colonel.*
Cus, *a curse* ; also, *a pitiful fellow.*

D

Darsn't, used indiscriminately, either in
 singular or plural number, for *dare not,
 dares not,* and *dared not.*
Deacon off, *to give the cue to* ; derived from
 a custom, once universal, but now extinct,
 in our New England Congregational
 churches. An important part of the
 office of deacon was to read aloud the
 hymns *given out* by the minister, one
 line at a time, the congregation singing
 each line as soon as read.
Demmercrat, leadin', *one in favour of extend-
 ing slavery* ; *a free-trade lecturer maintained in the custom-house.*
Desput, *desperate.*
Doos, *does.*
Doughface, *a contented lick-spittle* ; a common variety of Northern politician.
Dror, *draw.*

Du, *do.*

Dunno, dno, *do not or does not know.*

Dut, *dirt.*

E

Eend, *end.*

Ef, *if.*

Emptins, *yeast.*

Env'y, *envoy.*

Everlasting, an intensive, without reference to duration.

Ev'y, *every.*

Ez, *as.*

F

Fence, on the; said of one who halts between two opinions; a trimmer.

Fer, *for.*

Ferfle, ferful, *fearful*; also an intensive.

Fin', *find.*

Fish-skin, used in New England to clarify coffee.

Fix, *a difficulty, a nonplus.*

Foller, folly, *to follow.*

Forrerd, *forward.*

Frum, *from.*

Fur, *far.*

Furder, *farther.*

Furrer, *furrow.* Metaphorically, *to draw a straight furrow* is to live uprightly or decorously.

Fust, *first.*

G

Gin, *gave.*

Git, *get.*

Gret, *great.*

Grit, *spirit, energy, pluck.*

Grout, *to sulk.*

Grouty, *crabbed, surly.*

Gum, *to impose on.*

Gump, *a foolish fellow, a dullard.*

Gut, *got.*

H

Hed, *had.*

Heern, *heard.*

Hellum, *helm.*

Hendy, *handy.*

Het, *heated.*

Hev, *have.*

Hez, *has.*

Holl, *whole.*

Holt, *hold.*

Huf, *hoof.*

Hull, *whole.*

Hum, *home.*

Humbug, *General Taylor's antislavery.*

Hut, *hurt.*

I

Idno, *I do not know.*

In'my, *enemy.*

Insines, *ensigns*; used to designate both the officer who carries the standard, and the standard itself.

Inter, intu, *into.*

J

Jedge, *judge.*

Jest, *just.*

Jine, *join.*

Jint, *joint.*

Junk, *a fragment of any solid substance.*

K

Keer, *care.*

Kep', *kept.*

Killock, *a small anchor.*

Kin', kin' o', kinder, *kind, kind of.*

L

Lawth, *loath.*

Less, *let's, let us.*

Let daylight into, *to shoot.*

Let on, *to hint, to confess, to own.*

Lick, *to beat, to overcome.*

Lights, *the bowels.*

Lily-pads, *leaves of the water-lily.*

Long-sweetening, *molasses.*

Loon, *the northern diver.* (Eng. ed.)

M

Mash, *marsh.*

Mean, *stingy, ill-natured.*

Min', *mind.*

N

Ned, a slang phrase, going it like Ned, equivalent to our 'going like old Harry.' (Eng. ed.)

Nimepunce, *ninepence, twelve and a half cents.*

Nowers, *nowhere.*

O

Offen, *often.*

Ole, *old.*

Ollers, olluz, *always.*

On, *of*; used before *it* or *them*, or at the end of a sentence, as *on't, on'em, nut ez ever I heerd on.*

On'y, *only.*

Ossifer, *officer* (seldom heard).

P

Peaked, *pointed.*

Peek, *to peep.*

Pickerel, *the pike, a fish.*

Pint, *point.*

Pocket full of rocks, *plenty of money.*
Pooty, *pretty.*
Pop'ler, *conceited, popular.*
Pus, *purse.*
Put out, *troubled, vexed.*

Q

Quarter, *a quarter-dollar.*
Queen's-arm, *a musket.*

R

Resh, *rush.*
Revelee, *the réveille.*
Rile, *to trouble.*
Riled, *angry ; disturbed,* as the sediment in any liquid.
Riz, *risen.*
Row, a long row to hoe, *a difficult task.*
Row-de-dow, *troublesome talk.* (Eng. ed.)
Rugged, *robust.*

S

Sarse, *abuse, impertinence.*
Sartin, *certain.*
Saxon, *sacristan, sexton.*
Scaliest, *worst.*
Scringe, *cringe.*
Scrouge, *to crowd.*
Sech, *such.*
Set by, *valued.*
Shakes, great, *of considerable consequence.*
Shappoes, *chapeaux, cocked-hats.*
Sheer, *share.*
Shet, *shut.*
Shine, *a fancy or liking,* also written *shindy.* (Eng. ed.)
Shut, *shirt.*
Skeered, *scared.*
Skeeter, *mosquito.*
Skooting, *running,* or *moving swiftly.*
Slarterin', *slaughtering.*
Slim, *contemptible.*
Snake, *crawled like a snake ;* but *to snake any one out* is to track him to his hiding-place ; *to snake a thing out* is to snatch it out.
Soffies, *sofas.*
Sogerin', *soldiering ;* a barbarous amusement common among men in the savage state.
Som'ers, *somewhere.*
So'st, *so as that.*
Sot, *set, obstinate, resolute.*
Spiles, *spoils ; objects of political ambition.*
Spry, *active.*
Staddles, *stout stakes driven into the salt marshes,* on which the hay-ricks are set, and thus raised out of the reach of high tides.

Streaked, *uncomfortable, discomfited.*
Suckle, *circle.*
Sutthin', *something.*
Suttin, *certain.*
Swan, *to swear.* (Eng. ed.)

T

Take on, *to sorrow.*
Talents, *talons.*
Taters, *potatoes.*
Tell, *till.*
Tetch, *touch.*
Tetch tu, *to be able ;* used always after a negative in this sense.
Tollable, *tolerable.*
Toot, used derisively for *playing on any wind instrument.*
Thru, *through.*
Thundering, a euphemism common in New England, for the profane English expression *devilish.* Perhaps derived from the belief, common formerly, that thunder was caused by the Prince of the Air, for some of whose accomplishments consult Cotton Mather.
Tu, *to, too ;* commonly has this sound when used emphatically, or at the end of a sentence. At other times it has the sound of *t* in *tough,* as, *Ware ye goin' to ? Goin' ta Boston.*

U

Ugly, *ill-tempered, intractable.*
Uncle Sam, *United States ;* the largest boaster of liberty and owner of slaves.
Unrizzest, applied to dough or bread ; *heavy, most unrisen,* or *most incapable of rising.*

V

V-spot, *a five-dollar bill.*
Vally, *value.*

W

Wake snakes, *to get into trouble.*
Wal, *well ;* spoken with great deliberation, and sometimes with the *a* very much flattened, sometimes (but more seldom) very much broadened.
Wannut, *walnut (hickory).*
Ware, *where.*
Ware, *were.*
Whopper, *an uncommonly large lie ;* as, that General Taylor is in favour of the Wilmot Proviso.
Wig, *Whig ;* a party now dissolved.
Wiz, *to whiz ; go off* (like a rocket). (Eng. ed.)

Wunt, *will not.*
Wus, *worse.*
Wut, *what.*
Wuth, *worth*; as, *Antislavery perfessions 'fore 'lection aint wuth a Bungtown copper.*
Wuz, *was*, sometimes *were.*

Y

Yaller, *yellow.*

Yeller, *yellow.*
Yellers, *a disease of peach-trees.*

Z

Zack, Ole, *a second Washington, an antislavery slaveholder, a humane buyer and seller of men and women, a Christian hero generally.*

INDEX

THE UNHAPPY LOT OF MR. KNOTT

(1850)

PART I

SHOWING HOW HE BUILT HIS HOUSE
AND HIS WIFE MOVED INTO IT

My worthy friend, A. Gordon Knott,
  From business snug withdrawn,
Was much contented with a lot
That would contain a Tudor cot
'Twixt twelve feet square of garden-
    plot,
  And twelve feet more of lawn.

He had laid business on the shelf
  To give his taste expansion,
And, since no man, retired with pelf,
  The building mania can shun,   10
Knott, being middle-aged himself,
Resolved to build (unhappy elf !)
  A mediæval mansion.

He called an architect in counsel ;
  ' I want,' said he, ' a—you know
    what,
(You are a builder, I am Knott,)
A thing complete from chimney-pot
Down to the very grounsel ;
  Here 's a half-acre of good land ;
  Just have it nicely mapped and
    planned   20
And make your workmen drive on ;
  Meadow there is, and upland too,
  And I should like a water-view,
D' you think you could contrive one ?
  (Perhaps the pump and trough
    would do,
  If painted a judicious blue ?)
  The woodland I 've attended to ' ;
  (He meant three pines stuck up
    askew,
Two dead ones and a live one.)

' A pocket-full of rocks 't would
  take   30
To build a house of freestone,
  But then it is not hard to make
What nowadays is *the* stone ;
  The cunning painter in a trice
  Your house's outside petrifies,
  And people think it very gneiss
Without inquiring deeper ;
  My money never shall be thrown
  Away on such a deal of stone,
When stone of deal is cheaper.'   40

And so the greenest of antiques
  Was reared for Knott to dwell in :
The architect worked hard for weeks
In venting all his private peaks
Upon the roof, whose crop of leaks
  Had satisfied Fluellen ;
Whatever anybody had
Out of the common, good or bad,
  Knott had it all worked well in ;
A donjon-keep, where clothes might
    dry,   50
A porter's lodge that was a sty,
A campanile slim and high,
  Too small to hang a bell in ;
All up and down and here and there,
With Lord-knows-whats of round and
    square
Stuck on at random everywhere,—
  It was a house to make one stare,
  All corners and all gables ;
Like dogs let loose upon a bear,
Ten emulous styles *staboyed* with
    care,   60
The whole among them seemed to
    tear,
And all the oddities to spare
  Were set upon the stables.

Knott was delighted with a pile
  Approved by fashion's leaders :
(Only he made the builder smile,
By asking every little while,
Why that was called the Twodoor
    style,
  Which certainly had *three* doors ?)
Yet better for this luckless man   70
If he had put a downright ban
  Upon the thing *in limine* ;
For, though to quit affairs his plan,
Ere many days, poor Knott began
Perforce accepting draughts, that ran
  All ways—except up chimney ;
The house, though painted stone to
    mock,
With nice white lines round every
    block,
  Some trepidation stood in,   79
When tempests (with petrific shock,
So to speak,) made it really rock,
  Though not a whit less wooden ;
And painted stone, how'er well
    done,
Will not take in the prodigal sun
Whose beams are never quite at one
  With our terrestrial lumber ;
So the wood shrank around the knots,
And gaped in disconcerting spots,
And there were lots of dots and rots
  And crannies without number,   90
Wherethrough, as you may well pre-
    sume,
The wind, like water through a flume,
  Came rushing in ecstatic,
Leaving, in all three floors, no room
  That was not a rheumatic ;
And, what with points and squares
    and rounds
  Grown shaky on their poises,
The house at nights was full of
    pounds,
Thumps, bumps, creaks, scratchings,
    raps—till—' Zounds ! '
Cried Knott, ' this goes beyond all
    bounds ;   100
I do not deal in tongues and sounds,
Nor have I let my house and grounds
  To a family of Noyeses ! '

But, though Knott's house was full
    of airs,
  He had but one,—a daughter ;
And, as he owned much stocks and
    shares,
Many who wished to render theirs
Such vain, unsatisfying cares,
And needed wives to sew their tears,
  In matrimony sought her ;   110
They vowed her gold they wanted
    not
  Their faith would never falter,
They longed to tie this single Knott
  In the Hymeneal halter ;
So daily at the door they rang,
  Cards for the belle delivering,
Or in the choir at her they sang,
Achieving such a rapturous twang
  As set her nerves ashivering.

Now Knott had quite made up his
    mind   120
  That Colonel Jones should have
    her ;
No beauty he, but oft we find
Sweet kernels 'neath a roughish rind,
So hoped his Jenny 'd be resigned
  And make no more palaver ;
Glanced at the fact that love was
    blind,
That girls were ratherish inclined
  To pet their little crosses,
Then nosologically defined   129
The rate at which the system pined
In those unfortunates who dined
Upon that metaphoric kind
  Of dish—their own proboscis.

But she, with many tears and moans,
  Besought him not to mock her,
Said 't was too much for flesh and
    bones
To marry mortgages and loans,
That fathers' hearts were stocks and
    stones,
And that she 'd go, when Mrs. Jones,
  To Davy Jones's locker ;   140
Then gave her head a little toss
That said as plain as ever was,

If men are always at a loss
  Mere womankind to bridle—
To try the thing on woman cross
  Were fifty times as idle ;
For she a strict resolve had made
  And registered in private,
That either she would die a maid,
Or else be Mrs. Doctor Slade,   150
  If woman could contrive it ;
And, though the wedding-day was
    set,
  Jenny was more so, rather,
Declaring, in a pretty pet,
That, howsoe'er they spread their net,
She would out-Jennyral them yet,
  The colonel and her father.

Just at this time the Public's eyes
  Were keenly on the watch, a stir
Beginning slowly to arise   160
  About those questions and replies,
Those raps that unwrapped mysteries
  So rapidly at Rochester,
And Knott, already nervous grown
By lying much awake alone,
And listening, sometimes to a moan,
  And sometimes to a clatter,
Whene'er the wind at night would
    rouse   168
The gingerbread-work on his house,
Or when some hasty-tempered mouse,
Behind the plastering, made a towse
  About a family matter,
Began to wonder if his wife,
A paralytic half her life,
  Which made it more surprising,
Might not to rule him from her urn,
Have taken a peripatetic turn
  For want of exorcising.

This thought, once nestled in his
    head,   179
Erelong contagious grew, and spread
Infecting all his mind with dread,
Until at last he lay in bed
And heard his wife, with well-known
    tread,
Entering the kitchen through the
    shed,

(Or was 't his fancy, mocking ?)
Opening the pantry, cutting bread,
And then (she 'd been some ten years
    dead)
  Closets and drawers unlocking ;
Or, in his room (his breath grew
    thick)   189
He heard the long-familiar click
Of slender needles flying quick,
  As if she knit a stocking ;
For whom ?—he prayed that years
    might flit
With pains rheumatic shooting,
Before those ghostly things she knit
Upon his unfleshed sole might fit,
He did not fancy it a bit,
  To stand upon that footing ;   198
At other times, his frightened hairs
  Above the bedclothes trusting,
He heard her, full of household cares,
(No dream entrapped in supper's
    snares,
The foal of horrible nightmares,
But broad awake, as he declares,)
Go bustling up and down the stairs,
Or setting back last evening's chairs,
  Or with the poker thrusting
The raked-up sea-coal's hardened
    crust—   208
And—what ! impossible ! it must !
He knew she had returned to dust,
And yet could scarce his senses trust,
  Hearing her as she poked and fussed
    About the parlour, dusting !

Night after night he strove to sleep
  And take his ease in spite of it ;
But still his flesh would chill and creep,
And, though two night-lamps he
    might keep,
  He could not so make light of it.
At last, quite desperate, he goes
And tells his neighbours all his woes,
  Which did but their amount
    enhance ;   221
They made such mockery of his fears
That soon his days were of all jeers,
  His nights of the rueful counten-
    ance ;

'I thought most folks,' one neighbour
   said,
'Gave up the ghost when they were
   dead ? '
Another gravely shook his head,
  Adding, ' From all we hear, it 's
Quite plain poor Knott is going
   mad—   229
For how can he at once be sad
And think he 's full of spirits ? '
A third declared he knew a knife
  Would cut this Knott much quicker,
' The surest way to end all strife,
And lay the spirit of a wife,
  Is just to take and lick her ! '
A temperance man caught up the
   word,
' Ah, yes,' he groaned, ' I 've always
   heard   238
Our poor friend somewhat slanted
Tow'rd taking liquor overmuch ;
I fear these spirits may be Dutch,
(A sort of gins, or something such,)
  With which his house is haunted ;
I see the thing as clear as light,—
If Knott would give up getting tight,
  Naught farther would be wanted ':
So all his neighbours stood aloof
And, that the spirits 'neath his roof
Were not entirely up to proof,
  Unanimously granted.   250

Knott knew that cocks and sprites
   were foes,
And so bought up, Heaven only knows
How many, though he wanted crows
To give ghosts caws, as I suppose,
  To think that day was breaking ;
Moreover what he called his park
He turned into a kind of ark
For dogs, because a little bark
Is a good tonic in the dark,
  If one is given to waking ;   260
But things went on from bad to worse,
His curs were nothing but a curse,
  And, what was still more shocking,
Foul ghosts of living fowl made scoff
And would not think of going off
  In spite of all his cocking.

Shanghais, Bucks-counties, Domi-
   niques,   267
Malays (that did n't lay for weeks,)
  Polanders, Bantams, Dorkings,
(Waiving the cost, no trifling ill,
Since each brought in his little bill,)
By day or night were never still,
But every thought of rest would kill
  With cacklings and with quorkings;
Henry the Eighth of wives got free
By a way he had of axing ;
But poor Knott's Tudor henery
Was not so fortunate, and he
  Still found his trouble waxing;
As for the dogs, the rows they made,
And how they howled, snarled,
   barked and bayed,   281
  Beyond all human knowledge is ;
All night, as wide awake as gnats,
The terriers rumpused after rats,
Or, just for practice, taught their
   brats
To worry cast-off shoes and hats,
The bull-dogs settled private spats,
All chased imaginary cats,
Or raved behind the fence's slats
At real ones, or, from their mats,
With friends, miles off, held pleasant
   chats,   291
Or, like some folks in white cravats,
Contemptuous of sharps and flats,
  Sat up and sang dogsologies.
Meanwhile the cats set up a squall,
And, safe upon the garden-wall,
  All night kept cat-a-walling,
As if the feline race were all,
In one wild cataleptic sprawl,
  Into love's tortures falling.   300

PART II

SHOWING WHAT IS MEANT BY A FLOW OF SPIRITS

At first the ghosts were somewhat
   shy,
Coming when none but Knott was
   nigh,
And people said 't was all their eye,
(Or rather his) a flam, the sly

Digestion's machination :
Some recommended a wet sheet,
Some a nice broth of pounded peat,
Some a cold flat-iron to the feet,
Some a decoction of lamb's-bleat,
Some a southwesterly grain of wheat ;
Meat was by some pronounced un-
    meet,   11
Others thought fish most indiscreet,
And that 't was worse than all to eat
Of vegetables, sour or sweet,
(Except, perhaps, the skin of beet,)
  In such a concatenation :
One quack his button gently plucks
And murmurs, ' Biliary ducks ! '
  Says Knott, ' I never ate one ' ;
But all, though brimming full of
    wrath,   20
Homœo, Allo, Hydropath,
Concurred in this—that t' other's
    path
  To death's door was the straight
    one.
Still, spite of medical advice,
The ghosts came thicker, and a spice
  Of mischief grew apparent ;
Nor did they only come at night,
But seemed to fancy broad daylight,
Till Knott, in horror and affright,
  His unoffending hair rent ;   30
Whene'er with handkerchief on lap,
He made his elbow-chair a trap,
To catch an after-dinner nap,
The spirits, always on the tap,
Would make a sudden *rap, rap, rap*,
The half-spun cord of sleep to snap,
(And what is life without its nap
But threadbareness and mere mis-
    hap ?)   38
As 't were with a percussion cap
  The trouble's climax capping ;
It seemed a party dried and grim
Of mummies had come to visit him,
Each getting off from every limb
  Its multitudinous wrapping ;
Scratchings sometimes the walls ran
    round,
The merest penny-weights of sound ;
Sometimes 't was only by the pound

They carried on their dealing,
A thumping 'neath the parlour floor,
Thump-bump-thump-bumping   o'er
    and o'er,   50
As if the vegetables in store
(Quiet and orderly before)
  Were all together peeling ;
You would have thought the thing
    was done
By the spirit of some son of a gun,
  And that a forty-two-pounder,
Or that the ghost which made such
    sounds
Could be none other than John
    Pounds,   58
  Of Ragged Schools the founder.
Through three gradations of affright,
The awful noises reached their height;
  At first they knocked nocturnally,
Then, for some reason, changing
    quite,
(As mourners, after six months'
    flight,)
Turn suddenly from dark to light,)
  Began to knock diurnally,
And last, combining all their stocks,
  (Scotland was ne'er so full of Knox,)
Into one Chaos (father of Nox,)   69
Nocte pluit—they showered knocks,
  And knocked, knocked, knocked,
    eternally ;
Ever upon the go, like buoys,
(Wooden sea-urchins,) all Knott's
    joys,
They turned to troubles and a noise
  That preyed on him internally.

Soon they grew wider in their scope ;
Whenever Knott a door would ope,
It would ope not, or else elope
And fly back (curbless as a trope
Once started down a stanza's slope
By a bard that gave it too much
    rope—)   81
  Like a clap of thunder slamming ;
And, when kind Jenny brought his
    hat,
(She always, when he walked, did
    that,)

Just as upon his head it sat,
Submitting to his settling pat,
Some unseen hand would jam it flat,
Or give it such a furious bat
  That eyes and nose went cramming
Up out of sight, and consequently,
As when in life it paddled free,   91
  His beaver caused much damning ;
If these things seem o'er-strained to
    be,
Read the account of Doctor Dee,
'T is in our college library ;
Read Wesley's circumstantial plea,
And Mrs. Crowe, more like a bee,
Suckling the nightshade's honeyed fee,
And Stilling's Pneumatology ;   99
Consult Scot, Glanvil, grave Wie-
rus, and both Mathers ; further see,
Webster, Casaubon, James First's
    trea-
tise, a right royal Q. E. D.
Writ with the moon in perigee,
Bodin de la Demonomanie—
(Accent that last line gingerly)
All full of learning as the sea
Of fishes, and all disagree,
Save in *Sathanas apage !*
Or, what will surely put a flea   110
In unbelieving ears—with glee,
Out of a paper (sent to me
By some friend who forgot to P...
A...Y...—I use cryptography
Lest I his vengeful pen should dree—
His P...O...S...T...A...G...E...)
  Things to the same effect I cut,
About the tantrums of a ghost,
Not more than three weeks since, at
    most,   119
  Near Stratford, in Connecticut.

Knott's Upas daily spread its roots,
Sent up on all sides livelier shoots
And bore more pestilential fruits ;
The ghosts behaved like downright
    brutes,
They snipped holes in his Sunday
    suits,
Practised all night on octave flutes,
Put peas (not peace) into his boots,

Whereof grew corns in season,
They scotched his sheets, and, what
    was worse,   129
Stuck his silk nightcap full of burs,
Till he, in language plain and terse,
(But much unlike a Bible verse.)
Swore he should lose his reason.

The tables took to spinning, too,
Perpetual yarns, and arm-chairs grew
  To prophets and apostles ;
One footstool vowed that only he
Of law and gospel held the key,   138
That teachers of whate'er degree
To whom opinion bows the knee
Wern't fit to teach Truth's a b c,
And were (the whole lot) to a T
  Mere fogies all and fossils ;
A teapoy, late the property
  Of Knox's Aunt Keziah,
(Whom Jenny most irreverently
Had nicknamed her aunt-tipathy)
With tips emphatic claimed to be
  The prophet Jeremiah ;
The tins upon the kitchen-wall,
Turned tintinnabulators all,   151
And things that used to come at call
  For simple household services
Began to hop and whirl and prance,
Fit to put out of countenance
The *Commis* and *Grisettes* of France
  Or Turkey's dancing Dervises.

Of course such doings, far and wide,
With rumours filled the country-side,
And (as it is our nation's pride   160
To think a Truth not verified
Till with majorities allied)
Parties sprung up, affirmed, denied,
And candidates with questions plied,
Who, like the circus-riders, tried
At once both hobbies to bestride,
And each with his opponent vied
  In being inexplicit.
Earnest inquirers multiplied ;   169
Folks, whose tenth cousins lately died,
Wrote letters long, and Knott replied ;
All who could either walk or ride
Gathered to wonder or deride,

And paid the house a visit ;
Horses were to his pine-trees tied,
Mourners in every corner sighed,
Widows brought children there that
    cried,
Swarms of lean Seekers, eager-eyed,
(People Knott never could abide,)
Into each hole and cranny pried 180
With strings of questions cut and dried
From the Devout Inquirer's Guide,
For the wise spirits to decide—
    As, for example, is it
True that the damned are fried or
    boiled ?
Was the Earth's axis greased or oiled ?
Who cleaned the moon when it was
    soiled ?
How baldness might be cured or
    foiled ?
    How heal diseased potatoes ?   189
Did spirits have the sense of smell ?
Where would departed spinsters
    dwell ?
If the late Zenas Smith were well ?
If Earth were solid or a shell ?
Were spirits fond of Doctor Fell ?
Did the bull toll Cock-Robin's knell ?
What remedy would bugs expel ?
If Paine's invention were a sell ?
Did spirits by Webster's system spell?
Was it a sin to be a belle ?   199
Did dancing sentence folks to hell ?
If so, then where most torture fell—
    On little toes or great toes ?
If life's true seat were in the brain ?
Did Ensign mean to marry Jane ?
By whom, in fact, was Morgan slain ?
Could matter ever suffer pain ?
What would take out a cherry-stain ?
Who picked the pocket of Seth Crane,
Of Waldo precinct, State of Maine ?
Was Sir John Franklin sought in
    vain ?   210
Did primitive Christians ever train ?
What was the family-name of Cain ?
Them spoons, were they by Betty
    ta'en ?
Would earth-worm poultice cure a
    sprain ?

Was Socrates so dreadful plain ?
What teamster guided Charles's
    wain ?
Was Uncle Ethan mad or sane,
And could his will in force remain ?
If not, what counsel to retain ?   219
Did Le Sage steal Gil Blas from Spain ?
Was Junius writ by Thomas Paine ?
Were ducks discomforted by rain ?
How did Britannia rule the main ?
Was Jonas coming back again ?
Was vital truth upon the wane ?
Did ghosts, to scare folks, drag a
    chain ?
Who was our Huldah's chosen swain ?
Did none have teeth pulled without
    payin',
    Ere ether was invented ?   229
Whether mankind would not agree,
If the universe were tuned in C ?
What was it ailed Lucindy's knee ?
Whether folks eat folks in Feejee ?
Whether *his* name would end with
    T ?
If Saturn's rings were two or three,
And what bump in Phrenology
    They truly represented ?
These problems dark, wherein they
    groped,
Wherewith man's reason vainly coped,
Now that the spirit-world was oped,
In all humility they hoped   241
    Would be resolved *instanter* ;
Each of the miscellaneous rout
Brought his, or her, own little doubt,
And wished to pump the spirits out,
Through his or her own private spout,
    Into his or her decanter.

PART III

WHEREIN IT IS SHOWN THAT THE
MOST ARDENT SPIRITS ARE MORE
ORNAMENTAL THAN USEFUL.

MANY a speculating wight
Came by express-trains, day and
    night,
To see if Knott would ' sell his right,'
Meaning to make the ghosts a sight—

What they called a ' meenaygerie ' ;
One threatened, if he would not
  ' trade,'
His run of custom to invade,
(He could not these sharp folks per-
  suade
That he was not, in some way, paid,)
  And stamp him as a plagiary,   10
By coming down, at one fell swoop,
With THE ORIGINAL KNOCKING
    TROUPE,
Come recently from Hades,
Who (for a quarter-dollar heard)
Would ne'er rap out a hasty word
Whence any blame might be in-
  curred
From the most fastidious ladies ;
The late lamented Jesse Soule
To stir the ghosts up with a pole
And be director of the whole,   20
  Who was engaged the rather
For the rare merits he'd combine,
Having been in the spirit line,
Which trade he only did resign,
With general applause, to shine,
Awful in mail of cotton fine,
  As ghost of Hamlet's father !
Another a fair plan reveals   28
Never yet hit on, which, he feels,
To Knott's religious sense appeals—
' We 'll have your house set up on
  wheels,
A speculation pious ;
For music, we can shortly find
A barrel-organ that will grind
Psalm-tunes,—an instrument de-
  signed
For the New England tour—refined
From secular drosses, and inclined
To an unwordly turn, (combined
  With no sectarian bias ;)
Then, travelling by stages slow,   40
Under the style of Knott & Co.,
I would accompany the show
As moral lecturer, the foe
Of Rationalism ; while you could
  throw
The rappings in, and make them go
Strict Puritan principles, you know,

(How *do* you make 'em ? with your
  toe ?)
And the receipts which thence might
  flow,
  We could divide between us :   49
Still more attractions to combine,
Beside these services of mine,
I will throw in a very fine
(It would do nicely for a sign)
  Original Titian's Venus.'
Another offered handsome fees
If Knott would get Demosthenes
(Nay, his mere knuckles, for more
  ease)
To rap a few short sentences ;
Or if, for want of proper keys,   59
  His Greek might make confusion,
Then just to get a rap from Burke,
To recommend a little work
  On Public Elocution.
Meanwhile, the spirits made replies
To all the reverent *whats* and *whys*,
Resolving doubts of every size,
And giving seekers grave and wise,
Who came to know their destinies,
  A rap-turous reception ;   69
When unbelievers void of grace
Came to investigate the place,
(Creatures of Sadducistic race,
With grovelling intellects and base,)
They could not find the slightest trace
  To indicate deception ;
Indeed, it is declared by some
That spirits (of this sort) are glum,
Almost, or wholly, deaf and dumb,
And (out of self-respect) quite mum
To sceptic natures cold and numb,
Who of *this* kind of Kingdom Come
  Have not a just conception :   82
True, there were people who de-
  murred
That, though the raps no doubt were
  heard
Both under them and o'er them,
Yet, somehow, when a search they
  made,
They found Miss Jenny sore afraid,
Or Jenny's lover, Doctor Slade,
Equally awe-struck and dismayed,

Or Deborah, the chamber-maid, 90
Whose terrors not to be gainsaid,
In laughs hysteric were displayed,
    Was always there before them ;
This had its due effect with some
Who straight departed, muttering,
    Hum !
    Transparent hoax ! and Gammon !
But these were few : believing souls
Came, day by day, in larger shoals,
As the ancients to the windy holes
'Neath Delphi's tripod brought their
    doles,   100
    Or to the shrine of Ammon.

The spirits seemed exceeding tame,
Call whom you fancied, and he
    came ;
The shades august of eldest fame
    You summoned with an awful
    ease ;
As grosser spirits gurgled out
From chair and table with a spout,
In Auerbach's cellar once, to flout
The senses of the rabble rout,   109
Where'er the gimlet twirled about
    Of cunning Mephistopheles,
So did these spirits seem in store,
Behind the wainscot or the door,
Ready to thrill the being's core
Of every enterprising bore
    With their astounding glamour ;
Whatever ghost one wished to hear,
By strange coincidence, was near
To make the past or future clear
    (Sometimes in shocking grammar)
By raps and taps, now there, now
    here—   121
It seemed as if the spirit queer
Of some departed auctioneer
Were doomed to practise by the year
    With the spirit of his hammer :
Whate'er you asked was answered,
    yet
One could not very deeply get
Into the obliging spirits' debt,
Because they used the alphabet
    In all communications,   130
And new revealings (though sublime)

Rapped out, one letter at a time,
    With boggles, hesitations,
Stoppings, beginnings o'er again,
And getting matters into train,
Could hardly overload the brain
    With too excessive rations,
Since just to ask *if two and two
Really make four ?* or, *How d' ye do ?*
And get the fit replies thereto   140
In the tramundane rat-tat-too,
    Might ask a whole day's patience.

'T was strange ('mongst other things)
    to find
In what odd sets the ghosts combined,
    Happy forthwith to thump any
Piece of intelligence inspired,
The truth whereof had been inquired
    By some one of the company ;
For instance, Fielding, Mirabeau,
Orator Henley, Cicero,   150
Paley, John Zisca, Marivaux,
Melancthon, Robertson, Junot,
Scaliger, Chesterfield, Rousseau,
Hakluyt, Boccaccio, South, De Foe,
Diaz, Josephus, Richard Roe,
Odin, Arminius, Charles *le gros*,
Tiresias, the late James Crow,
Casabianca, Grose, Prideaux,
Old Grimes, Young Norval, Swift,
    Brissot,   159
Maimonides, the Chevalier D'O,
Socrates, Fenelon, Job, Stow,
The inventor of *Elixir pro*,
Euripides, Spinoza, Poe,
Confucius, Hiram Smith, and Fo,
Came (as it seemed, somewhat *de trop*)
With a disembodied Esquimaux,
To say that it was so and so.
    With Franklin's expedition ;
One testified to ice and snow,
One that the mercury was low,   170
One that his progress was quite slow,
One that he much desired to go,
One that the cook had frozen his toe,
(Dissented from by Dandolo,
Wordsworth, Cynaegirus, Boileau,
La Hontan, and Sir Thomas Roe,)
One saw twelve white bears in a row,

One saw eleven and a crow,
With other things we could not know
(Of great statistic value, though,)
    By our mere mortal vision.   181

Sometimes the spirits made mis-
        takes,
And seemed to play at ducks and
    · drakes
With bold inquiry's heaviest stakes
    In science or in mystery ;
They knew so little (and that wrong)
Yet rapped it out so bold and strong,
One would have said the unnumbered
        throng   188
    Had been Professors of History ;
What made it odder was, that those
Who, you would naturally suppose,
Could solve a question, if they chose,
As easily as count their toes,
    Were just the ones that blundered ;
One day, Ulysses happening down,
A reader of Sir Thomas Browne
    And who (with him) had wondered
What song it was the Sirens sang,
Asked the shrewd Ithacan—*bang !
    bang !*   199
With this response the chamber rang,
    ' I guess it was Old Hundred.'
And Franklin, being asked to name
The reason why the lightning came,
Replied, ' Because it thundered.'

On one sole point the ghosts agreed,
One fearful point, than which, indeed,
    Nothing could seem absurder ;
Poor Colonel Jones they all abused,
And finally downright accused   209
    The poor old man of murder ;
'T was thus ; by dreadful raps was
        shown
Some spirit's longing to make
        known
A bloody fact, which he alone
Was privy to, (such ghosts more
        prone
    In Earth's affairs to meddle are ;)
Who are you ? with awe-stricken
        looks,

All ask : his airy knuckles he crooks,
And raps, ' I *was* Eliab Snooks,
    That used to be a pedler ;   219
Some on ye still are on my books ! '
Whereat, to inconspicuous nooks,
(More fearing this than common
        spooks,)
    Shrank each indebted meddler ;
Further the vengeful ghost declared
That while his earthly life was spared,
About the country he had fared,
    A duly licensed follower
Of that much-wandering trade that
        wins   228
Slow profit from the sale of tins
    And various kinds of hollow-ware ;
That Colonel Jones enticed him in,
Pretending that he wanted tin,
There slew him with a rolling-pin,
    Hid him in a potato-bin,
    And (the same night) him ferried
Across Great Pond to t' other shore,
And there, on land of Widow Moore,
Just where you turn to Larkin's store,
    Under a rock him buried ;   239
Some friends (who happened to be by)
He called upon to testify
That what he said was not a lie,
    And that he did not stir this
Foul matter, out of any spite
But from a simple love of right ;—
    Which statements the Nine Wor-
        thies,
Rabbi Akiba, Charlemagne,
Seth, Colley Cibber, General Wayne,
Cambyses, Tasso, Tubal-Cain,
The owner of a castle in Spain,   250
Jehanghire, and the Widow of Nain,
(The friends aforesaid,) made more
        plain
    And by loud raps attested ;
To the same purport testified
Plato, John Wilkes, and Colonel Pride
Who knew said Snooks before he
        died,
    Had in his wares invested,
Thought him entitled to belief
And freely could concur, in brief,
    In everything the rest did.   260

Eliab this occasion seized,
(Distinctly here the spirit sneezed,)
To say that he should ne'er be eased
Till Jenny married whom she pleased,
  Free from all checks and urgin's,
(This spirit dropt his final g's)
And that, unless Knott quickly sees
This done, the spirits to appease,
They would come back his life to
  tease,   269
As thick as mites in ancient cheese,
And let his house on an endless lease
To the ghosts (terrific rappers these
And veritable Eumenides)
  Of the Eleven Thousand Virgins !

Knott was perplexed and shook his
  head,
He did not wish his child to wed
  With a suspected murderer,
(For, true or false, the rumour spread,)
But as for this roiled life he led,
' It would not answer,' so he said,
  ' To have it go no furderer.'   281
At last, scarce knowing what it
  meant,
Reluctantly he gave consent
That Jenny, since 't was evident
That she *would* follow her own bent,
  Should make her own election ;
For that appeared the only way
These frightful noises to allay
Which had already turned him grey
  And plunged him in dejection.

Accordingly, this artless maid   291
Her father's ordinance obeyed,
And, all in whitest crape arrayed,
(Miss Pulsifer the dresses made
And wishes here the fact displayed
That she still carries on the trade,
The third door south from Bagg's
  Arcade,)
A very faint ' I do ' essayed
And gave her hand to Hiram Slade,
From which time forth, the ghosts
  were laid,   300
  And ne'er gave trouble after ;
But the Selectmen, be it known,

Dug underneath the aforesaid stone,
Where the poor pedler's corpse was
  thrown,
And found thereunder a jaw-bone,
Though, when the crowner sat there-
  on,
He nothing hatched, except alone
  Successive broods of laughter ;
It was a frail and dingy thing,   309
In which a grinder or two did cling,
  In colour like molasses,
Which surgeons, called from far and
  wide,
Upon the horror to decide,
  Having put on their glasses,
Reported thus—' To judge by looks,
These bones, by some queer hooks or
  crooks,
May have belonged to Mr. Snooks,
But, as men deepest-read in books
  Are perfectly aware, bones,
If buried fifty years or so,   320
Lose their identity and grow
  From human bones to bare bones.'

Still, if to Jaalam you go down,
You 'll find two parties in the town,
One headed by Benaiah Brown,
  And one by Perez Tinkham ;
The first believe the ghosts all through
And vow that they shall never rue
The happy chance by which they
  knew   329
That people in Jupiter are blue,
And very fond of Irish stew,
Two curious facts which Prince Lee
  Boo
Rapped clearly to a chosen few—
  Whereas the others think 'em
A trick got up by Doctor Slade
With Deborah the chamber-maid
  And that sly cretur Jinny.
That all the revelations wise,
At which the Brownites made big
  eyes,
Might have been given by Jared
  Keyes,   340
  A natural fool and ninny,
And, last week, did n't Eliab Snooks

Come back with never better looks,
As sharp as new-bought mackerel
    hooks,
    And bright as a new pin, eh ?
Good Parson Wilbur, too, avers
(Though to be mixed in parish stirs
Is worse than handling chestnut-
    burrs)
That no case to his mind occurs
Where spirits ever did converse,
Save in a kind of guttural Erse.   351

(So say the best authorities ;)
And that a charge by raps conveyed
Should be most scrupulously weighed
    And searched into, before it is
Made public, since it may give pain
That cannot soon be cured again,
And one word may infix a stain
    Which ten cannot gloss over,   359
Though speaking for his private part,
He is rejoiced with all his heart
    Miss Knott missed not her lover.

AN ORIENTAL APOLOGUE

I

Somewhere in India, upon a time,
(Read it not Injah, or you spoil the verse,)
   There dwelt two saints whose privilege sublime
It was to sit and watch the world grow worse,
   Their only care (in that delicious clime)
At proper intervals to pray and curse ;
     Pracrit the dialect each prudent brother
     Used for himself, Damnonian for the other.

II

One half the time of each was spent in praying
For blessings on his own unworthy head,
   The other half in fearfully portraying
Where certain folks would go when they were dead ;
   This system of exchanges—there 's no saying
To what more solid barter 't would have led,
     But that a river, vext with boils and swellings
     At rainy times, kept peace between their dwellings.

III

So they two played at wordy battledore
And kept a curse forever in the air,
   Flying this way or that from shore to shore ;
Nor other labour did this holy pair,
   Clothed and supported from the lavish store
Which crowds lanigerous brought with daily care ;
     They toiled not neither did they spin ; their bias
     Was tow'rd the harder task of being pious.

IV

Each from his hut rushed six score times a day,
Like a great canon of the Church full-rammed
   With cartridge theologic, (so to say,)
Touched himself off, and then, recoiling, slammed
   His hovel's door behind him in a way
That to his foe said plainly,—*you'll* be damned ;
     And so like Potts and Wainwright, shrill and strong
     The two D—D'd each other all day long.

V

One was a dancing Dervise, a Mohammedan,
The other was a Hindoo, a gymnosophist ;
  One kept his whatd'yecallit and his Ramadan,
Laughing to scorn the sacred rites and laws of his
    Transfluvial rival, who, in turn, called Admed an
Old top, and, as a clincher, shook across a fist
    With nails six inches long, yet lifted not
    His eyes from off his navel's mystic knot.

VI

' Who whirls not round six thousand times an hour
Will go,' screamed Ahmed, ' to the evil place ;
  May he eat dirt, and may the dog and Giaour
Defile the graves of him and all his race ;
    Allah loves faithful souls and gives them power
To spin till they are purple in the face ;
    Some folks get you know what, but he that pure is
    Earns Paradise and ninety thousand houries.'

VII

' Upon the silver mountain, South by East,
Sits Brahma fed upon the sacred bean ;
  He loves those men whose nails are still increased,
Who all their lives keep ugly, foul, and lean ;
    'T is of his grace that not a bird or beast
Adorned with claws like mine was ever seen ;
    The suns and stars are Brahma's thoughts divine
    Even as these trees I seem to see are mine.'

VIII

' Thou seem'st to see, indeed ! ' roared Ahmed back ;
' Were I but once across this plaguy stream,
  With a stout sapling in my hand, one whack
On those lank ribs would rid thee of that dream !
    Thy Brahma-blasphemy is ipecac
To my soul's stomach ; couldst thou grasp the scheme
    Of true redemption, thou wouldst know that Deity
    Whirls by a kind of blessed spontaneity.

IX

' And this it is which keeps our earth here going
With all the stars.'—' O, vile ! but there 's a place
  Prepared for such ; to think of Brahma throwing
Worlds like a juggler's balls up into Space !
    Why, not so much as a smooth lotos blowing
Is e'er allowed that silence to efface
    Which broods round Brahma, and our earth, 't is known,
    Rests on a tortoise, moveless as this stone.'

X

So they kept up their banning amœbæan,
When suddenly came floating down the stream
A youth whose face like an incarnate pæan
Glowed, 't was so full of grandeur and of gleam ;
    ' If there *be* gods, then, doubtless, this must be one,'
Thought both at once, and then began to scream,
      ' Surely, whate'er immortals know, thou knowest,
      Decide between us twain before thou goest ! '

XI

The youth was drifting in a slim canoe
Most like a huge white waterlily's petal,
    But neither of our theologians knew
Whereof 't was made ; whether of heavenly metal
    Unknown, or of a vast pearl split in two
And hollowed, was a point they could not settle ;
      'T was good debate-seed, though, and bore large fruit
      In after years of many a tart dispute.

XII

There were no wings upon the stranger's shoulders
And yet he seemed so capable of rising
    That, had he soared like thistledown, beholders
Had thought the circumstance noways surprising ;
    Enough that he remained, and, when the scolders
Hailed him as umpire in their vocal prize-ring,
      The painter of his boat he lightly threw
      Around a lotos-stem, and brought her to.

XIII

The strange youth had a look as if he might
Have trod far planets where the atmosphere
    (Of nobler temper) steeps the face with light,
Just as our skins are tanned and freckled here ;
    His air was that of a cosmopolite
In the wide universe from sphere to sphere ;
      Perhaps he was (his face had such grave beauty)
      An officer of Saturn's guards off duty.

XIV

Both saints began to unfold their tales at once,
Both wished their tales, like simial ones, prehensile,
    That they might seize his ear ; *fool ! knave !* and *dunce !*
Flew zigzag back and forth, like strokes of pencil
    In a child's fingers ; voluble as duns,
They jabbered like the stones on that immense hill
      In the Arabian Nights ; until the stranger
      Began to think his ear-drums in some danger.

xv

In general those who nothing have to say
Contrive to spend the longest time in doing it ;
    They turn and vary it in every way,
Hashing it, stewing it, mincing it, *ragouting* it ;
    Sometimes they keep it purposely at bay,
Then let it slip to be again pursuing it ;
    They drone it, groan it, whisper it and shout it,
    Refute it, flout it, swear to 't, prove it, doubt it.

xvi

Our saints had practised for some thirty years ;
Their talk, beginning with a single stem,
    Spread like a banyan, sending down live piers,
Colonies of digression, and, in them,
    Germs of yet new dispersion ; once by the ears,
They could convey damnation in a hem,
    And blow the pinch of premise-priming off
    Long syllogistic batteries, with a cough.

xvii

Each had a theory that the human ear
A providential tunnel was, which led
    To a huge vacuum (and surely here
They showed some knowledge of the general head),
    For cant to be decanted through, a mere
Auricular canal or mill-race fed
    All day and night, in sunshine and in shower,
    From their vast heads of milk-and-water-power.

xviii

The present being a peculiar case,
Each with unwonted zeal the other scouted,
    Put his spurred hobby through its every pace,
Pished, pshawed, poohed, horribled, bahed, jeered, sneered, flouted,
    Sniffed, nonsensed, infideled, fudged, with his face
Looked scorn too nicely shaded to be shouted,
    And, with each inch of person and of vesture,
    Contrived to hint some most disdainful gesture.

xix

At length, when their breath's end was come about,
And both could, now and then, just gasp ' impostor ! '
    Holding their heads thrust menacingly out,
As staggering cocks keep up their fighting posture,
    The stranger smiled and said, ' Beyond a doubt
'T is fortunate, my friends, that you have lost your
    United parts of speech, or it had been
    Impossible for me to get between.

XX

'Produce ! says Nature,—what have you produced ?
A new strait-waistcoat for the human mind ;
   Are you not limbed, nerved, jointed, arteried, juiced,
As other men ? yet, faithless to your kind,
   Rather like noxious insects you are used
To puncture life's fair fruit, beneath the rind
      Laying your creed-eggs whence in time there spring
      Consumers new to eat and buzz and sting.

XXI

'Work ! you have no conception how 't will sweeten
Your views of Life and Nature, God and Man ;
   Had you been forced to earn what you have eaten,
Your heaven had shown a less dyspeptic plan ;
   At present your whole function is to eat ten
And talk ten times as rapidly as you can ;
      Were your shape true to cosmogonic laws,
      You would be nothing but a pair of jaws.

XXII

'Of all the useless beings in creation
The earth could spare most easily you bakers
   Of little clay gods, formed in shape and fashion
Precisely in the image of their makers ;
   Why, it would almost move a saint to passion,
To see these blind and deaf, the hourly breakers
      Of God's own image in their brother men,
      Set themselves up to tell the how, where, when,

XXIII

'Of God's existence ; one's digestion 's worse—
So makes a god of vengeance and of blood ;
   Another,—but no matter, they reverse
Creation's plan, out of their own vile mud
   Pat up a god, and burn, drown, hang, or curse
Whoever worships not ; each keeps his stud
      Of texts which wait with saddle on and bridle
      To hunt down atheists to their ugly idol.

XXIV

'This, I perceive, has been your occupation ;
You should have been more usefully employed ;
   All men are bound to earn their daily ration,
Where States make not that primal contract void
   By cramps and limits ; simple devastation
Is the worm's task, and what he has destroyed
      His monument ; creating is man's work
      And that, too, something more than mist and murk.'

XXV

So having said, the youth was seen no more,
And straightway our sage Brahmin, the philosopher,
  Cried, ' That was aimed at thee, thou endless bore,
Idle and useless as the growth of moss over
  A rotting tree-trunk ! ' ' I would square that score
Full soon,' replied the Dervise, ' could I cross over
    And catch thee by the beard. Thy nails I 'd trim
    And make thee work, as was advised by him.'

XXVI

' Work ?   Am I not at work from morn till night
Sounding the deeps of oracles umbilical
  Which for man's guidance never come to light,
With all their various aptitudes, until I call ? '
  ' And I, do I not twirl from left to right
For conscience' sake ? Is that no work ? Thou silly gull,
    He had thee in his eye ; 't was Gabriel
    Sent to reward my faith, I know him well.'

XXVII

' 'T was Vishnu, thou vile whirligig ! ' and so
The good old quarrel was begun anew ;
  One would have sworn the sky was black as sloe,
Had but the other dared to call it blue ;
  Nor were the followers who fed them slow
To treat each other with their curses, too,
    Each hating t' other (moves it tears or laughter ?)
    Because he thought him sure of hell hereafter.

XXVIII

At last some genius built a bridge of boats
Over the stream, and Ahmed's zealots filed
  Across, upon a mission to (cut throats
And) spread religion pure and undefiled ;
  They sowed the propagandist's wildest oats,
Cutting off all, down to the smallest child,
    And came back, giving thanks for such fat mercies,
    To find their harvest gone past prayers or curses.

XXIX

All gone except their saint's religious hops,
Which he kept up with more than common flourish ;
  But these, however satisfying crops
For the inner man, were not enough to nourish
  The body politic, which quickly drops
Reserve in such sad junctures, and turns currish ;
    So Ahmed soon got cursed for all the famine
    Where'er the popular voice could edge a damn in.

XXX

At first he pledged a miracle quite boldly,
And, for a day or two, they growled and waited ;
  But, finding that this kind of manna coldiy
Sat on their stomachs, they erelong berated
  The saint for still persisting in that old lie,
Till soon the whole machine of saintship grated,
    Ran slow, creaked, stopped, and, wishing him in Tophet,
    They gathered strength enough to stone the prophet.

XXXI

Some stronger ones contrived (by eating leather,
Their weaker friends, and one thing or another)
  The winter months of scarcity to weather ;
Among these was the late saint's younger brother,
  Who, in the spring, collecting them together,
Persuaded them that Ahmed's holy pother
    Had wrought in their behalf, and that the place
    Of Saint should be continued to his race.

XXXII

Accordingly, 't was settled on the spot
That Allah favoured that peculiar breed ;
  Beside, as all were satisfied, 't would not
Be quite respectable to have the need
  Of public spiritual food forgot ;
And so the tribe, with proper forms, decreed
    That he, and, failing him, his next of kin,
    Forever for the people's good should spin.

UNDER THE WILLOWS, AND OTHER POEMS

(1869)

TO CHARLES ELIOT NORTON

AGRO DOLCE

THE wind is roistering out of doors,
My windows shake and my chimney roars ;
My Elmwood chimneys seem crooning to me,
As of old, in their moody, minor key,
And out of the past the hoarse wind blows,
As I sit in my arm-chair, and toast my toes.

' Ho ! ho ! nine-and-forty,' they seem to sing,
' We saw you a little toddling thing.
We knew you child and youth and man,
A wonderful fellow to dream and plan,
With a great thing always to come,—who knows ?
Well, well ! 't is some comfort to toast one's toes.

' How many times have you sat at gaze
Till the mouldering fire forgot to blaze,
Shaping among the whimsical coals
Fancies and figures and shining goals !
What matters the ashes that cover those ?
While hickory lasts you can toast your toes.

' O dream-ship-builder ! where are they all,
Your grand three-deckers, deep-chested and tall,
That should crush the waves under canvas piles,
And anchor at last by the Fortunate Isles ?
There 's grey in your beard, the years turn foes,
While you muse in your arm-chair, and toast your toes.

I sit and dream that I hear, as of yore,
My Elmwood chimneys' deep-throated roar ;
If much be gone, there is much remains ;
By the embers of loss I count my gains,
You and yours with the best, till the old hope glows
In the fanciful flame, as I toast my toes.

Instead of a fleet of broad-browed ships,
To send a child's armada of chips !
Instead of the great guns, tier on tier,
A freight of pebbles and grass-blades sere !
' Well, maybe more love with the less gift goes,'
I growl, as, half moody, I toast my toes.

UNDER THE WILLOWS

FRANK-HEARTED hostess of the field and wood,
Gypsy, whose roof is every spreading tree,
June is the pearl of our New England year.
Still a surprisal, though expected long,
Her coming startles. Long she lies in wait,
Makes many a feint, peeps forth, draws coyly back,
Then, from some southern ambush in the sky,
With one great gush of blossom storms the world.
A week ago the sparrow was divine ;
The bluebird, shifting his light load of song   10
From post to post along the cheerless fence,
Was as a rhymer ere the poet come ;
But now, O rapture ! sunshine winged and voiced,
Pipe blown through by the warm wild breath of the West
Shepherding his soft droves of fleecy cloud,
Gladness of woods, skies, waters, all in one,
The bobolink has come, and, like the soul
Of the sweet season vocal in a bird,
Gurgles in ecstasy we know not what
Save *June ! Dear June ! Now God be praised for June.*   20

May is a pious fraud of the almanac,
A ghastly parody of real Spring
Shaped out of snow and breathed with eastern wind ;
Or if, o'er-confident, she trust the date,
And, with her handful of anemones,
Herself as shivery, steal into the sun,
The season need but turn his hourglass round,
And Winter suddenly, like crazy Lear,
Reels back, and brings the dead May in his arms,
Her budding breasts and wan dislustred front   30
With frosty streaks and drifts of his white beard
All overblown. Then, warmly walled with books,
While my wood-fire supplies the sun's defect,
Whispering old forest-sagas in its dreams,
I take my May down from the happy shelf
Where perch the world's rare song-birds in a row,
Waiting my choice to open with full breast,
And beg an alms of spring-time, ne'er denied
In-doors by vernal Chaucer, whose fresh woods
Throb thick with merle and mavis all the year.   40

July breathes hot, sallows the crispy fields,
Curls up the wan leaves of the lilac-hedge,
And every eve cheats us with show of clouds
That braze the horizon's western rim, or hang

Motionless, with heaped canvas drooping idly,
Like a dim fleet by starving men besieged,
Conjectured half, and half descried afar,
Helpless of wind, and seeming to slip back
Adown the smooth curve of the oily sea.

But June is full of invitations sweet,   50
Forth from the chimney's yawn and thrice-read tomes
To leisurely delights and sauntering thoughts
That brook no ceiling narrower than the blue
The cherry, drest for bridal, at my pane
Brushes, then listens, *Will he come ?* The bee,
All dusty as a miller, takes his toll
Of powdery gold, and grumbles. What a day
To sun me and do nothing ! Nay, I think
Merely to bask and ripen is sometimes
The student's wiser business ; the brain   60
That forages all climes to line its cells,
Ranging both worlds on lightest wings of wish
Will not distil the juices it has sucked
To the sweet substance of pellucid thought,
Except for him who hath the secret learned
To mix his blood with sunshine, and to take
The winds into his pulses. Hush ! 't is he !
My oriole, my glance of summer fire,
Is come at last, and, ever on the watch,
Twitches the pack-thread I had lightly wound   70
About the bough to help his housekeeping,—
Twitches and scouts by turns, blessing his luck,
Yet fearing me who laid it in his way,
Nor, more than wiser we in our affairs,
Divines the providence that hides and helps.
Heave, ho ! Heave, ho ! he whistles as the twine
Slackens its hold ; *once more, now !* and a flash
Lightens across the sunlight to the elm
Where his mate dangles at her cup of felt.
Nor all his booty is the thread ; he trails   80
My loosened thought with it along the air,
And I must follow, would I ever find
The inward rhyme to all this wealth of life.

I care not how men trace their ancestry,
To ape or Adam ; let them please their whim ;
But I in June am midway to believe
A tree among my far progenitors,
Such sympathy is mine with all the race,
Such mutual recognition vaguely sweet
There is between us. Surely there are times   90
When they consent to own me of their kin,
And condescend to me, and call me cousin,

Murmuring faint lullabies of eldest time,
Forgotten, and yet dumbly felt with thrills
Moving the lips, though fruitless of the words.
And I have many a lifelong leafy friend,
Never estranged nor careful of my soul,
That knows I hate the axe, and welcomes me
Within his tent as if I were a bird,
Or other free companion of the earth,   100
Yet undegenerate to the shifts of men.
Among them one, an ancient willow, spreads
Eight balanced limbs, springing at once all round
His deep-ridged trunk with upward slant diverse,
In outline like enormous beaker, fit
For hand of Jotun, where mid snow and mist
He holds unwieldy revel.   This tree, spared,
I know not by what grace,—for in the blood
Of our New World subduers lingers yet
Hereditary feud with trees, they being   110
(They and the red-man most) our fathers' foes,—
Is one of six, a willow Pleiades,
The seventh fallen, that lean along the brink
Where the steep upland dips into the marsh,
Their roots, like molten metal cooled in flowing,
Stiffened in coils and runnels down the bank.
The friend of all the winds, wide-armed he towers
And glints his steely aglets in the sun,
Or whitens fitfully with sudden bloom
Of leaves breeze-lifted, much as when a shoal   120
Of devious minnows wheel from where a pike
Lurks balanced 'neath the lily-pads, and whirl
A rood of silver bellies to the day.

Alas ! no acorn from the British oak
'Neath which slim fairies tripping wrought those rings
Of greenest emerald, wherewith fireside life
Did with the invisible spirit of Nature wed,
Was ever planted here !   No darnel fancy
Might choke one useful blade in Puritan fields ;
With horn and hoof the good old Devil came,   130
The witch's broomstick was not contraband,
But all that superstition had of fair,
Or piety of native sweet, was doomed.
And if there be who nurse unholy faiths,
Fearing their god as if he were a wolf
That snuffed round every home and was not seen,
There should be some to watch and keep alive
All beautiful beliefs.   And such was that,—
By solitary shepherd first surmised
Under Thessalian oaks, loved by some maid   140

Of royal stirp, that silent came and vanished,
As near her nest the hermit thrush, nor dared
Confess a mortal name,—that faith which gave
A Hamadryad to each tree ; and I
Will hold it true that in this willow dwells
The open-handed spirit, frank and blithe,
Of ancient Hospitality, long since,
With ceremonious thrift, bowed out of doors.

In June 't is good to lie beneath a tree
While the blithe season comforts every sense,   150
Steeps all the brain in rest, and heals the heart,
Brimming it o'er with sweetness unawares,
Fragrant and silent as that rosy snow
Wherewith the pitying apple-tree fills up
And tenderly lines some last-year robin's nest.
There muse I of old times, old hopes, old friends,—
Old friends ! The writing of those words has borne
My fancy backward to the gracious past,
The generous past, when all was possible,
For all was then untried ; the years between   160
Have taught some sweet, some bitter lessons, none
Wiser than this,—to spend in all things else,
But of old friends to be most miserly.
Each year to ancient friendships adds a ring,
As to an oak, and precious more and more,
Without deservingness or help of ours,
They grow, and, silent, wider spread, each year,
Their unbought ring of shelter or of shade.
Sacred to me the lichens on the bark,
Which Nature's milliners would scrape away ;   170
Most dear and sacred every withered limb !
'T is good to set them early, for our faith
Pines as we age, and, after wrinkles come,
Few plant, but water dead ones with vain tears.

This willow is as old to me as life ;
And under it full often have I stretched,
Feeling the warm earth like a thing alive,
And gathering virtue in at every pore
Till it possessed me wholly, and thought ceased,
Or was transfused in something to which thought   180
Is coarse and dull of sense. Myself was lost,
Gone from me like an ache, and what remained
Become a part of the universal joy.
My soul went forth, and, mingling with the tree,
Danced in the leaves ; or, floating in the cloud,
Saw its white double in the stream below ;
Or else, sublimed to purer ecstasy,

Dilated in the broad blue over all.
I was the wind that dappled the lush grass,
The tide that crept with coolness to its roots,   190
The thin-winged swallow skating on the air ;
The life that gladdened everything was mine.
Was I then truly all that I beheld ?
Or is this stream of being but a glass
Where the mind sees its visionary self,
As, when the kingfisher flits o'er his bay,
Across the river's hollow heaven below
His picture flits,—another, yet the same ?
But suddenly the sound of human voice
Or footfall, like the drop a chemist pours,   200
Doth in opacous cloud precipitate
The consciousness that seemed but now dissolved
Into an essence rarer than its own,
And I am narrowed to myself once more.

For here not long is solitude secure,
Nor Fantasy left vacant to her spell.
Here, sometimes, in this paradise of shade,
Rippled with western winds, the dusty Tramp,
Seeing the treeless causey burn beyond,
Halts to unroll his bundle of strange food   210
And munch an unearned meal. I cannot help
Liking this creature, lavish Summer's bedesman,
Who from the almshouse steals when nights grow warm,
Himself his large estate and only charge,
To be the guest of haystack or of hedge,
Nobly superior to the household gear
That forfeits us our privilege of nature.
I bait him with my match-box and my pouch,
Nor grudge the uncostly sympathy of smoke,
His equal now, divinely unemployed.   220
Some smack of Robin Hood is in the man,
Some secret league with wild wood-wandering things ;
He is our ragged Duke, our barefoot Earl,
By right of birth exonerate from toil,
Who levies rent from us his tenants all,
And serves the state by merely being. Here
The Scissors-grinder, pausing, doffs his hat,
And lets the kind breeze, with its delicate fan,
Winnow the heat from out his dank grey hair,—
A grimy Ulysses, a much-wandered man,   230
Whose feet are known to all the populous ways.
And many men and manners he hath seen,
Not without fruit of solitary thought.
He, as the habit is of lonely men,—
Unused to try the temper of their mind

In fence with others,—positive and shy,
Yet knows to put an edge upon his speech,
Pithily Saxon in unwilling talk.
Him I entrap with my long-suffering knife,
And, while its poor blade hums away in sparks,   240
Sharpen my wit upon his gritty mind,
In motion set obsequious to his wheel,
And in its quality not much unlike.

Nor wants my tree more punctual visitors.
The children, they who are the only rich,
Creating for the moment, and possessing
Whate'er they choose to feign,—for still with them
Kind Fancy plays the fairy godmother,
Strewing their lives with cheap material
For wingèd horses and Aladdin's lamps,   250
Pure elfin-gold, by manhood's touch profane
To dead leaves disenchanted,—long ago
Between the branches of the tree fixed seats,
Making an o'erturned box their table.   Oft
The shrilling girls sit here between school hours,
And play at *What's my thought like?* while the boys,
With whom the age chivalric ever bides,
Pricked on by knightly spur of female eyes,
Climb high to swing and shout on perilous boughs,
Or, from the willow's armory equipped   260
With musket dumb, green banner, edgeless sword,
Make good the rampart of their tree-redoubt
'Gainst eager British storming from below,
And keep alive the tale of Bunker's Hill.

Here, too, the men that mend our village ways,
Vexing McAdam's ghost with pounded slate,
Their nooning take ; much noisy talk they spend
On horses and their ills ; and, as John Bull
Tells of Lord This or That, who was his friend,
So these make boast of intimacies long   270
With famous teams, and add large estimates,
By competition swelled from mouth to mouth,
Of how much they could draw, till one, ill pleased
To have his legend overbid, retorts :
' You take and stretch truck-horses in a string
From here to Long Wharf end, one thing I know
Not heavy neither, they could never draw,—
Ensign's long bow ! '   Then laughter loud and long.
So they in their leaf-shadowed microcosm
Image the larger world ; for wheresoe'er   280
Ten men are gathered, the observant eye
Will find mankind in little, as the stars

Glide up and set, and all the heavens revolve
In the small welkin of a drop of dew.

I love to enter pleasure by a postern,
Not the broad popular gate that gulps the mob ;
To find my theatres in roadside nooks,
Where men are actors, and suspect it not ;
Where Nature all unconscious works her will,
And every passion moves with human gait,   290
Unhampered by the buskin or the train.
Hating the crowd, where we gregarious men
Lead lonely lives, I love society,
Nor seldom find the best with simple souls
Unswerved by culture from their native bent,
The ground we meet on being primal man
And nearer the deep bases of our lives.

But O, half heavenly, earthly half, my soul,
Canst thou from those late ecstasies descend,
Thy lips still wet with the miraculous wine   300
That transubstantiates all thy baser stuff
To such divinity that soul and sense,
Once more commingled in their source, are lost,—
Canst thou descend to quench a vulgar thirst
With the mere dregs and rinsings of the world ?
Well, if my nature find her pleasure so,
I am content, nor need to blush ; I take
My little gift of being clean from God,
Not haggling for a better, holding it
Good as was ever any in the world,   310
My days as good and full of miracle.
I pluck my nutriment from any bush,
Finding out poison as the first men did
By tasting and then suffering, if I must.
Sometimes my bush burns, and sometimes it is
A leafless wilding shivering by the wall ;
But I have known when winter barberries
Pricked the effeminate palate with surprise
Of savour whose mere harshness seemed divine.

O, benediction of the higher mood   320
And human-kindness of the lower ! for both
I will be grateful while I live, nor question
The wisdom that hath made us what we are,
With such large range as from the alehouse bench
Can reach the stars and be with both at home.
They tell us we have fallen on prosy days,
Condemned to glean the leavings of earth's feast
Where gods and heroes took delight of old ;

But though our lives, moving in one dull round
Of repetition infinite, become   330
Stale as a newspaper once read, and though
History herself, seen in her workshop, seem
To have lost the art that dyed those glorious panes,
Rich with memorial shapes of saint and sage,
That pave with splendour the Past's dusky aisles,—
Panes that enchant the light of common day
With colours costly as the blood of kings,
Till with ideal hues it edge our thought,—
Yet while the world is left, while nature lasts,
And man the best of nature, there shall be   340
Somewhere contentment for these human hearts,
Some freshness, some unused material
For wonder and for song.   I lose myself
In other ways where solemn guide-posts say,
This way to Knowledge, This way to Repose,
But here, here only, I am ne'er betrayed,
For every by-path leads me to my love.

God's passionless reformers, influences,
That purify and heal and are not seen,
Shall man say whence your virtue is, or how   350
Ye make medicinal the wayside weed ?
I know that sunshine, through whatever rift
How shaped it matters not, upon my walls
Paints disks as perfect-rounded as its source,
And, like its antitype, the ray divine,
However finding entrance, perfect still,
Repeats the image unimpaired of God.

We, who by shipwreck only find the shores
Of divine wisdom, can but kneel at first ;
Can but exult to feel beneath our feet,   360
That long stretched vainly down the yielding deeps,
The shock and sustenance of solid earth ;
Inland afar we see what temples gleam
Through immemorial stems of sacred groves,
And we conjecture shining shapes therein ;
Yet for a space we love to wonder here
Among the shells and sea-weed of the beach.

So mused I once within my willow-tent
One brave June morning, when the bluff northwest,
Thrusting aside a dank and snuffling day   370
That made us bitter at our neighbours' sins,
Brimmed the great cup of heaven with sparkling cheer
And roared a lusty stave ; the sliding Charles,
Blue toward the west, and bluer and more blue,

Living and lustrous as a woman's eyes
Look once and look no more, with southward curve
Ran crinkling sunniness, like Helen's hair
Glimpsed in Elysium, insubstantial gold ;
From blossom-clouded orchards, far away
The bobolink tinkled ; the deep meadows flowed 380
With multitudinous pulse of light and shade
Against the bases of the southern hills,
While here and there a drowsy island rick
Slept and its shadow slept ; the wooden bridge
Thundered, and then was silent ; on the roofs
The sun-warped shingles rippled with the heat ;
Summer on field and hill, in heart and brain,
All life washed clean in this high tide of June.

DARA

WHEN Persia's sceptre trembled in a hand
Wilted with harem-heats, and all the land
Was hovered over by those vulture ills
That snuff decaying empire from afar,
Then, with a nature balanced as a star,
Dara arose, a shepherd of the hills.

He who had governed fleecy subjects well
Made his own village by the selfsame spell
Secure and quiet as a guarded fold ;
Then, gathering strength by slow and wise degrees
Under his sway, to neighbour villages
Order returned, and faith and justice old.

Now when it fortuned that a king more wise
Endued the realm with brain and hands and eyes,
He sought on every side men brave and just ;
And having heard our mountain shepherd's praise,
How he refilled the mould of elder days,
To Dara gave a satrapy in trust.

So Dara shepherded a province wide,
Nor in his viceroy's sceptre took more pride
Than in his crook before ; but envy finds
More food in cities than on mountains bare ;
And the frank sun of natures clear and rare
Breeds poisonous fogs in low and marish minds.

Soon it was hissed into the royal ear,
That, though wise Dara's province, year by year,

Like a great sponge, sucked wealth and plenty up,
Yet, when he squeezed it at the king's behest,
Some yellow drops, more rich than all the rest,
Went to the filling of his private cup.

For proof, they said, that, wheresoe'er he went,
A chest, beneath whose weight the camel bent,
Went with him ; and no mortal eye had seen
What was therein, save only Dara's own ;
But, when 't was opened, all his tent was known
To glow and lighten with heaped jewels' sheen.

The King set forth for Dara's province straight ;
There, as was fit, outside the city's gate,
The viceroy met him with a stately train,
And there, with archers circled, close at hand,
A camel with the chest was seen to stand :
The King's brow reddened, for the guilt was plain.

' Open me here,' he cried, ' this treasure-chest ! '
'T was done ; and only a worn shepherd's vest
Was found therein. Some blushed and hung the head ;
Not Dara ; open as the sky's blue roof
He stood, and ' O my lord, behold the proof
That I was faithful to my trust,' he said.

' To govern men, lo all the spell I had !
My soul in these rude vestments ever clad
Still to the unstained past kept true and leal,
Still on these plains could breathe her mountain air,
And fortune's heaviest gifts serenely bear,
Which bend men from their truth and make them reel.

' For ruling wisely I should have small skill,
Were I not lord of simple Dara still ;
That sceptre kept, I could not lose my way.'
Strange dew in royal eyes grew round and bright,
And strained the throbbing lids ; before 't was night
Two added provinces blest Dara's sway.

THE FIRST SNOW-FALL

THE snow had begun in the gloaming,
  And busily all the night
Had been heaping field and highway
  With a silence deep and white.

Every pine and fir and hemlock
  Wore ermine too dear for an earl,
And the poorest twig on the elm-tree
  Was ridged inch deep with pearl.

From sheds new-roofed with Carrara
  Came Chanticleer's muffled crow,
The stiff rails softened to swan's-
    down,
  And still fluttered down the snow.

I stood and watched by the window
  The noiseless work of the sky,
And the sudden flurries of snow-birds,
  Like brown leaves whirling by.

I thought of a mound in sweet
    Auburn
  Where a little headstone stood ;
How the flakes were folding it gently,
  As did robins the babes in the wood.

Up spoke our own little Mabel,
  Saying, 'Father, who makes it
    snow ? '
And I told of the good All-father
  Who cares for us here below.

Again I looked at the snow-fall,
  And thought of the leaden sky
That arched o'er our first great sorrow,
  When that mound was heaped so
    high.

I remembered the gradual patience
  That fell from that cloud like snow,
Flake by flake, healing and hiding
  The scar of our deep-plunged woe.

And again to the child I whispered,
  'The snow that husheth all,
Darling, the merciful Father
  Alone can make it fall ! '

Then, with eyes that saw not, I kissed
  her ;
  And she, kissing back, could not
    know
That *my* kiss was given to her sister,
  Folded close under deepening snow.

THE SINGING LEAVES

A BALLAD

I

' WHAT fairings will ye that **I** bring ? '
  Said the King to his daughters
    three ;
' For I to Vanity Fair am boun,
  Now say what shall they be ? '

Then up and spake the eldest daugh-
    ter,
  That lady tall and grand :
' O, bring me pearls and diamonds
    great,
  And gold rings for my hand.'

Thereafter spake the second daughter,
  That was both white and red :
' For me bring silks that will stand
    alone,
  And a gold comb for my head.'

Then came the turn of the least
    daughter,
  That was whiter than thistle-down,
And among the gold of her blithe-
    some hair
  Dim shone the golden crown.

' There came a bird this morning,
  And sang 'neath my bower eaves,
Till I dreamed, as his music made me,
  "Ask thou for the Singing Leaves."'

Then the brow of the King swelled
    crimson
  With a flush of angry scorn :
' Well have ye spoken, my two eldest,
  And chosen as ye were born ;

' But she like a thing of peasant race,
  That is happy binding the sheaves';
Then he saw her dead mother in her
    face,
  And said, ' Thou shalt have thy
    leaves.'

II

He mounted and rode three days and
    nights
  Till he came to Vanity Fair,
And 't was easy to buy the gems and
    the silk,
  But no Singing Leaves were there.

Then deep in the greenwood rode he,
  And asked of every tree,
' O, if you have ever a Singing Leaf,
  I pray you give it me ! '

But the trees all kept their counsel,
  And never a word said they,
Only there sighed from the pine-tops
  A music of seas far away.

Only the pattering aspen
  Made a sound of growing rain,
That fell ever faster and faster,
  Then faltered to silence again.

' O, where shall I find a little foot-
    page
  That would win both hose and
    shoon,
And will bring to me the Singing
    Leaves
  If they grow under the moon ? '

Then lightly turned him Walter the
    page,
  By the stirrup as he ran :
' Now pledge you me the truesome
    word
  Of a king and gentleman,

' That you will give me the first, first
    thing
  You meet at your castle-gate,
And the Princess shall get the Singing
    Leaves,
  Or mine be a traitor's fate.'

The King's head dropt upon his breast
  A moment, as it might be ;
'T will be my dog, he thought, and
    said,
  ' My faith I plight to thee.'

Then Walter took from next his heart
  A packet small and thin,
' Now give you this to the Princess
    Anne,
  The Singing Leaves are therein.'

III

As the King rode in at his castle-gate,
  A maiden to meet him ran,
And ' Welcome, father ! ' she laughed
    and cried
  Together, the Princess Anne.

' Lo, here the Singing Leaves,' quoth
    he,
  ' And woe, but they cost me dear ! '
She took the packet, and the smile
  Deepened down beneath the tear.

It deepened down till it reached her
    heart,
  And then gushed up again,
And lighted her tears as the sudden
    sun
  Transfigures the summer rain.

And the first Leaf, when it was opened,
  Sang : ' I am Walter the page,
And the songs I sing 'neath thy
    window
  Are my only heritage.'

And the second Leaf sang : ' But in
    the land
  That is neither on earth or sea,
My lute and I are lords of more
  Than thrice this kingdom's fee.'

And the third Leaf sang, ' Be mine !
    Be mine ! '
  And ever it sang, ' Be mine ! '
Then sweeter it sang and ever sweeter,
  And said, 'I am thine, thine, thine!'

At the first Leaf she grew pale enough,
  At the second she turned aside,
At the third, 't was as if a lily flushed
  With a rose's red heart's tide.

' Good counsel gave the bird,' said
    she,
  ' I have my hope thrice o'er,
For they sing to my very heart,' she
    said,
  ' And it sings to them evermore.'

She brought to him her beauty and
    truth,
  But and broad earldoms three,
And he made her queen of the broader
    lands
  He held of his lute in fee.

SEA-WEED

Not always unimpeded can I pray,
Nor, pitying saint, thine intercession claim ;
Too closely clings the burden of the day,
And all the mint and anise that I pay
But swells my debt and deepens my self-blame.

Shall I less patience have than Thou, who know
That Thou revisit'st all who wait for thee,
Nor only fill'st the unsounded deeps below,
But dost refresh with punctual overflow
The rifts where unregarded mosses be ?

The drooping sea-weed hears, in night abyssed,
Far and more far the wave's receding shocks,
Nor doubts, for all the darkness and the mist,
That the pale shepherdess will keep her tryst,
And shoreward lead again her foam-fleeced flocks.

For the same wave that rims the Carib shore
With momentary brede of pearl and gold,
Goes hurrying thence to gladden with its roar
Lorn weeds bound fast on rocks of Labrador,
By love divine on one sweet errand rolled.

And, though Thy healing waters far withdraw,
I, too, can wait and feed on hope of Thee
And of the dear recurrence of Thy law,
Sure that the parting grace my morning saw
Abides its time to come in search of me.

THE FINDING OF THE LYRE

There lay upon the ocean's shore
What once a tortoise served to cover.
A year and more, with rush and roar,
The surf had rolled it over,
Had played with it, and flung it by,
As wind and weather might decide it,
Then tossed it high where sand-drifts dry
Cheap burial might provide it.

It rested there to bleach or tan,
The rains had soaked, the suns had burned it ;
With many a ban the fisherman
Had stumbled o'er and spurned it ;
And there the fisher-girl would stay,
Conjecturing with her brother
How in their play the poor estray
Might serve some use or other.

So there it lay, through wet and dry,
As empty as the last new sonnet,
Till by and by came Mercury,
And, having mused upon it,
' Why, here,' cried he, ' the thing of things
In shape, material, and dimension !
Give it but strings, and, lo, it sings,
A wonderful invention ! '

So said, so done ; the chords he strained,
And, as his fingers o'er them hovered,
The shell disdained a soul had gained,
The lyre had been discovered.
O empty world that round us lies,
Dead shell, of soul and thought forsaken,
Brought we but eyes like Mercury's,
In thee what songs should waken !

P 3

NEW YEAR'S EVE.   1850

THIS is the midnight of the century,—hark !
Through aisle and arch of Godminster have gone
Twelve throbs that tolled the zenith of the dark,
And mornward now the starry hands move on ;
' Mornward ! ' the angelic watchers say,
' Passed is the sorest trial ;
No plot of man can stay
The hand upon the dial ;
Night is the dark stem of the lily Day.'

If we, who watched in valleys here below,
Toward streaks, misdeemed of morn, our faces turned
When volcan glares set all the east aglow,—
We are not poorer that we wept and yearned ;
Though earth swing wide from God's intent,
And though no man nor nation
Will move with full consent
In heavenly gravitation,
Yet by one Sun is every orbit bent.

FOR AN AUTOGRAPH

THOUGH old the thought and oft exprest,
'T is his at last who says it best,—
I 'll try my fortune with the rest.

Muse not which way the pen to hold,
Luck hates the slow and loves the bold,
Soon come the darkness and the cold.

Life is a leaf of paper white
Whereon each one of us may write
His word or two, and then comes night.

Greatly begin ! though thou have time
But for a line, be that sublime,—
Not failure, but low aim, is crime.

' Lo, time and space enough,' we cry,
' To write an epic ! ' so we try
Our nibs upon the edge, and die.

Ah, with what lofty hope we came !
But we forget it, dream of fame,
And scrawl, as I do here, a name.

AL FRESCO

THE dandelions and buttercups
Gild all the lawn ; the drowsy bee
Stumbles among the clover-tops,
And summer sweetens all but me :
Away, unfruitful lore of books,
For whose vain idiom we reject
The soul's more native dialect,
Aliens among the birds and brooks,
Dull to interpret or conceive
What gospels lost the woods retrieve !

Away, ye critics, city-bred,   11
Who set man-traps of thus and so,
And in the first man's footsteps tread,
Like those who toil through drifted snow !
Away, my poets, whose sweet spell
Can make a garden of a cell !
I need ye not, for I to-day
Will make one long sweet verse of play.

Snap, chord of manhood's tenser
  strain !
To-day I will be a boy again ;   20
The mind's pursuing element,
Like a bow slackened and unbent,
In some dark corner shall be leant.
The robin sings, as of old, from the
  limb !
The catbird croons in the lilac-bush !
Through the dim arbour, himself more
  dim,
Silently hops the hermit-thrush,
The withered leaves keep dumb for
  him ;
The irreverent buccaneering bee
Hath stormed and rifled the nunnery
Of the lily, and scattered the sacred
  floor   31
With haste-dropt gold from shrine to
  door ;
There, as of yore,
The rich, milk-tingeing buttercup
Its tiny polished urn holds up,
Filled with ripe summer to the edge,
The sun in his own wine to pledge ;
And our tall elm, this hundredth year
Doge of our leafy Venice here,
Who, with an annual ring, doth wed
The blue Adriatic overhead,   41
Shadows with his palatial mass
The deep canals of flowing grass.

O unestrangèd birds and bees !
O face of Nature always true !
O never-unsympathizing trees !
O never-rejecting roof of blue,
Whose rash disherison never falls
On us unthinking prodigals,
Yet who convictest all our ill,   50
So grand and unappeasable !
Methinks my heart from each of these
Plucks part of childhood back again,
Long there imprisoned, as the breeze
Doth every hidden odour seize
Of wood and water, hill and plain ;
Once more am I admitted peer
In the upper house of Nature here,
And feel through all my pulses run
The royal blood of breeze and sun.

Upon these elm-arched solitudes
No hum of neighbour toil intrudes ;
The only hammer that I hear   63
Is wielded by the woodpecker,
The single noisy calling his
In all our leaf-hid Sybaris ;
The good old time, close-hidden here,
Persists, a loyal cavalier,
While Roundheads prim, with point
  of fox,
Probe wainscot-chink and empty box ;
Here no hoarse-voiced iconoclast   71
Insults thy statues, royal Past ;
Myself too prone the axe to wield,
I touch the silver side of the shield
With lance reversed, and challenge
  peace,
A willing convert of the trees.

How chanced it that so long I tost
A cable's length from this rich coast,
With foolish anchors hugging close
The beckoning weeds and lazy ooze,
Nor had the wit to wreck before   81
On this enchanted island's shore,
Whither the current of the sea,
With wiser drift, persuaded me ?

O, might we but of such rare days
Build up the spirit's dwelling-place !
A temple of so Parian stone
Would brook a marble god alone,
The statue of a perfect life,
Far-shrined from earth's bestaining
  strife.   90
Alas ! though such felicity
In our vext world here may not be,
Yet, as sometimes the peasant's hut
Shows stones which old religion cut
With text inspired, or mystic sign
Of the Eternal and Divine,
Torn from the consecration deep
Of some fallen nunnery's mossy sleep,
So, from the ruins of this day   99
Crumbling in golden dust away,
The soul one gracious block may draw,
Carved with some fragment of the law,
Which, set in life's uneven wall,
Old benedictions may recall,
And lure some nunlike thoughts to take
Their dwelling here for memory's sake.

MASACCIO

(IN THE BRANCACCI CHAPEL)

HE came to Florence long ago,
And painted here these walls, that
    shone
For Raphael and for Angelo,
With secrets deeper than his own,
Then shrank into the dark again,
And died, we know not how or when.

The shadows deepened, and I turned
Half sadly from the fresco grand ;
' And is this,' mused I, ' all ye earned,
High-vaulted brain and cunning hand,
That ye to greater men could teach
The skill yourselves could never
    reach ? '

' And who were they,' I mused, ' that
    wrought
Through pathless wilds, with labour
    long,
The highways of our daily thought ?
Who reared those towers of earliest
    song
That lift us from the throng to peace
Remote in sunny silences ? '

Out clanged the Ave Mary bells,
And to my heart this message came :
Each clamorous throat among them
    tells
What strong-souled martyrs died in
    flame
To make it possible that thou
Shouldst here with brother sinners
    bow.

Thoughts that great hearts once
    broke for, we
Breathe cheaply in the common air ;
The dust we trample heedlessly
Throbbed once in saints and heroes
    rare,
Who perished, opening for their race
New pathways to the commonplace.

Henceforth, when rings the health to
    those
Who live in story and in song,
O nameless dead, that now repose
Safe in Oblivion's chambers strong,
One cup of recognition true
Shall silently be drained to you !

WITHOUT AND WITHIN

My coachman, in the moonlight there,
    Looks through the side-light of the
      door ;
I hear him with his brethren swear,
    As I could do,—but only more.

Flattening his nose against the pane,
    He envies me my brilliant lot,
Breathes on his aching fists in vain,
    And dooms me to a place more hot.

He sees me in to supper go,
    A silken wonder by my side,
Bare arms, bare shoulders, and a row
    Of flounces, for the door too wide.

He thinks how happy is my arm
    'Neath its white-gloved and jewelled
      load ;
And wishes me some dreadful harm,
    Hearing the merry corks explode.

Meanwhile I inly curse the bore
    Of hunting still the same old coon,
And envy him, outside the door,
    In golden quiets of the moon.

The winter wind is not so cold
    As the bright smile he sees me
      win,
Nor the host's oldest wine so old
    As our poor gabble sour and thin.

I envy him the ungyved prance
    By which his freezing feet he warms,
And drag my lady's-chains and dance
    The galley-slaves of dreary forms.

O, could he have my share of din,
    And I his quiet !—past a doubt
'T would still be one man bored
      within,
    And just another bored without.

GODMINSTER CHIMES

WRITTEN IN AID OF A CHIME OF BELLS FOR
CHRIST CHURCH, CAMBRIDGE

GODMINSTER ? Is it Fancy's play ?
  I know not, but the word
Sings in my heart, nor can I say
  Whether 't was dreamed or heard ;
Yet fragrant in my mind it clings
  As blossoms after rain,
And builds of half-remembered things
  This vision in my brain.

Through aisles of long-drawn cen-
    turies
  My spirit walks in thought,
And to that symbol lifts its eyes
  Which God's own pity wrought ;
From Calvary shines the altar's
    gleam,
  The Church's East is there,
The Ages one great minster seem,
  That throbs with praise and prayer.

And all the way from Calvary down
  The carven pavement shows
Their graves who won the martyr's
    crown
  And safe in God repose ;
The saints of many a warring creed
  Who now in heaven have learned
That all paths to the Father lead
  Where Self the feet have spurned.

And, as the mystic aisles I pace,
  By aureoled workmen built,
Lives ending at the Cross I trace
  Alike through grace and guilt

One Mary bathes the blessed feet
  With ointment from her eyes,
With spikenard one, and both are
    sweet,
  For both are sacrifice.

Moravian hymn and Roman chant
  In one devotion blend,   .
To speak the soul's eternal want
  Of Him, the inmost friend ;
One prayer soars cleansed with martyr
    fire,
  One choked with sinner's tears,
In heaven both meet in one desire,
  And God one music hears.

Whilst thus I dream, the bells clash
    out
  Upon the Sabbath air,
Each seems a hostile faith to shout,
  A selfish form of prayer ;
My dream is shattered, yet who knows
  But in that heaven so near
These discords find harmonious close
  In God's atoning ear ?

O chime of sweet Saint Charity,
  Peal soon that Easter morn
When Christ for all shall risen be,
  And in all hearts new-born !
That Pentecost when utterance clear
  To all men shall be given,
When all shall say *My Brother* here,
  And hear *My Son* in heaven !

THE PARTING OF THE WAYS

WHO hath not been a poet ? Who hath not,
With life's new quiver full of wingèd years,
Shot at a venture, and then, following on,
Stood doubtful at the Parting of the Ways ?

There once I stood in dream, and as I paused,
Looking this way and that, came forth to me
The figure of a woman veiled, that said,
' My name is Duty, turn and follow me ' ;

Something there was that chilled me in her voice ;
I felt Youth's hand grow slack and cold in mine,   10
As if to be withdrawn, and I replied :
' O, leave the hot wild heart within my breast !
Duty comes soon enough, too soon comes Death ;
This slippery globe of life whirls of itself,
Hasting our youth away into the dark ;
These senses, quivering with electric heats,
Too soon will show, like nests on wintry boughs
Obtrusive emptiness, too palpable wreck,
Which whistling north-winds line with downy snow
Sometimes, or fringe with foliaged rime, in vain,   20
Thither the singing birds no more return.'

Then glowed to me a maiden from the left,
With bosom half disclosed, and naked arms
More white and undulant than necks of swans ;
And all before her steps an influence ran
Warm as the whispering South that opens buds
And swells the laggard sails of Northern May.
' I am called Pleasure, come with me ! ' she said,
Then laughed, and shook out sunshine from her hair,
Not only that, but, so it seemed, shook out   30
All memory too, and all the moonlit past,
Old loves, old aspirations, and old dreams,
More beautiful for being old and gone.

So we two went together ; downward sloped
The path through yellow meads, or so I dreamed,
Yellow with sunshine and young green, but I
Saw naught nor heard, shut up in one close joy ;
I only felt the hand within my own,
Transmuting all my blood to golden fire,
Dissolving all my brain in throbbing mist.   40

Suddenly shrank the hand ; suddenly burst
A cry that split the torpor of my brain,
And as the first sharp thrust of lightning loosens
From the heaped cloud its rain, loosened my sense :
' Save me ! ' it thrilled ; ' O, hide me ! there is Death !
Death the divider, the unmerciful,
That digs his pitfalls under Love and Youth
And covers Beauty up in the cold ground ;
Horrible Death ! bringer of endless dark ;
Let him not see me ! hide me in thy breast ! '   50
Thereat I strove to clasp her, but my arms
Met only what slipped crumbling down, and fell,
A handful of grey ashes, at my feet.

I would have fled, I would have followed back
That pleasant path we came, but all was changed ;
Rocky the way, abrupt, and hard to find ;
Yet I toiled on, and, toiling on, I thought,
' That way lies Youth, and Wisdom, and all Good ;
For only by unlearning Wisdom comes
And climbing backward to diviner Youth ;   60
What the world teaches profits to the world,
What the soul teaches profits to the soul,
Which then first stands erect with Godward face,
When she lets fall her pack of withered facts,
The gleanings of the outward eye and ear,
And looks and listens with her finer sense ;
Nor Truth nor Knowledge cometh from without.'

After long weary days I stood again
And waited at the Parting of the Ways ;
Again the figure of a woman veiled   70
Stood forth and beckoned, and I followed now :
Down to no bower of roses led the path,
But through the streets of towns where chattering Cold
Hewed wood for fires whose glow was owned and fenced,
Where Nakedness wove garments of warm wool
Not for itself ;—or through the fields it led
Where Hunger reaped the unattainable grain,
Where Idleness enforced saw idle lands,
Leagues of unpeopled soil, the common earth,
Walled round with paper against God and Man.   80
' I cannot look,' I groaned, ' at only these ;
The heart grows hardened with perpetual wont,
And palters with a feigned necessity,
Bargaining with itself to be content ;
Let me behold thy face.'
                The Form replied :
' Men follow Duty, never overtake ;
Duty nor lifts her veil nor looks behind.'
But, as she spake, a loosened lock of hair
Slipped from beneath her hood, and I, who looked
To see it grey and thin, saw amplest gold ;   90
Not that dull metal dug from sordid earth,
But such as the retiring sunset flood
Leaves heaped on bays and capes of island cloud.
' O Guide divine,' I prayed, ' although not yet
I may repair the virtue which I feel
Gone out at touch of untuned things and foul
With draughts of Beauty, yet declare how soon ! '

' Faithless and faint of heart,' the voice returned,
' Thou see'st no beauty save thou make it first ;

Man, Woman, Nature, each is but a glass   100
Where the soul sees the image of herself,
Visible echoes, offsprings of herself.
But, since thou need'st assurance of how soon,
Wait till that angel comes who opens all,
The reconciler, he who lifts the veil,
The reuniter, the rest-bringer, Death.'

I waited, and methought he came ; but how,
Or in what shape, I doubted, for no sign,
By touch or mark, he gave me as he passed :
Only I knew a lily that I held   .   110
Snapt short below the head and shrivelled up ;
Then turned my Guide and looked at me unveiled,
And I beheld no face of matron stern,
But that enchantment I had followed erst,
Only more fair, more clear to eye and brain,
Heightened and chastened by a household charm ;
She smiled, and ' Which is fairer,' said her eyes,
' The hag's unreal Florimel or mine ? '

ALADDIN

When I was a beggarly boy,
    And lived in a cellar damp,
I had not a friend nor a toy,
    But I had Aladdin's lamp ;
When I could not sleep for cold,
    I had fire enough in my brain,
And builded, with roofs of gold,
    My beautiful castles in Spain !

Since then I have toiled day and night,
    I have money and power good store,
But I 'd give all my lamps of silver bright,
    For the one that is mine no more ;
Take, Fortune, whatever you choose,
    You gave, and may snatch again ;
I have nothing 't would pain me to lose,
    For I own no more castles in Spain !

AN INVITATION

Nine years have slipt like hour-glass sand
From life's still-emptying globe away,
Since last, dear friend, I clasped your hand,
And stood upon the impoverished land,
Watching the steamer down the bay.

I held the token which you gave,
While slowly the smoke-pennon curled
O'er the vague rim 'tween sky and wave,
And shut the distance like a grave,
Leaving me in the colder world.

The old worn world of hurry and heat,
The young, fresh world of thought
  and scope,
While you, where beckoning billows
  fleet
Climb far sky-beaches still and sweet,
Sank wavering down the ocean-slope.

You sought the new world in the old,
I found the old world in the new,
All that our human hearts can hold,
The inward world of deathless mould,
The same that Father Adam knew.

He needs no ship to cross the tide,
Who, in the lives about him, sees
Fair window-prospects opening wide
O'er history's fields on every side,
To Ind and Egypt, Rome and Greece.

Whatever moulds of various brain
E'er shaped the world to weal or woe,
Whatever empires' wax and wane,
To him that hath not eyes in vain,
Our village-microcosm can show.

Come back our ancient walks to tread,
Dear haunts of lost or scattered friends,
Old Harvard's scholar-factories red,
Where song and smoke and laughter
  sped
The nights to proctor-haunted ends.

Constant are all our former loves,
Unchanged the icehouse-girdled pond,
Its hemlock glooms, its shadowy
  coves,
Where floats the coot and never
  moves,
Its slopes of long-tamed green beyond.

Our old familiars are not laid,
Though snapt our wands and sunk
  our books ;
They beckon, not to be gainsaid,
Where, round broad meads that
  mowers wade,
The Charles his steel-blue sickle
  crooks.

Where, as the cloudbergs eastward
  blow,
From glow to gloom the hillsides shift
Their plumps of orchard-trees arow,
Their lakes of rye that wave and flow,
Their snowy whiteweed's summer
  drift.

There have we watched the West
  unfurl
A cloud Byzantium newly born,
With flickering spires and domes of
  pearl,
And vapoury surfs that crowd and curl
Into the sunset's Golden Horn.

There, as the flaming occident
Burned slowly down to ashes grey,
Night pitched o'erhead her silent tent,
And glimmering gold from Hesper
  sprent
Upon the darkened river lay,

Where a twin sky but just before
Deepened, and double swallows
  skimmed,
And, from a visionary shore,
Hung visioned trees, that more and
  more
Grew dusk as those above were
  dimmed.

Then eastward saw we slowly grow
Clear-edged the lines of roof and spire,
While great elm-masses blacken slow,
And linden-ricks their round heads
  show
Against a flush of widening fire.

Doubtful at first and far away,
The moon-flood creeps more wide and
  wide ;
Up a ridged beach of cloudy grey,
Curved round the east as round a bay,
It slips and spreads its gradual tide.

Then suddenly, in lurid mood,
The moon looms large o'er town and
  field
As upon Adam, red like blood,
'Tween him and Eden's happy wood,
Glared the commissioned angel's shield.

Or let us seek the seaside, there
To wander idly as we list,
Whether, on rocky headlands bare,
Sharp cedar-horns, like breakers, tear
The trailing fringes of grey mist,

Or whether, under skies full flown,
The brightening surfs, with foamy din,
Their breeze-caught forelocks back-
    ward blown,
Against the beach's yellow zone,
Curl slow, and plunge forever in.

And, as we watch those canvas towers
That lean along the horizon's rim,
'Sail on,' I'll say; 'may sunniest
    hours
Convoy you from this land of ours,
Since from my side you bear not him!'

For years thrice three, wise Horace
    said,
A poem rare let silence bind;
And love may ripen in the shade,
Like ours, for nine long seasons laid
In deepest arches of the mind.

Come back! Not ours the Old
    World's good,
The Old World's ill, thank God, not
    ours;

But here, far better understood,
The days enforce our native mood,
And challenge all our manlier powers.

Kindlier to me the place of birth
That first my tottering footsteps trod;
There may be fairer spots of earth,
But all their glories are not worth
The virtue of the native sod.

Thence climbs an influence more
    benign
Through pulse and nerve, through
    heart and brain;
Sacred to me those fibres fine
That first clasped earth. O, ne'er be
    mine
The alien sun and alien rain!

These nourish not like homelier glows
Or waterings of familiar skies,
And nature fairer blooms bestows
On the heaped hush of wintry snows,
In pastures dear to childhood's eyes,

Than where Italian earth receives
The partial sunshine's ampler boons,
Where vines carve friezes 'neath the
    eaves,
And, in dark firmaments of leaves,
The orange lifts its golden moons.

THE NOMADES

WHAT Nature makes in any mood
To me is warranted for good,
Though long before I learned to see
She did not set us moral theses,
And scorned to have her sweet caprices
Strait-waistcoated in you or me.

I, who take root and firmly cling,
Thought fixedness the only thing;
Why Nature made the butterflies,
(Those dreams of wings that float and
    hover
At noon the slumberous poppies over,)
Was something hidden from mine
    eyes,

Till once, upon a rock's brown bosom,
Bright as a thorny cactus-blossom,
I saw a butterfly at rest;
Then first of both I felt the beauty;
The airy whim, the grim-set duty,
Each from the other took its best.

Clearer it grew than winter sky
That Nature still had reasons why;
And, shifting sudden as a breeze,
My fancy found no satisfaction,
No antithetic sweet attraction,
So great as in the Nomades.

Scythians, with Nature not at strife,
Light Arabs of our complex life,

They build no houses, plant no mills
To utilize Time's sliding river,
Content that it flow waste forever,
If they, like it, may have their wills.

An hour they pitch their shifting tents
In thoughts, in feelings, and events ;
Beneath the palm-trees, on the grass,
They sing, they dance, make love, and chatter,
Vex the grim temples with their clatter,
And make Truth's fount their looking-glass.

A picnic life ; from love to love,
From faith to faith they lightly move,
And yet, hard-eyed philosopher,
The flightiest maid that ever hovered
To me your thought-webs fine discovered,
No lens to see them through like her.

So witchingly her finger-tips
To Wisdom, as away she trips,
She kisses, waves such sweet farewells
To Duty, as she laughs ' To-morrow ! '

That both from that mad contrast borrow
A perfectness found nowhere else.

The beach-bird on its pearly verge
Follows and flies the whispering surge,
While, in his tent, the rock-stayed shell
Awaits the flood's star-timed vibrations,
And both, the flutter and the patience,
The sauntering poet loves them well.

Fulfil so much of God's decree
As works its problem out in thee,
Nor dream that in thy breast alone
The conscience of the changeful seasons,
The Will that in the planets reasons
With space-wide logic, has its throne.

Thy virtue makes not vice of mine,
Unlike, but none the less divine ;
Thy toil adorns, not chides, my play ;
Nature of sameness is so chary,
With such wild whim the freakish fairy
Picks presents for the christening-day.

SELF-STUDY

A PRESENCE both by night and day,
That made my life seem just begun,
Yet scarce a presence, rather say
The warning aureole of one.

And yet I felt it everywhere ;
Walked I the woodland's aisles along,
It seemed to brush me with its hair ;
Bathed I, I heard a mermaid's song.

How sweet it was ! A buttercup
Could hold for me a day's delight,
A bird could lift my fancy up
To ether free from cloud or blight.

Who was the nymph ? Nay, I will see,
Methought, and I will know her near ;

If such, divined, her charm can be,
Seen and possessed, how triply dear !

So every magic art I tried,
And spells as numberless as sand,
Until, one evening, by my side
I saw her glowing fullness stand.

I turned to clasp her, but ' Farewell,'
Parting she sighed, 'we meet no more;
Not by my hand the curtain fell
That leaves you conscious, wise, and poor.

' Since you have found me out, I go ;
Another lover I must find,
Content his happiness to know,
Nor strive its secret to unwind.'

I

A HEAP of bare and splintery crags
Tumbled about by lightning and
frost,
With rifts and chasms and storm-
bleached jags,
That wait and growl for a ship to be
lost ;
No island, but rather the skeleton
Of a wrecked and vengeance-smitten
one,
Where, æons ago, with half-shut eye,
The sluggish saurian crawled to die,
Gasping under titanic ferns ;
Ribs of rock that seaward jut,   10
Granite shoulders and boulders and
snags,
Round which, though the winds in
heaven be shut,
The nightmared ocean murmurs and
yearns,
Welters, and swashes, and tosses, and
turns,
And the dreary black sea-weed lolls
and wags ;
Only rock from shore to shore,
Only a moan through the bleak clefts
blown,
With sobs in the rifts where the coarse
kelp shifts,
Falling and lifting, tossing and drift-
ing,
And under all a deep, dull roar,   20
Dying and swelling, forevermore,—
Rock and moan and roar alone,
And the dread of some nameless thing
unknown,
These make Appledore.

These make Appledore by night :
Then there are monsters left and
right ;
Every rock is a different monster ;
All you have read of, fancied,
dreamed,
When you waked at night because
you screamed,

There they lie for half a mile,   30
Jumbled together in a pile,
And (though you know they never
once stir),
If you look long, they seem to be
moving
Just as plainly as plain can be,
Crushing and crowding, wading and
shoving
Out into the awful sea,
Where you can hear them snort and
spout
With pauses between, as if they were
listening,
Then tumult anon when the surf
breaks glistening
In the blackness where they wallow
about.   40

II

All this you would scarcely compre-
hend,
Should you see the isle on a sunny
day ;
Then it is simple enough in its way,—
Two rocky bulges, one at each end,
With a smaller bulge and a hollow
between :
Patches of whortleberry and bay ;
Accidents of open green,
Sprinkled with loose slabs square and
grey,
Like graveyards for ages deserted ;
a few
Unsocial thistles ; an elder or two,
Foamed over with blossoms white as
spray ;   51
And on the whole island never a tree
Save a score of sumachs, high as your
knee,
That crouch in hollows where they
may,
(The cellars where once stood a village,
men say,)
Huddling for warmth, and never grew
Tall enough for a peep at the sea ;
A general dazzle of open blue ;

A breeze always blowing and playing
    rat-tat
With the bow of the ribbon round
    your hat ;   60
A score of sheep that do nothing but
    stare
Up or down at you everywhere ;
Three or four cattle that chew the cud
Lying about in a listless despair ;
A medrick that makes you look over-
    head
With short, sharp scream, as he sights
    his prey,
And, dropping straight and swift as
    lead,
Splits the water with sudden thud ;—
This is Appledore by day.

A common island, you will say ;   70
But stay a moment : only climb
Up to the highest rock of the isle,
Stand there alone for a little while,
And with gentle approaches it grows
    sublime,
Dilating slowly as you win
A sense from the silence to take it in.
So wide the loneness, so lucid the air,
The granite beneath you so savagely
    bare,
You well might think you were look-
    ing down
From some sky-silenced mountain's
    crown,   80
Whose far-down pines are wont to
    tear
Locks of wool from the topmost cloud.
Only be sure you go alone,
For Grandeur is inaccessibly proud,
And never yet has backward thrown
Her veil to feed the stare of a crowd ;
To more than one was never shown
That awful front, nor is it fit
That she, Cothurnus-shod, stand
    bowed
Until the self-approving pit   90
Enjoy the gust of its own wit
In babbling plaudits cheaply loud ;
She hides her mountains and her sea
From the harriers of scenery,

Who hunt down sunsets, and huddle
    and bay,
Mouthing and mumbling the dying
    day.

Trust me, 't is something to be cast
Face to face with one's Self at last,
To be taken out of the fuss and strife,
The endless clatter of plate and knife,
The bore of books and the bores of
    the street,   101
From the singular mess we agree to
    call Life,
Where that is best which the most
    fools vote is,
And to be set down on one's own two
    feet
So nigh to the great warm heart of
    God,
You almost seem to feel it beat
Down from the sunshine and up from
    the sod ;
To be compelled, as it were, to notice
All the beautiful changes and chances
Through which the landscape flits and
    glances,   110
And to see how the face of common
    day
Is written all over with tender his-
    tories,
When you study it that intenser way
In which a lover looks at his mistress.

Till now you dreamed not what could
    be done
With a bit of rock and a ray of sun ;
But look, how fade the lights and
    shades
Of keen bare edge and crevice deep !
How doubtfully it fades and fades,
And glows again, yon craggy steep,
O'er which, through colour's dreamiest
    grades,   121
The yellow sunbeams pause and creep !
Now pink it blooms, now glimmers
    grey,
Now shadows to a filmy blue,
Tries one, tries all, and will not stay,
But flits from opal hue to hue,

And runs through every tenderest
range
Of change that seems not to be change
So rare the sweep, so nice the art,
That lays no stress on any part, 130
But shifts and lingers and persuades;
So soft that sun-brush in the west,
That asks no costlier pigments' aids,
But mingling knobs, flaws, angles,
dints,
Indifferent of worst or best,
Enchants the cliffs with wraiths and
hints
And gracious preludings of tints,
Where all seems fixed, yet all evades,
And indefinably pervades
Perpetual movement with perpetual
rest! 140

III

Away northeast is Boone Island light;
You might mistake it for a ship,
Only it stands too plumb upright,
And like the others does not slip
Behind the sea's unsteady brink;
Though, if a cloud-shade chance to dip
Upon it a moment, 't will suddenly
sink,
Levelled and lost in the darkened
main,
Till the sun builds it suddenly up
again,
As if with a rub of Aladdin's lamp.
On the mainland you see a misty
camp 151
Of mountains pitched tumultuously:
That one looming so long and large
Is Saddleback, and that point you see
Over yon low and rounded marge,
Like the boss of a sleeping giant's
targe
Laid over his breast, is Ossipee;
That shadow there may be Kearsarge;
That must be Great Haystack; I love
these names,
Wherewith the lonely farmer tames
Nature to mute companionship 161
With his own mind's domestic mood,
And strives the surly world to clip
In the arms of familiar habitude.

'T is well he could not contrive to
make
A Saxon of Agamenticus:
He glowers there to the north of us,
Wrapt in his blanket of blue haze,
Unconvertibly savage, and scorns to
take
The white man's baptism or his ways.
Him first on shore the coaster divines
Through the early grey, and sees him
shake 172
The morning mist from his scalp-lock
of pines;
Him first the skipper makes out in the
west,
Ere the earliest sunstreak shoots
tremulous,
Plashing with orange the palpitant
lines
Of mutable billow, crest after crest,
And murmurs *Agamenticus!*
As if it were the name of a saint.
But is that a mountain playing cloud,
Or a cloud playing mountain, just
there, so faint? 181
Lookalong over the low right shoulder
Of Agamenticus into that crowd
Of brassy thunderheads behind it;
Now you have caught it, but, ere you
are older
By half an hour, you will lose it and
find it
A score of times; while you look 't is
gone,
And, just as you 've given it up, anon
It is there again, till your weary
eyes
Fancy they see it waver and rise,
With its brother clouds; it is
Agiochook, 191
There if you seek not, and gone if you
look,
Ninety miles off as the eagle flies.

But mountains make not all the shore
The mainland shows to Appledore;
Eight miles the heaving water spreads
To a long low coast with beaches and
heads

That run through unimagined mazes,
As the lights and shades and magical
    hazes
Put them away or bring them near,
Shimmering, sketched out for thirty
    miles   201
Between two capes that waver like
    threads,
And sink in the ocean, and reappear,
Crumbled and melted to little isles,
With filmy trees, that seem the mere
Half-fancies of drowsy atmosphere ;
And see the beach there, where it is
Flat as a threshing-floor, beaten and
    packed
With the flashing flails of weariless
    seas,
How it lifts and looms to a precipice,
O'er whose square front, a dream, no
    more,   211
The steepened sand-stripes seem to
    pour,
A murmurless vision of cataract ;
You almost fancy you hear a roar,
Fitful and faint from the distance
    wandering ;
But 't is only the blind old ocean
    maundering,
Raking the shingle to and fro,
Aimlessly clutching and letting go
The kelp-haired sedges of Appledore,
Slipping down with a sleepy forget-
    ting,   220
And anon his ponderous shoulder
    setting,
With a deep, hoarse pant against
    Appledore.

IV

Eastward as far as the eye can see,
Still eastward, eastward, endlessly,
The sparkle and tremor of purple sea
That rises before you, a flickering hill,
On and on to the shut of the sky,
And beyond, you fancy it sloping
    until
The same multitudinous throb and
    thrill   229
That vibrate under your dizzy eye

In ripples of orange and pink are sent
Where the poppied sails doze on the
    yard,
And the clumsy junk and proa lie
Sunk deep with precious woods and
    nard,
Mid the palmy isles of the Orient.
Those leaning towers of clouded white
On the farthest brink of doubtful
    ocean,
That shorten and shorten out of sight,
Yet seem on the selfsame spot to stay,
Receding with a motionless motion,
Fading to dubious films of grey,
Lost, dimly found, then vanished
    wholly,   242
Will rise again, the great world under,
First films, then towers, then high-
    heaped clouds,
Whose nearing outlines sharpen
    slowly
Into tall ships with cobweb shrouds,
That fill long Mongol eyes with won-
    der,
Crushing the violet wave to spray
Past some low headland of Cathay ;—
What was that sigh which seemed so
    near,   250
Chilling your fancy to the core ?
'T is only the sad old sea you hear,
That seems to seek forevermore
Something it cannot find, and so,
Sighing, seeks on, and tells its woe
To the pitiless breakers of Appledore.

V

How looks Appledore in a storm ?
    I have seen it when its crags seemed
    frantic,
    Butting against the mad Atlantic,
When surge on surge would heap
    enorme,   260
    Cliffs of emerald topped with snow,
    That lifted and lifted, and then
    let go
A great white avalanche of thunder,
    A grinding, blinding, deafening ire
Monadnock might have trembled
    under ;

And the island, whose rock-roots
  pierce below
To where they are warmed with the
  central fire,
You could feel its granite fibres racked,
  As it seemed to plunge with
  a shudder and thrill
  Right at the breast of the swooping
  hill,   270
And to rise again snorting a cataract
Of rage-froth from every cranny and
  ledge,
  While the sea drew its breath in
  hoarse and deep,
And the next vast breaker curled its
  edge,
  Gathering itself for a mightier leap.

North, east, and south there are reefs
  and breakers
  You would never dream of in
  smooth weather,
That toss and gore the sea for acres,
  Bellowing and gnashing and snarl-
  ing together ;
Look northward, where Duck Island
  lies,   280
And over its crown you will see arise,
Against a background of slaty skies,
  A row of pillars still and white,
  That glimmer, and then are out of
  sight,
As if the moon should suddenly kiss,
  While you crossed the gusty desert
  by night,
The long colonnades of Persepolis ;
Look southward for White Island
  light,
  The lantern stands ninety feet o'er
  the tide ;
There is first a half-mile of tumult and
  fight,   290
Of dash and roar and tumble and
  fright,
  And surging bewilderment wild and
  wide,
Where the breakers struggle left and
  right,
  Then a mile or more of rushing sea,

And then the lighthouse slim and
  lone ;
And whenever the weight of ocean is
  thrown
Full and fair on White Island head,
  A great mist-jotun you will see
  Lifting himself up silently
High and huge o'er the lighthouse top,
With hands of wavering spray out-
  spread,   301
  Groping after the little tower,
  That seems to shrink and shorten
  and cower,
Till the monster's arms of a sudden
  drop,
  And silently and fruitlessly
  He sinks again into the sea.

You, meanwhile, where drenched you
  stand,
  Awaken once more to the rush and
  roar,
And on the rock-point tighten your
  hand,   309
As you turn and see a valley deep,
  That was not there a moment be-
  fore,
Suck rattling down between you and
  a heap
  Of toppling billow, whose instant fall
  Must sink the whole island once for
  all,
Or watch the silenter, stealthier seas
  Feeling their way to you more and
  more ;
If they once should clutch you high
  as the knees,
They would whirl you down like a
  sprig of kelp,   318
Beyond all reach of hope or help ;—
  And such in a storm is Appledore.

VI

'T is the sight of a lifetime to behold
The great shorn sun as you see it now,
Across eight miles of undulant gold
That widens landward, weltered and
  rolled,
With freaks of shadow and crimson
  stains ;

To see the solid mountain brow
As it notches the disk, and gains and
   gains
Until there comes, you scarce know
   when,
A tremble of fire o'er the parted lips
Of cloud and mountain, which
   vanishes ; then   330
From the body of day the sun-soul
   slips
And the face of earth darkens ; but
   now the strips
Of western vapour, straight and thin,
From which the horizon's swervings
   win
A grace of contrast, take fire and burn
Like splinters of touchwood, whose
   edges a mould
Of ashes o'erfeathers ; northward
   turn
For an instant, and let your eye grow
   cold
On Agamenticus, and when once more
You look, 't is as if the land-breeze,
   growing,   340
From the smouldering brands the film
   were blowing,
And brightening them down to the
   very core ;
Yet they momently cool and dampen
   and deaden,
The crimson turns golden, the gold
   turns leaden,
Hardening into one black bar
O'er which, from the hollow heaven
   afar,
Shoots a splinter of light like diamond,
Half seen, half fancied ; by and by
Beyond whatever is most beyond
In the uttermost waste of desert sky,
Grows a star ;   351
And over it, visible spirit of dew,—
Ah, stir not, speak not, hold your
   breath,
Or surely the miracle vanisheth,—
The new moon, tranced in unspeak-
   able blue !
No frail illusion ; this were true,
Rather, to call it the canoe

Hollowed out of a single pearl,
That floats us from the Present's whirl
Back to those beings which were ours,
When wishes were winged things like
   powers !   361
Call it not light, that mystery tender,
Which broods upon the brooding ocean,
That flush of ecstasied surrender
To indefinable emotion,
That glory, mellower than a mist
Of pearl dissolved with amethyst,
Which rims Square Rock, like what
   they paint
Of mitigated heavenly splendour
Round the stern forehead of a Saint !

No more a vision, reddened, largened,
The moon dips toward her mountain
   nest,   372
And, fringing it with palest argent,
Slow sheathes herself behind the
   margent
Of that long cloud-bar in the West,
Whose nether edge, erelong, you see
The silvery chrism in turn anoint,
And then the tiniest rosy point
Touched doubtfully and timidly
Into the dark blue's chilly strip, 380
As some mute, wondering thing below,
Awakened by the thrilling glow,
Might, looking up, see Dian dip
One lucent foot's delaying tip
In Latmian fountains long ago.

Knew you what silence was before ?
Here is no startle of dreaming bird
That sings in his sleep, or strives to
   sing ;
Here is no sough of branches stirred,
Nor noise of any living thing,   390
Such as one hears by night on shore ;
Only, now and then, a sigh,
With fickle intervals between,
Sometimes far, and sometimes nigh,
Such as Andromeda might have heard,
And fancied the huge sea-beast un-
   seen
Turning in sleep ; it is the sea
That welters and wavers uneasily
Round the lonely reefs of Appledore.

THE WIND-HARP

I TREASURE in secret some long, fine hair
　　Of tenderest brown, but so inwardly golden
I half used to fancy the sunshine there,
So shy, so shifting, so waywardly rare,
　　Was only caught for the moment and holden
While I could say *Dearest !* and kiss it, and then
In pity let go to the summer again.

I twisted this magic in gossamer strings
　　Over a wind-harp's Delphian hollow ;
Then called to the idle breeze that swings
All day in the pine-tops, and clings, and sings
　　Mid the musical leaves, and said, ' O, follow
The will of those tears that deepen my words,
And fly to my window to waken these chords.'

So they trembled to life, and, doubtfully
　　Feeling their way to my sense, sang, ' Say whether
They sit all day by the greenwood tree,
The lover and loved, as it wont to be,
　　When we——' but grief conquered, and all together
They swelled such weird murmur as haunts a shore
Of some planet dispeopled,—' Nevermore ! '

Then from deep in the past, as seemed to me,
　　The strings gathered sorrow and sang forsaken,
' One lover still waits 'neath the greenwood tree,
But 't is dark,' and they shuddered, ' where lieth she
　　Dark and cold !　Forever must one be taken ? '
But I groaned, ' O harp of all ruth bereft,
This Scripture is sadder,—" the other left " ! '

There murmured, as if one strove to speak,
　　And tears came instead ; then the sad tones wandered
And faltered among the uncertain chords
In a troubled doubt between sorrow and words ;
　　At last with themselves they questioned and pondered,
' Hereafter ?—who knoweth ? ' and so they sighed
Down the long steps that lead to silence and died.

AUF WIEDERSEHEN !

SUMMER

THE little gate was reached at last,
　　Half hid in lilacs down the lane ;
She pushed it wide, and, as she past,
A wistful look she backward cast,
　　And said,—' *Auf wiedersehen !* '

With hand on latch, a vision white
　　Lingered reluctant, and again
Half doubting if she did aright,
Soft as the dews that fell that night,
　　She said,—' *Auf wiedersehen !* '

The lamp's clear gleam flits up the stair ;
I linger in delicious pain ;
Ah, in that chamber, whose rich air
To breathe in thought I scarcely dare,
Thinks she,—' *Auf wiedersehen !* '

'T is thirteen years ; once more I press
The turf that silences the lane ;
I hear the rustle of her dress,
I smell the lilacs, and—ah, yes,
I hear ' *Auf wiedersehen !* '

Sweet piece of bashful maiden art !
The English words had seemed too fain,
But these—they drew us heart to heart,
Yet held us tenderly apart ;
She said, ' *Auf wiedersehen !* '

PALINODE

AUTUMN

STILL thirteen years : 't is autumn now
On field and hill, in heart and brain;
The naked trees at evening sough ;
The leaf to the forsaken bough
Sighs not,—' We meet again ! '

Two watched yon oriole's pendent dome,
That now is void, and dank with rain,
And one,—O, hope more frail than foam !
The bird to his deserted home
Sings not,—' We meet again ! '

The loath gate swings with rusty creak ;
Once, parting there, we played at pain ;
There came a parting, when the weak
And fading lips essayed to speak
Vainly,—' We meet again ! '

Somewhere is comfort, somewhere faith,
Though thou in outer dark remain ;
One sweet sad voice ennobles death,
And still, for eighteen centuries saith
Softly,—' Ye meet again ! '

If earth another grave must bear,
Yet heaven hath won a sweeter strain,
And something whispers my despair,
That, from an orient chamber there,
Floats down, ' We meet again ! '

AFTER THE BURIAL

YES, faith is a goodly anchor ;
When skies are sweet as a psalm,
At the bows it lolls so stalwart,
In bluff, broad-shouldered calm.

And when over breakers to leeward
The tattered surges are hurled,
It may keep our head to the tempest,
With its grip on the base of the world.

But, after the shipwreck, tell me
What help in its iron thews,
Still true to the broken hawser,
Deep down among sea-weed and ooze?

In the breaking gulfs of sorrow,
When the helpless feet stretch out
And find in the deeps of darkness
No footing so solid as doubt,

Then better one spar of Memory,
One broken plank of the Past,
That our human heart may cling to,
Though hopeless of shore at last !

To the spirit its splendid conjectures,
To the flesh its sweet despair,
Its tears o'er the thin-worn locket
With its anguish of deathless hair !

Immortal ?   I feel it and know it,
Who doubts it of such as she ?
But that is the pang's very secret,—
Immortal away from me.

There's a narrow ridge in the grave-
    yard
Would scarce stay a child in his race,
But to me and my thought it is wider
Than the star-sown vague of Space.

Your logic, my friend, is perfect,
Your morals most drearily true ;
But, since the earth clashed on *her*
    coffin,
I keep hearing that, and not you.

Console if you will, I can bear it ;
'T is a well-meant alms of breath ;

But not all the preaching since Adam
Has made Death other than Death.

It is pagan ; but wait till you feel it,—
That jar of our earth, that dull shock
When the ploughshare of deeper
    passion
Tears down to our primitive rock.

Communion in spirit !   Forgive me,
But I, who am earthy and weak,
Would give all my incomes from
    dreamland
For a touch of her hand on my cheek.

That little shoe in the corner,
So worn and wrinkled and brown,
With its emptiness confutes you,
And argues your wisdom down.

THE DEAD HOUSE

HERE once my step was quickened,
    Here beckoned the opening door,
And welcome thrilled from the
    threshold
    To the foot it had known before.

A glow came forth to meet me
    From the flame that laughed in the
    grate,
And shadows adance on the ceiling,
    Danced blither with mine for a
    mate.

' I claim you, old friend,' yawned the
    arm-chair,
    ' This corner, you know, is your
    seat ' ;
' Rest your slippers on me,' beamed
    the fender,
' I brighten at touch of your feet.'

' We know the practised finger,'
    Said the books, ' that seems like
    brain ' ;
And the shy page rustled the secret
    It had kept till I came again.

Sang the pillow, ' My down once
    quivered
    On nightingales' throats that flew
Through moonlit gardens of Hafiz
    To gather quaint dreams for you.'

Ah me, where the Past sowed heart's-
    ease,
    The Present plucks rue for us men !
I come back : that scar unhealing
    Was not in the churchyard then.

But, I think, the house is unaltered,
    I will go and beg to look
At the rooms that were once familiar
    To my life as its bed to a brook.

Unaltered !   Alas for the sameness
    That makes the change but more !
'T is a dead man I see in the mirrors,
    'T is his tread that chills the floor !

To learn such a simple lesson,
    Need I go to Paris and Rome,
That the many make the household,
    But only one the home ?

'T was just a womanly presence,
  An influence unexprest,
But a rose she had worn, on my grave-
    sod
  Were more than long life with the
    rest !

'T was a smile, 't was a garment's
    rustle,
  'T was nothing that I can phrase,
But the whole dumb dwelling grew
    conscious,
  And put on her looks and ways.

Were it mine I would close the
    shutters,
  Like lids when the life is fled,
And the funeral fire should wind it,
  This corpse of a home that is
    dead.

For it died that autumn morning
  When she, its soul, was borne
To lie all dark on the hillside
  That looks over woodland and
    corn.

A MOOD

I go to the ridge in the forest
I haunted in days gone by,
But thou, O Memory, pourest
No magical drop in mine eye,
Nor the gleam of the secret restorest
That hath faded from earth and sky :
A Presence autumnal and sober
Invests every rock and tree,
And the aureole of October
Lights the maples, but darkens me.

Pine in the distance,   11
Patient through sun or rain,
Meeting with graceful persistence,
With yielding but rooted resistance,
The northwind's wrench and strain,
No memory of past existence
Brings thee pain ;
Right for the zenith heading,
Friendly with heat or cold,
Thine arms to the influence spreading
Of the heavens, just from of old,
Thou only aspirest the more,   22
Unregretful the old leaves shedding
That fringed thee with music before,
And deeper thy roots embedding
In the grace and the beauty of yore ;

Thou sigh'st not, ' Alas, I am older,
The green of last summer is sear ! '
But loftier, hopefuller, bolder,
Winnest broader horizons each year.

To me 't is not cheer thou art singing :
There 's a sound of the sea,   32
O mournful tree,
In thy boughs forever clinging,
And the far-off roar
Of waves on the shore
A shattered vessel flinging.

As thou musest still of the ocean
On which thou must float at last,
And seem'st to foreknow   40
The shipwreck's woe
And the sailor wrenched from the
    broken mast,
Do I, in this vague emotion,
This sadness that will not pass,
Though the air throbs with wings,
And the field laughs and sings,
Do I forebode, alas !
The ship-building longer and wearier,
The voyage's struggle and strife,
And then the darker and drearier
Wreck of a broken life ?   51

I

BIÖRN'S BECKONERS

Now Biörn, the son of Heriulf, had ill days
Because the heart within him seethed with blood
That would not be allayed with any toil,
Whether of war or hunting or the oar,
But was anhungered for some joy untried:
For the brain grew not weary with the limbs,
But, while they slept, still hammered like a Troll,
Building all night a bridge of solid dream
Between him and some purpose of his soul,
Or will to find a purpose. With the dawn   10
The sleep-laid timbers, crumbled to soft mist,
Denied all foothold. But the dream remained,
And every night with yellow-bearded kings
His sleep was haunted,—mighty men of old,
Once young as he, now ancient like the gods,
And safe as stars in all men's memories.
Strange sagas read he in their sea-blue eyes
Cold as the sea, grandly compassionless ;
Like life, they made him eager and then mocked.
Nay, broad awake, they would not let him be ;   20
They shaped themselves gigantic in the mist,
They rose far-beckoning in the lamps of heaven,
They whispered invitation in the winds,
And breath came from them, mightier than the wind,
To strain the lagging sails of his resolve,
Till that grew passion which before was wish,
And youth seemed all too costly to be staked
On the soiled cards wherewith men played their game,
Letting Time pocket up the larger life,
Lost with base gain of raiment, food, and roof.   30
' What helpeth lightness of the feet ? ' they said,
' Oblivion runs with swifter foot than they ;
Or strength of sinew ?   New men come as strong,
And those sleep nameless ; or renown in war ?
Swords grave no name on the long-memoried rock
But moss shall hide it ; they alone who wring
Some secret purpose from the unwilling gods
Survive in song for yet a little while
To vex, like us, the dreams of later men,
Ourselves a dream, and dreamlike all we did.'   40

II

THORWALD'S LAY

So Biörn went comfortless but for his thought,
And by his thought the more discomforted,

Till Eric Thurlson kept his Yule-tide feast :
And thither came he, called among the rest,
Silent, lone-minded, a church-door to mirth :
But, ere deep draughts forbade such serious song
As the grave Skald might chant nor after blush,
Then Eric looked at Thorwald where he sat
Mute as a cloud amid the stormy hall,
And said : ' O Skald, sing now an olden song,   10
Such as our fathers heard who led great lives ;
And, as the bravest on a shield is borne
Along the waving host that shouts him king,
So rode their thrones upon the thronging seas ! '
Then the old man arose ; white-haired he stood,
White-bearded, and with eyes that looked afar
From their still region of perpetual snow,
Beyond the little smokes and stirs of men :
His head was bowed with gathered flakes of years,
As winter bends the sea-foreboding pine,   20
But something triumphed in his brow and eye,
Which whoso saw it could not see and crouch :
Loud rang the emptied beakers as he mused,
Brooding his eyried thoughts ; then, as an eagle
Circles smooth-winged above the wind-vexed woods,
So wheeled his soul into the air of song
High o'er the stormy hall ; and thus he sang :
' The fletcher for his arrow-shaft picks out
Wood closest-grained, long-seasoned, straight as light ;
And from a quiver full of such as these   30
The wary bowman, matched against his peers,
Long doubting, singles yet once more the best.
Who is it needs such flawless shafts as Fate ?
What archer of his arrows is so choice,
Or hits the white so surely ?   They are men,
The chosen of her quiver ; nor for her
Will every reed suffice, or cross-grained stick
At random from life's vulgar fagot plucked :
Such answer household ends ; but she will have
Souls straight and clear, of toughest fibre, sound   40
Down to the heart of heart ; from these she strips
All needless stuff, all sapwood ; seasons them ;
From circumstance untoward feathers plucks
Crumpled and cheap ; and barbs with iron will :
The hour that passes is her quiver-boy :
When she draws bow, 't is not across the wind,
Nor 'gainst the sun her haste-snatched arrow sings,
For sun and wind have plighted faith to her :
Ere men have heard the sinew twang, behold
In the butt's heart her trembling messenger !   50

'The song is old and simple that I sing ;
But old and simple are despised as cheap,
Though hardest to achieve of human things :
Good were the days of yore, when men were tried
By ring of shields, as now by ring of words ;
But while the gods are left, and hearts of men,
And wide-doored ocean, still the days are good.
Still o'er the earth hastes Opportunity,
Seeking the hardy soul that seeks for her.
Be not abroad, nor deaf with household cares   60
That chatter loudest as they mean the least ;
Swift-willed is thrice-willed ; late means nevermore ;
Impatient is her foot, nor turns again.'
He ceased ; upon his bosom sank his beard
Sadly, as one who oft had seen her pass
Nor stayed her : and forthwith the frothy tide
Of interrupted wassail roared along ;
But Biörn, the son of Heriulf, sat apart
Musing, and, with his eyes upon the fire,
Saw shapes of arrows, lost as soon as seen.   70
'A ship,' he muttered, 'is a wingèd bridge
That leadeth every way to man's desire,
And ocean the wide gate to manful luck ' ;
And then with that resolve his heart was bent,
Which, like a humming shaft, through many a stripe
Of day and night, across the unpathwayed seas
Shot the brave prow that cut on Vinland sands
The first rune in the Saga of the West.

III

GUDRIDA'S PROPHECY

Four weeks they sailed, a speck in sky-shut seas,
Life, where was never life that knew itself,
But tumbled lubber-like in blowing whales ;
Thought, where the like had never been before
Since Thought primeval brooded the abyss ;
Alone as men were never in the world.
They saw the icy foundlings of the sea,
White cliffs of silence, beautiful by day,
Or looming, sudden-perilous, at night
In monstrous hush ; or sometimes in the dark   10
The waves broke ominous with paly gleams
Crushed by the prow in sparkles of cold fire.
Then came green stripes of sea that promised land
But brought it not, and on the thirtieth day
Low in the West were wooded shores like cloud.
They shouted as men shout with sudden hope ;
But Biörn was silent, such strange loss there is

Between the dream's fulfilment and the dream,
Such sad abatement in the goal attained.
Then Gudrida, that was a prophetess,   20
Rapt with strange influence from Atlantis, sang :
Her words : the vision was the dreaming shore's.

Looms there the New Land :
Locked in the shadow
Long the gods shut it,
Niggards of newness
They, the o'er-old.

Little it looks there,
Slim as a cloud-streak ;
It shall fold peoples
Even as a shepherd
Foldeth his flock.

Silent it sleeps now ;
Great ships shall seek it,
Swarming as salmon ;
Noise of its numbers
Two seas shall hear.

Men from the Northland,
Men from the Southland,
Haste empty-handed ;
No more than manhood
Bring they, and hands.

Dark hair and fair hair,
Red blood and blue blood,
There shall be mingled ;
Force of the ferment
Makes the New Man.

Pick of all kindreds,
King's blood shall theirs be,
Shoots of the eldest
Stock upon Midgard,
Sons of the poor.

Them waits the New Land ;
They shall subdue it,
Leaving their sons' sons
Space for the body,
Space for the soul.

Leaving their sons' sons
All things save song-craft,
Plant long in growing,
Thrusting its tap-root
Deep in the Gone.

Here men shall grow up
Strong from self-helping ;
Eyes for the present
Bring they as eagles',
Blind to the Past.

They shall make over
Creed, law, and custom ;
Driving-men, doughty
Builders of empire,
Builders of men.

Here is no singer ;
What should they sing of ?
They, the unresting ?
Labour is ugly,
Loathsome is change.

These the old gods hate,
Dwellers in dream-land,
Drinking delusion
Out of the empty
Skull of the Past.

These hate the old gods,
Warring against them ;
Fatal to Odin,
Here the wolf Fenrir
Lieth in wait.

Here the gods' Twilight
Gathers, earth-gulfing ;
Blackness of battle,
Fierce till the Old World
Flares up in fire.

Doubt not, my Northmen ;
Fate loves the fearless ;
Fools, when their roof-tree
Falls, think it doomsday ;
Firm stands the sky.

Over the ruin
See I the promise ;
Crisp waves the cornfield,
Peace-walled, the homestead
Waits open-doored.

LOWELL   Q

There lies the New Land ;
Yours to behold it,
Not to possess it ;
Slowly Fate's perfect
Fullness shall come.

Then from your strong loins
Seed shall be scattered,
Men to the marrow,
Wilderness tamers,
Walkers of waves.

Jealous, the old gods
Shut it in shadow,
Wisely they ward it,
Egg of the serpent,
Bane to them all.

Stronger and sweeter
New gods shall seek it
Fill it with man-folk
Wise for the future,
Wise from the past.

Here all is all men's,
Save only Wisdom ;
King he that wins her ;
Him hail they helmsman,
Highest of heart.

Might makes no master
Here any longer ;
Sword is not swayer ;
Here e'en the gods are
Selfish no more.

Walking the New Earth,
Lo, a divine One
Greets all men godlike,
Calls them his kindred,
He, the Divine.

Is it Thor's hammer
Rays in his right hand ?
Weaponless walks he ;
It is the White Christ,
Stronger than Thor.

Here shall a realm rise
Mighty in manhood ;
Justice and Mercy
Here set a stronghold
Safe without spear.

Weak was the Old World,
Wearily war-fenced ;
Out of its ashes,
Strong as the morning,
Springeth the New.

Beauty of promise,
Promise of beauty,
Safe in the silence
Sleep thou, till cometh
Light to thy lids !

Thee shall awaken
Flame from the furnace,
Bath of all brave ones,
Cleanser of conscience,
Welder of will.

Lowly shall love thee,
Thee, open-handed !
Stalwart shall shield thee,
Thee, worth their best blood,
Waif of the West !

Then shall come singers,
Singing no swan-song,
Birth-carols, rather,
Meet for the man child
Mighty of bone.

MAHMOOD THE IMAGE-BREAKER

OLD events have modern meanings ; only that survives
Of past history which finds kindred in all hearts and lives.

Mahmood once, the idol-breaker, spreader of the Faith,
Was at Sumnat tempted sorely, as the legend saith.

In the great pagoda's centre, monstrous and abhorred,
Granite on a throne of granite, sat the temple's lord.

Mahmood paused a moment, silenced by the silent face
That, with eyes of stone unwavering, awed the ancient place.

Then the Brahmins knelt before him, by his doubt made bold,
Pledging for their idol's ransom countless gems and gold.

Gold was yellow dirt to Mahmood, but of precious use,
Since from it the roots of power suck a potent juice.

' Were yon stone alone in question, this would please me well,'
Mahmood said ; ' but, with the block there, I my truth must sell.

' Wealth and rule slip down with Fortune, as her wheel turns round ;
He who keeps his faith, he only cannot be discrowned.

' Little were a change of station, loss of life or crown,
But the wreck were past retrieving if the Man fell down.'

So his iron mace he lifted, smote with might and main,
And the idol, on the pavement tumbling, burst in twain.

Luck obeys the downright striker ; from the hollow core,
Fifty times the Brahmins' offer deluged all the floor.

INVITA MINERVA

THE Bardling came where by a river grew
The pennoned reeds, that, as the westwind blew,
Gleamed and sighed plaintively, as if they knew
What music slept enchanted in each stem,
Till Pan should choose some happy one of them,
And with wise lips enlife it through and through.

The Bardling thought, ' A pipe is all I need ;
Once I have sought me out a clear, smooth reed,
And shaped it to my fancy, I proceed
To breathe such strains as, yonder mid the rocks,
The strange youth blows, that tends Admetus' flocks,
And all the maidens shall to me pay heed.'

The summer day he spent in questful round,
And many a reed he marred, but never found
A conjuring-spell to free the imprisoned sound ;
At last his vainly wearied limbs he laid
Beneath a sacred laurel's flickering shade,
And sleep about his brain her cobweb wound.

Then strode the mighty Mother through his dreams,
Saying : ' The reeds along a thousand streams
Are mine, and who is he that plots and schemes
To snare the melodies wherewith my breath
Sounds through the double pipes of Life and Death
Atoning what to men mad discord seems ?

' He seeks not me, but I seek oft in vain
For him who shall my voiceful reeds constrain,
And make them utter their melodious pain ;
He flies the immortal gift, for well he knows
His life of life must with its overflows
Flood the unthankful pipe, nor come again.

' Thou fool, who dost my harmless subjects wrong,
'T is not the singer's wish that makes the song :
The rhythmic beauty wanders dumb, how long,
Nor stoops to any daintiest instrument,
Till, found its mated lips, their sweet consent
Makes mortal breath than Time and Fate more strong.'

THE FOUNTAIN OF YOUTH

I

'T IS a woodland enchanted !
By no sadder spirit
Than blackbirds and thrushes,
That whistle to cheer it
All day in the bushes,
This woodland is haunted :
And in a small clearing,
Beyond sight or hearing
Of human annoyance,
The little fount gushes   10
First smoothly, then dashes
And gurgles and flashes,
To the maples and ashes
Confiding its joyance ;
Unconscious confiding,
Then, silent and glossy,
Slips winding and hiding
Through alder-stems mossy,
Through gossamer roots
Fine as nerves,   20
That tremble, as shoots
Through their magnetized curves
The allurement delicious
Of the water's capricious
Thrills, gushes, and swerves.

II

'T is a woodland enchanted !
I am writing no fiction ;
And this fount, its sole daughter,
To the woodland was granted
To pour holy water   30

And win benediction ;
In summer-noon flushes,
When all the wood hushes,
Blue dragon-flies knitting
To and fro in the sun,
With sidelong jerk flitting
Sink down on the rushes,
And, motionless sitting,
Hear it bubble and run,
Hear its low inward singing,   40
With level wings swinging
On green tasselled rushes,
To dream in the sun.

III

'T is a woodland enchanted !
The great August noonlight,
Through myriad rifts slanted,
Leaf and bole thickly sprinkles
With flickering gold ;
There, in warm August gloaming,
With quick, silent brightenings,   50
From meadow-lands roaming,
The firefly twinkles
His fitful heat-lightnings ;
There the magical moonlight
With meek, saintly glory
Steeps summit and wold ;
There whippoorwills plain in the
    solitudes hoary
With lone cries that wander
Now hither, now yonder,
Like souls doomed of old   60

To a mild purgatory ;
But through noonlight and moonlight
The little fount tinkles
Its silver saints'-bells,
That no sprite ill-boding
May make his abode in
Those innocent dells.

IV

'T is a woodland enchanted !
When the phebe scarce whistles
Once an hour to his fellow,   70
And, where red lilies flaunted,
Balloons from the thistles
Tell summer's disasters,
The butterflies yellow,
As caught in an eddy
Of air's silent ocean,
Sink, waver, and steady
O'er goats'-beard and asters,
Like souls of dead flowers,
With aimless emotion   80
Still lingering unready
To leave their old bowers ;
And the fount is no dumber,
But still gleams and flashes,
And gurgles and plashes,
To the measure of summer ;
The butterflies hear it,
And spell-bound are holden,
Still balancing near it
O'er the goats'-beard so golden.   90

V

'T is a woodland enchanted !
A vast silver willow,
I know not how planted,
(This wood is enchanted,
And full of surprises,)
Stands stemming a billow,
A motionless billow
Of ankle-deep mosses ;
Two great roots it crosses
To make a round basin,   100
And there the Fount rises ;
Ah, too pure a mirror
For one sick of error
To see his sad face in !
No dew-drop is stiller

In its lupin-leaf setting
Than this water moss-bounded ;
But a tiny sand-pillar
From the bottom keeps jetting,
And mermaid ne'er sounded   110
Through the wreaths of a shell,
Down amid crimson dulses
In some dell of the ocean,
A melody sweeter
Than the delicate pulses,
The soft, noiseless metre,
The pause and the swell
Of that musical motion :
I recall it, not see it ;
Could vision be clearer ?   120
Half I 'm fain to draw nearer,
Half tempted to flee it ;
The sleeping Past wake not,
Beware !
One forward step take not,
Ah ! break not
That quietude rare !
By my step unaffrighted
A thrush hops before it,
And o'er it   130
A birch hangs delighted,
Dipping, dipping, dipping its tremu-
          lous hair ;
Pure as the fountain, once
I came to the place,
(How dare I draw nearer ?)
I bent o'er its mirror,
And saw a child's face
Mid locks of bright gold in it ;
Yes, pure as this fountain once,—
Since, how much error !   140
Too holy a mirror
For the man to behold in it
His harsh, bearded countenance !

VI

'T is a woodland enchanted !
Ah, fly unreturning !
Yet stay ;—
'T is a woodland enchanted,
Where wonderful chances
Have sway ;
Luck flees from the cold one   150
But leaps to the bold one

Half-way ;
Why should I be daunted ?
Still the smooth mirror glances,
Still the amber sand dances,
One look,—then away !
O magical glass !
Canst keep in thy bosom
Shades of leaf and of blossom
When summer days pass,   160
So that when thy wave hardens
It shapes as it pleases,
Unharmed by the breezes,
Its fine hanging gardens ?
Hast those in thy keeping,
And canst not uncover,
Enchantedly sleeping,
The old shade of thy lover ?
It is there !   I have found it !
He wakes, the long sleeper !   170
The pool is grown deeper,
The sand dance is ending,
The white floor sinks, blending
With skies that below me
Are deepening and bending,
And a child's face alone
That seems not to know me,
With hair that fades golden
In the heaven-glow round it,
Looks up at my own :   180
Ah, glimpse through the portal
That leads to the throne,
That opes the child's olden
Regions Elysian !
Ah, too holy vision
For thy skirts to be holden
By soiled hand of mortal !
It wavers, it scatters,
'T is gone past recalling !
A tear's sudden falling   190
The magic cup shatters,
Breaks the spell of the waters,
And the sand cone once more,
With a ceaseless renewing,
Its dance is pursuing

On the silvery floor,
O'er and o'er,
With a noiseless and ceaseless renewing.

VII

'T is a woodland enchanted !
If you ask me, *Where is it ?*   200
I only can answer,
'T is past my disclosing ;
Not to choice is it granted
By sure paths to visit
The still pool enclosing
Its blithe little dancer ;
But in some day, the rarest
Of many Septembers,
When the pulses of air rest,
And all things lie dreaming   210
In drowsy haze steaming
From the wood's glowing embers,
Then, sometimes, unheeding,
And asking not whither,
By a sweet inward leading
My feet are drawn thither,
And, looking with awe in the magical
       mirror,
I see through my tears,
Half doubtful of seeing,
The face unperverted,   220
The warm golden being
Of a child of five years ;
And spite of the mists and the error,
And the days overcast,
Can feel that I walk undeserted,
But forever attended
By the glad heavens that bended
O'er the innocent past ;
Toward fancy or truth
Doth the sweet vision win me ?   230
Dare I think that I cast
In the fountain of youth
The fleeting reflection
Of some bygone perfection
That still lingers in me ?

YUSSOUF

A STRANGER came one night to Yussouf's tent,
Saying, ' Behold one outcast and in dread,
Against whose life the bow of power is bent,
Who flies, and hath not where to lay his head ;
I come to thee for shelter and for food,
To Yussouf, called through all our tribes " The Good." '

' This tent is mine,' said Yussouf, ' but no more
Than it is God's ; come in, and be at peace ;
Freely shalt thou partake of all my store
As I of His who buildeth over these
Our tents His glorious roof of night and day,
And at whose door none ever yet heard Nay.'

So Yussouf entertained his guest that night,
And, waking him ere day, said : ' Here is gold ;
My swiftest horse is saddled for thy flight ;
Depart before the prying day grow bold.'
As one lamp lights another, nor grows less,
So nobleness enkindleth nobleness.

That inward light the stranger's face made grand,
Which shines from all self-conquest ; kneeling low,
He bowed his forehead upon Yussouf's hand,
Sobbing : ' O Sheik, I cannot leave thee so ;
I will repay thee ; all this thou hast done
Unto that Ibrahim who slew thy son ! '

' Take thrice the gold,' said Yussouf, ' for with thee
Into the desert, never to return,
My one black thought shall ride away from me ;
First-born, for whom by day and night I yearn,
Balanced and just are all of God's decrees ;
Thou art avenged, my first-born, sleep in peace ! '

THE DARKENED MIND

THE fire is burning clear and blithely,
Pleasantly whistles the winter wind ;
We are about thee, thy friends and kindred,
On us all flickers the firelight kind ;
There thou sittest in thy wonted corner
Lone and awful in thy darkened mind.

There thou sittest ; now and then thou moanest ;
Thou dost talk with what we cannot see,
Lookest at us with an eye so doubtful,
It doth put us very far from thee ;
There thou sittest ; we would fain be nigh thee,
But we know that it can never be.

We can touch thee, still we are no nearer ;
Gather round thee, still thou art alone ;
The wide chasm of reason is between us ;
Thou confutest kindness with a moan ;
We can speak to thee, and thou canst answer,
Like two prisoners through a wall of stone.

Hardest heart would call it very awful
When thou look'st at us and seest—Oh, what ?
If we move away, thou sittest gazing
With those vague eyes at the selfsame spot,
And thou mutterest, thy hands thou wringest,
Seeing something,—us thou seëst not.

Strange it is that, in this open brightness,
Thou shouldst sit in such a narrow cell ;
Strange it is that thou shouldst be so lonesome
Where those are who love thee all so well ;
Not so much of thee is left among us
As the hum outliving the hushed bell.

WHAT RABBI JEHOSHA SAID

RABBI JEHOSHA used to say
That God made angels every day,
Perfect as Michael and the rest
First brooded in creation's nest,
Whose only office was to cry
Hosanna ! once, and then to die ,
Or rather, with Life's essence blent,
To be led home from banishment.

Rabbi Jehosha had the skill   9
To know that Heaven is in God's will ;
And doing that, though for a space
One heart-beat long, may win a grace
As full of grandeur and of glow
As Princes of the Chariot know.

'T were glorious, no doubt, to be
One of the strong-winged Hierarchy,
To burn with Seraphs, or to shine
With Cherubs, deathlessly divine ;
Yet I, perhaps, poor earthly clod,
Could I forget myself in God,   20
Could I but find my nature's clue
Simply as birds and blossoms do,
And but for one rapt moment know
'T is Heaven must come, not we must go,
Should win my place as near the throne
As the pearl-angel of its zone,
And God would listen mid the throng
For my one breath of perfect song,
That, in its simple human way,
Said all the Host of Heaven could say.   30

ALL-SAINTS

ONE feast, of holy days the crest,
  I, though no Churchman, love to
    keep,
All-Saints,—the unknown good that
    rest
  In God's still memory folded deep ;
The bravely dumb that did their deed,
  And scorned to blot it with a name,
Men of the plain heroic breed,
  That loved Heaven's silence more
    than fame.

Such lived not in the past alone,
  But thread to-day the unheeding
    street,
And stairs to Sin and Famine known
  Sing with the welcome of their feet ;

The den they enter grows a shrine,
  The grimy sash an oriel burns,
Their cup of water warms like wine,
  Their speech is filled from heavenly
    urns.

About their brows to me appears
  And aureole traced in tenderest
    light,
The rainbow-gleam of smiles through
    tears
In dying eyes, by them made bright,
  Of souls that shivered on the edge
  Of that chill ford repassed no more,
And in their mercy felt the pledge
  And sweetness of the farther shore.

A WINTER-EVENING HYMN TO MY FIRE

I

BEAUTY on my hearth-stone blazing !
To-night the triple Zoroaster
Shall my prophet be and master :
To-night will I pure Magian be,
Hymns to thy sole honour raising,
While thou leapest fast and faster,
Wild with self-delighted glee,
Or sink'st low and glowest faintly
As an aureole still and saintly,
Keeping cadence to my praising   10
Thee ! still thee ! and only thee !

II

Elfish daughter of Apollo !
Thee, from thy father stolen and bound
To serve in Vulcan's clangorous
    smithy
Prometheus (primal Yankee) found,
And, when he had tampered with thee,
(Too confiding little maid !)
In a reed's precarious hollow
To our frozen earth conveyed :
For he swore I know not what ;   20
Endless ease should be thy lot,
Pleasure that should never falter,
Lifelong play, and not a duty
Save to hover o'er the altar,

Vision of celestial beauty,
Fed with precious woods and spices ;
Then, perfidious ! having got
Thee in the net of his devices,
Sold thee into endless slavery,   29
Made thee a drudge to boil the pot,
Thee, Helios' daughter, who dost bear
His likeness in thy golden hair ;
Thee, by nature wild and wavery,
Palpitating, evanescent
As the shade of Dian's crescent,
Life, motion, gladness, everywhere !

III

Fathom deep men bury thee
In the furnace dark and still,
There, with dreariest mockery,
Making thee eat, against thy will,
Blackest Pennsylvanian stone ;   41
But thou dost avenge thy doom,
For, from out thy catacomb,
Day and night thy wrath is blown
In a withering simoom,
And, adown that cavern drear,
Thy black pitfall in the floor,
Staggers the lusty antique cheer,
Despairing, and is seen no more !

IV

Elfish I may rightly name thee ;   50
We enslave, but cannot tame thee ;
With fierce snatches, now and then,
Thou pluckest at thy right again,
And thy down-trod instincts savage
To stealthy insurrection creep,
While thy wittol masters sleep,
And burst in undiscerning ravage :
Then how thou shak'st thy bacchant
    locks !
While brazen pulses, far and near,
Throb thick and thicker, wild with
    fear   60
And dread conjecture, till the drear
Disordered clangour every steeple
    rocks !

V

But when we make a friend of thee,
And admit thee to the hall
On our nights of festival,
Then, Cinderella, who could see
In thee the kitchen's stunted thrall ?
Once more a Princess lithe and tall,
Thou dancest with a whispering tread,
While the bright marvel of thy head
In crinkling gold floats all abroad,
And gloriously dost vindicate   72
The legend of thy lineage great,
Earth-exiled daughter of the Pythian
    god !
Now in the ample chimney-place,
To honour thy acknowledged race,
We crown thee high with laurel good,
Thy shining father's sacred wood,   78
Which, guessing thy ancestral right,
Sparkles and snaps his dumb delight,
And, at thy touch, poor outcast one,
Feels through his gladdened fibres go
The tingle and thrill and vassal glow
Of instincts loyal to the sun.

VI

O thou of home the guardian Lar,
And, when our earth hath wandered
    far
Into the cold, and deep snow covers
The walks of our New England lovers,

Their sweet secluded evening-star !
'T was with thy rays the English
    Muse   90
Ripened her mild domestic hues ;
'T was by thy flicker that she conned
The fireside wisdom that enrings
With light from heaven familiar
    things ;
By thee she found the homely faith
In whose mild eyes thy comfort
    stay'th,
When Death, extinguishing his torch,
Gropes for the latch-string in the
    porch ;
The love that wanders not beyond
His earliest nest, but sits and sings
While children smooth his patient
    wings ;   101
Therefore with thee I love to read
Our brave old poets : at thy touch
    how stirs
Life in the withered words ! how swift
    recede
Time's shadows ! and how glows
    again
Through its dead mass the incandes-
    cent verse,
As when upon the anvils of the brain
It glittering lay, cyclopically wrought
By the fast-throbbing hammers of the
    poet's thought !
Thou murmurest, too, divinely stirred,
The aspirations unattained,   111
The rhythms so rathe and delicate,
They bent and strained
And broke, beneath the sombre
    weight
Of any airiest mortal word.

VII

What warm protection dost thou bend
Round curtained talk of friend with
    friend,
While the grey snow-storm, held
    aloof,
To softest outline rounds the roof,
Or the rude North with baffled strain
Shoulders the frost-starred window-
    pane !   121

Now the kind nymph to Bacchus born
By Morpheus' daughter, she that
    seems
Gifted upon her natal morn
By him with fire, by her with dreams,
Nicotia, dearer to the Muse
Than all the grape's bewildering juice,
We worship, unforbid of thee;
And, as her incense floats and curls
In airy spires and wayward whirls,
Or poises on its tremulous stalk   131
A flower of frailest reverie,
So winds and loiters, idly free,
The current of unguided talk,
Now laughter-rippled, and now
    caught
In smooth, dark pools of deeper
    thought.
Meanwhile thou mellowest every
    word,
A sweetly unobtrusive third;
For thou hast magic beyond wine,
To unlock natures each to each;   140
The unspoken thought thou canst
    divine;
Thou fill'st the pauses of the speech
With whispers that to dream-land
    reach
And frozen fancy-springs unchain
In Arctic outskirts of the brain;
Sun of all inmost confidences,
To thy rays doth the heart unclose
Its formal calyx of pretences,
That close against rude day's offences,
And open its shy midnight rose! 150

VIII

Thou holdest not the master key
With which thy Sire sets free the
    mystic gates
Of Past and Future: not for common
    fates
Do they wide open fling,
And, with a far-heard ring,
Swing back their willing valves
    melodiously;

Only to ceremonial days,
And great processions of imperial song
That set the world at gaze,   159
Doth such high privilege belong:
But thou a postern-door canst ope
To humbler chambers of the selfsame
    palace
Where Memory lodges, and her sister
    Hope,
Whose being is but as a crystal chalice
Which, with her various mood, the
    elder fills
Of joy or sorrow,
So colouring as she wills
With hues of yesterday the uncon-
    scious morrow.

IX

Thou sinkest, and my fancy sinks
    with thee:
For thee I took the idle shell,   170
And struck the unused chords again,
But they are gone who listened well;
Some are in heaven, and all are far
    from me:
Even as I sing, it turns to pain,
And with vain tears my eyelids throb
    and swell:
Enough; I come not of the race
That hawk their sorrows in the
    market-place.
Earth stops the ears I best had loved
    to please;
Then break, ye untuned chords, or
    rust in peace!
As if a white-haired actor should come
    back   180
Some midnight to the theatre void
    and black,
And there rehearse his youth's great
    part
Mid thin applauses of the ghosts,
So seems it now: ye crowd upon my
    heart,
And I bow down in silence, shadowy
    hosts!

FANCY'S CASUISTRY

How struggles with the tempest's
    swells
That warning of tumultuous bells !
The fire is loose ! and frantic knells
    Throb fast and faster,
As tower to tower confusedly tells
    News of disaster.

But on my far-off solitude
No harsh alarums can intrude ;
The terror comes to me subdued
    And charmed by distance,
To deepen the habitual mood
    Of my existence.

Are those, I muse, the Easter
    chimes ?
And listen, weaving careless rhymes
While the loud city's griefs and crimes
    Pay gentle allegiance
To the fine quiet that sublimes
    These dreamy regions.

And when the storm o'erwhelms the
    shore,
I watch entranced as, o'er and o'er,
The light revolves amid the roar
    So still and saintly,
Now large and near, now more and
    more
    Withdrawing faintly.

This, too, despairing sailors see
Flash out the breakers 'neath their
    lee
In sudden snow, then lingeringly
    Wane tow'rd eclipse,
While through the dark the shudder-
    ing sea
    Gropes for the ships.

And is it right, this mood of mind
That thus, in reverie enshrined,
Can in the world mere topics find
    For musing stricture,
Seeing the life of humankind
    Only as picture ?

The events in line of battle go ;
In vain for me their trumpets blow
As unto him that lieth low
    In death's dark arches,
And through the sod hears throbbing
    slow
    The muffled marches.

O Duty, am I dead to thee
In this my cloistered ecstasy,
In this lone shallop on the sea
    That drifts tow'rd Silence ?
And are those visioned shores I see
    But sirens' islands ?

My Dante frowns with lip-locked mien,
As who would say, ' 'T is those, I
    ween,
Whom lifelong armour-chafe makes
    lean
    That win the laurel ' ;
But where *is* Truth ?　What does it
    mean,
    The world-old quarrel ?

Such questionings are idle air :
Leave what to do and what to spare
To the inspiring moment's care,
    Nor ask for payment
Of fame or gold, but just to wear
    Unspotted raiment.

TO MR. JOHN BARTLETT

WHO HAD SENT ME A SEVEN-POUND TROUT

Fit for an Abbot of Theleme,
    For the whole Cardinals' College,
        or
The Pope himself to see in dream
Before his lenten vision gleam,
    He lies there, the sogdologer !

His precious flanks with stars be-
    sprent,
    Worthy to swim in Castaly !
The friend by whom such gifts are sent,
For him shall bumpers full be spent,
    His health ! be Luck his fast ally !

I see him trace the wayward brook
  Amid the forest mysteries,
Whereat their shades shy aspens look,
Or where, with many a gurgling crook,
  It croons its woodland histories.

I see leaf-shade and sun-fleck lend
  Their tremulous, sweet vicissitude
To smooth, dark pool, to crinkling
  bend,—
(O, stew him, Ann, as 't were your
  friend,
  With amorous solicitude !)

I see him step with caution due,
  Soft as if shod with moccasins,
Grave as in church, for who plies you,
Sweet craft, is safe as in a pew
  From all our common stock o'
  sins.

The unerring fly I see him cast,
  That as a rose-leaf falls as soft,
A flash ! a whirl ! he has him fast !
We tyros, how that struggle last
  Confuses and appalls us oft.

Unfluttered he : calm as the sky
  Looks on our tragi-comedies,

This way and that he lets him fly,
A sunbeam-shuttle, then to die
  Lands him, with cool *aplomb*, at
  ease.

The friend who gave our board such
  gust,
  Life's care may he o'erstep it
  half,
And, when Death hooks him, as he
  must,
He 'll do it handsomely, I trust,
  And John H—— write his
  epitaph !

O, born beneath the Fishes' sign,
  Of constellations happiest,
May he somewhere with Walton dine,
May Horace send him Massic wine,
  And Burns Scotch drink, the
  nappiest !

And when they come his deeds to
  weigh,
  And how he used the talents his,
One trout-scale in the scales he 'll lay
(If trout had scales), and 't will
  outsway
  The wrong side of the balances.

ODE TO HAPPINESS

SPIRIT, that rarely comest now
  And only to contrast my gloom,
  Like rainbow-feathered birds that
  bloom
A moment on some autumn bough
That, with the spurn of their farewell,
Sheds its last leaves,—thou once
  didst dwell
  With me year-long, and make
  intense
To boyhood's wisely vacant days
Their fleet but all-sufficing grace
  Of trustful inexperience,   10
  While soul could still transfigure
  sense,

And thrill, as with love's first
  caress,
At life's mere unexpectedness.
  Days when my blood would leap
  and run
  As full of sunshine as a breeze,
  Or spray tossed up by Summer
  seas
That doubts if it be sea or sun !
Days that flew swiftly like the band
  That played in Grecian games at
  strife,
And passed from eager hand to
  hand   20
  The onward-dancing torch of life !

Wing-footed ! thou abid'st with him
  Who asks it not ; but he who hath
  Watched o'er the waves thy
    waning path,
Shall nevermore behold returning
Thy high-heaped canvas shoreward
  yearning !
Thou first reveal'st to us thy face
Turned o'er the shoulder's parting
    grace,
  A moment glimpsed, then seen no
    more,—
Thou whose swift footsteps we can
  trace   30
  Away from every mortal door.

Nymph of the unreturning feet,
  How may I win thee back ? But
    no,
I do thee wrong to call thee so ;
'T is I am changed, not thou art fleet :
The man thy presence feels again,
Not in the blood, but in the brain,
Spirit, that lov'st the upper air
Serene and passionless and rare,
  Such as on mountain heights we
    find   40
  And wide-viewed uplands of the
    mind ;
Or such as scorns to coil and sing
Round any but the eagle's wing
  Of souls that with long upward
    beat
  Have won an undisturbed retreat
Where, poised like wingèd victories,
They mirror in relentless eyes
  The life broad-basking 'neath their
    feet,—
Man ever with his Now at strife,
  Pained with first gasps of earthly
    air,   50
  Then praying Death the last to
    spare,
Still fearful of the ampler life.

Not unto them dost thou consent
  Who, passionless, can lead at ease
A life of unalloyed content
  A life like that of land-locked seas,

Who feel no elemental gush
Of tidal forces, no fierce rush
  Of storm deep-grasping scarcely
    spent   59
'Twixt continent and continent.
Such quiet souls have never known
  Thy truer inspiration, thou
Who lov'st to feel upon thy brow
Spray from the plunging vessel thrown
  Grazing the tusked lee shore, the
    cliff
That o'er the abrupt gorge holds its
    breath,
  Where the frail hair-breadth of an *if*
Is all that sunders life and death :
These, too, are cared-for, and round
    these
Bends her mild crook thy sister
  Peace ;   70
These in unvexed dependence lie,
  Each 'neath his strip of household
    sky ;
O'er these clouds wander, and the blue
Hangs motionless the whole day
    through ;
  Stars rise for them, and moons
    grow large
And lessen in such tranquil wise
As joys and sorrows do that rise
  Within their nature's sheltered
    marge ;
Their hours into each other flit
  Like the leaf-shadows of the vine
And fig-tree under which they sit,
  And their still lives to heaven in-
    cline   82
With an unconscious habitude,
  Unhistoried as smokes that rise
From happy hearths and sight elude
  In kindred blue of morning skies.

Wayward ! when once we feel thy
    lack,
'Tis worse than vain to woo thee back !
  Yet there is one who seems to be
Thine elder sister, in whose eyes 90
A faint far northern light will rise
  Sometimes, and bring a dream of
    thee ;

She is not that for which youth hoped,
But she hath blessings all her own,
Thoughts pure as lilies newly oped,
And faith to sorrow given alone :
Almost I deem that it is thou
Come back with graver matron brow,
With deepened eyes and bated breath,
Like one that somewhere hath met Death,   100
But ' No,' she answers, ' I am she
Whom the gods love, Tranquillity :
That other whom you seek forlorn
Half earthly was ; but I am born
Of the immortals, and our race

Wears still some sadness on its face :
He wins me late, but keeps me long,
Who, dowered with every gift of passion,
In that fierce flame can forge and fashion   109
Of sin and self the anchor strong ;
Can thence compel the driving force
Of daily life's mechanic course,
Nor less the nobler energies
Of needful toil and culture wise ;
Whose soul is worth the tempter's lure
Who can renounce, and yet endure,
To him I come, not lightly wooed,
But won by silent fortitude.'

VILLA FRANCA

1859

Wait a little : do *we* not wait ?
Louis Napoleon is not Fate,
Francis Joseph is not Time ;
There 's One hath swifter feet than Crime ;
Cannon-parliaments settle naught ;
Venice is Austria's,—whose is Thought ?
Minié is good, but, spite of change,
Gutenberg's gun has the longest range.
Spin, spin, Clotho, spin !
Lachesis, twist ! and, Atropos, sever !
In the shadow, year out, year in,
The silent headsman waits forever.

Wait, we say : our years are long ;
Men are weak, but Man is strong ;
Since the stars first curved their rings,
We have looked on many things ;
Great wars come and great wars go,
Wolf-tracks light on polar snow ;
We shall see him come and gone,
This second-hand Napoleon.
Spin, spin, Clotho, spin !
Lachesis, twist ! and, Atropos, sever !
In the shadow, year out, year in,
The silent headsman waits forever.

We saw the elder Corsican,
And Clotho muttered as she span,
While crowned lackeys bore the train,
Of the pinchbeck Charlemagne :
' Sister, stint not length of thread !
Sister, stay the scissors dread !
On Saint Helen's granite bleak,
Hark, the vulture whets his beak ! '
Spin, spin, Clotho, spin !
Lachesis, twist ! and, Atropos, sever !
In the shadow, year out, year in,
The silent headsman waits forever.

The Bonapartes, we know their bees
That wade in honey red to the knees ;
Their patent reaper, its sheaves sleep sound
In dreamless garners underground :
We know false glory's spendthrift race
Pawning nations for feathers and lace ;
It may be short, it may be long,
' 'T is reckoning day ! ' sneers unpaid Wrong.
Spin, spin, Clotho, spin !
Lachesis, twist ! and, Atropos, sever !
In the shadow, year out, year in,
The silent headsman waits forever.

The Cock that wears the Eagle's skin
Can promise what he ne'er could win ;
Slavery reaped for fine words sown,
System for all, and rights for none,
Despots atop, a wild clan below,
Such is the Gaul from long ago ;
Wash the black from the Ethiop's face,
Wash the past out of man or race !
  Spin, spin, Clotho, spin !
    Lachesis, twist ! and, Atropos, sever !
  In the shadow, year out, year in,
  The silent headsman waits forever.

'Neath Gregory's throne a spider swings,
And snares the people for the kings ;
' Luther is dead ; old quarrels pass ;
The stake's black scars are healed with grass ' ;
So dreamers prate ; did man ere live

Saw priest or woman yet forgive ?
But Luther's broom is left, and eyes
Peep o'er their creeds to where it lies.
  Spin, spin, Clotho, spin !
    Lachesis, twist ! and, Atropos, sever !
  In the shadow, year out, year in,
  The silent headsman waits forever.

Smooth sails the ship of either realm,
Kaiser and Jesuit at the helm ;
We look down the depths, and mark
Silent workers in the dark
Building slow the sharp-tusked reefs,
Old instincts hardening to new beliefs ;
Patience a little ; learn to wait ;
Hours are long on the clock of Fate.
  Spin, spin, Clotho, spin !
    Lachesis, twist ! and, Atropos, sever !
  Darkness is strong, and so is Sin,
  But surely God endures forever !

THE MINER

Down 'mid the tangled roots of things
  That coil about the central fire,
I seek for that which giveth wings
  To stoop, not soar, to my desire.

Sometimes I hear, as 't were a sigh,
  The sea's deep yearning far above,
' Thou hast the secret not,' I cry,
  ' In deeper deeps is hid my Love.'

They think I burrow from the sun,
  In darkness, all alone, and weak ;
Such loss were gain if He were won,
  For 't is the sun's own Sun I seek.

' The earth,' they murmur, ' is the tomb
  That vainly sought his life to prison ;
Why grovel longer in the gloom ?
  He is not here ; he hath arisen.'

More life for me where he hath lain
  Hidden while ye believed him dead,

Than in cathedrals cold and vain,
  Built on loose sands of *It is said*.

My search is for the living gold ;
  Him I desire who dwells recluse,
And not his image worn and old,
  Day-servant of our sordid use.

If him I find not, yet I find
  The ancient joy of cell and church,
The glimpse, the surety undefined,
  The unquenched ardour of the search.

Happier to chase a flying goal
  Than to sit counting laurelled gains,
To guess the Soul within the soul
  Than to be lord of what remains.

Hide still, best Good, in subtile wise,
  Beyond my nature's utmost scope ;
Be ever absent from mine eyes
  To be twice present in my hope !

GOLD EGG: A DREAM-FANTASY

HOW A STUDENT IN SEARCH OF THE BEAUTIFUL FELL ASLEEP IN DRESDEN
OVER HERR PROFESSOR DOCTOR VISCHER'S WISSENSCHAFT DES SCHÖNEN,
AND WHAT CAME THEREOF.

I SWAM with undulation soft,
  Adrift on Vischer's ocean,
And, from my cockboat up aloft,
Sent down my mental plummet oft
  In hope to reach a notion.

But from the metaphysic sea
  No bottom was forthcoming,
And all the while (how drearily!)
In one eternal note of B
  My German stove kept humming.

'What's Beauty?' mused I; 'is it
    told
  By synthesis? analysis?
Have you not made us lead of gold?
To feed your crucible, not sold
  Our temple's sacred chalices?'

Then o'er my senses came a change;
  My book seemed all traditions,
Old legends of profoundest range,
Diablery, and stories strange
  Of goblins, elves, magicians.

Old gods in modern saints I found,
  Old creeds in strange disguises;
I thought them safely underground,
And here they were, all safe and
    sound,
  Without a sign of phthisis.

Truth was, my outward eyes were
    closed,
  Although I did not know it;
Deep into dream-land I had dozed
And so was happily transposed
  From proser into poet.

So what I read took flesh and blood,
  And turned to living creatures:
The words were but the dingy bud
That bloomed, like Adam, from the
    mud,
  To human forms and features.

I saw how Zeus was lodged once more
  By Baucis and Philemon;
The text said, 'Not alone of yore,
But every day, at every door,
  Knocks still the masking Demon.'

DAIMON 't was printed in the book
  And, as I read it slowly,
The letters stirred and changed, and
    took
Jove's stature, the Olympian look
  Of painless melancholy.

He paused upon the threshold worn:
  'With coin I cannot pay you;
Yet would I fain make some return;
The gift for cheapness do not spurn,
  Accept this hen, I pray you.

'Plain feathers wears my Hemera,
  And has from ages olden;
She makes her nest in common hay,
And yet, of all the birds that lay,
  Her eggs alone are golden.'

He turned, and could no more be seen;
  Old Baucis stared a moment,
Then tossed poor Partlet on the green,
And with a tone, half jest, half spleen,
  Thus made her housewife's com-
    ment:

'The stranger had a queerish face,
  His smile was hardly pleasant,
And, though he meant it for a grace,
Yet this old hen of barnyard race
  Was but a stingy present.

'She's quite too old for laying eggs,
  Nay, even to make a soup of;
One only needs to see her legs,—
You might as well boil down the pegs
  I made the brood-hen's coop of!

'Some eighteen score of such do I
　　Raise every year, her sisters ;
Go, in the woods your fortunes try,
All day for one poor earthworm pry,
　　And scratch your toes to blisters ! '

Philemon found the rede was good,
　　And, turning on the poor hen,
He clapt his hands, and stamped, and
　　shooed,
Hunting the exile tow'rd the wood,
　　To house with snipe and moor-hen.

A poet saw and cried : ' Hold ! hold !
　　What are you doing, madman ?
Spurn you more wealth than can be
　　told,
The fowl that lays the eggs of gold,
　　Because she 's plainly clad, man ? '

To him Philemon : ' I 'll not balk
　　Thy will with any shackle ;
Wilt add a burden to thy walk ?
There ! take her without further talk ;
　　You 're both but fit to cackle ! '

But scarce the poet touched the bird,
　　It swelled to stature regal ;
And when her cloud-wide wings she
　　stirred,
A whisper as of doom was heard,
　　'T was Jove's bolt-bearing eagle.

As when from far-off cloud-bergs
　　springs
　　A crag, and, hurtling under,
From cliff to cliff the rumour flings,
So she from flight-foreboding wings
　　Shook out a murmurous thunder.

She gripped the poet to her breast,
　　And, ever upward soaring,
Earth seemed a new moon in the west,
And then one light among the rest
　　Where squadrons lie at mooring.

How tell to what heaven-hallowed
　　seat
　　The eagle bent his courses ?
The waves that on its bases beat,
The gales that round it weave and
　　fleet,
　　Are life's creative forces.

Here was the bird's primeval nest,
　　High on a promontory
Star-pharosed, where she takes her
　　rest
To brood new æons 'neath her breast,
　　The future's unfledged glory.

I know not how, but I was there
　　All feeling, hearing, seeing ;
It was not wind that stirred my hair
But living breath, the essence rare
　　Of unembodied being.

And in the nest an egg of gold
　　Lay soft in self-made lustre,
Gazing whereon, what depths untold
Within, what marvels manifold,
　　Seemed silently to muster !

Daily such splendours to confront
　　Is still to me and you sent ?
It glowed as when Saint Peter's front,
Illumed, forgets its stony wont,
　　And seems to throb translucent.

One saw therein the life of man,
　　(Or so the poet found it,)
The yolk and white, conceive who can,
Were the glad earth, that, floating,
　　span
　　In the glad heaven around it.

I knew this as one knows in dream,
　　Where no effects to causes
Are chained as in our work-day
　　scheme,
And then was wakened by a scream
　　That seemed to come from Baucis.

' Bless Zeus ! ' she cried, ' I 'm safe
　　below ! '
　　First pale, then red as coral ;
And I, still drowsy, pondered slow,
And seemed to find, but hardly know,
　　Something like this for moral.

Each day the world is born anew
　　For him who takes it rightly ;
Not fresher that which Adam knew,
Not sweeter that whose moonlit dew
　　Entranced Arcadia nightly.

Rightly ? That 's simply : 't is to see
  Some substance casts these shadows
Which we call Life and History,
That aimless seem to chase and flee
  Like wind-gleams over meadows.

Simply ? That 's nobly : 't is to
  know
  That God may still be met with,

Nor groweth old, nor doth bestow
These senses fine, this brain aglow,
  To grovel and forget with.

Beauty, Herr Doctor, trust in me,
  No chemistry will win you ;
Charis still rises from the sea :
If you can't find her, *might* it be
  Because you seek within you ?

A FAMILIAR EPISTLE TO A FRIEND

ALIKE I hate to be your debtor,
Or write a mere perfunctory letter ;
For letters, so it seems to me,
Our careless quintessence should be,
Our real nature's truant play
When Consciousness looks t' other
  way
Not drop by drop, with watchful skill,
Gathered in Art's deliberate still,
But life's insensible completeness
Got as the ripe grape gets its sweet-
  ness,   10
As if it had a way to fuse
The golden sunlight into juice.
Hopeless my mental pump I try ;
The boxes hiss, the tube is dry ;
As those petroleum wells that spout
Awhile like M. C.'s, then give out,
My spring, once full as Arethusa,
Is a mere bore as dry 's Creusa ;
And yet you ask me why I 'm glum,
And why my graver Muse is dumb.
Ah me ! I 've reasons manifold   21
Condensed in one,—I 'm getting old !

When life, once past its fortieth year,
Wheels up its evening hemisphere,
The mind's own shadow, which the
  boy
Saw onward point to hope and joy,
Shifts round, irrevocably set
Tow'rd morning's loss and vain regret,
And, argue with it as we will,
The clock is unconverted still.   30

'But count the gains,' I hear you say,
'Which far the seeming loss outweigh ;

Friendships built firm 'gainst flood
  and wind
On rock-foundations of the mind ;
Knowledge instead of scheming hope ;
For wild adventure, settled scope ;
Talents, from surface-ore profuse,
Tempered and edged to tools for use ;
Judgement, for passion's headlong
  whirls ;   39
Old sorrows crystalled into pearls ;
Losses by patience turned to gains,
Possessions now, that once were pains ;
Joy's blossom gone, as go it must,
To ripen seeds of faith and trust ;
Why heed a snow-flake on the roof
If fire within keep Age aloof
Though blundering north-winds push
  and strain
With palms benumbed against the
  pane ? '

My dear old Friend, you 're very wise;
We always are with others' eyes,   50
And see *so* clear ! (our neighbour's
  deck on)
What reef the idiot's sure to wreck on ;
Folks when they learn how life has
  quizzed 'em
Are fain to make a shift with Wisdom,
And, finding she nor breaks nor bends,
Give her a letter to their friends.
Draw passion's torrent whoso will
Through sluices smooth to turn a mill,
And, taking solid toll of grist,
Forget the rainbow in the mist,   60
The exulting leap, the aimless haste
Scattered in iridescent waste ;

Prefer who likes the sure esteem
To cheated youth's midsummer dream,
When every friend was more than Damon,
Each quicksand safe to build a fame on ;
Believe that prudence snug excels
Youth's gross of verdant spectacles,
Through which earth's withered stubble seen
Looks autumn-proof as painted green,—   70
I side with Moses 'gainst the masses,
Take you the drudge, give me the glasses !
And, for your talents shaped with practice,
Convince me first that such the fact is ;
Let whoso like be beat, poor fool,
On life's hard stithy to a tool,
Be whoso will a ploughshare made,
Let me remain a jolly blade !
What 's Knowledge, with her stocks and lands,
To gay Conjecture's yellow strands ?
What 's watching her slow flocks increase   81
To ventures for the golden fleece ?
What her deep ships, safe under lee,
To youth's light craft, that drinks the sea,
For Flying Islands making sail,
And failing where 't is gain to fail ?
Ah me ! Experience (so we 're told),
Time's crucible, turns lead to gold ;
Yet what 's experience won but dross,
Cloud-gold transmuted to our loss ?
What but base coin the best event
To the untried experiment ?   92

'T was an old couple, says the poet,
That lodged the gods and did not know it ;
Youth sees and knows them as they were
Before Olympus' top was bare ;
From Swampscot's flats his eye divine
Sees Venus rocking on the brine,
With lucent limbs, that somehow scatter a   99
Charm that turns Doll to Cleopatra ;
Bacchus (that now is scarce induced
To give Eld's lagging blood a boost),
With cymbals' clang and pards to draw him,
Divine as Ariadne saw him,
Storms through Youth's pulse with all his train
And wins new Indies in his brain ;
Apollo (with the old a trope,
A sort of finer Mister Pope),
Apollo—but the Muse forbids ;   109
At his approach cast down thy lids,
And think it joy enough to hear
Far off his arrows singing clear ;
He knows enough who silent knows
The quiver chiming as he goes ;
He tells too much who e'er betrays
The shining Archer's secret ways.

Dear Friend, you 're right and I am wrong ;
My quibbles are not worth a song,
And I sophistically tease   119
My fancy sad to tricks like these.
I could not cheat you if I would ;
You know me and my jesting mood,
Mere surface-foam, for pride concealing
The purpose of my deeper feeling.
I have not spilt one drop of joy
Poured in the senses of the boy,
Nor Nature fails my walks to bless
With all her golden inwardness ;
And as blind nestlings, unafraid,
Stretch up wide-mouthed to every shade   130
By which their downy dream is stirred,
Taking it for the mother-bird,
So, when God's shadow, which is light,
Unheralded, by day or night,
My wakening instincts falls across,
Silent as sunbeams over moss,
In my heart's nest half-conscious things
Stir with a helpless sense of wings,

Lift themselves up, and tremble long
With premonitions sweet of song.

Be patient, and perhaps (who knows?)
These may be winged one day like
    those ;   142
If thrushes, close-embowered to sing,
Pierced through with June's delicious
    sting ;
If swallows, their half-hour to run
Star-breasted in the setting sun.
At first they 're but the unfledged
    proem,
Or songless schedule of a poem ;
When from the shell they 're hardly
    dry
If some folks thrust them forth,
    must I ?   150

But let me end with a comparison
Never yet hit upon by e'er a son
Of our American Apollo,
(And there 's where I shall beat them
    hollow,
If he is not a courtly St. John,
But, as West said, a Mohawk Injun.)
A poem's like a cruise for whales :
Through untried seas the hunter sails,
His prow dividing waters known
To the blue iceberg's hulk alone ; 160
At last, on farthest edge of day,
He marks the smoky puff of spray ;
Then with bent oars the shallop flies
To where the basking quarry lies ;

Then the excitement of the strife,
The crimsoned waves,—ah, this is life!

But, the dead plunder once secured
And safe beside the vessel moored,
All that had stirred the blood before
Is so much blubber, nothing more,
(I mean no pun, nor image so 171
Mere sentimental verse, you know,)
And all is tedium, smoke, and soil,
In trying out the noisome oil.

Yes, this *is* life ! And so the bard
Through briny deserts, never scarred
Since Noah's keel, a subject seeks,
And lies upon the watch for weeks ;
That once harpooned and helpless
    lying,
What follows is but weary trying.

Now I 've a notion, if a poet 181
Beat up for themes, his verse will
    show it ;
I wait for subjects that hunt me,
By day or night won't let me be,
And hang about me like a curse,
Till they have made me into verse,
From line to line my fingers tease
Beyond my knowledge, as the bees
Build no new cell till those before
With limpid summer-sweet run o'er ;
Then, if I neither sing nor shine, 191
Is it the subject's fault, or mine ?

AN EMBER PICTURE

How strange are the freaks of
    memory !
  The lessons of life we forget,
While a trifle, a trick of colour,
  In the wonderful web is set,—

Set by some mordant of fancy,
  And, spite of the wear and tear
Of time or distance or trouble,
  Insists on its right to be there.

A chance had brought us together ;
  Our talk was of matters-of-course ;
We were nothing, one to the other,
  But a short half-hour's resource.

We spoke of French acting and actors,
  And their easy, natural way :
Of the weather, for it was raining
  As we drove home from the play.

We debated the social nothings
  We bore ourselves so to discuss ;
The thunderous rumours of battle
  Were silent the while for us.

Arrived at her door, we left her
  With a drippingly hurried adieu,
And our wheels went crunching the
    gravel
  Of the oak-darkened avenue.

As we drove away through the
    shadow,
  The candle she held in the door
From rain-varnished tree-trunk to
    tree-trunk
  Flashed fainter, and flashed no
    more ;—

Flashed fainter, then wholly faded
  Before we had passed the wood ;
But the light of the face behind it
  Went with me and stayed for good.

The vision of scarce a moment,
  And hardly marked at the time,
It comes unbidden to haunt me,
  Like a scrap of ballad-rhyme.

Had she beauty ? Well, not what
    they call so ;
  You may find a thousand as fair ;

And yet there's her face in my
    memory
  With no special claim to be there.

As I sit sometimes in the twilight,
  And call back to life in the coals
Old faces and hopes and fancies
    Long buried, (good rest to their
    souls !)

Her face shines out in the embers ;
  I see her holding the light,
And hear the crunch of the gravel
  And the sweep of the rain that
    night.

'T is a face that can never grow older,
  That never can part with its
    gleam,
'T is a gracious possession forever,
  For is it not all a dream ?

TO H. W. L.

ON HIS BIRTHDAY, 27TH FEBRUARY, 1867

I NEED not praise the sweetness of his song,
  Where limpid verse to limpid verse succeeds
Smooth as our Charles, when, fearing lest he wrong
The new moon's mirrored skiff, he slides along,
  Full without noise, and whispers in his reeds.

With loving breath of all the winds his name
  Is blown about the world, but to his friends
A sweeter secret hides behind his fame,
And Love steals shyly through the loud acclaim
  To murmur a *God bless you !* and there ends.

As I muse backward up the chequered years
  Wherein so much was given, so much was lost,
Blessings in both kinds, such as cheapen tears,—
But hush ! this is not for profaner ears ;
  Let them drink molten pearls nor dream the cost.

Some suck up poison from a sorrow's core,
  As naught but nightshade grew upon earth's ground ;
Love turned all his to heart's-ease, and the more
Fate tried his bastions, she but forced a door
  Leading to sweeter manhood and more sound.

Even as a wind-waved fountain's swaying shade
   Seems of mixed race, a grey wraith shot with sun,
So through his trial faith translucent rayed
Till darkness, half disnatured so, betrayed
   A heart of sunshine that would fain o'errun.

Surely if skill in song the shears may stay
   And of its purpose cheat the charmed abyss,
If our poor life be lengthened by a lay,
He shall not go, although his presence may,
   And the next age in praise shall double this.

Long days be his, and each as lusty-sweet
   As gracious natures find his song to be ;
May Age steal on with softly-cadenced feet
Falling in music, as for him were meet
   Whose choicest verse is harsher-toned than he !

THE NIGHTINGALE IN THE STUDY

'Come forth ! ' my catbird calls to me,
   ' And hear me sing a cavatina
That, in this old familiar tree,
   Shall hang a garden of Alcina.

' These buttercups shall brim with wine
   Beyond all Lesbian juice or Massic;
May not New England be divine ?
   My ode to ripening summer classic ?

' Or, if to me you will not hark,
   By Beaver Brook a thrush is ringing
Till all the alder-coverts dark
   Seem sunshine-dappled with his singing.

' Come out beneath the unmastered sky,
   With its emancipating spaces,
And learn to sing as well as I,
   Without premeditated graces.

' What boot your many-volumed gains,
   Those withered leaves forever turning,
To win, at best, for all your pains,
   A nature mummy-wrapt in learning ?

' The leaves wherein true wisdom lies
   On living trees the sun are drinking;
Those white clouds, drowsing through the skies,
   Grew not so beautiful by thinking.

' Come out ! with me the oriole cries,
   Escape the demon that pursues you !
And, hark, the cuckoo weatherwise,
   Still hiding, farther onward wooes you.'

' Alas, dear friend, that, all my days,
   Has poured from that syringa thicket
The quaintly discontinuous lays
   To which I hold a season-ticket,

' A season-ticket cheaply bought
   With a dessert of pilfered berries,
And who so oft my soul hast caught
   With morn and evening voluntaries,

' Deem me not faithless, if all day
   Among my dusty books I linger,
No pipe, like thee, for June to play
   With fancy-led, half-conscious finger.

' A bird is singing in my brain
    And bubbling o'er with mingled
        fancies,
Gay, tragic, rapt, right heart of Spain
    Fed with the sap of old romances.

' I ask no ampler skies than those
    His magic music rears above me,
No falser friends, no truer foes,—
    And does not Doña Clara love me ?

' Cloaked shapes, a twanging of
        guitars,
    A rush of feet, and rapiers clashing,
Then silence deep with breathless
        stars,
    And overhead a white hand flashing.

' O music of all moods and climes,
    Vengeful,   forgiving,   sensuous,
        saintly,

Where still, between the Christian
        chimes,
    The moorish cymbal tinkles faintly !

' O life borne lightly in the hand,
    For   friend   or   foe   with   grace
        Castilian !
O valley safe in Fancy's land,
    Not tramped to mud yet by the
        million !

' Bird of to-day, thy songs are stale
    To his, my singer of all weathers,
My Calderon, my nightingale,
    My Arab soul in Spanish feathers.

' Ah, friend, these singers dead so
        long,
    And still, God knows, in purgatory,
Give its best sweetness to all song,
    To Nature's self her better glory.'

IN THE TWILIGHT

Men say the sullen instrument,
    That, from the Master's bow,
    With pangs of joy or woe,
Feels music's soul through every fibre
        sent,
    Whispers the ravished strings
More than he knew or meant ;
    Old summers in its memory glow ;
    The secrets of the wind it sings ;
    It hears the April-loosened springs ;
    And mixes with its mood   10
    All it dreamed when it stood
    In the murmurous pine-wood
        Long ago !

The magical moonlight then
    Steeped every bough and cone ;
The roar of the brook in the glen
Came dim from the distance blown ;
The wind through its glooms sang low,
    And it swayed to and fro
        With delight as it stood,   20
        In the wonderful wood,
        Long ago !

O my life, have we not had seasons
    That only said, Live and rejoice ?
That asked not for causes and reasons,
    But made us all feeling and voice ?
When we went with the winds in their
        blowing,
    When Nature and we were peers,
And we seemed to share in the flowing
    Of the inexhaustible years ?   30
    Have we not from the earth drawn
        juices
    Too fine for earth's sordid uses ?
        Have I heard, have I seen
        All I feel and I know ?
        Doth my heart overween ?
        Or could it have been
            Long ago ?

Sometimes a breath floats by me,
    An odour from Dreamland sent,
That makes the ghost seem nigh me
    Of a splendour that came and went,
Of a life lived somewhere, I know not
    In what diviner sphere,   43

Of memories that stay not and go not,
  Like music heard once by an ear
    That cannot forget or reclaim it,
    A something so shy, it would
        shame it
      To make it a show,
    A something too vague, could
        I name it,
      For others to know, 50
As if I had lived it or dreamed it,
As if I had acted or schemed it,
      Long ago !

And yet, could I live it over,
  This life that stirs in my brain,
Could I be both maiden and lover,
Moon and tide, bee and clover,
  As I seem to have been, once again,
Could I but speak and show it,
  This pleasure more sharp than pain,
    That baffles and lures me so,
The world should not lack a poet,
    Such as it had 63
    In the ages glad,
      Long ago !

THE FOOT-PATH

It mounts athwart the windy hill
  Through sallow slopes of upland
      bare,
And Fancy climbs with foot-fall still
  Its narrowing curves that end in air.

By day, a warmer-hearted blue
  Stoops softly to that topmost swell;
Its thread-like windings seem a clue
  To gracious climes where all is well.

By night, far yonder, I surmise
  An ampler world than clips my ken,
Where the great stars of happier skies
  Commingle nobler fates of men.

I look and long, then haste me home,
  Still master of my secret rare ;
Once tried, the path would end in
      Rome,
  But now it leads me everywhere.

Forever to the new it guides,
  From former good, old overmuch ;
What Nature for her poets hides,
  'T is wiser to divine than clutch.

The bird I list hath never come
  Within the scope of mortal ear ;
My prying step would make him
      dumb,
  And the fair tree, his shelter, sear.

Behind the hill, behind the sky,
  Behind my inmost thought, he
      sings ;
No feet avail ; to hear it nigh,
  The song itself must lend the wings.

Sing on, sweet bird, close hid, and raise
  Those angel stairways in my brain,
That climb from these low-vaulted
      days
    To spacious sunshines far from pain.

Sing when thou wilt, enchantment
      fleet,
  I leave thy covert haunt untrod,
And envy Science not her feat,
  To make a twice-told tale of God.

They said the fairies tript no more,
  And long ago that Pan was dead ;
'T was but that fools preferred to bore
  Earth's rind inch-deep for truth
      instead.

Pan leaps and pipes all summer long,
  The fairies dance each full-mooned
      night,
Would we but doff our lenses strong,
  And trust our wiser eyes' delight.

City of Elf-land, just without
  Our seeing, marvel ever new,

Glimpsed in fair weather, a sweet
    doubt
  Sketched-in, mirage-like, on the
    blue.

I build thee in yon sunset cloud,
  Whose edge allures to climb the
    height ;
I hear thy drowned bells, inly-loud,
  From still pools dusk with dreams
    of night.

Thy gates are shut to hardiest will,
  Thy countersign of long-lost
    speech,—

Those fountained courts, those cham-
    bers still,
  Fronting Time's far East, who shall
    reach ?

I know not, and will never pry,
  But trust our human heart for all ;
Wonders that from the seeker fly
  Into an open sense may fall.

Hide in thine own soul, and surprise
  The password of the unwary elves ;
Seek it, thou canst not bribe their
    spies ;
  Unsought, they whisper it them-
    selves.

POEMS OF THE WAR

THE WASHERS OF THE SHROUD

October, 1861

Along a river-side, I know not where,
I walked one night in mystery of dream ;
A chill creeps curdling yet beneath my hair,
To think what chanced me by the pallid gleam
Of a moon-wraith that waned through haunted air.

Pale fireflies pulsed within the meadow-mist
Their halos, wavering thistledowns of light ;
The loon, that seemed to mock some goblin tryst,
Laughed ; and the echoes, huddling in affright,
Like Odin's hounds, fled baying down the night.

Then all was silent, till there smote my ear
A movement in the stream that checked my breath :
Was it the slow plash of a wading deer ?
But something said, ' This water is of Death !
The Sisters wash a shroud,—ill thing to hear ! '

I, looking then, beheld the ancient Three
Known to the Greek's and to the Northman's creed,
That sit in shadow of the mystic Tree,
Still crooning, as they weave their endless brede,
One song : ' Time was, Time is, and Time shall be.'

No wrinkled crones were they, as I had deemed,
But fair as yesterday, to-day, to-morrow,
To mourner, lover, poet, ever seemed ;
Something too high for joy, too deep for sorrow,
Thrilled in their tones, and from their faces gleamed.

' Still men and nations reap as they have strawn,'
So sang they, working at their task the while ;
' The fatal raiment must be cleansed ere dawn :
For Austria ?   Italy ?   the Sea-Queen's isle ?
O'er what quenched grandeur must our shroud be drawn ?

' Or is it for a younger, fairer corse,
That gathered States like children round his knees,
That tamed the wave to be his posting-horse,
Feller of forests, linker of the seas,
Bridge-builder, hammerer, youngest son of Thor's ?

' What make we, murmur'st thou ? and what are we ?
When empires must be wound, we bring the shroud,
The time-old web of the implacable Three :
Is it too coarse for him, the young and proud ?
Earth's mightiest deigned to wear it,—why not he ?

' Is there no hope ? ' I moaned, ' so strong, so fair !
Our Fowler whose proud bird would brook erewhile
No rival's swoop in all our western air !
Gather the ravens, then, in funeral file
For him, life's morn yet golden in his hair ?

' Leave me not hopeless, ye unpitying dames !
I see, half seeing. Tell me, ye who scanned
The stars, Earth's elders, still must noblest aims
Be traced upon oblivious ocean-sands ?
Must Hesper join the wailing ghosts of names ? '

' When grass-blades stiffen with red battle-dew,
Ye deem we choose the victor and the slain :
Say, choose we them that shall be leal and true
To the heart's longing, the high faith of brain ?
Yet there the victory lies, if ye but knew.

' Three roots bear up Dominion : Knowledge, Will,—
These twain are strong, but stronger yet the third,—
Obedience,—'tis the great tap-root that still,
Knit round the rock of Duty, is not stirred,
Though Heaven-loosed tempests spend their utmost skill.

' Is the doom sealed for Hesper ? 'T is not we
Denounce it, but the Law before all time :
The brave makes danger opportunity ;
The waverer, paltering with the chance sublime,
Dwarfs it to peril : which shall Hesper be ?

' Hath he let vultures climb his eagle's seat
To make Jove's bolts purveyors of their maw ?
Hath he the Many's plaudits found more sweet
Than Wisdom ? held Opinion's wind for Law ?
Then let him hearken for the doomster's feet !

' Rough are the steps, slow-hewn in flintiest rock,
States climb to power by ; slippery those with gold
Down which they stumble to eternal mock :
No chafferer's hand shall long the sceptre hold,
Who, given a Fate to shape, would sell the block.

' We sing old Sagas, songs of weal and woe,
Mystic because too cheaply understood ;
Dark sayings are not ours ; men hear and know,
See Evil weak, see strength alone in Good,
Yet hope to stem God's fire with walls of tow.

' Time Was unlocks the riddle of Time Is,
That offers choice of glory or of gloom ;
The solver makes Time Shall Be surely his.
But hasten, Sisters ! for even now the tomb
Grates its slow hinge and calls from the abyss.'

' But not for him,' I cried, ' not yet for him,
Whose large horizon, westering, star by star
Wins from the void to where on Ocean's rim
The sunset shuts the world with golden bar,
Not yet his thews shall fail, his eye grow dim !

' His shall be larger manhood, saved for those
That walk unblenching through the trial-fires ;
Not suffering, but faint heart, is worst of woes,
And he no base-born son of craven sires,
Whose eye need blench confronted with his foes.

' Tears may be ours, but proud, for those who win
Death's royal purple in the foeman's lines ;
Peace, too, brings tears ; and mid the battle-din,
The wiser ear some text of God divines,
For the sheathed blade may rust with darker sin.

' God, give us peace ! not such as lulls to sleep,
But sword on thigh, and brow with purpose knit !
And let our Ship of State to harbour sweep,
Her ports all up, her battle-lanterns lit,
And her leashed thunders gathering for their leap ! '

So cried I with clenched hands and passionate pain,
Thinking of dear ones by Potomac's side ;
Again the loon laughed mocking, and again
The echoes bayed far down the night and died,
While waking I recalled my wandering brain.

TWO SCENES FROM THE LIFE OF BLONDEL

Autumn, 1863

Scene I.—*Near a castle in Germany*

'T were no hard task, perchance, to win
The popular laurel for my song ;
'T were only to comply with sin,
And own the crown, though snatched by wrong :
Rather Truth's chaplet let me wear,
Though sharp as death its thorns may sting ;
Loyal to Loyalty, I bear
No badge but of my rightful king.

Patient by town and tower I wait,
Or o'er the blustering moorland go ;
I buy no praise at cheaper rate,
Or what faint hearts may fancy so ;
For me, no joy in lady's bower,
Or hall, or tourney, will I sing,
Till the slow stars wheel round the hour
That crowns my hero and my king.

While all the land runs red with strife,
  And wealth is won by pedler-crimes,
Let who will find content in life
  And tinkle in unmanly rhymes;
I wait and seek; through dark and
    light,
  Safe in my heart my hope I bring,
Till I once more my faith may plight
  To him my whole soul owns her king.

When power is filched by drone and
    dolt,
  And, with caught breath and flash-
    ing eye,
Her knuckles whitening round the bolt,
  Vengeance leans eager from the sky,
While this and that the people guess,
  And to the skirts of praters cling,
Who court the crowd they should
    compress,
  I turn in scorn to seek my king.

Shut in what tower of darkling chance
  Or dungeon of a narrow doom,
Dream'st thou of battle-axe and lance
  That for the Cross make crashing
    room?
Come! with hushed breath the
    battle waits
  In the wild van thy mace's swing;
While doubters parley with their
    fates,
  Make thou thine own and ours, my
    king!

O, strong to keep upright the old,
  And wise to buttress with the new,
Prudent, as only are the bold,
  Clear-eyed, as only are the true,
To foes benign, to friendship stern,
  Intent to imp Law's broken wing,
Who would not die, if death might earn
  The right to kiss thy hand, my king?

SCENE II.—*An Inn near the Château of Chalus*

WELL, the whole thing is over, and here I sit
  With one arm in a sling and a milkscore of gashes,
And this flagon of Cyprus must e'en warm my wit,
  Since what's left of youth's flame is a head flecked with ashes.
I remember I sat in this very same inn,—
  I was young then, and one young man thought I was handsome,—
I had found out what prison King Richard was in,
  And was spurring for England to push on the ransom.

How I scorned the dull souls that sat guzzling around
  And knew not my secret nor recked my derision!
Let the world sink or swim, John or Richard be crowned,
  All one, so the beer-tax got lenient revision.
How little I dreamed, as I tramped up and down,
  That granting our wish one of Fate's saddest jokes is!
I had mine with a vengeance,—my king got his crown,
  And made his whole business to break other folks's.

I might as well join in the safe old *tum, tum* :
  A hero's an excellent loadstar,—but, bless ye,
What infinite odds 'twixt a hero to come
  And your only too palpable hero *in esse* !
Precisely the odds (such examples are rife)
  'Twixt the poem conceived and the rhyme we make show of,
'Twixt the boy's morning dream and the wake-up of life,
  'Twixt the Blondel God meant and a Blondel I know of !

But the world's better off, I 'm convinced of it now,
  Than if heroes, like buns, could be bought for a penny
To regard all mankind as their haltered milch-cow,
  And just care for themselves. Well, God cares for the many ;
For somehow the poor old Earth blunders along,
  Each son of hers adding his mite of unfitness,
And, choosing the sure way of coming out wrong,
  Gets to port as the next generation will witness.

You think her old ribs have come all crashing through,
  If a whisk of Fate's broom snap your cobweb asunder ;
But her rivets were clinched by a wiser than you,
  And our sins cannot push the Lord's right hand from under.
Better one honest man who can wait for God's mind
  In our poor shifting scene here though heroes were plenty !
Better one bite, at forty, of Truth's bitter rind,
  Than the hot wine that gushed from the vintage of twenty !

I see it all now : when I wanted a king,
  'T was the kingship that failed in myself I was seeking,—
'T is so much less easy to do than to sing,
  So much simpler to reign by a proxy than *be* king !
Yes, I think I *do* see : after all 's said and sung,
  Take this one rule of life and you never will rue it,—
'T is but do your own duty and hold your own tongue
  And Blondel were royal himself, if he knew it !

MEMORIAE POSITUM

R. G. S.

I

BENEATH the trees,
  My lifelong friends in this dear spot,
  Sad now for eyes that see them not,
I hear the autumnal breeze
Wake the sear leaves to sigh for glad-
      ness gone,
Whispering hoarse presage of ob-
      livion,—
  Hear, restless as the seas,
Time's grim feet rustling through the
      withered grace
Of many a spreading realm and
      strong-stemmed race,
  Even as my own through these.

  Why make we moan
For loss that doth enrich us yet
With upward yearnings of regret ?

Bleaker than unmossed stone
Our lives were but for this immortal
      gain
Of unstilled longing and inspiring
      pain !
As thrills of long-hushed tone
Live in the viol, so our souls grow fine
With keen vibrations from the touch
      divine
  Of noble natures gone.

  'T were indiscreet
To vex the shy and sacred grief
With harsh obtrusions of relief ;
  Yet, Verse, with noiseless feet,
Go whisper : ' *This* death hath far
      choicer ends
Than slowly to impearl in hearts of
      friends ;

These obsequies 't is meet
Not to seclude in closets of the heart,
But, church-like, with wide doorways,
    to impart
    Even to the heedless street.'

II

Brave, good, and true,
I see him stand before me now,
And read again on that young brow,
    Where every hope was new,
How sweet were life! Yet, by the
    mouth firm-set,
And look made up for Duty's utmost
    debt,
    I could divine he knew
That death within the sulphurous
    hostile lines,
In the mere wreck of nobly-pitched
    designs,
    Plucks heart's-ease, and not rue.

Happy their end
Who vanish down life's evening
    stream
    Placid as swans that drift in dream
    Round the next river-bend !
Happy long life, with honour at the
    close,
Friends' painless tears, the softened
    thought of foes !
    And yet, like him, to spend
All at a gush, keeping our first faith
    sure
From mid-life's doubt and eld's
    contentment poor,—
    What more could Fortune send ?

Right in the van,
On the red rampart's slippery swell,
With heart that beat a charge, he
    fell
    Foeward, as fits a man ;
But the high soul burns on to light
    men's feet
Where death for noble ends makes
    dying sweet ;
    His life her crescent's span
Orbs full with share in their un-
    darkening days

Who ever climbed the battailous
    steeps of praise
    Since valour's praise began.

III

His life's expense
Hath won for him coeval youth
With the immaculate prime of
    Truth ;
    While we, who make pretence
At living on, and wake and eat and
    sleep,
And life's stale trick by repetition keep,
    Our fickle permanence
(A poor leaf-shadow on a brook, whose
    play
Of busy idlesse ceases with our day)
    Is the mere cheat of sense.

We bide our chance,
Unhappy, and make terms with Fate
    A little more to let us wait ;
    He leads for aye the advance,
Hope's forlorn-hopes that plant the
    desperate good
For nobler Earths and days of man-
    lier mood ;
    Our wall of circumstance
Cleared at a bound, he flashes o'er the
    fight,
A saintly shape of fame, to cheer the
    right
    And steel each wavering glance.

I write of one,
While with dim eyes I think of
    three ;
    Who weeps not others fair and
    brave as he ?
    Ah, when the fight is won,
Dear Land, whom triflers now make
    bold to scorn,
(Thee ! from whose forehead Earth
    awaits her morn,)
    How nobler shall the sun
Flame in thy sky, how braver breathe
    thy air,
That thou bred'st children who for
    thee could dare
    And die as thine have done !

1863.

ON BOARD THE '76

WRITTEN FOR MR. BRYANT'S SEVENTIETH BIRTHDAY

NOVEMBER 3, 1864

OUR ship lay tumbling in an angry sea,
　　Her rudder gone, her mainmast o'er the side ;
Her scuppers, from the waves' clutch staggering free,
　　Trailed threads of priceless crimson through the tide ;
Sails, shrouds, and spars with pirate cannon torn,
　　　　We lay, awaiting morn.

Awaiting morn, such morn as mocks despair ;
　　And she that bore the promise of the world
Within her sides, now hopeless, helmless, bare,
　　At random o'er the wildering waters hurled ;
The reek of battle drifting slow alee
　　　　Not sullener than we.

Morn came at last to peer into our woe,
　　When lo, a sail ! Now surely help was nigh ;
The red cross flames aloft, Christ's pledge ; but no,
　　Her black guns grinning hate, she rushes by
And hails us :—' Gains the leak ! Aye, so we thought !
　　　　Sink, then, with curses fraught ! '

I leaned against my gun still angry-hot,
　　And my lids tingled with the tears held back ;
This scorn methought was crueller than shot :
　　The manly death-grip in the battle-wrack,
Yard-arm to yard-arm, were more friendly far
　　　　Than such fear-smothered war.

There our foe wallowed, like a wounded brute
　　The fiercer for his hurt. What now were best ?
Once more tug bravely at the peril's root,
　　Though death came with it ? Or evade the test
If right or wrong in this God's world of ours
　　　　Be leagued with higher powers ?

Some, faintly loyal, felt their pulses lag
　　With the slow beat that doubts and then despairs ;
Some, caitiff, would have struck the starry flag
　　That knits us with our past, and makes us heirs
Of deeds high-hearted as were ever done
　　　　'Neath the all-seeing sun.

But there was one, the Singer of our crew,
　　Upon whose head Age waved his peaceful sign,
But whose red heart's-blood no surrender knew ;
　　And couchant under brows of massive line,
The eyes, like guns beneath a parapet,
　　　　Watched, charged with lightnings yet.

LOWELL   R

The voices of the hills did his obey ;
        The torrents flashed and tumbled in his song ;
He brought our native fields from far away,
        Or set us 'mid the innumerable throng
Of dateless woods, or where we heard the calm
        Old homestead's evening psalm.

But now he sang of faith to things unseen,
        Of freedom's birthright given to us in trust ;
And words of doughty cheer he spoke between,
        That made all earthly fortune seem as dust,
Matched with that duty, old as Time and new,
        Of being brave and true.

We, listening, learned what makes the might of words,—
        Manhood to back them, constant as a star ;
His voice rammed home our cannon, edged our swords,
        And sent our boarders shouting ; shroud and spar
Heard him and stiffened ; the sails heard, and wooed
        The winds with loftier mood.

In our dark hours he manned our guns again ;
        Remanned ourselves from his own manhood's store ;
Pride, honour, country, throbbed through all his strain ;
        And shall we praise ?   God's praise was his before ;
And on our futile laurels he looks down,
        Himself our bravest crown.

ODE RECITED AT THE HARVARD COMMEMORATION

JULY 21, 1865

I

WEAK-WINGED is song,
Nor aims at that clear-ethered height
Whither the brave deed climbs for light :
        We seem to do them wrong,
Bringing our robin's-leaf to deck their hearse
Who in warm life-blood wrote their nobler verse,
Our trivial song to honour those who come
With ears attuned to strenuous trump and drum,
And shaped in squadron-strophes their desire,
Live battle-odes whose lines were steel and fire :
        Yet sometimes feathered words are strong,
A gracious memory to buoy up and save
From Lethe's dreamless ooze, the common grave
        Of the unventurous throng.

II

To-day our Reverend Mother welcomes back
　Her wisest Scholars, those who understood
The deeper teaching of her mystic tome,
　　And offered their fresh lives to make it good :
　　　　No lore of Greece or Rome,
No science peddling with the names of things,　　　　　20
Or reading stars to find inglorious fates,
　　　　Can lift our life with wings
Far from Death's idle gulf that for the many waits,
　　　　And lengthen out our dates
With that clear fame whose memory sings
In manly hearts to come, and nerves them and dilates :
Nor such thy teaching, Mother of us all !
　　　　Not such the trumpet-call
　　　　Of thy diviner mood,
　　　　That could thy sons entice　　　　　　　30
From happy homes and toils, the fruitful nest
Of those half-virtues which the world calls best,
　　　　Into War's tumult rude ;
　　　　But rather far that stern device
The sponsors chose that round thy cradle stood
　　　　In the dim, unventured wood,
　　　　The VERITAS that lurks beneath
　　　　The letter's unprolific sheath,
　Life of whate'er makes life worth living,
Seed-grain of high emprise, immortal food,　　　　　40
　　One heavenly thing whereof earth hath the giving.

III

Many loved Truth, and lavished life's best oil
　Amid the dust of books to find her,
Content at last, for guerdon of their toil,
　With the cast mantle she hath left behind her.
　　Many in sad faith sought for her,
　　Many with crossed hands sighed for her ;
　　But these, our brothers, fought for her
　　At life's dear peril wrought for her,
　　So loved her that they died for her,　　　　　50
　　Tasting the raptured fleetness
　　Of her divine completeness :
　　　Their higher instinct knew
Those love her best who to themselves are true,
And what they dare to dream of, dare to do ;
　　They followed her and found her
　　Where all may hope to find,
Not in the ashes of the burnt-out mind,
But beautiful, with danger's sweetness round her.
　　Where faith made whole with deed　　　　60

Breathes its awakening breath
Into the lifeless creed,
They saw her plumed and mailed,
With sweet, stern face unveiled,
And all-repaying eyes, look proud on them in death.

IV

Our slender life runs rippling by, and glides
Into the silent hollow of the past ;
What is there that abides
To make the next age better for the last ?
Is earth too poor to give us   70
Something to live for here that shall outlive us ?
Some more substantial boon
Than such as flows and ebbs with Fortune's fickle moon ?
The little that we see
From doubt is never free ;
The little that we do
Is but half-nobly true ;
With our laborious hiving
What men call treasure, and the gods call dross,
Life seems a jest of Fate's contriving,   80
Only secure in every one's conniving,
A long account of nothings paid with loss,
Where we poor puppets, jerked by unseen wires,
After our little hour of strut and rave,
With all our pasteboard passions and desires,
Loves, hates, ambitions, and immortal fires,
Are tossed pell-mell together in the grave.
But stay ! no age was e'er degenerate,
Unless men held it at too cheap a rate,
For in our likeness still we shape our fate.   90
Ah, there is something here
Unfathomed by the cynic's sneer,
Something that gives our feeble light
A high immunity from Night,
Something that leaps life's narrow bars
To claim its birthright with the hosts of heaven ;
A seed of sunshine that doth leaven
Our earthy dullness with the beams of stars,
And glorify our clay
With light from fountains elder than the Day ;   100
A conscience more divine than we,
A gladness fed with secret tears,
A vexing, forward-reaching sense
Of some more noble permanence ;
A light across the sea,
Which haunts the soul and will not let it be,
Still glimmering from the heights of undegenerate years.

V

Whither leads the path
To ampler fates that leads ?
Not down through flowery meads,   110
To reap an aftermath
Of youth's vainglorious weeds,
But up the steep, amid the wrath
And shock of deadly-hostile creeds,
Where the world's best hope and stay
By battle's flashes gropes a desperate way,
And every turf the fierce foot clings to bleeds.
Peace hath her not ignoble wreath,
Ere yet the sharp, decisive word
Light the black lips of cannon, and the sword   120
Dreams in its easeful sheath ;
But some day the live coal behind the thought,
Whether from Baäl's stone obscene,
Or from the shrine serene
Of God's pure altar brought,
Bursts up in flame ; the war of tongue and pen
Learns with what deadly purpose it was fraught,
And, helpless in the fiery passion caught,
Shakes all the pillared state with shock of men :
Some day the soft Ideal that we wooed   130
Confronts us fiercely, foe-beset, pursued,
And cries reproachful : ' Was it, then, my praise,
And not myself was loved ? Prove now thy truth ;
I claim of thee the promise of thy youth ;
Give me thy life, or cower in empty phrase,
The victim of thy genius, not its mate ! '
Life may be given in many ways,
And loyalty to Truth be sealed
As bravely in the closet as the field,
So bountiful is Fate ;   140
But then to stand beside her,
When craven churls deride her,
To front a lie in arms and not to yield,
This shows, methinks, God's plan
And measure of a stalwart man,
Limbed like the old heroic breeds,
Who stands self-poised on manhood's solid earth,
Not forced to frame excuses for his birth,
Fed from within with all the strength he needs.

VI

Such was he, our Martyr-Chief,   150
Whom late the Nation he had led,
With ashes on her head,
Wept with the passion of an angry grief :

Forgive me, if from present things I turn
To speak what in my heart will beat and burn,
And hang my wreath on his world-honoured urn.
    Nature, they say, doth dote,
    And cannot make a man
    Save on some worn-out plan,
    Repeating us by rote :   160
For him her Old-World moulds aside she threw,
    And, choosing sweet clay from the breast
        Of the unexhausted West,
With stuff untainted shaped a hero new,
Wise, steadfast in the strength of God, and true.
    How beautiful to see
Once more a shepherd of mankind indeed,
Who loved his charge, but never loved to lead ;
One whose meek flock the people joyed to be,
    Not lured by any cheat of birth,   170
    But by his clear-grained human worth,
And brave old wisdom of sincerity !
    They knew that outward grace is dust ;
    They could not choose but trust
In that sure-footed mind's unfaltering skill,
    And supple-tempered will
That bent like perfect steel to spring again and thrust.
    His was no lonely mountain-peak of mind,
    Thrusting to thin air o'er our cloudy bars,
    A sea-mark now, now lost in vapours blind ;   180
    Broad prairie rather, genial, level-lined,
    Fruitful and friendly for all human kind,
Yet also nigh to heaven and loved of loftiest stars.
    Nothing of Europe here,
Or, then, of Europe fronting mornward still,
    Ere any names of Serf and Peer
    Could Nature's equal scheme deface ;
    And thwart her genial will ;
Here was a type of the true elder race,
And one of Plutarch's men talked with us face to face.   190
    I praise him not ; it were too late ;
And some innative weakness there must be
In him who condescends to victory
Such as the Present gives, and cannot wait,
    Safe in himself as in a fate.
    So always firmly he :
    He knew to bide his time,
    And can his fame abide,
Still patient in his simple faith sublime,
    Till the wise years decide.   200
  Great captains, with their guns and drums,
    Disturb our judgement for the hour,

But at last silence comes;
These all are gone, and, standing like a tower,
Our children shall behold his fame,
The kindly-earnest, brave, foreseeing man,
Sagacious, patient, dreading praise, not blame,
New birth of our new soil, the first American.

VII

Long as man's hope insatiate can discern
Or only guess some more inspiring goal   210
Outside of Self, enduring as the pole,
Along whose course the flying axles burn
Of spirits bravely-pitched, earth's manlier brood;
Long as below we cannot find
The meed that stills the inexorable mind;
So long this faith to some ideal Good,
Under whatever mortal names it masks,
Freedom, Law, Country, this ethereal mood
That thanks the Fates for their severer tasks,
Feeling its challenged pulses leap,   220
While others skulk in subterfuges cheap,
And, set in Danger's van, has all the boon it asks,
Shall win man's praise and woman's love,
Shall be a wisdom that we set above
All other skills and gifts to culture dear,
A virtue round whose forehead we inwreathe
Laurels that with a living passion breathe
When other crowns grow, while we twine them, sear
What brings us thronging these high rites to pay,
And seal these hours the noblest of our year,   230
Save that our brothers found this better way?

VIII

We sit here in the Promised Land
That flows with Freedom's honey and milk;
But 't was they won it, sword in hand,
Making the nettle danger soft for us as silk.
We welcome back our bravest and our best;—
Ah me! not all! some come not with the rest,
Who went forth brave and bright as any here!
I strive to mix some gladness with my strain,
But the sad strings complain,   240
And will not please the ear:
I sweep them for a pæan, but they wane
Again and yet again
Into a dirge, and die away, in pain.
In these brave ranks I only see the gaps,
Thinking of dear ones whom the dumb turf wraps
Dark to the triumph which they died to gain:

Fitlier may others greet the living,
For me the past is unforgiving;
   I with uncovered head   250
    Salute the sacred dead,
Who went, and who return not.—Say not so
'T is not the grapes of Canaan that repay,
But the high faith that failed not by the way;
Virtue treads paths that end not in the grave;
No bar of endless night exiles the brave;
     And to the saner mind
We rather seem the dead that stayed behind.
Blow, trumpets, all your exultations blow!
For never shall their aureoled presence lack: 260
I see them muster in a gleaming row,
With ever-youthful brows that nobler show;
We find in our dull road their shining track;
    In every nobler mood
We feel the orient of their spirit glow,
Part of our life's unalterable good,
Of all our saintlier aspiration;
    They come transfigured back,
Secure from change in their high-hearted ways,
Beautiful evermore, and with the rays   270
Of morn on their white Shields of Expectation!

IX

   But is there hope to save
Even this ethereal essence from the grave?
What ever 'scaped Oblivion's subtle wrong
Save a few clarion names, or golden threads of song?
    Before my musing eye
  The mighty ones of old sweep by,
Disvoicèd now and insubstantial things,
As noisy once as we; poor ghosts of kings,
Shadows of empire wholly gone to dust,   280
And many races, nameless long ago,
To darkness driven by that imperious gust
Of ever-rushing Time that here doth blow:
O visionary world, condition strange,
Where naught abiding is but only Change,
Where the deep-bolted stars themselves still shift and range!
Shall we to more continuance make pretence?
Renown builds tombs; a life-estate is Wit;
   And, bit by bit,
The cunning years steal all from us but woe;   290
  Leaves are we, whose decays no harvest sow.
   But, when we vanish hence,
Shall they lie forceless in the dark below,

Save to make green their little length of sods,
Or deepen pansies for a year or two,
Who now to us are shining-sweet as gods ?
Was dying all they had the skill to do ?
That were not fruitless : but the Soul resents
Such short-lived service, as if blind events
Ruled without her, or earth could so endure ;   300
She claims a more divine investiture
Of longer tenure than Fame's airy rents ;
Whate'er she touches doth her nature share ;
Her inspiration haunts the ennobled air,
        Gives eyes to mountains blind,
Ears to the deaf earth, voices to the wind,
And her clear trump sings succour everywhere
By lonely bivouacs to the wakeful mind ;
For soul inherits all that soul could dare :
        Yea, Manhood hath a wider span   310
And larger privilege of life than man.
The single deed, the private sacrifice,
So radiant now through proudly-hidden tears,
Is covered up erelong from mortal eyes
With thoughtless drift of the deciduous years ;
But that high privilege that makes all men peers,
That leap of heart whereby a people rise
        Up to a noble anger's height,
And, flamed on by the Fates, not shrink, but grow more bright,
        That swift validity in noble veins,   320
        Of choosing danger and disdaining shame,
            Of being set on flame
        By the pure fire that flies all contact base,
But wraps its chosen with angelic might,
        These are imperishable gains,
    Sure as the sun, medicinal as light,
    These hold great futures in their lusty reins
And certify to earth a new imperial race.

X

        Who now shall sneer ?
    Who dare again to say we trace   330
    Our lines to a plebeian race ?
        Roundhead and Cavalier !
Dumb are those names erewhile in battle loud ;
Dream-footed as the shadow of a cloud,
    They flit across the ear :
That is best blood that hath most iron in 't,
To edge resolve with, pouring without stint
        For what makes manhood dear.
    Tell us not of Plantagenets,

Hapsburgs, and Guelfs, whose thin bloods crawl   340
Down from some victor in a border-brawl !
  How poor their outworn coronets,
Matched with one leaf of that plain civic wreath
Our brave for honour's blazon shall bequeath,
  Through whose desert a rescued Nation sets
Her heel on treason, and the trumpet hears
Shout victory, tingling Europe's sullen ears
  With vain resentments and more vain regrets !

XI

    Not in anger, not in pride,
    Pure from passion's mixture rude   350
    Ever to base earth allied,
    But with far-heard gratitude,
    Still with heart and voice renewed,
To heroes living and dear martyrs dead,
The strain should close that consecrates our brave.
  Lift the heart and lift the head !
      Lofty be its mood and grave,
      Not without a martial ring,
      Not without a prouder tread
      And a peal of exultation :   360
      Little right has he to sing
      Through whose heart in such an hour
      Beats no march of conscious power,
      Sweeps no tumult of elation !
      'T is no Man we celebrate,
      By his country's victories great,
    A hero half, and half the whim of Fate,
      But the pith and marrow of a Nation
      Drawing force from all her men,
      Highest, humblest, weakest, all,   370
      For her time of need, and then
      Pulsing it again through them,
Till the basest can no longer cower,
Feeling his soul spring up divinely tall,
Touched but in passing by her mantle-hem.
Come back, then, noble pride, for 't is her dower !
      How could poet ever tower,
      If his passions, hopes, and fears,
      If his triumphs and his tears,
      Kept not measure with his people ?   380
Boom, cannon, boom to all the winds and waves !
Clash out, glad bells, from every rocking steeple !
Banners, adance with triumph, bend your staves !
    And from every mountain-peak
    Let beacon-fire to answering beacon speak,

Katahdin tell Monadnock, Whiteface he,
And so leap on in light from sea to sea,
  Till the glad news be sent
  Across a kindling continent,
Making earth feel more firm and air breathe braver : 390
' Be proud ! for she is saved, and all have helped to save her !
  She that lifts up the manhood of the poor,
  She of the open soul and open door,
  With room about her hearth for all mankind !
  The fire is dreadful in her eyes no more ;
  From her bold front the helm she doth unbind,
  Sends all her handmaid armies back to spin,
  And bids her navies, that so lately hurled
  Their crashing battle, hold their thunders in,
  Swimming like birds of calm along the unharmful shore. 400
  No challenge sends she to the elder world,
  That looked askance and hated ; a light scorn
  Plays o'er her mouth, as round her mighty knees
  She calls her children back, and waits the morn
Of nobler day, enthroned between her subject seas.'

XII

Bow down, dear Land, for thou hast found release !
 Thy God, in these distempered days,
 Hath taught thee the sure wisdom of His ways,
And through thine enemies hath wrought thy peace !
  Bow down in prayer and praise ! 410
No poorest in thy borders but may now
Lift to the juster skies a man's enfranchised brow,
O Beautiful ! my Country ! ours once more !
Smoothing thy gold of war-dishevelled hair
O'er such sweet brows as never other wore,
  And letting thy set lips,
  Freed from wrath's pale eclipse,
The rosy edges of their smile lay bare,
What words divine of lover or of poet
Could tell our love and make thee know it, 420
Among the Nations bright beyond compare ?
  What were our lives without thee ?
  What all our lives to save thee ?
  We reck not what we gave thee ;
  We will not dare to doubt thee,
But ask whatever else, and we will dare !

L'ENVOI

TO THE MUSE

WHITHER ?   Albeit I follow fast,
   In all life's circuit I but find,
Not where thou art, but where thou wast,
   Sweet beckoner, more fleet than wind !
I haunt the pine-dark solitudes,
   With soft brown silence carpeted,
And plot to snare thee in the woods :
   Peace I o'ertake, but thou art fled !
I find the rock where thou didst rest,
The moss thy skimming foot hath prest ;   10
   All Nature with thy parting thrills,
Like branches after birds new-flown ;
   Thy passage hill and hollow fills
With hints of virtue not their own ;
In dimples still the water slips
Where thou hast dipt thy finger-tips ;
   Just, just beyond, forever burn
   Gleams of a grace without return ;
   Upon thy shade I plant my foot,
And through my frame strange raptures shoot ;   20
All of thee but thyself I grasp ;
   I seem to fold thy luring shape,
And vague air to my bosom clasp,
   Thou lithe, perpetual Escape !

One mask and then another drops,
And thou art secret as before :
   Sometimes with flooded ear I list,
   And hear thee, wondrous organist,
From mighty continental stops
A thunder of new music pour ;   30
Through pipes of earth and air and stone
Thy inspiration deep is blown ;
Through mountains, forests, open downs,
Lakes, railroads, prairies, states, and towns,
Thy gathering fugue goes rolling on
From Maine to utmost Oregon ;
The factory-wheels in cadence hum,
From brawling parties concords come ;
All this I hear, or seem to hear,
But when, enchanted, I draw near   40

To mate with words the various theme,
Life seems a whiff of kitchen steam,
History an organ-grinder's thrum,
 For thou hast slipt from it and me
And all thine organ-pipes left dumb,
 Most mutable Perversity !

Not weary yet, I still must seek,
And hope for luck next day, next week ;
I go to see the great man ride,
Shiplike, the swelling human tide   50
That floods to bear him into port,
Trophied from Senate-hall and Court ;
Thy magnetism, I feel it there,
Thy rhythmic presence fleet and rare,
Making the Mob a moment fine
With glimpses of their own Divine,
As in their demigod they see
 Their cramped ideal soaring free ;
'T was thou didst bear the fire about,
 That, like the springing of a mine   60
Sent up to heaven the street-long shout ;
Full well I know that thou wast here,
It was thy breath that brushed my ear ;
But vainly in the stress and whirl
I dive for thee, the moment's pearl.

Through every shape thou well canst run,
Proteus, 'twixt rise and set of sun,
Well pleased with logger-camps in Maine
 As where Milan's pale Duomo lies
A stranded glacier on the plain,   70
 Its peaks and pinnacles of ice
 Melted in many a quaint device,
And sees, above the city's din,
Afar its silent Alpine kin :
I track thee over carpets deep
To wealth's and beauty's inmost keep ;
Across the sand of bar-room floors
Mid the stale reek of boosing boors ;
Where drowse the hay-field's fragrant heats,
Or the flail-heart of Autumn beats ;   80
I dog thee through the market's throngs
To where the sea with myriad tongues
Laps the green edges of the pier,
And the tall ships that eastward steer,
Curtsy their farewells to the town,
O'er the curved distance lessening down ;

I follow allwhere for thy sake.
Touch thy robe's hem, but ne'er o'ertake,
Find where, scarce yet unmoving, lies,
Warm from thy limbs, thy last disguise ;   90
But thou another shape hast donned,
And lurest still just, just beyond !

But here a voice, I know not whence,
Thrills clearly through my inward sense,
Saying : ' See where she sits at home
While thou in search of her dost roam !
All summer long her ancient wheel
  Whirls humming by the open door,
Or, when the hickory's social zeal
  Sets the wide chimney in a roar,   100
Close-nestled by the tinkling hearth,
It modulates the household mirth
With that sweet serious undertone
Of duty, music all her own ;
Still as of old she sits and spins
Our hopes, our sorrows, and our sins ;
With equal care she twines the fates
Of cottages and mighty states ;
She spins the earth, the air, the sea,
The maiden's unschooled fancy free,   110
The boy's first love, the man's first grief,
The budding and the fall o' the leaf ;
The piping west-wind's snowy care
For her their cloudy fleeces spare,
Or from the thorns of evil times
She can glean wool to twist her rhymes ;
Morning and noon and eve supply
To her their fairest tints for dye,
But ever through her twirling thread
There spires one line of warmest red,   120
Tinged from the homestead's genial heart,
The stamp and warrant of her art ;
With this Time's sickle she outwears,
And blunts the Sisters' baffled shears.

' Harass her not : thy heat and stir
But greater coyness breed in her ;
Yet thou mayst find, ere Age's frost,
Thy long apprenticeship not lost,
Learning at last that Stygian Fate
Unbends to him that knows to wait.   130
The Muse is womanish, nor deigns
Her love to him that pules and plains ;

With proud, averted face she stands
To him that wooes with empty hands.
Make thyself free of Manhood's guild ;
Pull down thy barns and greater build ;
The wood, the mountain, and the plain
Wave breast-deep with the poet's grain ;
Pluck thou the sunset's fruit of gold,
Glean from the heavens and ocean old ;   140
From fireside lone and trampling street
Let thy life garner daily wheat ;
The epic of a man rehearse,
Be something better than thy verse ;
Make thyself rich, and then the Muse
Shall court thy precious interviews,
Shall take thy head upon her knee,
And such enchantment lilt to thee,
That thou shalt hear the life-blood flow
From farthest stars to grass-blades low,   150
And find the Listener's science still
Transcends the Singer's deepest skill ! '

THE CATHEDRAL

TO

MR. JAMES T. FIELDS

MY DEAR FIELDS :

Dr. Johnson's sturdy self-respect led him to invent the Bookseller as a substitute for the Patron. My relations with you have enabled me to discover how pleasantly the Friend may replace the Bookseller. Let me record my sense of many thoughtful services by associating your name with a poem which owes its appearance in this form to your partiality.

Cordially yours,

J. R. LOWELL.

CAMBRIDGE, *November* 29, 1869.

Οὐδὲν σοφιζώμεσθα τοῖσι δαίμοισιν.
πατρίους παραδοχάς, ἅς θ᾽ ὁμήλικας χρόνῳ
κεκτήμεθ᾽, οὐδεὶς αὐτὰ καταβαλεῖ λόγος,
οὐδ᾽ ἢν δι᾽ ἄκρων τὸ σορὸν εὔρεται φρενῶν.

EURIPIDES, *Bacchae* 196-9.

FAR through the memory shines a happy day,
Cloudless of care, down-shod to every sense,
And simply perfect from its own resource,
As to a bee the new campanula's
Illuminate seclusion swung in air.
Such days are not the prey of setting suns,
Nor ever blurred with mist of after-thought ;
Like words made magical by poets dead,
Wherein the music of all meaning is
The sense hath garnered or the soul divined,   10
They mingle with our life's ethereal part,
Sweetening and gathering sweetness evermore,
By beauty's franchise disenthralled of time.

I can recall, nay, they are present still,
Parts of myself, the perfume of my mind,
Days that seem farther off than Homer's now
Ere yet the child had loudened to the boy,
And I, recluse from playmates, found perforce
Companionship in things that not denied
Nor granted wholly ; as is Nature's wont,   20

Who, safe in uncontaminate reserve,
Lets us mistake our longing for her love,
And mocks with various echo of ourselves.

These first sweet frauds upon our consciousness,
That blend the sensual with its imaged world,
These virginal cognitions, gifts of morn,
Ere life grow noisy, and slower-footed thought
Can overtake the rapture of the sense,
To thrust between ourselves and what we feel,
Have something in them secretly divine.   30
Vainly the eye, once schooled to serve the brain,
With pains deliberate studies to renew
The ideal vision : second-thoughts are prose ;
For beauty's acme hath a term as brief
As the wave's poise before it break in pearl.
Our own breath dims the mirror of the sense,
Looking too long and closely : at a flash
We snatch the essential grace of meaning out,
And that first passion beggars all behind,
Heirs of a tamer transport prepossessed.   40
Who, seeing once, has truly seen again
The grey vague of unsympathizing sea
That dragged his Fancy from her moorings back
To shores inhospitable of eldest time,
Till blank foreboding of earth-gendered powers,
Pitiless seignories in the elements,
Omnipotences blind that darkling smite,
Misgave him, and repaganized the world ?
Yet, by some subtler touch of sympathy,
These primal apprehensions, dimly stirred,   50
Perplex the eye with pictures from within.
This hath made poets dream of lives foregone
In worlds fantastical, more fair than ours ;
So Memory cheats us, glimpsing half-revealed.
Even as I write she tries her wonted spell
In that continuous redbreast boding rain :
The bird I hear sings not from yonder elm ;
But the flown ecstasy my childhood heard
Is vocal in my mind, renewed by him,
Haply made sweeter by the accumulate thrill   60
That threads my undivided life and steals
A pathos from the years and graves between.

I know not how it is with other men,
Whom I but guess, deciphering myself ;
For me, once felt is so felt nevermore.
The fleeting relish at sensation's brim
Had in it the best ferment of the wine.

One spring I knew as never any since:
All night the surges of the warm south-west
Boomed intermittent through the shuddering elms,   70
And brought a morning from the Gulf adrift,
Omnipotent with sunshine, whose quick charm
Startled with crocuses the sullen turf
And wiled the bluebird to his whiff of song:
One summer hour abides, what time I perched,
Dappled with noonday, under simmering leaves,
And pulled the pulpy oxhearts, while aloof
An oriole clattered and the robins shrilled,
Denouncing me an alien and a thief:
One morn of autumn lords it o'er the rest,   80
When in the lane I watched the ash-leaves fall,
Balancing softly earthward without wind,
Or twirling with directer impulse down
On those fallen yesterday, now barbed with frost,
While I grew pensive with the pensive year:
And once I learned how marvellous winter was,
When past the fence-rails, downy-grey with rime,
I creaked adventurous o'er the spangled crust
That made familiar fields seem far and strange
As those stark wastes that whiten endlessly   90
In ghastly solitude about the pole,
And gleam relentless to the unsetting sun:
Instant the candid chambers of my brain
Were painted with these sovran images;
And later visions seem but copies pale
From those unfading frescoes of the past,
Which I, young savage, in my age of flint,
Gazed at, and dimly felt a power in me
Parted from Nature by the joy in her
That doubtfully revealed me to myself.   100
Thenceforward I must stand outside the gate;
And paradise was paradise the more,
Known once and barred against satiety.

What we call Nature, all outside ourselves,
Is but our own conceit of what we see,
Our own reaction upon what we feel;
The world's a woman to our shifting mood,
Feeling with us, or making due pretence;
And therefore we the more persuade ourselves
To make all things our thought's confederates,   110
Conniving with us in whate'er we dream.
So when our Fancy seeks analogies,
Though she have hidden what she after finds,
She loves to cheat herself with feigned surprise.
I find my own complexion everywhere:

No rose, I doubt, was ever, like the first,
A marvel to the bush it dawned upon,
The rapture of its life made visible,
The mystery of its yearning realized,
As the first babe to the first woman born ; 120
No falcon ever felt delight of wings
As when, an eyas, from the stolid cliff
Loosing himself, he followed his high heart
To swim on sunshine, masterless as wind ;
And I believe the brown earth takes delight
In the new snowdrop looking back at her,
To think that by some vernal alchemy
It could transmute her darkness into pearl ;
What is the buxom peony after that,
With its coarse constancy of hoyden blush ? 130
What the full summer to that wonder new ?

But, if in nothing else, in us there is
A sense fastidious hardly reconciled
To the poor makeshifts of life's scenery,
Where the same slide must double all its parts,
Shoved in for Tarsus and hitched back for Tyre.
I blame not in the soul this daintiness,
Rasher of surfeit than a humming-bird,
In things indifferent by sense purveyed ;
It argues her an immortality . 140
And dateless incomes of experience,
This unthrift housekeeping that will not brook
A dish warmed-over at the feast of life,
And finds Twice stale, served with whatever sauce.
Nor matters much how it may go with me
Who dwell in Grub Street and am proud to drudge
Where men, my betters, wet their crust with tears :
Use can make sweet the peach's shady side,
That only by reflection tastes of sun.

But she, my Princess, who will sometimes deign 150
My garret to illumine till the walls,
Narrow and dingy, scrawled with hackneyed thought
(Poor Richard slowly elbowing Plato out),
Dilate and drape themselves with tapestries
Nausikaa might have stooped o'er, while, between,
Mirrors, effaced in their own clearness, send
Her only image on through deepening deeps
With endless repercussion of delight,—
Bringer of life, witching each sense to soul,
That sometimes almost gives me to believe 160
I might have been a poet, gives at least
A brain desaxonized, an ear that makes

Music where none is, and a keener pang
Of exquisite surmise outleaping thought,—
Her will I pamper in her luxury:
No crumpled rose-leaf of too careless choice
Shall bring a northern nightmare to her dreams,
Vexing with sense of exile; hers shall be
The invitiate firstlings of experience,
Vibrations felt but once and felt life-long:					170
O, more than half-way turn that Grecian front
Upon me, while with self-rebuke I spell,
On the plain fillet that confines thy hair
In conscious bounds of seeming unconstraint,
The *Naught in overplus*, thy race's badge!

One feast for her I secretly designed
In that Old World so strangely beautiful
To us the disinherited of eld,—
A day at Chartres, with no soul beside
To roil with pedant prate my joy serene					180
And make the minster shy of confidence.
I went, and, with the Saxon's pious care,
First ordered dinner at the pea-green inn,
The flies and I its only customers,
Till by and by there came two Englishmen,
Who made me feel, in their engaging way,
I was a poacher on their self-preserve,
Intent constructively on lèse-anglicism.
To them (in those old razor-ridden days)
My beard translated me to hostile French;					190
So they, desiring guidance in the town,
Half condescended to my baser sphere,
And, clubbing in one mess their lack of phrase,
Set their best man to grapple with the Gaul.
'Esker vous ate a nabitang?' he asked;
'I never ate one; are they good?' asked I;
Whereat they stared, then laughed, and we were friends,
The seas, the wars, the centuries interposed,
Abolished in the truce of common speech
And mutual comfort of the mother-tongue.					200
Like escaped convicts of Propriety,
They furtively partook the joys of men,
Glancing behind when buzzed some louder fly.

Eluding these, I loitered through the town
With hope to take my minster unawares
In its grave solitude of memory.
A pretty burgh, and such as Fancy loves
For bygone grandeurs, faintly rumorous now
Upon the mind's horizon, as of storm

Brooding its dreamy thunders far aloof, 210
That mingle with our mood, but not disturb.
Its once grim bulwarks, tamed to lovers' walks,
Look down unwatchful on the sliding Eure,
Whose listless leisure suits the quiet place,
Lisping among his shallows homelike sounds
At Concord and by Bankside heard before.
Chance led me to a public pleasure-ground,
Where I grew kindly with the merry groups,
And blessed the Frenchman for his simple art,
Of being domestic in the light of day. 220
His language has no word, we growl, for Home ;
But he can find a fireside in the sun,
Play with his child, make love, and shriek his mind,
By throngs of strangers undisprivacied.
He makes his life a public gallery,
Nor feels himself till what he feels comes back
In manifold reflection from without ;
While we, each pore alert with consciousness,
Hide our best selves as we had stolen them,
And each bystander a detective were, 230
Keen-eyed for every chink of undisguise.

So, musing o'er the problem which was best,—
A life wide-windowed, shining all abroad,
Or curtains drawn to shield from sight profane
The rites we pay to the mysterious I,—
With outward senses furloughed and head bowed
I followed some fine instinct in my feet,
Till, to unbend me from the loom of thought,
Looking up suddenly, I found mine eyes
Confronted with the minster's vast repose. 240
Silent and grey as forest-leaguered cliff
Left inland by the ocean's slow retreat,
That hears afar the breeze-borne rote and longs,
Remembering shocks of surf that clomb and fell,
Spume-sliding down the baffled decuman,
It rose before me, patiently remote
From the great tides of life it breasted once,
Hearing the noise of men as in a dream.
I stood before the triple northern port,
Where dedicated shapes of saints and kings, 250
Stern faces bleared with immemorial watch,
Looked down benignly grave and seemed to say,
Ye come and go incessant ; we remain
Safe in the hallowed quiets of the past ;
Be reverent, ye who flit and are forgot,
Of faith so nobly realized as this.
I seem to have heard it said by learnèd folk

Who drench you with aesthetics till you feel
As if all beauty were a ghastly bore,
The faucet to let loose a wash of words,   260
That Gothic is not Grecian, therefore worse ;
But, being convinced by much experiment
How little inventiveness there is in man,
Grave copier of copies, I give thanks
For a new relish, careless to inquire
My pleasure's pedigree, if so it please,
Nobly, I mean, nor renegade to art.
The Grecian gluts me with its perfectness,
Unanswerable as Euclid, self-contained,
The one thing finished in this hasty world,   270
Forever finished, though the barbarous pit,
Fanatical on hearsay, stamp and shout
As if a miracle could be encored.
But ah ! this other, this that never ends,
Still climbing, luring fancy still to climb,
As full of morals half-divined as life,
Graceful, grotesque, with ever new surprise
Of hazardous caprices sure to please,
Heavy as nightmare, airy-light as fern,
Imagination's very self in stone !   280
With one long sigh of infinite release
From pedantries past, present, or to come,
I looked, and owned myself a happy Goth.
Your blood is mine, ye architects of dream,
Builders of aspiration incomplete,
So more consummate, souls self-confident,
Who felt your own thought worthy of record
In monumental pomp ! No Grecian drop
Rebukes these veins that leap with kindred thrill,
After long exile, to the mother-tongue.   290

Ovid in Pontus, puling for his Rome
Of men invirile and disnatured dames
That poison sucked from the Attic bloom decayed,
Shrank with a shudder from the blue-eyed race
Whose force rough-handed should renew the world,
And from the dregs of Romulus express
Such wine as Dante poured, or he who blew
Roland's vain blast, or sang the Campeador
In verse that clanks like armour in the charge,—
Homeric juice, if brimmed in Odin's horn.   300
And they could build, if not the columned fane
That from the height gleamed seaward many-hued,
Something more friendly with their ruder skies :
The grey spire, molten now in driving mist,
Now lulled with the incommunicable blue ;

The carvings touched to meanings new with snow,
Or commented with fleeting grace of shade;
The statues, motley as man's memory,
Partial as that, so mixed of true and false,
History and legend meeting with a kiss   310
Across this bound-mark where their realms confine;
The painted windows, freaking gloom with glow,
Dusking the sunshine which they seem to cheer,
Meet symbol of the senses and the soul,
And the whole pile, grim with the Northman's thought
Of life and death, and doom, life's equal fee,—
These were before me: and I gazed abashed,
Child of an age that lectures, not creates,
Plastering our swallow-nests on the awful Past,
And twittering round the work of larger men,   320
As we had builded what we but deface.
Far up the great bells wallowed in delight,
Tossing their clangours o'er the heedless town,
To call the worshippers who never came,
Or women mostly, in loath twos and threes.
I entered, reverent of whatever shrine
Guards piety and solace for my kind
Or gives the soul a moment's truce of God,
And shared decorous in the ancient rite
My sterner fathers held idolatrous.   330
The service over, I was tranced in thought:
Solemn the deepening vaults, and most to me,
Fresh from the fragile realm of deal and paint,
Or brick mock-pious with a marble front;
Solemn the lift of high-embowered roof,
The clustered stems that spread in boughs disleaved,
Through which the organ blew a dream of storm,—
Though not more potent to sublime with awe
And shut the heart up in tranquillity,
Than aisles to me familiar that o'er-arch   340
The conscious silences of brooding woods,
Centurial shadows, cloisters of the elk:
Yet here was sense of undefined regret,
Irreparable loss, uncertain what:
Was all this grandeur but anachronism,—
A shell divorced of its informing life,
Where the priest housed him like a hermit-crab,
An alien to that faith of elder days
That gathered round it this fair shape of stone?
Is old Religion but a spectre now,   350
Haunting the solitude of darkened minds,
Mocked out of memory by the sceptic day?
Is there no corner safe from peeping Doubt,
Since Gutenberg made thought cosmopolite

And stretched electric threads from mind to mind ?
Nay, did Faith build this wonder ? or did Fear,
That makes a fetish and misnames it God
(Blockish or metaphysic, matters not),
Contrive this coop to shut its tyrant in,
Appeased with playthings, that he might not harm ?   360

I turned and saw a beldame on her knees ;
With eyes astray, she told mechanic beads
Before some shrine of saintly womanhood,
Bribed intercessor with the far-off Judge :
Such my first thought, by kindlier soon rebuked,
Pleading for whatsoever touches life
With upward impulse : be He nowhere else,
God is in all that liberates and lifts,
In all that humbles, sweetens, and consoles :
Blessèd the natures shored on every side   370
With landmarks of hereditary thought !
Thrice happy they that wander not lifelong
Beyond near succour of the household faith,
The guarded fold that shelters, not confines !
Their steps find patience in familiar paths,
Printed with hope by loved feet gone before
Of parent, child, or lover, glorified
By simple magic of dividing Time.
My lids were moistened as the woman knelt,
And—was it will, or some vibration faint   380
Of sacred Nature, deeper than the will ?—
My heart occultly felt itself in hers,
Through mutual intercession gently leagued.

Or was it not mere sympathy of brain ?
A sweetness intellectually conceived
In simpler creeds to me impossible ?
A juggle of that pity for ourselves
In others, which puts on such pretty masks
And snares self-love with bait of charity ?
Something of all it might be, or of none :   390
Yet for a moment I was snatched away
And had the evidence of things not seen ;
For one rapt moment ; then it all came back,
This age that blots out life with question-marks,
This nineteenth century with its knife and glass
That make thought physical, and thrust far off
The Heaven, so neighbourly with man of old,
To voids sparse-sown with alienated stars.

'T is irrecoverable, that ancient faith,
Homely and wholesome, suited to the time,   400

With rod or candy for child-minded men :
No theologic tube, with lens on lens
Of syllogism transparent, brings it near,—
At best resolving some new nebula,
Or blurring some fixed-star of hope to mist.
Science was Faith once ; Faith were Science now,
Would she but lay her bow and arrows by
And arm her with the weapons of the time.
Nothing that keeps thought out is safe from thought
For there 's no virgin-fort but self-respect,   410
And Truth defensive hath lost hold on God.
Shall we treat Him as if He were a child
That knew not His own purpose ? nor dare trust
The Rock of Ages to their chemic tests,
Lest some day the all-sustaining base divine
Should fail from under us, dissolved in gas ?
The armèd eye that with a glance discerns
In a dry blood-speck between ox and man,
Stares helpless at this miracle called life,
This shaping potency behind the egg,   420
This circulation swift of deity,
Where suns and systems inconspicuous float
As the poor blood-disks in our mortal veins.
Each age must worship its own thought of God,
More or less earthy, clarifying still
With subsidence continuous of the dregs ;
Nor saint nor sage could fix immutably
The fluent image of the unstable Best,
Still changing in their very hands that wrought :
To-day's eternal truth To-morrow proved   430
Frail as frost-landscapes on a window-pane.
Meanwhile Thou smiledst, inaccessible,
At Thought's own substance made a cage for Thought,
And Truth locked fast with her own master-key ;
Nor didst Thou reck what image man might make
Of his own shadow on the flowing world ;
The climbing instinct was enough for Thee.
Or wast Thou, then, an ebbing tide that left
Strewn with dead miracle those eldest shores,
For men to dry, and dryly lecture on,   440
Thyself thenceforth incapable of flood ?
Idle who hopes with prophets to be snatched
By virtue in their mantles left below ;
Shall the soul live on other men's report,
Herself a pleasing fable of herself ?
Man cannot be God's outlaw if he would,
Nor so abscond him in the caves of sense
But Nature still shall search some crevice out
With messages of splendour from that Source

Which, dive he, soar he, baffles still and lures.   450
This life were brutish did we not sometimes
Have intimation clear of wider scope,
Hints of occasion infinite, to keep
The soul alert with noble discontent
And onward yearnings of unstilled desire ;
Fruitless, except we now and then divined
A mystery of Purpose, gleaming through
The secular confusions of the world,
Whose will we darkly accomplish, doing ours.
No man can think nor in himself perceive,   460
Sometimes at waking, in the street sometimes,
Or on the hillside, always unforewarned,
A grace of being, finer than himself,
That beckons and is gone,—a larger life
Upon his own impinging, with swift glimpse
Of spacious circles luminous with mind,
To which the ethereal substance of his own
Seems but gross cloud to make that visible,
Touched to a sudden glory round the edge.
Who that hath known these visitations fleet   470
Would strive to make them trite and ritual ?
I, that still pray at morning and at eve,
Loving those roots that feed us from the past,
And prizing more than Plato things I learned
At that best academe, a mother's knee,
Thrice in my life perhaps have truly prayed,
Thrice, stirred below my conscious self, have felt
That perfect disenthralment which is God ;
Nor know I which to hold worst enemy,—
Him who on speculation's windy waste   480
Would turn me loose, stript of the raiment warm
By Faith contrived against our nakedness,
Or him who, cruel-kind, would fain obscure,
With painted saints and paraphrase of God,
The soul's east-window of divine surprise,
Where others worship I but look and long ;
For, though not recreant to my fathers' faith,
Its forms to me are weariness, and most
That drony vacuum of compulsory prayer,
Still pumping phrases for the Ineffable,   490
Though all the valves of memory gasp and wheeze.
Words that have drawn transcendent meanings up
From the best passion of all bygone time,
Steeped through with tears of triumph and remorse,
Sweet with all sainthood, cleansed in martyr-fires,
Can they, so consecrate and so inspired,
By repetition wane to vexing wind ?
Alas ! we cannot draw habitual breath

In the thin air of life's supremer heights,
We cannot make each meal a sacrament,   500
Nor with our tailors be disbodied souls,—
We men, too conscious of earth's comedy,
Who see two sides, with our posed selves debate,
And only for great stakes can be sublime !
Let us be thankful when, as I do here,
We can read Bethel on a pile of stones,
And, seeing where God *has* been, trust in Him.

Brave Peter Fischer there in Nuremberg,
Moulding Saint Sebald's miracles in bronze,
Put saint and stander-by in that quaint garb   510
Familiar to him in his daily walk,
Not doubting God could grant a miracle
Then and in Nuremberg, if so He would ;
But never artist for three hundred years
Hath dared the contradiction ludicrous
Of supernatural in modern clothes.
Perhaps the deeper faith that is to come
Will see God rather in the strenuous doubt,
Than in the creed held as an infant's hand
Holds purposeless whatso is placed therein.   520

Say it is drift, not progress, none the less,
With the old sextant of the fathers' creed,
We shape our courses by new-risen stars,
And, still lip-loyal to what once was truth,
Smuggle new meanings under ancient names,
Unconscious perverts of the Jesuit, Time.
Change is the mask that all Continuance wears
To keep us youngsters harmlessly amused ;
Meanwhile some ailing or more watchful child,
Sitting apart, sees the old eyes gleam out,   530
Stern, and yet soft with humorous pity too.
Whilere, men burnt men for a doubtful point,
As if the mind were quenchable with fire,
And Faith danced round them with her war-paint on,
Devoutly savage as an Iroquois ;
Now Calvin and Servetus at one board
Snuff in grave sympathy a milder roast,
And o'er their claret settle Comte unread.
Faggot and stake were desperately sincere :
Our cooler martyrdoms are done in types ;   540
And flames that shine in controversial eyes
Burn out no brains but his who kindles them.
This is no age to get cathedrals built :
Did God, then, wait for one in Bethlehem ?
Worst is not yet : lo, where his coming looms,

Of Earth's anarchic children latest born,
Democracy, a Titan who hath learned
To laugh at Jove's old-fashioned thunderbolts,—
Could he not also forge them, if he would ?
He, better skilled, with solvents merciless,   550
Loosened in air and borne on every wind,
Saps unperceived : the calm Olympian height
Of ancient order feels its bases yield,
And pale gods glance for help to gods as pale.
What will be left of good or worshipful,
Of spiritual secrets, mysteries,
Of fair religion's guarded heritage,
Heirlooms of soul, passed downward unprofaned
From eldest Ind ? This Western giant coarse,
Scorning refinements which he lacks himself,   560
Loves not nor heeds the ancestral hierarchies,
Each rank dependent on the next above
In orderly gradation fixed as fate.
King by mere manhood, nor allowing aught
Of holier unction than the sweat of toil ;
In his own strength sufficient ; called to solve,
On the rough edges of society,
Problems long sacred to the choicer few,
And improvise what elsewhere men receive
As gifts of deity ; tough foundling reared   570
Where every man 's his own Melchisedek,
How make him reverent of a King of kings ?
Or Judge self-made, executor of laws
By him not first discussed and voted on ?
For him no tree of knowledge is forbid,
Or sweeter if forbid.   How save the ark,
Or holy of holies, unprofaned a day
From his unscrupulous curiosity
That handles everything as if to buy,
Tossing aside what fabrics delicate   580
Suit not the rough-and-tumble of his ways ?
What hope for those fine-nerved humanities
That made earth gracious once with gentler arts,
Now the rude hands have caught the trick of thought
And claim an equal suffrage with the brain ?

The born disciple of an elder time
(To me sufficient, friendlier than the new),
Who in my blood feel motions of the Past,
I thank benignant Nature most for this,—
A force of sympathy, or call it lack   590
Of character firm-planted, loosing me
From the pent chamber of habitual self
To dwell enlarged in alien modes of thought,

Haply distasteful, wholesomer for that,
And through imagination to possess,
As they were mine, the lives of other men.
This growth original of virgin soil,
By fascination felt in opposites,
Pleases and shocks, entices and perturbs.
In this brown-fisted rough, this shirt-sleeved Cid,   600
This backwoods Charlemagne of empires new,
Whose blundering heel instinctively finds out
The goutier foot of speechless dignities,
Who, meeting Caesar's self, would slap his back,
Call him ' Old Horse,' and challenge to a drink,
My lungs draw braver air, my breast dilates
With ampler manhood, and I front both worlds,
Of sense and spirit, as my natural fiefs,
To shape and then reshape them as I will.
It was the first man's charter ; why not mine ?   610
How forfeit ? when deposed in other hands ?

Thou shudder'st, Ovid ? Dost in him forebode
A new avatar of the large-limbed Goth,
To break, or seem to break, tradition's clue,
And chase to dreamland back thy gods dethroned ?
I think man's soul dwells nearer to the east,
Nearer to morning's fountains than the sun ;
Herself the source whence all tradition sprang,
Herself at once both labyrinth and clue.
The miracle fades out of history,   620
But faith and wonder and the primal earth
Are born into the world with every child.
Shall this self-maker with the prying eyes,
This creature disenchanted of respect
By the New World's new fiend, Publicity,
Whose testing thumb leaves everywhere its smutch,
Not one day feel within himself the need
Of loyalty to better than himself,
That shall ennoble him with the upward look ?
Shall he not catch the Voice that wanders earth,   630
With spiritual summons, dreamed or heard,
As sometimes, just ere sleep seals up the sense,
We hear our mother call from deeps of Time,
And, waking, find it vision,—none the less
The benediction bides, old skies return,
And that unreal thing, pre-eminent,
Makes air and dream of all we see and feel ?
Shall he divine no strength unmade of votes,
Inward, impregnable, found soon as sought,
Not cognizable of sense, o'er sense supreme ?   640
His holy places may not be of stone,

Nor made with hands, yet fairer far than aught
By artist feigned or pious ardour reared,
Fit altars for who guards inviolate
God's chosen seat, the sacred form of man.
Doubtless his church will be no hospital
For superannuate forms and mumping shams,
No parlour where men issue policies
Of life-assurance on the Eternal Mind,
Nor his religion but an ambulance   650
To fetch life's wounded and malingerers in,
Scorned by the strong ; yet he, unconscious heir
To the influence sweet of Athens and of Rome,
And old Judaea's gift of secret fire,
Spite of himself shall surely learn to know
And worship some ideal of himself,
Some divine thing, large-hearted, brotherly,
Not nice in trifles, a soft creditor,
Pleased with his world, and hating only cant.
And, if his Church be doubtful, it is sure   660
That, in a world, made for whatever else,
Not made for mere enjoyment—in a world
Of toil but half-requited, or, at best,
Paid in some futile currency of breath,
A world of incompleteness, sorrow swift
And consolation laggard, whatsoe'er
The form of building or the creed professed,
The Cross, bold type of shame to homage turned,
Of an unfinished life that sways the world,
Shall tower as sovereign emblem over all.   670

The kobold Thought moves with us when we shift
Our dwelling to escape him ; perched aloft
On the first load of household-stuff he went ;
For, where the mind goes, goes old furniture.
I, who to Chartres came to feed my eye
And give to Fancy one clear holiday,
Scarce saw the minster for the thoughts it stirred
Buzzing o'er past and future with vain quest.
Here once there stood a homely wooden church,
Which slow devotion nobly changed for this   680
That echoes vaguely to my modern steps.
By suffrage universal it was built,
As practised then, for all the country came
From far as Rouen, to give votes for God,
Each vote a block of stone securely laid
Obedient to the master's deep-mused plan.
Will what our ballots rear, responsible
To no grave forethought, stand so long as this ?—
Delight like this the eye of after days

Brightening with pride that here, at least, were men   690
Who meant and did the noblest thing they knew ?
Can our religion cope with deeds like this ?
We, too, build Gothic contract-shams, because
Our deacons have discovered that it pays,
And pews sell better under vaulted roofs
Of plaster painted like an Indian squaw.
Shall not that Western Goth, of whom we spoke,
So fiercely practical, so keen of eye,
Find out, some day, that nothing pays but God,
Served whether on the smoke-shut battle-field,   700
In work obscure done honestly, or vote
For truth unpopular, or faith maintained
To ruinous convictions, or good deeds
Wrought for good's sake, mindless of heaven or hell ?
Shall he not learn that all prosperity,
Whose bases stretch not deeper than the sense,
Is but a trick of this world's atmosphere,
A desert-born mirage of spire and dome,
Or find too late, the Past's long lesson missed,
That dust the prophets shake from off their feet   710
Grows heavy to drag down both tower and wall ?
I know not ; but, sustained by sure belief
That man still rises level with the height
Of noblest opportunities, or makes
Such, if the time supply not, I can wait.
I gaze round on the windows, pride of France,
Each the bright gift of some mechanic guild
Who loved their city and thought gold well spent
To make her beautiful with piety ;
I pause, transfigured by some stripe of bloom,   720
And my mind throngs with shining auguries,
Circle on circle, bright as seraphim,
With golden trumpets, silent, that await
The signal to blow news of good to men.

Then the revulsion came that always comes
After these dizzy elations of the mind :
And with a passionate pang of doubt I cried,
' O mountain-born, sweet with snow-filtered air
From uncontaminate wells of ether drawn
And never-broken secrecies of sky,   730
Freedom, with anguish won, misprized till lost,
They keep thee not who from thy sacred eyes
Catch the consuming lust of sensual good
And the brute's licence of unfettered will.
Far from the popular shout and venal breath
Of Cleon blowing the mob's baser mind
To bubbles of wind-piloted conceit,

Thou shrinkest, gathering up thy skirts, to hide
In fortresses of solitary thought
And private virtue strong in self-restraint.   740
Must we too forfeit thee misunderstood,
Content with names, nor inly wise to know
That best things perish of their own excess,
And quality o'er-driven becomes defect ?
Nay, is it thou indeed that we have glimpsed,
Or rather such illusion as of old
Through Athens glided maenadlike and Rome,
A shape of vapour, mother of vain dreams
And mutinous traditions, specious plea
Of the glaived tyrant and long-memoried priest ? '   750

I walked forth saddened ; for all thought is sad,
And leaves a bitterish savour in the brain,—
Tonic, it may be, not delectable,—
And turned, reluctant, for a parting look
At those old weather-pitted images
Of bygone struggle, now so sternly calm.
About their shoulders sparrows had built nests,
And fluttered, chirping, from grey perch to perch,
Now on a mitre poising, now a crown,
Irreverently happy.   While I thought   760
How confident they were, what, careless hearts
Flew on those lightsome wings and shared the sun,
A larger shadow crossed ; and looking up,
I saw where, nesting in the hoary towers,
The sparrow-hawk slid forth on noiseless air,
With sidelong head that watched the joy below,
Grim Norman baron o'er this clan of Kelts.
Enduring Nature, force conservative,
Indifferent to our noisy whims ! Men prate
Of all heads to an equal grade cashiered   770
On level with the dullest, and expect
(Sick of no worse distemper than themselves)
A wondrous cure-all in equality ;
They reason that To-morrow must be wise
Because To-day was not, nor Yesterday,
As if good days were shapen of themselves,
Not of the very lifeblood of men's souls ;
Meanwhile, long-suffering, imperturbable,
Thou quietly complet'st thy syllogism,
And from the premise sparrow here below   780
Draw'st sure conclusion of the hawk above,
Pleased with the soft-billed songster, pleased no less
With the fierce beak of natures aquiline.

Thou beautiful Old Time, now hid away
In the Past's valley of Avilion,

Haply, like Arthur, till thy wound be healed,
Then to reclaim the sword and crown again !
Thrice beautiful to us ; perchance less fair
To who possessed thee, as a mountain seems
To dwellers round its bases but a heap 790
Of barren obstacle that lairs the storm
And the avalanche's silent bolt holds back
Leashed with a hair,—meanwhile some far-off clown,
Hereditary delver of the plain,
Sees it an unmoved vision of repose,
Nest of the morning, and conjectures there
The dance of streams to idle shepherds' pipes,
And fairer habitations softly hung
On breezy slopes, or hid in valleys cool,
For happier men. No mortal ever dreams 800
That the scant isthmus he encamps upon
Between two oceans, one, the Stormy, passed,
And one, the Peaceful, yet to venture on,
Has been that future whereto prophets yearned
For the fulfilment of Earth's cheated hope,
Shall be that past which nerveless poets moan
As the lost opportunity of song.

O Power, more near my life than life itself
(Or what seems life to us in sense immured),
Even as the roots, shut in the darksome earth, 810
Share in the tree-top's joyance, and conceive
Of sunshine and wide air and wingèd things
By sympathy of nature, so do I
Have evidence of Thee so far above,
Yet in and of me ! Rather Thou the root
Invisibly sustaining, hid in light,
Not darkness, or in darkness made by us.
If sometimes I must hear good men debate
Of other witness of Thyself than Thou,
As if there needed any help of ours 820
To nurse Thy flickering life, that else must cease,
Blown out, as 't were a candle, by men's breath,
My soul shall not be taken in their snare,
To change her inward surety for their doubt
Muffled from sight in formal robes of proof :
While she can only feel herself through Thee,
I fear not Thy withdrawal ; more I fear,
Seeing, to know Thee not, hoodwinked with dreams
Of signs and wonders, while, unnoticed, Thou,
Walking Thy garden still, commun'st with men, 830
Missed in the commonplace of miracle.

THREE MEMORIAL POEMS

Εἷς οἰωνὸς ἄριστος ἀμύνεσθαι περὶ πάτρης.

'Coscienza fusca
O della propria o dell' altrui vergogna
Pur sentirà la tua parola brusca.'

If I let fall a word of bitter mirth
When public shames more shameful pardon won,
Some have misjudged me, and my service done,
If small, yet faithful, deemed of little worth:
Through veins that drew their life from Western earth
Two hundred years and more my blood hath run
In no polluted course from sire to son;
And thus was I predestined ere my birth
To love the soil wherewith my fibres own
Instinctive sympathies; yet love it so
As honour would, nor lightly to dethrone
Judgement, the stamp of manhood, nor forgo
The son's right to a mother dearer grown
With growing knowledge and more chaste than snow.

TO

E. L. GODKIN

IN CORDIAL ACKNOWLEDGEMENT OF HIS EMINENT SERVICE
IN HEIGHTENING AND PURIFYING THE TONE
OF OUR POLITICAL THOUGHT,

This Volume

IS DEDICATED

*** Readers, it is hoped, will remember that, by his Ode at the Harvard Commemoration, the author had precluded himself from many of the natural outlets of thought and feeling common to such occasions as are celebrated in this little volume.

ODE

READ AT THE ONE HUNDREDTH ANNI-
VERSARY OF THE FIGHT AT CONCORD
BRIDGE.

19TH APRIL, 1875.

I

WHO cometh over the hills,
Her garments with morning sweet,
The dance of a thousand rills
Making music before her feet?
Her presence freshens the air;
Sunshine steals light from her face;
The leaden footstep of Care
Leaps to the tune of her pace,
Fairness of all that is fair,
Grace at the heart of all grace,   10
Sweetener of hut and of hall,
Bringer of life out of naught,
Freedom, oh, fairest of all
The daughters of Time and Thought!

II

She cometh, cometh to-day :
Hark ! hear ye not her tread,
Sending a thrill through your clay,
Under the sod there, ye dead,
Her nurslings and champions ?
Do ye not hear, as she comes,   20
The bay of the deep-mouthed guns,
The gathering buzz of the drums ?
The bells that called ye to prayer,
How wildly they clamour on her,
Crying, ' She cometh ! prepare
Her to praise and her to honour,
That a hundred years ago
Scattered here in blood and tears
Potent seeds wherefrom should grow
Gladness for a hundred years ! '   30

III

Tell me, young men, have ye seen,
Creature of diviner mien
For true hearts to long and cry for,
Manly hearts to live and die for ?
What hath she that others want ?
Brows that all endearments haunt,
Eyes that make it sweet to dare,
Smiles that glad untimely death,
Looks that fortify despair,
Tones more brave than trumpet's
    breath ;   40
Tell me, maidens, have ye known
Household charm more sweetly rare,
Grace of woman ampler blown,
Modesty more debonair,
Younger heart with wit full grown ?
Oh for an hour of my prime,
The pulse of my hotter years,
That I might praise her in rhyme
Would tingle your eyelids to tears,
Our sweetness, our strength, and our
    star,   50
Our hope, our joy, and our trust,
Who lifted us out of the dust,
And made us whatever we are !

IV

Whiter than moonshine upon snow
Her raiment is, but round the hem
Crimson stained ; and, as to and fro
Her sandals flash, we see on them,
And on her instep veined with blue,
Flecks of crimson, on those fair feet,
High-arched, Diana-like, and fleet,
Fit for no grosser stain than dew :
Oh, call them rather chrisms than
    stains,   62
Sacred and from heroic veins !
For, in the glory-guarded pass,
Her haughty and far-shining head
She bowed to shrive Leonidas
With his imperishable dead ;
Her, too, Morgarten saw,
Where the Swiss lion fleshed his icy
    paw ;
She followed Cromwell's quenchless
    star   70
Where the grim Puritan tread
Shook Marston, Naseby, and Dunbar :
Yea, on her feet are dearer dyes
Yet fresh, nor looked on with untear-
    ful eyes.

V

Our fathers found her in the woods
Where Nature meditates and broods,
The seeds of unexampled things
Which Time to consummation brings
Through life and death and man's
    unstable moods ;   79
They met her here, not recognized,
A sylvan huntress clothed in furs,
To whose chaste wants her bow suf-
    ficed,
Nor dreamed what destinies were
    hers :
She taught them bee-like to create
Their simpler forms of Church and
    State ;
She taught them to endue
The past with other functions than it
    knew,
And turn in channels strange the un-
    certain stream of Fate ;
Better than all, she fenced them in
    their need
With iron-handed Duty's sternest
    creed,   90
'Gainst Self's lean wolf that ravens
    word and deed.

VI

Why cometh she hither to-day
To this low village of the plain,
Far from the Present's loud highway,
From Trade's cool heart and seething
    brain ?
Why cometh she ? She was not far
    away.
Since the soul touched it, not in vain,
With pathos of immortal gain,
'T is here her fondest memories stay.
She loves yon pine-bemurmured ridge
Where now our broad-browed poet
    sleeps,   101
Dear to both Englands ; near him he
Who wore the ring of Canace ;
But most her heart to rapture leaps
Where stood that era-parting bridge,
O'er which, with footfall still as dew,
The Old Time passed into the New ;
Where, as your stealthy river creeps,
He whispers to his listening weeds
Tales of sublimest homespun deeds.
Here English law and English thought
'Gainst the self-will of England
    fought ;   112
And here were men (coequal with
    their fate)
Who did great things, unconscious
    they were great.
They dreamed not what a die was
    cast
With that first answering shot ; what
    then ?
There was their duty ; they were men
Schooled the soul's inward gospel to
    obey,
Though leading to the lion's den.
They felt the habit-hallowed world
    give way   120
Beneath their lives, and on went they,
Unhappy who was last.
When Buttrick gave the word,
That awful idol of the unchallenged
    Past,
Strong in their love, and in their
    lineage strong,
Fell crashing : if they heard it not,
Yet the earth heard,

Nor ever hath forgot,
As on from startled throne to throne,
Where Superstition sate or conscious
    Wrong,   130
A shudder ran of some dread birth
    unknown.
Thrice venerable spot !
River more fateful than the Rubicon !
O'er those red planks, to snatch her
    diadem,
Man's Hope, star-girdled, sprang with
    them,
And over ways untried the feet of
    Doom strode on.

VII

Think you these felt no charms
In their grey homesteads and em-
    bowered farms ?
In household faces waiting at the door
Their evening step should lighten up
    no more ?   140
In fields their boyish feet had known ?
In trees their fathers' hands had set,
And which with them had grown,
Widening each year their leafy coro-
    net ?
Felt they no pang of passionate regret
For those unsolid goods that seem so
    much our own ?
These things are dear to every man
    that lives,
And life prized more for what it lends
    than gives.
Yea, many a tie, through iteration
    sweet,
Strove to detain their fatal feet ; 150
And yet the enduring half they chose,
Whose choice decides a man life's slave
    or king,
The invisible things of God before the
    seen and known :
Therefore their memory inspiration
    blows
With echoes gathering on from zone
    to zone ;
For manhood is the one immortal
    thing
Beneath Time's changeful sky,

And, where it lightened once, from
age to age,
Men come to learn, in grateful pilgrimage,
That length of days is knowing when
to die. 160

VIII

What marvellous change of things
and men !
She, a world-wandering orphan then,
So mighty now ! Those are her
streams
That whirl the myriad, myriad wheels
Of all that does, and all that dreams,
Of all that thinks, and all that feels,
Through spaces stretched from sea to
sea ;
By idle tongues and busy brains,
By who doth right, and who refrains,
Hers are our losses and our gains ;
Our maker and our victim she. 171

IX

Maiden half mortal, half divine,
We triumphed in thy coming ; to the
brinks
Our hearts were filled with pride's
tumultuous wine ;
Better to-day who rather feels than
thinks.
Yet will some graver thoughts intrude,
And cares of sterner mood ;
They won thee : who shall keep thee ?
From the deeps
Where discrowned empires o'er their
ruins brood,
And many a thwarted hope wrings
its weak hands and weeps, 180
I hear the voice as of a mighty wind
From all heaven's caverns rushing
unconfined,
' I, Freedom, dwell with Knowledge :
I abide
With men whom dust of faction can-
not blind
To the slow tracings of the Eternal
Mind ;

With men by culture trained and
fortified,
Who bitter duty to sweet lusts prefer,
Fearless to counsel and obey.
Conscience my sceptre is, and law my
sword, 189
Not to be drawn in passion or in play,
But terrible to punish and deter ;
Implacable as God's word,
Like it, a shepherd's crook to them
that blindly err.
Your firm-pulsed sires, my martyrs
and my saints,
Shoots of that only race whose patient
sense
Hath known to mingle flux with per-
manence,
Rated my chaste denials and re-
straints
Above the moment's dear-paid para-
dise :
Beware lest, shifting with Time's
gradual creep,
The light that guided shine into your
eyes. 200
The envious Powers of ill nor wink
nor sleep :
Be therefore timely wise,
Nor laugh when this one steals, and
that one lies,
As if your luck could cheat those
sleepless spies,
Till the deaf Fury comes your house
to sweep ! '
I hear the voice, and unaffrighted
bow ;
Ye shall not be prophetic now,
Heralds of ill, that darkening fly
Between my vision and the rain-
bowed sky,
Or on the left your hoarse forebodings
croak 210
From many a blasted bough
On Yggdrasil's storm-sinewed oak,
That once was green, Hope of the
West, as thou :
Yet pardon if I tremble while I boast ;
For I have loved as those who pardon
most.

X

Away, ungrateful doubt, away !
At least she is our own to-day.
Break into rapture, my song,
Verses, leap forth in the sun,
Bearing the joyance along   220
Like a train of fire as ye run !
Pause not for choosing of words,
Let them but blossom and sing
Blithe as the orchards and birds
With the new coming of spring !
Dance in your jollity, bells ;
Shout, cannon ; cease not, ye drums ;
Answer, ye hillside and dells ;
Bow, all ye people ! She comes,
Radiant, calm-fronted, as when   230
She hallowed that April day.
Stay with us ! Yes, thou shalt stay,
Softener and strengthener of men,
Freedom, not won by the vain,
Not to be courted in play,
Not to be kept without pain.
Stay with us ! Yes, thou wilt stay,
Handmaid and mistress of all,
Kindler of deed and of thought,
Thou that to hut and to hall   240
Equal deliverance brought !
Souls of her martyrs, draw near,
Touch our dull lips with your fire,
That we may praise without fear
Her our delight, our desire,
Our faith's inextinguishable star,
Our hope, our remembrance, our trust,
Our present, our past, our to be,
Who will mingle her life with our dust
And makes us deserve to be free !

UNDER THE OLD ELM

POEM READ AT CAMBRIDGE ON THE HUNDREDTH ANNIVERSARY OF WASHING-
TON'S TAKING COMMAND OF THE AMERICAN ARMY, 3RD JULY, 1775

I

1

WORDS pass as wind, but where great deeds were done
A power abides transfused from sire to son :
The boy feels deeper meanings thrill his ear,
That tingling through his pulse life-long shall run,
With sure impulsion to keep honour clear,
When, pointing down, his father whispers, ' Here,
Here, where we stand, stood he, the purely Great,
Whose soul no siren passion could unsphere,
Then nameless, now a power and mixed with fate.'
Historic town, thou holdest sacred dust,   10
Once known to men as pious, learnèd, just,
And one memorial pile that dares to last ;
But Memory greets with reverential kiss
No spot in all thy circuit sweet as this,
Touched by that modest glory as it past,
O'er which yon elm hath piously displayed
These hundred years its monumental shade.

2

Of our swift passage through this scenery
Of life and death, more durable than we,
What landmark so congenial as a tree   20

Repeating its green legend every spring,
And, with a yearly ring,
Recording the fair seasons as they flee,
Type of our brief but still-renewed mortality ?
We fall as leaves : the immortal trunk remains,
Builded with costly juice of hearts and brains
Gone to the mould now, whither all that be
Vanish returnless, yet are procreant still
In human lives to come of good or ill,
And feed unseen the roots of Destiny.   30

II

1

Men's monuments, grown old, forget their names
They should eternize, but the place
Where shining souls have passed imbibes a grace
Beyond mere earth ; some sweetness of their fame
Leaves in the soil its unextinguished trace,
Pungent, pathetic, sad with nobler aims,
That penetrates our lives and heightens them or shames.
This insubstantial world and fleet
Seems solid for a moment when we stand
On dust ennobled by heroic feet   40
Once mighty to sustain a tottering land,
And mighty still such burthen to upbear,
Nor doomed to tread the path of things that merely were :
Our sense, refined with virtue of the spot,
Across the mists of Lethe's sleepy stream
Recalls him, the sole chief without a blot,
No more a pallid image and a dream,
But as he dwelt with men decorously supreme.

2

Our grosser minds need this terrestrial hint
To raise long-buried days from tombs of print :   . 50
' Here stood he,' softly we repeat,
And lo, the statue shrined and still
In that grey minster-front we call the Past,
Feels in its frozen veins our pulses thrill,
Breathes living air and mocks at Death's deceit.
It warms, it stirs, comes down to us at last,
Its features human with familiar light,
A man, beyond the historian's art to kill,
Or sculptor's to efface with patient chisel-blight.

3

Sure the dumb earth hath memory, nor for naught   60
Was Fancy given, on whose enchanted loom
Present and Past commingle, fruit and bloom
Of one fair bough, inseparably wrought

Into the seamless tapestry of thought.
So charmed, with undeluded eye we see
In history's fragmentary tale
Bright clues of continuity,
Learn that high natures over Time prevail,
And feel ourselves a link in that entail
That binds all ages past with all that are to be.   70

III

1

Beneath our consecrated elm
A century ago he stood,
Famed vaguely for that old fight in the wood
Whose red surge sought, but could not overwhelm
The life foredoomed to wield our rough-hewn helm :
From colleges, where now the gown
To arms had yielded, from the town,
Our rude self-summoned levies flocked to see
The new-come chiefs and wonder which was he.
No need to question long ; close-lipped and tall,   80
Long trained in murder-brooding forests lone
To bridle others' clamours and his own,
Firmly erect, he towered above them all,
The incarnate discipline that was to free
With iron curb that armed democracy.

2

A motley rout was that which came to stare,
In raiment tanned by years of sun and storm,
Of every shape that was not uniform,
Dotted with regimentals here and there ;
An army all of captains, used to pray   90
And stiff in fight, but serious drill's despair,
Skilled to debate their orders, not obey ;
Deacons were there, selectmen, men of note
In half-tamed hamlets ambushed round with woods,
Ready to settle Freewill by a vote,
But largely liberal to its private moods ;
Prompt to assert by manners, voice, or pen,
Or ruder arms, their rights as Englishmen,
Nor much fastidious as to how and when :
Yet seasoned stuff and fittest to create   100
A thought-staid army or a lasting state :
Haughty they said he was, at first ; severe ;
But owned, as all men own, the steady hand
Upon the bridle, patient to command,
Prized, as all prize, the justice pure from fear,
And learned to honour first, then love him, then revere.
Such power there is in clear-eyed self-restraint
And purpose clean as light from every selfish taint.

3

Musing beneath the legendary tree,
The years between furl off: I seem to see   110
The sun-flecks, shaken the stirred foliage through,
Dapple with gold his sober buff and blue
And weave prophetic aureoles round the head
That shines our beacon now nor darkens with the dead.
O, man of silent mood,
A stranger among strangers then,
How art thou since renowned the Great, the Good
Familiar as the day in all the homes of men !
The wingèd years, that winnow praise and blame,
Blow many names out: they but fan to flame   120
The self-renewing splendours of thy fame.

IV

1

How many subtlest influences unite,
With spiritual touch of joy or pain,
Invisible as air and soft as light,
To body forth that image of the brain
We call our Country, visionary shape,
Loved more than woman, fuller of fire than wine,
Whose charm can none define,
Nor any, though he flee it, can escape !
All party-coloured threads the weaver Time   130
Sets in his web, now trivial, now sublime,
All memories, all forebodings, hopes and fears,
Mountain and river, forest, prairie, sea,
A hill, a rock, a homestead, field, or tree,
The casual gleanings of unreckoned years,
Take goddess-shape at last and there is She,
Old at our birth, new as the springing hours,
Shrine of our weakness, fortress of our powers,
Consoler, kindler, peerless 'mid her peers,
A force that 'neath our conscious being stirs,   140
A life to give ours permanence, when we
Are borne to mingle our poor earth with hers,
And all this glowing world goes with us on our biers.

2

Nations are long results, by ruder ways
Gathering the might that warrants length of days ;
They may be pieced of half-reluctant shares
Welded by hammer-strokes of broad-brained kings,
Or from a doughty people grow, the heirs
Of wise traditions widening cautious rings ;
At best they are computable things,   150

A strength behind us making us feel bold
In right, or, as may chance, in wrong ;
Whose force by figures may be summed and told,
So many soldiers, ships, and dollars strong,
And we but drops that bear compulsory part
In the dumb throb of a mechanic heart ;
But Country is a shape of each man's mind
Sacred from definition, unconfined
By the cramped walls where daily drudgeries grind ;
An inward vision, yet an outward birth   160
Of sweet familiar heaven and earth ;
A brooding Presence that stirs motions blind
Of wings within our embryo being's shell
That wait but her completer spell
To make us eagle-natured, fit to dare
Life's nobler spaces and untarnished air.

3

You, who hold dear this self-conceived ideal,
Whose faith and works alone can make it real,
Bring all your fairest gifts to deck her shrine
Who lifts our lives away from Thine and Mine   170
And feeds the lamp of manhood more divine
With fragrant oils of quenchless constancy.
When all have done their utmost, surely he
Hath given the best who gives a character
Erect and constant, which nor any shock
Of loosened elements, nor the forceful sea
Of flowing or of ebbing fates, can stir
From its deep bases in the living rock
Of ancient manhood's sweet security :
And this he gave, serenely far from pride   180
As baseness, boon with prosperous stars allied,
Part of what nobler seed shall in our loins abide.

4

No bond of men as common pride so strong,
In names time-filtered for the lips of song,
Still operant, with the primal Forces bound
Whose currents, on their spiritual round,
Transfuse our mortal will nor are gainsaid :
These are their arsenals, these the exhaustless mines
That give a constant heart in great designs ;
These are the stuff whereof such dreams are made   190
As make heroic men : thus surely he
Still holds in place the massy blocks he laid
'Neath our new frame, enforcing soberly
The self-control that makes and keeps a people free.

V

1

O, for a drop of that Cornelian ink
Which gave Agricola dateless length of days,
To celebrate him fitly, neither swerve
To phrase unkempt, nor pass discretion's brink,
With him so statue-like in sad reserve,
So diffident to claim, so forward to deserve !   200
Nor need I shun due influence of his fame
Who, mortal among mortals, seemed as now
The equestrian shape with unimpassioned brow,
That paces silent on through vistas of acclaim.

2

What figure more immovably august
Than that grave strength so patient and so pure,
Calm in good fortune, when it wavered, sure,
That mind serene, impenetrably just,
Modelled on classic lines so simple they endure ?
That soul so softly radiant and so white   210
The track it left seems less of fire than light,
Cold but to such as love distemperature ?
And if pure light, as some deem, be the force
That drives rejoicing planets on their course,
Why for his power benign seek an impurer source ?
His was the true enthusiasm that burns long,
Domestically bright,
Fed from itself and shy of human sight,
The hidden force that makes a lifetime strong,
And not the short-lived fuel of a song.   220
Passionless, say you ? What is passion for
But to sublime our natures and control
To front heroic toils with late return,
Or none, or such as shames the conqueror ?
That fire was fed with substance of the soul
And not with holiday stubble, that could burn,
Unpraised of men who after bonfires run,
Through seven slow years of unadvancing war,
Equal when fields were lost or fields were won,
With breath of popular applause or blame,   230
Nor fanned nor damped, unquenchably the same,
Too inward to be reached by flaws of idle fame.

3

Soldier and statesman, rarest unison ;
High-poised example of great duties done
Simply as breathing, a world's honours worn
As life's indifferent gifts to all men born ;

Dumb for himself, unless it were to God,
But for his barefoot soldiers eloquent,
Tramping the snow to coral where they trod,
Held by his awe in hollow-eyed content;   240
Modest, yet firm as Nature's self; unblamed
Save by the men his nobler temper shamed;
Never seduced through show of present good
By other than unsetting lights to steer
New-trimmed in Heaven, nor than his steadfast mood
More steadfast, far from rashness as from fear;
Rigid, but with himself first, grasping still
In swerveless poise the wave-beat helm of will;
Not honoured then or now because he wooed
The popular voice, but that he still withstood;   250
Broad-minded, higher-souled, there is but one
Who was all this and ours, and all men's,—WASHINGTON.

4

Minds strong by fits, irregularly great,
That flash and darken like revolving lights,
Catch more the vulgar eye unschooled to wait
On the long curve of patient days and nights
Rounding a whole life to the circle fair
Of orbed fulfilment; and this balanced soul,
So simple in its grandeur, coldly bare
Of draperies theatric, standing there   260
In perfect symmetry of self-control,
Seems not so great at first, but greater grows
Still as we look, and by experience learn
How grand this quiet is, how nobly stern
The discipline that wrought through lifelong throes
That energetic passion of repose.

5

A nature too decorous and severe,
Too self-respectful in its griefs and joys,
For ardent girls and boys
Who find no genius in a mind so clear   270
That its grave depths seem obvious and near,
Nor a soul great that made so little noise.
They feel no force in that calm-cadenced phrase,
The habitual full-dress of his well-bred mind,
That seems to pace the minuet's courtly maze
And tell of ampler leisures, roomier length of days.
His firm-based brain, to self so little kind
That no tumultuary blood could blind,
Formed to control men, not amaze,

Looms not like those that borrow height of haze :   280
It was a world of statelier movement then
Than this we fret in, he a denizen
Of that ideal Rome that made a man for men.

VI

1

The longer on this earth we live
And weigh the various qualities of men,
Seeing how most are fugitive,
Or fitful gifts, at best, of now and then,
Wind-wavered corpse-lights, daughters of the fen,
The more we feel the high stern-featured beauty
Of plain devotedness to duty,   290
Steadfast and still, nor paid with mortal praise,
But finding amplest recompense
For life's ungarlanded expense
In work done squarely and unwasted days.
For this we honour him, that he could know
How sweet the service and how free
Of her, God's eldest daughter here below,
And choose in meanest raiment which was she.

2

Placid completeness, life without a fall
From faith or highest aims, truth's breachless wall,   300
Surely if any fame can bear the touch,
His will say ' Here ! ' at the last trumpet's call,
The unexpressive man whose life expressed so much.

VII

1

Never to see a nation born
Hath been given to mortal man,
Unless to those who, on that summer morn,
Gazed silent when the great Virginian
Unsheathed the sword whose fatal flash
Shot union through the incoherent clash
Of our loose atoms, crystallizing them   310
Around a single will's unpliant stem,
And making purpose of emotion rash.
Out of that scabbard sprang, as from its womb,
Nebulous at first but hardening to a star,
Through mutual share of sunburst and of gloom,
The common faith that made us what we are.

2

That lifted blade transformed our jangling clans,
Till then provincial, to Americans,
And made a unity of wildering plans ;
Here was the doom fixed : here is marked the date   320
When this New World awoke to man's estate,
Burnt its last ship and ceased to look behind :
Nor thoughtless was the choice ; no love or hate
Could from its poise move that deliberate mind,
Weighing between too early and too late
Those pitfalls of the man refused by Fate :
His was the impartial vision of the great
Who see not as they wish, but as they find.
He saw the dangers of defeat, nor less
The incomputable perils of success ;   330
The sacred past thrown by, an empty rind ;
The future, cloud-land, snare of prophets blind ;
The waste of war, the ignominy of peace ;
On either hand a sullen rear of woes,
Whose garnered lightnings none could guess,
Piling its thunder-heads and muttering ' Cease ! '
Yet drew not back his hand, but gravely chose
The seeming-desperate task whence our new nation rose.

3

A noble choice and of immortal seed !
Nor deem that acts heroic wait on chance   340
Or easy were as in a boy's romance ;
The man's whole life preludes the single deed
That shall decide if his inheritance
Be with the sifted few of matchless breed,
Our race's sap and sustenance,
Or with the unmotived herd that only sleep and feed.
Choice seems a thing indifferent ; thus or so,
What matters it ? The Fates with mocking face
Look on inexorable, nor seem to know
Where the lot lurks that gives life's foremost place.   350
Yet Duty's leaden casket holds it still,
And but two ways are offered to our will,
Toil with rare triumph, ease with safe disgrace,
The problem still for us and all of human race.
He chose, as men choose, where most danger showed,
Nor ever faltered 'neath the load
Of petty cares, that gall great hearts the most,
But kept right on the strenuous up-hill road,
Strong to the end, above complaint or boast :
The popular tempest on his rock-mailed coast   360
Wasted its wind-borne spray,
The noisy marvel of a day ;
His soul sate still in its unstormed abode.

VIII

Virginia gave us this imperial man
Cast in the massive mould
Of those high-statured ages old
Which into grander forms our mortal metal ran ;
She gave us this unblemished gentleman :
What shall we give her back but love and praise
As in the dear old unestrangèd days   370
Before the inevitable wrong began ?
Mother of States and undiminished men,
Thou gavest us a country, giving him,
And we owe alway what we owed thee then :
The boon thou wouldst have snatched from us agen
Shines as before with no abatement dim.
A great man's memory is the only thing
With influence to outlast the present whim
And bind us as when here he knit our golden ring.
All of him that was subject to the hours   380
Lies in thy soil and makes it part of ours :
Across more recent graves,
Where unresentful Nature waves
Her pennons o'er the shot-ploughed sod,
Proclaiming the sweet Truce of God,
We from this consecrated plain stretch out
Our hands as free from afterthought or doubt
As here the united North
Poured her embrownèd manhood forth
In welcome of our saviour and thy son.   390
Through battle we have better learned thy worth,
The long-breathed valour and undaunted will,
Which, like his own, the day's disaster done,
Could, safe in manhood, suffer and be still.
Both thine and ours the victory hardly won ;
If ever with distempered voice or pen
We have misdeemed thee, here we take it back,
And for the dead of both don common black.
Be to us evermore as thou wast then,
As we forget thou hast not always been,   400
Mother of States and unpolluted men,
Virginia, fitly named from England's manly queen !

AN ODE

FOR THE FOURTH OF JULY, 1876

I

1

ENTRANCED I saw a vision in the cloud
That loitered dreaming in yon sunset sky,
Full of fair shapes, half creatures of the eye,

Half chance-evoked by the wind's fantasy
In golden mist, an ever-shifting crowd :
There, 'mid unreal forms came and went
In robes air-spun, of evanescent dye,
A woman's semblance shone pre-eminent ;
Not armed like Pallas, not like Hera proud,
But, as on household diligence intent,　　　　10
Beside her visionary wheel she bent
Like Aretë or Bertha, nor than they
Less queenly in her port : about her knee
Glad children clustered confident in play :
Placid her pose, the calm of energy ;
And over her broad brow in many a round
(That loosened would have gilt her garment's hem),
Succinct, as toil prescribes, the hair was wound
In lustrous coils, a natural diadem.
The cloud changed shape, obsequious to the whim　　20
Of some transmuting influence felt in me,
And, looking now, a wolf I seemed to see
Limned in that vapour, gaunt and hunger-bold,
Threatening her charge : resolve in every limb,
Erect she flamed in mail of sun-wove gold,
Penthesilea's self for battle dight ;
One arm uplifted braced a flickering spear,
And one her adamantine shield made light ;
Her face, helm-shadowed, grew a thing to fear,
And her fierce eyes, by danger challenged, took　　30
Her trident-sceptred mother's dauntless look.
' I know thee now, O goddess-born ! ' I cried,
And turned with loftier brow and firmer stride ;
For in that spectral cloud-work I had seen
Her image, bodied forth by love and pride,
The fearless, the benign, the mother-eyed,
The fairer world's toil-consecrated queen.

2

What shape by exile dreamed elates the mind
Like hers whose hand, a fortress of the poor,
No blood in lawful vengeance spilt bestains ?　　40
Who never turned a suppliant from her door ?
Whose conquests are the gains of all mankind ?
To-day her thanks shall fly on every wind,
Unstinted, unrebuked, from shore to shore,
One love, one hope, and not a doubt behind !
Cannon to cannon shall repeat her praise,
Banner to banner flap it forth in flame ;
Her children shall rise up to bless her name,
And wish her harmless length of days,
The mighty mother of a mighty brood,　　50

Blessed in all tongues and dear to every blood,
The beautiful, the strong, and, best of all, the good !

3

Seven years long was the bow
Of battle bent, and the heightening
Storm-heaps convulsed with the throe
Of their uncontainable lightning ;
Seven years long heard the sea
Crash of navies and wave-borne thunder ;
Then drifted the cloud-rack a-lee,
And new stars were seen, a world's wonder ;   60
Each by her sisters made bright,
All binding all to their stations,
Cluster of manifold light
Startling the old constellations :
Men looked up and grew pale :
Was it a comet or star,
Omen of blessing or bale,
Hung o'er the ocean afar ?

4

Stormy the day of her birth :
Was she not born of the strong,   70
She, the last ripeness of earth,
Beautiful, prophesied long ?
Stormy the days of her prime :
Hers are the pulses that beat
Higher for perils sublime,
Making them fawn at her feet.
Was she not born of the strong ?
Was she not born of the wise ?
Daring and counsel belong
Of right to her confident eyes :   80
Human and motherly they,
Careless of station or race :
Hearken ! her children to-day
Shout for the joy of her face.

II

1

No praises of the past are hers,
No fanes by hallowing time caressed,
No broken arch that ministers
To some sad instinct in the breast :
She has not gathered from the years
Grandeur of tragedies and tears,   90

Nor from long leisure the unrest
That finds repose in forms of classic grace:
These may delight the coming race
Who haply shall not count it to our crime
That we who fain would sing are here before our time.
She also hath her monuments;
Not such as stand decrepitly resigned
To ruin-mark the path of dead events
That left no seed of better days behind,
The tourist's pensioners that show their scars   100
And maunder of forgotten wars;
She builds not on the ground, but in the mind,
Her open-hearted palaces
For larger-thoughted men with heaven and earth at ease:
Her march the plump mow marks, the sleepless wheel,
The golden sheaf, the self-swayed commonweal;
The happy homesteads hid in orchard trees
Whose sacrificial smokes through peaceful air
Rise lost in heaven, the household's silent prayer;
What architect hath bettered these?   110
With softened eye the westward traveller sees
A thousand miles of neighbours side by side,
Holding by toil-won titles fresh from God
The lands no serf or seigneur ever trod,
With manhood latent in the very sod,
Where the long billow of the wheat-field's tide
Flows to the sky across the prairie wide,
A sweeter vision than the castled Rhine,
Kindly with thoughts of Ruth and Bible-days benign.

2

O ancient commonwealths, that we revere   120
Haply because we could not know you near,
Your deeds like statues down the aisles of Time
Shine peerless in memorial calm sublime,
And Athens is a trumpet still, and Rome;
Yet which of your achievements is not foam
Weighed with this one of hers (below you far
In fame, and born beneath a milder star),
That to Earth's orphans, far as curves the dome
Of death-deaf sky, the bounteous West means home,
With dear precedency of natural ties   130
That stretch from roof to roof and make men gently wise?
And if the nobler passions wane,
Distorted to base use, if the near goal
Of insubstantial gain
Tempt from the proper race-course of the soul
That crowns their patient breath
Whose feet, song-pinioned, are too fleet for Death,

Yet may she claim one privilege urbane
And haply first upon the civic roll,
That none can breathe her air nor grow humane. 140

3

O, better far the briefest hour
Of Athens self-consumed, whose plastic power
Hid Beauty safe from Death in words or stone ;
Of Rome, fair quarry where those eagles crowd
Whose fulgurous vans about the world had blown
Triumphant storm and seeds of polity ;
Of Venice, fading o'er her shipless sea,
Last iridescence of a sunset cloud ;
Than this inert prosperity,
This bovine comfort in the sense alone ! 150
Yet art came slowly even to such as those,
Whom no past genius cheated of their own
With prudence of o'ermastering precedent ;
Petal by petal spreads the perfect rose,
Secure of the divine event ;
And only children rend the bud half-blown
To forestall Nature in her calm intent :
Time hath a quiver full of purposes
Which miss not of their aim, to us unknown,
And brings about the impossible with ease : 160
Haply for us the ideal dawn shall break
From where in legend-tinted line
The peaks of Hellas drink the morning's wine,
To tremble on our lids with mystic sign
Till the drowsed ichor in our veins awake
And set our pulse in tune with moods divine ;
Long the day lingered in its sea-fringed nest,
Then touched the Tuscan hills with golden lance
And paused ; then on to Spain and France
The splendour flew, and Albion's misty crest : 170
Shall Ocean bar him from his destined West ?
Or are we, then, arrived too late,
Doomed with the rest to grope disconsolate,
Foreclosed of Beauty by our modern date ?

III

1

POETS, as their heads grow grey,
Look from too far behind the eyes,
Too long-experienced to be wise
In guileless youth's diviner way ;
Life sings not now, but prophesies ;
Time's shadows they no more behold, 180
But, under them, the riddle old

That mocks, bewilders, and defies :
In childhood's face the seed of shame,
In the green tree an ambushed flame,
In Phosphor a vaunt-guard of Night,
They, though against their will, divine,
And dread the care-dispelling wine
Stored from the Muse's vintage bright,
By age imbued with second-sight.
From Faith's own eyelids there peeps out,					190
Even as they look, the leer of doubt ;
The festal wreath their fancy loads
With care that whispers and forebodes :
Nor this our triumph-day can blunt Megaera's goads.

2

Murmur of many voices in the air
Denounces us degenerate,
Unfaithful guardians of a noble fate,
And prompts indifference or despair :
Is this the country that we dreamed in youth,
Where wisdom and not numbers should have weight,					200
Seed-field of simpler manners, braver truth,
Where shams should cease to dominate
In household, church, and state ?
Is this Atlantis ? This the unpoisoned soil,
Sea-whelmed for ages and recovered late,
Where parasitic greed no more should coil
Round Freedom's stem to bend awry and blight
What grew so fair, sole plant of love and light ?
Who sit where once in crowned seclusion sate
The long-proved athletes of debate,					210
Trained from their youth, as none thinks needful now ?
Is this debating-club, where boys dispute
And wrangle o'er their stolen fruit,
The Senate, erewhile cloister of the few,
Where Clay once flashed and Webster's cloudy brow
Brooded those bolts of thought that all the horizon knew ?

3

Oh, as this pensive moonlight blurs my pines,
Here while I sit and meditate these lines,
To grey-green dreams of what they are by day,
So would some light, not reason's sharp-edged ray,					220
Trance me in moonshine as before the flight
Of years had won me this unwelcome right
To see things as they are, or shall be soon,
In the frank prose of undissembling noon !

4

Back to my breast, ungrateful sigh!
Whoever fails, whoever errs,
The penalty be ours, not hers!
The present still seems vulgar, seen too nigh;
The golden age is still the age that's past:
I ask no drowsy opiate   230
To dull my vision of that only state
Founded on faith in man, and therefore sure to last.
For, O my country, touched by thee,
The grey hairs gather back their gold;
Thy thought sets all my pulses free;
The heart refuses to be old;
The love is all that I can see.
Not to thy natal-day belong
Time's prudent doubt or age's wrong,
But gifts of gratitude and song: 240
Unsummoned crowd the thankful words,
As sap in spring-time floods the tree,
Foreboding the return of birds,
For all that thou hast been to me!

IV

1

FLAWLESS his heart and tempered to the core
Who, beckoned by the forward-leaning wave,
First left behind him the firm-footed shore,
And, urged by every nerve of sail and oar,
Steered for the Unknown which gods to mortals gave,
Of thought and action the mysterious door,   250
Bugbear of fools, a summons to the brave:
Strength found he in the unsympathizing sun,
And strange stars from beneath the horizon won,
And the dumb ocean pitilessly grave:
High-hearted surely he;
But bolder they who first off-cast
Their moorings from the habitable Past
And ventured chartless on the sea
Of storm-engendering Liberty:
For all earth's width of waters is a span,   260
And their convulsed existence mere repose,
Matched with the unstable heart of man,
Shoreless in wants, mist-girt in all it knows,
Open to every wind of sect or clan,
And sudden-passionate in ebbs and flows.

2

They steered by stars the elder shipmen knew,
And laid their courses where the currents draw
Of ancient wisdom channelled deep in law,
The undaunted few
Who changed the Old World for the New,   270
And more devoutly prized
Than all perfection theorized
The more imperfect that had roots and grew.
They founded deep and well,
Those danger-chosen chiefs of men,
Who still believed in Heaven and Hell,
Nor hoped to find a spell
In some fine flourish of a pen
To make a better man
Than long-considering Nature will or can,   280
Secure against his own mistakes,
Content with what life gives or takes,
And acting still on some fore-ordered plan,
A cog of iron in an iron wheel,
Too nicely poised to think or feel,
Dumb motor in a clock-like commonweal.
They wasted not their brain in schemes
Of what man might be in some bubble-sphere,
As if he must be other than he seems
Because he was not what he should be here,   290
Postponing Time's slow proof to petulant dreams:
Yet herein they were great
Beyond the incredulous lawgivers of yore,
And wiser than the wisdom of the shelf,
That they conceived a deeper-rooted state,
Of hardier growth, alive from rind to core,
By making man sole sponsor of himself.

3

God of our fathers, Thou who wast,
Art, and shalt be when those eye-wise who flout
Thy secret presence shall be lost   300
In the great light that dazzles them to doubt,
We, sprung from loins of stalwart men
Whose strength was in their trust
That Thou wouldst make Thy dwelling in their dust
And walk with them a fellow-citizen
Who build a city of the just,
We, who believe Life's bases rest
Beyond the probe of chemic test,
Still, like our fathers, feel Thee near,
Sure that, while lasts the immutable decree,   310
The land to Human Nature dear
Shall not be unbeloved of Thee.

MISCELLANEOUS POEMS

LETTER FROM BOSTON

[From *Anti-Slavery Advocate*, January 2, 1858; *Atlantic Monthly*, April, 1884.]

' By far the wittiest of all English living poets is an American and an abolitionist, and " the three first letters of his name " are JAMES RUSSELL LOWELL. In an old newspaper, printed about ten years ago, we found the following *jeu d'esprit*, which is now as fresh and as racy as if it were written yesterday, and that is much to say for anything ten years old in the way of *vers de société*. But WILLIAM LLOYD GARRISON, MRS. CHAPMAN, MRS. FOLLEN, EDMUND QUINCY, WENDELL PHILLIPS, PARKER PILLSBURY, STEPHEN FOSTER, and ABBY KELLEY, now MRS. FOSTER, have all survived through the decade, and are still as earnest, as industrious, and as hostile against slavery as ever. We wish they were all as unscathed, as vigorous, and as young. Lowell has sketched them with a master's hand in this letter from Boston to our friend James Miller M'Kim of Philadelphia.'

DEAR M.——
   By way of saving time,
I'll do this letter up in rhyme,
Whose slim stream through four
 pages flows,
Ere one is packed with tight-screwed
 prose,
Threading the tube of an epistle,
Smooth as a child's breath through
 a whistle.

The great attraction now of all
Is the ' Bazaar ' at Faneuil Hall,
Where swarm the anti-slavery folks
As thick, dear Miller, as your jokes.
There 's GARRISON, his features very
Benign for an incendiary, 12
Beaming forth sunshine through his
 glasses,
On the surrounding lads and lasses,
(No bee could blither be, or brisker,)
A Pickwick somehow turned John
 Ziska ;
His bump of firmness swelling up
Like a rye cupcake from its cup.

And there, too, was his English tea-
 set, 19
Which in his ear a kind of flea set,—
His Uncle Samuel, for its beauty,
Demanding sixty dollars duty !
('Twas natural Sam should serve his
 trunk ill,
For G., you know, has cut his uncle,)
Whereas, had he but once made tea
 in it,
His Uncle's ear had had the flea in it ;
There being not a cent of duty
On any pot that ever drew tea.[1]

There was MARIA CHAPMAN, too,
With her swift eyes of clear steel-
 blue, 30
The coiled up mainspring of the Fair,
Originating everywhere
The expansive force, without a sound,
That whirls a hundred wheels around;
Herself meanwhile as calm and still
As the bare crown of Prospect Hill ;
A noble woman, brave and apt,
Cumaea's sibyl not more rapt,

[1] When Mr. Garrison visited Edinburgh in 1846 he was presented with a handsome silver tea-set by his friends in that city. On the arrival of this gift at the Boston custom-house it was charged with an enormous entrance duty, which would have been evaded if the articles had ever been *used*. It was supposed that if the owner had not been the leader of the unpopular abolitionists this heavy impost would not have been laid upon a friendly British acknowledgement to an eminent American.

Who might, with those fair tresses
 shorn,
The Maid of Orleans' casque have worn;
Herself the Joan of our Arc,   41
For every shaft a shining mark.

And there, too, was ELIZA FOLLEN,
Who scatters fruit creating pollen
Where'er a blossom she can find
Hardy enough for Truth's northwind,
Each several point of all her face
Tremblingly bright with the inward
 grace,
As if all motion gave it light,
Like phosphorescent seas at night. 50

There jokes our EDMUND, plainly son
Of him who bearded Jefferson ;
A non-resistant by conviction,
But with a bump in contradiction,
So that, whene'er it gets a chance,
His pen delights to play the lance,
And—you may doubt it, or believe
 it—
Full at the head of Joshua Leavitt
The very calumet he'd launch,
And scourge him with the olive
 branch.   60
A master with the foils of wit,
'Tis natural he should love a hit :
A gentleman, withal, and scholar,
Only base things excite his choler.
And then his satire 's keen and thin
As the little blade of Saladin.
Good letters are a gift apart,
And his are gems of Flemish art,
True offspring of the fireside muse,
Not a chip gathering of news, 70
Like a new hopfield which is all poles,
But of one blood with Horace Wal-
 pole's.

There, with one hand behind his back,
Stands PHILLIPS, buttoned in a sack,

Our Attic orator, our Chatham ;
Old fogies, when he lightens at 'em,
Shrivel like leaves ; to him 'tis
 granted
Always to say the word that 's
 wanted,   78
So that he seems but speaking clearer
The tiptop thought of every hearer ;
Each flash his brooding heart lets fall,
Fires what 's combustible in all,
And sends the applauses bursting in,
Like an exploded magazine.
His eloquence no frothy show,
The gutter's street-polluted flow ;
No Mississippi's yellow flood,
Whose shoalness can't be seen for
 mud ;
So simply clear, serenely deep, 89
So silent, strong, its graceful sweep ;
None measures its unrippling force,
Who has not striven to stem its
 course.
How fare their barques, who think to
 play
With smooth Niagara's mane of spray,
Let Austin's total shipwreck say ! [1]
He never spoke a word too much—
Except of Story or some such,
Whom, though condemned by ethics
 strict,
The heart refuses to convict.

Beyond, a crater in each eye, 100
Sways, brown, broad-shouldered
 PILLSBURY ;
Who tears up words, like trees, by the
 roots,—
A Theseus in stout cowhide boots;
The wager of eternal war
Against that loathsome Minotaur,
To whom we sacrifice each year
The best blood of our Athens here,
(Dear M., pray brush up your Lem-
 priere.)

[1] On the occasion of the murder of Rev. Elijah P. Lovejoy, editor of an anti-slavery
newspaper at Alton, State of Illinois, an indignation meeting was held in Boston, at
which Austin, Attorney-General of Massachusetts, made an atrocious pro-slavery speech,
which called forth a crushing reply from Wendell Phillips, who from thenceforth has been
a main pillar of abolitionism.

A terrible denouncer, he!
Old Sinai burns unquenchably   110
Upon his lips; he well might be a
Hot-blazing soul from fierce Judea,
Habakkuk, Ezra, or Hosea.
His words burn as with iron searers,
And, nightmare-like, he mounts his
    hearers,
Spurring them like avenging fate, or
As Waterton his alligator.

Hard by, as calm as summer even,
Smiles the reviled and pelted
    STEPHEN,
The unappeasable Boanerges,   120
To all the churches and the clergies;
Who studied mineralogy,
Not with soft book upon the knee,
But learned the properties of stones
By contact sharp of flesh and bones,
And made the *experimentum crucis*
With his own body's vital juices.
A man with caoutchouc endurance,
A perfect gem for life insurance;
A kind of maddened John the Bap-
    tist,   130
To whom the harshest word comes
    aptest;
Who, struck by stone or brick ill-
    starred,
Hurls back an epithet as hard,
Which, deadlier than stone or brick,
Has a propensity to stick.
His oratory is like the scream
Of the iron-horse's frenzied steam,
Which warns the world to leave wide
    space
For the black engine's swerveless race.
Ye men with neckcloths white, I
    warn you,   140
Habet a whole haymow *in cornu*.

A Judith, there, turned Quakeress,
Sits Abby in her modest dress,
Serving a table quietly,
As if that mild and downcast eye
Flashed never with its scorn intense
More than Medea's eloquence.

So the same force which shakes its
    dread
Far-blazing locks o'er Aetna's head,
Along the wires in silence fares,   150
And messages of commerce bears.
No nobler gift of heart and brain,
No life more white from spot or stain,
Was e'er on Freedom's altar laid
Than hers, the simple Quaker maid.

These last three (leaving in the lurch
Some other themes) assault the
    church,
Who therefore writes them in her lists
As Satan's limbs, and atheists;
For each sect has one argument   160
Whereby the rest to hell are sent,
Which serves them like the Graine's
    tooth,
Passed round in turn from mouth to
    mouth.
If any *ism* should arise,
They look on it with constable's eyes,
Tie round its neck a heavy *athe*—
And give it kitten's hydropathy.
This trick, with other (useful very)
    tricks,   168
Is laid to the Babylonian *meretrix*,
But 'twas in vogue before her day,
Wherever priesthoods had their way;
And Buddha's Popes with this struck
    dumb
The followers of Fi and Fum.

Well, if the world, with prudent fear,
Pays God a seventh of the year,
And as a farmer, who would pack
All his religion in one stack,
For this world works six days in
    seven,   178
And on the seventh works for heaven,
Expecting, for his Sunday's sowing,
In the next world to go a-mowing
The crop of all his meeting going:
If the poor church, by power enticed,
Finds none so infidel as Christ,
Quite backward reads his gospel meek,
(As 'twere in Hebrew writ, not
    Greek,)

Fencing the gallows and the sword
With conscripts drafted from his
    word,
And makes one gate of heaven so wide,
That the rich orthodox might ride
Through on their camels, while the
    poor   191
Squeeze through the scant, unyielding
    door,
Which, of the gospel's straitest size,
Is narrower than bead-needles' eyes,—
What wonder World and Church
    should call
The true faith atheistical ?

Yet, after all, 'twixt you and me,
Dear Miller, I could never see
That Sin's and Error's ugly smirch
Stained the walls only of the church;—
There are good priests, and men who
    take   201
Freedom's torn cloak for lucre's sake.
I can't believe the church so strong,
As some men do, for Right or Wrong.
But, for this subject, (long and vext,)
I must refer you to my next,
As also for a list exact
Of goods with which the hall was
    packed.   208

OUR OWN

HIS WANDERINGS AND PERSONAL ADVENTURES

[From Putnam's *Monthly Magazine*, April–June, 1853.]

Πολλῶν δ᾽ ανθρώπων ἴδην ἄστεα, καὶ νοον ἔγνω

Quae regio in terris NOSTRI non plena laboris ?

Full many cities he hath seen and many great men known ;
What place on earth but testifies the labours of OUR OWN ?

DIGRESSION A

Our Own in mounting Pegasus,
   ´Takes such impetuous stride
That, with a downcome ominous,
   He falls o' the other side.

SIRS, Editors of Putnam's (if it's right to use the plural),
I wish to recommend myself to—*tooral, looral, looral !*
This strikes you as an oddish way of winding up a distich ?
As something rather wild, incomprehensible, and mystic ?
Well, to confess the truth at once, I'm something new at verses,
No fairy gave me rhymes at birth in Fortunatus-purses ;
Rhymes, I opine, like Plato's souls, are born in incompleteness,
Pining, mere bachelors, till they meet their destined linkéd sweetness ;
And some men, never finding halves *sans* those they should be pinned to,
Scrawl rhyme as easily as Jack Frost scrawls rime upon a window :   10
That's not my luck ;—the prior verse, before I've time to think, 's at hand,
While that which ought to marry it plays spinster in my inkstand,

Immovable as the proverb's horse that can both nod and wink stand ;
So, having written my first line, and ended it with *plural*,
I could not light on any mate but *Ural, mural, crural*,
All very crooked sticks (just try yourselves, good Messieurs Editors,—
When you have turned it twenty ways, you'll own I might have said it
    worse) ;
So baffled like poor Nap. the Third, for fear of worse miscarriage,
I sought some friendly assonance, a morganatic marriage ;
Failing in that, with Butler's rule I can my weakness bolster,   20
And 'gainst a lock-less pistol match the flask in t'other holster,
Or, better yet, with Tennyson's authority can cure all,—
If *he* says *tirra-lirra*, why mayn't *I* say *tooral-looral* ?

DIGRESSION B

> With foot in stirrup, hand on mane,
>   Our Own makes prudent pause,
> Swings o'er the careful leg again,
>   And tight the curb-rein draws.

There's naught so hard, Lord Byron says, as getting under way ;
The wilted sails droop from the yard, oil-smooth the windless bay,
The tide slips wimpling by, the same that weeks ago, perhaps,
Round coral-reefs in Indian seas, shimmered with whispering lapse ;
The same that, sweeping northward still, to Arctic snows may bear
Great leaves, scarce disenchanted yet of drowsy tropic air,
Such as may vex stout Franklin's dreams, where unrelenting lines
Of icepeaks whitening endlessly o'ertop his useless pines ;—
The tide slips by and there you lie, the anchor at the peak,
The captain swearing inwardly, the mate with quid in cheek ;   10
There's not a hope of any breeze before, beside, behind,
And, though with ingots laden deep, you cannot raise the wind ;
Fair cousins, kissed and bid good-bye, gaze awkward from the pier,
Sorry they wiped their eyes so soon, because their second tear
Declines to fill the other's place ; the cambric from the bags
Is taken once again and waved ; the slow time drags and dra-a-ags ;
He (whom in childhood's guileless prime, you used to lick), your brother,
Spells this exhausted leg, or that, with the exhausted other ;
The children go too near the edge, and fuss, and screw, and wriggle ;
Tommy's best cap falls overboard and no one dares to giggle ;   20
You strive to make the feeling stay that misted both your eyes,
But thoughts of luggage intervene, and the tired feeling dies ;
The farewell, mixed of smiles and tears, so painful-sweet before,
Drawn out into an hour, becomes impertinence and bore,
As if too literal Jove should grant the lovers' prayed-for bliss,
And glue them Siamesely tight in one eternal kiss ;
In such case what do captains, even of clippers swift as arrows ?
They take a prosy steam-tug till they get beyond the Narrows ;
That's what I've done, and, being now safe in the open main,
Set stu'nsails (that is, mend my pen), and take my start again.   30

Progression A.—The Invocation

He now, with wise spurs so inclined
That each the flank evades,
Nor gives a mettle undesigned,
Invokes two mighty blades.

Sirs, Editors of Putnam's, then, if you indeed be plural,
Or if you the Howadji be, who, sitting crucicrural
(A habit learned in Egypt), through the anaconda coils,
Of his *effendi* sucks the rare *ulemah's* fragrant spoils,
And on the best papyrus with a split reed splutters down
An article on Banking that will startle half the town,
(Proving our system all is due to some old Coptic file
Because before that Ramsay reigned, who helped at Babel's pile,
Deposits constantly were made on both banks of the Nile) ;
Then claps hands languidly (hands lotus-soft) to bring A lad in,   10
Allah ed deen he calls him—'tis a dyed Milesian clad in
A bloomer bought in Chatham-street and a bandanna turban,
Pure Saracenic in his style like certain cots suburban :—
Or if you Harry Franco be, who, though he e'er so far goes,
Remembers in his secret heart the dear, flat, dull sea's Argos,
And, as a mild suggestion of the customs of Nantucket,
To any kind of elbow-chair prefers an o'erturned bucket ;
Who (as the Persian Envoy to old Louis the Magnificent
A turf brought with him piously, that he might always sniff a scent
Of the *natale solum*) keeps an oilcask in the closet,   20
(One that has made a v'y'ge, too), lays a harpoon across it,
And with strange rites, left wisely to the fancy of my Reader,
Consults the bunghole's Delphic deeps before he writes a leader ;—
Or if you be that gentle youth, so tall and slim and pale,
Who fitted to his Pegasus a Scandinavian Tale,
Who the Pathfinder's leaders made, yet could not find the way
With next-day-after-never to displace our poor to-day,
And nothing met but humbergs, where Charles Fourier (on his slate)
Had cleared the Northwest Passage to a better Social State ;—
Or if you be that Moses who, from Modern Egypt's wrecks adust,   30
Unto their Canaan of Brook Farm the New Lights safely Exodused ;
Where life's clean page was never more to be defaced with fresh spots,
As soon as Theory could be made as fattening as the flesh-pots ;
Where the new manner, dropt from heaven, should so nerve hand and brain
That he who nothing did before, should do't as well again ;
Where with fresh water from the spring they warmed their stoic lunch,
Biding the time when Fourier said the sea would be milk-punch,
When gold into the public chest like water was to run
For phalansterian beets (that cost two shillings every one),
And Time should wander Ripleying along o'er golden sand,   40
When forty heads could dig as well as one experienced hand ;—
If you are one or all, or if you're ne'er a one of those,
Hear, by what title suits you best, the plan I now propose !

Progression B leading to Digression C

Our Own then states his business,
Sets forth the why and how,
Begins in safety to progress
But brings up in a slough.

I am a man of forty, sirs, a native of East Haddam,
And have some reason to surmise that I descend from Adam;
But what's my pedigree to you? That I will soon unravel;
I've sucked my Haddam-Eden dry, therefore desire to travel,
And, as a natural consequence, presume I needn't say,
I wish to write some letters home and have those letters * * *
[I spare the word suggestive of those grim Next thorns that mount,
Clump, clump, the stairways of the brain with—*sir, my small account*,
That, after every good we gain—Love, Fame, Wealth, Wisdom—still,
As punctual as a cuckoo clock, hold up their little bill,   10
The *garçons* in our Café of Life, by dreaming us forgot—
Sitting, like Homer's heroes, full and musing God knows what,—
Till they say, bowing, *s'il vous plait, voilà, Messieurs, la note !*]
I should not hint at this so soon, but in our callous day,
The tollman Debt, who drops the bar across the world's highway,
Great Caesar in mid-march would stop if Caesar could not pay;
Pilgriming's dearer than it was: men cannot travel now
Scot-free from Dan to Beersheba upon a simple vow;
Nay, as long back as Bess's time, when Walsingham went over
Ambassador to Cousin France, at Canterbury and Dover   20
He was so fleeced by innkeepers that, ere he quitted land,
He wrote to the Prime Minister to take the knaves in hand: [1]
If I with staff and scallop-shell should try my way to win,
Would Bonifaces quarrel as to who should take me in?
Or would my pilgrim's progress end where Bunyan started his on,
And my grand tour be round and round the backyard of a prison?
I give you here a saying deep and therefore, haply true;
'Tis out of Merlin's prophecies, but quite as good as new:
𝔗𝔥𝔢 question boath for men and meates longe bopages p' beginne
𝔏pes in a notshell, rather saue lpes in a case of tinne.   30
But, though men may not travel now, as in the middle ages,
With self-sustaining retinues of little gilt-edged pages,
Yet one may manage pleasantly, where'er he likes to roam,
By sending his small pages (at so much per small page) home;
And if a staff and scallop-shell won't serve so well as then,
Our outlay is about as small—just paper, ink, and pen.
Be thankful! Humbugs never die, more than the wandering Jew;
Bankrupt, they publish their own deaths, slink for a while from view,
Then take an *alias*, change the sign, and the old trade renew;
Indeed, 'tis wondrous how each Age, though laughing at the Past,   40
Insists on having its tight shoe made on the same old last;

---

[1] See the Compleat Ambassador, 1655, p. 21.

How it is sure its system would break up at once without
The bunnian which it *will* believe hereditary gout;
How it takes all its swans for geese, nay, stranger yet and sadder,
Sees in its treadmill's fruitless jog a heavenward Jacob's-ladder,
Shouts—*Lo, the Shining Heights are reached! One moment more aspire!*
Trots into cramps its poor, dear legs, gets never an inch the higher,
And, like the others, ends with pipe and mug beside the fire.
There, 'tween each doze, it whiffs and sips and watches with a sneer
The green recruits that trudge and sweat where it had swinked whilere,
And sighs to think this soon spent zeal should be in simple truth   51
The only interval between old Fogyhood and Youth:
' Well,' thus it muses, ' well, what odds? 'Tis not for us to warn;
' 'Twill be the same when we are dead, and was ere we were born;
Without the Treadmill, too, how grind our store of winter's corn?
Had we no stock, nor twelve *per cent.* received from Treadmill shares,
We might . . . . but these poor devils at last will get our easy-chairs;
High aims and hopes have great rewards, they, too, serene and snug,
Shall one day have their—soothing pipe and their enlivening mug;
From Adam, empty-handed Youth hath always heard the hum   60
Of Good Times Coming, and will hear until the last day come;
Young ears hear forward, old ones back, and, while the earth rolls on,
Full-handed Eld shall hear recede the steps of Good Times Gone;
Ah what a cackle we set up whene'er an egg was laid!
Cack-cack-cack-cackle! rang around, the scratch for worms was stayed,
Cut-cut-ca-dah-cut! from *this* egg the coming cock shall stalk!
The great New Era dawns, the age of Deeds and not of Talk!
And every stupid hen of us hugged close his egg of chalk,
Thought,—sure, I feel life stir within, each day with greater strength,
I have not sat these years in vain, the world is saved at length;—   70
When lo, the chick! from former chicks he differed not a jot,
But grew and crew and scratched and went, like those before, to pot!'
So muse the dim *Emeriti,* and, mournful though it be,
I must confess a kindred thought hath sometimes come to me,
Who, though but just of forty turned, have heard the rumorous fame
Of nine and ninety Coming Men, all—coming till they came.
Pure Mephistophiles all this? the vulgar nature jeers;
Good friend, while I was writing it, my eyes were dim with tears;
Thrice happy he who cannot see, or who his eyes can shut,
Life's deepest sorrow is contained in that small word there—But!   80

DIGRESSION D

Caught in the mire, he argufies,
Shows how 'twas done by rules,
And proves outright that nonsense lies
Beyond the reach of fools.

That's pure digression, then, you think? Now, just to prove 'tis *not*,
I shall begin a bigger one upon this very spot:
At any rate, 'tis naught, you say; precisely, I admit it,
For, in convicting it of that, you virtually acquit it;

You have conjectured, I suppose,—(come, never look despondent !)
That I intend to offer as an OUR OWN CORRESPONDENT,
And by what method more direct could I avouch my fitness
Than by exhibiting such art as the above may witness ?
I had one Nothing ; and, by dint of turning and displaying it,
I've occupied the time thus far in seeming to be saying it,   10
And have it, good as new, till comes the moment for conveying it.
Each creature must get forward in his own peculiar sort ;
The crab slants sideway to his end, and finds the way as short,
You'd make him go forth rightly, eh ? pray try your hand, Sir dab,—
Well, you have bettered Providence, but Nature wants her crab ;
Sir, in that awful Congress there, where sit th' assembled Fates,
Of which the unconscious newspapers report the slow debates,
Thank God, you can't be lobbying, log-rolling, and all that ;—
A world that suited you, O Smith, might be a trifle flat.
Fate, Idiosyncrasy, or what is just the same thing, custom,   20
Leads every mortal by the ear, though he be strong as Rustem,
Makes him do quite impossible things,—then, with a spear of grass
Marks the thin line none else can see, but which he cannot pass ;
That son of yours, so pale and slim, with whom the master fails,
What claps him in the fo'c'stle rude, and sends him after whales ?
And Samson, there, your burly boy, what takes him by the nape
And sets him at the counter's back to measure thread and tape ?
The servant-man you hired last year, who, for a paltry fee
Surrendered all his nature up, and would if he'd had three,
To suit your whimsies, and who seemed to find all drudgery sweet,   30
Left you in tears,—he could not take *that* bundle through the street ;
Centripetal, centrifugal, these the conditions two,
Some cling like moss, and other some fling off, their whole lives through ;
My style's centrifugal ; mark plain the settled boundary-line,
And, till it gets on t'other side, 'twill fret and fume and pine :
Or call 't the polypean style ; each verse contains, at any rate,
A polypus that in its turn new polypi can generate,
And if I the temptation strong that lurks in any verse shun,
'Tis certain that the next will breed new centres of dispersion ;
A brief attempt would shortly prove that I should be much worse if   40
I tried to curb my natural bent of being too discursive,
But I forbear, I spare you this *experimentum crucis,*
And shall, instead, proceed to show that Nonsense hath its uses ;
I mean good nonsense, there are men enough who have a leaning to
Write nonsense in great solemn tomes, nor have the wit of meaning to—
Tomes, the hop-pillows of the mind, that vanquish readers stout,
And which no gentleman's library can be complete without,
Pernoctent nobis, bedward turned, take one and feel no doubt ;
What a profound narcotic spell your fading senses greets,
'Tis just like getting into bed to look between their sheets ;   50
[I mean to make a list of them, some rainy day, to be a
Fasciculus first to my complete *librorum Pharmacopœia.*]
And now, because so hard of faith, this omnibus and gas age,

From an old author I translate the following deep passage ;
(See preface to the *Moriae Encomium* of Erasmus,
Recensuit et præfationem addidit Gelasmus :)

'Tis the easiest matter, in one sense,[1]
To write very passable nonsense ;
There are those who do naught but create your
Poor stuff from mere thinness of nature ;   60
But to do it with art and intention,
To never let fancy or pen shun
Any kind of odd lurches, twists, waggeries,
Absurdities, quibbles, and vagaries ;
To roll your Diogenes-puncheon
The vext reader's toes with a crunch on,
Making one quip the mere cotyledon
For the seed of another to feed on,
Is a matter—why, just reckon how many
Have fared well enough with Melpomene,   70
And how very few have come by a
Mere prosperous look from Thalia ;
Who since has contrived to hit off an ease
That in hard work will match A——s ?[2]
Hath even great Swift in his shabby lays
Come near the hop-skip prose of R——s ?
The deep-quibbling, sage-clown of S——e,
From among all the wits can you rake his peer ?
Are they not, my dear sir, *rari nantes*
Who can jingle the bells with C——s ?   80
How many great clerks in one turn could
Be both zany and wise man as S——e could ?
And who could with such a wise knack array
Great Jeames's phonetics as T——y ?
Your head is too small if it happen
That you can't keep the noble fool's-cap on.

So he goes maundering on and on, he's almost worse than I am,
And every line he writes begets as many sons as Priam ;
All this, good Messieurs Editors, is simply introduction
To show how nothing could be said in endless reproduction ;   90
I also wished to smooth the way for scribbling off some jolly
Good, topsy-turvy, head-o'er-heels, unmeaning, wholesome folly ;
We're pretty nearly crazy here with change and go-ahead,
With flinging our caught bird away for two ne'er caught instead,

[1] ' Nullitates scribere tam facile est quam bibere ; sed scribere intelligenter quod sit
inintelligibile ; insanire perfrequenter, motu proprio, libenter ; vertere in risibile quod
planè impossibile, sic ut titillat imum pectus,—hoc est summum intellectûs,' *et caetera.*
Praefatio Gelasmi pp. XCIX. *et seqq.*

[2] To avoid all suspicion of personality, I have omitted the names here. Though dead
for centuries, an enraged satirist might revenge himself on me, nowadays, through the
columns of the *Spiritual Telegraph*, or the legs of some dithyrambic centre-table.

With butting 'gainst the wall which we declare shall be a portal,
And questioning Deeps that never yet have said a word to mortal;
We're growing pale and hollow-eyed, and out of all condition,
With *mediums* and prophetic chairs, and crickets with a mission,
(The most astounding oracles since Balaam's donkey spoke,
'T would seem our furniture was all of Dodonean oak).   100
Make but the public laugh, be sure, 'twill take you to be somebody;
'Twill wrench its button from your clutch, my densely-earnest, glum body;
'Tis good, this noble earnestness, good in its place, but why
Make great Achilles' shield the pan to bake a penny pie?
Why, when we have a kitchen-range, insist that we shall stop,
And bore clear down to central fires to broil our daily chop?
Excalibur and Durandart are swords of price, but then
Why draw them sternly when you wish to cut your nails or pen?
Small gulf between the ape and man; you bridge it with your staff;
But it will be impassable until the ape can laugh;—   110
No, no, be common now and then, be sensible, be funny,
And, as Siberians bait their traps for bears with pots of honey,
From which ere they'll withdraw their snouts, they'll suffer many a club-lick,
So bait your moral figure-of-fours to catch the Orson public.
Look how the dead leaves melt their way down through deep-drifted snow;
They take the sun-warmth down with them—pearls could not conquer so;
There *is* a moral here, you see; if you would preach, you must
Steep all your truths in sun that they may melt down through the crust;
Brave Jeremiah, you are grand and terrible, a sign
And wonder, but were never quite a popular divine;   120
Fancy the figure you would cut among the nuts and wine!
I, on occasion, too, could preach, but hold it wiser far
To give the public sermons it will take with its cigar,
And morals fugitive, and vague as are these smoke-wreaths light
In which . . . . I trace . . . a . . . . let me see—bless me! 'tis out of sight.
When I my commentators have (who serve dead authors brave
As Turks do bodies that are sworn to stir within the grave,—
Unbury, make minced-meat of them, and bury them again),
They'll find deep meanings underneath each sputter of my pen,
Which I, a blissful shade (perhaps in teapoy pent, by process   130
Of these new moves in furniture, this wooden metempsychosis),
Accept for mine, unquestioning, as prudent Göthe choused
The critics out of all the thoughts they found for him in Faust.

PROGRESSION C

Our Own displays him just the man
To do the thing proposed,
Though what that thing is, nor his plan,
He hath not yet disclosed.

Travel (my theory is) suits least the race called Anglo-Saxon,
They come back loaded from each land they set their foolish tracks on
With every folly they can pile their mental and bodily backs on;
So at the outset let me state I do not mean to budge

LOWELL   T

And see the persons, places, things, I shall describe and judge,
Because when men have cheated you, or when they've tea'd and fed you, 'tis
The hardest thing to feel unbribed and clear the mind of prejudice ;
Therefore, 'tis wasting honest time, this squandering round the earth,
And I, who once sold wooden clocks, should know what time is worth.
Next as to how I'm qualified,—but let us first agree 10
What things deserve a wise man's eyes and ears across the sea ;
PERSONS : I'm forty, and have led, as you will see ere long,
A multifarious Yankee life, so there I'm rather strong ;
I've tended bar, worked farms to halves, been twice to the South seas,
Sold clocks (I mentioned that before), done something in herb teas,
Hawked books, kept district school (and thus, inspired with thirst for knowledge,
Pegged shoes till I had saved enough to put me through Yale College),
Invented a cheap stove (the famed *Antidotum Gehennae*,
So fuel-saving that no skill could coax it to burn any—
If you have lectured in small towns, you've probably seen many), 20
Driven stage, sold patent strops, by dint of interest at the White House,
Got nominated keeper of the Finback Island Light-house,
Where, just before a Northeast blow, the clockwork got ungeared,
And I revolved the light myself nine nights until it cleared ;
(I took it as a quiet place to invent perpetual motion,—
This large dose of the real thing quite cured me of the notion ;
It was, perhaps, the bitterest drop e'er mingled in my cup,
I rowed ashore so thoroughly sick, I threw the light-house up ;)
Then I went through the Bankrupt Act, merely from general caution—
For, if you're prudent, you'll take heed, and every chance's claws shun,
Nor leave old blankets lying about for adverse fates to toss ye on ; 31
Then I stood round a spell, and then bought out an Indian Doctor,
Then—but I have a faint surmise your credence may be shocked, or
I might go on, but I have said enough, no doubt, to show
That, to judge characters and men, I need not wait to grow ;—
PERSONS thus well provided for, the next thing is the strictures
On works of Art in general ; and first, we'll take the PICTURES.
Even here you cannot turn my flank,—I began life a painter,
Worked 'prentice first, then journeyman, with Major-General Taintor,
And did, myself, the sausages and the great round of beef 40
On the new market-house's sign, still prized for bold relief ;—
SCULPTURE : I think that more than half the Sculptors that have risen
Should hammer stone to some good end, sent all to Sing Sing prison ;
I'm sick of endless copyings of what were always bores,
Their dreary women on one toe, their Venuses by scores ;
(That's in the ignorant, slashing style,—if you prefer a judge
Mildly appreciative, deep,—just give my tap a nudge,
'Twill run aesthetic folderol, and best high-German fudge ;)—
MUSIC : when cousin Arad Cox at muster hurt his hand,
I played the bass-drum twice or more in the East Haddam band ;— 50
BUILDINGS : I saved them till the last, for there I feel at home—
Perhaps you never heard about the city of New Rome ?

'Twould not disgrace you deeply if you hadn't, for, you see,
It stayed in the potential mood, and was but going to be ;
We merely staked a pasture out, christened the poor thing Forum,
And chose two natural architects—OUR OWN was *unus horum ;*
'Twas he who planned the Meeting-house, a structure pure and winning,
With specimens of every style 'twixt vane and underpinning ;
Unhappily it ne'er was built ; New Rome, with nine good hills,
Remains unsettled to this day,—so do, alas ! its bills,—   60
But the experience thus obtained entitles me to hope
My architectural criticism will be allowed full scope.

PROGRESSION D

Our Own, his various qualities
  And aptitudes defined,
Descends, and makes more close replies
  To the inquiring mind.

But what, in these your voyagings, do you propose to do ?
I might retort, O, highborn Smythe, with—what is that to you ?
These twenty times I've bit my nails, and my left ear-tip scratched,
Wondering why *you* should wish to count *my* chickens ere they're hatched ;
But, if you further will insist, I'll answer (if I can) ;
My plan is—let me see—my plan is just to have no plan ;
In laying out a pleasure-ground (the rule is not in Price),
Be tipsy when you mark the paths, or you'll be too precise ;
And do it upon Burgundy, 'twill give a curvi-line
More sure of gentlemanly grace than any thinner wine ;   10
Precision is a right good thing, like olives, in its place,
But (still like olives) it comes in a long way after Grace.
Suppose I told you that I meant (as vines do, when they climb)
To wander where my clasp was wooed by any jutting rhyme ?
Or said that, like a river deep, lost first in bogs and sedges,
I soon should march to meet the sea with cities on my edges ?
(This seemingly mixed simile, at which the Highborn frowns,
Refers to sketches I shall give of European towns ;)
However, you shall have a peep ; come, children, form a ring,
I'll lift the crust, and let you see the birds are there to sing ;   20
Now then—I shall appear to go from capital to capital,
Pick up what's worth the picking up, and in my letters clap it all ;
When aught of interest shall occur, as certain as a star,
I, in our happy western phrase, shall be precisely *thar ;*
If Paris, for example, which is very likely, chooses
To have the periodic fit she's subject to—the Blouses,
And there should be a general row, I, from the very thick of it,
Shall send home thrilling narratives till you are fairly sick of it ;
I shall have interviews with kings and men of lower stations,
(Authors—of course,) and send reports of all the conversations ;   30
Shall visit the cathedrals, and, for fear of any blunder,
Call each the finest in the world, a mountain of carved wonder ;

Of every building, thing, and scene, that comes within my view,
I shall say something different, something so simply new,
The very Is upon my page shall with surprise grow round,—
And, by the way, lest any one should base enough be found
To steal the phrases got by me at cost of thought profuse,
I here put in a *caveat*, for some I mean to use,—

As—*Architecture's music cooled to zero point of Reaumur ;*

A statue is a song in stone (the chisel was its Homer) ;   40

*St. Peter's has an epic dome, beneath whose deeps profound
The papal choir, on Easter eve, build up a dome of sound ;*

*Art is the soul's horizon broad, and, as we onward go,
It moves with us and still recedes, until life's sun is low ;*

You call those rather goodish thoughts ? I have them by the score,
Ne'er yet by mortal man or maid put into words before ;
Life's sun I feel quite sure is new ; I got it by hard thinking
Only last night at half-past five, just as the sun was sinking ;
With these and other ornaments I shall enrich my text,
When, far across the Atlantic wave, I have to write my next.   50

PROGRESSION E

Our Own unfolds another coil
Of his portentous tale,
And shows the torture and the toil
Of riding on a rail.

I left East Haddam by the train—a mode of torture worse
Than any Dante conjured up—the case I will rehearse :
I found the car, then, occupied (I got in rather late,
And 'twas hermetically closed) by victims fifty-eight,
Each one of whom looked headachy and parboiledy and pale,
Having less air a-piece, perhaps, than Jonah in his whale ;
They seemed a troop of convict souls let out in search of bail
And, lest they might a mouthful get of unbedevilled air,
A Stygian sheriff's officer went with them every where,
Whose duty was to see that they no atmosphere should know   10
Cooler than that which Minos' tail had doomed them to below :
In shape he seemed a kind of stove, but by degrees my head
Was squeezed into an iron cap and screwed till I was dead
(Or thought I was), and then there came strange lights into my brain,
And 'neath his thin sheet-iron mask the tipstaff imp was plain.
At intervals another fiend—by mortals Brakeman hight—
Would rouse his fellow-torturer into a fierce delight,
Punching his ribs, and feeding him with lumps of anthracite ;
The demon's single eye grew red, and with unholy glee
Exulted as it shrivelled up the very soul in me.   20
I would have shrieked a maniac shriek, but that I did not dare ;
I thought of turning madly round, and seizing by the hair

A soul unblest that sat by me, only somehow I got
A notion that his treacherous scalp would prove to be red-hot.
I sprang to raise the window, but a female spirit of ill
Who all the space around her soured, sharp-nosed, close-lipped, and still,
(A vinegar-cruet incarnate) said, ' No *gentleman* would place
A lady in a thorough-draught that had a swollen face ! '
If you have ever chanced to bite a nice unripe persimmon,
You'll have some notion of her tone, but still a faint and dim one   30
No patent stove can radiate a chill more like the pole
Than such a lady, whose each act true views of grace control,
In doubt about her bonnet-box, secure about her soul.
Thenceforward all is phantasm dire ; I dimly recollect
A something 'twixt a nose and voice that said ' 'most there, I 'xpect,'——
Heavens ! almost WHERE ? a pang, a flash of fire through either eye shoots,
And I looked momently to see the last scene of Der Frieschutz ;
The bland conductor will become that flame-clad individual
Who stamping, Earth will gape, and ' Gentlemen, I bid you all,'
He'll shriek, ' to lava tea at six,' then crashing through the floor   40
With a strong smell of brimstone,—but all swam, I saw no more,
Only I vaguely seem to have seen the attendant fiend excite
His principal with further pokes and lumps of anthracite,
While faces featureless as dough, looked on serene and placid,
And nine and fifty pair of lungs evolved carbonic acid.
There was a scream, but whether 'twas the engine, or the last
Wild prayer for mercy of those eight and fifty as they passed
Down to their several torturings in deepest Malebolge,
As I myself am still in doubt, can't certainly be told ye ;
I only know they vanished all, the silent ghastly crew,   50
But whither, how, why, when,—these things I never fully knew ;
I stood with carpet-bag in hand, when the strange spell unbound me,
And five score yelling cabmen danced their frenzied war-dance round me.

PROGRESSION F

Our Own, howe'er with Byron's verse
   He may enchanted be,
Finds that he likes the ocean worse,
   When trying it *per se.*

When I was a beggarly boy,
   And lived in a cellar damp,
I had not a friend nor a toy,
   But I had Aladdin's lamp ;
When I could not sleep for cold,
   I had fire enough in my brain,
And built, with a roof of gold,
   My beautiful castles in Spain !

Since then I have toiled day and night,
   I have money and power good store,   10
But I'd give all my lamps of silver bright
   For the one that is mine no more ;

> Take, Fortune, whatever you choose,
> You gave, and may snatch again;
> I have nothing 'twould pain me to lose,
> For I own no more castles in Spain!

So mused a poet, quite as wise as either you or I,
Coughing with dust, as Crassus' coach rolled smoothly-swinging by;
And, if I understand his thought, which may be something trite,
He was (which for a poet's much) within two-thirds of right;   20
Fond youth, be abstinent, pull not that Hesperidean fruit,
One bite, and you repent too late, and lame your jaw to boot:
Thank God for the Unattainable, it leaves you still a boy,
The wishing for the wishing-cap is that which makes the joy;
Privation gives their charm to things, the glory and the grace,
Beckon and flee—ah, fool, that would'st their frozen zones embrace!
In winter, summer seems most fair, and what enchantment glows
In August o'er those mountain-peaks, ermined with rounding snows!
The frozen Samoiede makes his heaven a place of endless fire,
And, when kind fortune heaps the board, to glut the soul's desire,   30
Apicius Bufo starves and sighs, and wonders what it means,—
Nectar? Ambrosia?—hum, so-so, but no pig's head and greens?
And thou, oh hero, who hast climbed to scarce-dreamed fame and power,
Think'st only of a little mound which dusky yews embower,
And, sighing, musest what are all these idle sands to me
Since those blue eyes are closed with dust that should be here to see?
Ah, happy eyes that shut so soon, ye only have the might
To keep undimmed the olden spell, for ever warm and bright!
Had village Alice lived, poor fool, thou would'st without remorse
Be sighing for a bride of State, and planning a divorce.   40

This train of thought I've fallen on, far out here on the sea,
Coiled up, half-frozen underneath the weather-bulwark's lee,
And (faith that last wave soused me through)—and writing on my knee;
The application of it is, that when you're on the land
The sea is every thing that's bright, and broad, and blue, and grand,
And that you'd change what Wordsworth calls your glorious second berth
(Now that you've tried it) for a grave, because 'twould be firm earth;
Perhaps in some October night, when the roused south o'erwhelms,
With surge on surge rolled gathering down the night, the shuddering elms,
You have lain fancying what wild joy there must be in the motion   50
Of a brave vessel plunging through the broken coils of ocean;
Your mind ran forth and back again, like a fly-watching spider,
Upon that line in Byron of the *steed that knows its rider*,
And, in your bath next morning, you splash with double glee,
Humming, dear Barry Cornwall's song—*the sea! the o-pen sea!*
I wish that Barry and Byron both were only here with me!
All well enough this sentiment and stuff upon the shore,
But, when the sea is smoothest, 'tis an Erymanthian bore,
And when 'tis rough, my brace of bards, you'd neither of you sing
Of hands on manes, or blue and fresh, but quite another thing,—   60

Flat on your backs in jerking berths you scarce could keep your place in,
You'd moan an Amboean sad—*quick, steward! quick! a basin!*
(Queen's counsel most delectable, I still seem hearing thee
Sing *Camerière* through the rain along the Bieler sea.)

How easy 'tis to tyrannize over Taste's hapless lieges!
The poor *Achivi* still are plucked *quidquid delirant reges ;*
If Hamlet says he sees a whale, Polonius must follow,
And what A swears is beautiful, all down to Z will swallow ;
None dares confess he cannot see what great Flapdoddle spies,
And, like potatoes, fools are bred from one another's eyes ;   70
Dear Nyncombe, what sharp agonies I've seen you going through with
Before a statue which your soul had naught on earth to do with,
And what could e'er be finer than your awed, assenting ' Oh ! '
When I suggested that deep thought in the Apollo's toe ?
Don't come to Rome for nothing, man, with some likeminded crony,
Go valiantly and eat a steak down at the Gabione ;
'Tis in this way that men are made to say they like the sea,
Flam says he does, and all the rest will be as good as he.
I heard a great man once declare that he had never found
A sailor, yet, who loved the fate to which his life was bound,   80
And when I asked our brown first-mate, a seaman good and brave,
On shore as helpless as a fish, a viking on the wave,
What life would please him most ? he sighed, looked at his tattooed arm,
Studied its hieroglyphs awhile, and said—an inland farm.
And he was right ; I cannot, for example, see the least
Pleasure in walking on a deck that's drunk as any beast,
A wet plank, scarcely larger than a white bear's sloppy pen,
That tips you here and slips you there, and trips you back again ;
That cheats you with a moment's lull, and, when you think you feel
Quite sure of the companionway, half breaks you on the wheel,   90
Then slants until you need both hands to keep your hold on that,
And pins you helpless while the wind blows off your second hat.
The steed that *throws* his rider would be nearer to the fact :
To me it gives no pleasure to be swashed and washed and racked ;
To have a three weeks' tipsiness on cold saltwater merely,
With legs that seem like some one's else, they bother you so queerly
Taking you *here* when you mean *there*,—no, no, it has no charm,
Although the loveliest cousin may be hanging on your arm.
Of course, I am not seasick, for although that epidemic
(*Hic*) prostrates all my friends, yet (*hic*) I only pity them (*hic*).   100
Indeed, in this life's pilgrimage, I found this maxim true :
There are four common weaknesses no mortal ever knew,
A headache that was caused by wine, drowsiness late at night,
Seasickness, and a corn that came from wearing boots too tight.
A seasick man I never saw ; Our Own leans o'er the rail,
Muses awhile, and then comes back with features doughy pale ;
But he had only wandered aft, a Parthian glance to take
At those strange coils of moony fire that mark the writhing wake.

With ghastly calm he takes a pipe; in minutes five (or less) hence,
He'll feel again that ecstasy produced by phosphorescence.   110

  Conceive of an existence in which the great events
Are breakfast, luncheon, dinner, tea, in which, when Fate relents,
She sends a string of porpoises, perhaps a grampus, too,
Who blunders up beneath the stern, and gives a *poo-oo-ooh!*
While we immortal souls crowd aft and crush each other's toes
To see this stupid creature blow what he esteems a nose;
Why, I blew thrice my moral and accountable proboscis,
But found no fish so *blasé* that it ever came across his
Waterlogged brain that it was worth his while to turn and come anon,
Lest he should miss the witnessing of that sublime phenomenon;   120
Nor would it, though your nose were like fray John's, or even had you a
Verissimo fazzoletto of Saint Antony of Padua,
The Apostle who in Finland had a cure of souls, and sent
Conviction to his hearers that 'twas good to fry in Lent.
There are some goodish things at sea; for instance, one can feel
A grandeur in the silent man for ever at the wheel,
That bit of two-legged intellect, that particle of drill,
Who the huge floundering hulk inspires with reason, brain and will,
And makes the ship, though skies are black and headwinds whistle loud,
Obey her conscience there which feels the loadstar through the cloud;   130
And when by lusty western gales the full-sailed barque is hurled
Toward the great moon which, sitting on the silent underworld,
Rounds luridly up to look on ours, and shoots a broadening line,
Of palpitant light from crest to crest across the ridgy brine,
Then from the bows look back and feel a thrill that never stales
In that full-bosomed, swan-white pomp of onward-yearning sails;
Ah, when dear cousin Bull laments that you can't make a poem,
Take him aboard a clipper-ship, young Jonathan, and show him
A work of art that in its grace and grandeur may compare
With any thing that any race has fashioned any where;   140
'Tis not a statue, grumbles John; nay, if you come to that,
We think of Hyde Park corner, and concede you beat us flat
With your equestrian statue to a Nose and a Cocked-hat;
But 'tis not a cathedral; well, e'en that we will allow,
Both statues and cathedrals are anachronistic now;
Your minsters, coz, the monuments of men who conquered you,
You'd sell a bargain, if we'd take the deans and chapters too;
No; mortal men build now-a-days, as always heretofore,
Good temples to the gods which they in very truth adore;
The shepherds of this Broker Age, with all their willing flocks,   150
Although they bow to stones no more, do bend the knee to stocks,
And churches can't be beautiful though crowded, floor and gallery,
If people worship preacher, and if preacher worship salary;
'Tis well to look things in the face, the god o' the modern universe,
Hermes, cares naught for halls of art and libraries of puny verse,
If they don't sell, he notes them thus upon his ledger—say, *per*

Contra to loss of so much stone, best Russia duck and paper ;
And, after all, about this Art men talk a deal of fudge,
Each nation has its path marked out, from which it must not budge ;
The Romans had as little art as Noah in his ark, 160
Yet somehow on this globe contrived to make an epic mark ;
Religion, painting, sculpture, song—for these they ran up jolly ticks
With Greece and Egypt, but they were great artists in their politics,
And if we make no minsters, John, nor epics, yet the Fates
Are not entirely deaf to men who *can* build ships and states ;
(I waive the literary point, contented with observing
That *I* like Hawthorne, Longfellow, Emerson, Bryant, Irving,)
The arts are never pioneers, but men have strength and health
Who, called on suddenly, can improvise a commonwealth,
Nay, can more easily go on and frame them by the dozen, 170
Than you can make a dinner-speech, dear sympathizing cousin :
And, though our restless Jonathan have not your graver bent, sure he
Does represent this hand-to-mouth, pert, rapid, nineteenth century ;
This is the Age of Scramble ; men move faster than they did
When they pried up the imperial Past's deep-dusted coffin-lid,
Searching for scrolls of precedent ; the wire-tamed lightning now
Replaces Delphos—men don't leave the steamer for the scow ;
What hero, were they new to-day, would ever stop to read
The Iliad, the Shanàmeh, or the Nibelungenlied ?
Their public's gone, the artist Greek, the lettered Shah, the hairy Graf—
Folio and plesiosaur sleep well ; *we* weary o'er a paragraph ; 181
The mind moves planet-like no more, it fizzes, cracks, and bustles ;
From end to end with journals dry the land o'ershadowed rustles,
As with dead leaves a winter-beech, and, with their breath-roused jars
Amused, we care not if they hide the eternal skies and stars ;
Down to the general level of the Board of Brokers sinking,
The Age takes in the newspapers, or, to say sooth unshrinking,
The newspapers take in the Age, and Stocks do all the thinking.

THE ORIGIN OF DIDACTIC POETRY

[Atlantic Monthly, Nov. 1857.]

WHEN wise Minerva still was young
  And just the least romantic,
Soon after from Jove's head she flung
  That preternatural antic,
'T is said to keep from idleness
  Or flirting,—those twin curses,—
She spent her leisure, more or less,
  In writing po——, no, verses.

How nice they were ! to rhyme with *far*
  A kind *star* did not tarry ;

The metre, too, was regular
  As schoolboy's dot and carry ;
And full they were of pious plums,
  So extra-super-moral,—
For sucking Virtue's tender gums
  Most tooth-enticing coral.

A clean, fair copy she prepares,
  Makes sure of moods and tenses,
With her own hand,—for prudence spares
  A man- (or woman) -uensis ;

Complete, and tied with ribbons
   proud,
  She hinted soon how cosy a
Treat it would be to read them loud
  After next day's Ambrosia.

The Gods thought not it would amuse
  So much as Homer's Odyssees,
But could not very well refuse
  The properest of Goddesses :
So all sat round in attitudes
  Of various dejection,
As with a *hem !* the queen of prudes
  Began her grave prelection.

At the first pause Zeus said, ' Well
   sung !—
  I mean—ask Phoebus,—*he* knows.'
Says Phoebus, ' Zounds ! a wolf 's
   among
  Admetus's merinos !
Fine ! very fine ! but I must go ;
  They stand in need of me there ;
Excuse me ! ' snatched his stick, and
   so
  Plunged down the gladdened ether.

With the next gap, Mars said, ' For
   me
  Don't wait,—naught could be finer;
But I'm engaged at half past three,—
  A fight in Asia Minor ! '
Then Venus lisped, ' How very thad !
  It rainth down there in torrinth ;
But I *mutht* go, becauthe they've had
  A thacrifithe in Corinth ! '

Then Bacchus,—' With those slam-
   ming doors
  I lost the last half dist—(hic !)
Mos' bu'ful se'ments ! what 's the
   Chor's ?
  My voice shall not be missed—
   (hic !) '
His words woke Hermes ; ' Ah ! ' he
   said,

' I *so* love moral theses ! '
Then winked at Hebe, who turned
   red,
  And smoothed her apron's creases.

Just then Zeus snored,—the Eagle
   drew
  His head the wing from under ;
Zeus snored,—o'er startled Greece
   there flew
  The many-volumed thunder;
Some augurs counted nine,—some,
   ten,—
  Some said, 'twas war,—some,
   famine,—
And all, that other-minded men
  Would get a precious ——.

Proud Pallas sighed, ' It will not do ;
  Against the Muse I've sinned, oh ! '
And her torn rhymes sent flying
   through
  Olympus's back window.
Then, packing up a peplus clean,
  She took the shortest path thence,
And opened, with a mind serene,
  A Sunday-school in Athens.

The verses ? Some, in ocean swilled,
  Killed every fish that bit to 'em ;
Some Galen caught, and, when dis-
   tilled,
  Found morphine the residuum ;
But some that rotted on the earth
  Sprang up again in copies,
And gave two strong narcotics birth,—
  Didactic bards and poppies.

Years after, when a poet asked
  The Goddess's opinion,
As being one whose soul had basked
  In Art's clear-aired dominion,—
' Discriminate,' she said, ' betimes ;
  The Muse is unforgiving ;
Put all your beauty in your rhymes,
  Your morals in your living.'

THE MAPLE

[Atlantic Monthly, November, 1857.]

THE Maple puts her corals on in May,
While loitering frosts about the lowlands cling,
To be in tune with what the robins sing,
Plastering new log-huts 'mid her branches grey ;
But when the Autumn southward turns away,
Then in her veins burns most the blood of Spring,
And every leaf, intensely blossoming,
Makes the year's sunset pale the set of day.
O Youth unprescient, were it only so
With trees you plant, and in whose shade reclined,
Thinking their drifting blooms Fate's coldest snow,
You carve dear names upon the faithful rind,
Nor in that vernal stem the cross foreknow
That Age may bear, silent, yet unresigned !

MY PORTRAIT GALLERY

[Atlantic Monthly, December, 1857.]

OFT round my hall of portraiture I gaze,
By Memory reared, the artist wise and holy,
From stainless quarries of deep-buried days.
There, as I muse in soothing melancholy,
Your faces glow in more than mortal youth,
Companions of my prime, now vanished wholly,—
The loud, impetuous boy, the low-voiced maiden.
Ah, never master that drew mortal breath
Can match thy portraits, just and generous Death,
Whose brush with sweet regretful tints is laden !
Thou paintest that which struggled here below
Half understood, or understood for woe,
And, with a sweet forewarning,
Mak'st round the sacred front an aureole glow
Woven of that light that rose on Easter morning.

THE NEST

[Atlantic Monthly, March, 1858.]

MAY

WHEN oaken woods with buds are pink,
And new-come birds each morning
    sing,—
When fickle May on Summer's brink
    Pauses, and knows not which to
    fling,
Whether fresh bud and bloom again,
Or hoar-frost silvering hill and plain,—

Then from the honeysuckle grey
    The oriole with experienced quest
Twitches the fibrous bark away,
    The cordage of his hammock-nest
Cheering his labour with a note
Rich as the orange of his throat.

High o'er the loud and dusty road
    The soft grey cup in safety swings,

To brim ere August with its load
  Of downy breasts and throbbing
    wings,
O'er which the friendly elm-tree
  heaves
An emerald roof with sculptured
  eaves.

Below, the noisy World drags by
  In the old way, because it must,—
The bride with trouble in her eye,
  The mourner following hated dust:
Thy duty, wingèd flame of Spring,
Is but to love and fly and sing.

Oh, happy life, to soar and sway
  Above the life by mortals led,
Singing the merry months away,
  Master, not slave of daily bread,
And, when the Autumn comes, to flee
Wherever sunshine beckons thee!

PALINODE.—DECEMBER

Like some lorn abbey now, the wood
  Stands roofless in the bitter air;
In ruins on its floor is strewed
  The carven foliage quaint and rare,
And homeless winds complain along
The columned choir once thrilled with
  song.

And thou, dear nest, whence joy and
  praise
  The thankful oriole used to pour,
Swing'st empty while the north winds
  chase
  Their snowy swarms from Labra-
    dor:
But, loyal to the happy past,
I love thee still for what thou wast.

Ah, when the Summer graces flee
  From other nests more dear than
    thou,
And, where June crowded once, I see
  Only bare trunk and disleaved
    bough,
When springs of life that gleamed and
  gushed
Run chilled, and slower, and are
  hushed,—

I'll think, that, like the birds of
  Spring,
  Our good goes not without repair,
But only flies to soar and sing
  Far off in some diviner air,
Where we shall find it in the calms
Of that fair garden 'neath the palms.

BEATRICE

[*Atlantic Monthly*, June, 1858.]

How was I worthy so divine a loss,
  Deepening my midnights, kindling all my morns?
Why waste such precious wood to make my cross,
  Such far-sought roses for my crown of thorns?

And when she came, how earned I such a gift?
  Why spend on me, a poor earth-delving mole,
The fireside sweetnesses, the heavenward lift,
  The hourly mercy of a woman's soul?

Ah, did we know to give her all her right,
  What wonders even in our poor clay were done.
It is not Woman leaves us to our night,
  It is our earth that grovels from her sun.

Our nobler cultured fields and gracious domes
  We whirl too oft from her who still shines on
To light in vain our caves and clefts, the homes
  Of night-bird instincts pained till she be gone.

Still must this body starve our souls with shade ;
  But when Death makes us what we were before,
Then shall her sunshine all our depths invade,
  And not a shadow stain heaven's crystal floor.

IN THE HALF-WAY HOUSE

[Atlantic Monthly, January, 1863.]

I

At twenty we fancied the blest Middle Ages
  A spirited cross of romantic and grand,
All templars and minstrels and ladies and pages,
  And love and adventure in Outre-Mer land ;
But, ah, where the youth dreamed of building a minster,
  The man takes a pew and sits reckoning his pelf,
And the Graces wear fronts, the Muse thins to a spinster,
  When Middle-Age stares from one's glass at himself !

II

Do you twit me with days when I had an Ideal,
  And saw the sear future through spectacles green ?
Then find me some charm, while I look round and see all
  These fat friends of forty, shall keep me nineteen ;
Should we go on pining for chaplets of laurel
  Who 've paid a perruquier for mending our thatch,
Or, our feet swathed in baize, with our fate pick a quarrel,
  If, instead of cheap bay-leaves, she sent a dear scratch ?

III

We called it our Eden, that small patent-baker,
  When life was half moonshine and half Mary Jane ;
But the butcher, the baker, the candlestick-maker !—
  Did Adam have duns and slip down a back-lane ?
Nay, after the Fall did the modiste keep coming
  With last styles of fig-leaf to Madam Eve's bower ?
Did Jubal, or whoever taught the girls thrumming,
  Make the Patriarchs deaf at a dollar the hour ?

IV

As I think what I was, I sigh, *Desunt nonnulla !*
  Years are creditors Sheridan's self could not bilk ;
But then, as my boy says, ' What right has a fullah
  To ask for the cream, when himself spilled the milk ? '

Perhaps when you 're older, my lad, you 'll discover
 The secret with which Auld Lang Syne there is gilt,—
Superstition of old man, maid, poet, and lover,—
 That cream rises thickest on milk that was spilt!

V

We sailed for the moon, but, in sad disillusion,
 Snug under Point Comfort are glad to make fast,
And strive (sans our glasses) to make a confusion
 'Twixt our rind of green cheese and the moon of the past;
Ah, Might-have-been, Could-have-been, Would-have-been! rascals,
 He 's a genius or fool whom ye cheat at two-score,
And the man whose boy-promise was likened to Pascal's
 Is thankful at forty they don't call him bore!

VI

With what fumes of fame was each confident pate full!
 How rates of insurance should rise on the Charles!
And which of us now would not feel wisely grateful,
 If his rhymes sold as fast as the Emblems of Quarles?
E'en if won, what 's the good of Life's medals and prizes?
 The rapture 's in what never was or is gone;
That we missed them makes Helens of plain Ann Elizys,
 For the goose of To-day still is Memory's swan.

VII

And yet who would change the old dream for new treasure?
 Make not youth's sourest grapes the best wine of our life?
Need he reckon his date by the Almanac's measure
 Who is twenty life-long in the eyes of his wife?
Ah, Fate, should I live to be nonagenarian,
 Let me still take Hope's frail I. O. U.s upon trust,
Still talk of a trip to the Islands Macarian,
 And still climb the dream-tree for—ashes and dust!

THE BLACK PREACHER

A BRETON LEGEND

[Atlantic Monthly, April, 1864.]

At Carnac in Brittany, close on the bay,
They show you a church, or rather the grey
Ribs of a dead one, left there to bleach
With the wreck lying near on the crest of the beach;
Roofless and splintered with thunder-stone,
'Mid lichen-blurred gravestones all alone,
'T is the kind of ruin strange sights to see
That may have their teaching for you and me.

Something like this, then, my guide had to tell,
Perched on a saint cracked across when he fell,　　　　10
But since I might chance give his meaning a wrench,
He talking his *patois* and I English-French,
I 'll put what he told me, preserving the tone,
In a rhymed prose that makes it half his, half my own.

An abbey-church stood here, once on a time,
Built as a death-bed atonement for crime :
'T was for somebody's sins, I know not whose ;
But sinners are plenty, and you can choose.
Though a cloister now of the dusk-winged bat,
'T was rich enough once, and the brothers grew fat,　　　20
Looser in girdle and purpler in jowl,
Singing good rest to the founder's lost soul.
But one day came Northmen, and lithe tongues of fire
Lapped up the chapter-house, licked off the spire,
And left all a rubbish-heap, black and dreary,
Where only the wind sings *miserere*.
Of what the monks came by no legend runs,
At least they were lucky in not being nuns.

No priest has kneeled since at the altar's foot,
Whose crannies are searched by the nightshade's root,　　　30
Nor sound of service is ever heard,
Except from throat of the unclean bird,
Hooting to unassoiled shapes as they pass
In midnights unholy his witches' mass,
Or shouting 'Ho ! ho !' from the belfry high
As the Devil's sabbath-train whirls by ;
But once a year, on the eve of All-Souls,
Through these arches dishallowed the organ rolls,
Fingers long fleshless the bell-ropes work,
The chimes peal muffled with sea-mists mirk,　　　40
The skeleton windows are traced anew
On the baleful flicker of corpse-lights blue,
And the ghosts must come, so the legend saith,
To a preaching of Reverend Doctor Death.

Abbots, monks, barons, and ladies fair
Here the dull summons and gather there :
No rustle of silk now, no clink of mail,
Nor ever a one greets his church-mate pale ;
No knight whispers love in the *châtelaine's* ear,
His next-door neighbour this five hundred year ;　　　50
No monk has a sleek *benedicite*
For the great lord shadowy now as he ;
Nor needeth any to hold his breath,
Lest he lose the least word of Doctor Death.

He chooses his text in the Book Divine,
Tenth verse of the Preacher in chapter nine :—
' " Whatsoever thy hand shall find thee to do,
That do with thy whole might, or thou shalt rue ;
For no man is wealthy or wise or brave
In that quencher of might-bes and would-bes, the grave."   60
Bid by the Bridegroom, " To-morrow," ye said,
And To-morrow was digging a trench for your bed ;
Ye said, " God can wait ; let us finish our wine " ;
Ye had wearied Him, fools, and that last knock was mine ! '

But I can't pretend to give you the sermon,
Or say if the tongue were French, Latin, or German ;
Whatever he preached in, I give you my word
The meaning was easy to all that heard ;
Famous preachers there have been and be,
But never was one so convincing as he ;   70
So blunt was never a begging friar,
No Jesuit's tongue so barbed with fire,
Cameronian never, nor Methodist,
Wrung gall out of Scripture with such a twist.

And would you know who his hearers must be ?
I tell you just what my guide told me :
Excellent teaching men have, day and night,
From two earnest friars, a black and a white,
The Dominican Death and the Carmelite Life ;
And between these two there is never strife,   80
For each has his separate office and station,
And each his own work in the congregation ;
Whoso to the white brother deafens his ears,
And cannot be wrought on by blessings or tears,
Awake in his coffin must wait and wait,
In that blackness of darkness that means *too late*,
And come once a year, when the ghost-bell tolls,
As till Doomsday it shall on the eve of All-Souls,
To hear Doctor Death, whose words smart with the brine
Of the Preacher, the tenth verse of chapter nine.   90

' FROM *FIRESIDE TRAVELS*, 1864 '

DEDICATION TO W. W. STORY

WHO carves his thoughts in marble will not scorn
    These pictured bubbles, if so far they fly ;
They will recall days ruddy but with morn,
    Not red like those late past or drawing nigh !

DIFFUGERE NIVES

HERE lies, or lie,—decide the question, you,
If they were two in one or one in two,—
P. & S. Snow, whose memory shall not fade,
Castor and Pollux of the oyster-trade :
Hatched from one egg, at once the shell they burst,
(The last, perhaps, a P. S. to the first,)
So homoousian both in look and soul,
So undiscernibly a single whole,
That whether P. was S. or S. was P.
Surpassed all skill in etymology ;   10
One kept the shop at once, and all we know
Is that together they were *the* Great Snow,
A snow not deep, yet with a crust so thick
It never melted to the son of Tick ;
Perpetual ? nay, our region was too low,
Too warm, too Southern, for perpetual Snow ;
Still, like fair Leda's sons, to whom 'twas given
To take their turns in Hades and in Heaven,
Our new Dioscuri would bravely share
The cellar's darkness and the upper air ;   20
Twice every year would each the shades escape,
And, like a sea-bird, seek the wave-washed Cape,
Where (Rumour voiced) one spouse sufficed for both ;
No bigamist, for she upon her oath,
Unskilled in letters, could not make a guess
At any difference 'twixt P. and S.—
A thing not marvellous, since Fame agrees
They were as little different as two peas,
And she, like Paris, when his Helen laid
Her hand 'mid snows from Ida's top conveyed   30
To cool their wine of Chios, could not know,
Between those rival candours, which was Snow.
Whiche'er behind the counter chanced to be
Oped oysters oft, his clam-shells seldom he ;
If e'er he laughed, 'twas with no loud guffaw,
The fun warmed through him with a gradual thaw ;
The nicer shades of wit were not his gift,
Nor was it hard to sound Snow's simple drift ;
His were plain jokes, that many a time before
Had set his tarry messmates in a roar,   40
When floundering cod beslimed the deck's wet planks,—
The humorous specie of Newfoundland banks.
But Snow is gone, and, let us hope, sleeps well,
Buried (his last breath asked it) in a shell ;

Fate with an oyster-knife sawed off his thread,
And planted him upon his latest bed.

Him on the Stygian shore my fancy sees
Noting choice shoals for oyster colonies,
Or, at a board stuck full of ghostly forks,
Opening for practice visionary Yorks.   50
And whither he has gone, may we too go,—
Since no hot place were fit for keeping Snow !

FRAGMENT IN CONTINUATION OF 'OUR OWN' (see pp. 538-53)

MENENIUS, thou who fain wouldst know how calmly men can pass
Those biting portraits of themselves, disguised as fox or ass,—
Go borrow coin enough to buy a full-length psyche-glass,
Engage a rather darkish room in some well sought position,
And let the town break out with bills, so much per head admission,—
GREAT NATURAL CURIOSITY ! !   THE BIGGEST LIVING FOOL ! !
Arrange your mirror cleverly, before it set a stool,
Admit the public one by one, place each upon the seat,
Draw up the curtain, let him look his fill, and then retreat.
Smith mounts and takes a thorough view, then comes serenely down,   10
Goes home and tells his wife the thing is curiously like Brown ;
Brown goes and stares, and tells his wife the wonder's core and pith
Is that 'tis just the counterpart of that conceited Smith.
Life calls us all to such a show : Menenius, trust in me,
While thou to see thy neighbour smil'st, he does the same for thee.

DOCTOR LOBSTER

A PERCH, who had the toothache, once
Thus moaned, like any human dunce :
' Why must great souls exhaust so soon
Life's thin and unsubstantial boon ?
Existence on such sculpin terms,—
Their vulgar loves and hard-won worms,—
What is it all but dross to me,
Whose nature craves a larger sea ;
Whose inches, six from head to tail,
Enclose the spirit of a whale ;   10
Who, if great baits were still to win,
By watchful eye and fearless fin
Might with the Zodiac's awful twain
Room for a third immortal gain ?

Better the crowd's unthinking plan,—
The hook, the jerk, the frying-pan!
O Death, thou ever roaming shark,
Ingulf me in eternal dark!'

The speech was cut in two by flight:
A real shark had come in sight;   20
No metaphoric monster, one
It soothes despair to call upon,
But stealthy, sidelong, grim, I wis,
A bit of downright Nemesis;
While it recovered from the shock,
Our fish took shelter 'neath a rock:
This was an ancient lobster's house,
A lobster of prodigious *nous*,
So old that barnacles had spread
Their white encampments o'er its head,—   30
And of experience so stupend,
His claws were blunted at the end,
Turning life's iron pages o'er,
That shut and can be oped no more.

Stretching a hospitable claw,
' At once,' said he, ' the point I saw;
My dear young friend, your case I rue,
Your great-great-grandfather I knew;
He was a tried and tender friend
I know,—I ate him in the end: 40
In this vile sea a pilgrim long,
Still my sight's good, my memory strong;
The only sign that age is near
Is a slight deafness in this ear;
I understand your case as well
As this my old familiar shell;
This sorrow's a new-fangled notion,
Come in since first I knew the ocean;
We had no radicals, nor crimes,
Nor lobster-pots, in good old times;   50
Your traps and nets and hooks we owe
To Messieurs Louis Blanc and Co.;
I say to all my sons and daughters,
Shun Red Republican hot waters;
No lobster ever cast his lot
Among the reds, but went to pot:
Your trouble's in the jaw, you said?
Come, let me just nip off your head,
And, when a new one comes, the pain
Will never trouble you again: 60
Nay, nay, fear naught: 'tis nature's law;
Four times I've lost this starboard claw;

And still, ere long, another grew,
Good as the old,—and better too !'

The perch consented, and next day
An osprey, marketing that way,
Picked up a fish without a head,
Floating with belly up, stone dead.

MORAL

Sharp are the teeth of ancient saws,
And sauce for goose is gander's sauce ;   70
But perch's heads aren't lobster's claws.

AT SEA

AND I thus floating, lonely elf,
A kind of planet by myself,
The mists draw up and furl away,
And in the east a warming grey,
Faint as the tint of oaken woods
When o'er their buds May breathes and broods,
Tells that the golden sunrise-tide
Is lapsing up earth's thirsty side,
Each moment purpling on the crest
Of some stark billow farther west :   10
And as the sea-moss droops and hears
The gurgling flood that nears and nears,
And then with tremulous content
Floats out each thankful filament,
So waited I until it came,
God's daily miracle—O shame
That I had seen so many days
Unthankful, without wondering praise,
Not recking more this bliss of earth
Than the cheap fire that lights my hearth !   20
But now glad thoughts and holy pour
Into my heart, as once a year
To San Miniato's open door,
In long procession, chanting clear,
Through slopes of sun, through shadows hoar,
The coupled monks slow-climbing sing,
And like a golden censer swing
From rear to front, from front to rear
Their alternating bursts of praise,
Till the roof's fading seraphs gaze   30
Down through an odorous mist, that crawls
Lingeringly up the darkened walls,
And the dim arches, silent long,
Are startled with triumphant song.

THE RUINED TEMPLE OF FORTUNE AT PALESTRINA

COME hither, weary ghosts that wail
  O'er buried Nimroud's carven walls,
And ye whose nightly footsteps frail
  From the dread hush of Memphian halls
  Lead forth the whispering funerals !

Come hither, shade of ancient pain
  That, muffled sitting, hear'st the foam
To death-deaf Carthage shout in vain,
  And thou that in the Sibyl's tome
  Tear-stain'st the *never* after Rome !

Come, Marius, Wolsey, all ye great
  On whom proud Fortune stamped her heel,
And see herself the sport of Fate,
  Herself discrowned and made to feel
  The treason of her slippery wheel !

TO A FRIEND WHO SENT ME A MEERSCHAUM

[*Spirit of the Fair*, New York, April 12, 1864.]

WELL was it named *écume de mer*
The gracious earth so light and fair ;
Mysterious cross of foam and clay,
From both it stole the best away :
If clay, 'tis such as sense might doubt of,
The same Jove made the Naiads out of,
If foam, then such as crowns the glow
Of beakers brimmed with Veuve Clicquot,
And here combined they sure must be
The birth of some enchanted sea,   10
Shaped to immortal form, the type
And very Venus of a pipe !

For Fancy that : but since they say
We Yankees think it wrong to play,
And love a moral bench to squirm on
Harder than flint, I add a sermon.
Whene'er I fill it with the weed
From Lethe wharf, whose potent seed
Nicotia, child of Bacchus's age,
Heir of his cheer but not his rage,   20
In misty Indian summer bore
From Dreamland to Virginia's shore,

I'll think; so fill the costliest bowl,
And strange alembic of the soul,
With herbs far-sought that shall distill
Not fumes to slacken thought and will,
But gracious essences that nerve
To wait, to dare, to strive, to serve.

While curls the smoke in eddies soft,
Wreathing fantastic shapes aloft, 30
That give and take, though chance-designed,
The impress of the dreamer's mind,
And in a mild enchantment blends
The fireside thoughts of musing friends,
I'll think; so let the vapours bred
By passion in the heart or head,
Pass off and upward into space,
With bright farewells of tender grace,
Remembered in some happier time
To blend their beauty with my rhyme 40

While slowly through its candid grain
The colour deepens, as the brain
That burns in mortals leaves its trace
Of bale or blessing in the face,
I'll think; so let the virtue rare
Of life consuming make me fair,
So may its temperate fires imbue
My soul and sense with riper hue,
So 'gainst our earthly ills profuse
Steep me in some nepenthe-juice; 50
And if my years must part with all
That whiteness which men greenness call,
And the gods wisdom, if I must
Doubt where I grandly took on trust,
Grant me, Experience, this alone,—
Turn me to meerschaum, not to stone;
Smooth, grim Medusa, half thy frown,
Making me slowly, gently brown!
And while the ardour shrinks away
To hide itself in ashes grey; 60
When Eld's Ash Wednesday comes about
To strew my head from fires burnt out;
I'll think, as inward Life retreats,
And careful spares his wasting heats,
While one spark stays to light the eye
With a last flash of memory,
So may it be, till wholly gone,
But deeper in my heart withdrawn,
With kindling touch to make it glow
For the kind friend of long ago! 70

AT THE COMMENCEMENT DINNER, 1866, IN ACKNOWLEDGING
A TOAST TO THE SMITH PROFESSOR

[*Boston Evening Transcript*, July 20, 1866.]

I RISE, Mr. Chairman, as both of us know,
With the impromptu I promised you three weeks ago,
Dragged up to my doom by your might and my mane,
To do what I vowed I'd do never again ;
And I feel like your good honest dough when possest
By a stirring, impertinent devil of yeast.
' You must rise,' says the leaven.   ' I can't,' says the dough ;
' Just examine my bumps and you'll see it 's no go.'
' But you must,' the tormentor insists, ' 't is all right ;
You must rise when I bid you, and, what 's more, be light.'   10

'T is a dreadful oppression, this making men speak
What they 're sure to be sorry for all the next week ;
This asking some poor stick, like Aaron's, to bud
Into eloquence, pathos, or wit in cold blood,
As if the dull brain that you vented your spite on
Could be got, like an ox, by mere poking, to Brighton.

They say it is wholesome to rise with the sun,
And I dare say it may be if not overdone ;
(I think it was Thomson who made the remark
'T was an excellent thing in its way—for a lark ;)   20
But to rise after dinner and look down the meeting
On a distant (as Gray calls it) prospect of Eating,
With a stomach half full and a cerebrum hollow
As the tortoise-shell ere it was strung for Apollo,
Under contract to raise anerithmon gelasma
With rhymes so hard hunted they gasp with the asthma,
And jokes not much younger than Jethro's phylacteries,
Is something I leave you yourselves to characterize.

I 've a notion, I think, of a good dinner speech,
Tripping light as a sandpiper over the beach,   30
Swerving this way and that as the wave of the moment
Washes out its slight trace with a dash of whim's foam on 't,
And leaving on memory's edge just a sense
Something graceful had gone by, a live present tense ;
Not poetry,—no, not quite that, but as good,
A kind of winged prose that could fly if it would.
'T is a time for gay fancies as fleeting and vain
As the whisper of foam-beads on fresh-poured champagne,

For dinners are not perhaps strictly designed
For manœuvring the heavy dragoons of the mind.   40
When I hear your set speeches that start with a pop,
Then wander and maunder, too feeble to stop,
With a vague apprehension from popular rumour
There used to be something by mortals called humour,
Beginning again when you thought they were done,
Respectable, sensible, weighing a ton,
And as near to the present occasions of men
As a Fast Day discourse of the year eighteen ten,
I—well, I sit still, and my sentiments smother,
For am I not also a bore and a brother ?   50

And a toast,—what should that be ? Light, airy, and free,
The foam-Aphrodite of Bacchus's sea,
A fancy-tinged bubble, an orbed rainbow-stain,
That floats for an instant 'twixt goblet and brain ;
A breath-born perfection, half something, half naught,
And breaks if it strike the hard edge of a thought.
Do you ask me to make such ? Ah no, not so simple
Ask Apelles to paint you the ravishing dimple
Whose shifting enchantment lights Venus's cheek,
But the artist will tell you his skill is too weak ;   60
Once fix it, 't is naught, for the charm of it rises
From the sudden bopeeps of its smiling surprises.

I 've tried to define, but what mother's son
Could ever yet do what he knows should be done ?
My rocket has burst, and I watch in the air
Its fast-fading heart's-blood drop back in despair ;
Yet one chance is left me, and, if I am quick,
I can palm off, before you suspect me, the stick.

Now since I 've succeeded—I pray do not frown—
To Ticknor's and Longfellow's classical gown,   70
And profess four strange languages, which, luckless elf,
I speak like a native (of Cambridge) myself,
Let me beg, Mr. President, leave to propose
A sentiment treading on nobody's toes,
And give, in such ale as with pump-handles *we* brew,
Their memory who saved us from talking Hebrew,—
A toast that to deluge with water is good,
For in Scripture they come in just after the flood :
I give you the men but for whom, as *I* guess, sir,
Modern languages ne'er could have had a professor,   80
The builders of Babel, to whose zeal the lungs
Of the children of men owe confusion of tongues ;
And a name all-embracing I couple therewith,
Which is that of my founder—the late Mr. Smith.

FITZ ADAM'S STORY

[*Atlantic Monthly*, January, 1867.]

[The greater part of this poem was written many years ago, to form part of a larger one to be called 'The Nooning', made up of tales in verse, some of them grave, some comic.]

THE next whose fortune 't was a tale to tell
Was one whom men, before they thought, loved well,
And after thinking wondered why they did,
For half he seemed to let them, half forbid,
And wrapped him so in humours, sheath on sheath,
'T was hard to guess the mellow soul beneath;
But, once divined, you took him to your heart,
While he appeared to bear with you as part
Of life's impertinence, and once a year
Betrayed his true self by a smile or tear,   10
Or rather something sweetly-shy and loath,
Withdrawn ere fully shown, and mixed of both.
A cynic? Not precisely: one who thrust
Against a heart too prone to love and trust,
Who so despised false sentiment he knew
Scarce in himself to part the false and true,
And strove to hide, by roughening-o'er the skin,
Those cobweb nerves he could not dull within.
Gentle by birth, but of a stem decayed,
He shunned life's rivalries and hated trade;   20
On a small patrimony and larger pride,
He lived uneaseful on the Other Side
(So he called Europe), only coming West
To give his old-world appetite new zest;
A radical in thought, he puffed away
With shrewd contempt the dust of usage grey,
Yet loathed democracy as one who saw,
In what he longed to love, some vulgar flaw,
And, shocked through all his delicate reserves,
Remained a Tory by his taste and nerves.   30
His fancy's thrall, he drew all ergos thence,
And thought himself the type of common sense;
Misliking women, not from cross or whim,
But that his mother shared too much in him,
And he half felt that what in them was grace
Made the unlucky weakness of his race.
What powers he had he hardly cared to know,
But sauntered through the world as through a show,
A critic fine in his haphazard way,
A sort of mild La Bruyère on half-pay.   40

For comic weaknesses he had an eye
Keen as an acid for an alkali,
Yet you could feel, through his sardonic tone,
He loved them all, unless they were his own.
You might have called him, with his humorous twist,
A kind of human entomologist :
As these bring home, from every walk they take,
Their hat-crowns stuck with bugs of curious make,
So he filled all the lining of his head
With characters impaled and ticketed, 50
And had a cabinet behind his eyes
For all they caught of mortal oddities.
He might have been a poet—many worse—
But that he had, or feigned, contempt of verse,
Called it tattooing language, and held rhymes
The young world's lullaby of ruder times.
Bitter in words, too indolent for gall,
He satirized himself the first of all,
In men and their affairs could find no law,
And was the ill logic that he thought he saw. 60

Scratching a match to light his pipe anew,
With eyes half shut some musing whiffs he drew,
And thus began :—' I give you all my word,
I think this mock-Decameron absurd ;
Boccaccio's garden ! how bring that to pass
In our bleak clime save under double glass ?
The moral east-wind of New-England life
Would snip its gay luxuriance like a knife ;
These foreign plants are but half-hardy still,
Die on a south, and on a north wall chill ; 70
Had we stayed Puritans ! *They* had some heat
(Though whence derived, I have my own conceit),
But you have long ago raked up their fires ;
Where they had faith, you 've ten sham-Gothic spires.
Why more exotics ? Try your native vines,
And in some thousand years you *may* have wines ;
Your present grapes are harsh, all pulps and skins,
And want traditions of ancestral bins
That saved for evenings round the polished board
Old lava-fires, the sun-steeped hillside's hoard ; 80
Without a Past, you lack that southern wall
O'er which the vines of Poesy should crawl ;
Still they 're your only hope ; no midnight oil
Makes up for virtue wanting in the soil ;
Manure them well and prune them ; 't won't be France,
Nor Spain, nor Italy, but there 's your chance.
You have one story-teller worth a score
Of dead Boccaccios, nay, add twenty more,

A hawthorn asking spring's most southern breath,
And him you 're freezing pretty well to death.   90
However, since you say so, I will tease
My memory to a story by degrees,
Though you will cry, " Enough ! " I'm wellnigh sure,
Ere I have dreamed through half my overture.
Stories were good for men who had no books
(Fortunate race !), and built their nests like rooks
In lonely towers, to which the Jongleur brought
His pedler's-box of cheap and tawdry thought,
With here and there a fancy fit to see
Wrought to quaint grace in golden filigree ;   100
The morning newspaper has spoilt his trade,
(For better or for worse, I leave unsaid,)
And stories now, to suit a public nice,
Must be half epigram, half pleasant vice.

' All tourists know Shebagog County ; there
The summer idlers take their yearly stare,
Dress to see Nature in a well-bred way,
As 't were Italian opera, or play,
Encore the sunrise (if they're out of bed),
And pat the Mighty Mother on the head :   110
These have I seen,—all things are good to see,—
And wondered much at their complacency ;
This world's great show, that took in getting up
Millions of years, they finish ere they sup ;
Sights that God gleams through with soul-tingling force
They glance approvingly as things of course,
Say, " That 's a grand rock," " This a pretty fall,"
Not thinking, " Are we worthy ? " What if all
The scornful landscape should turn round and say,
" This is a fool, and that a popinjay " ?   120
I often wonder what the Mountain thinks
Of French boots creaking o'er his breathless brinks,
Or how the Sun would scare the chattering crowd,
If some fine day he chanced to think aloud.

' I, who love Nature much as sinners can,
Love her where she most grandeur shows,—in man ;
Here find I mountain, forest, cloud, and sun,
River and sea, and glows when day is done ;
Nay, where she makes grotesques, and moulds in jest
The clown's cheap clay, I find unfading zest.   130
The natural instincts year by year retire,
As deer shrink northward from the settler's fire,
And he who loves the wild game-flavour more
Than city-feasts, where every man 's a bore

To every other man, must seek it where
The steamer's throb and railway's iron blare
Have not yet startled with their punctual stir
The shy, wood-wandering brood of Character.
There is a village, once the county town,
Through which the weekly mail rolled dustily down,   140
Where the courts sat, it may be, twice a year,
And the one tavern reeked with rustic cheer ;
Cheeshogquesumscot erst, now Jethro hight,
Red-man and pale-face bore it equal spite.
The railway ruined it, the natives say,
That passed unwisely fifteen miles away,
And made a drain to which, with steady ooze,
Filtered away law, stage-coach, trade, and news.
The railway saved it, so at least think those
Who love old ways, old houses, old repose.   150
Of course the Tavern stayed : its genial host
Thought not of flitting more than did the post
On which high-hung the fading sign-board creaks,
Inscribed, " The Eagle Inn, by Ezra Weeks."

' If in life's journey you should ever find
An inn medicinal for body and mind,
'T is sure to be some drowsy-looking house
Whose easy landlord has a bustling spouse :
He, if he like you, will not long forego
Some bottle deep in cobwebbed dust laid low,   160
That, since the War we used to call the " Last,"
Has dozed and held its lang-syne memories fast ;
From him exhales that Indian-summer air
Of hazy, lazy welcome everywhere,
While with her toil the napery is white,
The china dustless, the keen knife-blades bright,
Salt dry as sand, and bread that seems as though
'T were rather sea-foam baked than vulgar dough.

' In our swift country, houses trim and white
Are pitched like tents, the lodging of a night ;   170
Each on its bank of baked turf mounted high
Perches impatient o'er the roadside dry,
While the wronged landscape coldly stands aloof,
Refusing friendship with the upstart roof.
Not so the Eagle ; on a grass-green swell
That toward the south with sweet concessions fell,
It dwelt retired, and half had grown to be
As aboriginal as rock or tree.
It nestled close to earth, and seemed to brood
O'er homely thoughts in a half-conscious mood,   180

As by the peat that rather fades than burns
The smouldering grandam nods and knits by turns,
Happy, although her newest news were old
Ere the first hostile drum at Concord rolled ;
If paint it e'er had known, it knew no more
Than yellow lichens spattered thickly o'er
That soft lead-grey, less dark beneath the eaves,
Which the slow brush of wind and weather leaves.
The ample roof sloped backward to the ground,
And vassal lean-tos gathered thickly round,   190
Patched on, as sire or son had felt the need,
Like chance growths sprouting from the old roof's seed,
Just as about a yellow-pine-tree spring
Its rough-barked darlings in a filial ring.
But the great chimney was the central thought
Whose gravitation through the cluster wrought,
For 't is not styles far-fetched from Greece or Rome,
But just the Fireside, that can make a home ;
None of your spindling things of modern style,
Like pins stuck through to stay the card-built pile,   200
It rose broad-shouldered, kindly, debonair,
Its warm breath whitening in the October air,
While on its front a heart in outline showed
The place it filled in that serene abode.

' When first I chanced the Eagle to explore,
Ezra sat listless by the open door ;
One chair careened him at an angle meet,
Another nursed his hugely-slippered feet ;
Upon a third reposed a shirt-sleeved arm,
And the whole man diffused tobacco's charm.   210
" Are you the landlord ? " " Wahl, I guess I be,"
Watching the smoke, he answered leisurely.
He was a stoutish man, and through the breast
Of his loose shirt there showed a brambly chest ;
Streaked redly as a wind-foreboding morn,
His tanned cheeks curved to temples closely shorn ;
Clean-shaved he was, save where a hedge of grey
Upon his brawny throat leaned every way
About an Adam's-apple that beneath
Bulged like a boulder from a furzy heath.   220
" Can I have lodging here ? " once more I said.
He blew a whiff, and, leaning back his head,
" You come a piece through Bailey's woods, I s'pose,
Acrost a bridge where a big swamp-oak grows ?
It don't grow neither ; it 's ben dead ten year,
Nor th' ain't a livin' creetur, fur nor near,
Can tell wut killed it ; but I some misdoubt
'T was borers, there 's sech heaps on 'em about ;

You did n' chance to run ag'inst my son,
A long, slab-sided youngster with a gun ?   230
He 'd oughto ben back more 'n an hour ago,
An' brought some birds to dress for supper—Sho !
There he comes now.   'Say, Obed, wut ye got ?
(He 'll hev some upland plover like as not.)
Wal, them 's real nice uns an 'll eat A 1,
Ef I can stop their bein' over-done ;
Nothin' riles *me* (I pledge my fastin' word)
Like cookin' out the natur' of a bird
(Obed, you pick 'em out o' sight an' sound,
Your ma'am don't love no feathers cluttrin' round) ;   240
Jes' scare 'em with the coals ; thet 's *my* idee."
Then, turning suddenly about on me,
" Wal, Square, I guess so.   Callilate to stay ?
I 'll ask Miss Weeks ; 'bout *thet* it 's hern to say."

' Well, there I lingered all October through,
In that sweet atmosphere of hazy blue,
So leisurely, so soothing, so forgiving,
That sometimes makes New England fit for living ;
I watched the landscape, erst so granite glum,
Bloom like the south side of a ripening plum,   250
And each rock-maple on the hillside make
His ten days' sunset doubled in the lake ;
The very stone walls draggling up the hills
Seemed touched, and wavered in their roundhead wills.
Ah ! there 's a deal of sugar in the sun !
Tap me in Indian-summer, I should run
A juice to make rock-candy of,—but then
We get such weather scarce one year in ten.

' There was a parlour in the house, a room
To make you shudder with its prudish gloom.   260
The furniture stood round with such an air,
There seemed an old maid's ghost in every chair ;
Each looked as it had scuttled to its place
And pulled extempore a Sunday face,
Too smugly proper for a world of sin,
Like boys on whom the minister comes in.
The table, fronting you with icy stare,
Strove to look witless that its legs were bare,
While the black sofa with its horse-hair pall
Gloomed like the bier for Comfort's funeral.   270
Two portraits graced the wall in grimmest truth,
Mister and Mistress W. in their youth,—
New England youth, that seems a sort of pill,
Half wish-I-dared, half Edwards on the Will,

Bitter to swallow, and which leaves a trace
Of Calvinistic cholic on the face.
Between them, o'er the mantel, hung in state
Solomon's temple, done in copperplate ;
Invention pure, but meant, we may presume,
To give some Scripture sanction to the room. 280
Facing this last, two samplers you might see,
Each, with its urn and stiffly-weeping tree,
Devoted to some memory long ago
More faded than their lines of worsted woe ;
Cut paper decked the frames against the flies,
Though none e'er dared an entrance who were wise,
And bushed asparagus in fading green
Added its shiver to the franklin clean.

'When first arrived, I chilled a half-hour there,
Nor dared deflower with use a single chair ; 290
I caught no cold, yet flying pains could find
For weeks in me,—a rheumatism of mind.
One thing alone imprisoned there had power
To hold me in the place that long half-hour,—
A scutcheon this, a helm-surmounted shield,
Three griffins argent on a sable field ;
A relic of the shipwrecked past was here,
And Ezra held some old-world lumber dear ;
Nay, do not smile, I love this kind of thing,
These cooped traditions with a broken wing, 300
This real estate in Fancy's pipe-blown ball,
This less than nothing that is more than all !
Have I not seen sweet natures kept alive
Amid the humdrum of your business hive,
Undowered spinsters shielded from all harms,
By force imagined of a coat of arms ? '

He paused a moment, and his features took
The flitting sweetness of that inward look
I hinted at before ; but, scarcely seen,
It shrank for shelter 'neath his harder mien, 310
And, rapping his black pipe of ashes clear,
He went on with a self-derisive sneer :—
'No doubt we make a part of God's design,
And break the forest-path for feet divine ;
To furnish foothold for this grand prevision
Is good,—and yet to be the mere transition,-
That, you will say, is also good, though I
Scarce like to feed the ogre By-and-by ;
My skull has somehow never closed the suture
That seems to bind yours firmly with the future, 320

So you 'll excuse me if I 'm sometimes fain
To tie the past's warm nightcap o'er my brain ;
I 'm quite aware 't is not in fashion here,
But then your north-east winds are *so* severe !

' But to my story ; though 't is truly naught
But a few hints in Memory's sketchbook caught,
And which may claim a value on the score
Of calling back some scenery now no more.
Shall I confess ? The tavern's only Lar
Seemed (be not shocked !) its homely-featured bar.   330
Here snapped a fire of beechen logs, that bred
Strange fancies in its embers golden-red,
And nursed the loggerhead whose hissing dip,
Timed by nice instinct, creamed the mug of flip
Which made from mouth to mouth its genial round,
Nor left one nature wholly winter-bound ;
Hence dropt the tinkling coal all mellow-ripe
For Uncle Reuben's talk-extinguished pipe ;
Hence rayed the heat, as from an indoor sun,
That wooed forth many a shoot of rustic fun.   340
Here Ezra ruled as king by right divine ;
No other face had such a wholesome shine,
No laugh like his so full of honest cheer ;
Above the rest it crowed like Chanticleer ;
No eye like his to value horse or cow,
Or gauge the contents of a stack or mow.
He could foretell the weather at a word,
He knew the haunt of every beast and bird,
Or where a two-pound trout was sure to lie
Waiting the flutter of his home-made fly ;   350
Nay, once in autumns fine, he had the luck
To drop at fair-play range a ten-tined buck.
Of sportsmen true he favoured every whim,
But never cockney found a guide in him.
A natural man, with all his instincts fresh,
Not buzzing helpless in Reflection's mesh,
Firm on its feet stood his broad-shouldered mind,
As bluffly honest as a northwest wind ;
Hard-headed and soft-hearted, you 'd scarce meet
A kinder mixture of the shrewd and sweet ;   360
Generous by birth, and ill at saying " No ",
Yet in a bargain he was all men's foe,
Would yield no inch of vantage in a trade,
And give away ere nightfall all he made.

' In this one room his dame you never saw,
Where reigned by custom old a salic law ;
Here coatless lolled he on his throne of oak,
And every tongue was muffled if he spoke ;

Due mirth he loved, yet was his sway severe,
No blear-eyed driveller got his stagger here; 370
" Measure was happiness; who wanted more,
Must buy his ruin at the Deacon's store; "
None but his lodgers after ten could stay,
Nor after nine on eves of Sabbath-day.
He had his favourites and his pensioners,
The same that gypsy Nature owns for hers,—
Loose-ended souls, whose skills bring scanty gold,
And whom the poor-house catches when they 're old :
Rude country-minstrels, men who doctor kine,
Or graft, and, out of scions ten, save nine; 380
Creatures of genius they, but never meant
To keep step with the civic regiment.
These Ezra welcomed, feeling in his mind
Perhaps some motions of the vagrant kind;
These paid no money, yet for them he drew
Special Jamaica from a tap they knew,
And, for their feelings, chalked behind the door
With solemn face a visionary score.
This warmed the one-eyed fiddler to his task,
Perched in the corner on an empty cask, 390
By whose shrill art rapt suddenly, some boor
Rattled a double-shuffle on the floor;
This thawed to life in Uncle Reuben's throat
A torpid shoal of jest and anecdote,
Like those queer fish that doze the droughts away,
And wait for moisture, wrapt in sun-baked clay.

' 'T was there I caught from Uncle Reuben's lips,
In dribbling monologue 'twixt whiffs and sips,
The story I so long have tried to tell;
The humour coarse, the persons common,—well, 400
From Nature only do I love to paint,
Whether she send a satyr or a saint;
To me Sincerity 's the one thing good,
Soiled though she be and lost to maidenhood.
Quompegan is a town some ten miles south
From Jethro, at Nagumscot river-mouth,—
A seaport town, and makes its title good
With lumber and dried fish and eastern wood.
Here Deacon Bitters dwelt and kept the Store,
The richest man for many a mile of shore; 410
In little less than everything dealt he,
From meeting-houses to a chest of tea,
So dextrous therewithal a flint to skin,
He could make profit on a single pin;
In business strict, to bring the balance true,
He had been known to cut a fig in two
And change a board-nail for a shingle-nail.
All that he had he ready held for sale,—

His house, his tomb, whate'er the law allows,
And he had gladly parted with his spouse.   420
His one ambition still to get and get,
He would arrest your very ghost for debt.
His store looked righteous, should the Parson come,
But in a dark back-room he peddled rum,
And eased Ma'am Conscience, if she e'er would scold,
By christening it with water ere he sold.
A small, dry man he was, who wore a queue,
And one white neckcloth all the week-days through,—
On Monday white, by Saturday as dun
As that worn homeward by the prodigal son ;   430
His earlocks grey, striped with a foxy brown,
Were braided up to hide a desert crown ;
His coat was brownish, black perhaps of yore ;
In summer-time a banyan loose he wore ;
His trousers short, through many a season true,
Made no pretence to hide his stockings blue ;
A waistcoat buff his chief adornment was,
Its porcelain buttons rimmed with dusky brass.
A deacon he, you saw it in each limb,
And well he knew to deacon-off a hymn,   440
Or lead the choir through all its wandering woes
With voice that gathered unction in his nose,
Wherein a constant snuffle you might hear,
As if with him 't were winter all the year.
At his pew-head he sat with decorous pains,
In sermon-time could foot his weekly gains,
Or, with closed eyes and heaven-abstracted air,
Could plan a new investment in long-prayer ;
A pious man and thrifty too, he made
The psalms and prophets partners in his trade,   450
And in his orthodoxy straitened more
As it enlarged the business at his store ;
He honoured Moses, but, when gain he planned,
Had his own notion of the Promised Land.

    ' Soon as the winter made the sledding good,
From far around the farmers hauled him wood,
For all the trade had gathered 'neath his thumb
He paid in groceries and New England rum,
Making two profits with a conscience clear,
Cheap all he bought, and all he paid with dear ;   460
With his own mete-wand measuring every load,
Each somehow had diminished on the road ;
An honest cord in Jethro still would fail
By a good foot upon the Deacon's scale,
And, more to abate the price, his gimlet eye
Would pierce to catsticks that none else could spy ;
Yet none dared grumble, for no farmer yet
But New Year found him in the Deacon's debt.

' While the first snow was mealy under feet,
A team drawled creaking down Quompegan street ;   470
Two cords of oak weighed down the grinding sled,
And cornstalk fodder rustled overhead ;
The oxen's muzzles, as they shouldered through,
Were silver-fringed ; the driver's own was blue
As the coarse frock that swung below his knee.
Behind his load for shelter waded he ;
His mittened hands now on his chest he beat,
Now stamped the stiffened cowhides of his feet
Hushed as a ghost's ; his armpit scarce could hold
The walnut whipstock slippery-bright with cold.   480
What wonder if, the tavern as he past,
He looked and longed, and stayed his beasts at last,
Who patient stood and veiled themselves in steam
While he explored the bar-room's ruddy gleam ?

' Before the fire, in want of thought profound,
There sat a brother-townsman weather-bound ;
A sturdy churl, crisp-headed, bristly-eared,
Red as a pepper ; 'twixt coarse brows and beard
His eyes lay ambushed on the watch for fools,
Clear, grey, and glittering like two bay-edged pools ;   490
A shifty creature, with a turn for fun,
Could swap a poor horse for a better one,—
He 'd a high-stepper always in his stall ;
Liked far and near, and dreaded therewithal.
To him the in-comer, " Perez, how d' ye do ? "
" Jest as I 'm mind to, Obed ; how do you ? "
Then, his eyes twinkling such swift gleams as run
Along the levelled barrel of a gun
Brought to his shoulder by a man you know
Will bring his game down, he continued, " So,   500
I s'pose you 're hauling wood ? But you 're too late ;
The Deacon 's off ; Old Splitfoot could n't wait ;
He made a bee-line last night in the storm
To where he won't need wood to keep him warm.
'Fore this he 's treasurer of a fund to train
Young imps as missionaries ; hopes to gain
That way a contract that he has in view
For fireproof pitchforks of a pattern new.
It must have tickled him, all drawbacks weighed,
To think he stuck the Old One in a trade ;   510
His soul, to start with, was n't worth a carrot,
And all he 'd left would hardly serve to swear at."

' By this time Obed had his wits thawed out,
And, looking at the other half in doubt,
Took off his fox-skin cap to scratch his head,
Donned it again, and drawled forth, " Mean he 's dead ? "

" Jes' so ; he's dead and tother *d* that follers
With folks that never love a thing but dollars ;
He pulled up stakes last evening, fair and square,
And ever since there's been a row Down There ;   520
The minute the old chap arrived, you see,
Comes the Boss-devil to him, and says he,
' What are you good at ? Little enough, I fear ;
We calculate to make folks useful here.'
' Well,' says old Bitters, ' I expect I can
Scale a fair load of wood with e'er a man.'
' Wood we don't deal in ; but perhaps you 'll suit,
Because we buy our brimstone by the foot :
Here, take this measuring rod, as smooth as sin,
And keep a reckoning of what loads come in,   530
You 'll not want business, for we need a lot
To keep the Yankees that you send us hot ;
At firing up they 're barely half as spry
As Spaniards or Italians, though they 're dry ;
At first we have to let the draught on stronger.
But, heat 'em through, they seem to hold it longer.'

' " Bitters he took the rod, and pretty soon
A teamster comes, whistling an ex-psalm tune.
A likelier chap you would n't ask to see,
No different, but his limp, from you or me—"   540
" No different, Perez ! Don't your memory fail ?
Why, where in thunder were his horns and tail ? "
" They 're only worn by some old-fashioned pokes ;
They mostly aim at looking just like folks.
Sech things are scarce as queues and top-boots here ;
'T would spoil their usefulness to look too queer.
If you could always know 'em when they come,
They 'd get no purchase on you : now be mum.
On come the teamster, smart as Davy Crockett,
Jinglin' the red-hot coppers in his pocket,   550
And close behind, ('t was gold-dust, you 'd ha' sworn,)
A load of sulphur yellower than seed-corn,—
To see it wasted as it is Down There
Would make a Friction Match Co. tear its hair !
' Hold on ! ' says Bitters, ' stop right where you be ;
You can't go in without a pass from me.'
' All right,' says t' other, ' only step round smart,
I must be home by noon-time with the cart.'
Bitters goes round it sharp-eyed as a rat,
Then with a scrap of paper on his hat   560
Pretends to cipher. ' By the public staff,
That load scarce rises twelve foot and a half.'
' There 's fourteen foot and over,' says the driver,
' Worth twenty dollars, if it 's worth a stiver,—

Good fourth-proof brimstone, that 'll make 'em squirm,
I leave it to the Headman of the Firm;
After we measure it, we always lay
Some on to allow for settling on the way;
Imp and full-grown, I 've carted sulphur here,
And given fair satisfaction, thirty year.' 570
With that they fell to quarrelling so loud
That in five minutes they had drawn a crowd,
And before long the Boss, who heard the row,
Comes elbowing in with ' What 's to pay here now ? '
Both parties heard, the measuring-rod he takes,
And of the load a careful survey makes.
' Since I have bossed the business here,' says he,
' No fairer load was ever seen by me;'
Then, turning to the Deacon, ' You mean cus,
None of your old Quompegan tricks with us! 580
They won't do here: we 're plain old-fashioned folks,
And don't quite understand that kind of jokes.
I know this teamster, and his pa before him,
And the hard-working Mrs. D. that bore him;
He would not soil his conscience with a lie,
Though he might get the custom-house thereby.
Here, constable, take Bitters by the queue
And clap him into furnace ninety-two,
And try this brimstone on him; if he 's bright,
He 'll find the measure honest before night. 590
He is n't worth his fuel, and I 'll bet
The parish poor-house has to take him yet ! ' "

' This is my tale, heard twenty years ago
From Uncle Reuben, as the logs burned low,
Touching the walls and ceiling with that bloom
That makes a rose's calyx of a room.
I could not give his language, wherethrough ran
The gamy flavour of the bookless man
Who shapes a word before the fancy cools,
As lonely Crusoe had to forge his tools. 600
I liked the tale, 't was like so many told
By Rutebeuf and his brother Trouvères bold;
Nor were the hearers much unlike to theirs,
Men unsophisticate, rude-nerved as bears.
Ezra is gone and his large-hearted kind,
The landlords of the hospitable mind;
Good Warriner of Springfield was the last.
An inn is now a vision of the past;
One yet surviving host my mind recalls,—
You 'll find him if you go to Trenton Falls.' 610

THE FLYING DUTCHMAN

[*Atlantic Monthly*, January, 1869.]

Don't believe in the Flying Dutch-
    man ?
  Well, I have known him for years;
My button I 've wrenched from his
    clutch, man :
  I shudder whenever he nears !

He 's a Rip van Winkle skipper,
  A Wandering Jew of the sea,
Who sails his bedevilled old clipper
  In the wind's eye, straight as a
    bee.

Back topsails ! you can't escape him ;
  The man-ropes stretch with his
    weight,
And the queerest old toggeries drape
    him—
  The Lord knows how far out of
    date !

Like a long-disembodied idea
  (A kind of ghost plentiful now),
He stands there ; you fancy you see a
  Coeval of Teniers or Douw.

He greets you ; would have you take
    letters :
  You scan the addresses with dread,
While he mutters his *donners* and
    wetters,—
  They 're all from the dead to the
    dead !

You seem taking time for reflection,
  But the heart fills your throat with
    a jam,
As you spell in each faded direction
  An ominous ending in *dam*.

Am I tagging my rhymes to a legend ?
  That were changing green turtle to
    mock :

No, thank you ! I 've found out
    which wedge-end
  Is meant for the head of a block.

The fellow I have in my mind's eye
  Plays the old Skipper's part upon
    shore,
And sticks like a burr, till he finds I
  Have got just the gauge of his bore.

This postman 'twixt one ghost and
    t' other,
  With last dates that smell of the
    mould,
I have met him (O man and brother,
  Forgive me !) in azure and gold.

In the pulpit I 've known of his
    preaching,
  Out of hearing behind the times,
Some statement of Balaam's impeach-
    ing,
  Giving Eve a due sense of her
    crimes.

I have seen him some poor ancient
    thrashing
  Into something (God save us !)
    more dry,
With the Water of Life itself washing
  The life out of earth, sea, and sky.

O dread fellow-mortal, get newer
  Dispatches to carry, or none !
We 're as quick as the Greek and the
    Jew were
  At knowing a loaf from a stone.

Till the Couriers of God fail in duty,
  We sha'n't ask a mummy for news,
Nor sate the soul's hunger for beauty
  With your drawings from casts of
    a Muse.

DEDICATION OF 'AMONG MY BOOKS', 1870

TO F. D. L.

LOVE comes and goes with music in his feet,
    And tunes young pulses to his roundelays ;
Love brings thee this : will it persuade thee, Sweet,
    That he turns proser when he comes and stays ?

AGASSIZ

[Atlantic Monthly, May, 1874.]

Come
Dicesti *egli ebbe ?* non viv' egli ancora ?
Non fiere gli occhi suoi lo dolce lome ?

I.

1

THE electric nerve, whose instantaneous thrill
Makes next-door gossips of the antipodes,
Confutes poor Hope's last fallacy of ease,—
The distance that divided her from ill :
Earth sentient seems again as when of old
    The horny foot of Pan
Stamped, and the conscious horror ran
Beneath men's feet through all her fibres cold :
Space's blue walls are mined ; we feel the throe
From underground of our night-mantled foe :   10
    The flame-winged feet
Of Trade's new Mercury, that dry-shod run
Through briny abysses dreamless of the sun,
    Are mercilessly fleet,
    And at a bound annihilate
Ocean's prerogative of short reprieve ;
    Surely ill news might wait,
And man be patient of delay to grieve :
    Letters have sympathies
    And tell-tale faces that reveal,   20
    To senses finer than the eyes,
Their errand's purport ere we break the seal ;
They wind a sorrow round with circumstance
To stay its feet, nor all unwarned displace
The veil that darkened from our sidelong glance
    The inexorable face :
    But now Fate stuns as with a mace ;

The savage of the skies, that men have caught
And some scant use of language taught,
  Tells only what he must,—   30
The steel-cold fact in one laconic thrust.

2

So thought I, as, with vague, mechanic eyes,
I scanned the festering news we half despise
  Yet scramble for no less,
And read of public scandal, private fraud,
Crime flaunting scot-free while the mob applaud,
Office made vile to bribe unworthiness,
  And all the unwholesome mess
The Land of Broken Promise serves of late
  To teach the Old World how to wait,   40
   When suddenly,
As happens if the brain, from over-weight
  Of blood, infect the eye,
Three tiny words grew lurid as I read,
And reeled commingling : *Agassiz is dead.*
  As when, beneath the street's familiar jar,
  An earthquake's alien omen rumbles far,
  Men listen and forebode, I hung my head,
   And strove the present to recall,
  As if the blow that stunned were yet to fall. 50

3

Uprooted is our mountain oak,
That promised long security of shade
And brooding-place for many a wingèd thought ;
  Not by Time's softly-warning stroke
  By pauses of relenting pity stayed,
But ere a root seemed sapt, a bough decayed,
From sudden ambush by the whirlwind caught
And in his broad maturity betrayed !

4

Well might I, as of old, appeal to you,
  O mountains, woods, and streams,   60
To help us mourn him, for ye loved him too ;
  But simpler moods befit our modern themes,
And no less perfect birth of nature can,
Though they yearn tow'rds him, sympathize with man,
Save as dumb fellow-prisoners through a wall ;
  Answer ye rather to my call,
Strong poets of a more outspoken day,
Too much for softer arts forgotten since
That teach our forthright tongue to lisp and mince,

Lead me some steps in your director way, 70
Teach me those words that strike a solid root
    Within the ears of men ;
Ye chiefly, virile both to think and feel,
Deep-chested Chapman and firm-footed Ben,—
For he was masculine from head to heel.
Nay, let himself stand undimished by
With those clear parts of him that will not die.
Himself from out the recent dark I claim
To hear, and, if I flatter him, to blame ;
To show himself, as still I seem to see, 80
A mortal, built upon the antique plan,
Brimful of lusty blood as ever ran,
And taking life as simply as a tree !
To claim my foiled good-bye let him appear,
Large-limbed and human as I saw him near,
Loosed from the stiffening uniform of fame :
And let me treat him largely : I should fear
(If with too prying lens I chanced to err,
Mistaking catalogue for character)
His wise forefinger raised in smiling blame. 90
Nor would I scant him with judicial breath
And turn mere critic in an epitaph ;
I choose the wheat, incurious of the chaff
That swells fame living, chokes it after death,
And would but memorize the shining half
Of his large nature that was turned to me :
Fain had I joined with those that honoured him
With eyes that darkened because his were dim,
And now been silent : but it might not be.

II.
1

In some the genius is a thing apart, 100
    A pillared hermit of the brain,
Hoarding with incommunicable art
    Its intellectual gain ;
    Man's web of circumstance and fate
    They from their perch of self observe,
Indifferent as the figures on a slate
    Are to the planet's sun-swung curve
    Whose bright returns they calculate ;
    Their nice adjustment, part to part,
Were shaken from its serviceable mood 110
By unpremeditated stirs of heart
    Or jar of human neighbourhood :
Some find their natural selves, and only then,
In furloughs of divine escape from men,

And when by that brief ecstasy left bare,
    Driven by some instinct of desire,
They wander worldward, 't is to blink and stare,
Like wild things of the wood about a fire,
Dazed by the social glow they cannot share ;
    His nature brooked no lonely lair,   120
But basked and bourgeoned in copartnery,
Companionship, and open-windowed glee :
    He knew, for he had tried,
    Those speculative heights that lure
The unpractised foot, impatient of a guide,
    Tow'rds ether too attenuately pure
For sweet unconscious breath, though dear to pride,
    But better loved the foothold sure
Of paths that wind by old abodes of men
Who hope at last the churchyard's peace secure,   130
And follow time-worn rules, that them suffice,
Learned from their sires, traditionally wise,
Careful of honest custom's how and when ;
His mind, too brave to look on Truth askance,
No more those habitudes of faith could share,
But, tinged with sweetness of the old Swiss manse,
Lingered around them still and fain would spare,
Patient to spy a sullen egg for weeks,
The enigma of creation to surprise,
His truer instinct sought the life that speaks   140
Without a mystery from kindly eyes ;
In no self-woven silk of prudence wound,
He by the touch of men was best inspired,
And caught his native greatness at rebound
From generosities itself had fired ;
Then how the heat through every fibre ran,
Felt in the gathering presence of the man,
While the apt word and gesture came unbid !
Virtues and faults it to one metal wrought,
    Fined all his blood to thought,   150
And ran the molten man in all he said or did.
All Tully's rules and all Quintilian's too
He by the light of listening faces knew,
And his rapt audience all unconscious lent
Their own roused force to make him eloquent ;
Persuasion fondled in his look and tone ;
Our speech (with strangers prudish) he could bring
To find new charm in accents not her own ;
Her coy constraints and icy hindrances
Melted upon his lips to natural ease,   160
As a brook's fetters swell the dance of spring.
Nor yet all sweetness : not in vain he wore,
Nor in the sheath of ceremony, controlled

By velvet courtesy or caution cold,
That sword of honest anger prized of old,
 But, with two-handed wrath,
If baseness or pretension crossed his path,
 Struck once nor needed to strike more.

2

 His magic was not far to seek,—
He was so human! Whether strong or weak, 170
Far from his kind he neither sank nor soared,
But sate an equal guest at every board:
No beggar ever felt him condescend,
No prince presume; for still himself he bare
At manhood's simple level, and where'er
He met a stranger, there he left a friend.
How large an aspect! nobly unsevere,
With freshness round him of Olympian cheer,
Like visits of those earthly gods he came;
His look, wherever its good-fortune fell, 180
Doubled the feast without a miracle,
And on the hearthstone danced a happier flame;
Philemon's crabbed vintage grew benign;
Amphitryon's gold-juice humanized to wine.

III.
1

 The garrulous memories
Gather again from all their far-flown nooks,
Singly at first, and then by twos and threes,
Then in a throng innumerable, as the rooks
 Thicken their twilight files
Tow'rds Tintern's grey repose of roofless aisles: 190
Once more I see him at the table's head
When Saturday her monthly banquet spread
 To scholars, poets, wits,
All choice, some famous, loving things, not names,
And so without a twinge at others' fames;
Such company as wisest moods befits,
Yet with no pedant blindness to the worth
 Of undeliberate mirth,
Natures benignly mixed of air and earth,
Now with the stars and now with equal zest 200
Tracing the eccentric orbit of a jest.

2

I see in vision the warm-lighted hall,
The living and the dead I see again,
And but my chair is empty of them all;—
'T is I that seem the dead: they all remain
Immortal, changeless creatures of the brain:

Wellnigh I doubt which world is real most,
Of sense or spirit, to the truly sane ;
In this abstraction it were light to deem
Myself the figment of some stronger dream ;   210
They are the real things, and I the ghost
That glide unhindered through the solid door,
Vainly for recognition seek from chair to chair,
And strive to speak and am but futile air,
As truly most of us are little more.

3

Him most I see whom we most dearly miss,
        The latest parted thence,
His features poised in genial armistice
And armed neutrality of self-defence
Beneath the forehead's walled preëminence,   220
While Tyro, plucking facts with careless reach,
Settles off-hand our human how and whence ;
The long-trained veteran scarcely wincing hears
The infallible strategy of volunteers
Making through Nature's walls its easy breach,
And seems to learn where he alone could teach.
Ample and ruddy, the room's end he fills
As he our fireside were, our light and heat,
Centre where minds diverse and various skills
Find their warm nook and stretch unhampered feet ;   230
I see the firm benignity of face,
Wide-smiling champaign without tameness sweet,
The mass Teutonic toned to Gallic grace,
The eyes whose sunshine runs before the lips
While Holmes's rockets curve their long ellipse,
And burst in seeds of fire that burst again
        To drop in scintillating rain.

4

There too the face half-rustic, half-divine,
Self-poised, sagacious, freaked with humour fine,
Of him who taught us not to mow and mope   240
About our fancied selves, but seek our scope
In Nature's world and Man's, nor fade to hollow trope ;
Listening with eyes averse I see him sit
Pricked with the cider of the judge's wit
(Ripe-hearted homebrew, fresh and fresh again),
While the wise nose's firm-built aquiline
        Curves sharper to restrain
The merriment whose most unruly moods
Pass not the dumb laugh learned in listening woods
        Of silence-shedding pine :   250

Hard by is he whose art's consoling spell
Hath given both worlds a whiff of asphodel,
His look still vernal 'mid the wintry ring
Of petals that remember, not foretell,
The paler primrose of a second spring.

5

And more there are : but other forms arise
And seen as clear, albeit with dimmer eyes :
First he from sympathy still held apart
By shrinking over-eagerness of heart,
Cloud charged with searching fire, whose shadow's sweep   260
Heightened mean things with sense of brooding ill,
And steeped in doom familiar field and hill,—
New England's poet, soul reserved and deep,
November nature with a name of May,
Whom high o'er Concord plains we laid to sleep,
While the orchards mocked us in their white array
And building robins wondered at our tears,
Snatched in his prime, the shape august
That should have stood unbent 'neath fourscore years,
The noble head, the eyes of furtive trust,   270
      All gone to speechless dust ;
      And he our passing guest,
Shy nature, too, and stung with life's unrest,
Whom we too briefly had but could not hold,
Who brought ripe Oxford's culture to our board,
      The Past's incalculable hoard,
Mellowed by scutcheoned panes in cloisters old,
Seclusions ivy-hushed, and pavements sweet
With immemorial lisp of musing feet ;
Young head time-tonsured smoother than a friar's,   280
Boy face, but grave with answerless desires,
Poet in all that poets have of best,
But foiled with riddles dark and cloudy aims,
      Who now hath found sure rest,
Not by still Isis or historic Thames,
Nor by the Charles he tried to love with me,
But, not misplaced, by Arno's hallowed brim,
Nor scorned by Santa Croce's neighbouring fames,
   Haply not mindless, wheresoe'er he be,
Of violets that to-day I scattered over him ;   290
      He, too, is there,
After the good centurion fitly named,
Whom learning dulled not, nor convention tamed,
Shaking with burly mirth his hyacinthine hair,
Our hearty Grecian of Homeric ways,
Still found the surer friend where least he hoped the praise.

6

Yea truly, as the sallowing years
Fall from us faster, like frost-loosened leaves
Pushed by the misty touch of shortening days,
　　And that unwakened winter nears, 300
'T is the void chair our surest guests receives,
'T is lips long cold that give the warmest kiss,
'T is the lost voice comes oftenest to our ears;
We count our rosary by the beads we miss:
　　To me, at least, it seemeth so,
An exile in the land once found divine,
　　While my starved fire burns low,
And homeless winds at the loose casement whine
Shrill ditties of the snow-roofed Apennine.

IV.

1

Now forth into the darkness all are gone, 310
But memory, still unsated, follows on,
Retracing step by step our homeward walk,
With many a laugh among our serious talk,
Across the bridge where, on the dimpling tide,
The long red streamers from the windows glide,
　　Or the dim western moon
Rocks her skiff's image on the broad lagoon,
And Boston shows a soft Venetian side
In that Arcadian light when roof and tree,
Hard prose by daylight, dream in Italy; 320
Or haply in the sky's cold chambers wide
Shivered the winter stars, while all below,
As if an end were come of human ill,
The world was wrapt in innocence of snow
And the cast-iron bay was blind and still;
These were our poetry; in him perhaps
Science had barred the gate that lets in dream,
And he would rather count the perch and bream
Than with the current's idle fancy lapse;
And yet he had the poet's open eye 330
That takes a frank delight in all it sees,
Nor was earth voiceless, nor the mystic sky,
To him the life-long friend of fields and trees:
Then came the prose of the suburban street,
Its silence deepened by our echoing feet,
And converse such as rambling hazard finds;
Then he who many cities knew and many minds,
And men once world-noised, now mere Ossian forms
Of misty memory, bade them live anew
As when they shared earth's manifold delight, 340
In shape, in gait, in voice, in gesture true,

And, with an accent heightening as he warms,
Would stop forgetful of the shortening night,
Drop my confining arm, and pour profuse
Much worldly wisdom kept for others' use,
Not for his own, for he was rash and free,
His purse or knowledge all men's, like the sea.
Still can I hear his voice's shrilling might
(With pauses broken, while the fitful spark
He blew more hotly rounded on the dark   350
To hint his features with a Rembrandt light)
Call Oken back, or Humboldt, or Lamarck,
Or Cuvier's taller shade, and many more
Whom he had seen, or knew from others' sight,
And make them men to me as ne'er before:
Not seldom, as the undeadened fibre stirred
Of noble friendships knit beyond the sea,
German or French thrust by the lagging word,
For a good leash of mother-tongues had he.
At last, arrived at where our paths divide,   360
' Good night ! ' and, ere the distance grew too wide,
' Good night ! ' again ; and now with cheated ear
I half hear his who mine shall never hear.

2

Sometimes it seemed as if New England air
For his large lungs too parsimonious were,
As if those empty rooms of dogma drear
Where the ghost shivers of a faith austere
    Counting the horns o'er of the Beast,
Still scaring those whose faith in it is least,
As if those snaps o' th' moral atmosphere   370
That sharpen all the needles of the East,
    Had been to him like death,
Accustomed to draw Europe's freer breath
    In a more stable element ;
Nay, even our landscape, half the year morose,
Our practical horizon grimly pent,
Our air, sincere of ceremonious haze,
Forcing hard outlines mercilessly close,
Our social monotone of level days,
    Might make our best seem banishment,   380
        But it was nothing so ;
    Haply his instinct might divine,
Beneath our drift of puritanic snow,
    The marvel sensitive and fine
Of sanguinaria over-rash to blow
And warm its shyness in an air benign ;
Well might he prize truth's warranty and pledge
In the grim outcrop of our granite edge,

The Hebrew fervour flashing forth at need
In the stiff sons of Calvin's iron breed,   390
As prompt to give as skilled to win and keep ;
But, though such intuitions might not cheer,
Yet life was good to him, and, there or here,
With that sufficing joy, the day was never cheap ;
Thereto his mind was its own ample sphere,
And, like those buildings great that through the year
Carry one temperature, his nature large
Made its own climate, nor could any marge
Traced by convention stay him from his bent :
He had a habitude of mountain air ;   400
He brought wide outlook where he went,
   And could on sunny uplands dwell
Of prospect sweeter than the pastures fair
   High-hung of viny Neufchâtel ;
      Nor, surely, did he miss
      Some pale, imaginary bliss
Of earlier sights whose inner landscape still was Swiss.

v.

1

I cannot think he wished so soon to die
With all his senses full of eager heat,
And rosy years that stood expectant by   410
To buckle the winged sandals on their feet,
He that was friends with earth, and all her sweet
Took with both hands unsparingly :
Truly this life is precious to the root,
And good the feel of grass beneath the foot ;
To lie in buttercups and clover-bloom,
   Tenants in common with the bees,
And watch the white clouds drift through gulfs of trees,
Is better than long waiting in the tomb ;
Only once more to feel the coming spring   420
As the birds feel it when it makes them sing,
   Only once more to see the moon
Through leaf-fringed abbey-arches of the elms
   Curve her mild sickle in the West
Sweet with the breath of hay-cocks, were a boon
Worth any promise of soothsayer realms
Or casual hope of being elsewhere blest ;
   To take December by the beard
And crush the creaking snow with springy foot,
While overheard the North's dumb streamers shoot,   430
Till Winter fawn upon the cheek endeared ;
   Then the long evening ends
   Lingered by cosy chimney-nooks,
With high companionship of books

Or slippered talk of friends
And sweet habitual looks,—
Is better than to stop the ears with dust:
Too soon the spectre comes to say, ' Thou must ! '

2

When toil-crooked hands are crost upon the breast,
 They comfort us with sense of rest ;   440
They must be glad to lie forever still ;
 Their work is ended with their day ;
Another fills their room ; 't is the World's ancient way,
 Whether for good or ill ;
 But the deft spinners of the brain,
 Tho love each added day and find it gain,
 Whem overtakes the doom
To snap the half-grown flower upon the loom
(Trophy that was to be of life-long pain),
The thread no other skill can ever knit again.   450
 'T was so with him, for he was glad to live,
 'T was doubly so, for he left work begue ;
Could not this eagerness of Fate forgive
 Till all the allotted flax was spun ?
It matters not ; for, go at night or noon,
A friend, whene'er he dies, has died too soon,
And, once we hear the hopeless *He is dead,*
So far as flesh hath knowledge, all is said.

VI.
1

I seem to see the black procession go :
That crawling prose of death too well I know,   460
The vulgar paraphrase of glorious woe ;
I see it wind through that unsightly grove,
Once beautiful, but long defaced
With granite permanence of cockney taste
And all those grim disfigurements we love :
There, then, we leave him : Him ? such costly waste
Nature rebels at : and it is not true
Of those most precious parts of him we knew :
 Could we be conscious but as dreamers be,
 'T were sweet to leave this shifting life of tents   470
Sunk in the changeless calm of Deity ;
Nay, to be mingled with the elements,
The fellow-servant of creative powers,
Partaker in the solemn year's events,
To share the work of busy-fingered hours
To be night's silent almoner of dew,
To rise again in plants and breathe and grow,
To stream as tides the ocean caverns through,
Or with the rapture of great winds to blow

About earth's shaken coignes, were not a fate   480
   To leave us all-disconsolate ;
Even endless slumber in the sweetening sod
   Of charitable earth
That takes out all our mortal stains,
And makes us clearlier neighbours of the clod,
   Methinks were better worth
Than the poor fruit of most men's wakeful pains,
   The heart's insatiable ache :
   But such was not his faith,
Nor mine : it may be he had trod   490
Outside the plain old path of *God thus spake*,
   But God to him was very God,
   And not a visionary wraith
Skulking in murky corners of the mind,
   And he was sure to be
Somehow, somewhere, imperishable as He,
Not with His essence mystically combined,
As some high spirits long, but whole and free,
   A perfected and conscious Agassiz.
And such I figure him : the wise of old   500
Welcome and own him of their peaceful fold,
   Not truly with the guild enrolled
   Of him who seeking inward guessed
   Diviner riddles than the rest,
   And groping in the darks of thought
   Touched the Great Hand and knew it not
   He rather shares the daily light,
   From reason's charier fountains won,
Of his great chief, the slow-paced Stagyrite,
And Cuvier clasps once more his long-lost son.   510

2

The shape erect is prone : forever stilled
The winning tongue ; the forehead's high-piled heap,
A cairn which every science helped to build,
Unvalued will its golden secrets keep :
He knows at last if Life or Death be best :
Wherever he be flown, whatever vest
The being hath put on which lately here
So many-friended was, so full of cheer
To make men feel the Seeker's noble zest,
We have not lost him all ; he is not gone   520
To the dumb herd of them that wholly die ;
The beauty of his better self lives on
In minds he touched with fire, in many an eye
He trained to Truth's exact severity ;
He was a Teacher : why be grieved for him

Whose living word still stimulates the air ?
In endless file shall loving scholars come
The glow of his transmitted touch to share,
And trace his features with an eye less dim
Than ours whose sense familiar wont makes numb.   530
FLORENCE, ITALY, *February*, 1874.

JEFFRIES WYMAN

DIED 4th SEPTEMBER, 1874.

[*Nation*, New York, October 8, 1874.]

THE wisest man could ask no more of Fate
Than to be simple, modest, manly, true,
Safe from the Many, honoured by the Few ;
Nothing to court in World, or Church, or State,
But inwardly in secret to be great ;
To feel mysterious Nature ever new,
To touch, if not to grasp, her endless clue,
And learn by each discovery how to wait ;
To widen knowledge and escape the praise ;
Wisely to teach, because more wise to learn ;
To toil for Science, not to draw men's gaze,
But for her lore of self-denial stern ;
That such a man could spring from our decays
Fans the soul's nobler faith until it burn.

SONNET

TO F. A.

[*Atlantic Monthly*, May, 1875.]

UNCONSCIOUS as the sunshine, simply sweet
And generous as that, thou dost not close
Thyself in art, as life were but a rose
To rumple bee-like with luxurious feet ;
Thy higher mind therein finds sure retreat,
But not from care of common hopes and woes ;
Thee the dark chamber, thee the unfriended knows,
Although no gaping crowds thy praise repeat :
Consummate artist, who life's landscape bleak
Hast brimmed with sun to many a clouded eye,
Touched to a brighter hue the beggar's cheek,
Hung over orphaned lives a gracious sky,
And traced for eyes, that else would vainly seek,
Fair pictures of an angel drawing nigh !
FLORENCE, ITALY, *January*, 1874.

JOSEPH WINLOCK

DIED JUNE 11, 1875.

[*Nation*, New York, June 17, 1875.]

SHY soul and stalwart, man of patient will
Through years one hair's-breadth on our Dark to gain,
Who, from the stars he studied not in vain,
Had learned their secret to be strong and still,
Careless of fames that earth's tin trumpets fill;
Born under Leo, broad of build and brain,
He watched while others slept, in that hushed fane
Of Science, only witness of his skill:
Sudden as falls a shooting-star he fell,
But inextinguishable his luminous trace
In mind and heart of all that knew him well.
Happy man's doom! To him the fates were known
Of orbs dim-hovering on the skirts of space,
Unprescient, through God's mercy, of his own!

SONNETS FROM OVER SEA

[*Atlantic Monthly*, July, 1875.]

I

ENGLISH BORDER

As sinks the sun behind yon alien hills
Whose heather-purpled slopes, in glory rolled,
Flush all my thought with momentary gold,
What pang of vague regret my fancy thrills?
Here 't is enchanted ground the peasant tills,
Where the shy ballad dared its blooms unfold,
And memory's glamour makes new sights seem old,
As when our life some vanished dream fulfils;
Yet not to thee belong these painless tears,
Land loved ere seen: before my darkened eyes,
From far beyond the waters and the years,
Horizons mute that wait their poet rise;
The stream before me fades and disappears,
And in the Charles the western splendour dies.

II

ON BEING ASKED FOR AN AUTOGRAPH IN VENICE

AMID these fragments of heroic days
When thought met deed with mutual passion's leap,
There sits a Fame whose silent trump makes cheap
What short-lived rumour of ourselves we raise ;
They had far other estimate of praise
Who stamped the signet of their souls so deep
In art and action, and whose memories keep
Their height like stars above our misty ways :
In this grave presence to record my name
Something within me hangs the head and shrinks ;
Dull were the soul without some joy in fame ;
Yet here to claim remembrance were, methinks,
Like him who, in the desert's awful frame,
Notches his cockney initials on the Sphinx.

TEMPORA MUTANTUR

[*Nation*, New York, August 26, 1875.]

THE world turns mild ; democracy, they say,
Rounds the sharp knobs of character away ;
And no great harm, unless at grave expense
Of what needs edge of proof, the moral sense ;
For man or race is on the downward path
Whose fibre grows too soft for honest wrath,
And there 's a subtle influence that springs
From words to modify our sense of things.
A plain distinction is obscured of late :
Men, if they will, may pardon ; but the State   10
Forgets its function if not fixed as Fate.
So thought our sires : a hundred years ago,
If men were knaves, why, people called them so,
And crime could see the prison-portal bend
Its brow severe at no long vista's end ;
In those days for plain things plain words would serve
Men had not learned to admire the graceful swerve
Wherewith the Esthetic Nature's genial mood
Makes public duty slope to private good ;
No muddled conscience raised the saving doubt   20
A soldier proved unworthy was drummed out,
An officer cashiered, a civil servant
(No matter though his piety were fervent)

Disgracefully dismissed, and through the land
Each bore for life a stigma from the brand,
Whose far-heard hiss made others more averse
To take the facile step from bad to worse.
The Ten Commandments had a meaning then
Felt in their bones by least considerate men,
Because behind them Public Conscience stood   30
And without wincing made their mandates good.
But now that 'Statesmanship' is just a way
To dodge the primal curse and make it pay ;
Since Office means a kind of patent drill
To force an entrance to the Nation's till,
And peculation something rather less
Risky than if you spelt it with an *s* ;
Now that to steal by law is grown an art,
Whom rogues the sires, their milder sons call smart,
And 'slightly irregular' dilutes the sham   40
Of what had once a somewhat blunter name ;
With generous curve we draw the moral line ;
Our swindlers are permitted to resign ;
Their guilt is wrapped in deferential names,
And twenty sympathize for one that blames.
Add national disgrace to private crime,
Confront mankind with brazen front sublime,
Steal but enough, the world is unsevere,—
Tweed is a statesman, Fisk a financier ;
Invent a mine, and be—the Lord knows what,   50
Secure, at any rate, with what you 've got.
The public servant who has stolen or lied,
If called on, may resign with honest pride :
As unjust favour put him in, why doubt
Disfavour as unjust has turned him out ?
Even if indicted, what is that but fudge
To him who counted-in the elective judge ?
Whitewashed, he quits the politician's strife
At ease in mind, with pockets filled for life :
His lady glares with gems whose vulgar blaze   60
The poor man through his heightened taxes pays,
Himself content if one huge Kohinoor
Bulge from a shirt-front ampler than before,—
But not too candid, lest it haply tend
To rouse suspicion of the People's Friend ;
A public meeting, treated at his cost,
Resolves him back more virtue than he lost ;
With character regilt, he counts his gains ;
What 's gone was air, the solid good remains ;
For what *is* good, except what friend and foe   70
Seem both unanimous in thinking so,
The stocks and bonds which in our age of loans

Replace the stupid pagan's stocks and stones ?
With choker white, wherein no cynic eye
Dares see idealized a hempen tie,
At parish-meetings he conducts in prayer,
And pays for missions—to be sent elsewhere ;
On 'Change respected, to his friends endeared,
Add but a Sunday-school class, he 's revered,
And his too early tomb will not be dumb   80
To point a moral for our youth to come.

THE DANCING BEAR

[*Atlantic Monthly*, September, 1875.]

FAR over Elf-land poets stretch their sway,
And win their dearest crowns beyond the goal
Of their own conscious purpose ; they control
With gossamer threads wide-flown our fancy's play,
And so our action.   On my walk to-day
A wallowing bear begged clumsily his toll,
When straight a vision rose of Atta Troll,
And scenes ideal witched mine eyes away.
' *Merci, Mossieu !* ' the astonished bear-ward cried,
Grateful for thrice his hope to me, the slave
Of partial memory, seeing at his side
A bear immortal ; the glad dole I gave
Was none of mine ; poor Heine o'er the wide
Atlantic welter reached it from his grave.
June 11, 1875.

A MISCONCEPTION

[*Nation*, New York, August 10, 1876.]

B—, TAUGHT by Pope to do his good by stealth,
  Nor 'twixt a noun or verb the difference feeling,
In office placed to serve the Commonwealth,
  Did himself all the good he could by stealing.

BIRTHDAY VERSES

WRITTEN IN A CHILD'S ALBUM

[*Atlantic Monthly*, January, 1877.]

'T WAS sung of old in hut and hall
How once a king in evil hour
Hung musing o'er his castle wall,
And, lost in idle dreams, let fall
Into the sea his ring of power.

Then, let him sorrow as he might,
And pledge his daughter and his
    throne
To who restored the jewel bright,
The broken spell would ne'er unite ;
The grim old ocean held his own.

Those awful powers on man that wait,
On man, the beggar or the king,
To hovel bare or hall of state
A magic ring that masters fate
With each succeeding birthday bring.

Therein are set four jewels rare :
Pearl winter, summer's ruby blaze,
Spring's emerald, and, than all more
    fair,
Fall's pensive opal, doomed to bear
A heart of fire bedreamed with haze.

To him the simple spell who knows
The spirits of the ring to sway,
Fresh power with every sunrise flows,
And royal pursuivants are those
That fly his mandates to obey.

But he that with a slackened will
Dreams of things past or things to be,
From him the charm is slipping still,
And drops, ere he suspect the ill,
Into the inexorable sea.

BANKSIDE

DEDHAM, MAY 21, 1877.

[*Nation*, New York, May 31, 1877.]

I

I CHRISTENED you in happier days, before
These grey forebodings on my brow were seen ;
You are still lovely in your new-leaved green ;
The brimming river soothes his grassy shore ;
The bridge is there ; the rock with lichens hoar
And the same shadows on the water lean,
Outlasting us.   How many graves between
That day and this !   How many shadows more
Darken my heart, their substance from these eyes
Hidden for ever !   So our world is made
Of life and death commingled ; and the sighs
Outweigh the smiles, in equal balance laid :
What compensation ?   None save that the Allwise
So schools us to love things that cannot fade.

II

Thank God, he saw you last in pomp of May,
Ere any leaf had felt the year's regret ;
Your latest image in his memory set
Was fair as when your landscape's peaceful sway
Charmed dearer eyes with his to make delay
On Hope's long prospect,—as if They forget
The happy, they, the unspeakable ones, whose debt,
Like the hawk's shadow, haunts our brightest day :
Better it is that ye should look so fair,
Slopes that he loved, and ever-murmuring pines
That make a music out of silent air,
And bloom-heaped orchard-trees in prosperous lines ;
In you the heart some sweeter hints divines,
And wiser, than in winter's dull despair.

III

Old friend, farewell ! Your kindly door again
I enter, but the master's hand in mine
No more clasps welcome, and the temperate wine,
That cheered our long nights, other lips must stain :
All is unchanged, but I expect in vain
The face alert, the manners free and fine,
The seventy years borne lightly as the pine
Wears its first down of snow in green disdain :
Much did he, and much well ; yet most of all
I prized his skill in leisure and the ease
Of a life flowing full without a plan ;
For most are idly busy ; him I call
Thrice fortunate who knew himself to please,
Learned in those arts that make a gentleman.

IV

Nor deem he lived unto himself alone ;
His was the public spirit of his sire,
And in those eyes, soft with domestic fire,
A quenchless light of fiercer temper shone
What time about the world our shame was blown
On every wind ; his soul would not conspire
With selfish men to soothe the mob's desire,
Veiling with garlands Moloch's bloody stone ;
The high-bred instincts of a better day
Ruled in his blood, when to be citizen
Rang Roman yet, and a Free People's sway
Was not the exchequer of impoverished men,
Nor statesmanship with loaded votes to play,
Nor public office a tramps' boosing-ken.

NIGHTWATCHES

[*Atlantic Monthly*, July, 1877.]

WHILE the slow clock, as they were miser's gold,
Counts and recounts the mornward steps of Time,
The darkness thrills with conscience of each crime
By Death committed, daily grown more bold;
Once more the list of all my wrongs is told,
And ghostly hands stretch to me from my prime
Helpless farewells, as from an alien clime;
For each new loss redoubles all the old:
This morn 't was May; the blossoms were astir
With southern wind; but now the boughs are bent
With snow instead of birds, and all things freeze:
How much of all my past is dumb with her,
And of my future, too, for with her went
Half of that world I ever cared to please!

RED TAPE

[*Masque of Poets*, 1878.]

WHAT countless years, what wealth of brain were spent
To bring us hither from our caves and huts,
And trace through pathless wilds the patient ruts
Of Faith and Habit, by whose deep indent
Prudence may guide if genius be not lent,—
Genius not always happy when it shuts
Its ears against the plodder's ifs and buts,
Thinking by some brave leap to snatch the event!
The coursers of the sun, whose hoofs of flame
Burn through morn's misty threshold, are exact
As bankers' clerks, and all this star-poised frame,
Self-will allowed, were with convulsion rackt;
The world would end, were Dullness not to tame
Wit's feathered heels in the stern stocks of fact.

'MY HEART, I CANNOT STILL IT'

[*Masque of Poets*, 1878.]

MY heart, I cannot still it,
Is a nest with song-birds in it;
And when the last shall go,
The dreary days, to fill it,
Instead of lark or linnet,
Will bring dead leaves and snow.

And were they swallows only,
Without the passion stronger
Of joy that soars and sings,
Woe 's me, I shall be lonely
When I can feel no longer
The impatience of their wings !

MERCEDES

June 26, 1878.

[*Harper's Magazine*, January, 1881.]

Hers all that life could promise or bestow :
Youth, beauty, love, a crown, the beckoning years,
Lids to be pearled with none but joyous tears,
A life unsoiled with any vulgar woe,
And by a nation's swelled to lordlier flow ;
What lurking-place, we thought, for doubts or fears
When, a white swan, she swam along the cheers
Of the Alcalá but five brief months ago ?
The cannon shouted hymeneals then
That on her birthday now denounce her doom ;
The same white steeds, that tossed their scorn of men ;
To-day as haughty drag her to the tomb.
Grim jest of Fate ! Yet who dare call it blind
Who knows what life is, what our human kind ?

THE PRISON OF CERVANTES

[*Harper's Magazine*, January, 1881.]

Were mine such cell ! Though nature's firm decree
The narrowing soul with narrowing dungeon bind,
Yet his was free of foot as any wind,
And held both worlds, of spirit and sense, in fee;
What mortals saw of him lay here, while he
In charmed communion with his dual mind
Was wandering Spain, himself both knight and hind,
Redressing wrongs he knew must ever be.
His humour wise could see life's long deceit,
Man's baffled aims, nor therefore both despise ;
His knightly nature could ill fortune greet
Like an old friend ; whose ever such kind eyes
That pierced so deep, such scope, save his whose feet
By Avon ceased 'neath the same April's skies ?

PHŒBE

[*Century Magazine*, November, 1881.]

ERE pales in Heaven the morning star,
A bird, the loneliest of its kind,
Hears Dawn's faint footfall from afar
While all its mates are dumb and blind.

It is a wee sad-coloured thing,
As shy and secret as a maid,
That, ere in choir the robins ring,
Pipes its own name like one afraid.

It seems pain-prompted to repeat
The story of some ancient ill,
But *Phœbe! Phœbe!* sadly sweet
Is all it says, and then is still.

It calls and listens: Earth and sky,
Hushed by the pathos of its fate,
Listen: no whisper of reply
Comes from its doom-dissevered
    mate.

Phœbe! it calls and calls again,
And Ovid, could he but have heard,
Had hung a legendary pain
About the memory of the bird;

A pain articulate so long
In penance of some mouldered crime
Whose ghost still flies the Furies'
    thong
Down the waste solitudes of Time;

Waif of the young World's wonder-
    hour,
When gods found mortal maidens fair,
And will malign was joined with power
Love's kindly laws to overbear,

Like Progne, did it feel the stress
And coil of the prevailing words
Close round its being and compress
Man's ampler nature to a bird's?

One only memory left of all
The motley crowd of vanished scenes,
Hers,—and vain impulse to recall
By repetition what it means.

Phœbe! is all it has to say
In plaintive cadence o'er and o'er,
Like children that have lost their way
And know their names, but nothing
    more.

Is it a type, since Nature's lyre
Vibrates to every note in man,
Of that insatiable desire,
Meant to be so, since life began?

I, in strange lands at grey of dawn,
Wakeful, have heard that fruitless
    plaint
Through Memory's chambers deep
    withdrawn
Renew its iterations faint.

So nigh! yet from remotest years
It seems to draw its magic, rife
With longings unappeased and tears
Drawn from the very source of life.

ESTRANGEMENT

[*Century Magazine*, May, 1882.]

THE path from me to you that led,
    Untrodden long, with grass is
        grown,
Mute carpet that his lieges spread
    Before the Prince Oblivion
When he goes visiting the dead.

And who are they but who forget?
    You, who my coming could surmise
Ere any hint of me as yet
Warned other ears and other eyes,
See the path blurred without regret.

But when I trace its windings sweet
    With saddened steps, at every spot
That feels the memory in my feet,
    Each grass-blade turns forget-me-
        not,
Where murmuring bees your name
    repeat.

CREDIDIMUS JOVEM REGNARE

[*Atlantic Monthly*, February, 1887.]

O DAYS endeared to every muse,
When nobody had any Views,
Nor, while the cloudscape of his mind
By every breeze was new designed,
Insisted all the world should see
Camels or whales where none there be!
O happy days, when men received
From sire to son what all believed,
And left the other world in bliss,
Too busy with bedevilling this !   10

Beset by doubts of every breed
In the last bastion of my creed,
With shot and shell for Sabbath-
      chime,
I watch the storming-party climb,
Panting (their prey in easy reach),
To pour triumphant through the
      breach
In walls that shed like snowflakes tons
Of missiles from old-fashioned guns,
But crumble 'neath the storm that
      pours
All day and night from bigger bores.
There, as I hopeless watch and wait   22
The last life-crushing coil of Fate,
Despair finds solace in the praise
Of those serene dawn-rosy days
Ere microscopes had made us heirs
To large estates of doubts and snares,
By proving that the title-deeds,
Once all-sufficient for men's needs,
Are palimpsests that scarce disguise
The tracings of still earlier lies,   30
Themselves as surely written o'er
An older fib erased before.

So from these days I fly to those
That in the landlocked Past repose,
Where no rude wind of doctrine
      shakes
From bloom-flushed boughs untimely
      flakes,
Where morning's eyes see nothing
      strange,
No crude perplexity of change,

And morrows trip along their ways
Secure as happy yesterdays.   40
Then there were rulers who could
      trace
Through heroes up to gods their race,
Pledged to fair fame and noble use
By veins from Odin filled or Zeus,
And under bonds to keep divine
The praise of a celestial line.
Then priests could pile the altar's
      sods,
With whom gods spake as they with
      gods,
And everywhere from haunted earth
Broke springs of wonder that had
      birth   50
In depths divine beyond the ken
And fatal scrutiny of men ;
Then hills and groves and streams and
      seas
Thrilled with immortal presences,
Not too ethereal for the scope
Of human passion's dream or hope.

Now Pan at last is surely dead,
And King No-Credit reigns instead,
Whose officers, morosely strict,
Poor Fancy's tenantry evict,   60
Chase the last Genius from the door,
And nothing dances any more.
Nothing ? Ah, yes, our tables do,
Drumming the Old One's own tattoo,
And, if the oracles are dumb,
Have we not mediums ? Why be
      glum ?

Fly thither ? Why, the very air
Is full of hindrance and despair !
Fly thither ? But I cannot fly ;
My doubts enmesh me if I try,   70
Each lilliputian, but, combined,
Potent a giant's limbs to bind ;
This world and that are growing dark;
A huge interrogation mark,
The Devil's crook episcopal,
Still borne before him since the Fall,

Blackens with its ill-omened sign
The old blue heaven of faith benign.
Whence ?   Whither ?   Wherefore ?
    How ?   Which ?   Why ?
All ask at once, all wait reply.   80
Men feel old systems cracking under
    'em ;
Life saddens to a mere conundrum
Which once Religion solved, but she
Has lost—has Science found ?—the
    key.

What was snow-bearded Odin, trow,
The mighty hunter long ago,
Whose horn and hounds the peasant
    hears
Still when the Northlights shake their
    spears ?
Science hath answers twain, I 've
    heard ;
Choose which you will, nor hope a
    third ;   90
Whichever box the truth be stowed in,
There 's not a sliver left of Odin.
Either he was a pinchbrowed thing,
With scarcely wit a stone to fling,
A creature both in size and shape
Nearer than we are to the ape,
Who hung sublime with brat and spouse
By tail prehensile from the boughs,
And, happier than his maimed de-
    scendants,
The culture-curtailed independents,
Could pluck his cherries with both
    paws,   101
And stuff with both his big-boned
    jaws ;—
Or else the core his name enveloped
Was from a solar myth developed,
Which, hunted to its primal shoot,
Takes refuge in a Sanskrit root,
Thereby to instant death explaining
The little poetry remaining.
Try it with Zeus, 't is just the same ;
The thing evades, we hug a name ;
Nay, scarcely that,—perhaps a vapour
Born of some atmospheric caper.   112
All Lempriere's fables blur together
In cloudy symbols of the weather,

And Aphrodite rose from frothy seas
But to illustrate such hypotheses.
With years enough behind his back,
Lincoln will take the selfsame track,
And prove, hulled fairly to the cob,
A mere vagary of Old Prob ;   120
Give the right man a solar myth,
And he 'll confute the sun therewith.

They make things admirably plain,
But one hard question *will* remain :
If one hypothesis you lose,
Another in its place you choose,
But, your faith gone, O man and
    brother,
Whose shop shall furnish you an-
    other—
One that will wash, I mean, and wear,
And wrap us warmly from despair ?
While they are clearing up our
    puzzles,   131
And clapping prophylactic muzzles
On the Actæon's hounds that sniff
Our devious track through But and If,
Would they explain away the Devil
And other facts that won't keep level,
But rise beneath our feet or fail
As doth a ship's deck in a gale !

God vanished long ago, iwis,
A mere subjective synthesis,   140
A doll, stuffed out with hopes and fears,
Too homely for us pretty dears,
Who want one that conviction carries,
Last make of London or of Paris.
He gone, I felt a moment's spasm,
But calmed myself with Protoplasm,
A finer name, and, what is more,
As enigmatic as before ;
Greek, too, and sure to fill with ease
Minds caught in the Symplegades
Of soul and sense, life's two condi-
    tions,   151
Each baffled with its own omni-
    science.
The men who labour to revise
Our Bibles will, I hope, be wise,
And print it without foolish qualms
Instead of God in David's psalms :

Noll had been more effective far
Could he have shouted at Dunbar,
' Rise, Protoplasm!' No dourest Scot
Had waited for another shot.　160

And yet I frankly must confess
A secret unforgivingness,
And shudder at the saving chrism
Whose best New Birth is Pessimism ;
My soul—I mean the bit of phosphorus,
That fills the place of what that was
　　for us—
Can't bid its inward bores defiance
With the new nursery-tales of science.
What profits me, though doubt by
　　doubt,
As nail by nail, be driven out,　170
When every new one, like the last,
Still holds my coffin-lid as fast ?
Would I find thought a moment's truce,
Give me the young world's Mother
　　Goose,
With life and joy in every limb,
The chimney-corner tales of Grimm !

Our dear and admirable Huxley
Cannot explain to me why ducks lay,
Or rather, how into their eggs
Blunder potential wings and legs　180
With will to move them and decide
Whether in air or lymph to glide.
Who gets a hair's-breadth on by
　　showing
That Something Else set all agoing ?
Farther and farther back we push
From Moses and his burning bush ;
Cry, ' Art Thou there ?' Above,
　　below,
All nature mutters yes and no !
'T is the old answer : we 're agreed
Being from Being must proceed,　190
Life be Life's source. I might as well
Obey the meeting-house's bell,
And listen while Old Hundred pours
Forth through the summer-opened
　　doors,
From old and young. I hear it yet,
Swelled by bass-viol and clarinet,
While the grey minister, with face
Radiant, let loose his noble bass.

If Heaven it reached not, yet its roll
Waked all the echoes of the soul,　200
And in it many a life found wings
To soar away from sordid things.
Church gone and singers too, the song
Sings to me voiceless all night long,
Till my soul beckons me afar,
Glowing and trembling like a star.
Will any scientific touch
With my worn strings achieve as much ?

I don't object, not I, to know
My sires were monkeys, if 't was so ;
I touch my ear's collusive tip　211
And own the poor-relationship.
That apes of various shapes and sizes
Contained their germs that all the
　　prizes
Of senate, pulpit, camp, and bar win
May give us hopes that sweeten
　　Darwin.
Who knows but from our loins may
　　spring
(Long hence) some winged sweet-
　　throated thing
As much superior to us
As we to Cynocephalus ?　220

This is consoling, but, alas,
It wipes no dimness from the glass
Where I am flattening my poor nose,
In hope to see beyond my toes.
Though I accept my pedigree,
Yet where, pray tell me, is the key
That should unlock a private door
To the Great Mystery, such no more ?
Each offers his, but one nor all
Are much persuasive with the wall
That rises now, as long ago,　231
Between I wonder and I know,
Nor will vouchsafe a pin-hole peep
At the veiled Isis in its keep.
Where is no door, I but produce
My key to find it of no use.
Yet better keep it, after all,
Since Nature 's economical,
And who can tell but some fine day
(If it occur to her) she may,　240
In her good-will to you and me,
Make door and lock to match the key ?

FANCY OR FACT?

[*Atlantic Monthly*, March, 1887.]

In town I hear, scarce wakened yet,
My neighbour's clock behind the wall
Record the day's increasing debt,
And *Cuckoo! Cuckoo!* faintly call.

Our senses run in deepening grooves,
Thrown out of which they lose their tact,
And consciousness with effort moves
From habit past to present fact.

So, in the country waked to-day,
I hear, unwitting of the change,
A cuckoo's throb from far away
Begin to strike, nor think it strange.

The sound creates its wonted frame:
My bed at home, the songster hid
Behind the wainscoting,—all came
As long association bid.

I count to learn how late it is,
Until, arrived at thirty-four,
I question, 'What strange world is this
Whose lavish hours would make me poor?'

Cuckoo! Cuckoo! Still on it went,
With hints of mockery in its tone;
How could such hoards of time be spent
By one poor mortal's wit alone?

I have it! Grant, ye kindly Powers,
I from this spot may never stir,
If only these uncounted hours
May pass, and seem too short, with Her!

But who She is, her form and face,
These to the world of dream belong;
She moves through fancy's visioned space,
Unbodied, like the cuckoo's song.

THE SECRET

[*Atlantic Monthly*, January, 1888.]

I have a fancy: how shall I bring it
Home to all mortals wherever they be?
Say it or sing it? Shoe it or wing it,
So it may outrun and outfly Me,
Merest cocoon-web whence it broke free?

Only one secret can save from disaster,
Only one magic is that of the Master:
Set it to music; give it a tune,—
Tune the brook sings you, tune the breeze brings you,
Tune that the columbines dance to in June!

This is the secret: so simple, you see!
Easy as loving, easy as kissing,
Easy as—well, let me ponder—as missing,
Known, since the world was, by scarce two or three.

ENDYMION

A MYSTICAL COMMENT ON TITIAN'S 'SACRED AND PROFANE LOVE'

[*Atlantic Monthly*, February, 1888.]

I

My day began not till the twilight fell,
And, lo, in ether from heaven's sweetest well,
The New Moon swam divinely isolate
In maiden silence, she that makes my fate
Haply not knowing it, or only so
As I the secrets of my sheep may know;
Nor ask I more, entirely blest if she,
In letting me adore, ennoble me
To height of what the Gods meant making man,
As only she and her best beauty can.   10
Mine be the love that in itself can find
Seed of white thoughts, the lilies of the mind,
Seed of that glad surrender of the will
That finds in service self's true purpose still;
Love that in outward fairness sees the tent
Pitched for an inmate far more excellent;
Love with a light irradiate to the core,
Lit at her lamp, but fed from inborn store;
Love thrice-requited with the single joy
Of an immaculate vision naught could cloy,   20
Dearer because, so high beyond my scope,
My life grew rich with her, unbribed by hope
Of other guerdon save to think she knew
One grateful votary paid her all her due;
Happy if she, high-radiant there, resigned
To his sure trust her image in his mind.
O fairer even than Peace is when she comes
Hushing War's tumult, and retreating drums
Fade to a murmur like the sough of bees
Hidden among the noon-stilled linden-trees,   30
Bringer of quiet, thou that canst allay
The dust and din and travail of the day,
Strewer of Silence, Giver of the dew
That doth our pastures and our souls renew,
Still dwell remote, still on thy shoreless sea
Float unattained in sacred empery,
Still light my thoughts, nor listen to a prayer
Would make thee less imperishably fair!

II

Can, then, my twofold nature find content
In vain conceits of airy blandishment?   40
Ask I no more? Since yesterday I task
My storm-strewn thoughts to tell me what I ask:

LOWELL   X

Faint premonitions of mutation strange
Steal o'er my perfect orb, and, with the change,
Myself am changed ; the shadow of my earth
Darkens the disc of that celestial worth
Which only yesterday could still suffice
Upwards to waft my thoughts in sacrifice ;
My heightened fancy with its touches warm
Moulds to a woman's that ideal form ;   50
Nor yet a woman's wholly, but divine
With awe her purer essence bred in mine.
Was it long brooding on their own surmise,
Which, of the eyes engendered, fools the eyes,
Or have I seen through that translucent air
A Presence shaped in its seclusions bare,
My Goddess looking on me from above
As look our russet maidens when they love,
But high-uplifted o'er our human heat
And passion-paths too rough for her pearl feet ?   60

Slowly the Shape took outline as I gazed
At her full-orbed or crescent, till, bedazed
With wonder-working light that subtly wrought
My brain to its own substance, steeping thought
In trances such as poppies give, I saw
Things shut from vision by sight's sober law,
Amorphous, changeful, but defined at last
Into the peerless Shape mine eyes hold fast.
This, too, at first I worshipt : soon, like wine,
Her eyes, in mine poured, frenzy-philtred mine ;   70
Passion put Worship's priestly raiment on
And to the woman knelt, the Goddess gone.
Was I, then, more than mortal made ? or she
Less than divine that she might mate with me ?

III

Long she abode aloof there in her heaven,
Far as the grape-bunch of the Pleiad seven
Beyond my madness' utmost leap ; but here
Mine eyes have feigned of late her rapture near,
Here in these shadowy woods and brook-lulled dells,
Moulded of mind-mist that broad day dispels.   80

Have no heaven-habitants e'er felt a void
In hearts sublimed with ichor unalloyed ?
E'er longed to mingle with a mortal fate
Intense with pathos of its briefer date ?
Could she partake, and live, our human stains ?
Even with the thought there tingles through my veins

Sense of unwarned renewal; I, the dead,
Receive and house again the ardour fled,
As once Alcestis; to the ruddy brim
Feel masculine virtue flooding every limb, 90
And life, like Spring returning, brings the key
That sets my senses from their winter free,
Dancing like naked fauns too glad for shame.
Her passion, purified to palest flame,
Can it thus kindle? Is her purpose this?
I will not argue, lest I lose a bliss
That makes me dream Tithonus' fortune mine,
(Or what of it was palpably divine
Ere came the fruitlessly immortal gift;)
I cannot curb my hope's imperious drift 100
That wings with fire my dull mortality;
Though fancy-forged, 't is all I feel or see.

IV

My Goddess sinks; round Latmos' darkening brow
Trembles the parting of her presence now,
Faint as the perfume left upon the grass
By her limbs' pressure or her feet that pass
By me conjectured, but conjectured so
As things I touch far fainter substance show.
Was it mine eyes' imposture I have seen
Flit with the moonbeams on from shade to sheen 110
Through the wood-openings? Nay, I see her now
Out of her heaven new-lighted, from her brow
The hair breeze-scattered, like loose mists that blow
Across her crescent, goldening as they go,
High-kirtled for the chase, and what was shown,
Of maiden rondure, like the rose half-blown.
If dream, turn real! If a vision, stay!
Take mortal shape, my philtre's spell obey!
If hags compel thee from thy secret sky
With gruesome incantations, why not I, 120
Whose only magic is that I distil
A potion, blent of passion, thought, and will,
Deeper in reach, in force of fate more rich,
Than e'er was juice wrung by Thessalian witch
From moon-enchanted herbs, a potion brewed
Of my best life in each diviner mood?
Myself the elixir am, myself the bowl
Seething and mantling with my soul of soul.
Taste and be humanized: what though the cup,
With thy lips frenzied, shatter? Drink it up! 130
If but these arms may clasp, o'erquited so,
My world, thy heaven, all life means I shall know.

V

Sure she hath heard my prayer and granted half,
As Gods do who at mortal madness laugh.
In sleep she comes; she visits me in dreams,
And, as her image in a thousand streams,
So in my veins, that her obey, she sees,
Floating and flaming there, her images
Borne to my little world's remotest zone
With messages of her, and her alone. 140
With silence-sandalled Sleep she comes to me,
(But softer-footed, sweeter-browed than she,)
In motion gracious as a seagull's wing,
And all her bright limbs, moving, seem to sing.
If life's most solid things illusion seem,
Why should not substance wear the mask of dream?
Let me believe so, then, if so I may
With the night's bounty feed my beggared day.
In dreams I see her lay the goddess down
With bow and quiver, and her crescent-crown 150
Flicker and fade away to dull eclipse
As down to mine she deigns her longed-for lips;
And as her neck my happy arms enfold,
Flooded and lustred with her loosened gold,
She whispers words each sweeter than a kiss:
Then, wakened with the shock of sudden bliss,
My arms are empty, my awakener fled,
And, silent in the silent sky o'erhead,
But coldly as on ice-plated snow, she gleams,
Herself the mother and the child of dreams. 160

VI

Gone is the time when phantasms could appease
My quest phantasmal and bring cheated ease;
When, if she glorified my dreams, I felt
Through all my limbs a change immortal melt
At touch of hers illuminate with soul.
Not long could I be stilled with Fancy's dole;
Too soon the mortal mixture in me caught
Red fire from her celestial flame, and fought
For tyrannous control in all my veins:
My fool's prayer was accepted; what remains? 170
Or was it some eidolon merely, sent
By her who rules the shades in banishment,
To mock me with her semblance? Were it thus,
How 'scape I shame, whose will was traitorous?
What shall compensate an ideal dimmed?
How blanch again my statue virgin-limbed,

Soiled with the incense-smoke her chosen priest
Poured more profusely as within decreased
The fire unearthly, fed with coals from far
Within the soul's shrine ? Could my fallen star   180
Be set in heaven again by prayers and tears
And quenchless sacrifice of all my years,
How would the victim to the flamen leap,
And life for life's redemption paid hold cheap !

But what resource when she herself descends
From her blue throne, and o'er her vassal bends
That shape thrice-deified by love, those eyes
Wherein the Lethe of all others lies ?
When my white queen of heaven's remoteness tires,
Herself against her other self conspires,   190
Takes woman's nature, walks in mortal ways,
And finds in my remorse her beauty's praise ?
Yet all would I renounce to dream again
The dream in dreams fulfilled that made my pain,
My noble pain that heightened all my years
With crowns to win and prowess-breeding tears ;
Nay, would that dream renounce once more to see
Her from her sky there looking down at me !

VII

Goddess, reclimb thy heaven, and be once more
An inaccessible splendour to adore,   200
A faith, a hope of such transcendent worth
As bred ennobling discontent with earth ;
Give back the longing, back the elated mood
That, fed with thee, spurned every meaner good ;
Give even the spur of impotent despair
That, without hope, still bade aspire and dare ;
Give back the need to worship that still pours
Down to the soul that virtue it adores !

Nay, brightest and most beautiful, deem naught
These frantic words, the reckless wind of thought ;   210
Still stoop, still grant,—I live but in thy will ;
Be what thou wilt, but be a woman still !
Vainly I cried, nor could myself believe
That what I prayed for I would fain receive.
My moon is set ; my vision set with her ;
No more can worship vain my pulses stir.
Goddess Triform, I own thy triple spell,
My heaven's queen,—queen, too, of my earth and hell !

INSCRIPTION

FOR A WINDOW DEDICATED TO THE MEMORY OF SIR WALTER RALEIGH, PLACED IN ST. MARGARET'S, WESTMINSTER, BY SUBSCRIPTIONS FROM THE UNITED STATES OF AMERICA, A.D. 1882

THE New World's sons, from England's breasts we drew
Such milk as bids remember whence we came ;
Proud of her Past wherefrom our Present grew,
This window we inscribe with Raleigh's name.

APPENDIX

EDITOR'S PREFACE[1]
TO THE ENGLISH EDITION
OF THE 'BIGLOW PAPERS', FIRST SERIES

I can safely say that few things in my life have pleased me more than the request of Messrs. Trübner, backed by the expressed wish of the author, that I would see the first English edition of the 'Biglow Papers' through the press. I fell in with the Papers about ten years ago, soon after their publication; and the impression they then made on me has been deepening and becoming more lively ever since. In fact, I do not think that, even in his own New England, Mr. Lowell can have a more constant or more grateful reader, though I cannot say that I go much beyond most of my own intimate friends over here in my love for his works. I may remark, in passing, that the impossibility of keeping a copy of the 'Biglow Papers' for more than a few weeks (of which many of us have had repeated and sorrowful proof[2]) shows how much an English Edition is needed.

Perhaps, strictly speaking, I should say a reprint, and not an edition. In fact, I am not clear (in spite of the wishes of author and publishers) that I have any right to call myself editor, for the book is as thoroughly edited already as a book need be. What between dear old Parson Wilbur—with his little vanities and pedantries, his 'infinite faculty of sermonizing', his simplicity and humour, and his deep and righteous views of life, and power of hard hitting when he has anything to say which needs driving home—and Father Ezekiel, 'the brown parchment-hided old man of the geoponic or bucolic species,' '76 year old cum next

tater diggin, and thair aint nowheres a kitting' (we readily believe) 'spryer 'n he be'; and that judicious and lazy sub-editor, 'Columbus Nye, pastor of a church in Bungtown Corner', whose acquaintance we make so thoroughly in the ten lines which he contributes—whatever of setting or framing was needed, or indeed possible, for the nine gems in verse of Mr. Hosea Biglow, has been so well done already in America by the hand best fitted for the task, that he must be a bold man who would meddle with the book now in the editing way. Even the humble satisfaction of adding a glossary and index has been denied to me, as there are already very good ones. I have merely added some half-dozen words to the glossary, at which I thought that English readers might perhaps stumble. When the proposal was first made to me, indeed, I thought of trying my hand at a sketch of American politics of thirteen years ago, the date of the Mexican war and of the first appearance of the 'Biglow Papers'. But I soon found out, first, that I was not, and had no ready means of making myself, competent for such a task; secondly, that the book did not need it. The very slight knowledge which every educated Englishman has of Transatlantic politics will be quite enough to make him enjoy the racy smack of the American soil, which is one of their great charms; and, as to the particular characters, they are most truly citizens of the world as well as Americans. If an Englishman cannot find

---

[1] By the Author of 'Tom Brown's School-Days' (Thomas Hughes). Published in 1859.

[2] Should this meet the eye of any persons who may have forgotten to return American copies of the 'Biglow Papers' to their respective owners, they are requested to forward them to the publishers. The strictest secrecy will be preserved, and an acknowledgment given in *The Times* if required.—*Note in English Edition*, 1859.

'Bird-o'-freedom Sawins', 'John P. Robinson's', 'pious editors', and candidates 'facin' south-by-north' at home—ay, and if he is not conscious of his own individual propensity to the meanness and duplicities of such, which come under the lash of Hosea—he knows little of the land we live in, or of his own heart, and is not worthy to read the 'Biglow Papers'.

Instead, therefore, of any attempt of my own, I will give Mr. Lowell's own account of how and why he came to write this book. 'All I can say is,' he writes, 'the book was *thar*. How it came is more than I can tell. I cannot, like the great Göthe, deliberately imagine what would have been a proper "Entstehungsweise" for my book, and then assume it as fact. I only know that I believed our war with Mexico (though we had as just ground for it as a strong nation ever had against a weak one) to be essentially a war of false pretences, and that it would result in widening the boundaries, and so prolonging the life of slavery. Believing that it is the manifest destiny of the English race to occupy this whole continent, and to display there that practical understanding in matters of government and colonization which no other race has given such proofs of possessing since the Romans, I hated to see a noble hope evaporated into a lying phrase to sweeten the foul breath of demagogues. Leaving the sin of it to God, I believed, and still believe, that slavery is the Achilles-heel of our own polity, that it is a temporary and false supremacy of the white races, sure to destroy that supremacy at last, because an enslaved people always prove themselves of more enduring fibre than their enslavers, as not suffering from the social vices sure to be engendered by oppression in the governing class. Against these and many other things I thought all honest men should protest. I was born and bred in the country, and the dialect was homely to me. I tried my first Biglow paper in a newspaper, and found that it had a great run. So I wrote the others from time to time during the year which followed, always very rapidly, and sometimes (as with "What Mr. Robinson thinks") at one sitting. When I came to collect them and publish them in a volume, I conceived my parson-editor, with his pedantry and verbosity, his amiable vanity and superiority to the verses he was editing, as a fitting artistic background and foil. He

gave me the chance, too, of glancing obliquely at many things which were beyond the horizon of my other characters.'

There are two American books, elder brethren of 'The Biglow Papers', which it would be unjust in an Englishman not to mention while introducing their big younger brother to his own countrymen,—I mean, of course, 'Major Downing's Letters,' and 'Sam Slick'; both of which are full of rare humour, and treat of the most exciting political questions of their day in a method and from points of view of which we are often reminded while reading the 'Biglow Papers'. In fact, Mr. Lowell borrows his name from the Major's Letters;—'Zekel Bigelow, Broker and Banker of Wall Street, New York,' is the friend who corrects the spelling, and certifies to the genuineness, of the honest Major's effusions,[1] and is one of the raciest characters in the book. No one, I am sure, would be so ready as Mr. Lowell to acknowledge whatever obligations he may have to other men, and no one can do it more safely. For though he may owe a name or an idea to others, he seems to me to stand quite alone amongst Americans, and to be the only one who is beyond question entitled to take his place in the first rank, by the side of the great political satirists of ancient and modern Europe.

Greece had her Aristophanes; Rome her Juvenal; Spain has had her Cervantes; France her Rabelais, her Molière, her Voltaire; Germany her Jean Paul, her Heine; England her Swift, her Thackeray; and America has her Lowell. By the side of all those great masters of satire, though kept somewhat in the rear by provincialism of style and subject, the author of the 'Biglow Papers' holds his own place distinct from each and all. The man who reads the book for the first time, and is capable of understanding it, has received a new sensation. In Lowell the American mind has for the first time flowered out into thoroughly original genius.

There is an airy grace about the best pieces of Washington Irving, which has no parallel amongst English writers, however closely modelled may be his style upon that of the Addisonian age. There is much original power, which will perhaps be better appreciated at a future day, about Fenimore Cooper's delineations of the physical and spiritual border-land, between white and red, between civilization and savagery.

[1] See the English Edition of 'Letters of Major Downing,' published by John Murray in 1835, pp. 22, 23; and Letters x. xi. xii. and xv.

There is dramatic power of a high order about Mr. Hawthorne, though mixed with a certain morbidness and bad taste, which debar him from ever attaining to the first rank. There is an originality of position about Mr. Emerson, in his resolute setting up of King Self against King Mob, which, coupled with a singular metallic glitter of style, and plenty of shrewd New England mother-wit, have made up together one of the best counterfeits of genius that has been seen for many a day; so good, indeed, that most men are taken by it for the first quarter of an hour at the least. But for real unmistakable genius,—for that glorious fullness of power which knocks a man down at a blow for sheer admiration, and then makes him rush into the arms of the knocker-down, and swear eternal friendship with him for sheer delight; the ' Biglow Papers' stand alone.

If I sought to describe their characteristics, I should say, the most exuberant and extravagant humour, coupled with strong, noble, Christian purpose,—a thorough scorn for all that is false and base, all the more withering because of the thorough geniality of the writer. Perhaps Jean Paul is of all the satirists I have named the one who at bottom presents most affinity with Lowell, but the differences are marked. The intellectual sphere of the German is vaster, but though with certain aims before him, he rather floats and tumbles about like a porpoise at play than follows any direct perceptible course. With Lowell, on the contrary, every word tells, every laugh is a blow; as if the god Momus had turned out as Mars, and were hard at work fighting every inch of him, grinning his broadest all the while.

Will some English readers be shocked by this combination of broad and keen humour with high Christian purpose—the association of humour and Christianity? I hope not. At any rate, I would remind any such of Luther, and of our own Latimer and Rowland Hill; are they prepared to condemn them and many more like them? Nay (though it is a question which can only be hinted at here), does not the Bible itself sanction the combination by its own example? Is there not humour mixed with the tremendous sarcasm of the old prophets —dread humour no doubt, but humour unmistakably—wherever they speak of the helplessness of idols, as in the forty-fourth and forty-sixth chapters of Isaiah, and in Elijah's mockery of the priests of Baal :—

' Cry aloud, for he is a God; either he is talking, or he is pursuing, or he is on a journey, or peradventure he sleepeth, and must be awakened.' Is not the book of Proverbs full of grave, dry, pungent humour? Consider only the following passage out of many of the same spirit: ' As the door turneth upon his hinges, so doth the slothful upon his bed. The slothful hideth his hand in his bosom, it grieveth him to bring it again to his mouth. The sluggard is wiser in his own conceit than seven men that can render a reason. He that passeth by and meddleth with strife belonging not to him, is like one that taketh a dog by the ears.'— Prov. xxvi. 14–17.

Or if it be objected that these things belong to an earlier covenant, that laughter and jesting are ' not convenient ' under the Gospel of Him who came not to destroy the law but to fulfil it, there is, perhaps, an answer to this also.

For a specimen of subdued humour in narrative, adhering in the most literal manner to facts, and yet contriving to bring them out by that graphic literalness under their most ludicrous aspect, what can equal St. Luke's description of the riot at Ephesus? The picture of the narrow trade selfishness of Demetrius—of polytheism reduced into a matter of business—of the inanity of a mob tumult in an enslaved country—of the mixed coaxing and bullying of its officials, was surely never brought out with a more vivid sense of the absurdity of the whole. ' And Gallio cared for none of these things,' is another touch of quiet humour, which at once brings out the ludicrous aspect of the punishment of the Jewish agitators by means of the very tumults which they raised.

I take it, therefore, that the exhibition of humour, in the pursuit, and as an aid for the attainment of a noble Christian purpose, is a means of action not only sanctioned by the very constitution of our natures (in which God has implanted so deeply the sense of the ludicrous, surely not that we might root it out), but by the very example of Holy Writ. The humour exhibited may be different in degree and in quality; the skies of Syria are not those of Germany, or of Spain, of England, whether old or new. But the gift in itself is a pure and precious one, if lawfully and rightfully used.

Military braggadocio, political and literary humbug, and slave-holding, are the three great butts at which Hosea Biglow and Parson Wilbur shoot, at point-blank range, and with shafts drawn well to the ear. The latter vice, indeed, includes both the others, or rather uses them as its instruments. Thus, the 'pious Editor' proclaims, as his creed,—

> I du believe in Freedom's cause
> 　Ez fur away ez Paris is ;
> I love to see her stick her claws
> 　In them infarnal Pharisees ;
>
> It's wal enough agin a king
> 　To dror resolves and triggers,
> But libbaty's a kind o' thing
> 　Thet dont agree with niggers.

No doubt they go further than this. I am quite aware that Mr. Lowell will be claimed as a champion by the peace party in this country ; and certainly no keener things have been said against war in general than are to be found in this book.

With our own peace-at-any-price party, no one has less sympathy than I ; and this leads me to urge on all English readers to bear in mind, that the ' Biglow Papers' were written for a New England audience, by a New Englander, and must be judged from a New England point of view. The citizen of a huge young mammoth country, divided by a whole ocean from the nearest enemy that it could fear, assailable only on the fringe of its seaboard (itself consisting chiefly of unapproachable swamp or barren sand wastes),surrounded by weak neighbours or thin wandering hordes, only too easy to bully, to subdue, to eat up ; from which bands of pirates, under the name of liberators, swarm forth year after year, almost unchecked, to neighbouring lands, and to which if defeated they only return to be caressed and applauded by their congeners ; where the getting up of war-fevers forms part of the stock-in-trade of too many of the leading politicians ; where in particular the grasping at new territories for slave labour, by means however foul, has become the special and avowed policy of the slavery party ; the citizen of such a country has a right to tell his countrymen that—

> 'Taint your eppyletts an' feathers
> 　Make the thing a grain more right ;
> 'Taint afollerin' your bell-wethers
> 　Will excuse ye in His sight ;
> Ef you take a sword an' dror it,
> 　An' go stick a feller thru,
> Guv'ment aint to answer for it,
> 　God 'll send the bill to you.

And the bravest officer in Her Majesty's service will laugh as heartily as you will, I take it, my dear reader, if you have never

heard it before, over a picture and a contrast such as the following :—

> Parson Wilbur sez *he* never heerd in his life
> 　Thet th' Apostles rigged out in their swaller-tail coats,
> An' marched round in front of a drum an' a fife,
> 　To git some on 'em office, an' some on 'em votes ;
> 　　　　But John P.
> 　　　　　Robinson he
> Sez they did n't know everythin' down in Judee.

But England is a small and wealthy country, whose best defence against a neighbour, always likely to become a foe, consists in a mere ocean canal ; where the question, I will not say of war, but of readiness for war, is one of life or death—in which the temptation, always so strong, to subordinate national honour to what is supposed to be policy, is in our day for most statesmen almost irresistible, because political influence is so evenly balanced, that a peace party of perhaps twenty votes has often the destinies of a ministry in its hands. Had Mr. Lowell been an Englishman, no one who knows his writings can believe for a moment that he would have swelled the cry or strengthened the hands of the vain and mischievous clique, who amongst us have of late years raised the cry of peace when there is no peace.

The same caution will apply to one marked peculiarity of style in the book, which may offend at first many persons otherwise most capable of entering into its spirit. I mean the constant, and so to speak, pervading use of Scripture language and incidents, not only side by side with the most grotesque effusions of humour, but as one main element of the ludicrous effects produced. This undoubtedly would be as really offensive as it would be untrue, from any other point of view perhaps than that of a New Englander bred in the country. The rural population of New England is still, happily for itself, tinctured in all its language, habits, modes of feeling and thought, by a strict Scriptural training—' Out of the fullness of the heart the mouth speaketh.' Look below the surface and you will see that there is no irreverence whatever beneath Hosea Biglow's daring use of Scripture ; only that ' perfect love which casteth out fear ' ; that the very purpose of the whole book is to set up Christ's Gospel as *the* standard by which alone all men are to be judged in all their acts. We may disagree from him in the conclusions which he draws from Scripture; of his earnest sincerity in enforcing those conclusions we cannot doubt.

It is satisfactory, indeed, to think that Mr. Lowell's shafts have already, in a great measure, ceased to be required, or would have to be aimed now at other bull's eyes. The servility of the Northern States to the South, which twelve years ago so raised his indignation, has wellnigh ceased to be. The vital importance of the slavery question is now thoroughly recognized by the great republican party, which I trust is year by year advancing towards an assured victory.

For that victory Mr. Lowell has done knight's-service by his other works, as well as by the ' Biglow Papers '. I need not do more than refer to these, however, as they have been published in a cheap form over here, and I believe have circulated largely. In his other poems he is by no means so equal as in the ' Biglow Papers '; but I cannot help thinking that (leaving out of sight altogether his satirical works) fifty years hence he will be recognized as the greatest American poet of our day, notwithstanding the contemporary judgement which has in England, and I believe in America, assigned that proud place to his friend and predecessor at Harvard College, H. W. Longfellow. To any reader who has not met with Lowell's Poems, and who may be induced to read them after a perusal of the present volume, I should recommend ' The Vision of Sir Launfal ', ' A Parable ', ' Stanzas on Freedom ', ' The Present Crisis ', and ' Hunger and Cold ', as specially fit to be read in connexion with the ' Biglow Papers '. It is only by looking at all sides of a man of this mould that you can get a notion of his size and power. Readers, therefore, should search out for themselves the exquisite little gems of a lighter kind, which lie about in the other poems comprised in the volume. I am only indicating those which, as it seems to me, when taken with the ' Biglow Papers ', give the best idea of the man, and what his purpose in life has been, and is.

I will not think so badly of my countrymen as to suppose for a moment that ' The Biglow Papers ' will not become the intimate friends of all good fellows in England; and when we have really made friends with a book, we like to know something about our friend's father; so I shall add the little I know of the history of James Russell Lowell.

He was born in 1819, at Cambridge, Massachusetts, so that he is some years younger than our own laureate, and we may hope to get out of him many another noble work, though we shall get no more ' Biglow Papers '—at least I fear not; for the sort of inspiration which finds voice in this way comes, I take it, only once in a man's life. And moreover, this is his own conviction. In a letter which I received from him as to the present publication, he writes : ' Friendly people say to me sometimes, " Write us more ' Biglow Papers ' " ; and I have even been simple enough to try, only to find that I could not. This has helped to persuade me that the book was a genuine growth, and not a manufacture, and that therefore I had an honest right to be pleased without blushing, if people liked it.' He was educated at Harvard College, Cambridge ; and, in fact, has never lived away from his native place. He read law, but never practised ; and in 1855 was chosen to succeed Longfellow as Professor of Modern Literature in Harvard College. He has visited Europe twice ; and I am sure that every one who knows his works must join with me in the hearty wish that he may come among us again as soon as possible.

INDEX OF TITLES

INDEX OF FIRST LINES

OXFORD: HORACE HART
PRINTER TO THE UNIVERSITY